"The Place Is Too Small for Us"

Sources for Biblical and Theological Study

General Editor:
David W. Baker
Ashland Theological Seminary

"The Place Is Too Small for Us"

The Israelite Prophets in Recent Scholarship

edited by

Robert P. Gordon

Eisenbrauns
Winona Lake, Indiana
1995

Library of Congress Cataloging-in-Publication Data

"The place is too small for us" : the Israelite prophets in recent scholarship /
   edited by Robert P. Gordon.
      p.   cm. — (Sources for biblical and theological study ; 5)
   Includes bibliographical references and indexes.
   ISBN 1-57506-000-0
   1. Bible. O.T. Prophets—Criticism, interpretation, etc.
   2. Prophets—Biblical teaching. I. Gordon, R. P. II. Series.
BS1505.2.P57   1995
224'.06—dc20   95-38977
                                                                   CIP

The paper used in this publication meets the minimum requirements of the
American National Standard for Information Sciences—Permanence of Paper
for Printed Library Materials, ANSI Z39.48-1984.♾

for Graham

CONTENTS

Part 4: Prophecy and Society

SERIES PREFACE

Old Testament scholarship is well served by several recent works which detail, to a greater or lesser extent, the progress made in the study of the Old Testament. Some survey the range of interpretation over long stretches of time, while others concern themselves with a smaller chronological or geographical segment of the field. There are also brief *entrés* into the various subdisciplines of Old Testament study included in the standard introductions as well as in several useful series. All of these provide secondary syntheses of various aspects of Old Testament research. All refer to, and base their discussions upon, various seminal works by Old Testament scholars which have proven pivotal in the development and flourishing of the various aspects of the discipline.

The main avenue into the various areas of Old Testament inquiry, especially for the beginner, has been until now mainly through the filter of these interpreters. Even on a pedagogical level, however, it is beneficial for a student to be able to interact with foundational works firsthand. This contact will not only provide insight into the content of an area, but hopefully will also lead to the sharpening of critical abilities through interaction with various viewpoints. This series seeks to address this need by including not only key, ground-breaking works, but also significant responses to these. This allows the student to appreciate the process of scholarly development through interaction.

The series is also directed toward scholars. In a period of burgeoning knowledge and significant publication in many places and languages around the world, this series will endeavor to make easily accessible significant, but at times hard to find, contributions. Each volume will contain essays, articles, extracts, and the like, presenting in a manageable scope the growth and development of one of a number of different aspects of Old Testament studies. Most volumes will contain previously published material, with synthetic essays by the editor(s) of the individual volume. Some volumes, however, are expected to contain significant, previously unpublished works. To facilitate access to students and scholars, all entries will appear in English and will be newly typeset. If students are excited by the study of Scripture and scholars are encouraged in amicable dialogue, this series would have fulfilled its purpose.

DAVID W. BAKER, *series editor*
Ashland Theological Seminary

Publisher's Note

Articles republished here are reprinted without alteration, except for minor matters of style not affecting meaning. Page numbers of the original publication are marked with double brackets (⟦267⟧, for example). Other editorial notes or supplementations are also marked with double brackets, including editorially-supplied translations of foreign words. Footnotes are numbered consecutively throughout each article, even when the original publication used another system. No attempt has been made to bring transliteration systems into conformity with a single style.

EDITOR'S PREFACE

The title of this volume is, of course, taken from 2 Kgs 6:1, where the prophetic group about Elisha point out that their accommodation is too cramped. It seemed an apt comment on the capacity of any proposed volume to house an adequate representation of the work that has recently been done on Israelite prophecy. To this I now have to add the all-too-ironic confession that the so-called pre-classical prophets (including Elisha and his colleagues) could not be accommodated in the present volume. Let no one complain about being misled by the subtitle when the title is so honest! Time, space and, to a certain extent, homogeneity were important considerations. Occasionally the pre-classical prophets slip in, but, if I may misuse the serious terminology of some recent prophets study, they are "peripheral" and the classical prophets are "central" to our study. The chief purpose of this assemblage is to provide the user with a sampling of issues and approaches in prophets study during the past couple of decades. So much of interest has been written that a compendium of this sort seemed both more desirable and more manageable than a digest of formative contributions to the subject since the publication of Bernhard Duhm's *Die Theologie der Propheten* in 1875. An account of the century since Duhm's book, with some updating, is attempted in the introductory chapter.

Apart from the framework chapters by the present writer, there are thirty-six items of varying length, and they divide almost equally between journal articles and excerpts from volumes (some of these of composite authorship). Naturally, they represent one individual's selection from within his personal reading, and this itself accounts for only a fraction of the vast scholarly output on the prophets, whether since 1875 or since 1975. A partial corrective to the inevitable distortions will be found in the "Additional Reading" lists which follow the short section introductions. The seriously disaffected may even be able to construct alternative prospectuses from them. I hope that my groupings of the selected items will be helpful. It will be apparent at several places in the volume that I take with great seriousness the study of Near Eastern (non-Israelite) prophecy as background to the Israelite phenomenon, so that the first short section

("The Near Eastern Background") was unavoidable. A proper treatment of "The Message of the Prophets" would, of course, require at least a volume of the present proportions. But though representation of this aspect of prophecy was essential, reasons are given in the appropriate place for confining part 2 to a couple of items. Without doubt, part 3 ("The Art of Prophecy") is the mixed bag in the volume. Equally, it conveys best of all an impression of the kaleidoscopic character of recent prophets study. Parts 4 ("Prophecy and Society") and 5 ("The Developing Tradition") likewise have their contents subdivided, though they are not so diverse in their subject matter. The question of the cessation or otherwise of prophecy and the interpretation of the biblical prophets in Jewish and Christian antiquity, addressed in part 6 ("Prophecy after the Prophets"), represent but one way in which the bridge-building commended in the final essay of part 7 ("Present Trends and Future Directions") might be achieved.

It is my pleasure to thank David Baker as series editor and Jim Eisenbraun as publisher for their warm encouragement since my enlisting, and for their gentle nudging when, at a safe transatlantic distance, I may have missed the occasional reveille. The volume is dedicated with affection and appreciation to my son Graham, who is in the second year of his Religious Studies course at Lancaster University.

ROBERT P. GORDON
University of Cambridge

ABBREVIATIONS

General

A	Preliminary Louvre Museum siglum for Mari tablets
Ant.	Josephus, *Antiquities*
ANE	Ancient Near East
AT	Alten Testament (German for Old Testament)
CH	Code of Hammurabi
ET	English translation
FS	Festschrift
JB	Jerusalem Bible
JPS(V)	Jewish Publication Society (Version)
LXX	Septuagint
MT	Masoretic Text
NEB	New English Bible
NIV	New International Version
RSV	Revised Standard Version

Books and Periodicals

AASF	Annales Academiae Scientiarum Fennicae
AB	Anchor Bible
ABL	R. F. Harper, *Assyrian and Babylonian Letters*
AfO	*Archiv für Orientforschung*
AHw	W. von Soden, *Akkadisches Handwörterbuch*
AJSL	*American Journal of Semitic Languages and Literature*
An(at.)St	*Anatolian Studies*
AnBib	Analecta Biblica
ANET	J. B. Pritchard (ed.), *Ancient Near Eastern Texts Relating to the Old Testament* (3d ed.)
AnOr	Analecta Orientalia
AO	*Der Alte Orient*
AOAT	Alter Orient und Altes Testament
AP	Cowley, *Aramaic Papyri of the Fifth Century* B.C.
ARM	Archives royales de Mari

ARMT	Archives royales de Mari Textes
ASTI	*Annual of the Swedish Theological Institute*
AT	D. J. Wiseman, *The Alalakh Tablets*
ATD	Das Alte Testament Deutsch
BA	*Biblical Archaeologist*
BASOR	*Bulletin of the American Schools of Oriental Research*
BETL	Bibliotheca ephemeridum theologicarum lovaniensium
BEvT(h)	Beiträge zur evangelischen Theologie
BHS	*Biblia Hebraica Stuttgartensia*
BibIll	*Biblical Illustrator*
BibOr	Biblica et Orientalia
B(i)K(i)	*Bibel und Kirche*
BiOr	*Bibliotheca orientalis*
BK(AT)	Biblischer Kommentar: Altes Testament
BN	*Biblische Notizen*
BRM	Babylonian Records in the Library of J. Pierpont Morgan
BTB	*Biblical Theology Bulletin*
BWANT	Beiträge zur Wissenschaft vom Alten und Neuen Testament
BWL	W. G. Lambert, *Babylonian Wisdom Literature*
BZ	*Biblische Zeitschrift*
BZAW	Beihefte zur ZAW
CAD	*The Assyrian Dictionary of the Oriental Institute of the University of Chicago*
CAT	Commentaire de l'Ancien Testament
CBOTS	Coniectanea Biblica Old Testament Series
CBQ	*Catholic Biblical Quarterly*
CBQMS	Catholic Biblical Quarterly Monograph Series
DISO	C.-F. Jean and J. Hoftijzer, *Dictionnaire des inscriptions sémitiques de l'ouest*
DSB	Daily Study Bible
Ebib	Études bibliques
Enc.	*Encounter*
Enc. Miqr.	*Encyclopaedia Miqra'it*
ErFor	Erträge der Forschung
E(r)I(sr)	Eretz-Israel
ETL	*Ephemerides theologicae lovanienses*
EvT(h)	*Evangelische Theologie*
E(xp)T(im)	*Expository Times*
FOTL	The Forms of Old Testament Literature
FRLANT	Forschungen zur Religion und Literatur des Alten und Neuen Testaments
F(z)B	Forschung zur Bibel
GGA	Göttingische Gelehrte Anzeigen
GK(C)	E. Kautzsch (ed.), *Gesenius' Hebrew Grammar* (trans. A. E. Cowley)
HAT	Handbuch zum Alten Testament
HKAT	Handkommentar zum Alten Testament

HSM	Harvard Semitic Monographs
HSS	*Harvard Semitic Studies*
HTR	*Harvard Theological Review*
HUCA	*Hebrew Union College Annual*
IB	*Interpreter's Bible*
ICC	International Critical Commentary
Int	*Interpretation*
ITS	*Innsbrucker theologische Studien*
JAAR	*Journal of the American Academy of Religion*
JANES(CU)	*Journal of the Ancient Near Eastern Society (of Columbia University)*
JAOS	*Journal of the American Oriental Society*
JBL	*Journal of Biblical Literature*
JCS	*Journal of Cuneiform Studies*
JEA	*Journal of Egyptian Archaeology*
JEN	Joint Expedition with the Iraq Museum at Nuzi
JJS	*Journal of Jewish Studies*
JNES	*Journal of Near Eastern Studies*
JNSL	*Journal of Northwest Semitic Languages*
JQR	*Jewish Quarterly Review*
JRAI	*Journal of the Royal Anthropological Institute of Great Britain and Ireland*
JSem	*Journal for Semitics*
JSOT	*Journal for the Study of the Old Testament*
JSOTS(up)(S)	Journal for the Study of the Old Testament Supplement Series
JTS	*Journal of Theological Studies*
KAI	H. Donner and W. Röllig, *Kanaanäische und aramäische Inschriften*
KAT	Kommentar zum Alten Testament
KB(L)	L. Koehler and W. Baumgartner, *Lexicon in Veteris Testamenti libros*
KUB	Keilschrifturkunden aus Boghazköi
LCL	Loeb Classical Library
MDB	*Monde du Bible*
NCB(C)	New Century Bible (Commentary)
NEB	Neue Echter Bibel
NICOT	New International Commentary on the Old Testament
NKZ	*Neue kirchliche Zeitschrift*
OBO	Orbis biblicus et orientalis
OTL	Old Testament Library
OTS	*Oudtestamentische Studiën*
OTWSA	Ou-Testamentiese Werkgemeenskap in Suid-Afrika (Pretoria)
RA	*Revue d'assyriologie et d'archéologie orientale*
RB	*Revue biblique*
R(el)S(t)R(ev)	*Religious Studies Review*
SBLASP	Society of Biblical Literature Abstracts and Seminar Papers
SBLDS	SBL Dissertation Series
SBLMS	SBL Monograph Series
SBLSP	SBL Seminar Papers
SBT(h)	Studies in Biblical Theology

SEÅ	*Svensk exegetisk Årsbok*
SEAsiaJT	*South East Asia Journal of Theology*
SJOT	*Scandinavian Journal of the Old Testament*
SJT	*Scottish Journal of Theology*
StBTh	*Studia Biblica et Theologica*
SVT	Vetus Testamentum Supplements
TB	*Tyndale Bulletin*
TD	*Theology Digest*
TDOT	G. J. Botterweck and H. Ringgren (eds.), *Theological Dictionary of the Old Testament*
T(h)B(ei)	*Theologische Beiträge*
T(h)LZ	*Theologische Literaturzeitung*
ThR	*Theologische Rundschau*
ThS(tud)	*Theologische Studiën*
TU	Texte und Untersuchungen
TUAT	Texte aus der Umwelt des Alten Testaments
TWAT	G. J. Botterweck and H. Ringgren (eds.), *Theologisches Wörterbuch zum Alten Testament*
TZ	*Theologische Zeitschrift*
UF	*Ugarit-Forschungen*
UT	C. H. Gordon, *Ugaritic Textbook*
UUÅ	Uppsala universitetsårsskrift
VF	*Verkündigung und Forschung*
VT	*Vetus Testamentum*
VTSup	Vetus Testamentum Supplements
WBC	Word Biblical Commentary
WMANT	Wissenschaftliche Monographien zum Alten und Neuen Testament
WO	*Die Welt des Orients*
WUNT	Wissenschaftliche Untersuchungen zum Neuen Testament
ZA	*Zeitschrift für Assyriologie*
ZAW	*Zeitschrift für die Alttestamentliche Wissenschaft*
ZB	Zürcher Bibelkommentare
ZDMG	*Zeitschrift der deutschen morgenländischen Gesellschaft*
ZDPV	*Zeitschrift des deutschen Palästina-Vereins*
ZT(h)K	*Zeitschrift für Theologie und Kirche*

Introduction

A Story of Two Paradigm Shifts

ROBERT P. GORDON

From 1875 to 1975

If we follow the story-line of the Old Testament, the prophets may be seen as representing a second phase in the development of Israelite religion. Many, and certainly the "classical" prophets, come from the period beginning in the mid–eighth century and ending with the Babylonian exile. In the late nineteenth century, however, nothing less than a paradigm shift—the first of two possible candidates that we shall observe in this review—occurred when the so-called Graf-Wellhausen hypothesis on Pentateuchal origins began to establish itself as the new orthodoxy. Now, following the earlier observations of scholars such as W. Vatke,[1] the law of Moses was seen as the starting-point for post-exilic Judaism rather than for the religion of pre-exilic Israel. The law was later than the prophets[2] and could not fulfil the role traditionally ascribed to it. Since the Psalter was not immune to the same centrifugal forces, with late and even Maccabean dates being proposed for many psalms, the overall effect was to leave the classical prophets in splendid isolation. They were no longer inheritors of long-established traditions of belief which it was their task to amplify and apply to the needs of their own generation. Rather, they were men of vision, the truly creative element in the development of Israelite religion, and those responsible,

---

1. Cf. his *Die biblische Theologie wissenschaftlich dargestellt*, vol. 1: *Die Religion des Alten Testamentes nach den kanonischen Büchern entwickelt* (Berlin: Bethge, 1835) 204, where the traditional role of the Pentateuchal laws in the establishing of Israelite religion is discounted.

2. Cf. J. Wellhausen, *Prolegomena to the History of Israel* (Edinburgh, 1885) 1 (Eng. trans. of *Prolegomena zur Geschichte Israels* [2d ed.; Berlin: Reimer, 1883], which first appeared as *Geschichte Israels*, vol. 1 [Berlin, 1878]).

in particular, for the emergence of "ethical monotheism" in Israel. Two excerpts from Wellhausen's *Prolegomena zur Geschichte Israels* will express this view in characteristically vivid terms:

> After the spirit of the oldest men of God, Moses at the head of them, had been in a fashion laid to sleep in institutions, it sought and found in the prophets a new opening; the old fire burst out like a volcano through the strata which once, too, rose fluid from the deep, but now were fixed and dead (Eng. trans., p. 398).

> It is a vain imagination to suppose that the prophets expounded and applied the law . . . the voice of the prophets, always sounding when there is need for it, occupies the place which, according to the prevailing view, should have been filled by the law: this living command of Jehovah is all he knows of, and not any testament given once for all (Eng. trans., p. 399).

Wellhausen's interest in Hebrew and the Old Testament owed much to the influence of Heinrich Ewald (1803–75), under whom he studied at Göttingen.[3] Ewald's views were given literary form in the two volumes of his *Die Propheten des Alten Bundes* (1840–41) and in his *Geschichte des Volkes Israel* (1843–59). Another student of Ewald's at that time was Bernhard Duhm, and, while Wellhausen may be regarded as the apostle of the new dispensation, his Göttingen contemporary was first into print on a major Old Testament theme—Wellhausen's earlier preoccupations were with the text of the books of Samuel (1871) and the Pharisees and Sadducees (1874)—and he also subsequently made more of the study of the prophets than did Wellhausen. Duhm's volume on prophecy, published in 1875, would have been not unworthy of Wellhausen. The prophets are here presented as seeking to break the cultic bonds which held Israelite religion prisoner, while Mic 6:1–8, with its apparent repudiation of the cult in favor of a kind of ethical idealism, is regarded as the most important section in all the prophets. Here we are permitted a glimpse into the innermost character of the Israelite prophetic movement.[4] Religion was about ethics and morality before God and in the life of the community. With Micah, Hebrew prophecy began to emphasize morality as a requirement laid upon the individual Israelite, and in that respect it anticipated the Christian emphasis on right relationship with God.[5] Duhm's portrayal of the prophets as self-consciously "theologians,"

3. See W. Zimmerli, *The Law and the Prophets: A Study of the Meaning of the Old Testament* (Oxford: Blackwell, 1965) 19–22.

4. *Die Theologie der Propheten als Grundlage für die innere Entwicklungsgeschichte der israelitischen Religion* (Bonn: Marcus, 1875) 183.

5. Ibid., 188.

as implied in the title of his book, is seriously overstated in this regard, but it is characteristic of the newer approach to prophecy. At about the same time the Dutch scholar Abraham Kuenen was writing in similar vein:

> What did the Israelitish prophets accomplish? What was the result of their work, and what value are we to assign to it? *Ethical monotheism* is their creation. They have themselves ascended to the belief in one only, holy, and righteous God, who realises his will, or moral good, in the world, and they have, by preaching and writing, made that belief the inalienable property of our race.[6]

This lionizing of the peerless prophets inevitably gave way to more realistic assessments of their importance for Israelite religion. For even if, for the sake of argument, the historical traditions of the Old Testament are not invoked, it remains clear that the eighth-century prophets are already acknowledging traditions and standards, to which, indeed, they appeal in their critique of contemporary social and religious practice. To that extent they are self-confessed inheritors of established tradition. Moreover, the discounting of priestly law as being largely post-prophetic—a truly self-denying ordinance in the light of our present understanding of priestly tradition—still leaves other representatives of Israelite law (in particular the Decalogue and the Book of the Covenant) that are capable of fulfilling the required role.[7] Again, various modern approaches to Old Testament study (e.g., tradition-history, form-criticism, archaeology) have sought to recover some of the geographical features lost to sight when the historical reliability of the pre-prophetic traditions came into question.

While it is impossible to do justice to all the aspects of modern prophets study that would rightly claim mention in a survey chapter of this kind, some attempt will be made to highlight the main developments since the late nineteenth century, and this by way of background to the presentation in this volume of a sampling of the more illuminative approaches to the subject that have been published since 1975.

Prophetic Psychology

The considerable interest in "prophetic psychology" that developed in the early decades of the twentieth century marked a shift from the more recent emphasis on the prophets as theologians and moralists. Of the

---

6. *The Prophets and Prophecy in Israel: An Historical and Critical Enquiry* (London: Longmans, Green, 1877) 585 (Eng. trans. of *De Profeten en de Profetie onder Israël* [2 vols; Leiden: Engels, 1875]).

7. Cf. Zimmerli, *The Law and the Prophets*, 30.

several reasons for this concern with what might be regarded as one of the more eccentric aspects of prophecy, the first is provided by the biblical texts themselves in that they associate a variety of conditions and experiences—for example ecstasy, dream, vision, translocation—with the exercise of prophecy. Even the Hebrew verb usually translated 'prophesy' (*nbʾ*) occasionally denotes some kind of ecstatic behavior (see 1 Sam 10:5–13; 18:10; 19:20–24), while in three places prophesying is even linked with madness (2 Kgs 9:11; Jer 29:26; Hos 9:7). Now, since ecstasy was evidently a common characteristic of Canaanite "prophecy," as is suggested by the story of the contest between Elijah and the Baalistic prophets in 1 Kings 18, the possibility of a Canaanite derivation for Hebrew prophecy had to be considered. Again, if ecstasy was a distinguishing feature of prophetic behavior, perhaps the explanation of the special insights associated with the prophets lies here? And, on the other hand, the fact that ecstasy figures little among the "classical" prophets—and not at all in some cases—would perhaps support a distinction between ecstatic prophets and "reform" prophets?

While the period 1914–50 may be seen as the heyday of the "prophetic psychology" quest, interest in the subject extends back into the previous century. In his 1892 commentary on Isaiah Duhm had given greater prominence to the inner life of the prophet(s) than he had allowed in his theologically focused study of seventeen years earlier.[8] Gustav Hölscher's 1914 volume on the prophets, influenced by the *Physiologische Psychologie* and *Völkerpsychologie* of Wilhelm Wundt, paid special attention to the question of prophetic psychology.[9] Hölscher regarded the whole Israelite prophetic tradition as exhibiting in various degrees the characteristics of ecstatic-mantic prophecy. Prophets, generally speaking, uttered their oracles while in a trance, which was sometimes brought on with the help of music (cf. 1 Sam 10:5; 2 Kgs 3:15) or mantic rites. Hölscher knew of the Egyptian Wen-Amon text, first published by W. Golénischeff in 1899, which recounts an ecstatic experience by a servant of the king of Byblos in the eleventh century B.C.,[10] and he was encouraged to think that the origins of Israelite ecstatic prophecy could be traced to Syria and Asia Minor. Israel therefore came upon "ecstasy"

---

8. B. Duhm, *Das Buch Jesaia* (HKAT 3/1; Göttingen: Vandenhoeck & Ruprecht, 1892 [5th ed. 1968]); cf. H. Gunkel, *The Expositor* 9/1 (1924) 357 (see n. 13 below), commenting on this aspect of Duhm's commentary.

9. *Die Profeten: Untersuchungen zur Religionsgeschichte Israels* (Leipzig: Hinrichs, 1914).

10. See W. Golénischeff, "Papyrus hiératique de la Collection W. Golénischeff contenant la description du voyage de l'égyptien Ounou-Amon en Phénicie," in *Recueil de travaux relatifs à la philologie et à l'archéologie égyptiennes et assyriennes* 21 (n.s. 5) (ed. G. Maspero; Paris: Librairie Emile Bouillon, 1899) 74–102.

after the settlement in Canaan, and that is why we hear of the "sons of the prophets" from the eleventh century onward. But the same movement gave birth to the higher forms of prophecy associated with the "classical" prophets. In a volume published in 1924 Hölscher applied his insights to Ezekiel who, as a good example of an ecstatic prophet, was believed to have expressed his ideas in poetic meter and so was credited with only a small proportion of the material in the canonical book.[11]

For Hermann Gunkel the essential element for the understanding of the prophets was an insight into the private, mystical experiences which they mediated to their hearers. Already in 1888 Gunkel had published a dissertation on conceptions of the Holy Spirit in the New Testament, in which he discussed the relationship between the "pneumatic" dimension of apostolic Christianity and the formation of early Christian doctrine.[12] In three essays published in 1914 on the subject of "the secret experiences of the prophets" Gunkel argued that ecstasy is basic to prophecy in all its manifestations, though he divided between the non-communicative ecstasy represented in a passage like 1 Sam 10:5–13 and more profound experiences which enabled prophets to deliver informative oracles on request or, at a still higher level, to speak in the manner of the classical prophets.[13] In the latter case, what a prophet announced as the word of God was first encountered in a mystical experience and then communicated in appropriate language to the prophet's hearers.

A succession of scholars pursued the psychology quest in the following decades. In the United Kingdom the names of T. H. Robinson[14] and his namesake H. Wheeler Robinson[15] are especially noteworthy. The former has also given us "a day in the life of a prophet":

> He might be mingling with the crowd, sometimes on ordinary days, sometimes on special occasions. Suddenly something would happen to him. His eye would become fixed, strange convulsions would seize upon his limbs, the form of his speech would change. Men would recognise that the Spirit had fallen upon him. The fit would pass, and he would

---

11. *Hesekiel, der Dichter und das Buch: Eine literarkritische Untersuchung* (BZAW 39; Giessen: Alfred Töpelmann, 1924).

12. *Die Wirkungen des heiligen Geistes nach der populären Anschauung der apostolischen Zeit und nach der Lehre des Apostels Paulus* (Göttingen: Vandenhoeck & Ruprecht, 1888).

13. "Die geheimen Erfahrungen der Propheten," pp. xvii–xxxiv of the Einleitungen written by Gunkel for H. Schmidt, *Die grossen Propheten* (Göttingen: Vandenhoeck & Ruprecht, 1914 [2d ed. 1923]). The section was published as three essays, in English translation, in *The Expositor* 9/1 (1924) 356–66, 427–35; 9/2 (1924) 23–32.

14. *Prophecy and the Prophets in Ancient Israel* (London: Duckworth, 1923 [2d ed. 1953]).

15. See his chapter entitled "The Psychology of Inspiration" in *Inspiration and Revelation in the Old Testament* (Oxford: Clarendon, 1946) 173–86.

tell to those who stood around the things which he had seen and
heard.[16]

In various studies published in the 1930s and 1940s Johannes Lindblom
attempted to unravel the term "ecstasy" in relation to Israelite prophecy.
In an article published in 1939 he distinguished between two kinds of
religious experience.[17] The "introspektive" is characteristic of the mystic, but the experiences of the Israelite prophets, for which Lindblom
uses the term "zirkumspektive," differ in that they do not involve the
same merging of the subject with the divine, being open to "objective"
divine revelation which may work through external agents such as sacred texts or historical events. Various distinguishing features between
the mystical and the prophetic are listed. Scholars like Sigmund Mowinckel,[18] H. H. Rowley[19] and G. Widengren[20] gave the subject their attention in the same period, but interest began to wane thereafter, so
that when Lindblom's 1962 volume devoted its first 65 pages to a discussion of the psychology and mechanics of prophecy, drawing upon many
extra-biblical comparisons, from Julian of Norwich to the "sleeping
preachers" of Finland, it came as a belated summary of a phase that
seemed to have run its course.[21] Throughout the period of the "prophetic psychology" quest there were those who, like Rowley, denied that
there was any significant ecstatic dimension to the bulk of classical biblical prophecy. And it has to be conceded that, when prophets are
represented as sometimes pleading and even arguing with God, the usefulness of ecstasy as an explanation of their experience becomes questionable. Even so, there has been, since the 1980s, a renewal of interest,
on the part of some scholars, in psychological aspects of prophecy,[22] and
to the extent that this may challenge a growing tendency to approach
the subject of prophecy in terms of prophetic books only, and to the exclusion of flesh and blood prophets, on the ground that their *ipsissima*

---

16. T. H. Robinson, *Prophecy*, 50. I owe this reference in the first instance to J. H.
Hayes, *An Introduction to Old Testament Study* (Nashville: Abingdon, 1979) 255–56.

17. "Die Religion der Propheten und die Mystik," *ZAW* n.s. 16 (1939) 65–74.

18. " 'The Spirit' and the 'Word' in the Pre-exilic Reforming Prophets," *JBL* 53 (1934)
199–227.

19. "The Nature of Prophecy in the Light of Recent Study," *HTR* 38 (1945) 1–38. Rowley plays down the psychological factor in prophecy: "What is really vital is the relation of
the prophet and of his word to God" (p. 38).

20. *Literary and Psychological Aspects of the Hebrew Prophets* (Uppsala: Almqvist & Wiksell,
1948).

21. *Prophecy in Ancient Israel* (Oxford: Blackwell, 1962); cf. his earlier *Profetismen i Israel*
(Uppsala: Almqvist & Wiksell, 1934).

22. See below ("The New Generation," pp. 19–26).

verba are no longer identifiable within the books, the interest may confer a more general benefit.

Prophecy and Cult

It appears from the prophetic books of the Old Testament that the prophets could be extremely critical of the cultic observances of their contemporaries (cf. Isa 1:11–17; Jer 7:21–28; Hos 6:6; Amos 5:21–27; Mic 6:6–8). On the other hand, 1 Sam 10:5 clearly links its band of ecstatic prophets with a cult center at Gibeath-elohim. Isaiah's "call" is located in a temple setting (Isa 6:1), and the prophets Jeremiah and Ezekiel are given priestly pedigrees in the books that bear their names (Jer 1:1; Ezek 1:3). Moreover, some of the prophets, and not least their post-exilic representatives, were very interested in the well-being of the temple and its worship (Hag 1:7–8; Zech 2:14–16[10–12]; Mal 1:6–2:9). There therefore seem to be grounds for questioning the simple prophet-priest polarity that has often been assumed on the basis of the prophetic diatribes against the cult. Again Hermann Gunkel made a decisive contribution when he observed the presence in certain psalms of oracular-sounding features more characteristic of the prophetic writings, though his conviction that the psalms were used mainly in private devotions prevented him from drawing conclusions about Israelite cultic praxis.[23] The point was, however, taken up by Mowinckel who provided a theoretical basis for the view, already expressed by William Robertson Smith and Hölscher,[24] that there were cult prophets in ancient Israel.[25] Mowinckel noted that in a number of psalms God speaks in the first person, in a manner reminiscent of the prophetic oracle (e.g., Psalms 60, 82), and he connected these first-person pronouncements with cult-prophets who addressed individuals or congregations of worshippers in the name of God on occasions of personal or national crisis or on festal and royal occasions.[26] (A narrative illustration of the function envisaged is provided by 2 Chr 20:14–17 where the Levite Jahaziel delivers an oracle of salvation in a time of national crisis.)

Mowinckel went on to identify certain of the "writing prophets" such as Habakkuk, Haggai and Zechariah as cultic prophets. Alfred Haldar,

23. H. Gunkel, "Psalmen," in *Die Religion in Geschichte und Gegenwart* ([1913]; 2d ed.; Tübingen: Mohr [Paul Siebeck], 1930) vol. 4, cols. 1609–27.

24. Cf. W. H. Bellinger, *Psalmody and Prophecy* (JSOTSup 27; Sheffield: JSOT Press, 1984) 13.

25. *Psalmenstudien*, vol. 3: *Kultprophetie und prophetische Psalmen* (Kristiania: Dybwad, 1923).

26. See also Mowinckel's *The Psalms in Israel's Worship* (Oxford: Blackwell, 1962) 2.53–73 (Eng. trans. of *Offersang og Sangoffer* [Oslo: Aschehoug, 1951]).

in his 1945 monograph, not only assumed the existence of cultic prophecy in Israel but also presented this as part of a "fundamentally homogeneous phenomenology" in the ancient Near East.[27] Ivan Engnell's study of the call of Isaiah, published in 1949, found supporting evidence for the view that the prophet's call is set in the context of the New Year festival, as this had been envisaged by a number of scholars.[28] The call of Jeremiah was treated in a not dissimilar fashion by H. Graf Reventlow fourteen years later when he argued that a cultic ceremony of ordination is reflected in Jeremiah 1.[29] In 1971, G. W. Ahlström argued that the book of Joel represents a collection of sayings by a cult-prophet living at the end of the sixth century B.C.[30]

The cult prophets have also been a major theme for A. R. Johnson who contended that they functioned in the dual role of intercessors for the congregation and as spokesmen for Yahweh.[31] Johnson's earlier views are rehearsed and developed in his 1979 volume where, as previously, he is mainly interested in cultic prophecy as it is reflected in the Psalter, rather than in drawing the "writing prophets" into the cultic orbit. Here he argues for pre-monarchical ("Settlement") dates for Psalms 81 and 95 and so makes the cultic prophet a functionary already in the earliest phases of Israelite history.[32] Interest in cultic prophecy persists, albeit on a limited scale, for, although the direct evidence in the form either of narrative attestation in the historical books or of clear rubrication in the Psalter is inconclusive, it remains the case that some features in the Psalter, for example the dramatic switches in mood in some psalms (cf. Pss 6:8/9[7/8]; 22:22/23[21/22]), are very satisfactorily explained by this hypothesis. Bellinger's 1984 monograph illustrates the point, for, in concentrating upon the "certainty-of-hearing" sections in certain individual and community laments in the psalms, Bellinger argues quite plausibly that a prophetic oracle is generally presupposed.[33] At the same time, he stresses that the title of the functionary is of little account in such cases; it is the function that is important.

27. *Associations of Cult Prophets among the Ancient Semites* (Uppsala: Almqvist & Wiksell, 1945).

28. *The Call of Isaiah: An Exegetical and Comparative Study* (Uppsala: Almqvist & Wiksell, 1949).

29. *Liturgie und prophetisches Ich bei Jeremia* (Gütersloh: Gerd Mohn, 1963) 24–77.

30. *Joel and the Temple Cult of Jerusalem* (VTSup 21; Leiden: Brill, 1971).

31. *The Cultic Prophet in Ancient Israel* ([1944]; 2d ed.; Cardiff: University of Wales Press, 1962) 58–59.

32. *The Cultic Prophet and Israel's Psalmody* (Cardiff: University of Wales Press, 1979) 5–22.

33. Bellinger, *Psalmody and Prophecy*, 78–82.

A cultic connection along another plane has been envisaged by those scholars who have seen the "national covenant" between God and Israel as a major structuring feature of prophetic thought. The hypothesis of a pre-monarchical tribal amphictyony in Israel, as first propounded by Martin Noth,[34] and the supposition that second millennium treaty texts offer a secular analogue to the Israelite covenant concept, and notably in its Sinaitic form, helped restore covenant for a time to its pre-Wellhausenian position at the head of the religious and theological traditions of Israel.[35] Despite the fact that specific references to a covenant between God and Israel are rare in the pre-exilic prophets, there is much else that could with goodwill be read against such a background. Taking Deut 18:15–19 as their basic text, a number of scholars have postulated the office of prophetic covenant mediator (or "law speaker") for the pre-monarchical period. The covenant mediator was thought to function in relation to the whole of the tribal federation as guardian of its legal traditions deriving from its covenant with Yahweh. The exercise of the office was specially linked with an annual covenant renewal festival. Some sort of cultic involvement on the part of this Mosaic prophet (cf. Deut 18:15) was therefore envisaged, and the residual evidence of this long-standing connection was found in various speech-forms that were identified in the books associated with the classical prophets. As partial compensation for the absence of explicit covenant references in these books, the so-called "prophetic law-suit" (cf. Isa 1:2–3, 10–20) was held to presuppose a national covenant to which the prophets made appeal as they called their hearers back to the requirements of the covenant faith. Current scholarship, however, has little space for the Nothian amphictyonic idea, and the relevance of the second-millennium Near Eastern treaties is widely regarded as having been somewhat neutralized in the course of further research which has given more attention to the treaties of the first millennium for the light that they may shed on the biblical covenant traditions. Such covenant presence as there may be in the prophets has even been attributed to Deuteronomistic theologizing, which itself is said to have taken inspiration from the secular treaty-making of the neo-Assyrian period.[36]

---

34. *Das System der zwölf Stämme Israels* (BWANT 4/1; Stuttgart: Kohlhammer, 1930).

35. For general discussion and evaluation see D. J. McCarthy, *Treaty and Covenant: A Study in Form in the Ancient Oriental Documents and in the Old Testament* (2d ed.; AnBib 21A; Rome: Pontifical Biblical Institute, 1978) 1–24.

36. See L. Perlitt, *Bundestheologie im Alten Testament* (WMANT 36; Neukirchen-Vluyn: Neukirchener Verlag, 1969) 282–83; R. E. Clements, *Prophecy and Tradition* (Oxford: Blackwell, 1975) 8–23, 41–57; E. W. Nicholson, *God and His People: Covenant and Theology in the Old Testament* (Oxford: Clarendon, 1986) 83–117.

Generally speaking, the notion of a fundamental opposition between prophecy and cult has fallen into disfavor in modern Old Testament scholarship, even if a clearly defined figure of "cult prophet" has
not been universally recognized. (Even so, already in 1951 Otto Eissfeldt
was deprecating a tendency in some quarters to treat all the biblical
prophets as cultic officials.[37]) The "writing prophets" have, in any case,
been perceived as probably more closely linked with the cult than their
anti-cult utterances would suggest, since these are interpreted more correctly as denunciations of malpractice than as expressions of outright rejection of the cult as such. On the other hand, the mere use of liturgical
forms by prophets is now less likely to be regarded as, by itself, the proof
of a prophet's close cultic attachment.

Prophetic Speech

It was Robert Lowth (1710–87), sometime Professor of Poetry at Oxford
and Bishop of London, who demonstrated that Hebrew poetry has a basic parallelistic structure,[38] and also that the prophetic books are largely
poetic in form.[39] Others had made observations of the sort before him,[40]
but it was Lowth who convincingly demonstrated the case and so exercised a decisive influence upon the study of Hebrew poetry in modern
biblical scholarship. And if modern scholarship has regressed into a
deep uncertainty as to how to describe Hebrew poetry or how, indeed,
to distinguish Hebrew poetry from Hebrew prose,[41] it is instructive to
note that, whereas some nineteenth-century scholars were happy to follow Lowth in his conclusions about the prophets—as, for example, Wilhelm Gesenius in his three-volume commentary on Isaiah[42]—others in
the same period were disinclined to do so. In the 1880s T. K. Cheyne was
not sufficiently persuaded by Lowth's insights to let them affect his com-

---

37. "The Prophetic Literature," in *The Old Testament and Modern Study* (ed. H. H. Rowley; Oxford: Clarendon, 1951) 159.

38. *De Sacra Poesi Hebraeorum: Praelectiones Academicae Oxonii Habitae* (Oxford: Clarendon, 1753).

39. *Isaiah: A New Translation; With a Preliminary Dissertation, and Notes Critical, Philological, and Explanatory* (London: Nichols, 1778); see also lectures 18–21 of *De Sacra Poesi*
(= pp. 166–215). For a biography of Lowth see B. Hepworth, *Robert Lowth* (Boston: Twayne
[G. K. Hall], 1978).

40. See R. P. Gordon, "'Isaiah's Wild Measure': R. M. McCheyne," *Expository Times* 103
(1992) 235–37 (235).

41. Cf. J . L. Kugel, *The Idea of Biblical Poetry: Parallelism and Its History* (New Haven: Yale
University Press, 1981).

42. *Der Prophet Jesaia: Philologisch-kritischer und historischer Commentar über den Jesaia*
(Leipzig: Vogel, 1820–21).

mentary on Isaiah.[43] Nor were the scholars responsible for the revision of the Old Testament in the Revised Version of 1885 convinced that Lowth's "poetry" was more than the elevated prose to which biblical speech tended to resort in its more exalted phases:

> In the poetical portions, besides the division into paragraphs, the Revisers have adopted an arrangement in lines, so as to exhibit the parallelism which is characteristic of Hebrew Poetry. But they have not extended this arrangement to the prophetical books, the language of which although frequently marked by parallelism is, except in purely lyrical passages, rather of the nature of lofty and impassioned prose.[44]

The field that Lowth had ploughed in parallel lines lay fairly fallow as far as the prophets were concerned until Duhm produced his commentary on Isaiah, in which he was able to apply his ideas on the metrical nature of Hebrew poetry to the demarcation of speech units and especially to the separation of what he deemed to be original and secondary material.[45] Joseph Blenkinsopp, in paying tribute to Duhm's skill, describes this volume as "the first genuinely modern commentary on a prophetic book."[46]

Gunkel's contribution in this area started with the simple observation that prophecy was originally spoken; figures like Elijah and Elisha are not associated with writing.

> Originally, the prophets were not writers, but became such towards the end of their history. They were originally orators, as can be seen from the expression "Hear!" with which their speeches begin. . . . Their public was the people, either in the market place or in the forecourt of the temple (Jer 7:2).[47]

The prophets received their messages by means of visions and "verbal revelations" (*Wortoffenbarungen*), these latter being expressed in terse and sometimes almost Delphic utterances such as "Lo-ammi" ('Not my people') and "Immanuel" ('God with us'). "In such mysterious words,"

43. *The Prophecies of Isaiah: A New Translation with Commentary and Appendices* (2 vols; London: Kegan Paul, 1880–82); see G. B. Gray, *Isaiah I–XXVII* (ICC; Edinburgh: T. & T. Clark, 1912) lix–lx.

44. "Revisers' Preface to the Old Testament," *The Holy Bible: The Revised Version* (Oxford: Oxford University Press, 1885).

45. Duhm, *Das Buch Jesaia* (5th ed.), 10–15.

46. *A History of Prophecy in Israel* (Philadelphia: Westminster, 1983) 13.

47. "Propheten," in *Die Religion in Geschichte und Gegenwart* (1913; 2d ed.; Tübingen: Mohr [Paul Siebeck], 1930), vol. 4, col. 1546 (Eng. trans. in *Twentieth Century Theology in the Making* [ed. J. Pelikan; London: Fontana / New York: Harper & Row, 1969] 1.61).

says Gunkel, "the literary prophets, imitating the cries of the ancient ecstatics, summed up their ideas."[48] From these laconic beginnings, prophecy developed into the well-fashioned oracles of the canonical books,
and many different speech-forms, from the fields of law and liturgy especially, were subsequently taken up by the prophets and used for the conveying of their message. Already the basic distinction between promise
(*Verheissung*) and threat (*Drohung*) is apparent in Gunkel's discussion.
The addition of the reproach (*Scheltrede*) in explanation of the threat he
regarded as a separate line of development which reflected the increasing prophetic preoccupation with the moral basis of God's dealings with
Israel.[49]

An influential observation of a different kind was made, apparently
independently, by Ludwig Köhler[50] and Johann Lindblom[51] in studies
published in 1923 and 1924. These two scholars identified the frequently
occurring "Thus says the Lord" as a messenger formula whose regular
occurrence in the prophetic writings derives from the conception of the
prophet as a (royal?) messenger announcing the decrees of Yahweh to
his people. The significance of this observation is reflected in von Rad's
comment that, though the messenger formula may not have been first in
time, it is first in importance among the many forms of prophetic
speech.[52] The idea was taken a step further by J. S. Holladay in 1970
when he sought to draw a comparison between Assyrian imperial proto-
col (including treaty-making) in the late ninth century B.C., and subsequently, and prophetic forms of address in Israel.[53] On this view, the
custom of the prophets from Amos onward of addressing not only the
king and court but also the general populace reflects a change in Assyrian imperial policy, beginning in the late ninth century, whereby the
emperor, through the royal heralds, addressed his demands both to the
vassal kings and also to the subject peoples whom they represented.

---

48. Gunkel, "Propheten," col. 1548 (Eng. trans., 65).
49. Gunkel, "Propheten," col. 1553 (Eng. trans., 74).
50. *Deuterojesaja (Jesaja 40–55) stilkritisch untersucht* (BZAW 37; Giessen: Alfred Töpelmann, 1923) 102–5.
51. "Die prophetische Orakelformel," appendix in *Die literarische Gattung der prophetischen Literatur: Eine literargeschichtliche Untersuchung zum Alten Testament* (Uppsala Universitets
Årsskrift, Teologi 1; Uppsala: Lundequistska, 1924) 97–115.
52. *The Message of the Prophets* (London: SCM, 1968) 18 (Eng. trans. of *Die Botschaft der
Propheten* [Munich: Siebenstern-Taschenbuch, 1967]). At the same time, G. M. Tucker notes
that the use of the formula is not restricted to "messages," and that messages do not necessarily begin (or end) with it ("Prophetic Speech," in *Interpreting the Prophets* [ed. J. L. Mays
and P. J. Achtemeier; Philadelphia: Fortress, 1987] 30–31).
53. "Assyrian Statecraft and the Prophets of Israel," *HTR* 63 (1970) 29–51.

Among those who have contributed most significantly on the subject of prophetic speech since Gunkel are C. Westermann,[54] K. Koch[55] and G. M. Tucker.[56] Much effort has gone into attempts to refine Gunkel's observations on the basic oracle form. Westermann, for example, avoids the use of "threat" because he regards the slight implication of hope suggested by the word as unwarranted. His preferred term is *Gerichts-ankündigung* ('announcement of judgment'). This, of course, touches on a basic question about the intentions of the prophets: whether in their preaching they offered their hearers any possibility of avoiding the judgment that they habitually announced in the pre-exilic period. The recognition of basic patterns of prophetic speech, as described by Westermann and Koch especially, has its uses, but the advantage is lost when oracles are bound too closely to form-critical stereotypes, for only a minority within the basic types conform to the original pattern as this is envisaged by the form-critics. The view that oracular forms develop from simplex to complex is the kind of assumption often made in the study of linguistic and literary units, but, as Tucker notes, this does not apply in the case of the "threat" since the "reproach" is a feature of the "threat" in all periods of prophecy.[57] Moreover, the "reproach" some-times features as part of the divine speech, and so cannot simply be re-garded as the prophet's own explanation of the judgment threatened.[58] Again, the tendency to limit oracles of salvation to the exilic and post-exilic periods has been a Procrustean commonplace upon which Wester-mann himself has more recently commented.[59] Questions may also legit-imately be asked about the significance of a prophet's use of this or that form of speech. In particular, does the use of a cultic lament make a prophet a cultic figure any more than his composing of a dirge makes him a professional wailer?[60] However, much more significant than all

54. *Grundformen prophetischer Rede* (Munich: Chr. Kaiser, 1960 [2d ed. 1964]) (Eng. trans. *Basic Forms of Prophetic Speech* [London: Lutterworth / Philadelphia: Westminster, 1967]).

55. *Was ist Formgeschichte? Neue Wege der Bibelexegese* (Neukirchen-Vluyn: Neukirchener Verlag [1964; 2d ed. 1967]; 3d ed. 1974) 223–70 (Eng. trans. *The Growth of the Biblical Tra-dition* (London: A. & C. Black / New York: Scribner's, 1969) 183–220.

56. *Form Criticism of the Old Testament* (Philadelphia: Fortress, 1971).

57. Ibid., 63.

58. Cf. Hayes, *An Introduction*, 277.

59. See his *Prophetische Heilsworte im Alten Testament* (FRLANT 145; Göttingen: Vanden-hoeck & Ruprecht, 1987) 5 (Eng. trans. *Prophetic Oracles of Salvation in the Old Testament* [Louisville: Westminster/John Knox, 1991] 7).

60. Cf. W. McKane in *Tradition and Interpretation* (ed. G. W. Anderson; Oxford: Claren-don, 1979) 168–69; G. Fohrer, "Die Propheten des Alten Testaments im Blickfeld neuer Forschung," in *Studien zur alttestamentlichen Prophetie (1949–1965)* (BZAW 99; Berlin: Alfred Töpelmann, 1967) 20.

this is the way in which the form-critical approach, while not restoring the prophets to their "pre-critical" position of inheritors and interpreters of the Mosaic tradition, has helped to locate them within the socio-religious traditions of Israel, from which they borrowed and upon which they built as they developed their great religious and social themes.

Prophetic Books

There are few clues in the Old Testament as to how the prophetic sayings and traditions were brought together to make up the canonical books with which we are familiar. Somewhat cryptically, Isa 8:16 talks about "fastening up the message" and "sealing the oracle," which may imply the committal to writing of certain of Isaiah's sayings at an early stage (cf. 30:8). Jer 36:1–2 has Yahweh tell Jeremiah to take a scroll and record on it all the oracles that he had received since his commissioning in the reign of Josiah. Thus, on the one hand the text is talking about the writing down of oracles, while on the other it implies that Jeremiah had not done this during his previous twenty years as a prophet. So how did prophetic books achieve their present shape? The question was addressed by T. H. Robinson in his 1923 volume, in which he envisaged four stages of development beginning with short oral units and progressing to "little booklets of oracular matter" (e.g., oracles against foreign nations) and thence to larger units comprising sayings and also traditions about the prophet in question, and finally to the canonical books (Isaiah, Jeremiah, Ezekiel, "The Twelve").[61] This is, then, a process of accretion or aggregation in which the prophetic oracles and traditions are assembled in increasingly large units of text. Scandinavian scholars especially emphasized the role of oral tradition in the process. Mowinckel's 1926 essay on Isaiah and his disciples assumed both a long-lived Isaiah tradition involving various of the other named Old Testament prophets, and a longish period of oral tradition during which the prophet's words were preserved and refashioned according to later circumstances and needs.[62] When he returned to the subject in 1946 Mowinckel reaffirmed the importance of the traditio-historical approach, but he also argued that oral tradition was complemented by written transmission, as in the case of Jeremiah (cf. chaps. 36, 45).[63]

This latter view was confirmed by Widengren in his study of literary and psychological aspects of prophecy, now on the basis of comparisons

---

61. T. H. Robinson, *Prophecy*, 50–59. There are close similarities between Robinson's approach and that outlined in Gunkel, "Propheten," col. 1547 (Eng. trans. 63–64).

62. *Jesaja-Disiplene: Profetien fra Jesaja til Jeremia* (Oslo: Aschehoug, 1926).

63. *Prophecy and Tradition: The Prophetic Books in the Light of the Study of the Growth and History of the Tradition* (Oslo: Dybwad, 1946) 60–62.

with pre-Islamic and early Islamic oral tradition and literary composition.[64] Engnell also found a place for written transmission of prophetic traditions.[65] He divided the prophetic literature into two main types, the liturgical and the *diwan*, the former representing books which give evidence of having been artistic compositions from the beginning. His examples include Joel and Nahum, and also "Deutero-Isaiah," about which Westermann later concluded that the chapters as we have them may go back basically to the prophet himself, and that certain longer poems such as 49:14–26 may have been literary productions from the beginning.[66] A. H. J. Gunneweg maintained the distinction between oral and written by treating them as separate lines of transmission to be attributed to different loci: oral transmission of prophetic sayings was "private" and home-based, while written transmission was "official" and cult-based.[67] Traditio-historical study of the prophets, tracing the prehistory of prophetic themes and traditions, sometimes to particular places or circles of influence, continued in the third quarter of the twentieth century with the German scholars Gerhard von Rad[68] and Hans Walter Wolff[69] prominent in the field.

Attention has also concentrated more recently, per redaction criticism, on the later editing of prophetic collections to reflect the concerns and interests of the receptor community. Discussion is then more likely to be in terms of strata, representing levels of intervention in the text whereby the original material is expanded and adapted to meet the needs of later generations. In his commentary on Amos, Wolff distinguishes three eighth-century literary strata—"all of which for the most part derive from Amos himself and his contemporary disciples"—and three additional strata which are recognizable "by their distinctive language and different intentions" and derive from the following centuries.[70] These last-named comprise Josianic (anti-Bethel) and Deuteronomistic levels

---

64. Widengren, *Literary and Psychological Aspects of the Hebrew Prophets*, 11–56.

65. Engnell, *The Call of Isaiah*, 60–61; idem, "Profetia och tradition: Några synpunkter på ett gammaltestamentligt centralproblem," *SEÅ* 12 (1947) 94–123 (112–13).

66. C. Westermann, *Das Buch Jesaia, 40–66* (ATD 19; Göttingen: Vandenhoeck & Ruprecht, 1966) 26 (Eng. trans. *Isaiah 40–66: A Commentary* [London: SCM, 1969] 28).

67. *Mündliche und schriftliche Tradition der vorexilischen Prophetenbücher als Problem der neueren Prophetenforschung* (FRLANT 73; Göttingen: Vandenhoeck & Ruprecht, 1959) 77–81.

68. Von Rad, *Theologie des Alten Testaments*, vol. 2: *Die Theologie der prophetischen Überlieferungen Israels* (Munich: Chr. Kaiser, 1960) (Eng. trans. *Old Testament Theology*, vol. 2 [Edinburgh and London: Oliver and Boyd, 1965]); idem, *Die Botschaft der Propheten*.

69. *Amos' geistige Heimat* (WMANT 18; Neukirchen-Vluyn: Neukirchener Verlag, 1964) (Eng. trans. *Amos the Prophet: The Man and His Background* [Philadelphia: Fortress, 1973]).

70. *Dodekapropheton 2: Joel und Amos* (BKAT 14/2; Neukirchen-Vluyn: Neukirchener Verlag, 1969) 130 (2d ed. 1975) (Eng. trans. *Joel and Amos* [Philadelphia: Fortress, 1977] 107).

of redaction and a post-exilic "eschatology of salvation," chiefly in 9:11–15. A similar redactional concern marks W. Zimmerli's two-volume commentary on Ezekiel in which much is made of a "school of Ezekiel" that is credited with the transmission and augmentation of the original prophetic core.[71] These two commentaries by Wolff and Zimmerli are representative of a wider interest in the redactional history of the prophetic books. The redactional afterlife of a prophecy becomes important inasmuch as it helps to explain how a prophet's words retain their relevance for generations following that to which they were first addressed. Thus, for example, the Assyrian prophecies of Isaiah are applied to the circumstances of the Babylonian exile,[72] and the message of Hosea to the Northern Kingdom is redirected towards the people of Judah after the fall of Samaria.[73] In certain respects the approach differs little from the long-established scholarly concern with separating prophetic core from scribal husk, but the difference consists in the higher valuation accorded the "husk." This altered outlook is fittingly summed up by W. McKane: "Disciples are also prophets and so the tradition is indivisible, and a prophetic book is the record of the on-going life of a prophetic community."[74] Concern with redactional history also has the obvious attraction of enabling the student of the prophetic books to keep faith with the final form of the biblical text over against the hypothetical reconstructions, on whatever scale, that may also have to be considered.

In the modern period there have been major developments in the study of individual prophetic books, notably in the separation of Isaiah 40–66 from (most of) the earlier chapters of Isaiah and therefore from the prophetic activity and utterances of the eighth-century Isaiah of Jerusalem. Plural authorship has been argued from the late eighteenth century by scholars such as J. B. Koppe and J. G. Eichhorn.[75] Duhm's isolation of the so-called "servant songs" within Isaiah 40–55 has also been determinative in much discussion of the identity of the servant and

---

71. *Ezechiel*, vols. 1–2 (BKAT 13; Neukirchen-Vluyn: Neukirchener Verlag, 1969) (Eng. trans. *Ezekiel*, vols. 1–2 [Philadelphia: Fortress, 1979–83]).

72. Cf. R. E. Clements, "The Prophecies of Isaiah and the Fall of Jerusalem in 587 B.C.," *VT* 30 (1980) 421–36.

73. Cf. G. I. Emmerson, *Hosea: An Israelite Prophet in Judean Perspective* (JSOTSup 28; Sheffield: JSOT Press, 1984) 56–116.

74. McKane, *Tradition and Interpretation*, 186. Cf. also G. I. Davies, *Hosea* (Old Testament Guides; Sheffield: JSOT Press, 1993) 102: "These later voices, too, are part of the prophetic tradition of Israel, and without them we should probably not have had the prophetic books at all."

75. See J. Rogerson, *Old Testament Criticism in the Nineteenth Century: England and Germany* (London: SPCK, 1984) 23.

of related issues in these chapters.[76] Likewise, the observations of Mowinckel on the diverse material in Jeremiah, formalized in his main
"sources" A, B and C, representing the poetry, biography and prose
speeches in the book, have been constitutive of the main stream of Jeremiah scholarship ever since.[77] In Mowinckel's 1946 volume the Deuteronomistic sermons are, however, explained in traditio-historical terms,
not now as representative of a source but as the product of a circle of
traditionists who transmitted sayings of Jeremiah in their own Deuteronomistic idiom: "they represent exactly a circle of tradition of their
own, within which certain of the sayings by Jeremiah have been transmitted and transformed according to the ideas and the style which prevailed in the circle, exactly the deuteronomistic ideas and forms of style
and interests."[78] The assumptions and methods of literary criticism and
tradition-history still feature prominently in prophets study, but they
have been supplemented by another generation of approaches, some of
them originally developed outside the biblical field, as we shall see in the
next section.

The New Generation

The face of prophets scholarship has altered substantially in the past
couple of decades. It is not simply that older preoccupations have been
abandoned and brash new approaches installed in their place. Not all
the newer emphases could be claimed as complete innovations as compared with previous work, if only because the texts remain the same and
must to some significant extent determine the approaches that are appropriate and the questions that are worth asking. Rather, the limitations of the older methods are more frankly acknowledged and the
desirability of a more sophisticatedly flexible approach to the biblical
texts is being recognized. The status of "the text," no less in religious
than in secular literature, has also been radically revised, with a greater
general awareness that the individual reader, by his or her interaction
with the text, is involved willy-nilly in the creation of meaning. However,
none of this means that the more excavative approaches to prophetic
texts are rendered redundant. Indeed, it is noticeable that, as well as the
current spate of "literarily correct" studies that deal in nothing but the

---

76. Duhm, *Das Buch Jesaia* (5th ed.), 14–15, 311, etc. See, however, T. N. D. Mettinger,
A Farewell to the Servant Songs: A Critical Examination of an Exegetical Axiom (Lund: CWK
Gleerup, 1983).

77. *Zur Komposition des Buches Jeremia* (Kristiania: Dybwad, 1914).

78. Mowinckel, *Prophecy and Tradition,* 62.

final form of the text, there are many others that involve historical reconstruction and/or the recreation of the social milieu in which prophets lived or in which their words were transmitted—though such are the penalties attaching to historical reconstruction in the present climate of academic scepticism, and so privileged is the final-form reading of biblical texts, that even excavative studies may be seen courting respectability in final-form dress.

We begin, then, by observing that, the newer emphases notwithstanding, the student of Israelite prophecy is obliged nowadays to take account of new *information.* The new "technology" must still include things like tablets and inscriptions, and even comparative philology, thanks to the ever-increasing number of relevant prophetic texts coming to light at various ancient Near Eastern sites.[79] These permit a very fragmentary account of a widespread phenomenon justifiably described as "Near Eastern prophecy," and one which gives evidence more and more of its cultural consanguinity with its Israelite counterpart. The main site is Mari in Syria, with its royal archive dating back to the national dynasty there in the eighteenth century B.C.[80] This is not the place to describe or even to summarize the contents of the several dozen Mari tablets from the period that attest the existence of oracular prophecy in Mari and related centers. But the profile of prophecy that is emerging from the growing number of published texts draws Mari ever nearer to Israel. At Mari the idea of prophetic access to the divine council and of the prophet's messenger status vis-à-vis the commissioning deity are firmly established, and already there are intimations of the concern of the Israelite prophets with justice and ethics in national affairs.[81] Furthermore, the recently-discovered existence of cognates, at Mari and also at thirteenth-century Emar, of the primary Hebrew term for 'prophet' (*nābî*) requires that Israelite prophecy be viewed in the context of Syro-Mesopotamian prophecy.[82] These extra-biblical texts, moreover, tend to support the idea of a western origin for their "*nabū*-prophecy." So despite the geographical and chronological gaps separating Mari and Israel, the points of contact are too substantial to be set aside. Prophecy at Mari, as

79. See R. P. Gordon, "From Mari to Moses: Prophecy at Mari and in Ancient Israel," in *Of Prophets' Visions and the Wisdom of Sages* (ed. H. A. McKay and D. J. A. Clines; JSOTSup 162; Sheffield: JSOT Press, 1993) 63–79.

80. Cf. A. Malamat, *Mari and the Early Israelite Experience* (The Schweich Lectures of the British Academy 1984; Oxford: Oxford University Press, 1989 [for an excerpt from Malamat's book, see pp. 50–73 in this volume]).

81. Cf. Gordon, "From Mari to Moses," 71–79.

82. Ibid., 65; for Emar see D. E. Fleming, "*Nābû* and *Munabbiātu*: Two New Syrian Religious Personnel," *JAOS* 113 (1993) 175–83; idem, "The Etymological Origins of the Hebrew *nābî*: The One Who Invokes God," *CBQ* 55 (1993) 217–24.

at the other Near Eastern centers referred to above, can illuminate Israelite prophecy (and *vice versa*), and, with its named prophets and sometimes very specific historical settings, may even serve as a useful reminder that behind prophetic oracles and even prophetic books stand flesh-and-blood prophets.

Interest in the prophets as prophets, and not just in prophecy as a literary phenomenon, is also reflected in a number of studies published in the 1970s and 1980s dealing with prophetic psychology.[83] R. R. Wilson, who is mainly interested in the sociology of prophecy, refers to passages in Jeremiah as evidence of the ecstatic nature of some prophecy (4:19; 23:9; 29:26).[84] As he notes, anthropologists now prefer to speak of "trance" rather than "ecstasy," and as a way of describing not a process of communication but the behavior of the "entranced" prophet. "Possession behavior" is also regarded as fairly stereotypical within particular groups or societies. The continuing publication of texts relating to ecstatic prophecy at Mari may help keep the subject alive, even though its importance in prophets studies "in real terms" is greatly reduced as compared with the first half of the twentieth century. The danger to be avoided, as Petersen notes, is that of turning the prophets generally into ecstatics such that they become isolated to an unjustifiable extent from the society of which they formed a part.[85]

Though productive of less historically specific evidence than the archival and epigraphic material considered above, the sociological-cum-anthropological study of prophecy as it has developed in the past twenty years nevertheless makes its own oblique kind of contribution to the profile of prophecy in Israel. Interest here focuses on the titles and roles of prophets, the authority by which they were able to function, and such other matters as the role of support groups, audience response, the distinction between "true" and "false" prophets, and the problem of unfulfilled prophecy.[86] In such studies, whether they are basically sociological or anthropological in their approach, society's familiarity with, and expectations of, the prophet figure are of crucial importance, and on at least two different levels. First, the success or failure of the claimed

---

83. Cf. S. B. Parker, "Possession Trance and Prophecy in Pre-exilic Israel," *VT* 28 (1978) 271–85; R. R. Wilson, "Prophecy and Ecstasy: A Reexamination," *JBL* 98 (1979) 321–37; B. Uffenheimer, "Prophecy, Ecstasy, and Sympathy," in *Congress Volume: Jerusalem 1986* (ed. J. A. Emerton; VTSup 40; Leiden: Brill, 1988) 257–69; P. Michaelsen, "Ecstasy and Possession in Ancient Israel: A Review of Some Recent Contributions," *SJOT* 2 (1989) 28–54.

84. "Prophecy and Ecstasy: A Reexamination," *JBL* 98 (1979) 323.

85. D. L. Petersen, *The Roles of Israel's Prophets* (JSOTSup 17; Sheffield: JSOT Press, 1981) 27.

86. See the group of essays in the section headed "Prophecy and Society," below, pp. 273–412.

prophet relates closely to his fulfilling the prophetic stereotype as this is
perceived by the society in which he operates—and here "stereotype"
should perhaps apply as much to a solitary or "peripheral" prophet as to
an official or "central" one. If a prophet does not conform in some way to
the popular conception of a prophet his credibility will diminish. Secondly, the social expectation that produced the formulation of the prophetic role in Israelite society should be a datum in the modern scholar's
investigation of prophecy in Israel. The biblical and extra-biblical information alike indicates societies in the Near East in which prophetic
modes of behavior were well-known and easily recognizable, and this applies no less to Israel in the eighth and seventh centuries B.C. When,
therefore, it is questioned whether the "classical" prophets of Israel self-
consciously functioned as prophets and were known by the term *nābîʾ*,[87]
the response to the first limb of the question may properly include, in addition to the internal evidence of prophetic books such as Amos and Hosea, the collateral evidence of the socially defined role of the prophet in
pre-exilic Israel. This, and not the mere use of a term for 'prophet', is the
deciding factor; there may indeed be evidence of a restrained use of the
term for the like of Isaiah and Amos in their own time, and it would not
be difficult to think of good reasons for its avoidance.[88] At the same time,
it would be truer to the genius of Hebrew prophecy to put the accent
upon the self-awareness of the prophets rather than upon any social role
thrust upon them, and the more so when the latter conflicted with the
higher purpose to which they felt called.

Much current discussion of Israelite prophecy is, for all that, predicated on the understanding that the prophets functioned self-
consciously as such throughout the period of the monarchy and on into
the post-exilic era. They called their contemporaries to observe ethical
standards of behavior in a God-conscious kind of way, and they issued
warnings of judgment in the event of their message being rejected.
Recent studies still seek to do justice to this "theological" dimension of
the prophetic message, and they enjoy representation in this volume.[89]

87. Cf. A. G. Auld, "Prophets Through the Looking Glass: Between Writings and
Moses," below, pp. 289–307.

88. Cf. R. P. Gordon, "Where Have All the Prophets Gone? The 'Disappearing'
Prophet against the Background of Ancient Near Eastern Prophecy," *Bulletin for Biblical Research* 5 (1995) 67–86.

89. See the section entitled "The Message of the Prophets," below, 75–104. Theological aspects of prophecy are, of course, frequently in evidence in other essays in this volume.
The volumes by K. Koch (*Die Profeten* [Stuttgart: Kohlhammer, 1978]; Eng. trans. *The Prophets* [2 vols., London: SCM, 1982–83]) and J. Blenkinsopp (*A History of Prophecy in Israel: From
the Settlement in the Land to the Hellenistic Period* [Philadelphia: Westminster, 1983]) deserve
special mention for their attention to the theology of the prophetic books of the Old
Testament.

There has, at the same time, been a very considerable interest in the ways in which prophecy, whether in its oral or its written phases, is crafted. Classical terms like rhetoric and drama will mingle with the more biblical-sounding "inner-biblical interpretation" and the modernisms of "language-event," "speech-act theory" and "audience reception" in any serious overview of recent prophets study. The prophets as undoubted poets deployed the skills of the poet, with serious rhetorical intention. Recent studies seek to do justice to this aspect of prophecy, whether by *rhetoric* we mean the linguistic and structural features of a finely-wrought composition or, as more in keeping with its original Aristotelian emphasis, the suasive effect that poets seek to achieve through their use of language.[90] To skill with words is sometimes added skill with texts, when later sections of the Old Testament use and adapt older texts to produce a kind of "inner-biblical exegesis." This can sometimes happen in a distinctly ironic way when an older text is turned against those who are all too complacently familiar with it.[91] While in theory such reworking of texts may be possible at either the oral or the written stage, the latter seems more likely for some of the more extended examples of this biblical phenomenon.[92] There is also an increased awareness in recent prophets study of the way in which the dialogue between a prophet and his audience may be reflected in the biblical text, where it may appear in the form of unrubricated dialogue, as evidently in the case of Jeremiah.[93] The not unrelated speech-form of the "prophetic disputation" implies such dialogue without necessarily itself being reportage of literal exchanges between a prophet and his audience.[94] Thus prophetic speech does not function simply as declamatory monologue, proceeding from prophet to hearer, but also involves quotation of, and response to, the questions and denials of the target audience.

Text dynamics operate at other levels, as recent prophets scholarship has sought to demonstrate. As in literary studies generally, so also in the

90. Cf. Y. Gitay, *Prophecy and Persuasion: A Study of Isaiah 40–48* (Bonn: Linguistica Biblica, 1981); idem, *Isaiah and His Audience: The Structure and Meaning of Isaiah 1–12* (Assen/Maastricht: Van Gorcum, 1991).

91. Cf. M. Fishbane, *Biblical Interpretation in Ancient Israel* (Oxford: Clarendon, 1985) 332–34 (reprinted as "*The Priestly Blessing and Its Aggadic Reuse*," below pp. 223–29).

92. Cf. J. Day, "A Case of Inner Scriptural Interpretation: The Dependence of Isaiah XXVI. 13–XXVII. 11 on Hosea XIII. 4–XIV. 10 (Eng. 9) and Its Relevance to Some Theories of the Redaction of the 'Isaiah Apocalypse,'" *JTS* n.s. 31 (1980) 309–19.

93. See J. T. Willis, "Dialogue between Prophet and Audience as a Rhetorical Device in the Book of Jeremiah," below, pp. 205–22; J. R. Lundbom, "Jeremiah and the Break-Away from Authority Preaching," *SEÅ* 56 (1991) 7–28.

94. Cf. A. Graffy, *A Prophet Confronts His People: The Disputation Speech in the Prophets* (AnBib 104; Rome: Pontifical Biblical Institute, 1984); D. F. Murray, "The Rhetoric of Disputation: Re-examination of a Prophetic Genre," *JSOT* 38 (1987) 95–121.

biblical field there has been an increased tendency to accord special
significance to the final form of texts, even if they are assumed to be of
composite authorship. This involves a willingness to recognize in the
final arrangement of material within the larger unit new structural patterns and phraseological relationships that by definition could not exist
in the constituent texts. Since these relationships of meaning may easily
exceed anything intended by the original authors, their operation tends
to be described in accordance with the looser canons of "intertextuality,"
where assumptions about authorial intention do not necessarily apply.
Where the situation is one of a developing tradition in which original
words and phrases are repeated and adapted in order to apply to new
situations, as is commonly envisaged nowadays for the book of Isaiah,[95]
the question remains, of course, very much one of authorial intention,
however else the phenomenon may be described. Something comparable to the situation in Isaiah seems to be implied in McKane's concept
of a "rolling corpus" in Jeremiah, according to which texts generate
other texts phraseologically or ideologically similar, though McKane
does not see the process in Jeremiah as particularly skilful or coherent.[96]
And, when once a collection of texts is viewed as a "canon" of authoritative scripture, the emphasis may again be not so much upon the internal
development that has produced the final form of the text as upon the
"canonical" meaning that may emerge from the finalized text. Moreover,
the canonical perspective makes it possible to treat not only the arrangement of the individual books but also their several relationships one to
another as interpretively significant. Thus the fact that the Christian
canon of the Old Testament differs from its Jewish counterpart in that it
ends with the prophetic books, climaxing with Haggai, Zechariah and
Malachi, is plausibly explained as the result of a deliberate striving after
an "eschatological canon" which, because of the expectations of the
Christ-event perceived in Zechariah 9–14 and Mal 4:1–6, is intended to
function as a *praeparatio* for the developments recounted in the New Testament. If such is the case, as it seems to be, "canon" functions here as a
significant interpretive factor not just in the way of a reading strategy

95. See the section entitled "The Developing Tradition," below, pp. 413–522.

96. *Jeremiah* (ICC; Edinburgh: T. & T. Clark, 1986) 1.1–lxxxiii. In his view of Jeremiah,
McKane stands somewhere between R. P. Carroll (*From Chaos to Covenant: Uses of Prophecy in
the Book of Jeremiah* [London: SCM, 1981]; *Jeremiah: A Commentary* [London: SCM, 1986]),
who thinks that certain identification of words of the historical Jeremiah is extremely
difficult, and W. L. Holladay (*Jeremiah 1* [Philadelphia: Fortress, 1986]; *Jeremiah 2* [Minnea-
polis: Fortress, 1989]), who reconstructs the career of the prophet on the basis of the data
in the biblical book.

but also as a pointer to objective realities in the final form of the biblical text.[97]

The final form of the text of the prophets has also been examined from a number of other perspectives developed in general literary studies, notably structuralist,[98] which concerns itself with patterns of human thought present but not expressly so in texts, deconstructionist,[99] which seeks to demonstrate that there are internal contradictions in any text and that these are subversive of the authority of texts as such, and "reader-response,"[100] of which feminist studies may be seen as a subcategory.[101] "Reader-response" is a catch-all term for reading strategies in which the participation of the reader is held to have a formative effect on meaning—regarded not as intrinsic to the text but as the product of interaction between text and reader. Legitimation of readings tends to be associated with interpretative communities, and indeed "reader-response" often functions in the way of a group hermeneutic meeting the needs of communities of interest, whether religious, social, ethnic or something else. Advocates of the approaches noted in this paragraph have generally, it should be said, found the narrative sections of the Old Testament more congenial to their interests. This is true not least of feminist studies.

The title of this introductory chapter refers to paradigm shifts in the study of the Israelite prophets. The first occurred in the later nineteenth century when the prophets were raised to new heights of eminence on account of their reconstructed role in the development of Israelite religion. The second is much more recent and will require further discussion, about how best to define it, in the final essay of this volume (pp. 600–605).

97. On this latter point as it affects the structuring of prophetic books, see R. E. Clements, *"Patterns in the Prophetic Canon,"* in *Canon and Authority: Essays in Old Testament Religion and Authority* (ed. G. W. Coats and B. O. Long; Philadelphia: Fortress, 1977) 42–55.

98. Cf. Y. Mazor, "Hosea 5:1–3: Between Compositional Rhetoric and Rhetorical Composition," *JSOT* 45 (1989) 115–26.

99. Cf. F. van Dijk-Hemmes, "The Imagination of Power and the Power of Imagination. An Intertextual Analysis of Two Biblical Love Songs: The Song of Songs and Hosea 2," *JSOT* 44 (1989) 75–88; D. J. A. Clines, "Haggai's Temple, Constructed, Deconstructed and Reconstructed," *SJOT* 7 (1993) 51–77.

100. Cf. Y. Gitay, " Isaiah and His Audience," *Prooftexts* 3 (1983) 223–30; E. W. Conrad, *Reading Isaiah* (Minneapolis: Fortress, 1991); F. O. García-Treto, "A Reader-Response Approach to Prophetic Conflict: The Case of Amos 7:10–17," in *The New Literary Criticism and the Hebrew Bible* (JSOTSup 143; ed. J. C. Exum and D. J. A. Clines; Sheffield: JSOT Press, 1993) 114–24.

101. See K. P. Darr, "Ezekiel's Justifications of God: Teaching Troubling Texts," *JSOT* 55 (1992) 97–117 (esp. 114–16), for discussion of the kind of issue that engages feminist (and other concerned) biblical criticism.

But, whereas both developments have occasioned fresh and insightful approaches to the prophetic traditions of the Old Testament, it is important not to overestimate their significance or their achievement. In the one case we have seen that the "splendid isolation" to which the prophets were elevated by the advocates of the newer approach in the late nineteenth century came to be recognized as an overstatement of the prophetic contribution to the formation of the Israelite ethico-religious consciousness. The overstatement was largely owing to an underestimation of what had preceded the great classical prophets in respect of both law and religion. The newer multifaceted approach to the prophetic books which warrants talk of a second paradigm shift bears its own testimony to the richness of the Israelite prophetic tradition. But it would be a pity if doctrinaire dismissals of older approaches were to turn the idea of "paradigm shift" into a euphemism for a neologistic tyranny which, in the familiar way of some Old Testament scholarship, assumed far more about what *cannot* be known about the workings of Israelite prophecy (for example) than the evidence justifies.

Part 1

The Near Eastern Background

Introduction

It is an irony of the present situation in Old Testament study that, just as newer methods of reading and discussing texts, prophetic and other, are being applied, our greatly increased knowledge of prophecy in its wider Near Eastern setting requires that we pay renewed attention to Israelite prophecy as an historical phenomenon with precursors and parallels in sibling Near Eastern cultures. The impetus for much present study comes from the discovery and publication of the Mari prophecies, but a number of other important texts, from such centers as Emar, Ugarit, Hamath and Deir ᶜAlla, attest to the existence of what is obviously a related phenomenon outside Israel in the second and first millennia B.C. The discussion of this composite testimony will become practicable and all the more necessary once the Mari material has been more thoroughly assessed. But the potential of this evidence is not restricted to the several dozen prophetic texts that have so far surfaced, for the Mari archive provides an almost encyclopedic account of Mari society in the mid-eighteenth century such as should make possible additional insights into the world of Mari prophecy. Already Malamat (1991) has illustrated how this may be done, by bringing together references in non-prophetic texts to the *piristum*, or royal council, which, in the Near East more widely, supplied the model for the mythological divine court or "council of the gods" that forms the background to the commissioning of a number of Near Eastern (including Israelite) prophets.

Although the article by Weinfeld reproduced below (pp. 32–49) touches on some matters that were more prominent in debate twenty years ago and more (e.g., covenant and prophetic lawsuit), it remains a very useful survey of the Near Eastern texts available in 1977 and especially of features that are paralleled in the prophetic literature of the Old Testament or that illuminate the biblical texts. It is proper, too, that evidence of ethical concern in Mesopotamian (non-prophetic) literature should be highlighted, especially since it has become commonplace to focus on the Admonitions and Instructions of the Egyptian wisdom literature as, at least chronologically, anticipating the ethically charged preaching of the Hebrew prophets. More recently the evidence of ethical concern specifically in Mari prophecy (represented here by the excerpt from Mala-mat's monograph, pp. 50–73 below) has been gathering, and it has now been supplemented by a text originating in Aleppo, according to which the god Adad demands of the king of Mari that he judge the case of anyone who cries out to him for justice (see Malamat 1993). With such glimmerings of ethical interest in evidence at Mari it is thus no longer satisfactory to claim that comparisons between Israelite and other proph-ecy exist only at a superficial level. Again, in drawing attention to the existence of a cognate for the Hebrew *nābîʾ* ('prophet') in the Emar texts Fleming (1993) has made a suggestion which, if substantiated, would pro-vide another point of correspondence between Israelite and non-Israelite prophecy, and which would at the same time remove what otherwise has strong title to be regarded as a "distinctive" of Israelite prophecy, viz., prophetic intercession. And although the etymology of the Emar cog-nate can be explained in other ways, the question of the exact relationship of ancient Hebrew prophecy to prophecy in its non-Israelite forms is one that will obviously require more attention.

Additional Reading

Charpin, D.
  1992   Le contexte historique et géographique des prophéties dans les textes retrouvés à Mari. *Canadian Society for Mesopotamian Studies Bulletin* 23: 21–31.
Dietrich, M. et al.
  1986   *Deutungen der Zukunft in Briefen, Orakeln und Omina.* Texte aus der Umwelt des Alten Testaments 2/1. Gütersloh: Mohn.
Ellis, M. de Jong
  1989   Observations on Mesopotamian Oracles and Prophetic Texts: Liter-ary and Historiographic Considerations. *Journal of Cuneiform Studies* 41–42: 127–86.
Fleming, D. E.
  1993   The Etymological Origins of the Hebrew *nābîʾ*: The One Who In-vokes God. *Catholic Biblical Quarterly* 55: 217–24.
Gordon, R. P.
  1993   From Mari to Moses: Prophecy at Mari and in Ancient Israel. Pp. 63–79 in *Prophets' Visions and the Wisdom of Sages* (R. N. Whybray Fest-schrift), edited by H. A. McKay and D. J. A. Clines. Journal for the Study of the Old Testament Supplement Series 162. Sheffield: Shef-field Academic Press.
  1995   Where Have All the Prophets Gone? The "Disappearing" Israelite Prophet against the Background of Ancient Near Eastern Prophecy. *Bulletin for Biblical Research* 5: 67–86.

Huffmon, H. B.

1976   The Origins of Prophecy. Pp. 171–86 in *Magnalia Dei—The Mighty Acts of God: Essays on the Bible and Archaeology in Memory of G. Ernest Wright,* edited by F. M. Cross, W. E. Lemke, and P. D. Miller. Garden City, New York: Doubleday.

Malamat, A.

1991   The Secret Council and Prophetic Involvement in Mari and Israel. Pp. 231–36 in *Prophetie und geschichtliche Wirklichkeit im alten Israel* (S. Herrmann Festschrift), edited by R. Liwak and S. Wagner. Stuttgart: Kohlhammer.

1993   A New Prophetic Message from Aleppo and Its Biblical Counterparts. Pp. 236–41 in *Understanding Poets and Prophets* (G. W. Anderson Festschrift), edited by A. G. Auld. Journal for the Study of the Old Testament Supplement Series 152. Sheffield: Sheffield Academic Press.

See also the various studies by Malamat listed in his bibliography (*Mari and the Early Israelite Experience,* 135–36).

Parker, S. B.

1993   Official Attitudes toward Prophecy at Mari and in Israel. *Vetus Testamentum* 43: 50–68.

1994   The Lachish Letters and Official Reactions to Prophecies. Pp. 65–78 in *Uncovering Ancient Stones: Essays in Memory of H. Neil Richardson,* edited by L. M. Hopfe. Winona Lake, Indiana: Eisenbrauns.

Ringgren, H.

1982   Prophecy in the Ancient Near East. Pp. 1–11 in *Israel's Prophetic Tradition* (P. R. Ackroyd Festschrift), edited by R. J. Coggins, A. Phillips, and M. A. Knibb. Cambridge: Cambridge University Press.

Weippert, M.

1991   The Balaam Text from Deir ʿAllā and the Study of the Old Testament. Pp. 151–84 (169–74) in *The Balaam Text from Deir ʿAlla Reevaluated,* edited by J. Hoftijzer and G. van der Kooij. Leiden: Brill.

Ancient Near Eastern Patterns in Prophetic Literature

MOSHE WEINFELD

[[178]] Almost every one of the literary types of the Old Testament has its prototype in the ancient Near Eastern literature. Law, epic, historiography, psalms, wisdom, all of them are established literary genres in the civilization of Mesopotamia and Egypt. Furthermorc in some cases it is even possible to prove direct dependence of the Biblical creation upon foreign sources as for example in the case of Prov 22:17–23:11 which is dependent on the Proverbs of Amen-em-opet. The only exception is Classical Prophecy which has always been considered an original creation of ancient Israel. Indeed there is no doubt that the religious moral pathos pervading classical prophecy as well as the prophetic ideas about the end of idolatry, universal peace and world salvation, reflect the genuine spirit of classical prophecy. The question is whether the literary conventions out of which classical prophecy has been formed were unique. Now, close investigation and constant follow-up of the ever growing literature of the ancient Near East show that basic forms as well as basic motifs of classical prophecy are rooted in the ancient Near-Eastern literature, and it is my purpose to illustrate and exemplify this thesis.

Let us start with a problem which lies at the roots of classical prophecy: *the prophet as a messenger.* Y. Kaufmann, for example, argued that the characteristic feature of the Israelite prophet was his total dependence upon God; he was a messenger sent to Israel by God in con-

Reprinted with permission from *Vetus Testamentum* 27 (1977) 178–95.

trast to the pagan prophet who acted by a divine power which had become embodied in him.[1] Now, the Mari texts from the 18th century B.C. which have been published in the last decades revealed to us a type of prophet-messenger not unlike the one familiar to us [[179]] from ancient Israel.[2] As A. Malamat has indicated, we find there the god Dagan sending prophets to convey messages to the king, and as in Israel the messages were delivered by means of prophetic frenzy[3] (cp. *ARM* II 90:19; III 40:13; *Rev. Ass.* 42 [1938], line 32).[4] W. L. Moran, however, still argues that the "mission" in Mari is secondary and even incidental.[5] But in respect to this problem attention should be paid to some key terms or conventions which are decisive. In the revelation of Dagan to Malikdagan his prophet we find a messenger-formula verbally identical with the mission-formula found in Exod 3:10 in the vision of the burning bush. There we read *w^cth lkh w^ʾšlḥk ʾl pr^ch* 'Now go, I send you to Pharaoh', and in the revelation to Malikdagan:[6] *inanna alik aštaparka ummami . . .*[7] 'Now go I send you, thus say . . . '. A similar convention is attested in the revelation to Isaiah: *ʾt my ʾšlḥ wmy ylk lnw* 'whom shall I send and who will go for us?' (6:8). This convention is found in the Akkadian Maqlu text and there also in connection with imposing a mission upon a man by the supreme gods Anu and Antu: *mannu lušpur* 'whom shall I send?'[8] which shows that the type of divine messenger was prevailing for a long time in Mesopotamia (cp. also Jer 1:7; Ezek 2:3ff.).

---

1. Y. Kaufmann, *The Religion of Israel*, translated and abridged by M. Greenberg (Chicago, 1960), 212ff.

2. Cp. A. Malamat, "Prophetic Revelations in New Documents from Mari and the Bible," *SVT* 15 (1966), 207ff.

3. Compare the *muḫḫum* in Mari whose function overlaps that of the Hebrew *mšg^c* [['crazed person']], *ʾyš hrwḥ* [['inspired man']] (= *mtnb^ʾ* [['speak in ecstasy']]) (Jer 29:26, Hos 9:7), and see Malamat, pp. 210–211, and note 4. *meḫû* in Akkadian is wind or storm, and the verb *maḫû* in the Nif^cal form: *namḫû* (cp. *ARM* X 7:6; 8:7) equals *hyh ^clyw hrwḥ* [['the spirit was upon him']] (= *htnb^ʾ*).

4. Cp. A. Malamat, p. 221.

5. W. L. Moran, "New Evidence from Mari on the History of Prophecy," *Biblica* 50 (1969), 26, n. 2. In a sense Moran strengthens Kaufmann's position; see esp. Kaufmann's reaction to the Mari discoveries in *Religion of Israel*, 215, n. 1.

6. *RA* 42 (1938), line 32.

7. From the grammatical point of view *aštaparka* equals *šlḥtyk* [['I have sent you']] (as in v. 12) and not *ʾšlḥk* [['I will send you']]. Functionally however there is no distinction; both refer to the present. *aštaparka* as well as *ašpurka* both express the *Koinzidenzfall* [['simultaneity']]: 'I hereby send you' (see Heimpel-Guidi, *ZDMG* 17 [1968], 151f.), and the same applies to the Hebrew *šlḥtyk* [['I send you']] —compare, e.g., in the message to Gideon (Judg 6:14): *lk . . . hl^ʾ šlḥtyk* [['Go . . . do not I send you?']].

8. Cp. G. Meier, *Maqlû, AfO*, Beiheft 2 (1937), 9, line 53.

Signs and Portents

In connection with his mission Moses is given signs or portents: *ʾōtôt* (Exod 4:1ff., 21; 7:8f.). These also play an important role in [[180]] the Mari prophecies,[9] and here again a similar literary convention is employed: *lū ittum* 'let it be a sign',[10] which is the equivalent of *wzh (lk) hʾwt* found in the revelation to Moses (Exod 3:12) and in other prophetic passages.[11] Furthermore the sign or portent is asked for in Mari (the verb *šaʾālu*)[12] as in the Bible (Isa 7:11), and is also awaited and longed for (*quʾû*),[13] a phenomenon encountered in Isa 8:17[14] and Hab 2:3.

Purification of the Mouth

Before undertaking his mission, Isaiah (chap. 6) undergoes a purification ceremony which is not unlike the ceremonies of *mīs pî*[15] known to us from Mesopotamia. A striking parallel to this is to be found in an Old Babylonian Prayer of a diviner (*barûm*) published recently by A. Goetze.[16] Thus we read at the beginning of the text:

> O Šamaš, I am placing in my mouth pure cedar (resin).[17] . . . I wiped (*akpur*) my mouth with . . . cedar (resin). . . . Being (now) clean, to the assembly of the gods I shall draw near.[18]

Like Isaiah, whose mouth has to be purged in order that he may participate in the divine council, the Babylonian prophet also declares that having cleansed his mouth he is ready to draw near to the divine assembly. Although no cedar is mentioned in Isaiah 6, we learn from Num 19:6 that 'cedar wood' (*ʿṣ ʾrz* = *iṣ erinni*) was used in purification ceremonies

---

9. For *ittum* [['sign']] in the Mari prophecies see Moran, *Biblica* 50, p. 39, n. 3; W. H. Ph. Römer, *Frauenbriefe*, AOAT 12 (1971), 30.

10. Moran. Cp. also in Nuzi: *annūtu lū ittu* = 'this is the sign' (*HSS* 15 291:4, 8 and 19); compare *CAD* I, p. 308, 3.

11. Cp. 1 Sam 2:34, 10:1 (LXX), 14:10; 2 Kgs 19:29, 20:9.

12. *ARM* X no. 4:6, 10. The verb appears frequently in connection with omina.

13. Cp. Römer, p. 50, n. 8, reading with von Soden apud Berger, *UF* 1, p. 221.

14. Note *wqwyty* [['I will trust']], *wḥkyty* [['I will wait']] associated with *ʾtwt wmwptym* [['signs and portents']] in the next verse.

15. Cp. G. Meier, "Die Ritualtafel der Serie 'Mundwaschung,'" *AfO* 12 (1937–39), 40ff. and see also E. Ebeling, *Tod und Leben* etc. (1931), 100ff. For the ritual in connection with idols as well as with diviners, cp. the references in Sjöberg, *JNES* 26 (1967), 211.

16. *JCS* 22 (1968), 25f.

17. (*iṣ*) *erinnam ellam* (obv. line 1); in the continuation we find *ša-bi-im iṣ erinnim* (line 6) which according to Goetze means compact/solid cedar (resin).

18. *ana puḫur ilī eteḫḫi* (line 9).

in Israel,[19] and it is quite possible that the live coal [[181]] which had been taken from the altar by the Saraph in order to touch with it the lips of the prophet came from burned cedar wood.[20] It is also significant that the altar out of which the coals were taken for the purification of Isaiah's mouth, as well as for the ceremony of the Day of Atonement (Exod 30:10), was made of cedar; cp. 1 Kgs 6:22f.[21]

Ecstasy

The mantic frenzy is also described in a similar manner in both cultures and one may even learn from the Biblical descriptions of the prophetic ecstasy about the proper nature of the activity of the *muḫḫû*, i.e., the Mari prophet. The literary convention in Mari for the ecstatic action is *imaḫḫi* (he went into a trance), *itbe*[22] (arose)[23] *kiʾam idbub ummami* (thus said).[24] The same situation is met in the Biblical descriptions of ecstasy, and even identical phraseology is employed here. The prophets and the divine men are seized by the spirit, and this is expressed by *hyh ʿlyw rwḥ* [['(the) spirit came upon him']], Num 24:2; Judg 3:10, 11:29; 2 Chr 20:14; *ṣlḥ ʿlyw rwḥ* [['(the) spirit rushed upon him']], Judg 14:6, 19; 15:14; 1 Sam 10:6, 10; 11:6; 16:13; *bʾ bw rwḥ* [['(the) spirit entered into him']] (Ezek 2:2, 3:24); *npl ʿlyw rwḥ* [['(the) spirit fell upon him']] (Ezekiel passim); *lbš rwḥ* [['(the) spirit took possession']] (2 Chr 24:20); *nḥḥ ʿlyw rwḥ* [['(the) spirit rested on him']] (Num 11:17, 25, 26), and as in the Mari texts we hear that the prophet rises (compare *itbe*) or stands up on

19. Compare the purification ceremony in Lev 14:4, 6, 49f., where together with cedar wood, crimson stuff (*šny twlᶜt*) is taken. For cedar and antimony in the covenant ceremony described in the Stele of the Vultures (Eannatum of Lagash) cp. M. Weinfeld, *Deuteronomy and the Deuteronomic School* (Oxford, 1972), 7, n. 5.

20. Cedar wood occurs as wood qualified for the altar in *Jub.* 21:12.

21. Noth's contention that *mzbḥ* [['altar']] here means *šlḥn* [['table']] and that it refers to the 'table of the bread' has no basis, see S. Yeivin, *Enc. Miqr.* s.v. *mqdš*, col. 342.

22. According to Moran (pp. 25f.) *itbe* is said of professionals and *imaḫḫi* of laity. This distinction is dubious however in the light of Biblical evidence quoted below. It seems that when the *muḫḫû* appears in the text, the act of going into trance (*namḫû*) is self-understood and only *itbe* is mentioned. On the other hand, *imaḫḫi* refers to the whole process and therefore when it occurs no *itbe* needs to be mentioned.

23. P.-R. Berger (*UF* 1 [1969], 209) compared this with *qm* [['arise']] in Deut 34:10; however *qm* in such contexts is interchangeable with *hyh* [['be']] (compare, e.g., 2 Kgs 18:5 with 23:25) and means just 'exist' (derived from *ex* + *sistere*). More relevant to *itbe* is the causative *hqym* [['raise up']] which is used in connection with appointing prophets and charismatic figures; cp. Deut 18:15, 18; Judg 2:18; Amos 2:11; Jer 29:15, although the same usage is also found in connection with kings and priests (1 Sam 2:35; Deut 28:36; 1 Kgs 14:16; Jer 30:9).

24. For this typology, cp. Moran, pp. 24–25.

his feet for hearing or delivering the word of God. This is clearly expressed in Ezekiel whose ecstatic activity is most vividly described: he
sees the vision, then falls upon his face, the spirit enters him, *wtʾ by rwḥ*
which equals *imaḫḫi*, and makes him stand on his feet *wtᶜmdny ᶜl rgly,*
which corresponds to *itbe* (1:28, 2:2, 3:22–24).

⟦182⟧ Similarly we read in 2 Chr 24:20 that the *spirit seized* (*rwḥ yhwh
lbš*) the prophet Zechariah and *he stood up* (*wyᶜmd*) above the people
and said. . . .

The traumatic experience of the prophet involved in ecstatic visions
comes to clear expression in Dan 8:17f., 10:4ff. There we read that
Daniel lay sick for a few days (8:27) or that his strength failed him and
no breath was left in him (10:17).[25] There we also find instructive details
about the way the prophet gets his vision, which recalls the visions of
Ezekiel and which might supply more evidence about going into trance
in Mari:

> I was left alone gazing at his great vision. . . . I became a sorry figure of
> a man, I retained no strength . . . I fell on the ground. . . . Suddenly a
> hand grasped me and pulled me up on to my hands and knees; he said
> to me: Daniel attend to the words I am speaking to you and stand up
> where you are. . . . I stood up trembling . . . and he said: Do not be
> afraid, etc.

Here again, as in the Mari letters and in Ezekiel, going into trance and
rising up, when the message is proclaimed, are presented conspicuously.

Moran is therefore quite correct when he contends that 'he arose'
(= *itbe* in the Mari prophecies) implies "that the professional was usually
sitting, kneeling or crouching until inspiration seized him. . . . Here we
may imagine him arise, and facing with the statue towards the worship-
ers. . . . For the witnesses this must have been an impressive and at times
even terrifying experience."[26]

Ecstatic activity amongst prophets in Mesopotamia (of later times) is
also reflected in terms like *zabbu* and *eššebu*. The former seems to be associated with dirt and self-inflicted wounds[27] while the latter was characterized by the way he let his hair grow.[28] Such attributes are indeed
ascribed to the ecstatic prophets in Israel (2 Kgs 1:8; Zech 13:4, 6; 1 Kgs
20:35ff.). Self-mutilation of ecstatic prophets is also attested in the
Canaanite milieu. In 1 Kgs 18:28 we read about the Canaanite prophets

---

25. Cp. Kaufmann, *Toledot haʾemunah hayisraʾelit* 1, p. 529, and see the apocryphal references there.
26. P. 26.
27. Cp. *CAD* Z, p. 7.
28. Cp. *CAD* E, p. 371.

mutilating themselves, a custom mentioned in the Ugaritic text about the Righteous Sufferer:

My brothers washed in their blood like the ecstatics.[29]

Salvation Oracle

[[183]] A full account of an oracle given in the precincts of the temple by a person who was seized by the spirit of God is found in 2 Chr 20:14ff. At the time of war with the Ammonites and Moabites, Jehoshaphat and the people gathered in the temple for prayer, and all of a sudden a Levite by the name of Yahziel was seized by the spirit of God in the midst of the assembly, *hyth ʿlyw rwḥ yhwh btwk hqhl*;[30] he said . . . "Thus said the Lord: Have no fear, do not be dismayed by the great horde, for the battle is in God's hands. . . . Go down to them tomorrow . . . you will find them at the end of the valley . . . stand firm and wait and you will see the deliverance." Next morning we hear Jehoshaphat saying to the people: "have faith in your God . . . , in his prophets and you will prosper."

This type of prophetic encouragement in war is found in the mouth of the prophet in the Mari letter *ARM* X 4:

> his (Išme-Dagan's) auxiliary troops will be scattered, furthermore, they will cut off the head of Išme-Dagan and put (it) under the foot of my lord. Thus (my lord may say): "the army of Išme-Dagan is large and if I (arrive), will his auxiliary troops be scattered from him?"[31] It is Dagan, Adad . . . who march at my lord's side . . . (lines 23–24).

The idea of God going out to war with the Israelites and marching at their side and saving them from the enemy's multitudes is very common in the Bible, and especially instructive in this context are the military exhortations in Exod 14:13; Deut 7:17ff.,[32] 20:1–4, 31:1–8, etc.[33] The promise of *scattering* (*sapāḫu*) the enemy's troops is also characteristic of the ancient salvation oracles of the holy war as for example in Num 10:35: 'Stand up, O Lord, may your enemies be *scattered*' *qwmh yhwh wypṣw ʾybyk*

---

29. *Aḫūa kīma mahḫê dāmišunu rāmku* (*Ugaritica* V, p. 267:11).

30. Compare, in a neo-Assyrian text: the prophetess prophesied (*raggimtu tartaggumu*) in the assembly of the land (*ina* UKKIN *ša* KUR) (*ABL* 437, rev. 1–2, cp. B. Landsberger, *Brief des Bischofs von Esagila* [1965] 48); compare also *ABL* 149:7, 121:9.

31. On the interrogative nature of the sentence, see Moran, p. 48, and n. 1 there.

32. Note the interrogative opening which recalls the Mari passage (see previous note).

33. See G. von Rad, *Studies in Deuteronomy* (London, 1953), 51ff., and cp. Weinfeld, *Deuteronomy*, 45ff.

(cp. Ps 68:2), Ps 144:6: "Make lightning flash and *scatter* them" (cp. 2 Sam 22:15 = Ps 18:15 and Ps 89:11).

The promise that the head of the enemy will be put under the foot ⟦184⟧ of the king in the letter just quoted[34] is also known to us from the Biblical sources: Deut 33:29; Ps 45:6, 18:39; Josh 10:24–25. In Josh 10:24 this is even executed in a dramatic way: Joshua calls his officers to put their feet on the necks of the defeated Kings and declares that so will God do to all the enemies of Israel (v. 25).[35]

Another literary convention found in the context of the prophetic salvation oracle in Mari is: 'I shall deliver your enemies into your hand' (*nakrēka ina qātīka umalla*) (*ARM* X 8:12–14),[36] an exact equivalent of the Hebrew *hnny ntn ʾt ʾwybyk bydyk* which is a stereotyped formula in the war oracles of ancient Israel (cp. 1 Sam 23:4, 24:5, 26:8; Judg 7:7; 1 Kgs 20:13, 28) and once even related to the Philistines (Judg 16:24).[37] This is accompanied in the Bible by *ʾl tyrʾ* 'do not fear', a phrase widely attested in the salvation oracles of the ancient Near East[38] and according to some also found in the prophetic texts of Mari (*ARM* XIII 114:13–16).[39]

False Prophets

An important point in the Mari letter quoted above (*ARM* X 4) is the sentence: 'I am not making them speak, on their (own) they agree' (*mimma ul ušadbabšunūti šunūma idabbubu, šunūma imtaḫḫaru*) (lines 37–39). This reminds us of the prophets who prophesy 'with one voice' (*ph ʾḥd*) to Ahab that (the enemy) will be given into the hands of the King (1 Kgs 22:13). The messenger of the king who comes to Micaiah in order to persuade him to predict favorably employs a device similar to that of Šibtu in her letter to Zimrilim. In order to disperse doubts about authenticity Šibtu adds "that nobody makes them speak." This tendency is also implied in the words of the messenger to Micaiah in 1 Kgs 22:13. In this respect one could learn something from neo-Assyrian texts. Esar-

34. Compare also *ARM* X 6:4′–8′: *u elīšu tazzaz* 'you will stand over him'.

35. This motif is most common in the Egyptian pictures of war and also in the written Sumerian, Akkadian and Phoenician sources; cp. Kramer, Weinfeld, *Beth Mikra* 57 (1974), 157–158.

36. Cp. *RA* 42 (1948), 128–132, lines 30–31; *ARM* X 7:20–22; *ARM* XIII 23:14–51. For an iconographic illustration of this idea in the ancient Near East cp. most recently O. Keel, *Wirkmächtige Siegeszeichen im AT* (1974), 47f. (note), and there also an Egyptian literary parallel.

37. See J. G. Heintz, *SVT* 17 (1969), 128.

38. Cp. Jonas C. Greenfield, "The Zakir Inscription and the Danklied," *Proceedings of the Fifth World Congress of Jewish Studies*, Jerusalem, 3–11 August 1969, pp. 180ff.

39. *lā iḫâš*, cp. also *lā taštanarrar* (*ARM* X 80:27); see Heintz, pp. 122f., but see Greenfield, p. 185, n. 28.

haddon tells [[185]] us[40] that before entering the *bīt mumme* (the temple workshop) he divided the shares (lists ?) between the diviners separately (*qātāte aḥennâ ukînma*)[41] and they gave identical answers, literally: 'they agreed with one voice' *kî pî išten indaḥarama* (= Gt √ *maḥāru*). The verb *maḥāru* is used as in the Mari passage, and the idiom: *pî išten* which is employed too in 1 Kgs 21:13: *ph ʾḥd*. This procedure of dividing the diviners into groups in order to get independent results is known to us also from other neo-Assyrian texts. Thus for example Sennacherib says that he divided the diviners into three groups in order to get the right answer.[42] It seems, therefore, that Ahab acted in a similar manner with his prophets and only after identical answers were given (*ph ʾḥd*) he decided to go to battle.

Dream and Vision

Another feature common to the prophecy in Mari and the Bible is the dream,[43] and here also identical conventions are employed. The opening formula for the dream revelation in Mari is: *ina šuttiya* 'in my dream'[44] which is exactly like the formula in the dreams of Pharaoh and his servants בחלומי (Gen 40:9, 16; 41:17, 22). And as in Pharaoh's dreams so also in Mari we find the repetition of the dream (*ARM* XII 112)[45] which implies a strong confirmation of the oracle.[46] This is even explicitly expressed in Gen 41:32: "As for Pharaoh having had the same dream twice it means that the matter has been confirmed by God נכון הדבר מעם האלהים and that God will soon carry it out." The word נכון used in this context is identical with the word *kīnu* used in connection with reliable dreams in Babylonia: *šunāt šarri kînā* = 'the dreams of the King are reliable'.[47]

This verse may also teach us that although the dreams of Pharaoh are not dreams of a prophet they nevertheless are of prophetic significance since they convey to Pharaoh the will of God, which is evident [[186]] from v. 28: "God has revealed to Pharaoh what he is about to do."[48]

40. Borger, *Asarhaddon*, 82:21f.

41. Cp. *CAD* A/1, *aḥennā*, p. 184; cp. *CAD* K *kānu* A 3a 4', p. 163.

42. H. Tadmor, *Eretz-Israel* 5, p. 156, rev. 7–8.

43. Cp. A. Malamat, *EI* 8 (1967), 237ff.

44. Cp., e.g., Moran, p. 28. After submitting this article, I came across the article of J. F. Craghan, *Journal of the ANE Society of Columbia Univ.* 6 (1974), 39ff., who brings up this analogy and elaborates the notion, suggested by M. Held, that *ina šuttiya* is a West Semitism, see pp. 43f., and n. 32 there.

45. Cp. A. Malamat, pp. 238ff.

46. Cp. the two dreams of Gudea; see Weinfeld, *Deuteronomy*, 248.

47. For references, cp. Moran, p. 23, n. 2.

48. Cp. also v. 25 *ʾt ʾšr hʾlhym ʿśh hgyd lprʿh* [['God has told Pharaoh what he is about to do']] which is to be compared with Amos 4:7 and Gen 18:17.

Another convention belonging to dream revelations in Mari is the figure in the vision which 'stands up' or 'steps up' beside the seer (*izziz*).[49] In one case it is a deity (*ARM* X 51:9), in the other it is a man (*ARM* X 94 rev. 6). This convention is similarly attested in the revelations in the Bible and likewise in reference to the deity (Gen 28:13 *nṣb* [['standing']], 1 Sam 3:10 *htyṣb* [['stood']]; cp. Exod 34:5; Amos 7:7, 9:1) as well as to a man or angel (Ezek 43:6; Zech 1:8, 10, 11; 3:5; Dan 10:16).

In the Bible dreams and visions go together (e.g., Num 12:6). In Mari too we find accounts of prophetic visions (*ARM* X 10)[50] and in one case (*ARM* X 9) it seems that we encounter a vision of the assembly of gods in heaven,[51] which is to be compared with the vision of Micaiah in 1 Kings 22 and the vision of Isaiah in chap. 6.

An interesting Biblical parallel to the way divination was practised in Mari may be found in the Balaam story in Numbers 23.[52] Balak and his entourage are said to be 'standing beside the sacrifice' *nṣb/htyṣb ᶜl ᶜltw* (Num 23:3, 6, 15, 17). This seems to be equivalent, in our opinion, to: *ina têrētim ittanazzaz* in connection with the prophetic utterances of the *āpilū*.[53] It seems that the persons on [[187]] whose behalf the sacrificial omens were prepared had "to stand," in other words "to be present" at the sacrifice while the diviner was watching and expecting the oracular response. (Compare the Rabbinic dictum in connection with the *mᶜmdwt*, i.e., people's representatives 'standing at' the daily services in the Temple: "how can a man's offering be offered while he does not stand by it?" [Mishnah Taᶜanit iv 2]). Indeed the sacrifices of Balaam and Balak

---

49. Moran, p. 28.

50. *ina bīt Itur-Mer imur ummami* (lines 6–7) = he saw '(the vision) in the temple of Itur-mer as follows'.

51. The gods and the goddesses drink and swear not to harm the brickwork of Mari; see Moran, *Biblica* 50, pp. 50–52. This is a kind of ordeal; see Weinfeld, "Ordeal," *Encycl. Judaica.*

52. On Mesopotamian parallels to Balaam's practice of divination see S. Daiches, *Hilprecht Anniversary Volume* (1909), 60–70; J. Liver, *EI* 3 (1954), 97ff. (especially p. 99 in connection with the sacrifices); R. de Largement, "Les Oracles de Bileam et la mantique suméro-akkadienne," *Mémorial du Cinquantenaire de l'École des langues orientales anciennes de l'Institut Catholique de Paris* (1964), 35–51. (Cf. also *Dict. de la Bible*, Suppl. 8, 904f.) Especially instructive are the parallels concerning the building of seven altars and the sacrificing of seven animals (Num 23:1, 4, 14; cp. *Anat. St.* 5, 104:108).

53. Cp. the text published by G. Dossin apud A. Lods in H. H. Rowley (ed.), *Studies in Old Testament Prophecy Presented to T. H. Robinson* (Edinburgh, 1950), 104, lines 24–25. The phrase occurs after "thus the prophets said" and has to be translated—in my opinion— 'while he (the representative of the King?) was standing at the omens'. Note that *ittanazzaz* (Gtn of *uzzuzu*) corresponds grammatically to *htyṣb* [['stood']], cp. E. A. Speiser, "The Durative Hithpaᶜel: A tan Form," *JAOS* 75 (1955), 118–121. For *têrtum* as sacrificial entrails, cp. *ARM* X 87:7: *têrētum lupputa* 'the entrails (liver) were stricken/infected' (compare *ngwᶜ* [['stricken']] in Hebrew); see also *Ludlul* I:51, and Lambert's remark in *BWL*, p. 284.

involve constant watching and looking out for the oracle (Num 23:3, 14, 28). This seems also to be implied in the Mari passage just referred to. Immediately after the indication of the *āpilū*'s prophetic utterances we read that the *āpilum* of Adad is watching (*inaṣṣar*) at the *maškānum* which according to A. Malamat equals *mškn* 'tabernacle'[54] (for the 'tabernacle' in Israel as an oracular pavilion compare Exod 33:7f.).

The *Rîb* Pattern

Prophetic admonition dressed in the form of a lawsuit has been recognized since the 1930's,[55] although the lawsuit convention has been limited to marital formulae. Hosea's proclamation: "Plead (*rybw*) the cause with your mother because she is not my wife and I am not her husband . . . or I will strip her naked and expose her as in the day of her birth" (3:2–3) had been seen as containing two formulaic elements: (1) the term *rîb* which has forensic overtones;[56] (2) stripping of the divorcee of her garments which is attested in the documents of Mari and Nuzi and in an almost identical context. Thus we find in an Old Babylonian document from Ḫana:[57] 'and if PN the woman says to PN her husband "you are not my husband" she shall go out naked and they shall take her up to the upper storey of the palace (i.e., expose her)', and in a Nuzi document:[58] '(if after my death she intends to contract another marriage) my sons will strip my wife of her garment and send her out of my house'. However a third formulaic [[188]] element is to be added and that is the *verba solemnia*: "She is not my wife and I am not her husband" which is now attested as a legal formula of divorce or of marriage—if put in the positive form—from Old Babylonian times[59] on and down to the Persian period.[60] This formula lies behind the phrase "I will be to you a God and

54. *JAOS* 82 (1962), 149, n. 30. However it is also possible to understand *maškanum* in its conventional meaning 'threshing floor' (*AHW*, p. 626) which also served for the purpose of hearing oracles (1 Kgs 22:10).

55. Cp. C. Kuhl, *ZAW* 52 (1934), 102–109, and C. Gordon, *ZAW* 54 (1936), 277–280.

56. Cp. J. Limburg, *JBL* 88 (1969), 301ff. See especially Jer 3:1–10, where Jeremiah develops more fully the Hoseanic theme and refers to a written legal document *spr krytwt*.

57. u šumma PN₁ aššassu ana PN₂ mutiša ul mutīmi atta iqabbi erišiša uṣṣi ana bīt rugbat ekallim ušellûši (*BRM* IV 52:14, cp. *CAD* E, p. 320); cp. for discussion, S. Greengus, *HUCA* 40 (1969), 41, n. 21.

58. ᵀᵁᴳ-šu ša aššatiya mārēja ihammaṣu u uštu bītiya ušeṣṣû (*JEN* 444:21 cp. *CAD* A/2, p. 464).

59. Cp. S. Greengus, "The Old Babylonian Marriage Contract," *JAOS* 89 (1969), 515ff.

60. Cp. A. Cowley, *Aramaic Papyri*, 15:3ff.; E. G. Kraeling, *Brooklyn Museum Aramaic Papyri*, 2:3ff.; 7:4; 14:3ff.

you will be a people to me," which appears in a covenantal context in the Law and in the Prophets.[61]

In the last fifteen years a new dimension has been added to the problem of *rîb* [['lawsuit']]. It has been argued that the *rîb* admonition reflects the lawsuit of the vassal type.[62] The prophets consider the violation of the covenant by Israel as the abrogation of the treaty with the sovereign God-King. This contention was based mostly on the witnesses in the *rîb* speech, which are the same as those of the vassal treaties: heaven and earth, mountains, etc.[63] But here again the decisive parallel should be the literary convention. In the Hittite treaties we find, in the context of keeping loyalty to the sovereign, the motif of "the cattle choosing (lit. recognizing) their stable,"[64] which is reproduced almost literally by Isaiah in the opening of his lawsuit: "the ox recognizes its master and the donkey its master's crib. Israel does not recognize, my people does not know . . ." (1:3).

Besides the images of husband-wife, master-vassal, a third image exists and that is the image of father-son, the relationship of which was also based on *verba sollemnia* [[lit. 'solemn words']]: "You are my son" creating adoption, and "You are not my son" when breaking it.[65] As in the marriage [[189]] dissolution so also in the case of the dissolution of parental relationship the son forfeits house and property and leaves the house naked.[66] This might be compared with Hos 9:15: "I hated them. . . . I will *drive them from my house,* I will love them no more."[67]

---

61. Cp. Weinfeld, *Deuteronomy,* pp. 80–81, and the reference to Y. Muffs there (p. 81, n. 1).

62. See J. Harvey, *Biblica* 43 (1962), 172–196, and, in more detail, in his book, *Le plaidoyer prophétique,* etc. (1967).

63. H. B. Huffmon, *JBL* 78 (1959), 286–295.

64. *alpē bit alpēšunu uwaddûnimmi* (Weidner, *Polit. Dokumente aus Kleinasien* [1923], no. 7, I:17f., 30f.). The correct interpretation of the phrase was seen by A. Goetze (*Kizuwatna* [1940] 36, note 38); *CAD* A/1, p. 372; A/2, p. 190; A/1, p. 32 misses the point. Compare also in the Hittite prayer to Arinna: "I am thy servant from of old, a heifer from thy stable" (KUB XXI, 27 I:8; see translation by A. Goetze, *ANET*[3], p. 393).

65. Cp. CH §170, where the father legitimizing children born by a slave girl says to them 'you are my children' (*mārū⁾a*), and the Sumerian family law (*ana ittišu* tablet 7 lines 34–39): 'if a father says to his son: "You are not my son"' (*ul māri atta*). For a thorough discussion of *verba sollemnia* in adoption see Greengus, *JAOS* 89 (1969), 517ff.

66. Cp. in the a.m. Sumerian family law: *ina bīti u igarum iteli* 'he forfeits house and wall'; and in a contract from Ugarit: *naḥlaptašu išakkanma ana sikkuri u ipaṭṭar ana sūqi* 'he (the son who shows disrespect) will put his garment on the (door) bolt and go out into the street' (Thureau-Dangin, *Syria* 18 [1937], 249, lines 22–23. Compare *Ugaritica* V, no. 83:8–10 [p. 177]). Cp. R. Yaron, *Journal of Juristic Papyrology* 15 (1965), 179ff. For the document of Alalaḫ (Wiseman, *AT* 1953, No. 16) where the son leaving is deprived of everything (*šaḥit*) see A. Draffkorn-Kilmer, *JAOS* 94 (1974), 177ff.

67. 'Love' and 'hate' are taken here in the sense of loyalty and disloyalty; cp. Moran, *CBQ* 25 (1963), 77ff., for 'love' and for 'hate' (*śn⁾*); cp. *śn⁾* in the Aramaic papyri in con-

Marriage, enslavement (= vassal relationship) and adoption representing not genetic-natural but artificial formalized relationship, suited well the depiction of the relationship between God and Israel which was formalized by Covenant and thus liable to dissolution following the breach of the Covenant.

We must admit however that beyond the judicial formulation which the prophets adopted for depicting the relationship between God and Israel, a strong emotional factor prevails. The love of God for Israel be it depicted as the love of a husband for his wife or of a father for his son is full of emotions and personal sentiments. We are dealing then with legal conventions which were turned into metaphors.[68]

Finally, it should be said that the lawsuit form is not limited to the classical prophets. It is found in ancient poetry (Deuteronomy 32) and in the Psalmodic literature: Psalms 50, 81, 95.

Furthermore, the lawsuit is also found in the prophetic messages ascribed to the times of the Judges (Judg 2:1–5, 6:8–10, 10:11–15; 1 Sam 7:3; 12:6ff.), and it indeed seems that the lawsuit type was crystallized amongst the popular, so called cultic prophets.[69]

The fact that the lawsuit is found in ancient poetry as well as in historiographical accounts would be sufficient to prove that it is not genuine in classical prophecy but was taken over by them from tradition although embellished with literary motifs of a different kind.

Morality versus Cult

In the lawsuit speeches we often find arguments against cultic [[190]] worship: Observing the moral commandment is the wish of God rather than sacrifice (Isa 1:11–17; Jer 6:20, 7:22; Mic 6:6–8 [cp. Ps 50:18ff.]; Amos 5:21–25). The arguments are usually dressed in the form of a rhetorical question: "To what purpose are all your sacrifices?" (Isa 1:11); "To what purpose is the incense which comes from Seba?" (Jer 6:20); "Does God want thousands of rams?" (Mic 6:6–7); "Do I consume the meat of oxen and blood of the goats?" (Ps 50:13f.); "Did you bring me sacrifices and gifts in the desert?" (Amos 5:25).

Now the idea of the primacy of morality is also known from Wisdom literature—e.g., Prov 15:8: "The sacrifice of the evildoer is an

---

nection with divorce (Cowley, *AP* 15:22–29, et al.); and *zêru* in Akkadian in connection with divorce as well as cancellation of adoption; see references in Greengus, *JAOS* 89 (1969), 518, n. 61.

68. Cp. M. Weinfeld, *Biblica* 56 (1975), 125.

69. Cp. J. Jeremias, *Kultprophetie und Gerichtsverkündigung*, etc. (1970).

abomination to God, the prayer of the upright is his wish";[70] "The doing
of right and justice is more pleasing to the Lord than sacrifice" (21:3);
"The wicked man's sacrifice is an abomination to the Lord, how much
more when he offers it with vileness" (21:27; cp. 28:9).

The same idea comes to expression in the Egyptian wisdom literature. Thus we read in the Instruction to King Merikare:

> Make firm your place (= grave) with uprightness and just dealing for it
> is on that which their hearts rely; more acceptable is a loaf[71] of the up-
> right than the ox of the wrongdoer.[72]

The futility of multiplying sacrifices and ritual is clearly expressed in the
admonition of the Egyptian sage Ipuwer:[73]

> All the amulets / carved figures (*twtw wḏȝw*) are insufficient and meaning-
> less. Is it by sacrifice and cleaving asunder to the crocodile?[74] Is it by slay-
> ing and roasting to the lion?[75] Is it by pouring libations 〚191〛 (and
> sacrificing) to the god Ptah? Why do you give it to him? it does not suffice
> for him.[76] It is misery/sadness (*indw*) that you give to him.

The idea is expressed in the most clear manner in the Egyptian story
of the shipwrecked sailor[77] which in the light of the comparison with the
psalms quoted below should be seen as a thanksgiving.[78] The sailor saved
from disaster says there:

70. *zbḥ ršʿym twʿbt yhwh wtplt yšrym rṣwnw.* Compare Isa 1:11ff., where *zbḥ* 〚'sacrifice'〛
and *tplh* 〚'prayer'〛 are juxtaposed (vv. 11, 15), and similarly *lʾ ḥpṣty* 〚'I do not delight'〛
and *śnʾh npšy* 〚'my soul hates'〛 (vv. 11, 19), coupled with *twʿbh* 〚'abomination'〛 (v. 13).

71. According to M. Lichtheim in *Ancient Egyptian Literature* I (1973), 109, n. 28, which
translates *bit* 'loaf' rather than 'character' (based on a suggestion of R. Williams, *Essays,*
p. 19).

72. "The Teaching for Merikare," *ANET*³, p. 417.

73. Translation: G. Fecht, *Zeitschrift für Ägypt. Spr.* 100 (1973), 12. According to Fecht
this passage is a quotation which shows that the theme was a prevalent one in Egyptian
literature.

74. The Crocodile-god (alluding to Osiris) before whom the dead are offered, see
Fecht, pp. 13–14.

75. Alluding to the goddess Sachmet, p. 14. As Fecht remarked (p. 15), it seems that
the author deliberately uses the pictures of crocodile and lion in order to indicate that the
offerings to the gods are like prey for the wild beasts. Compare the Midrashic saying ascribed to Rabbi Pinehas: "Just as the wolf snatches so the altar snatches the offerings" (*Be-
reschit Rabba,* ed. Ch. Albeck, p. 1276) and for the altar being called λύκος 'wolf' cp. Tosefta
Sukkah iv 28, and see S. Lieberman, *Tosefta Ki-fshutah* 4 (1962), 909.

76. Compare Isa 40:16: "And Lebanon is not sufficient to burn, nor are the beasts of it
enough for burnt offerings." It is of interest to note that after this verse comes a passage
about the vanity of carved figures and statues not unlike our Egyptian passage.

77. See Faulkner, Wente, Simpson, *The Literature of Ancient Egypt* (1972), 50ff.

78. The meaning and tendency of this story has not yet been established; cp. W. K.
Simpson, p. 50: "The real import of the tale perhaps escapes us." In my opinion, however,

I shall have brought to you . . . incense for the temples to satisfy every god. . . . You will be thanked in my town in the presence of the magistrates (*knbt*)[79] I shall sacrifice to you oxen as burnt offerings . . . and I shall wring the necks of birds for you. . . . Then he (the serpent-god) laughed at me and said: I am the Prince of Punt, myrrh belongs to me. . . . Place my good reputation in your town, this is all I ask from you. . . .

This passage is very close in its concepts and expressions to several passages in the thanksgiving Psalms in the Psalter. Thus we read in Ps 50:8ff.:

I do not reproach you for your sacrifices. . . . I claim no bull from your estate, no he goats from your pens, for mine is every animal of the forest, I know every bird of the mountains. . . . Were I hungry I would not tell you for mine is the world and all it holds. Do I eat the meat of bulls or drink the blood of he-goats? (cp. Mic 6:6ff.).

[[192]] Like the Egyptian text the Psalms which indulge in polemics against sacrifice also stress the idea that God wants to be praised and thanked rather than offered sacrifices. Thus we read in Ps 51:17–18:

O Lord, open my lips and let my mouth declare your praise. You do not want me to bring sacrifices. You do not desire burnt offerings.[80]

---

the tendency of the story is expressed by the recurring exhortations to praise and give thanks for salvation: "How happy is he who tells what he has experienced (lit. tasted)" (line 124); "I shall tell what happened to me, what I saw of your power, you will be praised in the city before the magistrates (*knbt*) of the whole land" (140f.); "Place my good repute in your town, this is all I ask from you" (line 160); "I placed myself upon my belly to thank him" (line 168); "I gave praise upon the shore to the lord of this island" (171f.). Thanksgiving psalms on the occasion of coming back alive from a dangerous journey by sea were common in the ancient world; cp. the Psalm of Jonah (2:3–10), and Ps 107:23–32 where the rescued person praises God in the presence of the congregation and the elders (v. 32) as in the Egyptian text quoted above (lines 170f.). Psalm 107, which enumerates four cases for thanksgiving, is paralleled by a passage in the Šamaš Hymn where Šamaš is extolled for saving the traveller on a difficult road, the seafarer in the dreadful waves, the prisoner in jail and the sick (Lambert, *Babylonian Wisdom Lit.*, p. 131, lines 65–78), the same cases found in Psalm 107. For miracles of the same type recorded in Roman Egypt (for the glory of the deities), cp. A. D. Nock, *Conversion* (1933), 83ff.

79. *Knbt* are the councillors and the judges, who parallel the *zqnym* [['elders']] in Ps 107:32; see previous note.

80. Following the translation in *The Book of Psalms* by Greenberg-Greenfield-Sarna, *JPS* (1972).

and in Ps 69:31:

> I will praise the name of God with a song and will extol him with
> thanksgiving (hymn) and this will be more favorable to him than
> an ox with horns and hooves.

It is not without significance that both in Israel and in Egypt the problem of the religious value of sacrifices is dealt with in Wisdom literature,
in texts of prophetic nature[81] and in hymnodic-thanksgiving literature.
What is common to all these sources is the juxtaposition of spiritual
worship with cultic worship and this is expressed by rhetorical questions
like "Do I eat them?" and "Why all the sacrifices and incense?" "Is it by
sacrifice (that one can satisfy God)?" It is worthwhile to note that in this
respect we encounter in the Psalmodic literature the same difficulties
which occur in the Egyptian texts. Thus we find immediately after the
passage quoted from the "Instruction for Merikare" about the loaf of the
just man which is more acceptable than the ox of the wrongdoer: "Serve
God . . . with offerings and with carving. . . . God is aware of whoever
serves him" (129–130). We face a similar problem in Psalm 50.[82] After
speaking about the vanity of multiplying sacrifices (vv. 8–13) the psalmist
states surprisingly: "Sacrifice a thank offering to God, etc." (v. 14); and
also at the end of this Psalm: "He who sacrifices a thank offering honors
me" (v. 23). It seems as if by these additions both authors wanted to make
themselves clear that they do not reject sacrifices totally. Their aim was
only to stress that sacrifice has no value when accompanied by evil.[83]

[193] One has to admit that there is a difference here between the
prophetic attitude and that of the Psalms. The prophets are concerned
with *morality* versus cult while the Psalmist is mostly concerned with *praise*
versus cult. But this difference can be explained by the very nature of
the Psalms. Songs and thanksgiving are the most characteristic part of
the Psalms (cp. the name *thlym* [['praises, psalms']]), and it is only natural that the problem of praise versus sacrifice should be given expression
here. In fact the moral issue comes to expression also in the Psalms
(50:16ff., 51:19) though in a less explicit way than in Prophecy.

---

81. For the messianic nature of the *Admonitions of Ipuwer*, cp. M. Lichtheim, *Ancient
Egyptian Literature*, I (1973), 149–150.

82. Ps 51:20–21, which also seems to contradict the previous section, has long been
recognized as an addition; see Ibn Ezra, ad loc. See, however, the next note.

83. S. Mowinckel, *The Psalms in Israel's Worship* 2 (Oxford, 1962), 21–22, explains
51:20–21 in like manner, and does not see any contradiction with what is said before:
"When God has looked in mercy upon the sinner and upon his people, and restored normal relations, then offerings, too, are a normal expression of the grateful homage and honour which the congregation owes to him" (p. 22).

In contradistinction to the Psalms the book of Proverbs like the Prophets juxtaposes morality versus cult. A similar difference actually exists in Egyptian literature. In the "Instruction for Merikare" the issue is *righteousness* versus sacrifices whereas in the "Shipwrecked Sailor" which bears the character of a thanksgiving, the issue is *praise* versus sacrifice.

It is clear then that the prophets were not the first to undermine the value of sacrifice in worshipping God: this was already stressed hundreds of years before the prophets by the Egyptians and also by the Psalmists and wise men in Israel.

Furthermore, in the light of the aforementioned parallels there is no basis for Gunkel's contention that the Psalms which take issue with sacrifices are prophetic. On the contrary it turns out that the prophets developed a motif which was current in popular admonition in Israel as well as in ancient Egypt.

Violation of Morality as Cause for Destruction

Another feature which has been seen as characteristic of classical prophecy was morality as a national historical factor. Kaufmann,[84] for example, argues that classical prophets were the first to consider sins of individual nature like deceit, bribery, exploiting the poor, etc., as determining the fate of the nation. According to Kaufmann, the Pentateuch and the Former Prophets see in idolatry and cultic deviation the cause for destruction while the prophets saw in the social crimes the main cause for destruction and exile. One must say that although this distinction is generally correct it cannot be seen as valid all along the line. For example, in the most ancient code we find that if the people maltreat widows and orphans they will be killed with the sword (Exod 22:23–24)—that is: they will perish in [[194]] battle, which is not unlike the prophetic warnings (e.g., Isa 9:15ff.).[85]

However, surprisingly enough the idea of moral behaviour as a decisive factor for the survival of the nation is found even in pagan literature.

Thus when describing the moral decay of Babylon before its destruction the Esarhaddon inscriptions[86] tell us:

---

84. *The Religion of Israel,* pp. 157ff.

85. Cp. also Gen 18:19, which clearly indicates that the realization of the promise to Abraham is conditioned by the establishment of righteousness and justice.

86. *niše āšib libbišu anna ulla aḫameš etappulu, idabuba sūrrati . . . enšu iḫabbilu, šarraku ana danni, ina qereb āli dullulu, maḫar katrê ibbasima, ūmišam la naparkā imšuʾu būšê ša aḫameš, māru ina sūqi itarrar abašu, igugma* ^dEnlil *. . . ana sapān māti ḫulluqu nišēša iktapud lemuttim* (R. Borger, *Die Inschriften Asarhaddons* [Graz, 1956], p. 12, Ep. 3, Fassung a, b, c, lines 7–14; p. 13).

the people living in it (Babylon) answered each other Yes, (in their
heart): No;[87] they plotted evil ... they (the Babylonians) were oppressing the weak/poor and putting them into the power of the mighty;
there was oppression and acceptance of bribes within the city daily
without ceasing; they were robbing each other's property; the son was
cursing his father in the street ... then the god (Enlil/Marduk) became
angry, he planned to overwhelm the land and to destroy its people.

This passage reminds us especially of the prophecy of Mic 7:1ff.:

there is no upright man, people hunt each other, the officer and
the judge ask for a bribe, the son despises the father, the daughter rises against her mother. . . .

The Isaianic concept of Jerusalem as the city of faithfulness and justice (ʿyr ḥṣdq qryh nʾmnh) is also not unique to classical prophecy. Similar
attributes were ascribed to Nippur the city of Enlil in the Sumerian
Hymns.

Thus we read in the Hymn to Enlil:[88]

Hypocrisy, distortion, abuse, malice ... enmity, oppression, envy, (brute)
force, libellous speech, arrogance, violation or agreement, breach of
contract, abuse of (a court) verdict, (all these) evils the city does not
tolerate ... the city endowed with truth where righteousness (and) justice are perpetuated.

The last sentence reminds us of ṣdq ylyn bh [['righteousness dwelled in
her']] in Isa 1:21. The phrase [[195]] 'city of justice, the faithful city' ʿyr
ḥṣdq qryh nʾmnh found in Isa 1:26 (cp. Jer 31:23 nwh ḥṣdq [['habitation of
righteousness']]) is also attested in the Assyrian literature in reference to
the Babylonian city Borsippa:

in Borsippa, the city of truth and justice (āl kitti u mišati).[89]

A similar attitude is reflected in the so-called "Advice to a Prince" in
the Babylonian literature.[90] There we read:

If a king does not heed justice, his people will fall into anarchy and his
land will be devastated ... if he does not heed his nobles, his life will be
cut short. If he does not heed his adviser, his land will rebel against

87. For this interpretation cp. Borger, p. 12.
88. Cp. S. N. Kramer, *ANET*³, pp. 573–574. For the Sumerian text (with translation
and annotations), cp. D. Reisman, *Two Neo-Sumerian Royal Hymns* (University Microfilms,
Ann Arbor, Michigan, 1969), 44f., lines 20ff.
89. See W. G. Lambert, *JAOS* 88 (1968), 126, lines 16f.
90. W. G. Lambert, *Babylonian Wisdom Lit.*, 112f.

him. . . . If citizens of Nippur are brought before him for judgment and he accepts bribes and treats them with injustice, Enlil, lord of the lands, will bring a foreign army against him. . . . If he takes the money of his citizens and puts it into his treasure . . . Marduk . . . will give his wealth and property to his enemy.

If he mobilized the whole of Sippar, Nippur and Babylon and imposed forced labour on the people . . . Marduk . . . will turn his land over to his enemy. . . .

This passage has broad implications for the law of the king in Deuteronomy 17, for the story of the disruption of the Kingdom in 1 Kings 12, and also for the admonition of Jeremiah in Jer 22:13ff., which cannot be discussed in the framework of the present study.[91]

It is true we lack in the Mesopotamian literature the moral pathos and the vehemence of expression found in classical prophecy and there is no indication that these ideas were disseminated there, not to speak of an ideology which shaped the life of the nation as it was the case in Israel. One must admit, however, that the very notion of social justice as determining the fate of a nation is found in Mesopotamian literature. We have seen that basic procedures of prophetic activity as well as basic patterns of the prophetic message are found in the ancient Near East, especially in Mesopotamia. We intend in the future to show that basic ideological concepts—such as the metropolis as world centre, messianic hopes, the appearance of the deity for world judgement—also have their roots in the ancient Near East, though their development and realization in Israel remain unique.

91. Cp. provisionally my article in *Leshonenu* 36 (Oct. 1971), 5–6.

Prophecy at Mari

ABRAHAM MALAMAT

Intuitive Prophecy

[[79]] A phenomenon attested only at Mari and in the Bible is intuitive prophecy—that is, prophetic revelation without resort to mantic or oracular devices and techniques. This is not "run-of-the-mill" haruspicy, or any similar variation of examining the entrails of sacrifices, which was in the province of the formal cult priests and sorcerers, and which generally served the royal courts throughout most of the ancient Near East. Indeed, one of the most remarkable disclosures at Mari is this informal type of divination, which existed alongside the more "academic" mantic practices. These Mariote diviner-prophets were spontaneously imbued with a certain consciousness of mission, and of a divine initiative.

In the religion of Israel, of course, prophecy held—and holds—a far greater significance than the somewhat ephemeral role evident at Mari. The prophetic utterances at Mari have almost nothing comparable to the socio-ethical or religious ideology of biblical prophecy (but see below, p. 83 [[54]]). Generally the Mari oracles are limited to a very mundane plane, placing before the king or his delegates divine demands of a most material nature and reflecting a clear *Lokalpatriotism*, concern solely for the king's personal well-being.

The corpus of known prophetic texts from Mari—that is, documents [[80]] conveying prophecies—presently numbers twenty-eight.[1] Several works have appeared which discuss this material (save one document,

Reprinted with permission from "Prophets, Ancestors and Kings," *Mari and the Early Israelite Experience* (Schweich Lectures 1984; Oxford: Oxford University Press, 1989) 79–96, 125–44.

1. See Malamat 1956, 1958, 1966, 1980 and 1987 (the latter including all the material published to about 1986).

published in 1975; and see below),[2] and we can now summarise our understanding of this topic as follows.

Two Types of Diviners at Mari

A Mari letter not directly related to our subject can serve as a key for understanding the reality behind prophecy at Mari. Baḫdi-Lim, the palace prefect, advised Zimri-Lim: "[Verily] you are the king of the Ḫaneans, [but s]econdly you are the king of the Akkadians! [My lord] should not ride a horse. Let my [lord] ride in a chariot or on a mule and he will thereby honour his royal head!" (*ARMT* VI 76:20–25). This is a clear reflection of the two strata comprising the population of Mari: West Semites (Ḫaneans, the dominant tribal federation of the kingdom), on the one hand; and a veteran Akkadian component, on the other hand.[3] As we have seen, the symbiosis between these two elements left a general imprint on every walk of life at Mari, including religion and cult.

It is in this context that we can understand at Mari (and for the present, with one late exception,[4] only at Mari) the coexistence of the two patterns noted above of predicting the future and revealing the divine word. As at every other Mesopotamian centre, we find here the typical Akkadian divination as practised by specially trained experts, above all the *bārûm* or haruspex. We are familiar with several such experts at Mari, the best known of whom was Asqudum, whose spacious mansion has recently been uncovered not far from Zimri-Lim's palace.[5] The activities of these "professionals" was usually confined to such crucial matters as omens for the security of the city.[6] Alongside this academic, supposedly "rational" system, we are confronted at Mari with an atypical phenomenon in Mesopotamia [[81]]—intuitive divination or prophecy, the informal acquiring of the word of god. Indeed, this is the earliest such

2. We cite here only general works on the entire corpus of "prophetic" materials and not studies of individual Mari documents: Ellermeier 1968; Moran 1969a; Moran, in *ANET*, 623–25, 629–32; Huffmon 1970; Craghan 1974; Noort 1977; Wilson 1980; Schmitt 1982; Nakata 1982a; Dietrich 1986; and van der Toorn 1987.

3. Charpin and Durand 1986 now suggest that the duality in the above text refers to two geographical components of Zimri-Lim's kingdom: Terqa and the Land of the Ḫaneans, and the land of Akkad.

4. I.e., Neo-Assyrian prophecy; see Weippert 1981, 1985; Hecker 1986; and see below, nn. 8, 25.

5. See Margueron 1982, 1983, 1984 (and above, p. 8 [[not included in this volume]]). On the archive of Asqudum discovered on the site, see Charpin 1985. Asqudum's wife, Yamama, was either the daughter or the sister of Yaḫdun-Lim.

6. The texts have recently been collected in Parpola 1983. For extispicy in Mesopotamia in general, and at Mari in particular, see Starr 1983: 107–8, and Index, s.v. *Mari* (p. 141 [[not reprinted here]]); and cf. the comprehensive Bottéro 1974.

manifestation known to us anywhere in the ancient Near East. This type of prophecy should properly be regarded as one of a chain of social and religious practices exclusive to Mari and, in part, similar to those found in the Bible.

This informal type of divination at Mari places biblical prophecy in a new perspective. Both phenomena bypass mantic or magic mechanisms, which require professional expertise; rather, they are the product of psychic, non-rational experience. The essential nature of prophecy of this type entails certain dominant characteristics, the three most significant of which, in my opinion, are delineated as follows:[7]

(a) Spontaneous prophetic manifestations resulting from inspiration or divine initiative (in contrast to mechanical, inductive divination, which was usually initiated by the king's request for signs from the deity). In this connection we may compare the utterance of Isaiah, communicating the word of God: "I was ready to be sought by those who didn't ask for me; I was ready to be found by those who didn't seek me. I said, 'Here am I, here am I . . .'" (Isa 65:1).

(b) A consciousness of mission, the prophets taking a stand before the authorities to present divinely inspired messages.

(c) An ecstatic component in prophecy, a somewhat problematic and complex characteristic. This concept should be allowed a broad, liberal definition, enabling it to apply to a wide range of phenomena from autosuggestion to the divinely infused dream. Only in rare instances did this quality appear as extreme frenzy, and even then it is not clear whether it was accompanied by loss of senses—for the prophets always appear sober and purposeful in thought, and far from spouting mere gibberish.

These particular characteristics—not necessarily found in conjunction—link the diviner-prophet at Mari with the Israelite prophet more than with any other divinatory type known in the ancient Near East.[8] Nevertheless, comparing Mari and the Bible, one cannot ignore the great differences between the two types of source-material: respectively first-hand documents, as against compositions which had undergone lengthy, complex literary processes. Furthermore, the documentation concerning prophecy at Mari is mostly restricted to a very short span of time, perhaps only to the final decade (or less) of Zimri-Lim's reign. In

7. Noort 1977: 24ff., rejects the characteristics mentioned below as typical of prophesying at Mari and accordingly denies any relationship to biblical prophecy. But his approach is too extreme in requiring every single characteristic to appear in each and every "prophetic" text. He has justifiably been criticized, for example, by Nakata 1982b: 166–68.

8. Except for the *rāgimu* (fem. *rāgintu*), 'the pronouncer', 'speaker' of the Neo-Assyrian period, addressing Esarhaddon and Ashurbanipal. See Weippert 1981. And see below, n. 25.

comparison, the activity [[82]] of the Israelite prophets extended over a period of centuries.[9] In other words, here too, Mari represents a synchronous picture, a cross-section at one particular point in time, while the Bible gives a diachronous view, tracing the development of the prophetic phenomenon over a period of time (and see lecture II, p. 35 [[not reprinted in this volume]]).

Prophecy at Mari and in the Bible: Similarities and Differences

Despite the external, formal similarity between the diviner-prophets at Mari and the Israelite prophets, there is an obvious discrepancy in content between the divine messages and in the function they assumed, as well as, apparently, in the status of the prophets within the respective societies and kingdoms. In Israelite society, the prophet seems usually to have enjoyed a more or less central position, though certain types of prophet were peripheral. At Mari, however, the prophets apparently played only a marginal role.[10] Admittedly, this distinction might merely be illusory, deriving from the nature of the respective source materials. In both societies many of the prophets, basing on their place of origin and locale of activity, came from rural communities: in Mari, from such towns as Terqa and Tuttul, and in Judah, from Tekoa (Amos), Moreshet (Micah), Anathot (Jeremiah) and Gibeon (Hananiah); but others resided in the respective capitals.

As for contents, the prophecies at Mari are limited to material demands on the king, such as the construction of a building or a city gate in some provincial town (*ARMT* III 78; XIII 112), the offering of funerary sacrifices (*ARMT* II 90; III 40; and see below, p. 96 [[not reprinted in this volume]]), the despatch of valuable objects to various temples (A 4260), or the request of property (*niḫlatum*) for a god (A 1121; the reference is

---

9. The lengthy span of prophecy in Israel is especially evident if we include, for our present purposes, both the early, "primitive" prophets as well as the late, "classical" ones, who were not so decidedly distinct from one another. This distinction has gained currency ever since the over-emphasis of the Canaanite origin of the early Israelite prophecy; cf. Hölscher 1914, and Lindblom 1962: 47 and 105ff. In contrast, subsequent scholars occasionally pointed out the continuity of certain early elements through the period of classical prophecy; see e.g., Haran 1977 (with earlier literature).

10. The question of centre and periphery in the status of the prophets has been raised only in recent years, under the influence of sociology. See Wilson 1980, where the peripheral role of all Mari prophets is emphasised, when compared with the central role of the *bārûm* [['diviner']]; and see most recently Petersen 1981. The author considers the *nābi²* [['prophet']] and the *ḥōzeh* [['one who sees visions']] to be "central" in both Israel and Judah, while the *rō²eh* [['seer']] and the *²iš hā²ēlōhîm* [['man of God']], as well as the *běnē něḇi²îm* ('sons of the prophets') are regarded as peripheral. For the latter see also Porter 1981.

surely to a landed estate sought by a sanctuary and its priestly staff).[11]
Many of the more recently published Mari prophecies refer to military
and political affairs, above all the welfare of the king [[83]] and his personal safety. He is warned against conspirators at home and enemies
abroad (*ARMT* X 7, 8, 50, 80), especially Ḫammurabi, king of Babylon
(see below), who was soon to conquer Mari. This sort of message is very
distinct from biblical prophecy, expressing a full-fledged religious ideology, a socio-ethical manifesto and a national purpose. But this glaring
contrast might actually be something of a distortion. At Mari nearly all the
"prophetic" texts were discovered in the royal-diplomatic archives of the
palace (Room 115), which would serve to explain their tendency to concentrate on the king. Prophecies directed at other persons presumably did
exist but, on account of their nature, have not been preserved. In comparison, had the historiographic books of the Bible (Samuel, Kings and
Chronicles) alone survived, we would be faced with a picture closely resembling that at Mari, in which Israelite prophecy, too, was oriented primarily toward the king and his politico-military enterprises.

A glimmer of social-moral concern can, however, be seen at Mari, in
a prophetic message which is contained in two recently joined fragments
(A 1121 + A 2731):[12] A diviner-prophet urges Zimri-Lim, in the name of
the god Adad of Aleppo: "When a wronged man or woman cries out to
you, stand and let his/her case be judged." This command has an exact
parallel in Jeremiah's sermon to kings: "Execute justice in the morning,
and deliver from the hand of the oppressor him who has been robbed"
(Jer 21:12; and cf. 22:3).

A tangible example of the imposition of obligations on the king at
Mari is found in one letter (*ARMT* X 100), in which a divinely imbued
woman writes to the king directly, with no intervention of a third party
(although a scribe may have been employed). The woman (whose name
is apparently to be read Yanana) addressed Zimri-Lim in the name of Dagan concerning a young lady (her own daughter, or perhaps a companion) who had been abducted when the two of them were on a journey.
Dagan appeared to the woman in a dream and decreed that only Zimri-
Lim could save and return the girl. Thus, a woman who was wronged
turned to the king in seeking redress, in the spirit of the prophetic commands adduced above.

11. Interestingly, the divine threat of Adad hanging over Zimri-Lim should he refuse
to donate the estate—"What I have given, I shall take away . . ." (A 1121, l. 18)—closely mirrors Job's words: "The Lord gave and the Lord has taken away . . ." (Job 1:27).

12. For the join (initially proposed by J.-M. Durand) of A 1121, published long ago,
and a fragment previously published only in translation, see Lafont 1984. For earlier treatments of the following passage, see, inter alia, Anbar 1975, and Malamat 1980: 73 and n. 6.

All told, the analogy between prophecy at Mari and that in Israel is presently still vague, the two being set apart by a gap of more than six centuries. Furthermore, all the intervening links are "missing." It would thus be premature to regard Mari as the prototype of prophecy in Israel.[13] But the earliest manifestation of intuitive prophecy among West Semitic tribes at Mari should not be belittled, notwithstanding its still enigmatic aspects. In this regard we can put forward two assumptions (which are not mutually exclusive):

(a) [[84]] Intuitive prophecy was basically the outcome of a specific social situation—an erstwhile non-urban, semi-nomadic, tribal society. Urban sophistication, no matter how primitive, naturally engenders institutionalized cult specialists, such as the *bārû* (haruspex), the foremost of the diviner types in Mesopotamia and part and parcel of the cult personnel of any self-respecting town or ruler.

(b) The phenomenon of intuitive prophecy was a characteristic of a particular *Kulturkreis* [['culture area']] which extended across the West, from Palestine and Syria to Anatolia, and as far as Mari in the east. This assumption is based mainly on the ecstatic element in prophecy, attested throughout this region (albeit rather sporadically). It is found outside the Bible in such cases as the prophets of the Hittite sources, at Byblos (as mentioned in the Egyptian Tale of Wen-Amon), in Syria (in the Aramaic inscription of Zakkur, king of Hamath), and in notations in classical literature.[14]

Let us now delve deeper into the data at hand concerning prophecy at Mari. Since 1948, twenty-eight letters addressed to the king and containing reports on prophecies and divine revelations have been published. The senders were high ranking officials and bureaucrats from all over the kingdom. About half were women, mostly ladies of the palace, headed by Šibtu, Zimri-Lim's principal queen. Several of the letters contain two individual visions and thus the total number of prophecies is some thirty-five. In several cases the correspondent was the prophet himself (though the letters *per se* may well have been written by scribes; one is reminded of Baruch son of Neriah, Jeremiah's amanuensis).

---

13. Here I fully agree with Noort 1977; see his summary on p. 109; I do reject, however, the remarks such as those of Schmitt 1982: 13.

14. The West as a separate *Kulturkreis* from the East (Southern Mesopotamia) with regard to certain basic religious elements has been appreciated by Oppenheim 1964: 221ff. Several scholars assume that prophecy in both Mari and Israel originated in the Arabian-Syrian desert; see, e.g., Rendtorff 1962: 146. For the ecstatic prophet in Hittite sources, see *ANET*, p. 395a; for the prophet from Byblos, see Cody 1979: 99–106. The author derives the Egyptian word ꜥ*dd* from the West Semitic ꜥ*dd*, which in the Aramaic inscription of Zakkur (see below [[not reprinted in this volume]]) designates a type of diviner-prophet; and see Malamat 1966: 209 and n. 2.

Thus, a prophet acting in the name of Šamaš of Sippar (A 4260); the court lady Addu-Duri (*ARMT* X 50); and a woman named Yanana (mentioned above; *ARMT* X 100). As already noted, the words of the diviner-prophets, whether transmitted through intermediaries or dispatched directly to the king, were generally formulated with utmost lucidity. This was perhaps due to the slight interval between the actual prophetic experience and the committing of the vision to writing. How much more is this so in connection with biblical prophecy, which generally has undergone repeated editing (though certain prophecies may well have been preserved in their pristine form).

This raises the possible conclusion (not usually considered),[15] that the messages of the diviner-prophets at Mari may originally have been pronounced in the West Semitic dialect conventionally designated "Amorite." Should this be the case in the documents before us, the original words [[85]] of the prophecies (or at least some of them) would have already been rendered into the language of the chancery, Akkadian—either by the officials writing or by their scribes. Such an assumption could also serve to explain why the "prophetic" texts at Mari display a relatively greater number of West Semitic idioms and linguistic forms than do the other Mari documents. If these assumptions are correct, the transmission of the prophetic word, *ipsissima verba* [['the very words']], to the king's ear, was considerably more complex than outwardly appears.

The diviner-prophets at Mari were of two types: professional or "accredited"—recognisable by distinctive titles (as were the biblical *rōʾeh* [['seer']], *ḥōzeh* [['seer of visions']], *nābîʾ* [['prophet']] and *ʾîš ʾĕlōhîm* [['man of God']]); and casual—lay persons who held no formal title (see below [[pp. 62–66]]). Thus far, five different titles are known at Mari designating "cult" prophets (if we may use a term current in Bible studies):

(1) A priest (*šangûm*) is mentioned once as a prophet (*ARMT* X 51), imbued with a prophetic dream containing a warning; in the Bible, too, Ezekiel was originally a priest, and so was Pashhur, son of Immer (Jer 20:1, 6).

(2) There are three references to the prophetic *assinnum* (*ARMT* X 6, 7, 80),[16] though this term is not entirely clear in meaning. Basing on later sources, it might refer to a eunuch, a male prostitute or a cult musician. One such functionary served in a temple at Mari and prophesied in the name of Annunītum (a goddess normally associated with women), apparently while disguised as a woman (perhaps in the manner of present-day transvestites).

---

15. An exception in Sasson 1980.
16. For this prophet, see Wilson 1980: 106–7, with bibliography.

(3) In one solitary instance (*ARMT* X 8), a prophetess bears the title *qabbātum* (or possibly *qamatum*),[17] a term undoubtedly derived from the Akkadian verb *qabûm*, 'to speak, proclaim'.[18]

(4) One of the best known of the "accredited" prophets at Mari is the *muḫḫûm* (fem. *muḫḫūtum*) who, as etymology would indicate, was some sort of ecstatic or frenetic.[19] The peculiar behaviour of this type of prophet led him to be perceived as a madman, similar to the biblical *mĕšuggāᶜ* [['crazy']], a term occasionally used as a synonym for *nābîʾ* [['prophet']] (2 Kgs 9:11; Jer 29:26; Hos 9:7).[20] We may also mention instances of the Akkadian verb *immaḫu* (3rd person preterite), derived from the same root as *muḫḫûm*, [[86]] and used in the N-stem, resembling Biblical Hebrew *nibbāʾ* [['prophesying']] (cf. also *hitnabbēʾ* [['prophesy']]). This word, *immaḫu*, means 'became insane', 'went into a trance' (*ARMT* X 7:5–7; 8:5–8). Besides the five unnamed *muḫḫûm*s mentioned in the "prophetic" documents, the recently published volumes of Mari documents[21] include new administrative material naming five *muḫḫûm*s, along with the deities they served. These documents are lists of personnel receiving clothes from the palace. In a previously published list, there is a reference to an *āpilum* (*ARMT* IX 22:14; and see below [[p. 58]]). This would imply that the *muḫḫûm* (as well as the *āpilum*) received material support from the royal court. A surprising feature here is that four of the named *muḫḫûm*s have strictly Akkadian (rather than West Semitic) names: Irra-gamil, *muḫḫûm* of Nergal; Ea-maṣi, *muḫḫûm* of Itur-Mer (*ARMT* XXI 333:33'/34'; XXIII 446:9', 19'); Ea-mudammiq, *muḫḫûm* of Ninhursag; and Anu-tabni, *muḫḫūtum* of the goddess Annunitum (*ARMT* XXII 167:8' and 326:8–10); the fifth was a *muḫḫûm* of Adad, mentioned with the intriguing notation that he received a silver ring "when (he) delivered an oracle for the king" (*ARMT* XXV 142:3'). Another *muḫḫūtum*

---

17. For this term, and additional bibliographical references, see *CAD* Q, p. 2b. It is tempting to link this term with the Hebrew root *qbb*, 'to curse', frequently applied in connection with the prophecy of Balaam, who announced: *māh ʾeqqōḇ lōʾ qabbōh ʾēl* . . . (the form *qabbōh* is irregular and resembles a possible root *qbh*), Num 23:8: "How can I curse whom God has not cursed?"

18. Cf. Renger 1969: 219ff.; and *CAD* M/1, p. 90a, which includes Old Babylonian references outside Mari.

19. The *purrusum* form of the noun is peculiar to Mari (in other Akkadian sources we find the form *maḫḫûm*). This nominal form designates bodily defects and functionally resembles the Hebrew *qiṭṭēl* form used in such words as *ᶜiwwēr*, 'blind', *pissēaḥ*, 'lame', and *gibbēn*, 'hunchback'. See Holma 1914 and Landsberger 1915: 363–66.

20. Malamat 1966: 210–11 and n. 4, for additional references and earlier bibliography on *muḫḫûm*.

21. *ARMT* XXI; *ARMT* XXII; *ARMT* XXIII; *ARMT* XXV (1986).

with court connections was named Ribatum; she sent an oracle to Zimri-Lim concerning the two tribal groups, the Simalites and the Yaminites.[22]

It is possible that on the whole these prophets, who were dependent on the royal court of Mari, had already been assimilated into Akkadian culture to a great extent, hence their Akkadian names. In any case, the direct contact with the royal court calls to mind the court prophets in Israel, such as Nathan the *nābî* [['prophet']] and Gad the *hōzeh* [['seer of visions']], who served David and Solomon, or the Baal and Ashera prophets functioning at the court of Ahab and Jezebel.

(5) Finally, there was the *āpilum* (fem. *āpiltum*), a prophetic title exclusive to Mari and meaning 'answerer, respondent' (derived from the verb *apālum*, 'to answer').[23] Unlike the other types of prophets, *āpilum*s on occasion acted in consort, in groups similar to the bands of prophets in the Bible (*hebel* or *lahăqat něbî*'*îm* [['band of prophets']]). The *āpilum* is attested in documents covering a broad geographical expanse, with a wider distribution than any other type of prophet—from Aleppo in northern Syria to Sippar near Babylon. Thus, an *āpilum* of Šamaš of Sippar, addressing the king of Mari directly, demanded a throne for Šamaš, as well as one of the king's daughters (?) for service in his temple.[24] He also demanded objects for other deities (including an *asakku* or consecrated object; see above, p. 72 [[not reprinted here]]): Adad of [[87]] Aleppo, Dagan of Terqa and Nergal of Ḫubšalum (A 4260). Another *āpilum* was in the Dagan temple at Tuttul (near the confluence of the Baliḫ and the Euphrates rivers) and there was an *āpiltum* in the Annunîtum temple in the city of Mari itself. And an *āpilum* of Dagan, bearing the strictly Akkadian name Qišatum, received bronze objects from the palace, like the "gifts" from the king noted above (*ARMT* XX 5:2′–3′).[25] It is noteworthy that the *muḫḫûm* and the *muḫḫūtum* functioned in these very same sanctuaries as well, indicating that two different types of diviner-

22. Charpin and Durand 1986: 151 and n. 7.

23. Malamat 1966: 212–13 and n. 2, for the various spellings *apillû, aplûm, āpilum*; and see *CAD* A/2, p. 170a; Malamat 1980: 68ff.; Anbar 1981: 91.

24. Interestingly, compliance with this prophetic demand seems to be alluded to in the female correspondence. Further on in our document the name of Zimri-Lim's daughter is given as Erišti-Aya. Indeed, a woman by this name sent several doleful letters to her royal parents from the temple at Sippar; see *ARMT* X 37:15; 43:16, etc. Cf. Kraus 1984: 98 and n. 224; and Charpin and Durand 1985: 332, 340.

25. Another *āpilum*, of Marduk (!), is mentioned in an unpublished Mari letter addressed to Išme-Dagan, king of Assyria, urging him to deliver a handsome ransom to the king of Elam (A 428:21–28); see Charpin 1987: 133. "Prophetic" documents of this same period have been discovered also at Ishchali, on the Lower Diyala river, seat of the goddess Kititum; her oracles, addressed to Ibal-pi-El, king of Ešnunna, a contemporary of the Mari kings, are similar in tone and message to those from Mari, but they are quite different in their mode of transmission, for they appear in the form of letters from the deity herself, with no prophetic intermediary involved. See Ellis 1987: 251–57.

prophets could be found side by side. Indeed, in the Dagan temple at Terqa, three types of prophet were at work simultaneously: a *muḫḫûm*, a *qabbātum* and a dreamer of dreams.

Affinities in Terminology and Contents: Mari and Israel

The terms *āpilum* and *muḫḫûm* would appear to have counterparts in Biblical Hebrew. The terms *ᶜānāh* and *ᶜōneh*, 'answer' and 'answerer', respectively, can refer to divine revelation.[26] Most significantly, the very verb *ᶜānāh* is used at times to describe the prophet's function as God's mouthpiece, whether actually responding to a query put to the deity or not. This is clearly seen, for instance, in 1 Sam 9:17: "When Samuel saw Saul, the Lord answered him, 'Here is the man of whom I spoke to you! He it is who shall rule over my people.' " This is also indicated by Jeremiah's condemnation (23:33ff.) of one Hebrew term for prophetic utterance, *maśśāᵓ* (cf., e.g., Lam 2:14 and 2 Kgs 9:25), and his commendation of the more "legitimate" *ᶜānāh* in its stead: "What has the Lord answered and what has the Lord said?" (Jer 23:37). The term *maᶜănēh ᵓĕlōhīm* (lit. 'God's answer'), meaning the word of the Lord, occurs once in the Bible, in Mic 3:7, which also elucidates the use of *ᶜnh* in connection with the oracles of Balaam: "Remember now, O my people, remember what Balak king of Moab devised and what Balaam the son of Beor *answered* him" (Mic 6:5). The verb *ᶜānāh* here does not indicate response to a specific question put forth to Balaam but, rather, the prophetic oracle which Balaam was compelled to deliver in Israel's favour. It is possible that this non-Israelite diviner, who is never designated *nābīᵓ*, was a prophet of the *āpilum* ('answerer') type. The analogy might be strengthened by the cultic acts performed by Balaam, on the one hand (Num 23:3, [[88]] 14–15, 29), and by the band of *āpilum*s on the other hand (A 1121, esp. lines 24–25)—both soliciting the divine word.[27]

It is of interest that the recently discovered "Balaam Inscription" from Tell Deir ᶜAlla in Transjordan, from the late 8th or early 7th century B.C. and written in either an Ammonite or "Israelite-Gileadite" dialect, enumerates various types of sorcerers, including a woman designated *ᶜnyh*. The latter term most likely means "(female) respondent," that

---

26. Malamat 1958: 72–73.

27. Balaam was certainly not a prophet of the *bārûm* type, as was long ago suggested in Daiches 1909: 60–70. This claim has often been refuted, correctly; see Rofé 1979: 32 n. 53. Offering sacrifices in preparation for deriving the word of the deity as is found in the Balaam pericope is similarly alluded to at the beginning of Mari texts *ARMT* XIII 23 and A 1221; it is explicitly mentioned in a "prophetic" document which has so far been published only in French translation—A 455: '. . . One head of cattle and six sheep I will sacrifice . . .', that is, seven sacrificial animals. In what follows, a *muḫḫûm* "arises" and prophesies in the name of Dagan. Compare the seven altars, seven bulls and seven rams which Balaam had Balak prepare before delivering his oracle (Num 23:29–30).

is, a semantic equivalent of the Mari term *āpiltum*.[28] This interpretation
gains cogency through the phrase following the reference to the woman:
rqḥt mr wkhnh, 'a perfumer of myrrh and priestess'. Even more significant
is the Aramaic inscription of Zakkur, king of Hamath, from about 800 B.C.
In his hour of peril, Zakkur turned to his gods, "and Baalšamayn responded to me (*wyᶜnny*) and Baalšamayn [spoke to me] through seers
and diviners" (*ᶜddn*; lines 11–12).[29]

A probable overlap of the prophetic activity of the *āpilum* and that of
the *muḫḫûm* is indicated in a letter containing the message of a *muḫḫūtum*,
imploring the king of Mari not to leave the capital to wage war at that
time; it declares: "I will *answer* you constantly" (*attanapal*; ARMT X 22–
26). In other words, there are cases where a *muḫḫûm* would be involved in
the act of 'answering' (*apālum*).

Before turning to the matter of lay prophets at Mari, let us examine
two prophecies of similar content, reminiscent of the biblical oracles
"against the nations": one of an *āpilum* (curiously spelled here *aplûm*);
and the other of 'the wife of a man', that is, a lay woman. Both reports
were transmitted through Kibri-Dagan, Zimri-Lim's governor at Terqa.
The *āpilum/aplûm* 'arose' in the name of Dagan of Tuttul, "and so he said
as follows: 'O Babylon! Why doest thou ever (evil)? I will gather thee into
〚89〛 a net! . . . The houses of the seven confederates and all their possessions I shall deliver into Zimri-Lim's hand!' " (ARMT XIII 23:6–15).
This prophecy, which contains several motifs well known in the biblical
prophecies of doom,[30] reflects the deteriorating relations between Mari
and Babylon, brought about by Ḥammurabi's expansionist aspirations.
The other prophecy explicitly mentions Ḥammurabi as an enemy of Mari

28. See the Deir ᶜAlla inscription, first combination, line 11; Hoftijzer and van der
Kooij 1976: 180, 212. The editors interpreted *ᶜnyh* as a female answerer, indicating a prophetess, following our conclusion concerning the title *āpilum* at Mari and its relationship to
biblical terminology. This opinion has been accepted by Rofé 1979: 67 and n. 33, among
others. Indeed, in the dialect of this inscription verbs with a third weak radical are spelled
preserving the *yod* before the final *he*, like Hebrew *bōḳiyāh* (I must thank B. Levine for this
information; and see his forthcoming study on this text 〚"The Plaster Inscriptions from
Deir ᶜAlla: General Interpretation," in *The Balaam Text from Deir ᶜAlla Re-evaluated* [Leiden,
1991]〛). This term has nothing to do with 'poor woman', despite the Hebrew homograph
ᶜnyh, as various scholars contend; see, e.g., Caquot and Lemaire 1977: 200; McCarter 1980:
58; Weippert 〚and Weippert〛 1982: 98; and Hackett 1984: 133 s.v. *ᶜnyh*.

29. See Gibson 1975: 8ff. The author there translates the word *ᶜddn* as '(prophetic?)
messengers' on the basis of *ᶜdd* in Ugaritic (p. 15), and cf. above, n. 14. For a possible connection between prophecy at Mari and that at Hamath, see Ross 1970.

30. Especially the motifs of gathering into a net and delivering into the hand, which
are found frequently in both ancient Near Eastern and biblical literature in connection
with vanquishing an enemy; Malamat 1980: 217–18, and cf. Heintz 1969, who relates these
motifs to the "Holy War" in the ancient Near East and the Bible.

(*ARMT* XIII 114). A divinely inspired woman approached Kibri-Dagan late one afternoon with the following words of consolation: "The god Dagan sent me. Send your lord; he shall not worry [. . .], he shall not worry. Ḫammurabi [king] of Babylon . . . [continuation broken]." The urgency of the matter is indicated by the fact that the letter bearing this encouraging message was dispatched the very day it was uttered.

From these two prophecies—and possibly from most of the visions concerning the king's safety—it is apparent that they were recorded at a time of political and military distress at Mari. This, too, would be analogous to Israelite prophecy, which thrived particularly in times of national emergency—such as during the Philistine threat in the days of Samuel and Saul, during Sennacherib's campaign against Jerusalem, and especially at the time of Nebuchadnezzar's moves against Judah. The crisis factor was certainly one of the principal forces engendering prophetic manifestations in both Mari and Israel.[31] However, in contrast to the Bible with its prophecies of doom and words of admonition against king and people, the messages at Mari were usually optimistic and sought to placate the king rather than rebuke or alert him. Such prophecies of success and salvation (see *ARMT* X 4, 9, 10, 51, 80), coloured by a touch of nationalism, liken the Mari prophets to the "false prophets" of the Bible. Surely, the corresponding prophecies are quite similar. Indeed, one of the prominent "false prophets" in the Bible, Hananiah of Gibeon, Jeremiah's rival, rashly proclaimed in the name of the Lord (and not in the name of a foreign god) the impending return of the Judean exiles from Babylonia: "for I will break the yoke of the king of Babylon" (Jer 28:4). How reminiscent is this of the *āpilum*'s prediction against Babylon (see above, *ARMT* XIII 23). In both instances the message is a whitewashing of the critical situation, for such prophets of peace served the "establishment" and expressed its interests (compare the four hundred prophets at Ahab's court, who prophesy "with one accord"; 1 Kgs 22:13).[32]

In contrast to Mari, the Bible is replete with prophecies unfavourable [[90]] to king and country; their heralds, the so-called prophets of doom (or "true" prophets), were constantly harassed by the authorities. One well-known case is that of Amos who, at the royal sanctuary at Bethel, foretold of King Jeroboam's death and the exile of the people (Amos 7:10–13). In reaction, the priest Amaziah, by order of the king, expelled the prophet to Judah in disgrace. Jeremiah provoked an even more

31. This has been indicated by, among others, Uffenheimer 1973: 27, 37; Noort 1977: 93, 109; and Blenkinsopp 1983: 45. Remarkably, just prior to Ḫammurabi's conquest of Mari there is a noticeable rise in future-telling activities of the *bārûm* [['diviner']]; see Starr 1983: 107.

32. For the "false" prophets and their dependence on the Israelite establishment, see, among others, Buber 1950: 253ff.; Hossfeld and Meyer 1973; DeVries 1978.

violent response, in the days of both Jehoiakim and Zedekiah. Pashhur (the priest in charge of the temple in Jerusalem), when confronted by the prophet's words of wrath, "beat Jeremiah the prophet, and put him in the stocks that were in the house of the Lord" (Jer 20:2).

At certain times, however, we do find close cooperation between king, priest and prophet. A priest occasionally officiated as an intermediary between the king and the prophet, as when Hezekiah sent emissaries to Isaiah (2 Kgs 19:20ff. = Isa 37:2ff.) and Zedekiah to Jeremiah (Jer 21:1ff.; 37:3ff.). Similarly, Hilkiahu, the high-priest, headed the royal delegation which Josiah sent to Huldah the prophetess (2 Kgs 22:12ff.). The roles are inverted at Mari, where a prophet's report could be conveyed to the king via a priest. According to two documents (*ARMT* VI 45 and X 8), prophetesses appeared before Aḫum the priest, who served in the temple of Annunitum in Mari proper. Once Aḫum reported the message to Baḫdi-Lim, palace prefect, who passed it on to the king; at another time he transmitted the prophetic words to the queen, Šibtu.[33] In the latter case, a new element appears, to which we have alluded only briefly above—the frenetic here was a mere maidservant named Aḫatum and had no prophetic title—that is, she was a simple lay-person.

Lay Prophets and Message Dreams

More than half the "prophetic" documents from Mari deal with lay-persons, "prophets" not "accredited" to any sanctuary. Among these we find such designations as "a man," "a woman," "a man's wife," "a youth" and "a young woman (or 'maidservant')," as well as several instances of persons who are merely mentioned by name. In one case a prophetic message was elicited from "a man and a woman" (lit. "male and female"), who prophesied jointly (*ARMT* X 4). Because this manner of prophecy was uncommon and surprising at Mari, it should be examined briefly.

Queen Šibtu wrote to her husband that she had asked a man and a woman to foretell the fortunes of Zimri-Lim's forthcoming military venture against Išme-Dagan, king of Ashur. As noted, the mode of divination here [[91]] is exceptional, and has led to various scholarly interpretations.[34] The key sentence at the opening of Šibtu's letter reads (according

---

33. Moran 1969a: 20, holds that *ARMT* VI 45 deals with the same event as *ARMT* X 50, while Sasson 1980: 131b, associates it with *ARMT* X 8. Neither suggestion is compelling. *ARMT* X 50 does not mention a priest by the name of Aḫum, but someone else, while *ARMT* X 8 mentions a prophetess by name but without title, and *ARMT* VI 45 speaks of an anonymous *muḫḫūtum*. It may be assumed, therefore, that both professional and lay prophets would occasionally appear before Aḫum, a priest in Mari.

34. On *ARMT* X 4, and the mode of prophesying, see the recent studies: Finet 1982; Durand 1982; Durand 1984: 150ff.; and Wilcke 1983: 93.

to a recent collation): "Concerning the report on the military campaign which my lord undertakes, I have asked a man and a woman about the signs (*ittātim*) when I plied (them with drink) and the oracle (*egerrûm*) for my lord is very favourable" (*ARMT* X 4:3–37). Šibtu immediately inquired of the fate of Išme-Dagan, and the oracle "was unfavourable." This query concerning the fate of the enemy recalls how king Ahab consulted the four-hundred prophets, prior to his battle against the Arameans (1 Kgs 22:6ff.). Further on, Šibtu cited the full prophecy proclaimed by the two persons, which contains several motifs found in biblical prophecies.[35] How are we to perceive this kind of divination? It has been suggested that the man and woman themselves served as a sign and portent, partly on the basis of the words of Isaiah (8:18): "Behold, I and the children the Lord has given me are signs and portents in Israel"—but such an interpretation seems forced. Rather, the queen seems to have selected a couple at random, offering them drink (perhaps wine) to loosen their tongues and thus obtained an *egerrûm*-oracle, based on "chance utterances." This type of divining, known as cledomancy, has been likened to the divinatory method known in Hebrew as *bat qōl* (literally 'a trace of a voice', usually translated 'echo'). The same Hebrew term is found in Talmudic sources, where it serves as an ersatz for prophecy *per se*.[36]

Among lay prophets as well as transmitters of prophetic reports, there was an unusually large proportion of women, mostly from Zimri-Lim's court. Indeed, one of the king's daughters explicitly stated to her father: "Now, though I am a (mere) woman, may my father the lord hearken unto my words. I will constantly send the word of the gods to my father" (*ARMT* X 31:7'–10'). Some prophetesses and female dreamers of dreams sent their prophecies directly to the king, without a mediator (*ARMT* X 50, 100). Šibtu, more than anyone else, served as an intermediary for conveying prophetic messages to her husband. This would call to mind rather bizarre episodes throughout history, where a "prophet" or mystic used or exploited a queen so as to bring his visions and message to the attention of her husband, the king. Among the

35. Note, above all, the motif of the gods marching alongside the king in time of war and saving him from his enemies, a motif resembling the intervention of the Lord in the wars of Israel. This involves also driving the enemy into flight; cf.: "Arise, O Lord, and let thy enemies be scattered . . ." (Num 10:35; and see also Ps 68:2) [in relation to the above-mentioned biblical parallel, note the utterance of the prophet Micaiah the son of Imlah concerning the dispersion of the Israelite army (1 Kgs 22:17)], and eventually decapitating the foe who would be trampled under the foot of the king of Mari (see, e.g., Josh 24:25). And see Weinfeld 1977.

36. For this type of oracle, see *CAD* E, s.v. *egirrû*, p. 45: ". . . oracular utterances . . . which are either accidental in origin (comp. with Greek *klēdōn*) or hallucinatory in nature. . . ." For the parallel with Hebrew *bat qōl*, see Sperling 1972.

"accredited" prophets, too—as we have ⟦92⟧ seen—there were many women, as there were in the Bible. The outstanding of these were Deborah, wife of Lapidoth (Judg 4:4) and Huldah, wife of Shallum (2 Kgs 22:14). In both instances the Bible specifically notes that they were married women, probably to stress their stability and reliability—as in the case of the "wife of a man," one of the Mari prophetesses (*ARMT* XIII 114:8).

Are there any characteristics which distinguish the "accredited" prophets from the lay ones? Two prominent features have been noticed by scholars: (a) Only in the case of the "accredited" are the actual messages preceded by the verb *tebû*, 'to arise' (e.g., "he/she arose and . . ."), somehow alluding to prophetic stimulation in the temple.[37] Synonymous expressions are used in connection with the biblical prophets, as well (Deut 13:2; 18:15, 18; 34:10; Jer 1:17; etc.); note in particular Ezekiel: "And set me upon my feet" (Ezek 2:2; and cf. Ezek 3:22–24; Dan 8:17–18; 10:10–11; 2 Chr 24:2). (b) Among the lay prophets, dreaming is prevalent as the prophetic means, while this medium is totally absent among the "accredited" prophets.

Almost half the published prophecies from Mari were revealed in dreams. Phenomenologically, we thus find two distinct categories of acquiring the divine word. "Accredited" prophets enjoyed direct revelation while fully conscious; whereas lay prophets often received revelations through dreams. The latter was a widespread phenomenon throughout the ancient Near East, including Israel.[38] At Mari, as in the Bible, we find a specific subcategory of "message dream" alongside ordinary revelatory dreams—that is, dreams in which the message was not intended for the dreamer himself, but rather for a third party (in the Bible, see Num 12:6; Jer 23:25ff.; 29:8; Zech 10:2; etc.).

The two above categories of prophecy now clarify a parallel distinction made in the Bible, especially in legal contexts: "If a prophet arises among you, or a dreamer of a dream, and gives you a sign or a wonder . . ." (Deut 13:1ff.). In an incident involving Saul, the Bible is explicit in differentiating between three distinct divinatory methods: "The Lord did not answer him, either by dreams or by Urim or by prophets" (1 Sam 28:6; and see v. 15).[39] Even Jeremiah regarded the dreamer as a distinct type of prophet (Jer 27:9), though he belittled this medium, contrasting it with "the word of God" and associating it with false prophets:

37. See, in particular, Moran 1969a: 25–26; and Weinfeld 1977: 181–82.

38. Malamat 1966: 221–22 and n. 1 on p. 222, for literature on the dream in the Bible. For the ancient Near East, see the basic study of Oppenheim 1956.

39. An exact parallel to these three alternative means of inquiring of the deity may be found in the Plague Prayers of the Hittite King Muršili II; see *ANET*, 394b–395a; and Herrmann 1965: 54–55.

"Let the prophet who has a dream tell the dream, but let him who has my word speak my word faithfully. What has straw in common with wheat?" (Jer 23:28). This deflated status of the dream as a source of prophetic [93] inspiration also finds clear expression in the Rabbinic dictum comparing sleep to death, just as 'a dream is a withered prophecy' (*nōḇelet nĕḇûʾāh ḥălōm*; Genesis Rabba 44:17).

The Mari letters reporting dream-revelations are usually structured on a regular scheme: (1) the male or female dreamer; (2) the opening formula of the dream—'(I saw) in my dream' (*ina šuttīya*—an obviously West Semitic form identical with Biblical Hebrew *baḥălōmī*; cf. Gen 40:9, 16; 41:17);[40] (3) the content of the dream, based on a visual or, more often, an auditory "experience"; and finally, (4) the communicator's comments, in many cases including a statement that a lock of the prophet/prophetess's hair and a piece of the hem of his/her garment are being sent to the king as well.

In one illuminating incident at Mari, where the same dream recurred on two successive nights, the dreamer was a mere youth (*ṣuḥārum*), to whom a god appeared in a nocturnal vision. The dream was eventually reported to the king by Kibri-Dagan: "Thus he saw (a vision) as follows: 'Build not this house . . . ; if that house will be built I will make it collapse into the river!' On the day he saw that dream he did not tell (it) to anyone. On the second day he saw again the dream as follows: 'It was a god (saying): "Build not this house; if you will build it, I will make it collapse into the river!"' Now, herewith the hem of his garment and a lock of hair of his head I have sent to my lord . . ." (*ARMT* XIII 112:1'–15'). The boy, who apparently had no previous prophetic experience, did not at first realize the source of his dream; only when it recurred the next night did he become aware of its divine origin and of the mission imposed upon him. This immediately calls to mind young Samuel's initial prophetic experience, while reposing in the temple at Shiloh (1 Sam 3:3ff.). The Lord informed him, in a nocturnal vision, of the impending demise of the Elide clan. In Samuel's case, it was only after the fourth beckoning (but on the same night) that he comprehended the divine nature of the vision.[41]

In general, novice and inexperienced prophets were unable to identify divine revelations when first encountered (as in the case of Samuel;

40. The West Semitic form was pointed out by M. Held, apud Craghan 1974: 43 n. 32. The standard Akkadian form would be *ina šuttim ša āmuru/aṭṭulu*; compare a similar West Semitic usage in one of the first prophecies published: *ina pānīya*, lit. 'in front of me', meaning 'on my way'; see Malamat 1956: 81.

41. See Malamat 1980: 223ff.; and Gnuse 1984; esp. 119ff. The phenomenon of an identical dream recurring several times is known especially from the Classical world; see Hanson 1978: 1411, and the passages from Cicero, *De divinatione*, cited there.

see 1 Sam 3:7). Hence we find the repetition of the manifestation, both at Mari and in the Bible. Jeremiah's initial call is also most illuminating: he too was reluctant to accept his prophetic calling, pleading youthfulness (Jer 1:6–7). After bolstering the youth's confidence, God tested him by a vision: "And the word of the Lord came to me saying: 'Jeremiah, what do you see?' and I said: 'I see a rod of almond (Hebrew: *šāqēd*).' [94] Then the Lord said to me: 'You have seen well for I am watching (*šōqēd*) over my word to perform it' " (Jer 1:11–12). God, in his response, expressly confirmed the reliability of the prophet's perception—a totally unique event in the realm of prophetic vision in the Bible—and thus proving Jeremiah's fitness to undertake his prophetic mission.[42]

Prophetic Credibility

In the most recently published "prophetic" text from Mari (A 222),[43] the name of the writer has been lost, as has been the name of the recipient (who was probably Zimri-Lim, recipient of the other letters). We read:

> The woman Ayala saw (*iṭṭul*) in her dream as follows:
> A woman from Šeḫrum (and) a woman from Mari in the gate of (the temple of) Annunitum . . . /line missing/ which is at the edge of the city—quarrelled among themselves. Thus (said) the woman from Šeḫrum to the woman from Mari: "Return to me my *position as high priestess* (*enūtum* may refer instead to 'equipment'); either you sit or I myself shall sit."
> By the *ḫurru*-bird I have examined this matter and she could see (*naṭlat*) (the dream). Now her hair and the hem of the garment I am sending along. May my lord investigate the matter!

The nature of the dispute between these two women is not entirely clear although it may involve rivalry over the office of the high priestess. The penultimate passage relates that the writer confirmed the validity of the vision by means of augury. This divinatory device, well known in the classical world, appeared at a very early period in Hither Asia.[44] In this instance, the examination "proved" that the woman actually did see (*naṭlat*), that is, she actually did see the vision she claimed to have seen. Inasmuch as the verb *amāru*, 'to see (a dream)', is synonymous and interchangeable with *naṭālu*, the intention here seems to be that the woman

---

42. See Malamat 1954: esp. 39–40.

43. The document was published by Dossin 1975 (attributed by him to King Yaḫdun-Lim!); and see the comments in Sasson 1983: 291. His interpretation of *enūtum* (see below [not reprinted here]) as 'utensils' rather than 'priesthood' is possible.

44. Divination by bird behaviour is a typically western practice; cf. Oppenheim 1964: 209–10. This practice was especially widespread among the Hittites; see Kammenhuber 1976, which deals only briefly (p. 11) with the kind of bird mentioned in our text: MUŠEN ḪURRI; for this bird, see Salonen 1973: 143–46; and cf. McEwan 1980.

was indeed competent and experienced in the art of dream oracles.[45] Thus, the meaning is precisely as the editor of the text translated: 'Elle a bien eu ce songe!'—just like God's words to Jeremiah: 'You have seen well' (*hēṭabtā lirʾōt*)! The writer did not suffice with his own examination of the dream, and [[95]] sent the woman's hair and the hem of her garment to the king—for his examination. This unique and somewhat puzzling practice, attested only in connection with the Mari prophets, is mentioned on nine different occasions; that is, in a third of all the "prophetic" letters. Several scholarly interpretations have been offered, all of which remain in the realm of speculation. This procedure was clearly related in some manner to the reliability of the diviner and of his message. In most of the cases, the prophet's words were presented to the king only as recommendations, the final decision to act upon them remaining in his hands: "Let my lord do what pleases him"; "Let my lord do what, in accordance with his deliberation, pleases him." (In this matter, these prophecies decidedly differ from biblical prophecy, which is absolute and "non-negotiable.") Several points should be noted in this context.

The lock of hair and the hem of the garment are unequivocally personal objects,[46] specific to their individual owners, and seem to have served as a sort of "identity card." In the Bible, we read how David took the fringe of Saul's robe in the cave near En-Gedi (1 Samuel 24), in order to show him that Saul had been entirely at his mercy. In other words, the Mari procedure may primarily have had a legal significance, more than a religio-magic meaning, as often suggested. These personal items may also have been sent to the king in order to serve as evidence for the very existence of a diviner, and that the message was not simply a fabrication of the reporting official, who may have had some particular motive for promoting a false report.[47] Surely *fraus pia*, 'pious fraud', was no rarer in that period than it was later. This aspect also emerges from a long text

45. See *CAD* A/2, s.v. *amāru* A2, p. 13: to learn by experience (especially stative . . .). The stative form with the meaning 'experienced, trained' is particularly prevalent in the Mari idiom, and we may therefore assume a similar nuance for the stative of *naṭālu: naṭlat* in our document.

46. For the hair (or lock of hair—*šārtum*) and the hem of a garment (*sissiktum*) see Liverani 1977; Malul 1986; the latter suggests that not merely the hem but the entire garment (or rather, undergarment, covering the private parts) was involved; and see n. 47 below.

47. Malamat 1956: 81, 84; Malamat, 1966: 225ff. and notes. For other explanations, see Uffenheimer 1973: 29–33; Ellermeier 1968; Moran 1969a: 19–22; Noort 1977: 83–86; and Craghan 1974: 53ff. Note in two documents (A 455: 25; and *ARMT* X 81:18), the illuminating but problematic addition appearing after the despatch of the hair and the hem; in the latter: "let them declare (me) clean (*lizakkû*)"; according to Moran 1969a: 22–23: ". . . it is the haruspex who 'tries the case' and it is his response that will in effect declare the prophetess clean." And cf. *ARMT* X, p. 267, ad loc.; Noort 1977: 85–86. See Dalley *et al.* 1976: 64–65, No. 65—for initial evidence for an identical procedure outside Mari (at Tell al-Rimaḥ).

(A 15) in which the writer specifically states of a dreamer-prophet: "since this man was trustworthy, I did not take any of his hair or the fringe of his garment."[48]

The credibility of prophetic revelation was obviously a sensitive matter, not to be taken for granted. Thus it was often verified and confirmed by the accepted mantic devices, considered more reliable means than intuitive prophecy *per se*.[49] Alongside the obscure practice of sending the hem [[96]] of a garment and a lock of the dreamer-prophet, we encounter the following features: Šibtu wrote to Zimri-Lim that she personally examined a prophet's message, prior to sending it on to him, and found the report to be trustworthy (*ARMT* X 6). In another letter, a lady of the royal household reported a vision, and advised the king: "Let my lord have the haruspex look into the matter . . ." (*ARMT* X 94). In a third letter, a woman implores the king to verify the vision of an *āpiltum* by divinatory means (*ARMT* X 81); the same woman advises the king, following the prophecy of a *qabbātum* (see above, p. 85 [[57]]), to be alert and not to enter the city without inquiring of the omens (*ARMT* X 80).

In contrast, in Israel the prophetic word—whether accepted or rejected by the king or the people—was never subjected to corroboration by mantic means, but was vindicated by the test of fulfilment (cf. Deut 18:21–22; Ezek 33:33).

In sum, the problem of reliability existed wherever intuitive prophecy flourished. It concerned the Mari authorities no less than the biblical lawmakers and "true" prophets, from Moses to Jeremiah—all of whom sought a yardstick for measuring prophetic authenticity. In the words of one expert: "The prophets who preceded you and me from ancient times prophesied war, famine and pestilence against many countries and great kingdoms. As for the prophet who prophesies peace, when the word of that prophet comes to pass, then it will be known that the Lord has truly sent the prophet" (Jer 28:8–9).

---

48. Dossin 1948: 132; in line 53 we read (with Oppenheim 1956: 195, and 1952: 134): *tāk-lu*, 'trustworthy' (rather than Dossin's *kal-lu*, a kind of official).
49. Moran 1969a: 22–23; Craghan 1974: 41–42; and Saggs 1978: 141.

Bibliography

Anbar, M.
    1975   Aspect moral dans un discours "prophétique" de Mari. *Ugarit-Forschungen* 7: 517–18.
    1981   Notes brèves. *Revue d'assyriologie et d'archéologie orientale* 75: 91.
Blenkinsopp, J.
    1983   *A History of Prophecy in Israel.* Philadelphia.

Bottéro, J.
1974   Pp. 70–197 in *Divination et Rationalité*, edited by J. P. Vernant et al. Paris.

Buber, M.
1950   *Der Glaube der Propheten*. Zurich.

Caquot, A., and A. Lemaire
1977   Les textes araméens de Deir ᶜAlla. *Syria* 54: 189–208.

Charpin, D.
1985   Les archives du devin Asqudum dans la résidence du chantier A. *MARI* 4: 453–62.
1987   Mari and the "Western Coast" during the Reign of Šamši-Addu. P. 3 in *American Oriental Society Meeting, Abstracts*, No. 7. Los Angeles.

Charpin, D., and J.-M. Durand
1985   La prise du pouvoir par Zimri-Lim. *MARI* 4: 293–343.
1986   "Fils de Sim'al": Les origines tribales des rois de Mari. *Revue d'assyriologie et d'archéologie orientale* 80: 141–83.

Cody, A.
1979   The Phoenician Ecstatic in Wenamun. *Journal of Egyptian Archaeology* 65: 99–106.

Craghan, J. F.
1974   The *ARM* X "Prophetic" Texts: Their Media, Style and Structure. *Journal of the Ancient Near Eastern Society of Columbia University* 6: 39–57.

Daiches, S.
1909   Balaam: A Babylonian *barû*. Pp. 60–70 in *Assyrian and Archaeological Studies (H. V. Hilprecht Anniversary Volume)*. Leipzig.

Dalley, S. et al.
1976   *The Old Babylonian Tablets from Tell al Rimah*. Hertford.

DeVries, S.
1978   *Prophet against Prophet*. Grand Rapids, Michigan.

Dietrich, M.
1986   Prophetenbriefe aus Mari. Pp. 83–93 in *Texte aus der Umwelt des Alten Testaments* 2/1. Gütersloh.

Dossin, G.
1948   Une revelation du dieu Dagan de Terqa. *Revue d'assyriologie et d'archéologie orientale* 42: 125–34.
1975   Le songe d'Ayala. *Revue d'assyriologie et d'archéologie orientale* 69: 28–30.

Durand, J. M.
1982   In vino veritas. *Revue d'assyriologie et d'archéologie orientale* 76: 43–50.
1984   Trois études sur Mari. *MARI* 3: 127–80.

Ellermeier, F.
1968   *Prophetie in Mari und Israel*. Herzberg.

Ellis, M. de Jong
1987   The Goddess Kititum Speaks to King Ibalpiel: Oracle Texts from Ishchali. *MARI* 5: 235–57.

Finet, A.
1982   Un cas de clédonomancie à Mari. Pp. 48–55 in *Zikir Šumim* (F. R. Kraus Festschrift), edited by G. van Driel et al. Leiden.

Gibson, J. C. L.
1975   *Textbook of Syrian Semitic Inscriptions II: Aramaic Inscriptions.* Oxford.

Gnuse, R. K.
1984   *The Dream Theophany of Samuel.* Lanham, New York.

Hackett, J. A.
1984   *The Balaam Text from Deir ʿAlla.* Harvard Semitic Monographs 31. Chico, California.

Hanson, J. S.
1978   Dreams and Visions in the Graeco-Roman World and Early Christianity. *Aufstieg und Niedergang der Römischen Welt* II 23/2, edited by H. Temporini and W. Haase. Berlin.

Haran, M.
1977   From Early to Classical Prophecy: Continuity and Change. *Vetus Testamentum* 27: 385–97.

Hecker, K.
1986   Assyrische Prophetien. Pp. 56ff. in Texte aus der Umwelt des Alten Testaments 2/1. Gütersloh.

Heintz, J. G.
1969   Oracles prophétiques et "guerre sainte" selon les archives royales de Mari et l'Ancien Testament. Pp. 112–38 in Vetus Testamentum Supplements 17. Leiden.

Herrmann, S.
1965   *Die prophetischen Heilserwartungen im Alten Testament.* Stuttgart.

Hoftijzer, J., and G. van der Kooij
1976   *Aramaic Texts from Deir ʿAlla.* Leiden.

Holma, H.
1914   *Die assyrisch-babylonischen Personennamen der Form quṭṭulu.* Helsingfors.

Hölscher, G.
1914   *Die Profeten.* Leipzig.

Hossfeld, F. L., and I. L. Meyer
1973   *Prophet gegen Prophet.* Fribourg and Göttingen.

Huffmon, H. B.
1970   "Prophecy in the Mari Letters." Pp. 199–224 in *Biblical Archaeologist Reader* 3. Garden City, New York.

Kammenhuber, A.
1976   *Orakelpraxis, Träume und Vorzeichenschau bei den Hethitern.* Heidelberg.

Kraus, F. R.
1984   *Königliche Verfügungen im altbabylonischer Zeit.* Leiden.

Lafont, B.
1984   Le roi de Mari et les prophètes du dieu Adad. *Revue d'assyriologie et d'archéologie orientale* 78: 7–18.

Landsberger, B.
1915   Review of Die assyrisch-babylonischen Personennamen der Form quṭṭulu, by H. Holma. *Göttingische Gelehrte Anzeigen* 117: 363–66.

Lindblom, J.
1962   *Prophecy in Ancient Israel.* Oxford.
Liverani, M.
1977   Segni Arcaici di Individuazione Personale. *Rivista di Filologia* 105: 106–18.
Malamat, A.
1954   Jeremiah Chapter One: The Call and the Visions. *Iyyunim* 21 [Hebrew]. Jerusalem.
1956   Prophecy in the Mari Documents. *Eretz-Israel* 4: 74–84 [Hebrew].
1958   History and Prophetic Vision in a Mari Letter. *Eretz-Israel* 5: 67–73 [Hebrew; English summary, pp. 86*–87*].
1966   Prophetic Revelations in New Documents from Mari and the Bible. Pp. 207–27 in Vetus Testamentum Supplements 15. Leiden.
1980   A Mari Prophecy and Nathan's Dynastic Oracle. Pp. 68–82 in *Prophecy: Essays Presented to G. Fohrer*, edited by J. A. Emerton. Berlin and New York.
1987   A Forerunner of Biblical Prophecy: The Mari Documents. Pp. 33–52 in *Ancient Israelite Religion: Essays in Honor of F. M. Cross*, edited by P. D. Miller, P. D. Hanson, and S. Dean McBride. Philadelphia.
Malul, M.
1986   "Sissiktu" and "sikku": Their Meaning and Function. *Bibliotheca orientalis* 43: 20–36.
Margueron, J. C.
1982   Rapport préliminaire sur la campagne de 1979. *MARI* 1: 9–30.
1983   Rapport préliminaire sur la campagne de 1980. *MARI* 2: 9–35.
1984   Rapport préliminaire sur la campagne de 1982. *MARI* 3: 7–39.
McCarter, P. K.
1980   The Balaam Texts from Deir ᶜAlla: The First Combination. *Bulletin of the American Schools of Oriental Research* 239: 49–60.
McEwan, J. P.
1980   A Seleucid Augural Request. *Zeitschrift für Assyriologie* 70: 58–69.
Moran, W. L.
1969a   New Evidence from Mari on the History of Prophecy. *Biblica* 50: 15–56.
1969b   Akkadian Letters. Pp. 623–32 in *Ancient Near Eastern Texts*, edited by J. B. Pritchard. Princeton.
Nakata, I.
1982a   Two Remarks on the So-Called Prophetic Texts from Mari. *Acta Sumerologica* 4: 143–48.
1982b   Rezension zu: Noort, Edward, *Untersuchungen zum Gottesbescheid in Mari*, AOAT 202, 1977. *Journal of the American Oriental Society* 102: 166–68.
Noort, E.
1977   *Untersuchungen zum Gottesbescheid in Mari.* Alter Orient und Altes Testament 202. Neukirchen-Vluyn.

Oppenheim, A. L.
1952   The Archives of the Palace of Mari: A Review Article. *Journal of Near Eastern Studies* 11: 129–34.
1956   *The Interpretation of Dreams in the Ancient Near East.* Transactions of the American Philosophical Society 46. Philadelphia.
1964   *Ancient Mesopotamia.* Chicago.
Parpola, S.
1983   Pp. 486–91 in *Letters from Assyrian Scholars to the Kings Esarhaddon and Assurbanipal,* volume 2. Alter Orient und Altes Testament 5/2. Neukirchen-Vluyn.
Petersen, D. L.
1981   *The Roles of Israel's Prophets.* Sheffield.
Porter, J. R.
1981   *bᵉnê hannᵉbîʾîm. Journal of Theological Studies* 32: 423–29.
Rendtorff, R.
1962   Erwägungen zur Frühgeschichte des Prophetentum in Israel. *Zeitschrift für katholische Theologie* 59: 145–67.
Renger, J.
1969   Untersuchungen zum Priestertum in der altbabylonischen Zeit. *Zeitschrift für Assyriologie* 59 (n.s. 25): 104–230.
Rofé, A.
1979   *The Book of Balaam.* Jerusalem [Hebrew].
Ross, J.
1970   Prophecy in Hamath, Israel and Mari. *Harvard Theological Review* 63: 1–28.
Saggs, H. W. F.
1978   *The Encounter with the Divine in Mesopotamia and Israel.* London.
Salonen, A.
1973   *Vögel und Vogelfang im alten Mesopotamien.* Helsinki.
Sasson, J. M.
1980   Two Recent Works on Mari. *Archiv für Orientforschung* 27: 127–35.
1983   Mari Dreams. *Journal of the American Oriental Society* 103: 283–93.
Schmitt, A.
1982   *Prophetischer Gottesbescheid in Mari und Israel.* Stuttgart.
Sperling, D.
1972   Akkadian *egirru* and Hebrew *bt qwl. Journal of the Ancient Near Eastern Society of Columbia University* 4: 63–74.
Starr, I.
1983   *The Ritual of the Diviner.* Bibliotheca Mesopotamica 12. Malibu, California.
van der Toorn, K.
1985   *Sin and Sanction in Israel and Mesopotamia.* Assen.
1987   L'oracle de victoire comme expression prophétique au Proche Orient ancien. *Revue biblique* 94: 63–97.
Uffenheimer, B.
1973   *Early Isaelite Prophecy.* Jerusalem [Hebrew].

Weinfeld, M.
1977   Ancient Near Eastern Patterns in Prophetic Literature. *Vetus Testamentum* 27: 178–95 [reprinted in this volume, pp. 32–49].

Weippert, M.
1981   Assyrische Prophetien der Zeit Asarhaddons und Assurbanipals. Pp. 71–115 in *Assyrian Royal Inscriptions: New Horizons*, edited by F. M. Fales. Orientis Antiqui Collectio 17. Rome.
1985   Die Bildsprache der neuassyrischen Prophetie. Pp. 55–93 in *Beiträge zur prophetischen Bildsprache in Israel und Assyrien*, edited by H. Weippert et al. Fribourg and Göttingen.

Weippert, M., and H. Weippert
1982   Die "Bileam" Inschrift von Tell Deir ᶜAlla. *Zeitschrift des deutschen Palästina-Vereins* 98: 77–103.

Wilcke, C.
1983   *ittātim ašqi aštāl*: Medien in Mari? *Revue d'assyriologie et d'archéologie orientale* 77: 93–94.

Wilson, R. R.
1980   *Prophecy and Society in Ancient Israel.* Philadelphia.

Part 2

The Message of the Prophets

J. Barton, "Ethics in Isaiah of Jerusalem"
C. Westermann, "Oracles of Salvation"

Introduction

Gerhard von Rad's *Message of the Prophets* (Eng. trans. [New York: Harper & Row, 1968] of *Die Botschaft der Propheten* [Munich: Siebenstern Taschenbuch, 1967]), from the far side of our 1975 watershed, makes an excellent introduction to the subject. Von Rad seeks to expound the message(s) of the prophets in the light of historical-critical conclusions, yet without letting the individual prophets or their messages suffer eclipse in the process. The more recent volume by Joseph Blenkinsopp (*A History of Prophecy in Israel* [Philadelphia: Westminster, 1983]) makes a fine complement to von Rad's volume, paying more attention to modern scholarly discussion of the prophets and interesting itself in a much wider range of issues relating to prophecy. Much of the recent literature concerned with the prophets could be said to relate in some way or other to the "message(s)" of these prophets. At the same time, it is certainly not the case that recent scholarship has been more attentive in this regard than have previous generations of scholars, if only because the multiplicity of approaches to the prophets currently being implemented has, if anything, distracted from this central concern. On the other hand, there is a limit to the number of times that the prophetic "message(s)" can usefully be restated according to the traditional categories, hence the present quest for fresh perspectives and new questions that will give rein to the full hermeneutic potential of the texts. In this section token acknowledgement is made of the fact that the "message(s)" of the prophets, in one respect or another, must always be at the center of the study of these books. Other lines of approach may from this perspective be valued for their centripetal effect as, in their illumination of smaller or larger portions of texts or in their exploration of particular reading strategies, they help to a profounder understanding of the central themes of the prophets and/or the books in question.

The passages selected for reproduction here illustrate two facets of study since 1975 that are specially worthy of highlighting. The ethical emphasis of Israelite prophecy has long been appreciated as one of its most important features. The actual basis upon which the prophets made their ethical appeal to their contemporaries or, as often, issued their condemnation of non-Israelite peoples has been less studied until recently. In particular, the idea of "natural law"—historically a specially British preoccupation—has been introduced into the discussion as helping to explain the grounds upon which eighth-century prophets like Amos and Isaiah judged their contemporaries of having deviated from acceptable standards of conduct. The subject will continue to be important as ethical aspects of non-Israelite prophecy come more prominently into view (see previous section). The other excerpt included here (pp. 98–104 below) deals with the oracle of salvation in the prophetic books. Westermann's monograph, from which it is taken, is the more welcome because it should help to correct a frequent distortion in the perception of pre-exilic prophecy, for, just as it makes sense to corral the prophetic judgment oracles generally into the pre-exilic period, so there has been a common tendency to restrict oracles of salvation to the exilic and post-exilic era. Westermann himself notes that his earlier study, *Basic Forms of Prophetic Speech* (Eng. trans. [Cambridge: Lutterworth, 1967] of *Grundformen prophetischer Rede* [2d ed.; Munich: Chr. Kaiser, 1964]), contributed to the imbalance by treating the judgment oracle as the archetypal utterance of the pre-exilic prophets. This has had much more serious effects than to exclude the prophets from everyone's party, affecting both the characterization of individual prophets and our perception of the development of such major themes as messianism and covenant in the pre-exilic period.

Additional Reading

Barton, J.
  1979   Natural Law and Poetic Justice in the Old Testament. *Journal of Theological Studies* n.s. 30: 1–14.
  1980   *Amos's Oracles against the Nations: A Study of Amos 1.3–2.5.* Cambridge: Cambridge University Press.
Brueggemann, W.
  1986   *Hopeful Imagination: Prophetic Voices in Exile.* Philadelphia: Fortress.
  1987   *Hope within History.* Atlanta: John Knox.
  1988   *To Pluck Up, To Tear Down: A Commentary on the Book of Jeremiah 1–25.* Grand Rapids: Eerdmans.
  1991   *To Build, To Plant: A Commentary on Jeremiah 26–52.* Grand Rapids: Eerdmans.
Carroll, M. D.
  1992   *Contexts for Amos: Prophetic Poetics in Latin American Perspective.* Journal for the Study of the Old Testament Supplement Series 132. Sheffield: JSOT Press.

Davies, E. W.
  1981   *Prophecy and Ethics: Isaiah and the Ethical Traditions of Israel.* Journal for the Study of the Old Testament Supplement Series 16. Sheffield: JSOT Press.
McConville, J. G.
  1993   *Judgment and Promise: An Interpretation of the Book of Jeremiah.* Leicester: Apollos / Winona Lake, Indiana: Eisenbrauns.
Prinsloo, W. S.
  1985   *The Theology of the Book of Joel.* Beihefte zur Zeitschrift für die Alttestamentliche Wissenschaft 163. Berlin: de Gruyter.
Stuhlmueller, C.
  1980   Deutero-Isaiah: Major Transitions in the Prophet's Theology and in Contemporary Scholarship. *Catholic Biblical Quarterly* 42: 1–29.
Westermann, C.
  1986   Zur Erforschung und zum Verständnis der prophetischen Heilsworte. *Zeitschrift für die Alttestamentliche Wissenschaft* 98: 1–13.
Wolff, H. W.
  1981   *Micah the Prophet.* Philadelphia: Fortress. English translation of *Mit Micha Reden: Prophetie einst und jetzt.* Munich: Chr. Kaiser, 1978.
  1983   *Confrontations with Prophets: Discovering the Old Testament's New and Contemporary Significance.* Philadelphia: Fortress. English translation of *Prophetische Alternativen: Entdeckungen des Neuen im Alten Testament.* Munich: Chr. Kaiser, 1982.
  1987   *Studien zur Prophetie: Probleme und Erträge.* Munich: Chr. Kaiser.
Williamson, H. G. M.
  1995   Isaiah and the Wise. Pp. 133–41 in *Wisdom in Ancient Israel* (J. A. Emerton Festschrift), edited by J. Day, R. P. Gordon, and H. G. M. Williamson. Cambridge: Cambridge University Press.

Ethics in Isaiah of Jerusalem

JOHN BARTON

〚1〛 This paper is intended as a modest contribution to the history of ideas. It attempts, like a paper I published in *JTS* in 1979,[1] to show that the natural-law tradition which has played a prominent role in Western moral philosophy and theology has roots not only (as is universally acknowledged) in the classical world, but also in the Hebrew tradition as that is preserved in the Old Testament. I shall try to show that the prophet Isaiah, working in Jerusalem in the eighth century B.C., already had a developed understanding of the basis of morality which has more affinities with Western theories of natural law than has usually been thought, and less in common with the notion of moral imperatives as "revealed" or positive law, given by God as the terms of a "covenant" or contract with the people of Israel, than is supposed by many Old Testament specialists.[2]

It cannot be said that the subject I intend to deal with is central to Isaiah's concerns, and it is no part of my purpose to suggest that it ought to be included in any statement of his "message." First, he is plainly more interested in the particular moral offences that he finds to condemn in his contemporaries than in abstract questions of moral philosophy, even though, as I shall hope to show, these particular denunciations reveal a cast of mind that assumes something like natural law as its starting-point. He is certainly not trying to convince his hearers that morality is a matter of natural law, but that their actions are evil and will bring down the

Reprinted with permission from *Journal of Theological Studies* n.s. 32 (1981) 1–18.

1. "Natural Law and Poetic Justice in the Old Testament," *JTS* n.s. 30 (1979), 1–14.

2. A major exception, to be discussed below, is H. H. Schmid, *Gerechtigkeit als Weltordnung* (Tübingen, 1968).

wrath of God. My concern is therefore with something taken for granted rather than with something that is being positively asserted or put forward for acceptance, and this of course makes the inquiry very speculative: indeed, it would be open to a critic to suggest that the questions I shall be asking simply do not admit of any answers, since there is not the evidence on which to decide them. But, secondly, Isaiah has many other concerns besides morality in any case: in particular, an intense interest in what the immediate (perhaps also the remote) future holds for his nation, which has rightly been of more concern to most commentators even since the rise of critical Old Testament scholarship rescued the moral teaching of the prophets from the [[2]] obscurity into which it had been thrown by the traditional Christian concentration on their role in predicting (as was thought) the coming of Christ. Despite this shift in emphasis, it is neither surprising nor regrettable that interest in the predictive side of Isaiah's teaching continues unabated, and that most commentators have little to say on the question of the basis of the prophet's moral teaching. Nevertheless, I hope that the topic, though thus far from being the most important one in the study of Isaiah, is an interesting one in itself, and appears sufficiently important in the general context of Old Testament studies as well as for the history of ethics to justify a short study. A study of Isaiah's ethical system is at least largely spared one of the greatest inconveniences of Isaiah scholarship: on the whole the authenticity of the passages in Isaiah 1–39 which deal with questions of morality is not disputed. The following list, which contains all the passages I shall be dealing with, should make this clear: a glance at any standard commentary will show that few of them are highly controversial from a literary-critical point of view, though in some cases there is no agreement about the period of the prophet's ministry to which they belong. The passages in question are: 1:2–3, 10–17, 21–23, 29–30; 2:6–22; 3:1–12, 13–15; 3:16–4:1; 5:8–23; 7:3–9; 8:5–8, 19; 9:8–21; 10:1–4, 5–19, 33–34; 17:7–11; 18:1–6; 19:11–15; 20:1–6; 22:8b–14, 15–19; 28:1–22; 29:11–12, 15–16, 20–21; 30:1–7, 15–17; 31:1–3, 6–7; 32:9–14.

I

Before setting out my own understanding of Isaiah's approach to ethics, which I shall present as a continuous whole, without detailed discussions of the many exegetical cruces on whose resolution it depends, let me briefly indicate the comparative novelty of the questions I am trying to ask. Broadly speaking, studies of prophetic ethics have concentrated on two types of question. First, there have been studies of the actual moral conduct deprecated or enjoined by the prophets, and attempts to set it in its social and historical context.[3] Thanks to studies ⟦3⟧ of this kind, we now know far more than we did about the political and social climate of eighth-century Israel and Judah, about the standards of public and administrative life, and about the lot of those oppressed members of Israelite society whom the prophets championed. Secondly, there has in recent years been a great interest in the *sources* of prophetic morality. We have seen a slow but steady back-pedalling from older views that seemed to make the prophets almost the discoverers of morality, and instead they have increasingly appeared (at least until very recently) as primarily links in a chain of tradition, handing on standards of morality long accepted as authoritative within the circles in which they themselves moved, and seeking to recall the people at large, who had lost touch with the roots of their own traditional culture, to a renewed allegiance to these uncompromising moral values. There has been conspicuously less agreement on where the sources of prophetic morality should correctly be located. Some see the prophets as appealing to values drawn from the legal and covenantal traditions,[4] with perhaps some mediation through the cult;[5]

3. A classic attempt is that of E. Troeltsch, "Das Ethos der hebräischen Propheten," *Logos* 6 (1916–17), 1–28; the most thorough recent study is that of H. J. Kraus, "Die prophetische Botschaft gegen das soziale Unrecht Israels," *EvTh* (1955), 295–307. There is useful material also in J. Lindblom, *Prophecy in Ancient Israel* (Oxford, 1962); A. Phillips, *Ancient Israel's Criminal Law* (Oxford, 1970); and N. W. Porteous, "The Care of the Poor in the Old Testament," in his *Living the Mystery* (Oxford, 1967). Two important attempts to relate the prophets' moral teaching to specific aspects of the social organization of ancient Israel are H. Donner, "Die soziale Botschaft der Propheten im Lichte der Gesellschaftsordnung in Israel," *Oriens Antiquus* 2 (1963), 229–45, and A. Alt, "Micah 2.1–5—ΓHC ANAΔACMOC in Juda," in *Interpretationes ad vetus testamentum pertinentes S. Mowinckel missae* (Oslo, 1955), 13–23, reprinted in his *Kleine Schriften* 3 (Munich, 1959), 373–81.

4. See, for example, L. Dürr, "Altorientalisches Recht bei Amos und Hosea," *BZ* 23 (1935–36), 150–57; M. A. Beek, "The Religious Background of Amos II. 6–8," *OS* 5 (1948), 132–41; R. Bach, "Gottesrecht und weltliches Recht in der Verkündigung des Propheten Amos," in *Festschrift für Günther Dehn*, ed. W. Schneemelcher (Neukirchen, 1957), 23–34; R. E. Clements, *Prophecy and Covenant*, SBTh I/43 (London, 1965); N. W. Porteous, "The Care of the Poor in the Old Testament," in his *Living the Mystery*; and W. Eichrodt, "Prophet and Covenant—Some Observations on the Exegesis of Isaiah," in *Proclamation and Presence*, ed. J. I. Durham and J. R. Porter (London, 1970). For an up-to-date survey of scholarly opinion about the prophets' reliance on legal traditions see the chapter "Prophecy and Law" by A. Phillips in the forthcoming Festschrift for Professor P. R. Ackroyd ⟦*Israel's Prophetic Tradition: Essays in Honour of Peter Ackroyd* (ed. R. J. Coggins et al.; Cambridge: Cambridge University Press, 1982) 217–32⟧.

5. Thus E. Würthwein, "Der Ursprung der prophetischen Gerichtsrede," *ZThK* 49 (1952), 1–16; H. J. Kraus, "Die prophetische Verkündigung des Rechts in Israel," *ThSt* 51 (1957); and E. Hammershaimb, "On the Ethics of the Old Testament Prophets," *SVT* 7 (1960), 75–101; N. W. Porteous, "The Prophets and the Problem of Continuity," in *Israel's Prophetic Tradition*, ed. B. W. Anderson and W. Harrelson (New York, 1962), discusses the possibility cautiously, but regards the prophets themselves as the main tradents of the ethical tradition in Israel.

others regard the traditions of "wisdom," in either its international or "folk" versions, as a more likely source.[6] It seems to me that a good case can be made out on both sides. [[4]] So far as Isaiah is concerned, if we leave aside "extrinsic" arguments such as that he was a scribe, and therefore prima facie more likely to be familiar with wisdom than with "covenant morality," and concentrate on the internal evidence of his moral teaching, we can easily find material to suggest that he appealed to the law in something like the form it has in the Book of the Covenant (Exodus 21–23): for example, his condemnations of murder (1:21), theft (1:21), oppression of widows and orphans (1:17b, 21–23; 3:14), bribery and corruption in the courts (1:23, 3:9a, 5:23, 10:1–2), perhaps also dispossession of the poor in the interests of enclosure (5:8–10).[7] On the other hand, there is no shortage of features that seem to confirm the prophet's indebtedness to the wisdom schools. Negatively, it may be argued that his condemnation of the pride of the Assyrians (10:5–15) cannot derive from any tradition of morality which is concerned purely with the moral imperatives binding on Israelites alone, such as the law, and hence must come from that interest in man as such which is generally held to characterize international wisdom;[8] and positively, it may be noted that both here and in other places Isaiah is concerned with actions or attitudes which either were not in fact mentioned in the law (e.g., excessive luxury, 3:16–4:1; drunkenness, 5:11–17, 22; 28:1–14) or could not be in the nature of the case (e.g., pride, 5:22; cynicism about moral values, 5:20; failure to trust in God, 22:8–14), but which do find an echo in many texts from the wisdom tradition. This case is argued by Whedbee,[9] and seems to me quite persuasive. It is possible that an attempt to do justice to both sides of the prophet's moral teaching might help us to avoid oversimplifying the means by which ethical norms and attitudes

6. See J. Fichtner, "Jesaja unter den Weisen," *TLZ* 78 (1949), cols. 75–80; R. T. Anderson, "Was Isaiah a Scribe?" *JBL* 79 (1960), 57–58; J. Lindblom, "Wisdom in the Old Testament Prophets," in *Israel's Prophetic Tradition*; J. W. Whedbee, *Isaiah and Wisdom* (Nashville, 1971); H. W. Wolff, *Amos' geistige Heimat* (Neukirchen, 1964) (translated as *Amos the Prophet: The Man and His Background* [Philadelphia, 1973]).

7. Whedbee, op. cit., 93–94, argues that Isaiah is here appealing simply to general ancient Near Eastern tradition deploring seizure of land and boundary-breaking, well attested in treaties and *kudurru*-inscriptions as well as in wisdom and legal texts throughout the area. However, there is no reason to suppose that those condemned by Isaiah were simply *seizing* land without observing even the form of law, and it seems to many commentators more likely that Isaiah is here implicitly appealing to the more specifically Israelite tradition of the inalienability of the family inheritance, which is being transgressed through compulsory purchase of land from poor debtors.

8. On the other hand, it could well be argued that 10:5–15 represents a sophisticated theological rationalization of an Israelite chauvinism that was the very reverse of internationalist.

9. Op. cit., 98ff.

were transmitted in ancient Israel, and incidentally to provide us with a little more information about the social and institutional background of the independent prophets, which in spite of much study remains relatively ill-defined and shadowy.[10]

[[5]] It is not, however, my purpose to pursue these lines of inquiry any further. My concern is not the content, nor the social setting, nor the source, of Isaiah's moral demands and strictures, but their basis: what he took or assumed to underlie the particular norms whose transgression he condemned, what he thought was so sinful about sins. It would certainly be presumptuous to claim that no one has asked this question before. Von Rad, in particular, often touches on it,[11] and there are many pages on the prophets in general in Hempel's classic work on Old Testament ethics[12] and in the "ethics" section of Eichrodt's *Theology*,[13] and on the basis of Isaiah's ethics in particular in Wildberger's commentary.[14] Nevertheless, I do not know of any systematic treatment of the matter; rather, it is generally broached piecemeal in connection with specific texts. It is for this reason that it seems best to state my own thesis in a straightforward way, at the risk of appearing somewhat assertive, rather than working patiently through each relevant text with a survey of the history of scholarly opinion and then systematizing the results.[15] Let me begin with a statement of the data to be accounted for, and then present one interpretation of them which seems to me to do them the most justice.

II

If one combs the prophetic books for information about the prophets' moral values, one soon notices that any simple list of sins condemned or courses of action commended blurs a number of significant distinctions.

---

10. Cf. the recent work of R. R. Wilson, *Prophecy and Society in Ancient Israel* (Philadelphia, 1980).

11. See G. von Rad, *Old Testament Theology*, vol. ii (London, 1965), 135–38, 149–55, 212–17.

12. J. Hempel, *Das Ethos des Alten Testaments*, BZAW lxvii 2nd edn. (1964), 109–35, 194–203.

13. W. Eichrodt, *Theology of the Old Testament*, vol. ii (London, 1967), 365–400.

14. H. Wildberger, *Jesaja 1–12* (BK 10) (Neukirchen, 1972), 15–17, 201ff. There is much useful material on this subject in U. Türck, *Die sittliche Forderung der israelitischen Propheten des 8. Jahrhunderts* (Göttingen, 1935), an undeservedly neglected work. N. W. Porteous's article "The Basis of the Ethical Teaching of the Prophets," in his *Living the Mystery*, is not (as might appear) on this subject, but is concerned with the sources of the prophets' moral teaching and the urgency with which they present it. E. Jacob, "Les bases théologiques de l'éthique de l'ancien testament," *SVT* 7 (1960), 39–51, has little to say about the prophets.

15. I hope to publish a more detailed account of the matter in the form of a monograph.

For example, one might say that Jeremiah condemns his contemporaries for oppression of the poor, failure to submit to the Babylonians, rejection of Yahweh's will, blindness to moral values, [[6]] adultery, inability to read the signs of the times, and ill treatment of slaves. But this would plainly be a very unsatisfactory classification of what Jeremiah has to say about the conduct of his hearers. One of these accusations, that of rejecting God's will, may be taken implicitly to include, or to function as a summary of, most of the others, and another—blindness to moral values—refers to attitudes of mind taken to cause or condition the specific sins being castigated; while failure to submit to the Babylonians is a particular error in political policy, taken by Jeremiah to flow from a general moral and religious decline in the nation, but not a sin such as could be included in a catalogue of ethical norms (say, the Decalogue) which was meant to be valid for life in society in many different periods. Obviously, the "sins" in our list are incommensurable, and resist arrangement in such a simple, linear form. Now, of all the prophets, it is Isaiah who presents the most complex case of this mixing of levels and categories in his comments on the behaviour and attitudes of those he criticizes, and it is abundantly clear that no list-like statement of his ethical concerns will do them justice. It seems to me that one can distinguish at least three different categories in Isaiah's comments on morality, though there is inevitably material whose correct classification must remain uncertain.[16]

First, Isaiah condemns a number of specific crimes, sins, and culpable errors in those he attacks, who seem to be chiefly the rulers of Judah as a whole, though he once singles out a specific member of the administration, Shebna (22:15–19), and also has oracles against the Assyrians (10:5–15) and against the wise men of Pharaoh (19:11–14) which many commentators regard as authentic. There are about a dozen types of sinful activity that can be readily distinguished, as follows. In the sphere of social relations: (1) oppressive treatment of widows and orphans (1:17, 21–23; 3:14); (2) theft (1:21); (3) murder (1:21); (4) perversion of the course of justice, especially by the acceptance of bribes (1:23, 3:9, 5:23, 10:1–2, 29:21); (5) expropriation of land belonging to the poor (5:8–10); (6) drunkenness (5:11–17, 22; 28:1–14); (7) excessive luxury and personal adornment, and the accumulation of wealth and status (3:16–4:1, 9:9–12, 22:15–19, 32:9–14). In the political sphere: (8) making preparations for national defence (7:3–9, 22:8–14, 28:14–18); (9) entering into foreign alliances (8:5–8, 18:4–5, 20:1–6, 30:1–5, 31:1–3); (10) boasting

16. It will be apparent that these categories do not correspond to any form-critical distinctions, but cut across differences of *Gattung* [['genre']]. The possible objection that this renders the investigation somewhat unscientific is discussed in Section IV.

of military conquests (10:5–15, against the Assyrians). In the religious sphere: (11) idolatry or cultic apostasy (1:29–30, 2:6–22, 8:19, 17:4–11, ⟦7⟧ 31:6–7); (12) the use of the sacrificial cultus (1:11–15).[17] In addition, there are passages which speak of people who (13) mock God (5:18–19) or (14) are sceptical of his power to act and to direct the course of events (5:20–21, 22:12–14), which may perhaps refer to specific and overt refusals to take into account God's power, probably by pouring scorn on the message of the prophet himself (cf. also 28:9–10). But with this we are already moving into the next major category.

Secondly, then, there are passages where Isaiah denounces attitudes and states of mind which are in themselves culpable, but the chief evidence for which is precisely those specific sins which have just been listed. (1) The first of these, which can be seen in the mockery of God and of his prophet, is the pride or arrogance of "those who are wise in their own eyes" (5:21) or who attribute their successes to their own power (10:5–15). (2) Closely related to this is the delight in prestige and self-aggrandizement: the sin of Shebna, "hewing himself out a tomb on high" (22:15–19), of the women of Jerusalem (3:16–4:1), and of the inhabitants of Samaria "who say in pride and arrogance of heart, 'The bricks have fallen, but we will build with dressed stones' " (9:9–10). Some commentators hold, indeed, that pride of this kind is the fundamental sin in Isaiah. Thus Eichrodt writes: "[for Isaiah,] the central sin of man lay in the overweening pride with which he set himself up against God . . . Luther's dictum 'omne peccatum est superbia,' all sin is pride, exactly sums up Isaiah's conviction."[18] And clearly this is at least part of the truth. (3) Thirdly, Isaiah identifies a failure or unwillingness to trust God alone as lying at the root of much that is wrong with the religious and political life of Judah: thus classically in 31:3 (against the Egyptian alliance), and also in 8:19 (on those who consult mediums). (4) Fourthly, he speaks of the contempt felt by the nation's rulers towards legitimate claims on them: contempt for the rights of the needy and those with no legal status, which were a commonplace of the moral tradition of the ancient Near East, and also contempt for the just claim of God to exact obedience as Israel's father and owner (1:2–3). (5) And, finally, in a number of places Isaiah speaks of folly or stupidity as the motive force behind human sin. This emerges clearly from the unfavourable comparison instituted in 1:3 between Israel and domestic animals: in Robert Lowth's words this verse is "an amplification of the gross insensibility of the disobedient Jews, by

17. Here, as generally with the pre-exilic prophets, the question arises how far this is condemned in itself, and how far it is regarded merely as an illicit attempt to avert the consequences of other sins.

18. W. Eichrodt, *Der Heilige in Israel (Jes. 1–12)* (Stuttgart, 1960), 56.

comparing them with the most heavy and stupid of all animals, yet not so insensible as they."[19] And [[8]] it may also be seen in the oracle on the wise men of Pharaoh (19:11–14), who are fools because they cannot perceive God's plans; how much more those Israelites who stupidly rely on them!

So much for denunciations of the attitudes that lie behind particular sins, which represent a second stratum in Isaiah's moral universe. A third category may be described as attempts to encapsulate, either by explicit formulation or (more commonly) by metaphors and analogies, what is the essence of both sinful actions and wrong attitudes: passages which therefore give us some hints of what Isaiah saw as the basis or essence of morality or of sin. Such attempts are naturally of a high order of generality, and it is to them—to what might be called third-order moral statements—that we need to look in trying to find organizing principles for ethics in Isaiah. There are five passages that seem to me to belong in this category: 2:6–22, 3:1–12, 5:8–10, 5:20, and 29:15–16. Let us examine the first of them in some detail, and then make some more summary comments on the others.

I have already mentioned that Isa 2:6–22 suggests to some commentators that human pride is being presented as the root of all sin: thus Eichrodt, in the passage already quoted, and Budde, in an article published in 1931:

> Pride and self-assertion, lack of humility before the exalted God, this is
> for Isaiah the cardinal sin of the creature, and it contains all other sin
> within itself. Hence his address begins with the highest thing to be found
> on earth, the forests which still crowned the mountains, and then passes
> to the mountains themselves, then to the proud works of man, and last
> to man himself.[20]

I have treated the pride which is undoubtedly the chief theme of these verses rather as an attitude producing sin than as what, in the last analysis, sin is. It seems to me that the very extraordinary suggestion that God will "punish" all the things in the natural world that are too high belongs to a rather subtle world of thought in which it is not merely asserted that pride is sinful, indeed the root of all other sins, but in which there is also some theory as to *why* it is sinful, *why* the created order should bow in humility before God. The reason is not simply that God occupies *de facto* the highest place in the world order, but that he does so *de jure*. The universe forms an ordered whole in which each creature should know its

19. R. Lowth, *Isaiah* (London, 1778), *ad loc.*
20. K. Budde, "Zu Jesaja 1–5," *ZAW* 49 (1931), 197.

place; and God's place, if we may speak so, is to be supreme. This world order is thus theological, in the sense that God both has a place in it, and also is the active force that keeps it in being; but it is not based on the idea of a potentially arbitrary divine lordship. I would suggest that the strictures on the mountains and trees [[9]] in [[Isa 2:]]13–15 are hard to account for by saying simply that pride is the root sin, if by that is meant self-assertion against God or the gods: their haughtiness is rebuked (of course mainly metaphorically, but still it must be seen as in some remote sense "sinful" for the analogy to work) because they step outside their proper place, that is, the place in which they most appropriately belong, by aspiring to scale the heavens.

If this admittedly nice distinction between humility and subordination, on the one hand, and acceptance of one's rightful place in the world, on the other, is accepted, it may be possible to fit in the references to the worship of idols in this passage ([[vv.]] 8, 20) without distorting the picture. With pride as the root sin, idolatry must be seen as some kind of self-assertion; and this is odd, since it seems on the face of it to involve precisely the opposite—reliance on things other than oneself even to the absurd extent (on the prophetic understanding of the use of images) of trusting in blocks of wood. If the chapter is simply a denunciation of human pride, the allusions to idols are out of place, and it is not surprising that they are sometimes excised, or explained away by rather strained exegesis.[21] But if we take both pride and idolatry as examples of the effect of failing to observe order in the world, the passage forms a unified whole. We might sum up the logical structure of the whole oracle according to this interpretation as follows. When men ignore the universal moral order, they become foolish, and lose both moral and practical insight. This produces two consequences in their ethical life. On the one hand, they come to overestimate their own importance, failing to keep to their appointed place in the world; and this pride leads to a delight in prestige and the accumulation of riches and status symbols. On the other hand, they fail to see where their trust and confidence should properly be placed, and rely on sources of strength other than God—for example on false foreign gods or on images of God, which they worship with blind idolatry.

With this example in mind, we may turn to examine the other passages more briefly. [[Isa]] 3:1–12 apparently sees both the social decay of eighth-century Judah, and Yahweh's probable punishment of it, as consisting in what we should call anarchy. Reversals of the proper order of

---

21. See the discussion by H. Wildberger, *Jesaja 1–12*, pp. 100f., 113–14; he himself accepts the authenticity of the material about idols.

society—rule by women and minors (⟦v.⟧ 12)—is punished in the same
coin (⟦v.⟧ 4), by an enforced breakdown of all natural social relationships; the usurpation of power by the unworthy leads, paradoxically, to
a time when men will refuse to accept power even when others try to
force it on them. This is a "poetic justice" text such as I have discussed
elsewhere.[22] ⟦10⟧ It seems to me to imply an ethical system which sets a
very high value on the received orders of society, and sees the processes
of history themselves, under God's hand, as operating according to similar orders and taking their vengeance on those who infringe them. Much
the same may be said of vv. 8–10, where those who build great houses by
expropriating land—thus contravening the old-established orders of Israelite society—will find that the defeat of their country in war leaves
their houses desolate; and those who join the fields of others into large
farms will be left with so little yield that their efforts will have been
wasted. (Compare 10:1–4 for a similar reversal.) Finally, 5:20 and 29:15–
16 are more straightforward statements of principle. 5:20 presents sin as
a challenge to the natural and true order of things: "Woe to those who
call evil good and good evil, who put darkness for light and light for
darkness, who put bitter for sweet and sweet for bitter!" And 29:15–16
presents us with a rhetorical question in which is made explicit what is
sinful about the action of those who "hide deep from the Lord their
counsel, and whose deeds are in the dark," viz. that it involves treating the
Creator as if he were a creature less perceptive even than oneself: "Shall
the potter be counted as the clay, that the thing made should say of its
maker, 'He did not make me'; or the thing formed say of him who
formed it, 'He has no understanding'?" The elliptical הָפְכְּכֶם at the beginning of this verse is translated with some freedom by the RSV 'You turn
things upside down'; whether this is justified or not, some such interpretation of the whole oracle seems legitimate.

So much, then, for the different types of material that deal with ethical issues in Isaiah's oracles. It seems clear that any adequate analysis of
this material must allow not only for the variety of actual moral norms
involved, but also for the distinction between first-, second-, and third-
order assertions about morality, as I have tried to present them. Ethics in
Isaiah cannot be adequately described by simply drawing up a list. This,
no doubt, is one reason why the quest for the *sources* of his moral teaching has proved somewhat inconclusive: it has necessarily had to work with
catalogues of sins condemned, and has found it hard to allow for higher-
order statements of moral principle or attitude. It may, of course, not be
wholly safe to assume that Isaiah's ethical teaching does in fact form an

22. Barton, art. cit., 9–13.

ordered whole—it might be that his occasional suggestions about the basis of morality were merely stray thoughts which have no real bearing on the practical questions of actual sin and transgression with which he had to deal; but to accept this is something of a counsel of despair, and I should like at least to attempt a description of an ethical system that would display an inner coherence and account for all the data so far discussed. I do not claim that we can ⟦11⟧ know Isaiah held it, but only that his extant oracles make more coherent sense if he did.

III

Isaiah, then, begins with a picture of the world in which God is the creator and preserver of all things, and occupies by right the supreme position over all that he has made. The essence of morality is cooperation in maintaining the ordered structure which prevails, under God's guidance, in the natural constitution of things, and the keynote of the whole system is order, a proper submission to one's assigned place in the scheme of things and the avoidance of any action that would challenge the supremacy of God or seek to subvert the orders he has established. Such is the basic premise from which all Isaiah's thinking about ethical obligation begins.

Sin takes its rise, therefore, in disregard for order and in a deliberate refusal to see the world in its true colours. The first and most obvious manifestation of this may be described as folly, ignorance, or perversity: a perversity which man alone seems capable of, for while the natural and animal worlds seem to observe order by instinct, man, in this respect more degraded than his own domestic animals, goes against the principles of his own nature. This moral blindness is culpable in itself because it refuses to God the respect that is his due, and prefers the purposes of mere men to those of their creator; and it is also the root of other evil attitudes, which in their turn produce the specific sinful acts which distort human life. Folly produces a disregard for the orders in society which should mirror God's ordering of the universe, and anarchy ensues, an anarchy in which those with power no longer feel any respect for the claims of others—especially of those who themselves have no power or legal means to assert their claims—nor for those positive laws which God has given to ensure that right prevails.[23] The practical effects of this dual failure in respect (for other people and for the law that pro-

---

23. It will be seen from this that the analysis presented here is quite compatible with the contention that Isaiah drew on the moral teaching of the law, and believed that it was being infringed; see above, p. 5 ⟦84⟧, on the distinction between the *source* and the *basis* of ethical norms appealed to by the prophets.

tects them) are the crimes against social order which were listed above: theft, murder, bribery and corruption, oppression of orphans and widows, enclosure of land. Folly, since it means blindness to the proper orders of the world, also naturally produces pride and arrogance, a "presumptuous neglection of degree," which affects all men, Israelites and foreigners, high and low alike. One of its cruder manifestations is the boastfulness that goes with too much drink: [[12]] drunkenness, indeed, is not only a typical mark of the fool, but can also serve as a paradigm of the befuddled mind that lies at the root of so many other sins. But cynicism about moral values, and mockery of God and his prophets, also flow from pride; so does that delight in prestige and status which are seen in the parvenu Shebna, with his elaborate tomb, and in the enjoyment of trivial self-adornment in the midst of a city threatened with famine and pillage that characterizes the women of Jerusalem. And at the other end of the scale, the boasting of the king of Assyria amounts to nothing more: he, too, is a fool, deluded by his own success into thinking he can vie with God, instead of recognizing that he is no more than a tool in God's hand. Symbolic of all these examples of overweening pride are the high mountains and tall cedars of Isaiah 2, which will be humbled on the day of Yahweh.

Folly also leads to a false estimate of where true security lies for man. In the true order of reality, man's only hope of safety lies in giving God his proper place; but human blindness and perversity seek protection in things that are not God. In the religious sphere, this produces idolatry, which for all its appearance of entailing submission to divine powers (even if false ones, as prophets like Elijah and Hosea had emphasized) is more correctly seen as a form of self-worship, reliance on the work of one's own hands; and it also produces a false confidence in the paraphernalia of cultic worship, which though apparently "Yahwistic" is, in fact, equally self-centred, as Amos had already suggested. The word "apostasy" would be a somewhat misleading one to describe either kind of cultic offence: the trouble with the sort of worship that is practised in a society blinded to reality is not that it involves disloyalty to God so much as that it simply ignores him, even while claiming to do him honour, and degenerates into a form of self-worship. Very similar consequences follow in the political sphere. It is not that treaties with foreign powers entail religious syncretism, but that they imply a reliance on what is ultimately unreliable (the Egyptians are men, and not God). A society which brings about its own downfall by its internal neglect of order and justice and its pursuit of self-interest, and then seeks to protect itself by inventing religious rites that happen to suit its own taste, and relying for aid on other merely human states which are in a condition of mental and moral confusion just as bad as its own, is simply walking in its sleep, and has lost its hold on reality. God can no longer get through to such a people, whose condition can best be summed up in two of Isaiah's most vivid images: the drunkard of [[chap.]] 28, staggering in his own vomit, to whom the more plainly one speaks, the more one's warnings will be dismissed as childish babblings; and the Kafkaesque sealed book of [[chap.]] 29, which the learned cannot read because it is sealed, [[13]] and the unlearned cannot read because they cannot read at all. The intolerable sense of frustration that such perversity produces in the prophet will reach its climax in Jeremiah, who (it has been suggested) seems almost to welcome the exile, however harsh, as a return to reality after two long centuries of delirium.

If this analysis of Isaiah's ethical teaching is correct, we have in him an early example of that way of approaching ethics which begins with a hierarchically ordered universe whose moral pattern ought to be apparent to all men whose reason is not hopelessly clouded, and derives all particular moral offences from the one great sin, a disregard for natural law. Of course, what we have in Isaiah is a theological form of natural law, as were most natural-law theories before the Enlightenment: one might perhaps speak equally well of a theory of "general revelation." It is the remote ancestor of one of the classic source texts for such theories, Rom 1:19–25:

> What can be known about God is plain to them, because God has shown it to them. Ever since the creation of the world his invisible nature, that is, his eternal power and deity, has been clearly perceived in the things that have been made. So they are without excuse; for although they knew God, they did not honour him as God or give thanks to him, but they became futile in their thinking, and their senseless minds were darkened. Claiming to be wise, they became fools . . . because they exchanged the truth about God for a lie, and worshipped and served the creature rather than the Creator.

IV

There are no doubt many objections that could be made to the thesis presented here, but two at least are so obvious that it seems right to deal with them at once.

(1) First, if morality was conceived in terms of what we might describe as "natural law" by both Isaiah and, as I have hinted, a good many other people in ancient Israel, then it is reasonable to ask why this has apparently left no mark on the Hebrew language. It is widely held that a concept akin to natural law was current in Egypt, but there is a term—

ma‘at—which in at least some of its uses provided a way of making the concept explicit.[24] H. H. Schmid, who holds that a belief in natural orders of roughly the kind I have been describing was ubiquitous in the ancient world—to such an extent, indeed, that there would be nothing [[14]] peculiar to Isaiah at all in the ethical approach here ascribed to him—argues that צֶדֶק/צְדָקָה [['justice, righteousness']] and also מִשְׁפָּט [['judgment, law']] function in Hebrew as approximate equivalents for *ma‘at*,[25] but it does not seem that this suggestion has commended itself very widely. At all events, if צְדָקָה can be used in this sense it can undoubtedly be used in narrower senses, too, and each alleged instance of a "natural order" use would require detailed demonstration. Isaiah, in fact, uses the word rather little by comparison with Deutero-Isaiah, in whom it is very frequent, and it would be hazardous to rest the present case on it.[26]

A more satisfactory reply to the objection would perhaps be that a lack of terms for abstract ideas like "order" is characteristic of biblical Hebrew in its extant texts in any case: a point on which, of course, very large theological constructions have been made in the past, but which needs to be examined very carefully before it is regarded as an index of "Hebrew mentality." If there are no noun-forms readily translated "order" in biblical Hebrew, nor are there terms for "history," "revelation," "event," or "ethics"; there are no modal verbs corresponding to "ought" or "must"; and it is hard to see how notions like "assumption," "theory," or "presupposition" could be expressed with the resources of the language known to us. But if this sort of observation tells against the suggestion that Isaiah saw ethics in terms of natural law, it tells equally against a great many other interpretative models in Old Testament ethics and Old Testament theology.[27] In fact, however, the importance of observing the very

24. Classic studies of this are R. Anthes, *Die Maat des Echnaton von Amarna*, Suppl. *JAOS* 14 (1952); *Lebensregeln und Lebensweisheit der alten Ägypter*, AO 32/2 (1933); see also S. Morenz, *Gott und Mensch im alten Ägypten* (Heidelberg, 1965); *Ägyptische Religion*, vol. 8 of *Die Religionen der Menschheit*, ed. C. M. Schröder (Stuttgart, 1960); H. Gese, *Lehre und Wirklichkeit in der alten Weisheit* (Tübingen, 1958).

25. *Gerechtigkeit als Weltordnung*, especially pp. 23–66. Schmid contends that צֶדֶק and צְדָקָה are often distinguished: צֶדֶק is the abstract quality which produces specific acts that can be described as צְדָקָה. But whichever word is used, the idea of cosmic order is always implicit, in his view.

26. In the passages with which we are concerned, the root צדק occurs in 1:21, 26, and 27; 5:7, 16, and 23; 10:22; and 28:17. מִשְׁפָּט and צְדָקָה together seem to function as general terms for "well-doing," but it is difficult to see how one could establish that a particular view of ethics lay behind them. There is now a large body of critical literature on both terms, most of it reviewed in Schmid's work.

27. For example, Eichrodt stresses that ethical obligation does *not* (in his view) stem from "natural" or rational considerations, but only from the absolute will of Yahweh, which

characteristic lack of abstract terminology in Hebrew is not that it shows
any given interpretation of the Israelite world-view to be impossible, but
rather that it reminds us of a truth which applies to *all* our interpretations, not just of ancient Israel, but of any culture. This is [[15]] the
entirely general point that we cannot explain the presuppositions of another culture to ourselves without some translation into terms and categories which did not have exact linguistic equivalents in the culture in
question: a point which is easily overlooked when dealing with cultures
nearer at hand and whose languages are closer to our own, but which is
in reality just as important in such cases as it is when we are handling apparently rather remote societies such as that of ancient Israel. Thus, although it is perfectly true that Isaiah's vocabulary contained no terms
corresponding to any of our normal categories for discussing ethics (or
indeed theology), this does not in itself mean that we cannot decide
which of these categories gives the most adequate impression of his assumptions. To argue against a particular interpretation of this kind on the
grounds that it uses terms untranslatable into biblical Hebrew is, in fact,
a subtle form of special pleading, since *all* our interpretations of the Old
Testament are subject to the same drawback: it is to present a quite general problem in hermeneutics, in social anthropology, and in the history
of ideas, as if it were a peculiar and specific objection to this one line of
interpretation. This is not to deny that the preference for "concrete"
forms of expression and the lack of "abstract" terms in Hebrew are interesting and important features. It is clear that they make the task of Old
Testament theology a peculiarly difficult and precarious one, in which in-
tuitions about the meaning of texts are often difficult to check or even to
assess. Nevertheless, there is no cause for undue alarm: difficulty is not
the same as impossibility.

(2) There is, however, another possible problem arising from the
characteristic mode in which Hebrew prophecy, in particular, is expressed which is less easily disposed of, and this leads to a fundamental
objection to the case I have been arguing. One of the great achievements
of modern critical study of the prophets has been to stress that their message was always addressed to a concrete historical situation, and that they
did not enunciate theological systems or lay down general principles, but
spoke rhetorically and with an awareness of the effect their words would
be likely to have on their immediate audience. Sometimes, indeed, this

---

brooks no rational probing, by speaking of "the Unconditional Ought" (*Man in the Old Testament, SBTh* I/4 [London, 1951]). Whether or not this is a fair way of describing Old Testament attitudes to morality, it clearly comes under the same condemnation as the present
paper in respect of its use of non-biblical terminology.

led them to express ideas which would have been mutually incompatible if they had been intended as parts of a coherent and timeless system. Furthermore, form-critical studies have insisted that one cannot understand the prophets' message by beginning from its content, as though that could be read off from their words without regard to the forms in which they are couched, but that one must begin from the *Gattungen* [['genres']] into which prophetic speech falls:[28] form-critics, in this like [[16]] more recent structuralist critics, are convinced that meaning inheres as much in the form and genre of a communication as in the overt information being communicated. Now both of these emphases in modern Old Testament scholarship may be thought to call in question the enterprise I have been engaged on in this paper. So far from Isaiah having expressed a belief in a *system* of natural law, it may be said, he did not even express a disapproval of *particular* sins and an adherence to *particular* moral norms in the way this paper has suggested: he was not condemning pride or drunkenness or political activism as such, drawing up as it were a moral code in which these things were proscribed, but speaking to the specific situation of eighth-century Judah. Furthermore, is it not methodologically unsound to extract information about ethics, as I have done, from many different kinds of oracle, ignoring the difference between a *Scheltwort* [['reproach']] (e.g., 3:14), a woe-oracle (e.g., 5:8), and a *Königsansprache* [['address to a king']] (e.g., 7:4–5)?

I believe that such an objection fails to understand the aim of the investigation undertaken here, but it helps to throw into relief what the issues actually are. The purpose, as mentioned briefly at the outset, is not to suggest that Isaiah was constructing a theoretical system of ethics, or writing a work of moral philosophy, but was unfortunately hindered in this by the conventions of prophetic style so that we have, as it were, to reconstruct his system for him. Isaiah was speaking highly specific words of rebuke, threat, and accusation to a particular group of people, and he was a successful prophet, not a systematic theologian *manqué*. What Isaiah was trying to tell his audience, his "message" as it is usually described, has been studied in minute detail, and I have nothing to add to existing summaries of it. But any message makes sense only against a background of unspoken assumptions, and it is these that this paper has attempted to draw out and make explicit. In this respect my presentation differs from the work of H. H. Schmid, who (if I understand him correctly) believes that the Old Testament is in some sense "about" natural law or cosmic

---

28. Hence the approach adopted by C. Westermann, *Basic Forms of Prophetic Speech* (London, 1967). A detailed statement of the belief that exegesis must always begin from a (structural) form-critical approach is to be found in K. Koch *et al.*, *Amos untersucht mit den Methoden einer strukturalen Formgeschichte* (Neukirchen-Vluyn, 1976).

order, that the existence of such orders is one of the truths it seeks to convey.[29] At least so far as Isaiah is concerned, this ⟦17⟧ seems to me incorrect. The argument here is that Isaiah takes some such notion as given, just as (most commentators would agree) he takes as given the idea that God is concerned about sin, not indifferent to it. It is one of what a sociologist might call his "domain assumptions."[30]

To deal properly with the form-critical point would require a much fuller discussion than can be undertaken here. But it ought to be said that, while form-criticism is a useful method for extracting certain kinds of information from Old Testament texts, it is not necessarily the only valid one, and on the whole it is difficult to see how one would move from a study of prophetic *Gattungen* ⟦'genres'⟧ to the type of question dealt with here. As I see it, the effect of approaching these questions in a form-critical way would probably tend not so much to invalidate the conclusions so far drawn about the assumptions underlying Isaiah's oracles, as to call in question the idea that they are peculiarly *Isaiah's*. Thus one might say that the "tit-for-tat" form of divine punishment, which may involve a "natural law" view of ethics, and the rhetorical questions such as 29:16 which seem to imply that sin is a reversal of natural orders, are conventional types of prophetic utterance; and if they do indeed reflect a distinctive understanding of morality this must have been widely diffused in the religious culture that gave birth to such traditional forms, rather than being the peculiar insight of a particular prophet, such as Isaiah. This, again, would tend to support Schmid's if anything *more* ambitious project of finding natural law everywhere in ancient Israel, rather than undermining the whole idea. Nevertheless, it would put a question-mark over the claim of this paper to have penetrated one specific prophet's mind, since the conventional character of the utterances he uses would make it

---

29. This is most clearly expressed in Schmid's article "Schöpfung, Gerechtigkeit und Heil," *ZThK* 70 (1973), 1–19. Against von Rad, he argues that creation is the central theme of the Old Testament, and makes it clear that by "creation" he understands the existence of order and pattern in the world, not just the idea that it had a beginning. Thus "wenn auch die Art des Auftretens der Propheten . . . ohne altorientalische Parallele dasteht . . . , so bleibt doch das Material, der Horizont und sogar die Logik ihrer Verkündigung die gemeinorientalische (Schöpfungs-) Ordnungsvorstellung" ⟦'even if the type of prophetic behavior . . . stands without ancient oriental parallel . . . the substance, the horizon, and the very logic of their preaching remains the general oriental (creation) idea of order'⟧ (p. 8); and again "Der Schöpfungsglaube, das heißt der Glaube, daß Gott die Welt mit ihren mannigfaltigen Ordnungen geschaffen hat und erhält, ist nicht ein Randthema biblischer Theologie, sondern im Grunde ihr Thema schlechthin" ⟦'The belief in creation, which means the belief that God created and maintains the world with its diverse systems, is not a peripheral theme of biblical theology, but is simply its basic theme.'⟧ (p. 15).

30. See R. P. Carroll, *When Prophecy Failed* (London, 1979), 12–15 for the application of this term to the prophets.

impossible to know whether he was conscious of their implications or not. In the end, much will depend on one's general attitude towards form-criticism, and one's assessment of the balance between conventional form and original or personal content in prophetic oracles of the classical prophets; and it will be obvious that my discussion of Isaiah stands in an English tradition, not only in its very interest in natural law, but also in its assumption that the balance comes down in favour of the individual writer and thinker even when due allowance has been made for the conventional speech-forms in which his thoughts are expressed. But I believe that some of my [[18]] conclusions could be defended even within a more rigorously and committedly form-critical environment; and since, as has been repeatedly stressed, the argument is about assumptions rather than assertions, it may, in the end, matter less than might appear on the surface whether one speaks of the presuppositions of Isaiah, or the culturally given conventions within which he was working. At all events, the fact that support for natural law in the Old Testament is now coming from a German-speaking scholar like Schmid, who stands firmly within a form-critical tradition of Old Testament scholarship and is sensitive, as few of us in this country can be, to the theological pressures that make such a notion highly suspect as a possible part of the scriptural witness, encourages me to think that it is neither a sign of methodological weakness nor hopeless anachronism to think that there are signs of it in the thought of Isaiah of Jerusalem.

Oracles of Salvation

C. WESTERMANN

Introduction

[[11]] Anyone who sets out to investigate the prophetic oracles of salvation in the Old Testament immediately encounters difficulty in defining them precisely and thus in arranging and grouping the many texts involved. A first reaction would be to investigate the oracles of each of the prophetic books separately and to group them according to the time periods we find in the history of prophecy in Israel. This was the method used by S. Herrmann in his *Die prophetischen Heilserwartungen im Alten Testament* (BWANT, n.s. 5, 1965). But in so doing one encounters the problem that even today there is no agreement as to which of the oracles that are contained in the book of the prophet Isaiah, or the prophet Hosea, were really spoken by that prophet. There is still uncertainty over what the presuppositions of such a study should be.

It has become clear to me (and the following study will corroborate it) that the oracles in the various prophetic books, both in their form and in their content, agree with one another to an astonishing degree or are at least quite similar. To be sure, they display characteristic differences, but the points at which they agree or are similar are clearly predominant. From this we may conclude that the oracles of salvation in the prophetic books belong to the same distinctive tradition, just as do the oracles to the nations. This tradition must then be studied as a whole, and the grouping [[12]] of the oracles of salvation must be based on the totality of the texts of salvation oracles in all the prophetic books.

In reality anyone who has even once read through all the salvation oracles in the various prophetic books must be struck by the extensive

Reprinted with permission from "Introduction," *Prophetic Oracles of Salvation in the Old Testament* (Louisville: Westminster/John Knox, 1991) 11–18.

agreement and the many similarities among them. That thus far no conclusions have been drawn from these similarities that would help with the
exegesis and closer definition of these oracles is the fault of the exegesis
conducted thus far. This exegesis is for the most part—though not always
consciously—determined by the literary-critical method and is dominated by the first question it poses, that of authorship. It immediately
becomes involved in the question of whether or not a passage is "genuine." The words that are deemed "genuine" are accorded precedence
over those that are not. Thus the dominant concern is always to identify
the major personalities involved (Herrmann, p. 5). And this evaluation is
then imposed on the texts. The unavoidable consequence is that the
scholar who has made this determination is more interested in the "genuine" passages in the specific prophetic book. The history of research in
the prophets reflects this evaluation in that attention devoted to the "non-
genuine" texts is much less than that given to the "genuine." As a consequence of this discounting of texts, commentaries on the individual
prophetic books give little or no attention to passages in other prophetic
books that are regarded as not coming from the prophet in question.

The literary-critical method has given rise to the conception that a
prophetic saying contains the thoughts of that prophet (R. Kittel, *Ge-
stalten und Gedanken in Israel*), which then found their literary expression
in the written oracles. But the sayings of the prophets are not simply statements; they are addressed to specific hearers. It is this that finds expression in their spoken form. They are words of a messenger (L. Koehler),
words that Yahweh gives to the prophet (*wayyehi debar yhwh ʾel* [['and the
word of the Lord came to . . .']]), so that he may speak them to the
people of Israel. The word of the prophet is a component in a procedure
that moves from God by way of the prophet to the people. Our task is to
investigate this procedure and its components: to discover the Hebrew
dabar [['word']] as an event in time, to which belong the starting point,
the goal, and that which is said in the progress from [[13]] the former to
the latter. But if the content of what is said is separated from this process,
the prophetic word as such can no longer be understood.

What has been said thus far applies to the prophetic oracles of judgment as well as to those of salvation. We must now investigate the distinction between them.

Oracles of judgment are limited to one part of the history of Israel,
but the oracles of salvation are found throughout that history. The prehistory of the prophetic oracles of salvation begins with the promises to
the patriarchs and continues in various forms of salvation oracles in the
early history of Israel. Its posthistory extends into apocalyptic literature.

The prophecies of judgment are confined to a particular time in Israel's history, the individual phases of which are defined by the activity of individual prophets, from Amos to Ezekiel.

The situation is quite different for the oracles of salvation. Only a few of them can be ascribed with certainty to one of the prophets of judgment. The greatest number arose anonymously in the period between Deutero-Isaiah (a few are probably earlier) and the conclusion of the prophetic canon. The context of the vast majority is not to be regarded as the work of an individual prophet unknown to us, but in the total tradition of this period. These anonymous oracles were, individually or in small collections, added to or inserted into the various prophetic books by those who transmitted them. This followed a process similar to that which shaped the folk proverbs. This is seen with particular clarity in those oracles of salvation which arose as supplements to specific prophecies of judgment from Isaiah, Hosea, or other prophets. But in terms of the history of tradition it is false to ascribe them to disciples of these prophets, for they arose only when the specific proclamations of judgment had been fulfilled.

The primary result of literary-critical exegesis is that to the present day the prophetic oracles of salvation have been classified together as "expectation of salvation," or "hope of salvation," as if that were obvious. In the collection of articles in *Eschatologie im Alten Testament* (ed. H. D. Preuss, 1978), for example, there is, so far as I can see, no exception to this procedure. On the other hand no one speaks of "expectation of judgment." A proclamation ⟦14⟧ (*Ankündigung*) is not the same thing as an expectation. In the Old Testament the semantic domain of hope and expectation belongs exclusively to the language of the Psalms, especially the confession of trust, and not to the language of prophecy. It can occur that a prophet is given a message to proclaim that contradicts his hope. The questionable nature of the designation "expectation of salvation" for the prophetic proclamation of salvation is clear in that it does not correspond to the terms for messages of judgment; the latter are appropriately termed "proclamations of judgment." This can be explained by the concept that lurks in the background that the messages of salvation are expressions of the thought or concepts of the specific prophet. In my opinion it is not responsible scholarship to take it for granted that the prophetic messages of salvation should be termed "expectation of salvation," when this is in direct contradiction to the language of these messages.

There is a further reason why it is important to recognize that the prophecies of salvation in the prophetic books are intended as proclamations. This identity as proclamation is clear and unambiguous at an earlier stage of prophecy, especially in Deutero-Isaiah, where in one group of messages there is a distinction between the announcement and the fulfillment of the proclamation. But we can see at a later stage the transition from proclamation of salvation to expectation of salvation. This can be observed in a variety of changes in the language of salvation oracles. This change from proclamation to expectation in late stages of the oracles cannot, however, be identified and taken into account if the exegete *a priori* equates proclamation of salvation with expectation of salvation. Although it is not always possible to draw a sharp distinction between the two, these stages in the history of the prophetic oracles of salvation are unmistakable.

An Analysis of the Oracles of Salvation

If the prophetic oracles of salvation constitute in themselves a fixed, independent tradition, then objective criteria for the exegesis of an individual oracle can be derived only from a survey of the total corpus of such oracles. A preliminary task is the investigation of the oracles of salvation scattered [[15]] in the individual prophetic books. But because the oracles in all the prophetic books are in extensive agreement, this in itself is not sufficient. In addition, it is necessary to develop from a survey of all the prophetic oracles of salvation a grouping of these oracles on the basis of their structure and content.

First, a distinction must be made between the preponderant majority of oracles of salvation found in collections of such oracles in Deutero-Isaiah, Jeremiah, Ezekiel, Trito-Isaiah, Micah, and Zephaniah, or as additions to or insertions into collections of oracles of judgment, on the one hand, and on the other hand those found in reports of a situation in which an oracle of salvation was given, as we find them in the historical books. We encounter the latter only in the books of Isaiah and Jeremiah, and possibly also in Ezekiel.

Second, as for the large number of salvation oracles in collections, we must distinguish between a major group (Group 1), and three secondary groups found in all the prophetic books.

Third, there is a further distinction between those oracles that are addressed to an individual and those addressed to a community. In the patriarchal narratives at the beginning of the history of these oracles as it stretches throughout the whole Old Testament, we find oracles of salvation addressed to an individual, even when by the individual the whole family is meant. In the prophetic books, the oracles are for the most part, and in Deutero-Isaiah exclusively, addressed to Israel, the people of God. But there are also oracles addressed to individuals. A further distinction is that after the catastrophe of 587 B.C. the prophetic oracles of salvation are addressed to the "remnant," those who have survived the catastrophe; in many cases the "remnant" is explicitly addressed. This presents a new aspect of the oracles.

Fourth, there is also a difference in the length of time between the giving of the announcement and the arrival of that which has been announced. If the oracle is addressed to an individual the lapse of time between proclamation and fulfillment is usually brief (for example in the promise of a son: "At this season, when the time comes round . . ."; 2 Kgs 4:16). In such cases a sign is often added to the promise, as in Isa 7:14–16. For this brief time span the perfect [[16]] tense is appropriate in such an oracle, which originally was given only to individuals. In oracles to the people, the lapse of time is greater; thus the future tense is used.

Fifth, it is also necessary to explore the content of what is proclaimed. Various things can be meant by the word "salvation"; it can be an act or a state (*Zustand*). The proclamation can be of an act of deliverance or a state of well-being, or of the two together. This difference is expressed in the form of the oracle, and thus form and content cannot be separated. This distinction enables us to group the main oracles according to objective criteria. A proclamation of deliverance follows a fixed, unvarying sequence: Distress; cry for help (lament); the cry is heard; deliverance. A large number of oracles of salvation consist solely of the proclamation of deliverance.

An oracle of salvation may be given not only in a threatening situation but also in a situation of misery and adversity. Here a proclamation of a future situation of well-being is appropriate. This can take two forms. First, a proclamation of blessing can follow one of deliverance, a promise that announces a time of blessing and prosperity. It is found early in Israel's history coupled with a proclamation of deliverance and has its own roots and its own history. Second, after the collapse of 587 B.C. we find the proclamation of the restoration of a state of well-being. Both these forms have in common, in contrast to a proclamation of deliverance, that the promise of blessing and the proclamation of the restoration of a state of well-being do not follow a fixed order of events, but the motifs are presented alongside each other. The proclamation can move into a description, in which the proclamation of the new course of events is either reduced to an introductory formula such as "In that day . . ." or is omitted completely. This distinction between the act of deliverance and the state of well-being is of basic importance for our understanding and analysis of the oracles of salvation. It goes back to the distinction between God's activity in deliverance and his activity in blessing. The two together constitute God's saving activity. Typical of *Group 1* are the oracles of Deutero-Isaiah, who proclaimed Cyrus, the ruler of a foreign nation, as Israel's liberator, commissioned by Yahweh (Isaiah 45). Since thereby Israel also acknowledged the political rule of the Persian [[17]] Empire as the will of Yahweh, this had consequences for Israel's relationship to the other nations. Those who survived the fall of the Babylonian Empire can be included in the invitation to accept deliverance and well-being. The additional oracles of salvation belonging to Group 1 also follow the pattern of Deutero-Isaiah's proclamation.

Next we consider the other groups of prophetic oracles of salvation. The extensive similarities among the oracles of salvation in all the prophetic books are also found in the three smaller secondary groups 2, 3, and 4. It is especially striking that in all the prophetic books there are only these four groups, and none of the groups is found only in one or two of the books. This confirms that all the oracles of salvation belong to one strand of tradition.

The texts of *Group 2* are for the most part short and are generally supplements to other texts, with which they agree in form and content. They always consist of two parts and are seldom expanded. They proclaim destruction of Israel's foes and at the same time salvation for Israel. The simple form underwent two developments. In one set of texts the motif is added that the destruction of the foes will be achieved explicitly by Judah-Israel, and in the other that Judah-Israel will take possession of the land of their foes. At a later stage the form of the twofold proclamation underwent two expansions in two steps, which mark the transition to apocalyptic. In the first expansion the approach of the foes precedes their destruction, and in the second the twofold proclamation is expanded into larger compositions that present an apocalyptic drama.

Strictly speaking, groups 3 and 4 cannot be included among the prophetic oracles of salvation. As for *Group 3*, in the majority of the prophetic books, but especially in Jeremiah, we encounter conditional proclamations of salvation, which are derived from deuteronomistic paraenesis, and have there their original and appropriate place. They show the transition from prophetic proclamation of salvation to deuteronomistic paraenesis.

Group 4 consists of texts in which the prophetic proclamation of salvation is combined with a motif of the piety of late Wisdom literature— the fate of the pious and the fate of the wicked, or in which this motif replaces the prophetic proclamation.

[[18]] This analysis enables us to delineate at least a few essential features of a history of the oracles of salvation in postexilic times. This, however, is possible only through the investigation of all the oracles in categories derived from the total corpus.

The oracles of salvation in the proper sense (group one) can be tabulated as follows:

Deutero-Isaiah	35 texts
Isaiah 1–39	29 texts
Minor Prophets	34 texts
Jeremiah	38 texts
Ezekiel	15 texts
Trito-Isaiah	6 texts
Total	157 texts

In addition there are 39 texts of Group 2 (the twofold proclamation), and texts that are related to the prophetic words of salvation but cannot be included among them. Group 3 (conditional proclamations of salvation) includes 34 texts; and Group 4, the pious and the wicked, 16 texts.

The prophetic books include collections of oracles of salvation: Isaiah 40–55; parts of Isaiah 56–66 (60–62), and perhaps also parts of Isaiah 32–35; Jeremiah 30–33, and perhaps also 3:6–4:4; Ezekiel 33–37 (38–39; 40–48); Amos 9:11–15; Micah 4–5; Zeph 3:11–20; parts of Zechariah. All the other oracles of salvation are scattered outside these collections, added to oracles of judgment or to folk proverbs, or inserted between them. They were first collected in the process of compilation of the prophetic books. This is illustrated by the oracles that are found in the same or similar form in different prophetic books (e.g., Isa 2:2–4 and Mic 4:1–3), or in the same book at different places (e.g., Jer 23:5–6 = 33:15–16).

It should be noted that prophetic oracles are also found in the Psalter, there transformed into praise of God. An example is Ps 147:2–3: "The Lord builds up Jerusalem; he gathers the outcasts of Israel. He heals the brokenhearted, and binds up their wounds."

Part 3

The Art of Prophecy

Introduction

The subtitles which appear under this general heading give some impression of the variety of methods currently being used to highlight the prophetic books as literary texts. The use of the word *art* in the heading applies whether a particular prophecy originated in oral delivery or was in written form from the beginning. In practice it can be extremely difficult to attribute artistic features with certainty to oral or written stages of a tradition, and even such a prosaic prophecy as Ezekiel contains wry comment on the way in which the very attractiveness of the prophet's oral presentation could work against its reception by his hearers (33:30–32). For all that, the prophecy of the Old Testament exists now only as literature and therefore requires to be read and interpreted according to the canons of normal literary practice. The prophetic books themselves clearly represent the work of craftsmen and rhetoricians who sought to influence not only by the content of the message but also by the literary form into which they molded it. This craftedness, far from diminishing when oral prophecy took on a literary shape, if anything found more opportunity for expression, and certainly relished a literary stagesetting that allowed more of its subtleties to be grasped by the "audience." On the other hand, this emphasis upon skill and technique may result in the interpreter of the prophetic word becoming conscious of a tension between the element of divine communication and the contribution made by human creativity (Geller, pp. 154–65 below). But, of course, prophets also performed symbolic *acts* which, even when the historical referents are clear enough, invite questions about what exactly is being effected by the act (Stacey, pp. 112–32 below). Similar questions, in point of fact, have also to be faced when the predictive utterances of the prophets are being considered (Houston, pp. 133–53 below).

The rhetoric of prophecy is rightly, in the light of what has already been said, a current focus of attention (Clines, pp. 166–75; Fox, pp. 176–90; Lundbom 1975, 1979, 1991). Sometimes the prophetic books give the impression of being anthologies of loosely connected fragments whose historical background and referents cannot any longer be known. Study

107

of the rhetoric of the books aims to discover the structures and structuring elements which give coherence to the text, sectionally or as a whole, and which extend its effectiveness as communication between author and reader. While it is true that much such study has had the limited objective of observing the anatomy of texts, that is, the devices by which they are structured, attention is gradually expanding to include the rhetorical intent behind the structures, insofar as this may be recoverable at this distance from the author and the original committal to writing (see especially Clines, pp. 166–75 below; Gitay 1981). Again, the study of metaphor is not a novelty in prophets research, but now, under the discipline of modern linguistic theory and with stricter adherence to the classical definition of metaphor, it offers new sophistications for the opening up of a text (see Newsom, pp. 191–204 below; Bourguet 1987; Nielsen 1989). Sometimes the text presents a kind of unrubricated dialogue, whence the possibility arises that dialogistic sections in the prophets represent more than mere dramatic form, giving insight into the very *modus operandi* of a prophet like Jeremiah as he engaged in exchanges with his hearers (Willis, pp. 205–22 below; Gordon 1994; Lundbom 1991; Petersen 1983). (This dialogistic element in prophecy is to be distinguished from the form-critical genre of disputation speech [see Graffy 1984; Murray 1987].)

In some respects the recent emphases represent a formalizing of approaches long since adopted by attentive readers of the Bible as, for example, they have observed one scripture adapting another scripture to a new situation (inner-biblical exegesis; cf. Fishbane, pp. 223–29 below; Day, pp. 230–46 below), or have sensed resonances, less specific and yet exegetically suggestive, between one text and another (intertextuality; cf. Carroll 1993; van Dijk-Hemmes 1989). The possibility of a background of cultic enactment has also been explored for certain prophetic texts (Eaton, pp. 247–51 below), as has the possibility of a framework of dramatic dialogue in the case of Zephaniah (House, pp. 252–62 below). Finally, in the book of Jonah we have a prophetic narrative which, for all the simplicity of its story-line and its language, continues to impress literary critics and interpreters by its capacity to create meaning. And, just as "reader response" approaches consider the relationship between a text and its modern reader, so also it makes sense to attempt to understand the way in which this particular text may have been received at the beginning, by its earliest "audience" (Payne, pp. 263–72).

Additional Reading

Section (i). Symbolic Action

Amsler, S.
1985   *Les Actes des Prophètes.* Geneva: Labor et Fides.

Section (ii). Speech Act Theory

Carroll, R. P.
1979   Interpreting the Prophetic Traditions. Pp. 55–84 in *When Prophecy Failed: Reactions and Responses to Failure in the Old Testament Prophetic Traditions.* London: SCM / New York: Seabury.

Section (iii). Prophecy and Poetry

Alter, R.
1985   Prophecy and Poetry. Pp. 137–62 (endnotes 217–18) in *The Art of Biblical Poetry.* New York: Basic Books.

Section (iv). Rhetoric

Davis, E. F.
1989   *Swallowing the Scroll: Textuality and the Dynamics of Discourse in Ezekiel's Prophecy.* Journal for the Study of the Old Testament Supplement Series 78. Sheffield: Almond Press.

Gitay, Y.
1980   A Study of Amos's Art of Speech: A Rhetorical Analysis of Amos 3:1–15. *Catholic Biblical Quarterly* 42: 293–309.
1981   *Prophecy and Persuasion: A Study of Isaiah 40–48.* Forschung zur Theologie und Literatur 14. Bonn: Linguistica Biblica.
1983   Reflections on the Study of the Prophetic Discourse: The Question of Isaiah I 2–20. *Vetus Testamentum* 33: 207–21.
1991   *Isaiah and His Audience: The Structure and Meaning of Isaiah 1–12.* Assen and Maastricht: Van Gorcum.

Graffy, A.
1984   *A Prophet Confronts His People: The Disputation Speech in the Prophets.* Analecta Biblica 104. Rome: Pontifical Biblical Institute.

Jemielity, T.
1992   *Satire and the Hebrew Prophets.* Louisville: Westminster/John Knox.

Lundbom, J. R.
1975   *Jeremiah: A Study in Ancient Hebrew Rhetoric.* Society of Biblical Literature Dissertation Series 18. Missoula, Montana: Scholars Press.
1979   Poetic Structure and Prophetic Rhetoric in Hosea. *Vetus Testamentum* 29: 300–308.

1991 Rhetorical Structures in Jeremiah 1. *Zeitschrift für die Alttestamentliche Wissenschaft* 103: 193–210.

Murray, D. F.
1987 The Rhetoric of Disputation: Re-examination of a Prophetic Genre. *Journal for the Study of the Old Testament* 38: 95–121.

O'Connell, R. H.
1994 *Concentricity and Continuity: The Literary Structure of Isaiah.* Journal for the Study of the Old Testament Supplement Series 188. Sheffield: Sheffield Academic Press.

Smith, P. A.
1995 *Rhetoric and Redaction in Trito-Isaiah: The Structure, Growth and Authorship of Isaiah 56–66.* Vetus Testamentum Supplements 62. Leiden: Brill.

Section (v). Metaphor

Bjørndalen, A. J.
1986 *Untersuchungen zur allegorischen Rede der Propheten Amos und Jesaja.* Beihefte zur Zeitschrift für die Alttestamentliche Wissenschaft 165. Berlin: de Gruyter.

Bourguet, D.
1987 *Des métaphores de Jérémie.* Paris: Gabalda.

Darr, K. P.
1994a *Isaiah's Vision and the Family of God.* Literary Currents in Biblical Interpretation. Louisville: Westminster/John Knox.
1994b Two Unifying Female Images in the Book of Isaiah. Pp. 17–30 in *Uncovering Ancient Stones: Essays in Memory of H. Neil Richardson,* edited by L. M. Hopfe. Winona Lake, Indiana: Eisenbrauns.

Exum, J. C.
1981 Of Broken Pots, Fluttering Birds, and Visions in the Night: Extended Simile and Poetic Technique in Isaiah. *Catholic Biblical Quarterly* 43: 331–52. Reprinted pp. 349–72 in *Beyond Form Criticism: Essays in Old Testament Literary Criticism,* edited by P. R. House. Sources for Biblical and Theological Study 2. Winona Lake, Indiana: Eisenbrauns, 1992.

Nielsen, K.
1989 *There Is Hope for a Tree: The Tree as Metaphor in Isaiah.* Journal for the Study of the Old Testament Supplement Series 65. Sheffield: JSOT Press.

Section (vi). Dialogue

Gordon, R. P.
1994 Dialogue and Disputation in the Targum to the Prophets. *Journal of Semitic Studies* 39: 7–17.

Lundbom, J.
1991   Jeremiah and the Break-Away from Authority Preaching. *Svensk exegetisk årsbok* 56: 7–28.

Petersen, D. L.
1983   The Prophetic Process Reconsidered. *Iliff Review* 40: 13–19.

Section (vii).   Inner-Biblical Interpretation

Carroll, R. P.
1993   Intertextuality and the Book of Jeremiah: Animadversions on Text and Theory. Pp. 55–78 in *The New Literary Criticism and the Hebrew Bible,* edited by J. C. Exum and D. J. A. Clines. Journal for the Study of the Old Testament Supplement Series 143. Sheffield: JSOT Press.

Day, J.
1980   A Case of Inner Scriptural Interpretation: The Dependence of Isaiah XXVI. 13–XXVII. 11 on Hosea XIII. 4–XIV 10 (Eng. 9) and Its Relevance to Some Theories of the Redaction of the "Isaiah Apocalypse." *Journal of Theological Studies* n.s. 31: 309–19.

van Dijk-Hemmes, F.
1989   The Imagination of Power and the Power of Imagination. An Intertextual Analysis of Two Biblical Love Songs: The Song of Songs and Hosea 2. *Journal for the Study of the Old Testament* 44: 75–88.

Section (viii).   Drama

Eaton, J. H.
1981   *Vision in Worship: The Relation of Prophecy and Liturgy in the Old Testament.* London: SPCK.

Section (ix).   Prophetic Narrative

Craig, K. M.
1990   Jonah and the Reading Process. *Journal for the Study of the Old Testament* 47: 103–14.

Kahn, P.
1994   An Analysis of the *Book of Jonah. Judaism* 43: 87–100.

Magonet, J.
1983   *Form and Meaning: Studies in Literary Techniques in the Book of Jonah.* 2d edition. Bible and Literature Series 8. Sheffield: Almond.

The Function of Prophetic Drama

W. DAVID STACEY

[[260]] When a prophetic drama takes place, an action, a person or persons, and possibly an object belonging to the everyday world are deliberately brought into relationship with some unseen event or reality, usually something on a much larger scale than the drama itself.[1] The dramas point away from themselves towards the unseen element in the conjunction. The purpose of this final chapter is to determine as precisely as possible the relationship between these two elements as it was understood by all those who, in their several ways, gave us the Old Testament.

It has to be recognized that a single and simple account that covers the relationship of all the dramas to all the realities is not possible. There is too much variation between the dramas themselves; there is variation between the original sense of the drama and the sense expressed in the later record; and there is very considerable variation in the way in which different people understood the dramas at the material time. That is to say nothing about how differently they have been understood since biblical times. If we keep within the Old Testament itself, at least five different kinds of people have to be considered: there is the prophet himself acting under a sense of divine compulsion; there is the uncomprehending, syncretizing Hebrew onlooker; there are the prophet's disciples who made the first record and who must have carried out some selection and

Reprinted with permission from *Prophetic Drama in the Old Testament* (London: Epworth, 1990) 260–82.

1. F. W. Dillistone speaks of "metaphorical conjunction between present situations and future events" (*Christianity and Symbolism* [[London, 1955]] 275). In this [[chapter]] the terms drama and reality have been used. The problem of the logic involved in these terms has been discussed in Chapter 2 [[not reprinted here]].

rejection; there are the theologically sophisticated editors of the prophetic text; and there are the believing communities that produced the
canon and inevitably interpreted the individual prophet's work in terms
of the whole. Even ⟦261⟧ this analysis is a patent over-simplification—
one cannot even talk about "the prophet" or "the editors" as if there
was a common mind among them—and yet it embraces some who see
the dramas as something near to sorcery and others who regard them as
a word of God, not only to the prophet's generation, but to their own. We
need to tread warily.

It needs to be noted, too, that modern interest is not divided equally
between the five groups. Because most people who read the Old Testament today read it for theological reasons, or hear it read in a liturgical
context, interest is concentrated on the first and fifth groups. We are
interested in what the prophet thought he was doing, and we are interested in what the Bible, the revered, holy, canonical text, represents as
the meaning of prophetic activity. The views of disciples and editors are
of interest only to biblical scholars, and the views of the unsophisticated
onlookers are of interest only to scholars whose approach to the biblical
text includes an anthropological element. This explains the proportions
displayed in this chapter. No doubt the second group was much larger
than the third or fourth, but it was less significant for later thinking.
There is also the question of evidence. The attitudes of the second
group find their way into Scripture by chance, whereas the whole text
gives evidence of the beliefs of the others.

The most obvious variation is that between what seems to be the
view of the earliest prophets and that of Jeremiah and Ezekiel. They are
separated by more than three centuries, centuries which included periods of intense theological activity. It would be possible to write down
the arrow dramas in 2 Kings 13 as acts of imitative magic designed to
influence the deity, and then to suggest a quite different explanation for
the actions of the great prophets.[2] In that case the difficulty becomes
one of continuity. A rough and ready way of solving that problem is to
say that the acts of the great prophets preserve the form of imitative
magic but not the content. The prophets act to arrest attention, to impress an audience, to reveal an idea, rather than to implant anything in
the mind of the deity. It remains awkwardly true, however, that the editors of the Deuteronomistic history still saw fit to preserve the earlier
stories, including those surrounding Elisha, so presumably it must have
been possible for Jews of the post-exilic age to see virtue in both kinds

2. See, for example, J. Gray, *I and II Kings* ⟦2d ed.; OTL; London, 1970⟧ 599f.; cf. J. F. A.
Sawyer, *Isaiah*, vol. 1 ⟦DSB; Edinburgh, 1984⟧ 180.

of activity. Von Rad explains the ⟦262⟧ development by saying that the earlier actions were directed to the future in a creative way, whereas the actions of the great prophets were more concerned with proclamation in the present. They not only prefigure the future but prepare the people to meet it.[3] In the case of Jeremiah's yoke, says von Rad, the concept underwent an even more radical change, for the drama concerns a possible future, not necessarily the actual one. The issue is thus forcibly pressed upon the onlookers, but, as far as creative action is concerned, the hope must have been that it would not operate at all.

The conclusion from this must be that a single explanation for all dramas will not do. We must take account of growth and theological change, and at the same time try to preserve some sense of continuity. It is not enough to say that the outward form of the action did not change. In view of the diverse nature of the actions at all periods, that statement is almost meaningless. What one hopes for is an explanation that gives a coherent account of both the diversity and the development of the understanding of dramatic action, and yet also pays due regard to the theology of the most profound prophets.

Broadly speaking, the explanations that have been given in the past fall into three groups. The first two are manifestly inadequate, the last more subtly so.

Some scholars of a previous generation concentrated their attention on the psychological condition of the prophet and thought little of what he himself thought he was doing and how his actions were understood by his contemporaries. These scholars did not scrutinize the dramatic acts for positive meaning but wrote them off as the products—sometimes interesting, often embarrassing—of an over-charged psyche. One has to recognize the pressures of the period. Earlier in this century Christianity, indeed all religious belief and behaviour, suffered an onslaught of reductionism from Freudian psychologists. Anything that appeared odd or irrational by contemporary standards was seized on and held to be evidence, not of divine influence, but of some deep-seated, psychological malady. In the field of prophecy, Hölscher's work of 1914 had used ecstasy as a sufficient explanation for much of what had previously been regarded as divine inspiration. Some Old Testament commentators all but surrendered to the pressure. O. R. Sellers of McCormick Theological Seminary, writing in 1924, diagnosed in Hosea introspection, an inferiority ⟦263⟧ complex, a martyr complex, sadism, exhibitionism, jealousy and a desire for revenge. He had married Gomer out of physical attraction but was then anxious to clothe his motives in religion. Sellers

---

3. G. von Rad, *Old Testament Theology*, vol. 2 ⟦Munich, 1960; Eng. trans. Edinburgh and London, 1965⟧ 97f.

was equally disgusted with Isaiah for exposing himself in the streets of Jerusalem, "a clear-cut case of exhibitionism, a tendency which may be observed at any bathing-beach."[4] Ezekiel was an even easier target. He was often suspected of instability and his behaviour was said to be due to a disturbed mind. W. F. Lofthouse, by no means a rash critic, also took the psychologists seriously. He concluded that Ezekiel, acting under deep, religious excitement, tended to behave impulsively and then to attribute the impulse to God. Jeremiah, too, performed some of his dramas as a way of finding relief from pent-up emotions. Lofthouse seems to surrender a lot of ground, but he also contends that the deeper level of consciousness in which these strange impulses originated was the point of true religious inspiration.[5]

At this point we are in danger of plunging into confusion. Three different contentions must be distinguished. It might be argued that the prophets were merely acting under psychological duress, and mistakenly supposing that their actions had some religious significance. It might be argued that the prophets' religious experience was the dominant factor, that they believed themselves to be obeying the word of Yahweh, and that the modern psychological reduction, though interesting, is best regarded as an irrelevance. And it might be argued that the prophets were indeed obeying the inscrutable word of God and that any "explanation" that takes no account of this is of no consequence whatever. The first is sceptical, the third theological, and both must be disregarded here because they depend upon highly determinative presuppositions. We must endeavour to seek the middle way and minimize our presuppositions. That means recognizing the importance of the theological convictions of prophets, onlookers, editors, and interpreting the actions in the light of these, while at the same time taking care not to invoke our own theological convictions. Difficult as that is, and, to be realistic, ultimately impossible, nevertheless that method is the only one to be adopted if we are to understand the Old Testament in its own terms. The theological—or the sceptical—enterprise has to follow after this work is done.

It follows that the psychological explanation of prophetic drama is [[264]] almost useless. Indeed it is not an explanation at all. It tells us what the modern psychologist thinks the prophets were doing. It does not tell us what the prophets themselves thought they were doing, which is what we really want to know. It implies that the dramas were by-products of prophecy, adding nothing and often subtracting from the dignity of the message. For our purposes the method is all wrong, because it is the product of distant observation. Disturbed or not, Ezekiel

4. O. R. Sellers, "Hosea's Motives," [[AJSL 41 (1925) 243–47]].
5. W. F. Lofthouse, "Thus Hath Jahveh Said," [[AJSL 40 (1924) 231–51]].

and all the other prophets were acting in a way that their contemporaries took seriously. What concerns us is how the behaviour was understood by those contemporaries, not how Ezekiel would have fared on a modern psychiatrist's couch.

The second attempt to explain prophetic drama is found in the contention that they were illustrations, visual aids, whose purpose was to make a difficult message more clear and more memorable. What is seen is more easily grasped than what is received verbally.[6] The prophets now appear, not as sufferers from a psychological malady, but as exponents of a psychological technique. This explanation of prophetic drama was expounded by Buzy in 1923 and it has found supporters here and there ever since.[7] Engnell suggests that the dramas were "consciously sensational."[8] So strong is the sense that any dramatic performance must have the purpose of making things clear that John Bright insists that Jeremiah's action with the waistcloth must have had an audience and Robert Wilson is convinced that, because Ezekiel's acts were too complex to be comprehensible, they could not have happened at all. The possibility that a drama might have a purpose other than communication is not even considered.[9] As recently as 1983 we find Bernhard Lang expounding the methods of prophetic communication and including, "the performance of street [[265]] theatre in which the prophet illustrates his word by game, mime and props." Several dramas are mentioned as means of "obtaining a hearing and giving weight to the word of their god." In this regard the prophets were "showmen"![10] Burke Long takes the same view, "It is

6. It is interesting to note that some scholars who could not bear to think that the dramas were actually performed were none the less willing to recognize their value as visual aids. As regards Ezekiel, for example, P. Fairbairn approved of the dramatic acts as long as they were understood to be "visions," perceived and thought about but not actually carried out (*Ezekiel and the Book of His Prophecy* [[Edinburgh, 1863]] 48f.). Similarly I. G. Matthews was happy if the narratives were "the literary product of a Babylonian editor." The historical Ezekiel could then be described as, "a normal, healthy-minded, vigorous prophet" (*Ezekiel* [[Philadelphia, 1939]] xxiif.).

7. D. Buzy, *Les Symboles de l'Ancien Testament* [[Paris, 1923]] 156; see also M. H. Farbridge, *Studies in Biblical and Semitic Symbolism* [[London, 1923]] 10; C. Kuhl, *The Prophets of Israel* [[Edinburgh, 1960]] 35; H. G. May, "Ezekiel," [[*IB* 6 (1956)]] 86; J. Gray, *Kings*, 599.

8. I. Engnell, "Prophets and Prophetism in the Old Testament" [[*Critical Essays on the Old Testament* (Stockholm, 1962; Eng. trans. London, 1970)]] 151.

9. J. Bright, *Jeremiah* [[AB 21; New York, 1965]] 96; R. R. Wilson, *Prophecy and Society in Ancient Israel* [[Philadelphia, 1980]] 283; see too E. R. Fraser, "Symbolic Acts of the Prophets," [[*StBTh* 4 (1974)]] 49.

10. B. Lang, *Monotheism and the Prophetic Minority* [[Sheffield, 1983]] 81f., 88f.; C. Uehlinger [["'Zeichne eine Stadt . . . und belagere sie!': Bild und Wort in einer Zeichenhandlung Ezechiels gegen Jerusalem (Ez. 4f.)," in *Jerusalem: Texte-Bilder-Steine* (ed. M. Küchler and C. Uehlinger; Göttingen, 1987) 111–200]] takes a similar view in his discussion of Ezekiel 4–5. Lang quotes with some approval the words of E. Renan, who describes the prophet as "un journaliste en plein air" [['an open-air journalist']], who gathers a crowd with

clear from the prophetic traditions that the acts were primarily used to dramatize and underscore what the prophets were saying."[11] To be fair to Lang, he does not think of "street theatre" purely in terms of a visual aid. For him the prophet is a political activist, not simply bringing news, but calling for decision and action; his aim is not simply to communicate, but to shock, to stir, to move. Involving onlookers in a piece of drama is a powerful way of furthering this aim.

All this is well said. This explanation, unlike the previous one, has the virtue of setting out what the prophet himself thought he was doing. It does not take the haughty line that we know what he was up to and he did not know himself. But the suspicion remains that this explanation wishes onto the prophets some very modern notions about the process of communication and persuasion; perhaps more to the point, this explanation is not sufficient to account for all the facts.

There are these objections. In the first place, the explanation fails to take account of those dramas that were not performed before an audience, or, equally important, that were not recorded as having taken place before an audience. This matter has already been discussed in Chapter 14 [not reprinted here]. Elisha did not tear his clothes nor Ezekiel eat his scroll in public (2 Kgs 2:12; Ezek 2:8–3:3). Was this because those actions related to themselves alone? Hosea may have married Gomer in public, but the significance of the action as prophetic drama was evident only to himself. Jeremiah had no audience for his performance with the waistcloth (Jeremiah 13) and Ezekiel had none for his performance with his hair (Ezek 5:1–4). The book on the doom of Babylon was not used as a visual aid (Jeremiah 51), and in several other stories an audience is either not mentioned or treated as an irrelevance.

Secondly, many dramatic acts are, in fact, less clear than the oracles [266] they are supposed to illustrate. Ezekiel's actions may arrest attention, but few of them can be said to communicate meaning more easily than words. Often oracles are necessary to make clear what the dramas mean. There may be some sense in which the performance of a drama represents an escalation in expression, but it is by no means always an escalation in clarity. Neither must we forget the actions where a visual aid is totally unnecessary. In every case where an audience of one person is involved the message would be simple and clear without any embellishment. How easy to tell Jeroboam that Yahweh will prosper his rebellion;

publicity-seeking tricks. Buffoonery was apparently put to the service of piety (*History of the People of Israel,* vol. 2 [Paris, 1893; Eng. trans. Boston, 1896], Book IV, Ch. 16, 356f.). Renan does not have to be taken too seriously. Nevertheless his low view of prophetic drama has proved convincing to many, even today.

11. B. O. Long, *I Kings with an Introduction to Historical Literature* [FOTL 9; Grand Rapids, Mich., 1984] 129.

how laborious and unnecessary to tear up a new cloak into all those pieces! Amsler's point must not be forgotten: why waste a valuable cloak?[12]

Thirdly, several dramas appear to involve contests. Leaving aside the competition on Mount Carmel, there are the clashes between Zedekiah and Micaiah ben Imlah (1 Kings 22), Jeremiah and Hananiah (Jeremiah 27–28) and Jeremiah and Jehoiakim (Jeremiah 36). The purpose of the contest is to establish which prophet is speaking the truth. In no case is there any doubt about the content of the message, the doubt concerns its reliability. So it is not enough for Hananiah to deny Jeremiah's contention or to make him go away; the yoke had to be broken. Similarly Jehoiakim's dramatic gesture was unnecessary for the purpose of communication, and Jeremiah's response—to have the scroll rewritten—was even more unnecessary for that purpose. It is evident that the dramatic acts were taken much more seriously than they would have been if their purpose had been simply to clarify the message.

Fourthly, in at least one case, the onlooker who was most concerned never really understood what was going on. Elisha does not communicate very well with Joash in 2 Kings 13, and the poor king is reprimanded in the end. In that example it almost appears that Joash was not meant to know the meaning of the drama until it was too late.

Fifthly, we have to remember those dramas that were not artificially contrived. The tearing of Samuel's robe, the work of the potter, the various afflictions of Ezekiel were neutral happenings before they were invested with prophetic significance. In no way can they be regarded as visual aids to elucidate a pre-determined message.

[[267]] Sixthly, the notion of language that lies behind this approach is at odds with what we find in the Bible. If words are simply a practical code for communicating intelligence from one person to another, then it is conceivable that the code might break down and a second interpretative medium be required. A modern observer might understand language and dramatic action in that way.[13] But that, of course, is not how the Hebrew understood words. As we have argued above, words were not simply a code for communication, they were centres of power. If they fell short, they needed to be fortified, not clarified.

---

12. It is only fair to point out that S. Amsler's own answer to this question is quite different from the one implied here. He says that the new cloak was torn, in true prophetic style, to shock the audience into taking notice. In other words, he sees the dramas as essentially aids to communication (*Les Actes des Prophètes* [[Essais Bibliques 9; Geneva, 1985]] 11, 61ff.).

13. Many modern observers *think* they understand language in this rational way, but do they? Many of us are haunted by the idea that words have power even when reason assures us they have not.

If a prophet resorts to dramatic action, it is much more likely to be because the word was not powerful enough rather than not clear enough. This is confirmed by the treatment of the drama narratives by later editors. Their additions frequently complicate the meaning of the action and never clarify it. The reason is that the action is not thought of primarily as a means of bringing home a message, but as a divine creation in its own right. The prophet was moved by God to perform this action; therefore the action will continue to have significance. If the original reality to which it bore witness is no longer relevant, then the action will move on to relate to something else. It does not exist to make a single message clear but to represent a divine initiative in the world, and as that initiative moves through history, so the drama comes to signify new meaning.

From time to time variations of this explanation appear. It is sometimes affirmed that the dramas were not intended to make the message more clear but more authentic. They were supposed to reveal the prophet as a peculiarly gifted person and thus to validate his message. No doubt a prophet engaged in drama was more impressive than a prophet declaiming oracles, and this factor may contribute something to the way the dramas were understood, but this explanation cannot have satisfied the more sophisticated onlookers and it clearly did not satisfy the prophetic editors. Two of the most impressive dramas in the Old Testament were the work of false prophets. Zedekiah made horns and Hananiah broke Jeremiah's yoke; they were in error, and the editors knew they were in error, but they still recount the actions in all their impressiveness. Impressiveness is evidently not the point. Impressiveness plays no part in the well-known test of prophecy in Deut 18:22. Thomas Overholt considers this question [[268]] in an article in 1982.[14] He contends that acts of power are intended to give authenticity to the prophet, but he distinguishes between dramas as we have defined them and actions that appear to abrogate "the laws of nature." The latter—largely associated with Elijah and Elisha—provide the ground for Overholt's argument. On the basis of texts like 1 Kgs 17:24, 2 Kgs 2:15, 4:37 and 8:4–6, it is easy for him to make his case, but they represent a different kind of narrative from those we are studying. These narratives raise quite different questions and would need to be treated in a different book.

Samuel Amsler takes a somewhat similar line.[15] He approaches the subject by way of the modern study of communication theory. That

---

14. T. W. Overholt, "Seeing Is Believing: The Social Setting of Prophetic Acts of Power," [[*JSOT* 23 (1982) 3–31]].

15. "Les prophètes et la Communication par les Actes," [[in *Werden und Wirken des Alten Testament* (ed. R. Albertz et al.; Göttingen, 1980) 194–201]].

means, in the first place, recognizing that a relationship already existed between the prophet and his audience, and that the relationship could easily become blocked. If the prophet's chief intention was to move, shock, disturb his audience, then some new means of producing an effect had to be devised, a non-verbal means which would draw the audience into the action and so make effective communication possible. While this hypothesis might well have a bearing on some of the drama narratives, it does not, for reasons already given, provide an explanation for them all; and, as far as the literary stage of the process is concerned, it has little to offer.

Some scholars in recent times have taken a different direction and produced a third explanation of prophetic drama. It has now become commonplace to suppose that, in the biblical world, words and actions were regarded as "dynamic." Making things clear may be a subsidiary purpose of dramatic actions, but the main significance is independent of the effect on the audience; it is to achieve a positive end. Consequently, the public dramas, often thought to be typical—Jeremiah's breaking of the flask, for example—may actually mislead, because they divert attention from the main point. This approach represents a complete reversal of the argument that the dramas were visual aids. Dramatic actions do not exist primarily to convey intelligence but to exert power. Many scholars are now inclined to refer to the creative power of the prophetic word and the prophetic action.[16]

[269] The dangers here are obvious. Is it seriously being implied that prophets thought that, by their own words and actions, they could cause great events to happen? Is prophetic drama, then, the Old Testament version of instrumental magic? Not really, for few argue that the words and actions are dynamic *in themselves.* The one who comes closest to this position is R. P. Carroll. He sees a clear link between prophetic drama and magic, and he does not confine himself to those actions that patently "abrogate the laws of nature," as Overholt does. Fohrer and many others see links in history and in outward appearance, but Carroll goes much further. Carroll holds that prophetic dramas "belong to an epistemological framework where divination and incantation represent power transmitted through words and gestures . . . These are not just actions which illustrate words with gestures but are part of the creation of the thing itself—they make things happen. The performed ac-

16. Bernhard Lang is one of relatively few scholars to protest at this suggestion. See his introduction to the collection of essays he himself edits, *Anthropological Approaches to the Old Testament* [Philadelphia, 1985] 7f. His resolution of the problem is scarcely an advance, however. See above n. 10. Perhaps the best antidote to the whole thesis is supplied by A. C. Thiselton in "The Supposed Power of Words in the Biblical Writings" [*JTS* 25 (1974) 283–99].

tion, accompanied by the ritualized words and gestures, is causal."[17] These words might just about be tolerated if Carroll were to allow that the true agent was not the prophet but Yahweh. However, he rejects such sophisticated theology. It "fails to allow for the extent to which belief in magic dominated the ancient world."[18] The Jeremiah tradition, he maintains, is full of magical elements.[19] They should be recognized and not dissolved away by anachronistic explanations. The weakness of this position is tied up in the two phrases "belief in magic" and "the ancient world." Enough has been said about the former to make it clear that such generalizations add little light to the question, but the second phrase is equally unhelpful. There certainly was belief in magic of various kinds in the ancient world and there are abundant texts to prove it, but one cannot infer any such belief where there are no texts to prove it, least of all where what texts do exist point the other way. The evidence of the prophetic dramas shows that similarities can be traced between some dramatic actions and some kinds of magic, but very few imply the kind of similarity to which Carroll refers.[20] As a [[270]] general explanation of the function of prophetic drama, therefore, Carroll's thesis is unacceptable.

Carroll, however, must be respected for his boldness. Many other commentators show a tendency to have it both ways at this point. On the one hand, in order to stress the vitality of the prophetic act, they speak of dramatic actions being effective and ensuring fulfilment; on the other, when considering the larger theological issue, they draw back from the brink, modify their language, and make Yahweh the true agent. It is necessary to be quite clear about this. Is the prophet effective because his actions are dynamic, or because Yahweh prompts him? And if Yahweh prompts him, is it necessary also to make use of the notion of the dynamic quality of prophetic action? This point must be cleared up before it can be said that prophetic drama has been explained.

Perhaps, then, those people who speak about word and drama as dynamic are being imprecise. It is not difficult to believe that some of the early dramatic actions were popularly understood as being instrumentally effective, but that explanation will not do for them all; and it will

---

17. R. P. Carroll, *Jeremiah* [[OTL; London, 1986]] 295.

18. Ibid., 296.

19. "Ritual magic is characteristic of the presentation of Jeremiah in certain strands of the tradition (e.g., 13:1–11; 19:1–2, 10–11; 25:15–17; 51:59–64). He creates and presides over the annihilation of the enemy (e.g., Judah, Jerusalem, Egypt, Babylon) by his performance of certain acts accompanied by incantations, curses and magical utterances" (ibid., 727).

20. Jer 51:59–64 might be an exception and a case can be argued regarding some of those recorded in Samuel and Kings.

not do for any once they are seen within the context of the whole prophetic corpus. Prophets had neither the power nor the intention to act in this way. Nevertheless it can fairly be said that a version of this theory of dynamic drama is the one that holds the field at the moment. In a sentence, the common thesis is that prophetic drama preserves the outward form of instrumental magic but the inner substance of Yahwist theology. Zimmerli's great commentary on Ezekiel provides an excellent example. In one column he states the thesis with great vigour, "By this action, which is more than mere symbolism, the prophet prefigures as an event what he proclaims through his word. More precisely this event is brought into effect by the prophet and is commanded to happen. By accomplishing this action the prophet guarantees the coming event."[21] If it were left at that, we should have to conclude that, according to Zimmerli, the prophet's actions were instrumentally effective. But in the next column he writes that, "the sign-action is not to be regarded as an 'actualizing' of the prophet's message which he has ingeniously devised, but that it is wholly given through God's sending and empowering him. Furthermore the sign-action is throughout only a living manifestation of the word of Yahweh."

[271] Prophetic dramas preserve the outward appearance of acts of instrumental magic, that is to say, they are performed by a specially gifted person, they frequently mimic the end sought after, they are attended by an air of mystery and by the belief that, once carried out, they will proceed irrevocably to their fulfilment.[22] At the same time the theology is Yahwist, that is to say, the prophet takes no initiative and has no power of his own. He performs his dramas in obedience to Yahweh and it is Yahweh's power that ensures their fulfilment. Prophetic dramas are, therefore, explained as an amalgam of Yahwist theology and magical form.[23] They are effective acts, but they fall within the concept of Yahweh's control of history. Fohrer argues in this way.[24] He reckons that the world of magic provides the historical context out of which the prophetic dramas arose and he allows that a magical element persists in some Old Testament narratives. His list of symbolic actions, however, excludes the magical and he denies that any act of the classical prophets

21. *Ezekiel*, vol. 1 [1969; Eng. trans. Hermeneia; Philadelphia, 1979] 156, col. 1.
22. J. Gray, *Kings*, 413, 449, 592, 599.
23. See Sawyer, *Prophecy* [*and the Prophets of the Old Testament* (Oxford, 1987)], 10f. and T. W. Overholt, "Prophecy: The Problem of Cross-Cultural Comparison" [*Semeia* 21; Chico, Calif., 1982; repr. in *Anthropological Approaches to the Old Testament* (ed. B. Lang; Philadelphia, 1985)] 63.
24. G. Fohrer, "Prophetie und Magie" [*ZAW* 78 (1966)] 25ff.; *Die symbolischen Handlungen der Propheten* [2d ed.; Zurich, 1968] 10ff.; *History of Israelite Religion* [Berlin, 1969; Eng. trans. London, 1973] 234, 241, 243, 286.

can legitimately be called magical. Nevertheless he spends a lot of time providing parallels between the prophetic actions and those from various other cultures around the world that can be called magical; these parallels are, of course, in appearance only; the Hebrew prophet acts by Yahweh's command and the power of the action depends on Yahweh alone.

Most of the writers who recognize prophetic drama to be more than a visual aid argue in this way. Yahweh's sovereignty does not make dramatic actions unnecessary, nor rob them of their effectiveness. On the contrary, he wills to speak and act in this way. The dramas are both necessary and effective. They depend for their proper functioning upon a proper relationship between Yahweh and the prophet, hence the emphasis laid on the prophet's call and on the command to perform the actions; but they remain, in appearance, much like magical acts, though exceptions have to be made in the case of actions that were burdensome to the performer. These exceptions are in fact illuminating because they reveal that the supreme actor was not the prophet but Yahweh. They also reveal that we have not quite reached the end of our journey.

This explanation gives an apparently satisfactory account of most of the data. It tends to represent the dramas as predictions that proceed [[272]] to fulfilment, which is appropriate for many of the narratives, but not all. It sheds a little light on the problematic fact that prophets often pronounce judgment without any call to repentance, even sometimes when the time for repentance is past. The word and the drama are the beginning of the doom; through them Yahweh moves on to the historical consummation on which he has decided. This explanation is also consistent with the idea—prevalent, so it seems, in the Old Testament—that the course of history might be diverted if the prophet was silenced and his drama annulled.[25] It may seem dangerous to try to interfere with God's will, but presumably the prophets' antagonists had a different idea of what God's will was. That, however, is not quite the point. The point is that everyone agreed that it was not enough to disbelieve or denounce the drama. The drama had inherent power—even those who did not believe in the direction of its thrust recognized that it had power—so it had to be destroyed.

This explanation also has the virtue of ambiguity, ambiguity which is not, perhaps, intended but which none the less helps us to interpret some of the different views that were held in Israel. Dramatic action is always impressive, the more so if the performer displays the mystique of otherworldly powers. Those with a profound trust in Yahweh would see through the performance to the power of Yahweh evidenced in it. Those with a

25. See, for example, 1 Kings 22; Jer 20:1f.; 28:10f.; 32:2–5; 36:23; 37:15, 21.

feeble grasp of the theology would simply be impressed by the mystique. Jeremiah's confrontation with Jehoiakim shows two people, both concerned with the same actions and realities, both aware of the significance of dramatic action and of divine will; but they differed in where they laid the stress. For Jeremiah, Yahweh's will was dominant and his own action was simply the expression of it. For Jehoiakim, the right action was all-important and Yahweh's will could be expected to conform to it. Broadly speaking, they both took the view that the prophetic drama was an amalgam of mysterious, impressive performance and a divine act to complement it.

This explanation is, therefore, valuable, but it is by no means perfect. In the first place, it is never quite clear whether the analysis belongs to a modern, theological approach to the data, or whether it is supposed that the prophets themselves thought in these terms. If, as one suspects, the former is the case, then the explanation does not answer the question we are raising. If the latter is the case, then it [[273]] seems that we are wishing onto the prophets a degree of analytical and theological sophistication that belongs to our world rather than theirs. This is not to deny theological depth to the prophets, but to suggest that their theological awareness needs to be set out in terms appropriate to their situation.

In the second place, it is not profitable to talk about prophetic drama having the outward appearance of magic. This question has been discussed at length in the previous chapter and there is little need to say more now. Magic, in the primary sense, is now understood as part of the social programme. A magical action takes place when the community, following community tradition, goes to work with the deity. Solitary actions by individuals, which, because they are solitary, may well be anti-communal, represent a debased form of magic and may even deserve the name of sorcery. The sorcerer is intent on fulfilling his own will and that of his client; he proceeds by traditional methods, for no sorcerer simply makes up a charm out of his own head. The prophet does not express his own will; in many cases the prophet's own wishes are not referred to, and when they are referred to, they are frequently set on one side. Equally, the prophet is not bound by tradition. He acts, believing himself to be under divine constraint, in all kinds of novel and imaginative ways. It may be that we do not know much about Israel's arcane tradition, but whatever it contained, we may be sure that marrying a prostitute, appearing in public naked or yoked, and burying a waistcloth were not included in it. To suggest, therefore, that prophetic dramas have the outward appearance of magic is, at best, to be imprecise.

The reference to magic, however, is not essential to the position under discussion, which is really concerned with the dynamic nature of

Yahweh's word through the prophet. Zimmerli makes out this case without mentioning magic at all. Nevertheless there are other serious weaknesses in this explanation of the function of prophetic drama. In the third place then, it tends to assume a simple, linear view of time and causation in which drama always precedes fulfilment. It may be remembered from Chapters 4 and 16 [not reprinted here] that cultic activity and some expressions of magic warn against this presumption, and as a matter of fact, there are many prophetic dramas that cannot be explained exhaustively, or even explained at all, if they are regarded as actions to introduce or bring about future events.

Some of the dramas are best understood, not as introductions of [274] future events, but as dramatic expressions of present ones. Hosea's unhappy alliance with Gomer is not a prediction of future infidelity; it is a powerful expression of how Yahweh relates to Israel. A universal fact is brought into dramatic focus in the marriage. Similarly the potter in Jeremiah 18 is expressing God's power over the nation. Only in a very reduced sense is that expression predictive. Again, Micah's announcement that he will go about naked is a response to a bleak situation. In one sense it initiates a future condition of mourning, but in another it is an actual mourning for Israel's present state. The action is weakened if it is reckoned to have only future reference. Again, the very complex drama of Jeremiah's waistcloth is, in the first instance, a theological reflection rather than a prediction. It is an eternal truth of Israel's existence that to be separated from Yahweh means corruption and ruin. Many of the dramatic actions of Ezekiel relate to events that are happening at a distance in space, not in time. Ezekiel in Babylon is living out the tragedy of Jerusalem, and some of his dramas express the agony of that city. The siege story of Ezekiel 4 makes little sense as a prediction, but it makes great sense if it is reckoned to express in Babylon the precise conditions in Judah. Similarly, Ezekiel, lying on his side (4:4–6) expresses a state of affairs that already is; he does not cause it. The eating of strange bread (4:9–17) is an attempt to reproduce the conditions of the siege and the two dramatic actions of Ezekiel 12 (replicating the scene when the captives are carried off and eating and drinking in fear), are an attempt to involve the exiles in the predicament of their compatriots in Zion. Some dramas look back as much as they look forward. In the robe-tearing scene at Gilgal (1 Sam 15:27f.), Saul has already been rejected when the incident happens. Elisha burning his plough and boiling his oxen (1 Kgs 19:21) is saying goodbye to the old life and, in tearing his clothes (2 Kgs 2:12f.), he is denying the old identity before he takes on the new. The naming of Hosea's children (Hos 1:4–9) involves the representation of past sins with their consequences much more than any prophecy about the future. An explanation that does not take account of these variations in the chronological relation of drama to reality is bound to be inadequate.

Fourthly, if God's dynamic activity through the prophet is understood through the model of instrumental magic, it must follow that a reality, once brought into being by prophetic drama, is bound to continue to its conclusion, for though magicians may fail, God [[275]] presumably may not. This is very dangerous ground.[26] Every Israelite knew that fulfilment of any dramatic act could be frustrated—for all Zedekiah's efforts, Ahab lost—and in at least one case, Ezek 37:15–28, the prophet was simply wrong. But more important, some dramas take place in circumstances where repentance is still possible and fulfilment not inevitable. Although the potter reworked the clay in Jeremiah 18, v. 8 shows that it is not certain that Israel will be "reworked." It depends upon whether Israel turns from its evil way.[27] Similarly, in Jeremiah 27 a choice is available to the people, though it is a dusty one: either submit to the yoke of Babylon or suffer from sword, famine and pestilence. The drama indicates the better way, though the choice is still open.[28]

From all this it is clear that a new hypothesis is necessary; one that is concerned with more than prediction and fulfilment; that is not so strong on the dynamic force of the dramas themselves, but allows for the fact that they frequently exist to express reality rather than to cause it; one that is more in touch with the notion of time revealed in the cult and less tied to the simple, linear notion of time and causation; one that allows for the possibility of variation in the reality, even when a predictive action has been carried out; and above all, one that is rooted in the Hebrew world and is not informed by twentieth-century attitudes.

In the work of A. Lods there is the suggestion of an interesting alternative. In his essay of 1927 it is only a hint, but it is raised again in just

26. The Old Testament is so far from this mechanistic view of the universe that it allows that God can change his mind: Gen 6:5–7; 18:16–33; Exod 32:11–14; 1 Sam 2:30f.; 15:11; Amos 7:1–6, etc.

27. Jeremiah "is convinced that he is proclaiming not an immutable decree of Yahweh but rather a plan that allows God to 'repent' if the people repent" (H. Gunkel, "The Prophets as Writers and Poets" [[Prophecy in Israel [ed. D. L. Petersen; Philadelphia, 1987]]] 62; the whole section, pp. 61–63, is interesting and provides many other references).

28. This human involvement in the course of history, whereby Israel co-operates or fails to co-operate, raises large theological questions about how God was understood to act. Israel was free to repent, but presumably Babylon was not free to call off the siege once it had been decreed from above. How much freedom had Assyria in Isa 10:5f.? Much discussion of so-called "divine events" in the Old Testament is beggared by this problem. It is too large a subject to be pursued here.

a few lines in his work on the prophets of 1937.[29] Lods asks whether prophetic dramas create the future or whether they are not best understood as unveiling realities that exist but are as yet unseen [[276]] or unappreciated. "One wonders whether the prophet's act was supposed to influence the future or whether the future was reflected in the action of 'the man of the spirit'." Lods goes no further and the hint has generally been ignored. Von Rad speaks of the fall of Jerusalem "casting its shadow before it," but he does not expand on the subject.[30] The evidence, however, suggests that these two scholars are looking in the right direction for a solution.

In modern discussion of the cult, it seems that the ritual drama played out at the festivals on Mount Zion is suspended between two great events in the story of God's dealings with his people. On one hand there is the ancient event—the creation, the escape from Egypt—which is being recalled; on the other hand there is a great victory of the future, which is being anticipated. Contemporary victories also come into the reckoning and hoped for victories in imminent battles. The celebration is not, therefore, just a memorial, nor just an anticipation, but a telescoping of history, a drawing together of all events, past, present and future in the cultic day. It is as though the divine action shows itself in the world in a number of different modes, by our categories mythological (the creation), historical (the battle just won), ritual (the cultic drama), and the eschatological (God's final triumph). All are drawn together and expressed in the same celebration. To ask which of these causes the others is to ask the wrong question, for all are manifestations of the divine will. Equally, to suppose that they are all separate entities is to miss the point, for they are all different expressions of the same divine triumph.[31]

Cultic celebration demands a modification of the straightforward linear view of past, present and future, and the notion of causation that goes with it. The past is not drifting ever further away and the future is not blankly inaccessible. They exist in the divine will and they are brought together on the great occasion. This biblical understanding has remained with the Jewish people ever since. The Passover is a different kind of memorial from the annual service at the Cenotaph. Each year the marchers in Whitehall get older, and one has the sense that gradually we are losing touch with the past. Nobody can recall Ladysmith now,

29. "Le Rôle des Idées Magiques dans la Mentalité Israélite" [[in *Old Testament Essays* (ed. D. C. Simpson; London, 1927]] 59; *The Prophets and the Rise of Judaism* [[Eng. trans. London, 1937]] 54.

30. Von Rad, *Theology II*, 232.

31. See above Chapter 5 [[not reprinted here]].

few the Somme, and before very long, few will recall El Alamein. Not so with the Passover. [[277]] The escape from Egypt, escape from the holocaust, the founding of the State of Israel, and many other events, ancient and modern, together with eschatological visions of a glorious future, coalesce in the one celebration. Two different conceptions of time inform these two examples. The Old Testament with its theocentric view of history sees events, not as a series of sequential happenings spread out along a line, but as different aspects of the great divine activity in history in which all times and all places are drawn together.

When we discuss the bearing of this on prophecy, a similar number of guises of the divine event appear. An event has an existence in the will of Yahweh, in the mind of the prophet, in his oracle, in his drama, in the arena of history, and in the historical record.[32] Which of these manifestations comes first in the chronological sense is unimportant. Because the will of Yahweh is hidden, the first appearance of an event may well be in the word or drama of the prophet, in which case we may be misled into speaking of the word or action of the prophet being dynamic and *causing* a certain outcome. But that is unfortunate, for in fact, the whole complex has one cause, the divine intention. This explanation holds good for those dramas that are not predictive. In the case of Hosea's marriage, the critical factor—Yahweh's constant love for his unfaithful people—in the current state of affairs is hidden. The drama expresses that critical factor. It may not communicate widely, but that is not the point. The reality is focused and manifested in the dramatic action even if it is unappreciated. If one asks, "What is the point, if it is unappreciated?" the answer is that what is must proceed into expression because of the very weight of its being. It is expressed because it is true, and truth demands expression, whether it is apprehended or not. Even if it is not apprehended by people, it is apprehended by God. Jeremiah's action with the waistcloth expresses what needed to be expressed. More obviously, Ezekiel's dramatic acts relating to the fall of Jerusalem extend to Babylon a reality that had its locus hundreds of miles away.

This hypothesis is strengthened by considerations from two different directions. In the first place, the discussion of terminology in Chapter 2 [[not reprinted here]] revealed something interesting about the meaning of the words *ʾôt* [['sign']] and *māšāl* [['example']]. In Isaiah 7 Isaiah prophesies the break-up of the [[278]] Syro-Ephraimite confederacy. He then offers Ahaz a sign of the fulfilment of his prophecy. The sign is the birth of a child, and as the child grows, the deliverance takes shape. The purpose of the sign is to bind together the prophecy and the deliver-

---

32. Susan Niditch makes a somewhat similar point in *Symbolic Vision in Biblical Tradition* [[Chico, Calif., 1983]] (pp. 33f.), but she unhelpfully ties it up with sympathetic magic.

ance, so that the word, the growing child and the departure of the two kings are seen as a single divine reality. Something not too dissimilar is true of the typical *māšal*. The *māšal* represents a concretization of a universal truth. That sounds very abstract, but if the universal truth is Yahweh's hatred of infidelity and Israel is being punished for infidelity, then Israel has become a *māšal*, a particular expression of a divine attitude. What exists in extension also exists at a particular point through the *māšal*. One element does not cause the other. They are both aspects of the same reality.

The second confirmation derives from what was said in the previous chapter about the modern understanding of magic. In many cases the magical performance is not seen as a mechanism to bring about a particular effect. Rather the performance and the reality to which it relates are seen as different aspects of the same entity. There is rain, but there is also need for rain and gratitude for rain. There is war, but there is also fear of war and experience of war. The rain and the war themselves cannot be brought under control, but the experience of them can. So the hopes, joys, fears are worked out in the magical ceremonies so that the realities, when they happen, can be enjoyed or endured positively, successfully and to the full. Rain and rain rites, war and war rites belong together. But to decode these things in terms of our own notions of time and causation is to impose the wrong pattern upon them. It is considerations like these that help to unlock the Hebrew mind.

If we are to keep in touch with biblical understanding, we need to think of events in the Bible as complex entities existing on different levels or in different modes. The fall of Jerusalem is a divine act, a prophetic oracle, a flask broken before the elders, an actual horror, a series of dramatic actions in Babylon, and a bitter record. The deliverance at the Red Sea is an actual happening, an oral record, a written text, a constantly renewed celebration, plus all those later deliverances in which the prototype is recapitulated and renewed, and finally the great Messianic deliverance of the future when all the promises will be fulfilled. That is some event, but if we are to understand the idea properly, we must look at the whole rather than ⟦279⟧ the parts.[33] The various elements are not to be logically disconnected. They are best understood as one integer with many different modes of expression. This way of thinking may seem strange, but it requires little effort to apply it to our own situation. What is marriage? It is a piece of paper, a gold ring, a ritual

---

33. To take an example from outside the Old Testament, the most complex biblical entity of all is probably the resurrection, which exists in history (the resurrection of Jesus, however understood), in story (the kerygma), in ritual sign (baptism), in personal experience (repentance and faith), in practical ethics (so Paul continually hopes) and in eschatology (the consummation).

drama, a series of spoken words, an emotional attitude, a social status, a sexual act, a prolonged cohabitation, a new family unit. In one sense, none of these *is* marriage, but they are all aspects or expressions of one complex entity. It is in this sense that we have to understand drama and reality in the Old Testament.

The simplest and easiest application of this principle to prophecy is, of course, in the divine will-oracle-drama-fulfilment sequence. We simply need to recognize that it is not the word or the drama, but the divine will, that is dynamic. Diagrammatically,

is more correct than divine will → oracle → drama → fulfilment.

When the circus comes to town, the first indication is the man who posts the bills and then the caravan from which the tickets are sold. The clowns and the animals are still a long way off. The first lorry brings the four posts of the big top; then comes the tent itself; then at last comes the procession, and the circus is here. The performance takes place; and then it all moves away, leaving behind a few men to clean the site. The bill-posters come first, but they do not *cause* the show. They and the performers are part of the same enterprise, and they are all under the control of the circus-master. He is not bound by the bill-posters—they are bound by him—but his circus needs them. The circus is a complex reality with many modes of existence, all interrelated, all necessary and all dependent upon the one who is in charge.

This illustration fails, however, in that it deals only with the simplest [[280]] and commonest case of prophetic drama; it links one element and the next in a linear and sequential, though not causal, way. A comprehensive account of the relationship of prophetic drama to reality is not so easily illustrated. Perhaps the word "drama" was a wise choice because of the complexity and elusiveness of the relation of all drama to reality. The drama stands over against reality; it holds up a mirror to it, it represents, it informs, it interprets; it heightens reality by highlighting it and revealing its inner nature; the drama affects the way that reality is experienced. And so we could go on. Prophetic drama hovers around the reality and gives it further "presence." It is another form of manifestation of the reality itself.

It is wise to point out that the hypothesis we are putting forward is not necessarily theological; it has to do with Hebrew thought-forms rather than with Hebrew faith, though the latter is included in the former. Jehoiakim would have shared these ideas with Jeremiah. There is, however, a difference in the way the two men operated the concept, and this difference *is* theological. The common element is that word, act, fulfilment, record, etc. are all parts of the same reality. Diagrammatically, we have a kind of wheel.

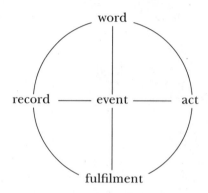

The theological question is where Yahweh fits into the diagram, where the dynamic force comes from, what turns the wheel. According to the "low" theology prevalent in Jehoiakim's court—and prevalent, without doubt, through much of Israel and most of the ancient Near East—the divine activity is but one more element in the event, and so is located on the circumference. The dynamic can be exerted through the word and the act; human agents can bear upon the divine and so bring about the fulfilment. According to the "high" Yahwist theology, no human being can exert control over the Holy One of Israel. The whole event belongs to him. If he wills it, all the elements happen; if [[281]] he does not, none of them do, or, if words are spoken and actions performed, they are powerless. There can be no dynamic from the circumference; if the wheel turns, it turns from the hub.

Some such conception alone allows us to take account of all the factors that have come to the surface in this study. It makes it possible to explain the shift in theology and the difference in understanding between the Jeremiahs and the Jehoiakims. The great prophets were possessed of an idea of the sovereignty of Yahweh that was not fully worked out in the earliest traditions nor comprehended by the mass of the people. To return to the circus illustration, the early stories imply too much power in the hands of the bill-poster, and Jehoiakim and his courtiers never got beyond this understanding. The great prophets recognized the power of the circus-master and realized that they themselves had no power of initiative at all. We can thus explain the sense of compulsion felt by the prophet. Yahweh called into being both the reality and the drama. We can also explain the relatively few cases where allowance must be made for possible repentance. Yahweh is not bound by the historical process as human beings are. The future is what he wills it to be, and his will constitutes reality, as nothing else does. That reality may break into human consciousness by prophetic act or word, and there is nothing spurious about these acts and words. If Yahweh's will changes, however, the future is different, and different acts and oracles are called for. In both cases the prophetic activity is authentic because it represents a reality that has its being in God. That only one future can actually happen does not invalidate either prophetic exercise. In a similar way dramas and oracles that are delivered when the time for repentance is past are explained. The work of the prophet is primarily related to Yahweh and his historical activity, not to his audience and their response. If Yahweh decrees that a reality is to be, then oracle and drama go with it, regardless of whether anyone is listening or watching. We have also to explain prophetic contests. On this reckoning there is an absolute difference between a true prophet and a false one, a difference that is not in any way diminished by the fact that, in any given instance, nobody can be sure which is which. The true prophet signifies a world-shattering reality. The false one signifies what is in his own imagination. The contest is an attempt, sometimes a vain attempt, to put the issue to the test. Even then, as 1 Kings 22 makes clear, nobody can be sure. Only time reveals the truth.

Drama and reality stand over against each other, mutually dependent [[282]] and interpreting each other. The drama presents, focuses, interprets and mediates the reality. It also modifies the reality, because, in so far as the attitude of the people is a significant element in the total event, response to the drama contributes something to the reality. Such a view of prophetic drama helps to unlock the world of the prophets and the thought of the Old Testament. It may also take us further. So much of the New Testament is written in Old Testament style, and Old Testament thought patterns persist in the New Testament. Beyond that, much Christian doctrine is conceived in terms of biblical ideas. It may be, then, that an enquiry of this kind has a bearing both on our understanding of the New Testament and on the starting-point of Christian doctrine. Perhaps the most interesting of the possibilities in this regard is in relation to the theology of the sacraments.

What Did the Prophets Think They Were Doing?

Speech Acts and Prophetic Discourse in the Old Testament

WALTER HOUSTON

[[167]] I try here to give an account of one type of prophetic discourse in the Hebrew Bible in terms of the theory of "speech acts" originally propounded by the Oxford philosopher J. L. Austin (Austin 1975) and developed by a number of successors, notably J. R. Searle (Searle 1969, 1979; Searle and Vanderveken 1985; a somewhat different account in Wolterstorff 1980: 200–231), according to which every utterance is interpreted as an intentional act of one or another kind in a particular situation: one "does things with words."[1] It has been taken up by linguists (such as Leech [1983]) as part of the theory of pragmatics ("the study of how utterances have meanings in situations" [Leech 1983: 10]), has attracted the attention of literary critics (e.g., Fish 1989) and has been made use of before now by theologians (Evans 1963) and biblical scholars (Carroll 1979: 69ff.; Caird 1980: 20–25). I hope that my

Reprinted with permission from *Biblical Interpretation* 1 (1993) 167–88.

Versions of this paper were read to the Durham conference on prophecy in December 1988 and to the Cambridge Old Testament Seminar in October 1991. I am grateful to all who participated in the discussions and so contributed towards its present shape, as well as to students at Westminster College and the Cambridge Federation of Theological Colleges, with whom its ideas were originally discussed over a number of years.

1. The terminology I use will broadly be that of Searle and Vanderveken, except when I am expounding works that use different terminology.

account may shed light on some current discussions of the function of
prophetic discourse in the Hebrew Bible, particularly the question
whether pronouncements of doom were intended to evoke repentance
and lead to reform.

I shall often refer, in old-fashioned style no doubt (cf. Auld 1983;
Carroll 1983, 1989), to "the prophets" as a designation of the figures to
whose activity the material of the books which go by that name is attributed editorially and implicitly. Whether or not this attribution is to any
extent correct, and whether or not these figures are correctly termed
prophets, does not really affect my argument, [[168]] which is concerned
with the character of the texts as utterances. Nevertheless I shall speak as
if the material is to some extent attributable to the activity of persons
with a public ministry addressing a contemporary audience. The theory
of speech acts has been criticized especially (see Derrida 1977 and Fish
1989) on the grounds that utterances may be separated from their original situation (otherwise writing and reading would be impossible), and
that in any case their precise relationship to the speaker's purposes and
situation is always more or less indeterminate; the necessity of interpretation, always open-ended, can never be short-circuited by an appeal to
the speech situation. In the case of the biblical prophets, whatever their
origins in a living speech situation, many (e.g., Carroll 1989) would argue
that they are to us simply texts, and they have to be interpreted as such.
Searle's reply to Derrida is that "*a meaningful sentence is just a standing
possibility of the corresponding (intentional) speech act.* To understand it, it is
necessary to know that anyone who said it and meant it would be performing that speech act determined by the rules of the languages that
give the sentence its meaning in the first place" (Searle 1977: 202, italics
in the original). In other words, even if we do not know the situation in
which the utterance originated, the structure of the utterance itself shows
us what kind of speech act it is. I do not agree with this in its entirety, because I accept Leech's contention (1983: 24–25) that the "illocutionary
force" of an utterance (what type of speech act it is: see below) is determined by the situation, not by the rules of language; this will become
clear later. Nevertheless, I would contend that however textual a text may
be, every sentence in it is a speech act of some kind and implies a situation, of course more or less indeterminately, and often more than one
situation, as for example the editor of Jeremiah addressing his readers,
the prophet addressing the people, God through the prophet addressing
the people. The identification of speech acts need not be excluded in
principle by the textuality of the text or the uncertainty of its origin.
Since one situation frequently implied is that of the prophet addressing
hearers, there is no reason why we should not assume it.

It is indeed worth recalling the memorable ways in which the origin of the prophetic books in an activity of speech is expressed in the accounts of commissioning. "The LORD put forth his hand and touched *my mouth*" (Jer 1:9); "Then flew one of the seraphs to me having in his hand a burning coal . . . and he touched *my mouth*" ⟦169⟧ (Isa 6:6–7). Even where prophets are represented as performing actions, such as walking naked for three years (Isaiah 20), buying a field (Jeremiah 32), digging a hole in the wall of his house (Ezek 12:7), these actions are understood as conveying a meaning: the effect they are intended to have is analogous to that of speech (Caird 1980: 22–23). Yet Jeremiah is told that with his words he is "to pluck up and to break down, to destroy and to overthrow, to build and to plant" (Jer 1:10). These words, it seems, are preternaturally powerful. A number of passages, as is well known, demonstrate the belief that the prophetic word is capable of itself of accomplishing the thing of which it speaks. E.g.,

I am making my words in your mouth a fire, and this people wood, and the fire shall devour them (Jer 5:14).

I have hewn them by the prophets, I have slain them by the words of my mouth (Hos 6:5).

So shall my word be that goes forth from my mouth; it shall not return to me empty, but shall accomplish that which I purpose, and prosper in the thing for which I sent it (Isa 55:11).

But it is worth stressing at this point that the word which accomplishes these things is always understood, and in most cases formulated, as the word of Yahweh. The most obvious role played by the prophets in their literary presentation is that of spokespersons for the Lord. Even where their words are not formulated as words of Yahweh (e.g., in Isa 2:6ff.), their context and content suggest that they are intended to represent God's judgement and will.

An earlier generation of scholars (Grether 1934: esp. 103–7; Dürr 1938; followed above all by von Rad, 1965: ii, 80ff.) took the view that the understanding of the prophetic word as effective in itself was simply a special case of an understanding of language in general in the ancient Near East, supposedly quite different from our present-day understanding in the West. Otto Procksch (1942: 90) coined the words "dynamic" and "dianoetic" to describe the distinct elements that he saw in the "word." Blessings and curses, for example, are typical "dynamic" words; they are words endued with power, which work automatically, as when Isaac blesses Jacob in mistake for Esau and then cannot change the

blessing even though it was extracted by fraud (Gen 27:35). The words
of priests and kings are more powerful than those of ordinary people,
and the word of God is most powerful of all. But in essence all words
are objective realities with power in the external world. In contrast, our
understanding is purely "dianoetic": it sees language as simply ⟦170⟧ referring to things and conveying information.

This view has been very effectively criticized—should I say plucked
up and broken down?—by A. C. Thiselton (1974).[2] Thiselton makes a
number of points, of which the most significant are these:

(a) The so-called "dynamic" and "dianoetic" views of languages are
not the only alternatives, but merely two out of a wide range of ways
in which language may function (1974: 287, 296ff.). We shall see shortly
what this full range actually covers. It is not Western people in general,
but just philosophers in a certain tradition who tend to assume that the
only proper use of language is referential and informative.

(b) In all the examples on which the "dynamic language" theory
relies, it is the words of God (or a god) which are in question (1974:
290ff.). Blessings and curses might be an exception, but it is surely reasonable to maintain that these depend on an implicit or explicit invocation of the deity. Hence one may ask whether the power of the word
discovered in these cases has much to do with the fact that it is a word,
and not rather with the fact that God has spoken it, or is appealed to
(cf. Caird 1980: 22).

(c) The power of blessings and curses depends on cultural convention involving accepted procedures and institutions. "They are effective,
in most cases, only when performed by the appropriate person in the appropriate situation" (Thiselton 1974: 294). Isaac cannot withdraw Esau's
blessing not because "his words are believed to be a grenade whose explosion can only be awaited," but because no convention exists by which
it may be revoked. In other situations, however, a curse may in fact be revoked or withdrawn (1974: 298f.); as in the case of Micah's mother who
cursed the thief of her life-savings, but when her son confessed to the
crime immediately replied "Blessed be my son by the LORD" (Judg 17:2).
This demonstrates sufficiently the falsity of the view that the Hebrews believed in an autonomous power inhering in words.

(d) An alternative and more useful explanation of such utterances
(Thiselton 1974: 293ff.) is to view them as "performatives," using the term
invented and expounded by Austin (1975), which develops the notion

2. Thiselton was to some extent anticipated by Evans (1963: 164); but Evans continues
to maintain an element of magic in the biblical conception.

already referred to of speech achieving its effect through a complex of conventions and institutional facts.

⟦171⟧ Austin shows that the idea of words achieving purposes, being effective, performing tasks, so far from being bound to an alien culture imbued with magical ideas, is part of our own understanding of how ordinary language works. The power of words is located in the social conventions which surround our own use of language. For example, "I appoint you my deputy," spoken by one who has the right to appoint a deputy, has the effect of making the person addressed the speaker's deputy. No act of appointment is required other than the bare words. The words "I take thee to be my lawful wedded wife" and "I take thee to be my lawful wedded husband," spoken in the appropriate circumstances, legally effect a marriage according to English law.

In each case the desired state of affairs is effected simply by the performance, in the appropriate circumstances, of the respective "speech act." In these examples the first person verb, "I appoint," "I take," simultaneously effects and describes the act. As Caird lucidly puts it (1980: 21), the speakers are not "reporting an action which has been accomplished by non-verbal means, but doing with words exactly what they say they are doing." This feature is true also of such sentences as "I promise to be there," "I bet you five pounds," though these are not thought of as effecting a state of affairs but as committing the speaker to some future action, either absolutely or conditionally. It is primarily this use of first person verbs which is known as "performative," and Searle and Vanderveken (1985: 3) restrict the word to this use, though it is used more loosely by Thiselton and by Caird and Carroll. But the extension is understandable, since it was Austin himself (1975: 56ff.) who pointed out that there was no essential difference between saying, "I promise to be there," and saying simply, "I'll be there." The latter is as much a promise as the former. If the convener of a meeting were to say, "The meeting stands adjourned," that is as much as to say, "I declare the meeting adjourned." In each case he or she adjourns the meeting by his or her words.

In this way Austin was led to offer a complete account of language as a set of speech acts, and to withdraw or blur his original distinction between "performatives" and "constatives." Of any utterance it is possible to ask "What is *being done* when that is said?" By that we may mean one of two crucially distinct things: "What are you doing *in* saying that?"—that is, what kind of speech act is it?—promising, warning, prohibiting, encouraging or whatever it may ⟦172⟧ be. These descriptions refer not to the causal effect of the words but to their significance as viewed by convention; or rather, as I should prefer to say with Leech, to their meaning in the situation. To refer to this meaning Austin coined the adjective *illocutionary*. The *illocutionary force* of the words, "I'll be there," is that of a promise.

But by the words, "What is being done?," we may alternatively mean "What are you doing *by* saying that?"—that is, what is causally effected by it, or what do you intend to effect by it? To denote this effect or intention Austin and his followers use the word *perlocutionary*. Perlocutionary acts are such as convincing, intimidating, astonishing, reassuring. These are not names of speech acts but effects which one may achieve by using particular speech acts. Obviously the illocutionary force of an utterance may be a significant factor in its perlocutionary effect. One may convince by argument, intimidate by threats, astonish by assertion, reassure by a promise. Some perlocutionary effects are very closely associated with particular illocutionary acts, as, for example, keeping a promise is with promising. Nevertheless, one can still promise and not keep one's promise: illocutionary force and perlocutionary effect must be distinguished. Indeed, one can make a promise without even intending to keep it. That would obviously be a defective sort of promise, but it would still be a promise. Austin (1975: 12ff.) spends much time in discussing different kinds of defect, or what he terms "infelicity," in illocutionary acts. But he takes care to distinguish between abuses such as insincerity, which do not make an act void, and "misfires" which mean that the act has not actually been performed, for example if someone other than the person in the chair were to declare the meeting adjourned. That would not be an adjournment, since the speaker would not be qualified to declare an adjournment. If such basic conditions as this are fulfilled, the act is said to be *successful* (Searle and Vanderveken 1985: 13).

Searle and Vanderveken, in their formal treatment of the subject (1985: 51ff., developing Searle's recasting of Austin's terminology in Searle 1979: 1–29), divide all illocutionary acts into five classes.

> One can say how things are (assertives), one can try to get other people to do things (directives), one can commit oneself to doing things (commissives), one can bring about changes in the world through one's utterances (declaratives), and one can express one's feelings and attitudes (expressives). Often one can do more than one of these things in the same utterance (52).

[[173]] Each of the classes may be further subdivided: directives, for example, include commands, requests, pleas and so forth. Leech, however (1983: 22–23), objects that this taxonomic approach, requiring all speech acts to be assigned to distinct categories, "represent[s] an unrealistic and unsubtle view of what communication by means of language is like." A particular utterance may have many interrelated or conflicting motivations and slide over the boundaries of many such categories. This objection is, I think, well taken, and it will have important effects in the course of our argument.

The declarative category requires some discussion, particularly because of the important place it will have in my discussion. This is the type of speech act with which we began, such as appointing or marrying, naming or legislating, in all of which the speech act, within an appropriate context, is seen to alter the state of affairs in reality. According to Searle, in most cases this can only happen because the speech act takes place within an extra-linguistic institution. "It is only given such institutions as the church, the law, private property, the state and a special position of the speaker and the hearer within these institutions that one can excommunicate, appoint, give and bequeath one's possessions or declare war" (Searle 1979: 18). Searle recognizes two exceptions to this rule. One is obvious enough: "declarations that concern language itself" (*ibid.*), such as naming or defining. But he also suggests (*ibid.*; cf. Searle and Vanderveken 1985: 57) that speech acts which produce results by means of supernatural power should be treated as declarations, as, for example, in the creation story when God says "Let there be light." Leech also (1983: 180) sees "a close connection between declarations and magical speech acts such as casting spells"—thus Ali Baba's "Open sesame" could be seen as a declaration, though in real life a declaration cannot achieve a physical effect such as opening a door. If this were correct, it might be a short cut to the conclusion of our discussion. But there is a fundamental difference between this case and the others. It is not in the same sense that the speech act is held to alter reality: the realm in which the words are said to work is that of physical nature rather than society. Moreover the semantic form of "Let there be light," or "Open sesame," is directive, not declarative; and in Genesis 1 "Let there be light" is paralleled by, for example, "Let the earth put forth vegetation," which is certainly directive. The context of Genesis 1 would in any case be a misleading one to start from. The use of language in the [[174]] creation account is *ex hypothesi* unique. The idea of speech which is heard and responded to either by inanimate creatures or by the void itself is an oddity in the theory we are discussing, because the very idea of such illocutionary forces as the directive, as well as the declarative, depends upon the existence of a social context.[3]

3. Evans, in his extensive treatment of the idea of creation by the word (1963: 145ff.) sees both "performative" (i.e., illocutionary) and causal elements; he avoids attributing the bare coming into being of the creature to any kind of illocutionary force, but notes nevertheless that "God's creative word . . . as a command . . . has Exercitive force [Evans follows Austin in using this word in a sense covering both Searle's directives and his declaratives] invoking a subordinate status of the creature so that the creature's very existence is 'obedience'" (1963: 27).

This does not prevent Leech from concluding that there is something odd about declarations as such, and that "there is reason for
arguing that they are not illocutionary acts at all. Instead, they are conventional rather than communicative acts: the linguistic parts of rituals"
(*ibid.*); and he excludes them from his discussion of performatives and
of illocutionary force. How ironic that anyone should conclude that the
very group of utterances which gave rise to the idea of illocutionary acts
in the first place is to be excluded from the ranks of genuine illocutionary acts! And it will not do. Not only are there such acts as naming and
defining to be considered, which are not institutional and not parts of
rituals, there are also expressions used in daily life, outside any institutional framework, which at least partake of the character of declarations.
One such is the utterance "I forgive you." Leech (1983: 212) lists this as
an expressive. But to say "I forgive you," or any equivalent ("You're for-
given," "Don't worry," "It's nothing"), is not primarily to express a mental
attitude to an offence, though the right mental attitude is needed to
make it sincere and (in this case) therefore effective: it *is* to forgive it.
(Saying "I forgive you" is a performative in the same way as "I apologize":
the pronouncement of the words is itself the act referred to.) Moreover,
the offence is annulled and a threatened relationship is restored simply
through the pronouncement of these words. They change the social
situation: therefore it would be entirely proper to term them a declaration. But if this is so, it undermines Searle's characterisation of declarations, and Leech's still more. They do not require an institutional
setting, only (like all speech acts) a relational one; they do not necessarily partake of the character of ritual. So far from being a unique and
separable variety of speech acts, they are ⟦175⟧ part of the general spectrum of illocutionary forces, and overlap with others as Leech rightly
points out others do, and as Searle sees is the case with his "assertive
declarations" (Searle 1979: 19f.).[4]

We return then to prophecy. If Thiselton can be held to have made
out his case as regards the general idea of words of power, what does this
mean for prophecy in particular? It is not impossible that prophecy, as
the word of God, should have been seen in a quite different way from
ordinary human words, and the prevalence of ideas in Israelite society
which look to us very like magic (the "signs" given by God to Moses in

---

4. Similar observations could be made on a number of the items in Searle's category of
expressives. Saying "thank you" is surely not primarily the expression of a grateful mind: it
is the passing of a verbal token in exchange for a favour received. To thank someone is a
social act, not the expression of an attitude. So also "I congratulate you" and many others.
Austin's treatment of such expressions (1975: 78ff.) is much sounder.

Exodus 4, for example) suggests that they could also have held a view of prophetic language not far removed from magic. In other words, the expressions such as "my word . . . shall accomplish that which I purpose" could have been understood literally. But Thiselton's success suggests to me that it would be fruitful to investigate the possibility that the power of the prophetic word could be understood as due to its illocutionary force, assuming that that idea does not cover words with supernatural power. This ought at least to be seriously considered as an alternative, and the following pages are an attempt to demonstrate its plausibility. Neither Thiselton nor Evans deals at any length with prophecy, and Caird's account, though suggestive, is altogether very brief. Nor does any of the contributions to an entire issue of *Semeia* (1988) devoted to the subject of speech acts and biblical interpretation mention prophecy other than in passing. In a recent symposium there is a *jeu d'esprit* by Terry Eagleton entitled "J. L. Austin and the Book of Jonah" (Eagleton 1990), and I shall look at that briefly in a moment, but the only extensive discussion known to me of the illocutionary force of prophetic language is by Robert Carroll in *When Prophecy Failed* (1979: 55ff., esp. 69ff.).

Carroll notes that the call-stories of prophets depict them as receiving the commission to *act* in various ways, as we have seen in the case of Jeremiah: "to pluck up and to break down . . . to build and to plant." This is true also of Isaiah: "make the heart of this people fat and dull their ears and smear over their eyes." In each [[176]] case the act is to be accomplished through their words. Carroll then goes on:

> The general terms used to describe the prophetic preaching such as proclamation, announcement, threat, warning, opposition, pardon all indicate that the very core of prophetic language was performative. In behaving in such ways the prophets performed the tasks of challenge, indictment of community, repudiation of its behaviour, conviction of crimes and offences, announced the people's guilt and passed sentence of death on it. On other occasions they commiserated with the community, pardoned it, promised it prosperity and blessed it. The perlocutionary aspects of their preaching may be seen in their encouragement and inspiration of the people, their persuasion of the people to act in certain ways and, on occasion, their deception of the community (Carroll 1979: 72).

However, he proceeds to qualify this judgement quite sharply. He argues that as performative language is bound to conventions, "to treat prophetic language as performative entails showing that it operated in terms of well-established conventions of linguistic use in ancient Israel" (*ibid.*). But according to Carroll, this is where the difficulties start. For according to the prophetic books themselves, the prophets were largely unsuccessful in persuading their contemporaries to heed their words and act in an appropriate manner. When King Jehoiakim heard the scroll of Jeremiah's prophecies read to him, we are told he cut off each few columns as they were read to him and threw them on the fire (Jer 36:21–23). The failure of both king and people to heed the testimony of the prophets is a very prominent theme of the books of Jeremiah and Kings, and in a different way it also emerges in Isaiah and Ezekiel. But "when a prophet declared the king to be illegitimate or doomed then whether that was a successful performative or otherwise will have depended upon the general acceptance of the prophet as a legitimate figure of authority in the community" (Carroll 1979: 74). But in fact there was no such general acceptance; indeed the prophets later accepted as canonical had to face the opposition of other prophets who took contrary political views, and "in such a context of prophetic conflict the effective prophet was one whose preaching influenced the community thereby confirming the performative force of the prophetic word" (*ibid.*).

A number of observations need to be made on this argument. It is at variance with Carroll's own reasonable point (Carroll 1981: 68–69) that Jeremiah's condemnation of his entire society as corrupt in each and every member, and therefore unwilling to listen to the word of the Lord, is rhetorical hyperbole. In fact, people did [[177]] listen to the prophets; they each had their support group, to use Wilson's terminology (Wilson 1980: 76ff., 226, etc.), one which is quite clearly delineated in the case of Jeremiah. If it were not so, it is difficult to imagine how their words could have been preserved or their memory honoured. The ineffectuality of the prophet's preaching became a dogma assiduously promoted by the Deuteronomists to account for the national disaster of the fall of the two kingdoms. In reality, there is every reason to suppose that not insignificant groups of people did share conventions of discourse with the prophets and were influenced by them in the way that the point of the discourse demanded. Moreover, the coming into being and continued existence of the prophetic books as literary works in itself demonstrates the existence of a receptive audience in succeeding generations, whatever might be said about the putative original audience.

But even if this were not so, the successful performance of an illocutionary act does not in general depend on the appropriate response of the hearers. It is necessary to distinguish, as Carroll has failed to do, between the illocutionary and the perlocutionary effects of an utterance. For example, if an officer gives an order to a mutinous army, the order may or may not be obeyed, but there can be no question that he has given an order (cf. Caird 1980: 24). The *illocutionary* act of giving an order has been successfully performed, even though the *perlocutionary* effect of getting them to obey it has not. As Searle puts it (1969: 47): "If I am trying to tell someone something, then . . . as soon as he recognizes that I am trying to tell him something and exactly what it is I am trying to tell him, I have succeeded in telling it to him." Whether he believes it or not is irrelevant to the illocutionary act. What Searle calls the "illocutionary effect" of the utterance "consists simply in the hearer understanding the utterance of the speaker" (*ibid.*). In these terms, as long as the prophets' hearers understood that they were warning them, calling for repentance or whatever the particular speech act might be, and understood the content of the warning or whatever it might be, then the prophets had *done* what they set out to do, even if they had not achieved the effect they had hoped for. There cannot be any reasonable doubt that such understanding was achieved, if even we, 2500 years later and reading their words in an imperfectly understood foreign language, can understand at least some of what they said. Or in the words of God to Ezekiel (2:4–5): "When you say to them, 'These are the words of the Lord GOD,' they will know that [[178]] they have a prophet among them, אם ישמעו ואם יחדלו (whether they listen or refuse to listen)." It is "knowing that they have a prophet among them" which constitutes the success of illocutionary prophetic acts. Whether they listen or refuse to listen, though a matter of life or death for them, is not relevant to the question of whether there was a shared understanding of what the prophet was doing.

In asserting the importance of conventional authority, Carroll could have been thinking of the conditions said to be essential to a declaration; yet in speaking of the illocutionary force of prophecy, he mentions proclamation, threat and warning, types of illocutionary force which certainly do not depend on authority. But in another way it is true that all prophetic acts depend on authority in that the fundamental presupposition of prophecy as we meet it in the OT is that the speaker has the authority of God. The prophets have often been understood as messengers, especially in the conventional designation of the formula כה אמר יהוה [['thus says the LORD']] as the "messenger formula." A better way of putting it is Caird's (1980: 24): prophecy is a verbal act performed by delegation. If someone has been delegated to speak on another's behalf, what he says has that person's authority, and the prophet may sincerely prefix "Thus says the Lord" to his own words. If a delegate does not observe the terms of his commission, or if someone purports to act as a delegate who has been given no commission, then he has not successfully performed an act by delegation; and if the prophet does not in truth have the authority of God for what he says then his speech acts are not successful ones. This is precisely the ground on which conflict between prophets is fought out. "I did not send these prophets, yet they went in haste; I did not speak to them, yet they prophesied" (Jer 23:21).

Now this appears to raise a difficulty for the point I made just now, that whether the prophets gained a hearing does not affect the illocutionary character of their speech. For if people's refusal to listen to a prophet means their failure or refusal to recognize divine authority in what they say, then on one essential point there is no shared understanding of the force of their words. In so far as they did gain a hearing, we may take it that this shared understanding did exist. However, even if it did not, it cannot in the end affect the illocutionary analysis of the prophets' words. It cannot be said that because people did not accept the prophets' words as divine, they are therefore not divine: the authority which they claim does not rest on popular acceptance or on the existence of appropriate social conventions. [[179]] Wolterstorff (1980: 204ff.) shows, against Searle (1969: 51–52), that in order for a particular act, such as an utterance, to count as for example an apology, it is not necessary for a rule or convention to that effect to exist—though that is often the case. For example, "a person may gesture in a certain fashion in a certain situation; and his doing so may count as his signalling for help" (Wolterstorff 1980: 216) even though no convention exists by which his gestures are to be interpreted in that way. According to Wolterstorff, for an act of one kind to count as an act of another kind, what is necessary is that the agent should on performing it acquire the rights and responsibilities associated with the latter (1980: 205). As a corollary, "one act may count as another even though no one counts it as the other" (1980: 213), for the agent may acquire the rights and responsibilities associated with the other act even though neither he nor anyone else recognizes them. Wolterstorff does not offer an example of this rather extreme situation, and it is not necessary to appeal to it here. What is necessary is to see that an utterance may have a certain authority in that it is performed by delegation, even though none of the hearers recognize the speaker as a delegate or the rights that accrue to him or her thereby. Equally, of course, the prophet's own belief in his authority may be false. The validity of the prophetic claim to divine authority is a theological question which is quite independent of the issues being discussed here. All that can be said here is that the prophets *claimed* divine authority, and that that claim was contested. Within the terms of the prophetic discourse itself, there is no way of challenging the claim, and we can only continue our analysis, having bypassed the theological question, by pragmatically accepting it.

The types of utterance in the prophetic books are many and various. It would take a whole volume to analyse them all. But many of them have the character of pronouncements of judgement, and many of these fall into the pattern designated form-critically as "oracles of judgement" and described as such by Westermann (1967). It is this broad group of utterances (not only the latter group technically described as "oracles of judgement") which I intend to deal with in this paper. A basic question of interpretation is constantly with us in relation to those prophetic collections that are dominated by this type of material. Generally it is raised in terms of the intention of the prophets: did they intend by their words to evoke repentance, and so lead the nation to mend its ways, or simply [180] to announce inexorable doom? This way of putting it is open to the rejoinder that we cannot possibly tell what the intention of these figures, who lie so dimly discerned behind the text, was. But it is possible to reformulate the question in terms of the theory of speech acts. In perlocutionary terms we could ask: is the effect of such words of judgement as we find in the prophetic books *repentance*, or is it the *destruction* of which they speak? But as similar problems of evidence affect this formulation of the question, it is better to put it in illocutionary terms: are these words to be described as—do they, in Wolterstorff's terminology, *count as*—calls for repentance (which would fall into the category of directive acts), or announcements of coming doom (which would presumably be assertive)?

Once we have the question stated in this way, there can only be one answer: although there are of course exhortations and calls for repentance in the prophetic literature, the material which we are now discussing has the character of assertion rather than direction. But to classify it simply as assertive fails to address the problem with which we started: the consciousness that these words are words of power which themselves bring into being the reality of which they speak. The case I shall argue is that the proclamation of judgement in the prophets is to be understood as *declarative*: for the essence of a declarative utterance is precisely that in the appropriate circumstances the speaking of the utterance in itself is held to bring a state of affairs into being. More precisely, I wish to suggest that it has the declarative force of a judicial sentence. (However, I do not wish to be understood as endorsing Westermann's suggestion [1967: 133ff.] that the form of the oracle of judgement was actually derived from usage in the courts. My argument does not depend on this rather precarious assertion.) My suggestion, then, is that the divine oracle of judgement in itself brings the hearers (or a third party) *under judgement.* It initiates an objective state of condemnation. When I say "objective" of course I do not mean that it is in some way materially determined, but rather that like the state of marriage, to use our earlier example, it is understood as existing in the public domain. In the courts we speak of a defendant on whom judgement has been passed as *convicted*. This is a fact brought about by the judge's words, regardless of whether the sentence has yet been carried out, or ever will be; so that it is reasonable to speak of the verdict and sentence, taken together, as a declarative act. If so, then it is possible to transfer the idea to the conceptually very similar oracle of judgement, [[181]] which likewise links a denunciation with the divine announcement of punishment, and to words of judgement in a more general sense.

At first sight, there is not a lot to be said for this suggestion. Generally speaking declarations are short, follow a standard form of words and announce the present existence or execution of that of which they are a declaration: "I take thee to be my lawful wedded wife," "I baptize you in the name of the Father, the Son and the Holy Spirit," "I forgive you for what you said." By contrast, prophetic oracles of judgement are extremely varied in wording, can sometimes be quite long, and generally announce an event in the external world which is to take place some time in the future. The event is frequently announced by Yahweh in the first person as a statement of intention: "Behold, I am bringing against you a nation . . . " (Jer 5:15); "I will not turn back the punishment . . . I will send fire . . . " (Amos 1:3–5). Often, however, the future state of affairs is described in the third person, whether the oracle is formally a word of Yahweh, as in Isa 5:8–10, or refers to him in the third person as in Isa 3:1–18. But it is also true that in such first person oracles as Jer 5:15–17 and Amos 1:3–5 the description of the punishment is developed in the third person. There does not seem to be any substantial difference in illocutionary force corresponding to these differences in grammatical form: all alike announce Yahweh's intended action, and therefore would appear to be in the commissive rather than the declarative field.

However, this may also be true of judicial sentences, which do not have to use the declarative words "I sentence you." It is, again, not always true that there is a standard form of words for a particular declarative act, for example opening a meeting—in my Church (the United Reformed Church in the UK) meetings are generally constituted by prayer, which has certain frequently occurring themes, but no fixed formula. It should in fact be recognized that a speech act may have a declarative effect even if it also partakes of the character of other types of speech act. This is simply a particular case of Leech's general point that the rigidly taxonomic approach to speech acts is inappropriate to the character of speech: but unlike Leech we have seen that it applies to declarations as well. Although I have here used the word "effect," I am still talking in illocutionary rather than perlocutionary terms. A meeting may be con-

stituted and yet not proceed, which would be the requisite perlocutionary effect; a sentence may not be carried out, but that would in no way
detract [[182]] from its character as a sentence. And a prophetic word of
judgement may remain unfulfilled, yet I would argue that it nevertheless
constitutes a bringing under judgement.

It is of course essential to most declarative acts that the person
making them should stand in the appropriate institutional or relational
position (for example, only a judge or magistrate can sentence, only
someone who has been offended can forgive—and can forgive only the
person who has offended her or him). As we have decided to treat prophetic oracles on their own terms as words proclaimed on the authority
of God to his people, this aspect is taken care of. This is not however the
sole condition for identifying a declarative act. We also need to have evidence that there was a recognized state of affairs brought into being by
these words—recognized, that is, by those who recognized their authority. We need to look at more than just the grammatical form of the words.
Austin declares (1975: 148) that "The total speech act in the total situation is the *only actual* phenomenon which . . . we are engaged in elucidating" (his italics). "The total situation" in this case must include evidence
of the appropriate or expected response to the words we are studying.
Not necessarily the actual response, even if that could be discovered in
any particular case; for it is the response as expected that marks for us
the presence of a declared state of affairs, and we have already seen how
varied and uncertain the real response might be.

We have numerous narratives about prophets in Samuel, Kings,
some parts of the prophetic collections, especially in Jeremiah, and the
book of Jonah. We may treat these as evidence of the appropriate response to words of judgement as understood by their authors. In the account of Jehoiakim's burning of Jeremiah's scroll in Jeremiah 36, the
author notes that there was a more appropriate response that the king
could have made. "Neither the king, nor any of his servants who heard
all these words, was afraid, nor did they rend their garments" (Jer
36:24). Why should they have torn their clothes? This gesture is well attested as a sign of mourning, though no one was dead—yet. Very similar
descriptions are given of the conduct of people who, unlike Jehoiakim,
responded correctly to the word of judgement—such as Ahab after his
denunciation by Elijah, who "rent his garments, wore sackcloth, fasted,
slept in sackcloth, and went about humbly" (1 Kgs 21:27) and as a result
secured a stay of execution until the time of his son (v. 29); or David,
after [[183]] Nathan's denunciation of his murder of Uriah for Bathsheba, who from the time his son fell ill, prayed for him, eating nothing
and lying on the floor, until his death (2 Sam 12:16–17). In the book of

Jonah the Ninevites react to Jonah's very bald announcement, "Yet forty days, and Nineveh will be overthrown," with similar acts of penance, which specifically include the renunciation of evil as well as the ritual acts of fasting and putting on sackcloth, and all this explicitly in the hope of God's changing his mind and deciding to spare the city—and in this case God does (Jonah 3).

The significance of these acts of response is not entirely unambiguous. The physical rites are all connected with mourning (cf. de Vaux 1961: 59), but they may also signify humiliation[5] and penance, while prominent also is the theme of prayer to avert the threatened disaster. On occasion this prayer is successful, or partially so. On the one hand, then, the hearers react to the word of doom in the same way as to a death; on the other they do not assume that their doom is inexorable, but that there is a possibility of mercy (2 Sam 12:22; Jonah 3:9, in both cases using מִי יוֹדֵעַ 'who knows?' 'perhaps'), so that prayer for mercy has some point.

Terry Eagleton (1990: 233) suggests, apropos of God's sparing of Nineveh in the book of Jonah, that:

> all good prophets are false prophets, undoing their own utterances in the very act of producing them. In the terms of J. L. Austin's *How to Do Things with Words*, prophetic utterances of Jonah's sort are "constative" (descriptive of some real or possible state of affairs) only in what one might call their "surface grammar"; as far as their "deep structure" goes they actually belong to Austin's class of "performatives," linguistic acts which get something done. What they get done is to produce a state of affairs in which the state of affairs they describe won't be the case. Effective declarations of imminent catastrophe cancel themselves out, containing as they do a contradiction between what they say and what they do.

This intriguing idea has a good deal of truth in it, but it is a little overdrawn. It does seem to be true of Jonah that this is the very thing which he objects to: that his prophetic announcement, having been heeded, fails of its material fulfilment (though Eagleton suggests that the real reason may be because Jonah suspects that God intended to spare Nineveh in any case, and consequently that his own prophetic activity was totally superfluous). But a look back over the examples I have quoted suggests that while the response of mourning-repentance [[184]] is treated as appropriate, it does not always secure a remission of the

---

5. Cf. the use of the verb עָנָה Pi. 'humiliate', in reference to fasting in Lev 16:29, 31; 23:27, 33; Isa 58:3, 5.

threatened penalty. Moreover, Eagleton seems to have fallen into the same confusion of perlocution and illocution as Carroll. That the effect of a prophetic oracle of judgement may be the remission of the judgement does not mean that the only successful prophetic oracle is one which achieves that effect. It is communicatively successful purely and simply if it is *understood* as a divinely guaranteed announcement of judgement. But what Jonah does show, as Eagleton has seen, is that such an utterance cannot be seen as assertive or commissive in any obvious sense. A prophetic utterance which produces the effect of repentance followed by remission of the punishment may not be the only "successful" kind of prophetic utterance, yet it has to be seen as successful in a perlocutionary sense even though the event announced does not occur. But in that case the word neither asserts a future state of affairs (assertive) nor commits its ultimate author, God, to future action (commissive). My suggestion that it declares a state of judgement is at least a possible alternative.

But of course a strong body of scholarly opinion today would dismiss this use of prophetic narratives as anachronistic. They offer, it is alleged, an understanding marked by hindsight at the time of the exile or later, when the question of repentance—its necessity and the failure of the pre-exilic generations to provide it—began to dominate thought about the relationship between Yahweh and Israel. It may be described as a dogma of the Deuteronomists that God's decrees are conditional (Jer 18:7–10) and that the purpose of prophetic proclamation is to awaken repentance; however, in the case of Israel and Judah, to whom the consistent proclamation of the prophets was addressed, there was no such response (2 Kgs 17:7–18). This theme determines the way in which the Deuteronomists present the prophets. A. V. Hunter, for example, writes (1982: 47):

> Dtr was interpreting Israel's past so that it would say something to his own time. What value could there be in prophetic judgement speeches that had already found fulfilment in historical event? The answer is that these same prophetic utterances could be used by people of any later generation as motivation for renewed obedience to Yahweh. Thus the prophetic judgement speeches, themselves delivered in the sometime distant past with one purpose, were now to serve another purpose as calls to repentance for Dtr's audience.

Most of the prophetic narratives I have quoted come from the Deuteronomistic history or from Jeremiah, which has undergone [[185]] Deuteronomistic editing; and a very late book like Jonah may be assumed to be influenced by the Deuteronomistic conception of prophecy which would already have been dominant in the developing prophetic

canon. It would be argued that a truer insight into the original purpose
of judgement prophecy in pre-exilic times is given by the terrible words
of Isa 6:9–10: "Make the heart of this people fat, and their ears heavy,
and shut their eyes; lest they see with their eyes and hear with their ears,
and understand with their hearts, and turn and be healed." No repentance, no healing, only the stroke of inexorable doom.

Whatever the truth of this perspective in a historical sense, it would
be misplaced criticism for our purposes. We are looking for insight into
the illocutionary force of a type of prophetic utterance. This is not likely
to be bound to a particular historical era. If a type of response is indicated in the literature which was certainly familiar with prophecy, that
is because it is appropriate to the type of utterance as such. It would
surely be a mistake to suppose that judgement prophecy as such was a
phenomenon of the monarchy which the people of the exile could only
look back on. And there is an ambiguity in the response, including both
mourning over an accomplished act of destruction, and prayer to avert
it; it is not tied exclusively to the Deuteronomistic view of prophecy.
There is an implicit tension, each side of which is developed at various
places in the tradition. The awakening of repentance is developed in
such passages as Jer 23:21–22, Amos 5:14–15, Isa 1:16–20. Passages of
this kind are, it is true, frequently seen as secondary (cf., e.g., on Amos,
Wolff 1977: 235), but what evidence is there for this beyond the dogma
that the pre-exilic prophets did not leave space for repentance? Hunter
(1982: 95) interprets them in an ironic sense, or (192ff.) as setting out
the principles on which Yahweh has already taken the decision for
judgement. In individual cases this may well be correct; but it is not successful in exorcising conditionality from pre-exilic prophecy, for ironical
or not, the idea is palpably there.

On the other hand, these passages are not oracles of doom, and the
bulk of such oracles either do not suggest the possibility of mercy or hint
at it as only a remote one. Some specifically exclude it, e.g., the series of
oracles against foreign nations at the beginning of Amos. "For three
transgressions of N, and for four, I will not revoke the punishment (לֹא
אֲשִׁיבֶנּוּ)" (Amos 1:3, 6, etc.). Others suggest that it was a now-vanished
opportunity of the past:

⟦186⟧ For thus said the Holy One of Israel, "In returning and in
rest you shall be saved; in quietness and confidence shall be your
strength." And you would not, but you said, "No! We will speed
upon horses," therefore you shall speed away, and, "We will ride
upon swift steeds," therefore your pursuers shall be swift (Isa
30:15–16).

Carroll (1979: 16ff.) sees a strong "dialectical" element in prophecy, surely rightly. But the dialectic not only subsists between different parts of the prophetic oeuvre, but is also inherent in the character of the dominant genre of that body of work. The whole range of possibilities suggested by the responses we find to the oracle of doom in narrative are also conceivable as responses to such oracles in the collections. They are not only conceivable, they are the actual range of responses whenever the prophetic words have been re-actualized and applied to contemporary situations by preachers in all ages. What has perhaps not always been observed is that when such words reject the possibility of mercy or refer to it as a no longer available opportunity they undermine the conception of the oracle of doom as a form of speech which of its nature excludes such a possibility. Even Isa 6:9–10 is not quite as unequivocal evidence against the theory that prophets might call for repentance as is sometimes thought, for the possibility of repentance is after all mentioned in order to be rejected: "lest they should turn and be healed." Striking though this passage is in its ruthless rejection of the possibility of "turning and being healed," it does not exist in a context where the ideas of repentance and of divine mercy are unheard of. Isaiah might in other circumstances have been given a mission to bring the people to repentance. Indeed, this fact enables Kaiser (1983: 120) to label this passage as dependent on Deuteronomistic ideas and hence exilic or post-exilic. Kaiser's argument has convinced no-one that I know of. But if we are not convinced by Kaiser, we should draw the logical conclusion and recognize that such ideas cannot be confined to a particular chronological period. The possibilities of inexorable doom and of mercy evoked by repentance were always implicit in the use of the genre of the oracle of doom.

What then does this attempt to reconstruct the expected or natural response to the oracle of doom imply for its illocutionary force? I would suggest that the ambiguous response of mourning-humiliation accompanied by prayer can naturally be understood as a response to a declaration putting the people under judgement.

In principle such a declaration is absolute. The state of condemnation it creates is a fact, not a mere expectation. But it is not in [[187]] principle unalterable. From a human sentence, appeal may lie to a higher court. There is no higher court than the Sovereign Lord's, but that does not mean that appeals cannot be entertained. Hence there is nothing inappropriate about the response of repentance and prayer for mercy alongside the mourning response. These two inextricably entwined strands of response are perlocutionary effects which follow naturally from the illocutionary force of the oracle of judgement, and attempts to deny the validity of one or the other are quite unnecessary. The question whether the intention of judgement prophecy is to condemn absolutely or to awaken repentance is transcended. Both possibilities exist within the single form of the judgement oracle and within reported responses to it, though as we have noted, only one theme may be dominant. The method of illocutionary analysis has placed the question within the appropriate context.

Bibliography

Auld, A. G.
1983   Prophets through the Looking Glass: Between Writings and Moses. *Journal for the Study of the Old Testament* 27: 3–23 ⟦reprinted in this volume, 289–307⟧.
Austin, J. L.
1975   *How to Do Things with Words.* 2d edition. Oxford: Clarendon.
Caird, G. B.
1980   *The Language and Imagery of the Bible.* London: Duckworth.
Carroll, R. P.
1979   *When Prophecy Failed.* London: SCM.
1981   *From Chaos to Covenant: Uses of Prophecy in the Book of Jeremiah.* London: SCM.
1983   Poets Not Prophets. *Journal for the Study of the Old Testament* 27: 25–31.
1989   Prophecy and Society. In *The World of Ancient Israel,* edited by R. E. Clements. Cambridge: Cambridge University Press.
Derrida, J.
1977   Signature Event Context. *Glyph* 1: 172–97.
Dürr, L.
1938   *Die Wertung des göttlichen Wortes im Alten Testament und im antiken Orient.* Mitteilungen der vorderasiatisch-aegyptischen Gesellschaft 42.1.
Eagleton, T.
1990   J. L. Austin and the Book of Jonah. In *The Book and the Text: The Bible and Literary Theory,* edited by R. M. Schwartz. Oxford: Blackwell.
Evans, D. D.
1963   *The Logic of Self-Involvement.* London: SCM Press.
Fish, S.
1989   With the Compliments Of the Author: Reflections on Austin and Derrida. Pp. 37–67 in *Doing What Comes Naturally.* Oxford: Clarendon.
Grether, O.
1934   *Name und Wort Gottes im Alten Testament.* Beihefte zur Zeitschrift für die Alttestamentliche Wissenschaft 64. Giessen: Alfred Töpelmann.
Hunter, A. V.
1982   *Seek the Lord! A Study of the Meaning and Function of the Exhortations in Amos, Hosea, Isaiah, Micah and Zephaniah.* Baltimore: St. Mary's Seminary and University Press.

Kaiser, O.
  1983   *Isaiah 1–12: A Commentary.* 2d edition. London: SCM Press (English translation of *Das Buch des Propheten Jesaja, Kapitel 1–12.* 5th edition Das Alte Testament Deutsch 17. Göttingen: Vandenhoeck & Ruprecht, 1981).
Leech, G. N.
  1983   *Principles of Pragmatics.* London and New York: Longman.
Procksch, O.
  1942   λέγω, C. Pp. 89–100 in *Theologisches Wörterbuch zum Neuen Testament.* Volume 4. Stuttgart: Kohlhammer.
von Rad, G.
  1965   *Old Testament Theology.* Volume 2. Edinburgh: Oliver & Boyd (English translation of *Theologie des Alten Testaments.* Volume 2. Munich: Chr. Kaiser, 1960).
Searle, J. R.
  1969   *Speech Acts.* Cambridge: Cambridge University Press.
  1977   Reiterating the Differences: A Reply to Derrida. *Glyph* 1: 198–208.
  1979   *Expression and Meaning: Studies in the Theory of Speech Acts.* Cambridge: Cambridge University Press.
Searle, J. R., and D. Vanderveken
  1985   *Foundations of Illocutionary Logic.* Cambridge: Cambridge University Press.
Semeia 41
  1988   *Speech Act Theory and Biblical Criticism,* edited by H. C. White.
Thiselton, A. C.
  1974   The Supposed Power of Words in the Biblical Writings. *Journal of Theological Studies* n.s. 25: 283–99.
de Vaux, R.
  1961   *Ancient Israel.* London: Darton, Longman & Todd (English translation of *Les institutions de l'Ancien Testament.* Paris: Cerf, 1958–60).
Westermann, C.
  1967   *Basic Forms of Prophetic Speech.* Philadelphia: Fortress (English translation of *Grundformen prophetischer Rede.* Munich: Chr. Kaiser, 1964).
Wilson, R. R.
  1980   *Prophecy and Society in Ancient Israel.* Philadelphia: Fortress.
Wolff, H.-W.
  1977   *Joel and Amos.* Hermeneia. Philadelphia: Fortress (English translation of *Dodekapropheton 2: Joel und Amos.* Biblischer Kommentar: Altes Testament 14/2. Neukirchen-Vluyn: Neukirchener Verlag, 1969).
Wolterstorff, N.
  1980   *Works and Worlds of Art.* Oxford: Clarendon.

Were the Prophets Poets?

STEPHEN A. GELLER

[[211]] Is the Bible literature? With the recent revival of interest in the literary study of the Hebrew Bible this question has again become the focus of debate. This essay does not intend to grapple directly with the theoretical and philosophical problems that enliven that debate. It will focus on a narrower issue which is yet an epitome of the wider problem: were the prophets also poets? In answer it will present a small exercise in literary exegesis of a prophetic text. The underlying hope is that the results of the exercise will be relevant to the discussion of the primary literary problem.

Were Israel's prophets also poets? This question resolves itself into two others: *can* they be poets and, if so, *may* they be? The former is a question of ability, the latter of propriety. This particular issue is so emblematic of the larger one because there has always been tension between the phenomena of prophecy and poetry. It is inherent even in the etymology of the terms. A prophet is a "(forth) speaker,"[1] the mouthpiece of a god. A poet is a "maker," a craftsman in words. The former is a medium, the latter an artist. A prophet who consciously molded his prophecy would be false. A poet whose verse did not reflect his personality would be no true artist.

The tension was perceptible to the Greeks. To be sure, they ascribed divine inspiration to both prophets and poets. The muse inspired the latter as Apollo did his Pythian oracle. But that prophetess delivered the

Reprinted with permission from *Prooftexts* 3 (1983) 211–21.

1. Cf. J. Lindblom, *Prophecy in Ancient Israel* (Philadelphia, 1967), 1. Reference is to the etymology of Greek *prophetes*, not Hebrew *navi*, whose root meaning is disputed.

god's message in a sacred babble. It was an attendant, crafty priest who translated it into poetry, understandable, if enigmatic, to humans. It was this second intermediary who was called a *prophetes*, Aaron to the oracle's Moses, so to speak. But who was the real prophet and who only a poet? Later Greeks declared all poets, like Cretans, to be liars. Their [[212]] chief lies were the stories about the gods, the sources of prophecy. Both prophecy and poetry were human fabrications.

Israel also felt the tension between prophecy and poetry. It may be perceived in Ezekiel's touchy complaint that the people view him as a mere maker of parables, a singer of love songs (Ezek 21:5; 33:32). He knows that to be called a poet is an accusation of false prophecy. Lying prophets composed their oracles consciously, *millibbam*, "from their own hearts." They were akin to poets. Poetry was probably viewed as a branch of Wisdom. To be sure, it was also divinely inspired, but only in a remoter sense. God put wisdom into Solomon's heart but the three thousand proverbs and thousand and five songs he spoke were his, not God's, achievement. A prophet who admitted to being a poet would stand self-condemned by his own mouth.

Later Jews, like Greeks, simplified the issue. Tradition absorbed poetry into prophecy. David's Psalms and Solomon's songs were uttered by the same Holy Spirit that spoke through Isaiah's oracles. The Rabbis "forgot" poetry in the Bible.[2] Some maintained that "the Torah speaks in human language"; that is, clothes itself in literary forms just as the divine Glory wraps itself in a cloud. Just as that cloud shields weak men from the searing Presence, so the literary garb of the Bible is a fabric of divine grace, to make comprehensible the love of an ineffable God. To view the Bible *as* literature betrays God's goodness. Aesthetic judgment of a sacred "poem" is inherently blasphemous, because it implies an assessment of the Author's skill. If the poem is declared beautiful it might have been declared ugly; but the divine can only be beautiful. So even if the Bible *can* be viewed as literature, it *may* not be. Its poetic aspect, like succulent but forbidden meats, is morally repugnant to the pious.

It is not surprising that when, in the eighteenth century, scholarship claimed the Bible for humanity, one of the first things "discovered" was biblical poetry. Yet even its first explorer, Bishop Lowth, despaired of uncovering the secrets of Hebrew meter because of our ignorance of the original pronunciation. For biblical scholarship the issue became one of possibility rather than propriety; not *may* the Bible be viewed as literature

---

2. On rabbinic "forgetting" of poetry, including parallelism, see most recently James L. Kugel, *The Idea of Biblical Poetry* (New Haven and London, 1981).

but *can* it be? Is the text sound enough for literary analysis? Can scholars reconstruct enough of ancient Israel's culture to allow literary communication between the ancient authors and ourselves? These are historical questions; and it was to historical research that biblical scholarship devoted itself for two centuries.

Most biblicists (but never the greatest ones) soon forgot the original literary questions that moved people like Lowth and Herder. Thirty years ago some scholars became more receptive to literary analysis, mainly because the historical study of the Bible seemed to have reached an impasse. It is ironic that general literary criticism had by that time [[213]] become incapable of providing sure guidance to inquiring biblicists. Literary critics were asking if the interpretation of *any* text is possible, or even advisable. Can we truly *understand* an author or, indeed, anyone other than ourselves? Others asked if it was proper to view texts through the prism of history. Why respect an author's presumed intentions?

Such disorienting questions were disturbing to those whose job it was to interpret an ancient text like the Bible. They felt they had to penetrate beyond their own prejudices into the mental world of a remote antiquity. Historical reconstruction seemed the only scholarly method of approach, even for literary analysis. How could one reconcile the claims of history and literature, science and art?

This essay cannot attempt to answer such large questions. As stated, it will limit itself to a small literary exercise in biblical interpretation, trying to determine if a brief prophetic passage can and ought to be considered poetry. Nevertheless, the type of analysis presented rests on a method that tries to be true to both historical and literary study. The essential assumption is that literature must be approached through language, that the goal of literary analysis is, as Schleiermacher said, to reconstruct the linguistic world of the author and his original audience. The following summary of the method is necessarily apodictic. It is a pastiche of the New Criticism, Russian formalism and other linguistically-oriented types of literary criticism. No claim is made that it represents the only proper way to approach texts. However, it has shown itself to be a useful one in dealing with ancient literature.

The basic principles are the following: a poet, as a literary artist, may be viewed as a kind of craftsman in words. One may judge his work more or less as one does that of any skilled artisan, by the "success" of his product. For example, a potter is judged by the skill with which he has formed material (clay) to fit certain functions (holding liquids, resisting heat) to produce a satisfying emotional reaction (attraction or repulsion, beauty or ugliness).[3] The latter aspect is the nettle. Emotional, aesthetic reaction is so idiosyncratic. One can only state that though a mystery it is still a fact. Man has been judging even tools for aesthetic features like symmetry ever since he first chipped a flint ax into a finer shape than that required for use. That was long before *homo* became *sapiens.*

Poems are judged by how well the poet has formed his material (words) to fit function (meaning) and affect our emotions. Poets must join words to meaning and feeling in a manner that arouses our awe at their skill. This virtuosity consists of the exploitation of the possibilities of language for establishing many lines of meaning. Linguistic richness is the major formal criterion of poetry. It must not be confused with [[214]] mere elaboration or ornamentation. Often the "simplest" poems are the most complex linguistically.

A formal clue to the link of meaning and emotion is often legitimate ambiguity. By "legitimate" is meant "allowed by language." In the case of ancient texts, for which we have no linguistic or literary "competence," this means historical reconstruction of the act of communication between author and audience. Ambiguities and other "problems" in a text often reveal inner tensions that can point the way to true meaning.[4]

For illustration I have chosen Isa 40:6–8. If it can be viewed as one does poetry, if its author displays a poet's skill in molding language to meaning and emotion, then he *can* be a poet. Then one may decide if he *may* be. The text is in relatively good shape and there are no real problems of basic meaning. This is a crucial point. The ambiguities one looks for must not be those engendered by textual corruption or other historical problems. Literary analysis can only plough a field that has been cleared of stumps and stones by historical criticism. This particular field has been ploughed often and well. It is one of the most familiar passages in the Hebrew Bible and is fully treated in innumerable commentaries. It is therefore a good test of the special contribution that literary analysis can make to the understanding of the Bible.

The three biblical verses resolve themselves into four couplets and eight lines:[5]

---

3. The conjunction of terms here and in D. N. Freedman's "Pottery, Poetry and Prophecy: An Essay on Biblical Poetry," *Journal of Biblical Literature* 96 (1977), is mainly coincidental.

4. A fuller presentation of the method and the theory validating it, as applied to biblical and other ancient texts, will be made elsewhere.

5. Of course, the division into lines and couplets assumes a prosodic analysis of the passage and so prejudges the issue of its status as "poetry." However, no details regarding

קוֹל אֹמֵר קְרָא	1. A voice says, Proclaim!
וָאֹמַר[6] מָה אֶקְרָא	2. And I said, What shall I proclaim?[6]
כָּל־הַבָּשָׂר חָצִיר	3. All flesh is grass,
וְכָל־חַסְדּוֹ כְּצִיץ הַשָּׂדֶה	4. And all its loyalty like flowers of the field.
יָבֵשׁ חָצִיר נָבֵל צִיץ	5. Grass withers, flowers droop
כִּי רוּחַ ה׳ נָשְׁבָה בּוֹ[7]	6. When the wind of the Lord blows on them;[7]
יָבֵשׁ חָצִיר נָבֵל צִיץ	7. Grass withers, flowers droop,
וּדְבַר אֱלֹהֵינוּ יָקוּם לְעוֹלָם	8. But the word of our God lasts forever!

All translations deceive; details regarding this one's perfidy will be presented below. First we must record some basic facts about the structure and meaning of the passage, paying special notice to ambiguities and problems.

These lines form part of a larger speech which begins in 40:1. The famous command "Comfort, comfort my people!" introduces the prophecy of the so-called Second Isaiah, a prophet who lived during the Babylonian Exile, the imminent end of which he is announcing here. The section that immediately precedes our passage declares the coming divine theophany. God will proceed along a miraculous road through the desert to rescue his people and lead them in a second exodus back to their land. This event will be witnessed by "all flesh," a phrase which is echoed by line three of our passage; just as its initial *kol omer kera*, "A [[215]] voice says, Proclaim!" recalls the proclaiming voice of v. 3; and "our God" of line 8 reiterates the same word in that verse. In short, the passage is well nested in its context.

Its distinctness from its environment is also clear. The eight lines are linked by form and meaning. The core structure is the quatrain of lines five to eight. Repetition serves to focus attention in the final, climactic word: *le'olam*, "forever." Repetition of "grass" and "flowers" also ties lines three and four to the quatrain. Lines one and two serve as an introduction, but also present a major structural ambiguity. They apparently re-

---

metrical structure and parallelism will be provided to further prejudice the case. I cannot refrain from taking note of the strong phonetic patterning, aside from that produced by the repetitions. Note especially the alliterations: *k* and *'* in lines one and two; the *s*'s of the following lines, especially those of *hasdo* [['its loyalty']] and *hassade* [['the field']]; the sequences of *v* and *sh* in *yavesh* [['withers']] and *nashva* [['blows']], etc.

6. Reading *va'omar* [['and I said']] with the Greek version and the Dead Sea Scroll (1QIsa) for the Massoretic text's *ve'amar* [['and he says']]. Even if one retains the latter reading poetic analysis would be little affected.

7. *Akhen hatsir ha'am*, "truly the people is grass," is certainly an ancient gloss and nonsensical from the literary point of view. One does not explain a metaphor while in the very process of presenting it! The words reflect one interpretation of the image; on which, see below.

cord a dialogue between a (presumably) angelic voice and a (presumably) prophetic respondent. Does that dialogue continue in the following lines? If so, who says what? Are lines three and four the angelic reply to "what shall I proclaim?" or an exclamation of despair by the prophet? Or are lines five through eight perhaps the angel's answer?

The meaning of the passage shows a similar tension between clarity and uncertainty. The dominant metaphor of withering vegetation, highlighted by the repetition quatrain, presents the following equations:

> the loyalty of flesh : grass/flowers
> the word of our God : lasts forever

The essential contrast is established by the pairs flesh : God and (withering) grass/flowers : forever. The logic is the opposition between human transitoriness and divine permanence; and also, to the ancient mind, between frailty and strength. Man ("flesh") is weak; like grass he soon shrivels (cf. Job 14:1ff.); God is powerful and eternal.

But here the metaphor of vegetation is modified by *ḥasdo*, "its loyalty." This word perhaps saves the image from triteness, but it also poses a serious problem of interpretation.[8] If it is specifically the *loyalty* of all flesh that is weak and impermanent, to what did it prove disloyal? To the word of God, to which it corresponds in the above equations? If so, what is meant by "word?" Hebrew *davar* also means "deed"; were man's words or deeds treasonous and/or weak? The clarity of the metaphor itself begins to wither.

The structure of the dominant quatrain, by the very power of its form, highlights another major ambiguity. Lines six and eight are placed in parallel positions. One is thus forced to consider the relationship between the two corresponding phrases *ruaḥ adonai* and *devar eloheinu*, "wind of the Lord" and "word of our God," respectively. The force of the quatrain and the logic of the metaphor demand a contrast between them, but every Israelite would recognize them as complementary terms. *Ruaḥ's* other sense is "spirit." When joined, as here, to *davar*, "word," the pair is almost diagnostic of the phenomenon of prophecy. The prophet, filled by the "spirit" delivers God's "word." The prophetic context of the passage

8. It seems intrusive only if one assumes the following statement: "the loyalty of flesh is like (the loyalty) of grass and flowers." That grass is loyal to its own greenness and luxuriance is a pleasant conceit—cf. the German folksong *O Tannenbaum*, which imputes a like loyalty to the fir tree and also, in the Bible, Jotham's riddle in Judg 9:6ff.—but arises here from a misunderstanding of the dynamics of the device of parallelism. The common emendations *ḥemdo, hodo* and *hadaro*, all meaning "beauty, glory" or the like, are all rooted in this misunderstanding; as is also the Greek version's *doxa* [['glory']]. The Targum's translation "strength" also reflects a particular interpretation; on all of which, see note 17.

seems to confirm this impression. Yet the *metaphor* requires that [[216]]
ruaḥ have its other, meteorological sense: the searing sirocco that blasts
vegetation. *Ruaḥ adonai* may even mean simply "mighty wind," a well-
known demotion of the deity, so to speak, to a grammatical superlative in
biblical Hebrew.[9] "Wind of the Lord" may also have an anthropomorphic
sense: the blast of God's wrath that incinerates his foes, an image familiar
to Bible readers (cf. Ps 18:16, etc.). The point of the metaphor would
then be punishment. Retribution, transience, prophetic inspiration: *ruaḥ
adonai*, like the arrow of a disoriented compass, swings in several directions. But if it is to mean punishment, who is being blasted, and for what
crime? Are "wind" and "spirit" simply a clever *double entendre*, or a play on
words somehow significant to interpretation?

Finally, what is meant by "all flesh?" In opposition to God it should
mean "mortal, human." But the proclamation of human frailty is here
qualified by *ḥasdo*, "its loyalty." *Ḥesed* is a cornucopia of meanings. The
old, beautiful translation "lovingkindness," a blend of love and mercy,
does not reflect the primarily covenantal associations of the term. *Ḥesed*
is the feeling of warm loyalty to one's covenant partner displayed by eager, ungrudging performance of one's obligations to him. It is a mixture
of love and law beyond any narrow legalism. If *davar* means both "word"
and "deed," *ḥesed* implies both emotion and action. If one emphasizes the
former aspect, it comes to mean "love"; if the latter, "act of love." If God
is expressing his *ḥesed* in mighty deeds, like the exodus and splitting of
the Reed Sea, it can mean "act of power." He can be addressed as *ḥasdi*,
"the one who displays *ḥesed* to me"; i.e., my protector, redeemer.[10] God's
ḥesed lasts forever: *ki leᶜolam ḥasdo*, the refrain of Psalm 136. Israel displays
its *ḥesed* by faithful performance of the covenantal commandments; that
is how it "loves" God. *Ḥesed*, as a covenantal term, implies a national
frame of reference, God's relationship to his people. In short, "all flesh"
in Isaiah 40, as modified by *ḥasdo*, "its loyalty," should refer to Israel.

"Withering" in line five can then have two meanings. It can refer to
the shrivelling of Israel's faith and obedience, its apostasy. As such it is a
statement of national sin, an echo of prophetic rebuke (*riv* [['lawsuit']],
tokheḥa [['rebuke']]). The "wind of the Lord" is then best taken literally,

---

9. So also *ruaḥ elohim* of Gen 1:2, probably, the most popular translation of which is
now: "mighty wind soared over the waters."

10. So in Ps 59:18 (and perhaps 11), 144:2; cf. L. J. Kuyper, "The Meaning of *ḥsdw* ISA.
XL 6," *Vetus Testamentum* 13 (1963): 489–92 and Dahood (Anchor Bible on *Psalms*) on
Ps 59:11. That "strength" or "permanence" is the root meaning of *ḥesed* is debatable and
probably irrelevant here, since it has such a meaning clearly only in the two places cited
above; and even they may reflect the semantic extension. *Ḥesed* is parallel to *oz*, "strength,"
only in Exod 15:13 and Ps 62:12–13. To Israelites *ḥesed* implied covenant and loyalty not
only to divine but also to human contracts; cf. 2 Sam 3:8, 9:1.

in terms of the metaphor: Israel's obedience was as impermanent as tender grass.

But the same line can also refer to Israel's punishment for its sin. In this case "wind of the Lord" most likely has its anthropomorphic connotation: God's blast of retribution. The resulting desiccation is then a metaphor for the exile. Israel lies parched and in despair; cf., with another metaphorical application of dryness, Ezek 37:2, 11—the famous valley of bones.

Both constructions point to the possibility of a strikingly negative interpretation of line 8: "and the word of our God lasts forever!" In truth, one expects not "word" but *ḥesed*, "loyalty of God"; cf. Ps 103:15ff.[11] In a context of rebuke and retribution "word" can easily [[217]] refer to the covenant curses for breach of contract, the *tokheḥot* of Deuteronomy 28 and Leviticus 26. Above, the initial conjunction in line eight was translated "but," implying contrast with the preceding lines. Line eight we took as positive in meaning, a reference to the coming salvation. But it can also be translated simply "and," continuing and complementing, not contrasting with, the grassy metaphor: God's curse will last forever!

Instinctively one feels that this negative interpretation is false; but what is the source of this "instinct?" Why is line eight so clearly a contrast with what precedes and so emphatically positive, almost ecstatic in tone? Perhaps it is only the contrast between the other parallel terms: "flesh" and "God," "grass/flowers" and "forever." But surely *ḥesed* and *davar*, "loyalty" and "word," are too heavy with biblical meaning to be mere adjuncts, deriving their power only from their propinquity to other terms!

I think that the positive construction of line eight derives from, or at least is confirmed by, the intersection of the covenantal line of meaning implied by *ḥasdo* with another, prophetic, line of meaning. The "problems" and ambiguities are a device, strategy and tactics to steer us toward a goal. The specific clue to the new prophetic line is the "unclear" use of the phrase *ruaḥ adonai* in a structure that makes it seem parallel to *devar eloheinu*. These intimations of a prophetic context would, I think, encourage the Hebrew ear to hear in these lines an echo of a famous prophetic genre, the inaugural vision.

A prophet's account of his call serves to validate his mission. The form is basically clear, despite the fact that there are only a few complete examples, all of which display significant variations. Two elements are crucial to this discussion: the prophetic demurral and divine

---

11. Ps 103:15ff. is similar in thought and language to Isa 40:6–8 and presents just such an equation. Man's days are like grass but God's *ḥesed* is forever to those who keep his covenant. The context is sin and punishment. So also Psalm 90, another famous use of the grass motif. Note also the traditional interpretation of *ḥatsir* as *reshaʿim*, "the wicked": so, for example, the Targum. See also Hos 6:4 for another metaphor with a similar meaning.

reassurance.[12] The prophet resists his call by protesting his unfitness for his mission. God then reassures him that he will be given the ability to fulfill his task.

In Isaiah 40 the call to "proclaim" in line one, followed by a response in line two, triggers one's perception of the inaugural context. *Ma ekra* is ambiguous. As "what shall I proclaim?" it is the prophet's request for the content of his commission. Lines three and four are then the angel's response. But the words may also mean "how can I proclaim?"—a protest or demurral.[13] The following lines would then be understood as the reason for his refusal, his human frailty: "I, like all flesh, am but as grass. . . . " The quatrain of lines five to eight are the angel's answer. The pun on the two meanings of *ruah* is the hinge device. The sense is "flesh, like grass, may be withered by the wind but you, filled by the spirit of the Lord, will deliver his eternal word."[14]

If one perceives the inaugural pattern, and the quatrain as reassurance to the prophet, a positive sense for line eight is guaranteed—also [[218]] on the level of covenantal meaning. This is the source of our "instinct" that the message of line eight is positive. It is the result of literary strategy, the intersection of complexes of form and meaning.

The implications are radical: this passage works on two levels at least. It refers to the prophet's call and simultaneously to Israel's relationship to God. Both lines of meaning, individual-prophetic and national-covenantal, merge in line eight. It is heard as encouragement to the prophet, a statement of his commission, and, on the covenantal level, as a proclamation that Israel's period of suffering is over, its redemption is at hand.[15]

Such a dual interpretation is feasible only if all the key terms work on all levels. An obvious thorn is *hasdo* in line three. What sense does it make in the inaugural context? Why should a prophet compare his *loyalty* to grass? Most likely it represents, like line eight, a merging of prophetic and national levels, through a shift in perspective, as some commentators have noticed. The prophet is identifying himself with the people's sin,

---

12. Exod 4:10ff.; Isa 6:5; Jer 1:6.

13. On *ma* as "how" see Gesenius 148a–b, Joüon 144e.

14. *Nashva* [['blows']] is a *hapax*, as is *nashaf* [['he blows']] of v. 24. Both are perhaps related to the common *nasham* [['breathe']]. *B/p* interchange is well attested, and *m* is also a labial. It is not unlikely that line six is to be heard in two ways: "the wind of the Lord blows against it (flesh)" and "the spirit of the Lord blows into him"; so that the whole line is a *double entendre* and not just the nouns.

15. The merging of "word" and "deed" in the sense of prophetic oracle and act of redemption probably also foreshadows Second Isaiah's famous "argument from prophecy." It is important to him that the coming act of salvation was predicted by past prophets. Its fulfillment is thus a sign of God's power and sovereignty as well as his loyalty and mercy. God's word, past as well as present, must find fulfillment; it never returns "empty" (55:11).

just as he shares their punishment in exile. So also the First Isaiah says
(6:5): "I am a man of unclean lips who dwells in the midst of a people of
unclean lips." The thorn is itself a rose: line four like line eight is en-
riched by the symbiosis of interpretations. The plural suffix of *eloheinu,*
"*our* God," seals the effect.

However, the truly climactic intersection of meanings is in the final
leᶜolam of line eight. If one has become attuned to the play of nuances,
and especially the relationship between *ḥasdo,* "his loyalty," and *davar,*
"word, deed," one must hear in the final *leᶜolam* an echo of the famous refrain *ki leᶜolam ḥasdo,* "his loyalty lasts forever!" The coming redemption
is the latest, and greatest, act of God's covenantal love. Indeed, this is the
true meaning of the entire passage: man's (the prophet's, Israel's) ability
to keep the covenant may have "withered," but despite the pattern of sin
and punishment God's covenantal ardor remains undiminished. He is
ready to begin again, as he did at the exodus, an event Second Isaiah uses
as a model for the return from exile. And once again prophet and people
merge; for the immediate sign of God's continuing *ḥesed* is his willingness
to speak again to Israel through his prophets.

The same duality of levels is also found in the opening words of Second Isaiah's mission, 40:1: "Comfort, comfort my people, says your God."
On the one hand, God directs his messengers, prophets or angelic heralds, to deliver their commission to Israel. On the other hand, he steps
outside this line of mediated discourse to address the people directly.
The unmediated message is covenantal. The clue is the relationship between the words "my people" and "your God." An Israelite would surely
have heard in them an echo of the classic covenant formulary, "You will
be my people and I shall be your God." The true sense of the verse lies in
the perceptual merger of prophetic and covenantal lines. [[219]] The real
"comfort" is precisely the renewal of the unbroken covenant relationship,
despite the exile, as signified by renewed prophetic activity. The meaning
is more subtle, but at the same time more effective emotionally and more
persuasive, because it is the result of simultaneous perceptions mediated
by language.[16]

If one accepts dual or even multi-leveled[17] interpretations of such
passages as the *peshat,* then one has, of course, conceded that their authors *can* be literary artists, perhaps even poets. They are using language

16. For a detailed analysis of these lines see my forthcoming article [["A Poetic Analysis
of Isaiah 40:1–2," *HTR* 77 (1984) 413–20]].

17. In fact, there is almost certainly yet a third level of meaning in Isa 40:6–8. "All
flesh" may refer not to man in general but to the nations (and their rulers). The trigger is
the occurrence of the phrase in verse five: *veraʾu kol basar yaḥdav,* "all flesh will see it together." Such witnessing of God's acts of redemption may apply to Israel (cf. 41:20) but

the way poets do, manipulating its potentialities, consciously or unconsciously, to produce structures rich in meaning and forceful in emotion. In Isa 40:6–7 the poetic intention is achieved by a coalescence of covenantal and prophetic lines of interpretation in the reader's mind. This duality of meaning is made possible by the "problems" and ambiguities of form and meaning: the indistinctness of the structural relationship of lines one and two to three through eight; the polyvalence of the metaphors "all flesh," "grass, flowers"; the double meanings of *ruaḥ*, "wind, spirit," and *davar*, "word, deed." The form of the repetition quatrain fuses these potentialities and focuses them on line eight, whose climactic emotional effect is like a thunderclap. This prophet *can* be a poet.

But *may* he be? The question of propriety must now be raised. Perhaps the prophet's poetic skill negates his claim to prophecy itself. Second Isaiah's claim to true prophetic inspiration has been considered suspect by many scholars. After all, he is an anonymous prophet. The form of the commissioning inaugural vision is only echoed, not boldly declared as it is by the first Isaiah, Jeremiah and Ezekiel. Perhaps this diffidence reflects his own suspicions in regard to his status as prophet.

One can perhaps save him from imputations of false prophecy by a dogmatic assertion that his work *may* not be viewed as poetry, even if it

---

most often to the nations; cf. 41:5; 52:10, 15, etc. The motif of vegetational impermanence is used of rulers in 40:24. If "all flesh" refers to them here, their "withering" may express their general vacuousness, a favorite theme of the prophet; or refer specifically to the fall of Babylon (so Ehrlich, although it is most unlikely that *haᶜam* [['the people']] of the gloss refers to the Chaldeans, as he suggests).

Ḥasdo, "loyalty," seems more intrusive here than in the other two lines of interpretation. In truth, the common emendation *ḥemdo* fits quite well (cf. *ḥemdat kol haggoyim* [['the desire of all the nations']] in Hag 2:7). "Beauty, pride, wealth, glory"—some such nuance corresponds to the standard crime of the nations in biblical literature, hubris; on the "withering" of prideful beauty (*tifʾeret*) cf. Isa 28:1. If one eliminates *ḥasdo* the covenantal line of meaning disappears. However, since there are still two simultaneous levels of meaning the basic point of this exercise remains unaffected.

Yet even *ḥasdo* [['its loyalty']] may not be impossible in regard to the nations. The suffix may be the logical subject: "the one from whom they expect acts of *ḥesed*, their source of confidence" or the like; cf. *ḥasdi* [['the one who displays loyalty to me']] in Ps 59:18 and 144:2, cited above. In line four it might refer to the gods of the nations, foreshadowing Second Isaiah's frequent polemic against idolatry. The Targum's *tqphwn*, "their strength," may reflect such an interpretation. Less likely, but not impossible, is that *ḥesed* has the meaning it has in Lev 20:17 and Prov 14:34: "abomination" or the like. The latter verse is cited by several medieval commentaries in connection with Isa 40:6; cf. perhaps also Jonah 2:9. *Ḥesed* in this sense is an "Aramaism" and may be an Aramaic-Hebrew pun; cf. *motsi* in 43:17 (Hebrew "bring out," Aramaic "destroy") and *oraḥ* in 41:3 (Hebrew "road," Aramaic "chain"). If one retains *ḥasdo* the passage then contains a triple meaning. It is the prophet's commission; reassurance to Israel (the promised "comfort" of 40:1); and a statement of the imminent act of redemption, the overthrow of Babylon.

can be. There can be no logical objection to such an assertion; but one must understand that it means beggaring his richness. For example, in 40:6–8 one must declare only one line of interpretation, covenantal or prophetic, to be the sole meaning of the passage, the unique bearer of the prophetic "intent." The lines are then not a true poem but a simple document transmitting a simple message for simple understanding.

This is, in fact, the standard procedure in most works of biblical exegesis, either because of religious dogmatism or a mistaken understanding of historical method as applied to literary study. Competing interpretations of a passage are often subjected to a ruthless process of amputation until only the "fittest" survives as bearer of the sole true meaning. Ambiguities are only problems to be eliminated, not opportunities for exegetical enrichment.

But what infallible standard of scientific judgment, what sensitive insight of literary feeling justifies such a process of deliberate impoverishment? How can one excise potential meanings if they are legitimate [[220]] in terms of language and Israel's known system of beliefs and traditions? To declare that a poem may not be studied as such violates the principles of science, literature and language.

Prophet or poet—if there is a conflict between them perhaps it will eventually be resolved by what they have in common: *davar*, the word. Poetry is art in words; the prophet transmits divine speech. But all words are divine creations; for if, according to Genesis, the first created thing was light, the first act in the process of creation itself was "And God said. . . . "

Language as Event

D. J. A. CLINES

Done by Saying: Language as Event

[[53]] Our study hitherto suggests that some approach to Isaiah 53 other than that of conventional historical criticism will be appropriate. Not only has the historical-critical method failed to provide acceptable solutions for the enigmas of the poem, but also our close reading of the poem's rhetoric has ruled out any merely objectivist approach to its meaning.

The outlook of the "new hermeneutic" school provides, I suggest, a framework within which some kind of justice may be done to the character and quality of this poem. A brief sketch of some aspects of the new hermeneutic particularly appropriate for our study thus seems to be called for.[1]

1. The new hermeneutic stresses that language can become event; that is, that language need not be mere talk *about* something, but that it can itself do something. E. Fuchs therefore commonly uses the term *Sprachereignis* "language event" for this understanding of language.[2] And G. Ebeling remarks: "We do not get at the nature of words by asking what they contain, but by asking what they effect, what they set going."[3]

Reprinted with permission from *I, He, We, and They: A Literary Approach to Isaiah 53* (Journal for the Study of the Old Testament Supplement 1; Sheffield: JSOT Press, 1976) 53–56 and 59–65.

1. I am much indebted to my colleague A. C. Thiselton for stimulating my interest in this approach to Biblical interpretation and for clarifying many issues. Of special value have been his papers, "The New Hermeneutic" in *New Testament Interpretation* (ed. I. H. Marshall; Exeter: Paternoster, 1976), and "The Parables as Language Event: Some Comments on Fuchs's Hermeneutics in the Light of Linguistic Philosophy," *SJT* 23 (1970) 437–68.

2. E. Fuchs, *Hermeneutik* (4th ed.; Tübingen: Mohr, 1970) 131; cf. R. W. Funk, *Language, Hermeneutic, and Word of God* (New York: Harper and Row, 1966) 51.

3. G. Ebeling, *The Nature of Faith* (London: Collins, 1961) 137.

2. This notion of language as *doing*—which goes against the conventional contrast between speech and action, between *logos* and *praxis*—is parallel, as Robert W. Funk has pointed out,[4] to the concept developed by J. L. Austin of "performative utterances," in which "the issuing of the utterance is the performing of an action."[5] Some well-known examples mentioned by Austin are: "I name this ship the *Queen Elizabeth*," "I give my watch to my brother" (in a will), "I bet you sixpence it will rain tomorrow."[6] Fuchs similarly ⟦54⟧ points out that to name a man "brother" performatively is thereby to admit him into a brotherly relationship.[7] Austin of course is interested primarily in performative utterances in ordinary language, Fuchs and Ebeling in "speech-events" in kerygmatic language, especially in the language of Jesus and in particular within his parabolic utterances, while I am interested in this functional aspect of literary language in general, and of high poetry in particular.

3. The next question concerns the *way* in which the language of parable or poem can be event. Here Austin's interest must of course drop out of sight, since he has established simply that one conventional use of language is as deed, thus providing the basic and irrefutable foundation for the more sophisticated superstructure of hermeneutical theory.

The *way* in which language is event is by its creating of an alternative *world* and thereby destroying the universal validity of the conventional "world." Thus Fuchs speaks of language as "world-forming and world-destroying."[8] "World" can be defined as "the total set of perception and participation in which we exist, the locus of historical being."[9] A literary text creates an alternative "world," another set of principles, values, relationships, and perceptions, which then confronts the reader. The result is a conflict between two worlds, two ways of seeing things, which puts the ball into the reader's court.

4. The world thus created invites the reader to enter it. It is not a world that can be viewed objectively, from the outside, as a spectator. One needs to be a participant in it, to experience it, in order to understand it. This is the way to more than mere knowledge (*Erkenntnis*), as

---

4. *Language, Hermeneutic, and Word of God* 26f.

5. *How to Do Things with Words* (2d ed., ed. J. O. Urmson and M. Sbisà; Oxford: Clarendon Press, 1975).

6. Austin, *op. cit.* 5.

7. *Studies of the Historical Jesus* (London: SCM, 1964) 209.

8. Quoted by W. G. Doty, *Contemporary New Testament Interpretation* (Englewood Cliffs, N.J.: Prentice-Hall, 1972) 42. C. S. Lewis speaks of the "unmaking of your mind" in a similar connection (*An Experiment in Criticism* [Cambridge: Cambridge University Press, 1961] 139).

9. Doty, *op. cit.* 37.

H.-G. Gadamer points out;[10] it leads to "understanding" (*Verstehen*), which is reached through "modes of experience in which truth comes to light" (*Erfahrungsweisen*) as one is [[55]] taken hold of by creative language or art. Unless one "enters" the alternative world created by language one cannot be gripped by its reality, but is condemned to remain a spectator. Gadamer is thinking of the analogy of a game, whose *reality* is experienced only by the players, and not by the spectators—however much they may know about its theory.

5. The process of moving from the one "world" to the other has been strikingly termed by Gadamer a "merging of horizons" (*Horizontverschmel-zung*).[11] One cannot abandon overnight one's original world, because it is only in that world that one has one's bearings and knows therefore one's own identity at the intersection of a three-dimensional grid of space and time and personal relationships. But also the "other" world may not sometimes be anything more than another perspective on the original world.

Hence the significance of the simile of "horizons." A. C. Thiselton has expressed Gadamer's concept of horizons thus:

> When language brings a new "world" into existence, the hearer who enters this world becomes aware of new horizons of meaning. But these necessarily differ from the horizons of understanding which have hitherto marked the extent of his own world. Thus, to begin with, two different worlds stand over against each other, each with its own horizon. Yet the peculiarity of horizons is that their positions are variable, in accordance with the position from which they are viewed. Hence adjustments can be made in the hearer's own understanding until the two horizons come to merge into one. A new comprehensive horizon now appears, which serves as the boundary of an enlarged world of integrated understanding.[12]

6. When the text is seen as creating a world which the reader is invited to "enter,"[13] it becomes obvious that the conventional model of the relation between a text and its interpreter has been made obsolete. No longer can it be said of a text such as poem or parable (though it may still properly be said of a legal document or technical manual or business letter) that it is the "object" of scrutiny by the "subject" (the interpreter)—the familiar Cartesian distinction [[56]]—but that the text as language-event,

---

10. H.-G. Gadamer, *Truth and Method* (New York: Seabury, 1975). See also Thiselton, "Parables as Language Event" 443–44, and cf. Lewis, *Experiment in Criticism* 139.

11. Gadamer, *Truth and Method* 269–73.

12. Thiselton, "Parables as Language Event" 445.

13. C. S. Lewis speaks of "cross[ing] the frontier into a new region" in the same connection (*Experiment in Criticism*).

world-creating and world-destroying, has the primacy over the interpreter. As James M. Robinson has put it:

> The flow of the traditional relation between subject and object, in which the subject interrogates the object, and, if he masters it, obtains from it his answer, has been significantly reversed. For it is now the object—which should henceforth be called the subject matter—that puts the subject [the interpreter] in question.[14]

It is significant that it is precisely in relation to art (the plastic or literary work of art) that it becomes clear that the categories of subject and object must be transcended. As Heidegger argued, if the dualist subject-object perspective is adopted, either art is reduced to the realm of the purely sensual, in which case it cannot be said to reveal truth; or else it is elevated into the realm of intellectual concepts, in which case it becomes reduced to the level of aesthetics.[15] Literary critics have, indeed, often recognized the primacy of the work of art, which interprets the critic rather than being interpreted by the critic, as the following remark shows:

> The first demand any work of any art makes upon us is surrender. Look. Listen. Receive. Get yourself out of the way.[16]

7. Another way of putting the relationship of the world of the text and the interpreter is to see the interpreter as "actively assum[ing] one of the concrete roles which it offers him." The interpreter is then "carried forward by a kind of inner logic of consequences which the chosen role brings with it."[17]

. . . .

Said and Doing: Isaiah 53 as Language-Event

[[59]] The relevance of the foregoing sketch for our understanding of Isaiah 53 is doubtless already obvious; nevertheless, some points of contact should perhaps be spelled out.

1. The impasse of historical-critical scholarship in the face of the enigmas of the poem can function heuristically in directing our attention away from a sense of "the poem as problem" to the poem as language-event.

14. *The New Hermeneutic* (ed. J. M. Robinson and J. B. Cobb; New Frontiers in Theology, 2; New York: Harper and Row, 1964) 23f.

15. A. C. Thiselton kindly drew my attention to this point. Heidegger's essay "The Origin of the Work of Art" is translated in *Philosophies of Art and Beauty* (ed. A. Hofstadter and R. Kuhns; New York: Random House, 1964).

16. Lewis, *Experiment in Criticism* 19.

17. Thiselton, "Parables as Language Event" 441.

It is remarkable that Old Testament scholarship has never made such a step, but has almost without exception taken an apparently masochistic delight in the intractability of the "problems" of the poem, as if it were primarily a brain-teaser, a puzzle for the most advanced students. Only Claus Westermann has recognised the insensitivity of such an approach, and has vigorously denied that quests for "identification"—i.e., problem-solving enquiries—are appropriate.[18] The language of the servant songs, he says, "at once reveals and conceals the servant."

> The veiled manner of speaking is intentional. . . . Exegesis must then be conscious of the limit thus imposed, and be careful to call a halt at those places where the distinctive nature of the songs demands this. . . . On principle, their exegesis must not be controlled by the question, "Who is this servant of God?" . . . Precisely this is what they neither tell nor intend to tell us. The questions which should control exegesis are: "What do the texts make known about what transpires, or is to transpire, between God, the servant, and those to whom his task pertains?"[19]

Westermann thus bars the way to a false path, but his suggestion of another direction in which exegesis should strike out is still too fixated by the concept of the text as information.

2. Once it is recognised that the text does not exist as a carrier of information, but has a life of its own, it becomes impossible to talk of *the* meaning of a text, as if it had only *one* proper meaning. Recognition of the hermeneutical circle, in which meaning is seen to reside not in the text but in what the text becomes for the [[60]] reader, also leads to the legitimacy of *multiple meanings.*[20]

A similar conclusion is reached, quite independently of the "new hermeneutic" school, by literary critics who stress, to one degree or another, the "autonomy of the work of art." While it is too extreme, I believe, to regard a literary work of art as totally autonomous of its author, and consequently to be understood independently of the circumstances of its origin,[21] there is truth in L. Alonso-Schökel's remark that when

---

18. C. Westermann [[*Isaiah 40–66* (London: SCM, 1969)]] 20.

19. Westermann, 93.

20. Cf. T. S. Eliot's remark that the meaning of a poem is "what the poem means to different sensitive readers" ("The Frontiers of Criticism," in *On Poetry and Poets* [London: Faber and Faber, 1957] 113).

21. See, for example, E. Staiger, *Die Kunst der Interpretation* (4th ed.; Zürich: Atlantis, 1963); M. Weiss, "Wege der neuen Dichtungswissenschaft in ihrer Auswendung auf die Psalmenforschung," *Bib* 42 (1961) 255–302 (259); R. E. Palmer, *Hermeneutics:* [[*Interpretation Theory in Schleiermacher, Dilthey, Heidegger, and Gadamer* (Evanston: Northwestern University Press, 1969]] 246f. For criticism of this approach, see for example Helen Gardner, *The Business of Criticism* (Oxford: Clarendon Press, 1959) 17–23.

an author produces a work the umbilical cord has to be cut and the work must go forth into the world on its own. Thus the original author's meaning, which is what is generally meant by *the* meaning of the text,[22] is by no means the only meaning a text may legitimately have (or rather, create). We cannot even be sure that a literary text (or any work of art) "originally"—whenever that was—meant one thing and one thing only to its author; even the author may have had multiple meanings in mind.

We may therefore prepare ourselves to recognize various meanings that our text, Isaiah 53, can create. When, for example, Philip the evangelist "begins" at that scripture and preaches Christ to the Ethiopian eunuch, we should not think so much of a *re-application* of the prophetic text which once meant something quite different, but of one of the vast variety of meanings the text itself can create. The text creates a world in which participants in the world of the text get to know their way around, and come to be able to say, like Wittgenstein, "Now I can go on."

Similarly we may reconcile ourselves to *not wishing* to identify the persons or groups of the fifth century B.C. to which the text may have alluded. Of course, if, for example, the "servant" is a code-name for Deutero-Isaiah, and his deliverance from "death" is a poetic expression for release from a Babylonian prison, and so on, [[61]] all other interpretations of the poem are *quite wrong*. On the understanding advanced here, it is not a matter of being quite wrong or even quite right: there are only more and less appropriate interpretations, no doubt, according to how well the world of the poem comes to expression in the new situation.

3. The poem is free to do its work by its very lack of specificity, its openness to a multiplicity of readings.

Of course, that lack of specificity, the enigmatic quality of the poem *could* perhaps be simply a historical accident. It *could* be that once there was a key to the enigmas of the poem, and that that key has been lost, so that *we* can never know what the poem means precisely and exactly—and, on this view, truly. Perhaps a line has dropped out at the beginning of chap. 53 which made clear who the "we" were;[23] perhaps it was "obvious" to the "original audience" (to use the language familiar to an unliterary historical-critical scholarship) who the servant was; perhaps in that case it was equally plain what the nature of his sufferings was, and whether he underwent death or not. Perhaps too it was clear whether his mission extended to the Gentiles or only to Israelites of the dispersion.

May it not be, however—and does not this approach respect the integrity of the text rather more than a circle of cautious "perhapses"?—that

22. See, for example, E. D. Hirsch, *Validity in Interpretation* (New Haven: Yale University Press, 1967).

23. So, for example, Whitehouse [[*Isaiah XL–LXVI* (Century Bible; Edinburgh: T. & T. Clark, 1908)]] 199.

the enigmas are part of what the poem must be in order to be itself? That is, that it exists to create another world, a world indeed that is recognizably our own, with brutality and suffering and God and a coming-to-see on the part of some, but not a world that simply once existed and is gone for good. The poem's very lack of specificity refuses to let it be tied down to one spot on the globe, or frozen at one point in history: it opens up the possibility that the poem can become true in a variety of circumstances—that is its work.

4. The world which the poem creates is a topsy-turvy world when judged by ordinary human standards.[24]

It is a world where a servant (*or*, slave) is elevated above kings, to the consternation of conventional wisdom; compare Prov 19:10: [[62]]

> It is not fitting for a fool to live in luxury,
>   much less for a servant to rule over princes.

It is a world where *one* achieves what the *many* cannot, and where the "intercession" of one avails for the many (53:12). It is a world where, so the poem makes out, the man God designates as his servant and as a hero is an object of loathing, so disfigured that he looks sub-human (*mošḥāt mēʾîš marʾēhû*, 52:14).[25] In this world, it is assumed with none too delicate irony, a man who serves God by "practising non-violence and never speaking dishonestly" (53:9) inevitably finds himself in the condemned cell (note the force of *ʿal* in 53:9b). Here too it is taken for granted in a mere half verse that the suffering of a righteous man is the will of God (53:10a), a breach with conventional theology so drastic that elsewhere a whole book is devoted to its ramifications (Job). So the social order, the strength of numbers, good taste, ordinary human decency, and the justice of God are all in turn called into question by this topsy-turvy, not to say shocking, poem.

This is the world that the reader is bidden to give his assent to—or rather, to enter. It is not an obviously appealing invitation. To allow the horizon of the poem to "merge" with any conventional horizon would almost seem to call for standing on one's head. But this is a poem precisely about horizons: it concerns perspectives, the way one *sees*, as we have noted above. It sets forth a vision of the world which is radically

---

24. This is made clear within the poem itself, which speaks of its own message as "something never heard before" (52:15).

25. The figure of Achilles, "bloom of the heroes, who grew up like a sprouting shoot, nourished like a plant in the luxuriant earth" (Iliad 18.437f.) is a convenient point of reference in the "real" world. Still closer to hand is Krt, "the beautiful one, servant of El" (*nʿmn ġlm ʾel*).

different from our prior expectations; it is a new "world" in that its scale of values differs from the conventional.

5. The means by which the reader of the poem is able to enter the world of the poem is by identification with the *personae* of the poem, that is, by an assumption of one of the roles presented in the poem.

If one identifies with the "they," who find the history of the servant unbelievable and his aspect revolting, one is still on the edge of the poem's world, an observer looking in on it but not committed to it. Yet the "they" are at least aware of the servant; they "see" and "ponder" the servant's fate. Though repelled, they [[63]] are at the same time fascinated by the servant, so they have made the first step towards the way of the servant. What is more, those who identify with the "they" of the poem find, by the time they reach 53:11–12, that the servant proves in their presence (*lārabbîm*) to be innocent and to have borne punishment on behalf of them, the many (*ḥēṭ² rabbîm nāśā²*).

If one accepts that the suffering of the innocent is in any way because of, for the sake of, or on behalf of, oneself who deserves to suffer, then one has joined the ranks of the "we." They are the group who once felt like the "they" but have had their eyes opened to the true relationship between themselves and the servant: "he was pierced because of our rebelliousness" (53:5). Identification with the "we" puts one entirely within the world of the poem; it involves a recognition that things are not what they seem and that one can have been dreadfully mistaken about the identity and nature of the true servant of the Lord. It requires also a questioning in order to discover who and where is the servant of Yahweh for oneself. No one can enter the world of the poem without becoming a participant in that world; no one truly understands who the "we" are and what they mean to say unless one has shared their experience of revulsion towards and rejection of the servant and their experience of "conversion," i.e., their recognition of being mistaken, their assurance that the servant is for them *the* significant other and not an insignificant being, despised and rejected.

There is yet another role in the poem which the reader is invited to assume: that of the servant himself. Naturally, if the servant *is* Deutero-Isaiah or some other historical figure, one may empathize with the servant; but I am arguing that the poem's lack of specificity about the servant's identity enables a relationship between the servant and the reader that is deeper than empathy to come into being. It is not simply that the reader may, by exercise of a vivid imagination, put himself in the servant's shoes, and empathetically share the servant's experience. It is rather that the figure of the servant presented by the poem has the potency to reach out from the confines of a historical past and from the poem itself and to "seize" the reader and bend him to a new understanding of himself and of the direction of his life. The reader can, in the presence of this, the central *persona* of the poem, cease to be [[64]] the active subject interrogating the text, and become the one who is questioned and changed by the text. It is the same case if the servant is, not a historical personage, but an ideal figure. Here again, the force of the poem is not simply to invite the reader to approximate his behaviour and life-style to that of the servant as best he can; it is rather that the figure of the servant seizes, imposes itself upon, a reader—with or without the reader's assent (so this is not the same thing as empathy)—and insists upon interpreting the reader rather than being interpreted by the reader. The assumption of the servant's role becomes, not the voluntary act of a dramatic role-playing, but a compulsion by the figure of the servant. The language becomes more than a tool for the conveyance of information or even emotion; it creates an event: it destroys a world and replaces it by a new one which it brings into being.

6. Cannot something more specific be said about the nature of this figure of the servant?

It can, but not perhaps in the style of an academic paper; perhaps only the language of testimony or confession, which the "we" of the poem find themselves using, can properly express what the servant is, for that means: what the servant is *for me.* Others are questioned and changed by different facets of the servant figure, but for me what is most compelling is that the servant of Yahweh in Isaiah 53 *does nothing and says nothing but lets everything happen to him.* We saw above, in looking at the verbal pattern of the poem (chapter 3c [[not reprinted here]]), that the servant is acted upon more often than he acts. Even his "actions" are by turns negative ("he did not open his mouth") or passive ("he bore the punishment"). There is, as we saw, no concrete action done by the servant; he suffers. Even his "intervention" (*yapgîaʿ*, 53:12) for the rebellious, and his "carrying" of punishment (*nāśāʾ, sābal,* 53:4, 11, 12), his "exposing" himself to death (*heʿĕrâ,* 53:12), are nothing more than his suffering; they are not the acts of a Superman intervening at the critical moment, of an Atlas carrying the world-guilt on his shoulders, of a hero of the trenches exposing himself to enemy fire. They are: his letting everything happen to him.

And, he says nothing (cf. above, chapter 3d [[not reprinted here]]): he does not open his mouth. What kind of silence that is I do not well know, for it is so rare in our world. It is not Stoic silence or insolent silence; it is not dumb brutish silence or dumbfounded amazed silence; it is [[65]] not heroic silence, for he has no one to betray by his speech, but neither is it the silence of ignorance, for he knows what he is doing.

It can only be the silence of suffering, his speech and his action mysteriously but deliberately absent.

In a religious culture such as our own, where commitment is measured almost quantitatively by speech and action, the servant of the Lord of Isaiah 53 is ill at ease, for his commitment to the "purposes of Yahweh" (53:10) lies entirely in his silent and unresisting suffering. No one wants to claim that there are no other servants of the Lord except this one of Isaiah 53, that this poem-parable is the only glimpse we have of the reality of servanthood. But this servant still walks among us, wordlessly calling in question our images of servanthood and with his suffering reproaching our easy activisms.

The Rhetoric of Ezekiel's Vision of the Valley of the Bones

MICHAEL V. FOX

[[1]] The movement within Bible studies known as rhetorical criticism[1] has, for reasons which are unclear, generally restricted itself to concerns that most [[2]] rhetorical critics do not usually associate with rhetorical criticism. Rhetorical criticism of the Bible has focused almost exclusively

Reprinted with permission from *Hebrew Union College Annual* 51 (1980) 1–15.

1. "Rhetorical criticism" was inaugurated as a movement in Bible studies and given its name by James Muilenburg in his presidential address to the Society of Biblical Literature in 1968, published as "Form Criticism and Beyond," *JBL* 88 (1969), 1–18 [[repr. *Beyond Form Criticism: Essays in Old Testament Literary Criticism* (SBTS 2; ed. P. R. House; Winona Lake, Ind.: Eisenbrauns, 1992) 49–69]]. Muilenburg's interest was in "understanding the nature of Hebrew literary composition, in exhibiting the structural patterns that are employed for the fashioning of a literary unit, whether in poetry or in prose, and in discerning the many and various devices by which the predications are formulated and ordered into a unified whole" (p. 8). He was concerned with the identification of formal "devices" such as parallelismus membrorum, strophic structure, particles and repetition. These devices were to be studied as components of the structure of the whole. In a programmatic article, M. Kessler urged that the term "rhetorical criticism" be used to include all synchronic literary analysis of the text ("A Methodological Setting for Rhetorical Criticism," *Semitics* 4 [1974], 22–36). I. Kikawada described the method of rhetorical criticism (as he practices it) as a study of the Hebrew Bible "from a synchronistic perspective, in an effort to appreciate the received text and to describe not only what the text says but also how it conveys the message" ("Some Proposals for the Definition of Rhetorical Criticism," *Semitics* 5 [1977], 67). This definition is closer to the traditional understanding of rhetorical criticism but still seems to me to miss the main point: suasion. Admittedly rhetoric has always been closely related to poetics, but a word loses value through inflation of its meaning.

Although I think that "rhetorical criticism" should be used in a more restricted fashion than it generally has been in Bible studies, I see no reason to restrict it to criticism of on revealing the formal structures of a text: schemata formed by repetitions of roots, words, phrases and themes. Some of these studies attempt to connect the formal data with the text's meaning, though many often seem to assume that once the details of the construction of the text are laid out, its rhetoric has been discovered. But even the discovery of meaning does not constitute rhetorical criticism as that term has been understood by the great majority of rhetorical theorists from Aristotle on:[2] Rhetoric is persuasive discourse (persuasive in intent if not in accomplishment). Rhetorical criticism may be defined first of all as the examination and evaluation of such discourse for the nature and quality of its suasive force. The term may legitimately be broadened to include examination of the suasive factors in discourse where the primary intent is not persuasion.

This definition accords with the programmatic statement of the Committee on the Advancement and Refinement of Rhetorical Criticism of the National Development Project in Rhetoric (1970). That committee urged that rhetorical criticism be identified by the *kinds of questions* posed by the critic. Studying discourse does not ipso facto make one a rhetorical critic. "The critic becomes rhetorical to the extent that he studies his subject in terms of its suasory potential or persuasive effect. So identified, rhetorical criticism may be applied to any human act, process, product or artifact which, in the critic's view, may formulate, sustain or modify attention, perceptions, attitudes, or behavior."[3] This definition would exclude a strictly aesthetic, stylistic, or formalistic study of, say, prophetic oratory, in spite of the suasive intent of the text.[4] A study becomes [[3]] rhetorical

---

the "received text." One can study the rhetoric of any stage of development he believes he can distinguish in the text, and the rhetoric of the redactional process is itself a legitimate object for rhetorical criticism (but such a study would probably be indistinguishable from redaction criticism).

2. See Edwin Black, *Rhetorical Criticism* (Madison, WI, 1978), 10–19 and Kenneth Burke, *A Rhetoric of Motives* (New York, 1950), 49–55.

3. L. F. Bitzer and E. Black, eds., *The Prospect of Rhetoric* (Englewood Cliffs, NJ, 1971), 220.

4. Ezekiel himself emphatically rejects an aesthetic or strictly literary approach to his prophecy as trivial and irrelevant. God tells him that his fellow countrymen flock to hear his words ". . . but they will not obey them, for they treat (them as) love-songs (?) in their mouths, while their hearts are set on nothing but gain. To them you are just a singer of love-songs who has a sweet voice and plays skillfully; they hear your words, but will not obey them" (33:31–32). Ezekiel's artistry was drawing crowds, and that presented him with a dilemma: The literary artistry a rhetor employs in order to achieve persuasion can detract from his persuasiveness by competing for the audience's attention. The rhetor's necessary instruments may interfere with his rhetoric. A similar competition occurs when people come to hear the voice of a protest singer but ignore the message—yet they would not listen at all if it were not for the voice. This passage reminds us that poetic and rhetoric are not synonymous, even though rhetoric may be poetical and poetry rhetorical. Ezekiel would

only when it removes a text from its "autonomy" and inquires into the transaction between rhetor and audience, focusing on suasive intentions, techniques, and effects. In practice, however, it is hardly possible and perhaps not desirable to distinguish strictly between rhetorical factors and stylistic-aesthetic factors. But emphasis on the suasory is the *sine qua non* of rhetorical criticism.[5]

Now I do think that diagrammable structural patterns in linguistic and thematic features can contribute to the suasory force of a discourse, especially the more obvious patterns that can impose themselves forcefully on the auditor's consciousness. I am not convinced, however, that they are so important as to deserve the near monopoly of attention they have been granted in rhetorical criticism of the Bible. In any case, if the formal structures that the critic claims to discover are indeed rhetorically effective, he should show not only that they exist but *what* they do and *how* they work. However, the real rhetorical force of a discourse will almost certainly lie in qualities that are harder to pin down and to describe than the formal patterns, and it would be unfortunate if the rhetorical critic were to stop his investigation before reaching them.

My other reservation about the sort of structural analysis commonly identified as rhetorical criticism is that it presents structure as static and synoptic, whereas in actual presentation—written as well as oral—it is dynamic and sequential. An introverted structure (*abccba*) for example,

---

agree with Kenneth Burke's distinction between the rhetorical function in language, which is instrumental, designed to produce effects "beyond" the speech-act, and the poetic function, which is consummatory, designed to exercise symbolic action in and for itself ("The Party Line," *Quarterly Journal of Speech* 62 [1976], 66). But these functions overlap, interact, reinforce each other and interfere with each other in discourse, so it may not be possible to keep them distinct in analysis.

5. Rhetorical theory is currently expanding its scope to include epistemology. Some theorists use "rhetoric" to encompass a mode (or *the* mode) of growth of knowledge. This understanding is "a radical break from the modern tradition" of rhetoric (M. C. Leff, "In Search of Ariadne's Thread: A Review of the Recent Literature on Rhetorical Theory," *Central States Speech Journal* 29 [1978], 77). Yet in general, rhetorical theory is still within the framework of the above definition, even as the meaning of "suasion" is reinterpreted and broadened. The epistemic approach to rhetoric has so far produced only extremely rarefied theorizing whose application to specific discourses is as yet unclear. But some types of epistemic rhetorical theory may turn out to be useful in investigating questions such as the effects of prophetic rhetoric on prophetic values and perceptions. (Traditional rhetoric would examine only how rhetoric transmitted those values. The new rhetoric regards the flow of rhetorical "energy" as two-directional.) Recent rhetorical theory may prove useful in analyzing modes of reasoning implicit in biblical discourse. Those modes of reasoning are not amenable to formal logical analysis but may be so to the more flexible types of analysis being developed in the context of rhetorical theory, e.g., by Ch. Perelman and L. Olbrechts-Tyteca, *The New Rhetoric* (Notre Dame, 1969).

if it is indeed grasped on some level by the audience, may help in organizing ideas and reinforcing them by repetition. But what will be far
more influential will be the way *a* leads into *b* and *b* flows into *c*, then the
effect of [[4]] hearing *c* repeated, and so on. The audience hears only sequence and movement. It is more important for the critic to show the direction of the movement (remembering that it need not be a straight
line) and its velocity (remembering that it may be variable and irregular) than to outline patterns discernible only in the completed and tran-
scribed discourse.

   The task of rhetorical criticism is thus to examine and evaluate the
interactions among the three constituents of the rhetorical transaction
that takes place between rhetor and audience: strategies, situations, and
effects (effects potential as well as real, ideal as well as actual, long-range
as well as immediate). Rhetorical criticism may be employed on a small
scale and on successively larger scales; it may be applied to an individual
discourse, to a rhetor's entire production, to a genre, and to a rhetorical
movement or stages thereof.

   The prophets offer excellent subjects for rhetorical criticism, for by
any definition prophecy is rhetoric. The prophets were intensely concerned with persuasion, and they are indeed persuasive. It is impossible
to gauge their effect on their immediate audiences, not only because the
sources offer little information on the question but because the prophets—for rhetorical and theological reasons—consistently presented their
audiences in the worst possible light. Yet they did gain followers, some of
whom preserved, transmitted and edited their works. Many of their contemporaries did take them seriously (and reacted either positively or negatively, both types of reaction testifying to the force of their words). As
time went on their rhetoric, in written form, imposed itself on the collective consciousness of the people and became a major force in shaping the
religion of postexilic Judaism. Beyond that, the rhetorician, as critic, is
not limited to recording the effect on the immediate audience. He may,
and should, assess for himself the rhetorical force of particular prophetic
orations and of the oratory of the prophetic movement in general. For
the rhetorical force of discourse is not to be identified with its immediate
effect. The limp response the Gettysburg Address evoked in its auditors,
for example, does not prove that it was a rhetorical failure. Conversely, a
speech that is rhetorically deficient may persuade an audience that is already inclined to its views.[6]

---

   6. The assumption that the immediate effects of a discourse are the only rhetorically
relevant ones is central to the Neo-Aristotelian view of rhetorical criticism. This view was
subjected to a trenchant and influential critique by Black, *Rhetorical Criticism, passim.*

It should be stressed that the effectiveness of a particular prophecy did not derive from that utterance alone. Factors external to the discourse in 〖5〗 question would bear strongly upon its effectiveness. These include the weight of the prophet's entire career, the theological and social contexts of prophecy, which predisposed the audience to a certain attentiveness (if not receptiveness) to prophecy as such, and the prophet's prior accuracy in prediction. This last factor is especially relevant to the oracle we will consider below, for Ezekiel had been prophesying the fall of Jerusalem for some time, and that prophecy was fulfilled shortly before this oracle was delivered.

Rhetorical criticism, with its concentration on rhetor-audience interaction, has much to offer Bible studies, especially with regard to prophecy. Perhaps nowhere did a rhetorical movement assume a more important role than in ancient Israel in the shaping of the national religion and in the molding of the nation's perception of itself. Conversely, it is possible that Bible studies have something to offer general rhetorical theory, for in Israel we have a well-documented major rhetorical movement entirely independent of the classical tradition from which Western rhetoric and rhetorical criticism descend.

An exceptionally effective work of Hebrew rhetorical artistry is Ezekiel's vision of the valley of the bones, Ezek 37:1–14.[7] Ezekiel's despair with his own generation and his concern for the broad-scale history of the people did not obviate his ministry to his immediate audience, the Jews exiled to Babylon in the first wave of deportation in 597. Here, more than in most of his speeches, Ezekiel's message is directed to his fellow exiles.

Rhetoric is created as a response to a rhetorical situation, a situation felt to need change of the sort that discourse may accomplish.[8] Ezekiel is responding to a rhetorical situation that (like all rhetorical situations) consists of objective and subjective factors.

There were two main objective factors: The nation was in exile; and the situation in exile was not so bad for the individual Jew as might have

---

7. Ezek 37:15–28 is probably a separate oracle joined editorially to vv. 1–14 because both speak of the future restoration of Israel. Verse 14 clearly is a climax and summary, bringing the first oracle to an end. The second oracle in the chapter is qualitatively different from the first. The second shows a natural, nonmiraculous act (the prophet holds two sticks together to symbolize the rejoining of the northern and southern kingdoms). This act was probably performed by the prophet as a visual device to reinforce his message. The vision of the first oracle could, of course, only be related verbally.

8. On the definition and components of the rhetorical situation see Lloyd F. Bitzer, "Functional Communication: A Situational Perspective," in *Rhetoric in Transition*, ed. Eugene White (University Park, PA, 1980), 21–38.

been expected. It was not nearly so bad as had been predicted in earlier covenant curses and prophetic threats. This oracle is not dated, but it certainly was delivered after 587. Previously Ezekiel had been fighting [[6]] hope—illusory hope—not despair, and the deep despair expressed in v. 11 does not fit the attitude of the people between 597 and 587, insofar as this is known from Jeremiah's and Ezekiel's words. The oracle probably was given not long after news of the disaster arrived, before the shock had begun to dull. Yet for all the despair and misery caused by the disaster, the realities of exile were not so horrendous as earlier prophecies of punishment had predicted (see, for example, Leviticus 26).[9] Life in exile did not consist of incessant disease, starvation, slaughter, terror, and persecution. Jeremiah's advice (Jer 29:4–7) shows that the exiles of 597 had the option of settling into a normal way of life in Babylonia, and there is no reason to think that that option was closed in 587. On the contrary, the silence of our sources is eloquent here, for the exilic prophets certainly would have described intense suffering, had it existed, in order to interpret it as foreseen punishment. The Jews, like other groups exiled to Babylonia, were settled according to the needs of Babylonian economic policy and more or less left to themselves.

Those were the objective factors in the rhetorical situation, to which a number of responses were possible. The factors of the situation decisive to the creation of this particular oracle were the subjective ones: Ezekiel's view of the situation and its possible consequences, and his valuation of those consequences. Ezekiel sees the situation as intolerable not because it is miserable, for the misery he regards as punishment well-deserved. He sees it as intolerable because it could so easily become permanent, and that would mean the end of Israel as a people. It could become permanent because a nation that despairs of its future will do nothing to insure its continuation. Despair is tantamount to surrender, meaning absorption of the nation into its new environment, and surrender would be all the easier because of the relative benignity of that environment. In the face of this attitude Ezekiel must both chastise and

---

9. Y. Kaufmann showed how the gap between the envisioned exile and the actual exile resulted in the prophecy of wrathful redemption in 20:32–44: If the conditions of exile are not sufficiently terrible to break the nation's obduracy and bring it to repentance, God will redeem Israel by force and purge it in the "desert of the peoples" (תולדות האמונה הישראלית) Jerusalem 1947 [1964], VI, pp. 556f. = *The Religion of Israel* [abridged translation by M. Greenberg], Chicago, 1960, pp. 440f.). See further M. Greenberg, יחזקאל כ׳ והגלות הרוחנית, *Jubilee Volume for David Ben-Gurion* (Jerusalem, 1964, pp. 433–42), who shows that all of chap. 20 is a reaction to the growing complacency of the exiles, which has led them to consider establishing a "high-place" in Babylonia. Despair and complacency may be contradictory attitudes but they are neighbors in the human heart, for the former can so easily lead to the latter.

encourage the people. The vision of the valley of the bones is a message
of encouragement. Hope has become essential for keeping the people
together until the time comes to return, and for giving them a belief in
national restoration strong enough ⟦7⟧ to move them to get up and return to the ruins of Judah when the call comes to do so.

Rational argumentation could not give the people this kind of hope.
Even if Ezekiel could convince the people that it was rational to expect
restoration, intellectual conviction alone would not give the people the
strength needed to carry them through the dark years. At any rate, there
was no rational basis for hope. A reasonable man could see that Judah
was in ruins and that only rags and tatters of the people were left in the
homeland, and that at the same time Jews were rapidly adjusting to the
conditions of exile. A young generation that scarcely knew the homeland had already grown up in exile. Since rational argumentation was
hopeless, Ezekiel chose a rhetorical strategy at its polar opposite. He
sought to create *irrational* expectations in his audience by making them
believe in the reality of the irrational, by getting them to expect the unexpected, to accept the plausibility of the absurd. To bring about such a
conviction the rhetor obviously must go deeper than conscious reason.
He must find a shortcut to the subconscious and implant there a new
perspective on reality strong enough to overcome the vision of reality
that usually imposes itself on the conscious. This strategy is analogous to
hypnosis, in which a suggestion impressed deeply below the conscious
can restructure the subject's vision of reality. Having chosen this rhetorical strategy, Ezekiel produced a speech of the genre Edwin Black labels
exhortation.[10] On the scale of the intensity of conviction promoted in
audiences, the exhortation is near the upper, more intense, end of the
scale. The exhortation is a genre of discourse "in which the evocation of
an emotional response in the audience induces belief in the situation to
which the emotion is appropriate. . . . Emotion can be said to produce
the belief, instead of the reverse."[11] In the exhortation the rhetor strives
to produce not so much a new opinion as a new way of viewing the world
and of reacting to it.

Let us look at how Ezekiel carries through this rhetorical strategy in
this vision.

The rhetor must select a stance, that is, a role and a point-of-view
and, unless he wants to bewilder his audience, maintain it with some consistency. Point-of-view has been discussed most extensively with regard to
fictional narrative,[12] but the issue is no less relevant to rhetoric, for point-

10. Black, *Rhetorical Criticism*, 138–147.
11. *Ibid.*, 138.
12. See N. Friedman, "Point of View in Fiction," *Pub. of the Modern Lang. Assoc.* 70
(1955), and W. Booth, *The Rhetoric of Fiction* (Chicago, 1971).

of-view at once creates and expresses the rhetor's relation to his ⟦8⟧ audience. In fiction the author may, for example, choose to make the narrator omniscient, giving him complete access to the characters' minds and to all events, past and future. In that case, the role of the narrator is usually identified with the author (although, as Wayne Booth has argued, we must still distinguish between the implied author [the author-in-the-work] and the real author).[13] Or the author may give the narrator the stance of a protagonist, in which case the role of the narrator is a specific character in the story and his point-of-view is limited to what that character sees, hears, and thinks. Since in oratory the rhetor usually speaks in his own voice, the question of stance may seem unnecessary. But the author of rhetoric too is creating a role for the speaker, whether or not that speaker is himself, and the speaker's point-of-view will be largely determined by that role. The rhetor may choose, for example, the role of "one of the people," in which he seeks to convince the audience that he shares their position in life and their outlook on the world. He hopes that if he aligns himself with them, they may believe that he speaks for them and come to align themselves with him. Or he may choose the "father" role, in which he speaks to them from a position of superior knowledge and moral wisdom, hoping that this stance will in itself increase his authority over his audience by putting them into a filial position. He may choose the "preacher" role, in which he claims that his propositions are deduced directly from the will of a higher, unquestioned authority (not necessarily God). This role allows him to stand above his audience while freeing him of some of the need for establishing his personal ethos. Or he may stand before them in the role of "reporter," in which he pretends neutrality in the issue at hand in order to enforce his implicit arguments with the appearance of objectivity.

The role taken by Israelite prophets is almost always that of messenger. This role is not just a rhetorical tactic, of course, but is the Israelite understanding of the actual nature of prophecy. Yet it does serve rhetorical purposes. The prophet claims to do nothing but transmit verbatim a message received from God. In effect the prophet identifies himself with God for the purpose of the rhetoric. The words he is speaking are God's, and the point-of-view is of course external to the audience and omniscient. The words are then spoken from the outside to the people. The rhetor as messenger stands (with God) outside and above the audience. The auditors are recipients of a message aimed *at* them. The desired effect of the messenger role is to imbue the speaker's ethos with absolute authority by identifying it with God's. Persuasion through authority is

---

13. See Booth, *Rhetoric of Fiction*, 70–76 and his fuller treatment, "Distance and Point-of-View," *Essays in Criticism* 11 (1961), 60–79.

[[9]] undoubtedly the fundamental rhetorical strategy in prophecy. But it is not the stance Ezekiel takes here.

Ezekiel's role is not messenger but *spectator.* Ezekiel is observing an event in which he is forcibly placed. Within that event he is indeed given a message to deliver (vv. 12–14), but that message is only part of the experience, and it will not be delivered until some time after the visionary experience. Here, as in chapters 8–11, the oracle is formally a narration of a visionary event. The prophet simply tells what he saw and heard. He is neutral insofar as he does not openly involve his own ego in the message. Ezekiel is an essentially passive spectator. It is true that he speaks the words that bring about the rising of the bones, but his part in the event is similar to that of a spectator invited up from the audience to "help" a stage magician by waving a wand over the magician's hat. Ezekiel carefully maintains a distance between himself and the events he saw.

By choosing this stance the rhetor steps into the audience, as it were, and aligns himself with them. He makes no explicit claims about the vision's plausibility. He does not request that the audience accept what he saw and certainly does not argue for the truth of his vision. Such a request would invite refusal, and such an argument would invite refutation. In effect the prophet says, "Here is what I saw. I too was surprised. Now believe it or not." This stance gives an impression of objectivity. More important, by taking the point-of-view of an audience the rhetor makes his audience's point-of-view congruent with his own. The audience looks over the rhetor's shoulder and watches the event unfold from the same angle of vision. Alignment of perspective encourages alignment of belief.

The most important rhetorical strategy of this vision is its central image. An image is a concentrated representation of reality. It makes the diffuse and abstract concrete and immediate. The most powerful images are foreign to our everyday experience. Images that conform to everyday experience have didactic value. They are useful in reinforcing accepted truths and in helping the auditor assimilate ideas that are complex or abstract. Strange, shocking, and bizarre images on the other hand are needed when one seeks to break down old frameworks of perception and to create new ones. They offer a way of transmitting the rhetor's fundamental perceptions of reality even when these perceptions are not amenable to rational exposition. Such images may attack our normal system of expectations in order to replace it with a new one.[14]

---

14. My analysis of Ezekiel's rhetorical use of imagery is indebted to R. C. Tannehill's analysis of Jesus' use of forceful imagery in the synoptic sayings to induce "imaginative shock" in order to challenge old structures of thought and to suggest new visions (*The Sword of His Mouth* [Philadelphia, 1975], 54 and *passim*).

〚10〛 Ezekiel does not merely predict the resurrection of the nation, for then all hope would rest on his listeners' confidence in his accuracy as forecaster, and there are more powerful forces working against hope. He is certainly not just relying on argumentation, for rational argumentation could hardly create belief in the absurd. Ezekiel's primary strategy is boldly to affirm the absurd. He does so by implanting within his auditors an image that will restructure their view of reality. He will seek to make them expect the unexpectable. What they are to expect is the resurrection of the "dead," i.e., exiled, nation and its return to its land. To achieve this (and not to teach the doctrine of individual resurrection) Ezekiel uses the image of the revival of bleached-out bones, the last remnants of rotted corpses.

Let us look carefully at the image and how it unfolds. The image is first of all dynamic, not static. The image is a configuration of a *process*. The process is movement from death to life. It is portrayed as movement from chaos to order, like the movement of the creation story. The scattered bones gather themselves together, sinews bind them together, flesh grows and skin covers it and thus binds it to sinew and bone. Then they are given the breath of life (which comes in from the four directions, thus reinforcing the centripetal movement of the overall imagery), and they finally stand up—not as separate individuals, but as a great army, an organized unit. The memorability of this image is increased by the double relation of the event, first as command (4–6), then as narration (7–10). Details are sparse, because it is a process the auditors are to picture and remember, and each step must be precise and distinct, with no unnecessary elaboration that might transfer attention from the process to the pictorial details of the envisioned objects.

The dramatic movement of the visionary event is carefully modulated to create suspense and intensify the imagery's impression. The dramatic movement unfolds through the dialogue between the first persona, Ezekiel, and the second persona, God, which is encompassed in the voice of the first.

God's actions markedly resemble those of a stage magician, who is out to awe his audience and convince them of his special powers or skills. Ultimately it is knowledge of God that he seeks to inculcate (v. 6b). Knowledge of God means not only cognitive knowledge of his identity, but full, personal awareness of his moral demands and of his control of history. Awe is a necessary element of this knowledge. God begins by giving Ezekiel a tour of the stage—the valley—showing him how many and how dry the bones are, in order to heighten his amazement at the feat God is about to perform. We may think of a Houdini showing spectators 〚11〛 the number and strength of the locks he is about to escape from.

God's question, "Can these bones come to life?" is likewise calculated to heighten wonder. The natural answer is no, but Ezekiel answers politely and ambiguously.

God does not make the bones rise immediately. He announces what will happen and then makes us wait for it to happen. To increase the suspense and draw the audience closer, he invites the spectator to participate. God orders Ezekiel to pronounce the "magic" words. (In this detail too there is a message, though it is kept carefully in the background: Prophets will be God's agents in the national resurrection when it comes.) Ezekiel just says that he prophesied as ordered (v. 7a) and does not quote his own words. He thus carefully keeps his own role in proper perspective. He is passive and not really affecting the outcome.

Ezekiel's narration of the resurrection in vv. 7–10 is a considerable expansion of God's command in 4–6. God, self-assured and certain of the outcome, is terse. Ezekiel, amazed at the scene unfolding before his eyes, is expansive. In the narration, but not in the prior command, the revival of the bodies is separated from the restoration of the life-breath. The bodies are reconstituted in vv. 7b–8a, but "there was no life-breath in them" (v. 8b). It is as if there were a hitch in the plans, for God had not prepared us for any such pause in the process. On the contrary, he began and ended his command to the bones with the declaration that he would put life-breath in them and they would come to life (vv. 5b–6aβ). By bracketing the resurrection of the bodies between two promises of the restoration of the spirit, God presented the process as a unity. So when the movement of events comes to a halt before the crucial step and God issues a new command to prophesy in order to bring in the spirit, it is as if he must put extra effort into achieving the hardest part of the task (v. 9). One is reminded of the magician who invariably "fails" once or twice in attempting his grand finale in order to intensify suspense and to focus attention on the climactic success to follow.

God's success goes beyond what was predicted. The scattered bones not only come to life, they rise as an army. They are organized and they have power.

The rhetorical use made of this image assumes that the audience regards corporeal resurrection as basically absurd. Ezekiel shares the attitude of the psalmist of Ps 88:11–12 who asks, "Will you perform a miracle for the dead? Will the Shades rise and praise you? Will your mercy be told in the grave, your faithfulness in Destruction?" The assumed answer is no, of course not. Ezekiel shows the dead rising, but not because he believes that actual corpses will do so. Rather he depicts the extreme [[12]] case of unpredictable salvation in order to enable the people to expect a salvation that though unlikely is yet less radical, the return of the nation from exile.

Yet he does show the dead rising, and it seems likely that this vision contributed to the formulation of the later doctrine of corporeal resurrection.[15] It would be a misinterpretation of Ezekiel 37 to see there a concept of individual resurrection, but that misinterpretation would be rooted in Ezekiel's own rhetoric. For Ezekiel takes the ultimate polarity, the archetypal polarity of life and death, and demonstrates that God can bridge the poles by a process similar to the process of creation. Now Ezekiel does this for rhetorical, not theological, purposes. The resurrection that he is really interested in is not from actual death but from figurative death. Yet his image does offer a new perspective on the life-death polarity, one in which death is not seen as final. I would surmise that this new perspective is one source of the rhetorical power of the imagery. The imagery of the vision appeals to one of the deepest and most widespread of human desires, the desire for individual immortality. A desire for immortality would combine with a hope for national continuation and reinforce it. The audience would link their desires to Ezekiel's vision so that they would participate in the process of their own persuasion. Ezekiel presents a vision of the reversal of death's disorder, and that vision is intrinsically appealing.

Clearly, the power of Ezekiel's rhetoric does not lie in rational argumentation. But rational argumentation does have a place in this oracle. The argument runs throughout the oracle, but its nature becomes clear in part II (vv. 11–14), which is God's explication of the vision of part I (vv. 1–10). God uses a sort of reverse enthymeme. He does not proceed from a common, unspoken premise. Rather he contradicts a universally accepted premise and constructs a new syllogism that directly confronts the people's unconscious, deep-rooted syllogism:

Israel:	*God:*
[Dry bones cannot come to life]	Dry bones *can* come to life (1–10)
Israel is dry bones (11bα)	Israel is dry bones (affirmed in 12a)
Therefore Israel cannot come to life (11bβ)	Therefore Israel can come to life (12–14)

[13] Let us consider how parts I and II interact in conveying and impressing the message of the oracle.

---

15. It is in fact not clear just what the doctrine of corporeal resurrection owes to Ezekiel 37. Dan 12:2–3 does not reflect Ezekiel's language, but the undoubted dependency of other parts of the visions in Daniel on Ezekiel (Dan 4:7–15, 7:9–10, 10:4–6 *et al.*) makes it likely that Ezekiel's vision is in the background here too. Somewhat surprisingly the rabbis did not use Ezekiel 37 as a major proof text for their resurrection belief.

Part II is more important than part I in communicating the content of the oracle, for part II tells explicitly what will happen in the nonvisionary reality. For the rhetorical strategy, on the other hand, part I is primary and II an appendage to it. The reader can test the relation between the two parts by asking what first comes to mind when recalling Ezek 37:1–14. Answering for myself (but the use of this theme in art and literature seems to confirm this answer), what always comes first and most prominently to mind is the scene depicted in part I. The dead arise from a battlefield, not from their graves (as II has it). But when asked to summarize the *message* of the oracle, I would paraphrase God's words in part II.

Part II is presentation as well as argumentation. God is presenting himself anew to the nation, which has just now experienced his wrath. Ezekiel shows God softening toward the forlorn and weary people. God indicates that the miracle he has just performed was in direct response to the mood of the people, to which he is sensitive (vv. 11–12). By presenting his actions as part of a dialogue with the people, God shows them that he is with them, meeting their needs in the present as well as in the future. And to stress that his bond with Israel continues, that they are not utterly cut off, he twice calls them "my people."

Black observes that one attribute of the exhortative style is the frequent substitution of *is* or *will be* for *should* or *should be*, for the exhorter aims to inculcate a belief that the world *is* a certain way rather than that it should be a certain way.[16] We may go further and say that in congregations of discourses high in Black's scale of intensity of conviction, *is* frequently substitutes for *will be*, for the speaker appropriates the future to himself and makes it his present. Thus within the vision proper (I), Ezekiel does not *predict* the national resurrection, he *sees* it imaged in a present event. The future tense comes in with God's words in part II, where God changes his role from magician to teacher and explains (with some didactic repetitiveness) the meaning of what Ezekiel saw. Part II is future tense, part I is present tense. Part II is argumentation, part I is demonstration. Part II is abstract and cognitive, part I is concrete and sensual. Part II puts the absurdity of part I into a rational framework. It asserts that the (previously) irrational hidden reality of the vision will be turned into a future manifest reality. Part II takes the emotions churned up by the bizarre and shocking imagery of part I and shapes them, redirecting them toward a new belief. It is as if there were present in the people a certain amount of [[14]] "belief energy," which is currently infusing their despair but which, once released by the detonation of their deepest assumptions and attitudes, can be deflected undiminished into new convictions.

16. *Rhetorical Criticism*, 143.

Underneath these two strategies—transformation of perception through imagery and argumentation by reverse enthymeme—there is another stratagem at work, one that is perhaps all the more powerful for being a clandestine operation. Ezekiel emphasizes the theme-word *rûaḥ* [['spirit']], repeating it (ten times, counting the plural[17]) and thrusting it before our eyes by the "hitch" in the plans in v. 8, as described above. At the same time that he keeps the term *rûaḥ* in the foreground of our consciousness and works to convince us of God's ability to put the *rûaḥ* in the lifeless nation, he does something less obvious but no less important: He permutes the meaning of the word *rûaḥ* in passing from part I to part II. The *rûaḥ* that God promises to put in the nation (v. 14aα) is not the same as the *rûaḥ* that he puts in the bones. In v. 1, God brings Ezekiel to the valley *bĕrûaḥ* Y_HWH_ 'by the spirit of the Lord', a term Ezekiel uses elsewhere to label the motivating power of his transportation visions. This occurrence begins the process of setting the theme-word in the audience's mind, but since the visionary spirit is and will be a property of prophets alone, it is really incidental in the "argument" borne by that theme-word.[18] What matters is the transformation in the use of *rûaḥ* between part I and part II.

17. A thematic number. Or, if we do not count the single occurrence of the plural (which refers to a different kind of *rûaḥ*), nine times—also a thematic number, three triads. Or, if we count only the occurrences of the singular between *rûaḥ* Y_HWH_ in v. 1 and *rûḥî* [['my spirit']] in v. 14 (taking those two as an inclusio), seven times—a *very* thematic number. In fact, it is rather hard not to find thematic numbers of occurrences, but the whole matter is of doubtful relevance to rhetoric.

18. It has been suggested to me that *rûḥî* (v. 14) forms an inclusio with *rûaḥ* Y_HWH_ (v. 1), for there alone does *rûaḥ* refer to the spirit of Yahweh. But is this really inclusio? To be a rhetorical inclusio, the terms must close off the unit by bringing the auditor's attention back to its beginning. Once the recurrence of a term or of similar terms has been observed it is necessary to make a subjective evaluation of their rhetorical effect. Would the occurrence of *rûḥî* at the end of the vision really make the auditor isolate *rûḥî* in v. 14 and *rûaḥ* Y_HWH_ in v. 1 from the other eight occurrences of *rûaḥ* and link up those two occurrences? I doubt it, but, more important, I do not see what *rhetorical* gain there would be in having the audience make that association. An inclusio, especially when it consists of a repeated and prominent idea and not of one word, can summarize the unit and reinforce memory. But here the *rûaḥ* that carries Ezekiel and the *rûaḥ* that God will place in the people, even if they are really the same thing (and not just two concepts with one name), function too differently to be able to combine into such a summary. The fact of the appearance of a term near the beginning and end of a unit need not be rhetorically relevant. J. Culler's remarks on Jakobson's attempt to use linguistics as an algorithm for the description of a poetic text can serve as a fundamental critique of rhetorical criticism as currently practiced in Bible studies: ". . . if one wishes to discover a pattern of symmetry in a text, one can always produce some class whose members will be appropriately arranged. If one wants to show, for example, that the first and last stanzas of a poem are related by a similar distribution of some linguistic item, one can always define a category such that its members will be symmetrically distributed between the two stanzas. Such patterns, needless to say, are

⟦15⟧ In part I (after v. 1) *rûaḥ* is the breath of life, the life-force common to all creatures. The naturalness and substantiality of this type of *rûaḥ* is emphasized by its being called from the four *rûḥôt* 'winds'. It is 'the wind' (vv. 1–10), something external to God that can be addressed and summoned. But at the very end (v. 14) God promises to put *rûḥî* 'my spirit' into the revivified Israel. Compare v. 14 ("And I will put my spirit [*rûḥî*] within you and you will live, . . . and you will know that I the Lord have done what I said") with v. 6 (". . . And I will put breath [*rûaḥ*] into you and you will live, and you will know that I am the Lord") to see how Ezekiel introduces a new idea by subterfuge just by adding the possessive suffix. Israel will get not the ordinary life-breath, but God's spirit. God's spirit transforms a man. It may make him a prophet as in the case of Ezekiel, but it may also transform a nation's moral character and remold its psychology. In 36:27 God says, "I will put my spirit in your midst and cause you to go in my laws and carefully to keep my ordinances." When one has God's spirit in him he does God's will because he *wants* to do God's will. Again in 39:29, "I will pour out my spirit upon the house of Israel" means a transformation of the nation's character. By permuting the meaning of his theme-word in this way Ezekiel takes advantage of the audience's new receptiveness in order to slip an additional message into his vision. The promised rebirth will not be merely a restoration of the nation to its former condition, but a fundamental restructuring of the national psychology.

The first two stratagems of this discourse, imagery and argumentation, are clearly directed to the accomplishment of Ezekiel's manifest goal in this chapter, the preservation of the nation's hope and thus its will to survive. The third stratagem, the permutation of the meaning of *rûaḥ*, points to a further goal—implanting in the people a particular understanding of the *meaning* of their survival.[19]

'objectively' present in the poem, but they are not for that reason alone of any importance" (*Structuralist Poetics*, Ithaca, NY, 1975, pp. 57f.).

19. Research for this study was aided by a grant from the Wisconsin Society for Jewish Learning.

A Maker of Metaphors:
Ezekiel's Oracles against Tyre

CAROL A. NEWSOM

[[151]] After having been charged by God to deliver an oracle in highly
figurative language, Ezekiel protested that he was developing something of a reputation. "Oh, Lord God, people are saying of me, 'He's just
a maker of metaphors!'" (*hălō* *mĕmaššēl mĕšālîm hû*; Ezek 21:5; Eng.
20:49). In truth Ezekiel deserved the reputation, though not the criticism
that it implied, for one finds in Ezekiel a greater number of elaborately
worked out metaphors, allegories, and symbolic speech than in any other
prophet. In the oracles against the nations (Ezekiel 25–32), Ezekiel en-
trusts a particularly large part of his argument to metaphorical language.
Here Ezekiel does not merely use striking metaphors to announce judgments. He often begins, rather, with an image by which a nation might
represent itself or one which Ezekiel's exilic audience might have applied
to that nation. Then Ezekiel subjects the metaphor to scrutiny. Does it
mean what it first appears to mean? Or does it reveal something about
the subject rather different from what the audience first thought? How
does it stand up to rival metaphors? Finally, Ezekiel uses the metaphor to
demonstrate the appropriateness and the inevitability of Yahweh's judgment on the nation in question.

While Ezekiel's original audience may have lacked appreciation of
his metaphorical style, the prophet stands a good chance of getting a
sympathetic hearing (for his rhetorical technique at least) from modern

Reprinted with permission from *Interpretation* 38 (1984) 151–64.
All translations are those of the author.

⟦152⟧ readers. During the past generation there has been a new perception of metaphor as more than elegant decoration of information
that could otherwise be communicated in a straightforward manner.[1] It
is now generally understood that far from being merely decorative, metaphors have real cognitive content. If one tries to paraphrase a metaphor,
what is lost is more than just a certain effect. What is lost is part of the
meaning itself, the insight which the metaphor alone can give.

One of the best explanations of how metaphor works to produce
meaning is given by Max Black.[2] Black takes a simple metaphorical statement as an example: "Man is a wolf." Here there are two subjects, a principal one ("Man") and a subsidiary one ("wolf"), the word which is used
metaphorically. The reader of the metaphor has at hand a body of common knowledge and attitudes concerning wolves—associated commonplaces, Black calls them—which may or may not be literally true but
which are readily brought to mind when one hears the word "wolf" (e.g.,
fierce, predatory, treacherous). In the statement "Man is a wolf" the
reader superimposes the wolf-system of associated commonplaces onto
the rather different system of commonplaces generally associated with
human beings. The metaphor, acting as a filter, brings into prominence
human characteristics that are wolf-like and suppresses those that are
not. What the metaphor accomplishes, Black says, is to *organize* our view
of human nature. Still, no literal paraphrase of wolf-like traits has the
power to give insight the way the wolf metaphor does. This is partly because a metaphor is always indeterminate. It is the reader who must actively, even if subliminally, decide which implications are relevant, and
how much relative weight each bears in producing the new perception of
human nature.

Nelson Goodman describes the way metaphor works in a similar manner.[3] He suggests that we have schemata by which we organize certain
parts of experience (e.g., plant life) and that we use various labels or
words by which we sort out this experience and make distinctions within

---

1. Critic Wayne Booth, commenting on the explosion of studies on metaphor in recent
years, wryly calculated that by the year 2039 there would be more students of metaphor
than people ("Metaphor as Rhetoric: The Problem of Evaluation" in S. Sacks, ed., *On Metaphor* [Chicago: Univ. of Chicago, 1978], 47). The following are some of the most significant
recent works: I. A. Richards, *The Philosophy of Rhetoric* (Oxford: Oxford Univ., 1936; reprinted 1965); Monroe Beardsley, *Aesthetics* (New York: Harcourt, Brace, 1958; reprinted
Indianapolis: Hackett, 1981); Philip Wheelwright, *Metaphor and Reality* (Bloomington, Ind.:
Indiana Univ., 1962); Max Black, *Models and Metaphors* (Ithaca, N.Y.: Cornell Univ., 1962);
Nelson Goodman, *Languages of Art* (Indianapolis: Bobbs-Merrill, 1968); Paul Ricoeur, *The
Rule of Metaphor* (Toronto: Univ. of Toronto, 1977).

2. Black, 38–44.

3. Goodman, 71–80.

it. If one [[153]] takes one of these labels from its home realm and applies it as a metaphor to an alien realm of experience (e.g., emotions), which one normally sorts out with a different set of labels, then one transfers not only a label, but the whole schematic system, a whole configuration of experience. One's perception of the realm of the emotions is then reorganized in a very different manner (as, e.g., in Andrew Marvell's lines, "My vegetable love should grow / vaster than empires, and more slow"). This transference and reorganization is the means by which metaphor creates new meaning which is not merely decorative but is a new perception of the relationships within one's world. Metaphor, says Paul Ricoeur, "is the rhetorical process by which discourse unleashes the power that certain fictions have to redescribe reality."[4]

As the recent philosophers of language have described it, to be a maker of metaphors is no insignificant thing. But because of the power which metaphors exercise over our sense of what is real, possible, or true, they have to be subjected to constant critique. The insight which metaphor gives into truth is properly tentative and hypothetical. It has what Ricoeur calls an is-and-is-not character.[5] Often, however, metaphors are absolutized, as though they provided literal descriptions of reality rather than suggestive glimpses. Metaphor derives much of its convincing power because it does not allow its hearers to be passive but requires them to participate in the construction of the metaphorical meaning. In this process, though, there is a sense of "virtual experience" (Ricoeur's phrase) which can be mistaken for literal truth. Perhaps more dangerous even than the brilliant metaphor is the dead one whose constructed character, whose is-and-is-not nature, has been forgotten. As Goodman provocatively says, "What was novel becomes commonplace, its past is forgotten, and metaphor fades to mere truth."[6] This may often be an innocent process, and one which is necessary to the development of everyday language; but where the metaphors in question guide our knowledge of fundamental human experience, they can be misleading and oppressive.[7] Consequently, the critique of metaphors is a business of equal importance to the making of them.

4. Ricoeur, 7. There is an inherently critical function in metaphor. As Ricoeur notes (p. 197), "the strategy of language at work in metaphor consists in obliterating the logical and established frontiers of language, in order to bring to light new resemblances the previous classification kept us from seeing."

5. Ricoeur, 7.

6. Goodman, 80.

7. See, e.g., Sallie McFague's *Metaphorical Theology: Models of God in Religious Language* (Philadelphia: Fortress, 1982), in which she employs recent research into the nature of metaphor in a searching critique of certain fundamental models and metaphors in Christian thought.

⟦154⟧ In his oracles against the nations, particularly in the collections of oracles against Tyre (chaps. 26–28) and Egypt (chaps. 29–32), Ezekiel both creates and criticizes metaphors that purport to give insight into the relationship between the power possessed by human nations and the sovereignty of Yahweh. Date formulae introducing the oracles indicate that with one exception (29:17–21, which comes from 571 B.C.), all the oracles were produced in the three years immediately before and after the fall of Jerusalem (26:1; 29:1; 30:20; 31:1; 32:1, 17). Except in 26:2, however, the oracles against Tyre and Egypt virtually ignore the political events of the fall of Jerusalem and its consequences. In fact these oracles are addressed, not to the political opponents of Judah, but to those of Babylon. The emphasis is easily understood, however. Since Ezekiel, like Jeremiah, was convinced that it was Yahweh's will to give political dominion to Nebuchadnezzar and to Babylon, opposition to Babylon was an implicit rejection of Yahweh's sovereignty. In the oracles against Tyre and Egypt Ezekiel scrutinizes metaphors which express the implicit self-understanding of these nations that underlies their defiant behavior.

Since it is not possible to look at all the oracles against the nations here, the relatively small and self-contained collection concerning Tyre provides an opportunity for examining in a limited way some of the techniques which Ezekiel uses in working with metaphor. This collection consists of four distinct oracles grouped by the use of a concluding refrain into three units, 26:1–21; 27:1–36; and 28:1–19, which pairs two separate oracles, 1–10 and 11–19.[8] There is general agreement about the structure of chapter 26 (vv. 2–6, 7–14, 15–18, 19–21), though disagreement about the relationship of the various parts.[9] What we are to focus on, however, is the figurative way in which judgment on Tyre is expressed in verses 3–5:

> See, I am against you, Tyre. And I will bring up many nations against you as the sea brings up its waves. And they will destroy the wall of Tyre and break down its towers; and I will scrape (*wĕsiḥêtî*) its soil from it, and I will make it a bare rock (*ṣĕḥîaḥ sālaᶜ*). A place for spreading nets shall it become in the midst of the sea.

8. Walther Zimmerli, *Ezekiel 2*, trans. R. E. Clements (Philadelphia: Fortress, 1983); German ed., BK 13/2 (Neukirchen-Vluyn: Neukirchener, 1969), 22.

9. Zimmerli, 33, is correct, I think, in seeing vv. 7–14 as an interpretive commentary on the figuratively expressed judgment in 2–6. Contrast J. W. Wevers, *Ezekiel*, New Century Bible (Greenwood, S.C.: Attic Press, 1969), 200, who thinks vv. 2–6 are secondary and based on 7–14. Verses 15–18 present a lament similar to the one in chap. 27. In vv. 19–21 the description of Tyre's descent to the netherworld recalls the more elaborate description of Egypt's descent in chap. 32.

To appreciate what Ezekiel is doing with this image of judgment, one has to keep in mind that the single most distinctive feature of the ancient ⟦155⟧ city of Tyre was its physical location on a rocky island just off the Phoenician coast. The island site with its natural and artificial harbors provided Tyre not only with economic advantages but with an easily defended position. Nebuchadnezzar's ultimately inconclusive siege of Tyre is said by Josephus (Ant. X 11, 1) to have lasted for thirteen years. The island city's defenses were not in fact decisively breached until 332 B.C. when Alexander the Great constructed an enormous mole from the mainland to the island. The significance of this physical location of Tyre seems to have captured the imagination of the ancient world, and in Egyptian, Assyrian, biblical, and classical writings references are repeatedly made to Tyre as the city "in the midst of the sea."[10] In the Egyptian Papyrus Anastasi I Tyre is described as follows: "They say another town is in the sea, named Tyre-the-Port. Water is taken to it by the boats, and it is richer in fish than in sand."[11]

There was reflection on the significance of Tyre's location in Phoenician lore, too, where it was said that Tyre had been founded on two floating rocks anchored to the bed of the sea.[12] In fact the very name Tyre is simply the common noun 'rock' (ṣōr). To call the physical location "rock" would be to make a fairly literal description. But to call the city "rock" is to speak metaphorically, to claim for the identity of the city the qualities of the ground on which it was built. To use Max Black's terms, "rock" forms the filter through which the city's existence and character are perceived. A contemporary and rather mundane example illustrates the same process. The use of the emblem of the rock of Gibraltar by the Prudential Life Insurance Company and their slogan, "Get a piece of the rock," associates with the company the qualities of enduring strength, soundness, dependability, and protection. One might object that the name Tyre is a frozen metaphor and should not be pushed for such connotations. But frozen metaphors can thaw rather quickly in the heat of an appropriate context, and Tyre, by its actions as well as by its name and symbols, represented itself as something of a Gibraltar in the early sixth century. It is this implicit metaphorical claim that Ezekiel attempts to refute by means of the metaphor he chooses to announce Tyre's judgment.

Tyre had relied on its situation "in the midst of the sea" to give it a kind of protection from besieging armies that mainland cities could not hope for. So Ezekiel frames a metaphor for destruction taken from Tyre's

10. H. J. Katzenstein, *The History of Tyre* (Jerusalem: Shocken, 1973), 9.
11. Adolf Erman, *Die Literatur der Aegypter* (Leipzig: Hinrichs, 1923), 288. ANET, 477, "richer in fish than the sands."
12. Nonnus, *Dionysiaca*, XL, 429–534.

image of its own security when he speaks of the "enmity" of sea and land. ⟦156⟧ The significant connotation of the phrase "as the sea brings up its waves" is not difficult to define. It is the utter relentlessness of the ocean. No one wave may bring full destruction, but it does not matter. It is the unending succession of waves that destroys even the strongest rock. The initial comparison is taken up again in the verbs where the two third person forms describe literally the destruction of the armies, and the final verb in the first person ("I will scrape bare") reverts to the metaphor of erosion. Though Ezekiel makes no explicit word play, one can scarcely avoid the sense of ironic transformation in which Tyre, the protecting rock, becomes the bare, eroded rock.[13] After Ezekiel's efforts to undermine the image of Tyre's island security, the concluding phrase "in the midst of the seas" in verse 5 has a strongly mocking character. The effect of the metaphor in the oracle is to reorganize one's sense of power. The apparent solidity and security of the island is revealed as an illusion of perspective, not a contradiction of Yahweh's power. Equally, the Babylonian opponents of Tyre, included as the "many nations," are imaged in such a way that they do not appear as independent powers but merely as episodes in Yahweh's patient, powerful sovereignty.

The second oracle against Tyre in Ezekiel 27 involves the use of a much more elaborately developed metaphor than the one in 26:1–6,[14] but it too explores the significance of Tyre's physical location and the special status which Tyre seems to claim from it. In this oracle Tyre is imaged as a ship. The first lines are somewhat corrupt but are probably to be read as follows: 'O Tyre, you are a ship, perfect in beauty. In the midst of the seas are your borders; your builders brought your beauty to perfection' (vv. 3b–4).[15] The basis for the metaphor is obvious—a ship, like an island, is surrounded by water, as the initial words of verse 4 underscore. One wonders if Tyrian poets and artists used this metaphor for their city. Certainly the reader gives immediate assent to the appropriateness of the metaphor.

Though the metaphor is obvious, it is not trite. The reader is invited to consider various connotations also associated with ships that can illu-

13. In light of Tyre's reputation as a fishing capital there may be further irony in the assertion that when Tyre is worn down by erosion it will become ideally suited for drying fishing nets.

14. See the article of E. M. Good, "Ezekiel's Ship: Some Extended Metaphors in the Old Testament," *Semitics* 1:79–103 (1970).

15. Reading, in v. 3, ʾatt ʾŏnî for MT ʾat ʾāmart ʾănî. See the remarks of Zimmerli, 42. Similar emendations are made by Georg Fohrer, *Ezechiel*, HAT 13 (Tübingen: J. C. B. Mohr, 1955), 153 and H. J. van Dijk, *Ezekiel's Prophecy on Tyre*, BibOr 29 (Rome: PBI, 1968), 56–57. Good, 82, defends the MT, remarking on the assonance of ʾŏniyyāh ʾănî. The metaphor of Tyre the ship is clear whether or not one accepts the emendation.

mine what Tyre is. Ships are instruments of trade. Since Tyre's wealth and
⟦157⟧ status—in short, its identity among the nations—derived from
trade, there is a special rightness in saying that Tyre *is* a ship. Ezekiel develops these connotations in verses 5–7 where the construction of the
ship from precious materials is described. It is not simply the luxurious-
ness of the materials that is at issue. They are rather examples of the
products of Tyrian trade, as the careful enumeration of their places of
origin suggests. The metaphor draws the reader to conclude that trade
indeed built Tyre.

Playing out the metaphor further, in verses 8ff.,[16] Ezekiel names the
leaders of the surrounding cities as those who row, navigate, and repair
the caulking of the ship. Very economically the metaphor suggests the political superiority that follows dominance in trade. Each detail enhances
one's sense of the aptness of the metaphor as an instrument for exploring
the situation of Tyre until the initial vision of the physical similarity of the
island Tyre with a ship seems weighted with significance. One is prepared
to concede that in a certain sense geography is destiny. Tyre's fortune
seems almost to be written into creation—literally and symbolically.

Ezekiel, though, was not a public relations agent hired by the Tyrian
chamber of commerce. He has played out the metaphor so that the
reader is deeply committed to its power to give insight into the reality of
Tyre's situation. But Ezekiel has done that with the intention of undermining the implications which first emerge from that metaphor. He
draws on other connotations of the metaphor, what Monroe Beardsley
would call lurking connotations,[17] which are not among the features one
would immediately associate with a ship but which one recognizes as true
when they are brought forward. After the long, slow description of the
construction of the ship and its staffing, Ezekiel simply takes the ship to
sea and sinks it in a single, sudden verse (v. 26). Immediately the sense
of the fragility of the ship dominates the connotations present to the
reader. The metaphoric schema through which the readers have been organizing their ideas of Tyre's wealth and power is itself reordered, so that
Tyre is seen to be vulnerable to sudden destruction even at the height
of its power. Ezekiel's rather risky rhetorical strategy seems worthwhile,
since the more one has become committed to the metaphor initially, the
more powerful is the reordering of its connotations.

Here, too, as in chapter 26, there is an ironic note in the way references are made to the phrase so closely associated with Tyre, "in the

---

16. There is general agreement that the prosaic list of those who traded with Tyre in
vv. 12–25 is secondary. Opinion is sharply divided as to the originality of vv. 9–11. The occurrence of "Tyre" in 8b is probably an error. See the commentaries *ad loc.*

17. "The Metaphorical Twist," *On Metaphor*, 113.

heart of the seas." It is first mentioned in describing the situation of Tyre in verse 4 and [[158]] recurs again in verse 26 when the destruction of the ship takes place, when "the east wind broke you in the heart of the seas." In the lament of the onlookers which concludes the oracle, the mourners ask, "Who was like Tyre in the midst of the sea?" (v. 32)[18] but say that "now she has been destroyed from the (high) seas in the depths of the waters" (v. 34). Through their related imagery the oracles in chapters 26 and 27 form a sort of diptych. The sea, the element from which Tyre drew its power and protection, is made the metaphor of Yahweh's judgment, slow but inevitable in the image of eroding waves, sudden and unexpected in the storm at sea.

As the first two oracles form a pair through their related imagery, so the latter two, 28:1–10 and 11–19, are connected by a common redactional conclusion, by being addressed to the ruler of Tyre, and by sharing similar mythological allusions. The third oracle (28:1–10), however, forms a bridge between the two pairs in that it too develops its metaphorical imagery from a reflection on Tyre's island location. The oracle begins with Ezekiel attributing an assertion of divinity to the prince of Tyre: "Your heart has grown proud and you have said, ' ʾēl ʾănî.' " The translation of that boast has been debated for some time: Should one understand 'I am a god' or 'I am El'. In Hebrew, of course, the word is ambiguous, and it is quite possible that Ezekiel is using the implications of both meanings in the oracle. Most of the oracle is concerned with a somewhat sarcastic argument about the divinity or mortality of the king of Tyre, suggesting the general appellative meaning. But since Ezekiel never uses the word ʾēl outside of this oracle, the reader naturally thinks of the proper name El as well. The critical statement is in the following phrase, however, when the king's reason for claiming divinity is apparently given. "I am a god/El; I live in a divine dwelling (*môšab ʾĕlōhîm*) in the heart of the seas." Marvin Pope has argued, correctly I think, that the geographical location of Tyre "in the heart of the seas" is being implicitly likened to El's dwelling place "at the springs of the (two) rivers, midst the channels of the (two) deeps."[19] Drawing attention to the physical similarity of the human city and the god's dwelling, the metaphor crystallizes an inchoate sense that there were ways in which Tyre's island location did

18. Reading *nidmāh* 'to be like', instead of MT *kĕdumāh* 'like silence'.
19. *El in the Ugaritic Texts*, VTS 2 (Leiden: E. J. Brill, 1955), 61, 98. It is not necessary to accept Pope's further suggestion of a deposed El in order to recognize here the rhetorical exploitation of a certain descriptive similarity on which to ground a metaphor. The references to the pit and to being "slain in the heart of the seas" in v. 8 do not refer to El but are part of the contrast between the prince's pretension to divinity and his real mortality. On the other hand those who would deny all allusion to El's abode in v. 2 are left with no basis for the reference to Tyre as a divine dwelling.

give it and its ruler at times an ⟦159⟧ almost superhuman exemption from the vicissitudes of ordinary political life as well as provide the conditions for its legendary wealth. Although verses 3–6 are probably secondary,[20] their concession that the king of Tyre is extraordinary in wealth, power, and splendor may give insight, I think, into the anxiety of the Judean exiles that Tyre and the power on which it drew might be qualitatively different from and greater than their own.

Ezekiel's purpose, of course, is not to create a perception of Tyre as superhuman but to argue against it. Consequently, he adopts a very particular rhetorical strategy with respect to the metaphor he has devised. The metaphorical identification of Tyre with El's dwelling says something true about Tyre's situation only so long as one remembers the tension between the "is and the is not" of metaphor. Ezekiel reduces the metaphor to false absurdity by having the prince of Tyre announce as an apparently literal truth, "I am a god/El; I live in a divine dwelling in the heart of the seas." Ezekiel makes short work of the assertion by emphasizing in verse 7 the "is not" side of the underlying metaphor—that the prince is not literally divine (as Tyre is not literally the dwelling of El).

Ezekiel is not finished with the metaphor yet, however, but indulges in a play on words between *ḥll* ('to pierce, slay') and *ḥll* ('to profane, pollute').

> See, I am bringing against you violent men,
> the most ruthless of the nations.
> And they will draw their swords against
>   the splendor of your wisdom
> and *profane* your beauty (v. 7).

> They will send you down to the pit
> and you will die the death of the *slain*
>   in the heart of the seas (v. 8).

> Will you then say, "I am a god"
>   before those who kill you?
> You are a mortal and not a god/El
>   in the hands of those who *profane* you (v. 9).

Commentators often note that after "draw their swords" in verse 7 and "those who kill you" in verse 9 one expects the parallel forms to be from *ḥll* ('slay'), not *ḥll* ('profane'), and many emend the text accordingly.[21] But it is precisely the frustration of the reader's expectation of a form of the word *ḥll* 'to slay' that makes one attend to the implications of the

---

20. So Zimmerli, 75, and Wevers, 213, though one could take the verses as an "aside."
21. E.g., Zimmerli, 75, and Fohrer, 161, on the authority of the versions.

unexpected reference to pollution. Just as the prince claimed to be a god [[160]] because of his divine dwelling "in the heart of the seas," so Ezekiel promises him that he will be one who is "slain in the heart of the seas." Since the presence of a corpse in a holy place profanes it and makes it unsuitable for the indwelling presence of deity,[22] Ezekiel is wryly telling the pretentious king of Tyre that once he is killed there, Tyre will be defiled and no longer a suitable residence for a god. One could almost say that Ezekiel undermines the claims of the metaphor first by demythologizing it and then by exorcising it. Though his rhetoric may not seem exactly "fair," it is certainly effective.

Ezek 28:11–19, the fourth oracle in the collection and the second against the king of Tyre, is the most intriguing. Textual difficulties, obscurities, and elusive allusions make it equally the most frustrating. Though I cannot pretend to solve all of its enigmas, close attention to the use of metaphor in the passage does clarify some features and illumines the function of the piece. Each of the other three oracles has featured some metaphorical play with the island location of Tyre, but there does not seem to be any such reference in the fourth oracle. Its connection with the other three depends more on its very close relationship with the oracle immediately preceding, 28:1–10. In addition to the connecting features mentioned above, there are a number of significant words and phrases that occur in both oracles: *gābāh lēb* (to be proud of heart, vv. 2, 17), *ḥokmāh* (wisdom, vv. 4, 12), *yŏpî* (beauty, vv. 7, 12), and *rĕkullāh* (trade, vv. 5, 16). Finally, there are related but contrasting images that form the basis for each oracle—the abode of El and the holy mountain of Yahweh. In the former oracle the extravagant claims of the prince of Tyre are reduced to nonsense and dismissed. In the latter a special status legitimately belonging to the king of Tyre is tragically lost.

What has attracted the most attention in the critical study of the fourth oracle against Tyre are the mythological materials used there, and various attempts have been made to show that Ezekiel presents here an ancient alternative version of the narrative of Genesis 2–3.[23] While there are undoubtedly mythological *allusions* in these verses, one cannot assume that Ezekiel is simply telling a well defined ancient myth. It seems more likely that Ezekiel is using such allusions, as he uses other materials, to create his own fictive situations for his own rhetorical purposes.

There seems to be no doubt that Ezekiel has chosen to represent the king of Tyre as an "Adamic" figure. Not only the explicit reference to "Eden, the garden of God" in verse 13 makes one think this, but also the

---

22. See Ezek 6:4–5; 2 Kgs 23:15–20.

23. The literature is conveniently reviewed in A. J. Williams, "The Mythological Background of Ezekiel 28:12–19?" *BTB* 6 (1976), 49–61.

[[161]] references to "the day you were created" (v. 13), the appearance of the guardian cherub (vv. 14, 16), and the motif of sin and expulsion (vv. 15–17). Before one tries to account for the details in which Ezek 28:11–19 differs from Genesis 2–3, it is worth inquiring how presenting the king of Tyre metaphorically as a figure like Adam affects Ezekiel's analysis of the situation of Tyre. How does it reorganize the reader's perceptions?

Perhaps the most obvious difference from the effect of the metaphors used in the preceding oracles is that another relationship between Yahweh and the king of Tyre is suggested besides that of simple enmity. In the previous oracles Ezekiel had countered the notion of Tyre's strength and invulnerability by undermining various ways in which Tyre's power might be imaged. Precisely by their argumentative quality, however, these oracles imply that Tyre's strength was theologically problematic. The imagery of the present oracle, however, goes beyond a claim of Yahweh's ability to break Tyre's power to assert that in some way Yahweh is the creator of all the advantages which Tyre possesses. It is not the sea that gives Tyre its access to wealth and magnificence and its special protection from foreign attack. Its paradisiacal situation is rather Yahweh's gift, imaged through the jewelled garment (v. 13) and the protecting cherub (v. 14). In this way the inescapable reality of Tyre's wealth and strength could be fully acknowledged and yet incorporated into a perception of the world which made that acknowledgement nonthreatening. The second advantage of the Adamic myth is that its plot provides for the guilt and punishment of the one who was once so favored. In this way the Adamic metaphor supplies a constellation of relationships very suggestive for what Ezekiel wishes to imply about Tyre's past and present situation and its coming fate.

There are a number of details in the oracle which do not seem dependent on a narrative of the first human beings as we have it from Genesis 2–3. Rather than postulate some variant form of the myth of which this oracle is the only surviving evidence, it seems better to suggest that Ezekiel, in his creative freedom, is exploiting a second, independent set of associations derived from the holy mountain / garden of God which have no direct relation to the Adamic myth. In Ezekiel, as in Israelite tradition in general, the mythic language of the mountain of God and the paradise garden is frequently used to describe Mount Zion and the temple.[24] The identification of Zion as Yahweh's cosmic mountain is

---

24. See the lengthy discussion in J. Levenson, "The Mountain of Ezekiel's Vision as Mount Zion," 7–24, and "The Mountain of Ezekiel's Vision as the Garden of Eden," 25–36, in *Theology of the Program of Restoration of Ezekiel 40–48*. See also Kalman Yaron, "The Dirge over the King of Tyre," *ASTI* 3:40–45 (1964).

particularly clear in [[162]] Ps 48:1–3: "Great is Yahweh and greatly to be praised, in the city of our God, His holy mountain. Beautiful in height, joy of all the earth, Mount Zion, the far reaches of Zaphon, city of the great king." Moreover, in the call vision of Isaiah the temple is assimilated to the place of the divine assembly on the cosmic mountain. In Ezekiel, too, Zion is alluded to as "my holy mountain" (20:40) and Jerusalem is called "the navel of the earth" (38:12). Like the garden of God, the temple is a place of paradisiacal abundance and the source of life-giving waters (Ps 36:9–10; Gen 2:6–10). The association of the river which rose in Eden with a river whose source is in the temple (cf. Ps 46:5–6; Zech 14:8; Joel 4:18) is particularly prominent in Ezekiel's vision of the restored temple (47:1–12). There the river which rises in the temple turns the waters of the Dead Sea fresh, supporting huge numbers of different kinds of fish and nurturing on its banks miraculous fruit trees, "whose leaves shall not wither nor shall their fruit fail. Every month they shall bear first-fruits, because the water for them flows from the sanctuary" (v. 12).

If the mountain/garden of God can suggest the temple, then there is another set of associations which can be applied to the figure in the oracles. He may be seen as a priest of the sanctuary. In suggesting this, one does not have to assume that there was a myth in which the first human being was a priest. Nor is it necessary to look for evidence that the kings of Tyre had priestly responsibilities. One need assume nothing more than that Ezekiel chose to exploit two parallel lines of imagery suggested by the mountain/garden of God: Eden/Adam and temple/priest. There is abundant evidence that Ezekiel did intend to present the figure in the garden as a priest. The statement in 28:13 that "of every precious stone was your *garment*"[25] evokes the image of the high priestly ephod with its rows of precious stones (Exodus 28). The list of gems which follows is without question drawn from the list of gems in Exodus 28. Even if the list is secondary, as many scholars think,[26] it at least indicates that an early audience identified the allusion as priestly. The end of verse 13 is difficult, but there appear to be references to gold work and to technical terms drawn from the jeweller's vocabulary which recall the gold filigree and engraving mentioned in Exodus 28.[27]

The mention of the cherub in Ezek 28:14 and 16 provides a point of connection between the imagery of Eden and of the temple. Here again

---

25. Heb. *měsukāh*. The most thorough recent discussion of the problematic words in this passage is to be found in Zimmerli's commentary.

26. Zimmerli, 82; Fohrer, 161; Wevers, 216.

27. See Zimmerli, 85.

there are textual difficulties,[28] but the cherub's function is evidently to
⟦163⟧ protect the garden and its occupant and later to expel him, much
as the cherub functions in Gen 3:24. One of the words describing the
cherub, however, *hassōkēk* 'shielding, covering, protecting' is a form of
the word regularly used to describe the wings of the cherubim which
cover the ark in the tabernacle and the temple (Exod 25:20; 37:9; 1 Kgs
8:7; 1 Chr 28:18). Such allusive and double functioning language aids
Ezekiel in keeping both frames of reference, Eden and temple, before
the reader.

Finally, the use of the language of pollution in connection with the
sin of the king suggests a priestly context. The accusation, "you profaned
your sanctuary" (v. 18), can scarcely be a comment on the literal level.
It could not be a matter of concern whether the pagan temples of Tyre
were defiled or not. This statement rather belongs to the metaphorical
conceit of the holy mountain/divine sanctuary and the king of Tyre as its
priest. The punishment of the king is similarly expressed in the language
of pollution, literally, "I defiled you from the mountain of God" (v. 16),
undoubtedly elliptical for "I expelled you as a defiled thing from the
mountain of God."

One has to keep a strong hold on the metaphorical quality of the
language. The image is a shocking one and perhaps intentionally provocative. Tyre was not, of course, literally the holy mountain/garden of
Yahweh, nor was the king of Tyre in any literal sense a priest of Yahweh;
but Ezekiel includes sufficient allusions to priestly vocabulary to make
one see the king *as* a priest in this fictive scene. The question, then, is
how one's perception of Tyre and its king are subtly reoriented by means
of the metaphor. One result is that the sense of Tyre's privileged position
is emphasized and seen as a blessedness which comes from the special in-
timacy with God which a priest experiences. But this much is accomplished by the "Adamic" metaphor. The priestly overtones of the oracle
are more important, I think, in reorienting one's understanding of the
nature of Tyre's sin. What the metaphor accomplishes is to take the political order and to reorganize it according to the schema of the sacral
order. A political action (whether the opposition of Tyre to Babylon or
its corruption through trade) is seen as a defilement of what is holy. The
significance of this reorientation can only be appreciated if one keeps in
mind how central the concept of Yahweh's holiness is to Ezekiel.[29] There

28. Two widely accepted emendations are to repoint the MT in agreement with the
versions, reading *ʾet-kěrûb* 'with a cherub', rather than *ʾat-kěrûb* 'you were a cherub', and to
delete the conjunction before the verb, reading 'with the . . . guardian cherub I placed
you'. One word, *mimšaḥ*, remains without convincing explanation.

29. It dominates, for example, Ezekiel's recounting of the history of Israel in chap. 20.

is one other way in which the sanctuary metaphor in chapter 28 may function, namely to underscore the certainty of Tyre's destruction. In the ⟦164⟧ long vision report in chapters 8–11 Ezekiel had detailed the way in which the profanation of the temple in Jerusalem had provoked Yahweh to leave the temple and to destroy both temple and city. If, as seems likely, the oracle against Tyre in 28:11–19 was announced after the destruction of Jerusalem, the exilic audience would have known from their own tragic experience that judgment against those who profaned Yahweh's holiness was not an empty word.

As this study of Ezekiel's oracles against Tyre has attempted to show, the analysis of the rhetoric of metaphor is an essential part of critical exegetical method. While it certainly does not replace traditional historical-critical investigations, the study of literary technique and its effect on meaning can both challenge the results of those investigations and produce new insights into the material.[30] Reflecting closely on Ezekiel's metaphors suggests something even more important, however. No less than the Tyrians and the Israelites, modern peoples perceive the realities of national power through metaphors, explicit and implicit. Ezekiel reminds one that it is a prophetic activity to define what these metaphors are, to subject them to critique, and to make new ones which can redescribe reality in a liberating manner.

---

30. See the important articles by Luis Alonso Schökel, "Die stilistiche Analyse bei den Propheten," *Congress Volume*, VTS 7 (Leiden: Brill, 1960), 154–64; and J. Cheryl Exum, "Of Broken Pots, Fluttering Birds and Visions in the Night: Extended Simile and Poetic Technique in Isaiah," *CBQ* 43:331–52 (1981) ⟦reprinted in *Beyond Form Criticism: Essays in Old Testament Literary Criticism* (ed. P. R. House; SBTS 2; Winona Lake, Ind.: Eisenbrauns, 1992), 349–72⟧.

Dialogue between Prophet and Audience as a Rhetorical Device in the Book of Jeremiah

JOHN T. WILLIS

〚63〛 In Jack Lundbom's study of Hebrew rhetoric in the book of Jeremiah, he declared that the two controlling structures both for the whole book and for the poems of Jeremiah were inclusio and chiasmus. He claimed that Jeremiah probably learned these structural patterns in the Jerusalem temple from the rhetorical tradition of Deuteronomy, and that his audiences were already quite familiar with them from frequent exposure to the same source.[1] The existence of these structures suggests a literary coherence in the book of Jeremiah, at least in portions of this prophetic work.

The purpose of the present study is to emphasize the presence of a third factor which has a bearing on the structure of the book of Jeremiah, a rhetorical device appearing with some degree of regularity in the book, namely, dialogue, in particular, dialogue between the prophet and his audience; and to stress that it should be taken into consideration in studying the structure of this book. Dialogue is a well established literary form throughout the Old Testament, both in prose narrative contexts (e.g., Abraham's dialogue with Yahweh over the impending fate of Sodom and Gomorrah, Gen 18:22–33; or the dialogue between the ten spies, Joshua and Caleb, and the Israelites after the twelve spies had trekked through the land of Canaan forty days, Num 13:25–14:10) and

Reprinted with permission from *Journal for the Study of the Old Testament* 33 (1985) 63–82.
    1. *Jeremiah: A Study in Ancient Hebrew Rhetoric* (SBLDS 18; Missoula: Scholars Press, 1975), 16–19, 23–24, 51, 113–14, 116.

in prose or poetic prophetic pericopes (e.g., the conversation between Isaiah and the leaders of Judah, Isa 28:7–13; or the discussion over Micah's lawsuit, Mic 6:1–8;[2] or virtually the entire book of Malachi).[3]

In Robert Gordis's efforts to interpret and elucidate the difficult problems in the book of Ecclesiastes, he has proposed that a fundamental key to understanding many of its enigmas is the [[64]] realization that the author frequently communicates his message by quoting a position which he considers to be erroneous, then responding to it by stating what he regards as the correct view.[4] Michael Fox has questioned the correctness of certain specifics of Gordis's suggestions, but agrees that this "quotation-countermand" pattern is indeed a viable explanation for the problems of this book.[5] Further, Burke Long has called attention to two types of question-answer schemata in the prophetic literature, especially in the book of Jeremiah.[6]

An examination of the book of Jeremiah reveals several contexts which present various viewpoints in dialogue form. There are dialogues between Yahweh and the prophet, as in the call narrative (1:4–19) and certain complaints of Jeremiah (12:1–6; 15:15–21); between Jeremiah and Judean leaders and groups, as the priests and prophets after the temple sermon (chap. 26), Hananiah the prophet (chap. 28), Shemaiah (29:24–32), Jeremiah's cousin Hanamel (32:6–8), the Rechabites (chap. 35), Irijah (37:1–15), Zedekiah (37:16–21; 38:14–28), Johanan and his

2. See J. T. Willis, "Review of *Micha 6,6–8. Studien zu Sprache, Form und Auslegung,* by Theodor Lescow," *VT* 18 (1968), 273–78.

3. See Egon Pfeiffer, "Die Disputationsworte in Buche Maleachi," *EvTh* 19 (1959), 546–68.

4. "Quotations in Wisdom Literature," *JQR* n.s. 30 (1939), 123–47; "Quotations as a Literary Usage in Biblical, Rabbinic and Oriental Literature," *HUCA* 22 (1949), 157–219; and *Koheleth—The Man and His World: A Study of Ecclesiastes* (3rd edn; New York: Schocken Books, 1968), "XII. The Style—His Use of Quotations," 95–108. Gordis has also dealt with this phenomenon in the book of Job, the Dead Sea Scrolls, and other ancient Oriental literature. See his *The Book of God and Man—A Study of Job* (Chicago: University of Chicago Press, 1965), "XIII. The Use of Quotations in Job," 174–87; *The Book of Job: Commentary, New Translation and Special Studies* (New York: The Jewish Theological Seminary of America, 1978), "17. On 21.17–33. The Use of Quotations in Argument," 529–30; "21. On 27.7–10, Job's Former Faith," 535; "29. Elihu's Apology (Chapter 32)," 553–54; and "Virtual Quotations in Job, Sumer and Qumran," *VT* 31 (1981), 410–27.

5. "The Identification of Quotations in Biblical Literature," *ZAW* 92 (1980), 416–31.

6. "Two Question and Answer Schemata in the Prophets," *JBL* 90 (1971), 129–39. See further William J. Horwitz, "Audience Reaction in Jeremiah," *CBQ* 32 (1970), 555–64 (who deals with passages in the latter half of the book, as 26:8–9; 32:3–5; 36:29; 38:4; 42:2–6, 20; 44:15–19; and only texts which specifically identify the respondents); Walter Brueggemann, "Jeremiah's Use of Rhetorical Questions," *JBL* 92 (1973), 358–74 (whose primary concern is possible Wisdom influence on rhetorical questions in the book of Jeremiah); and Thomas W. Overholt, "Jeremiah 2 and the Problem of 'Audience Reaction,'" *CBQ* 41 (1979), 262–73.

followers (42:1–43:7), and the Jews who fled to Egypt after Gedaliah had been murdered (chap. 44); and between individuals and groups other than Yahweh or Jeremiah, as Micaiah the son of Gemariah and the princes under Jehoiakim and Baruch (36:11–19), Zedekiah and some of his princes (38:1–6), and Gedaliah and Johanan and his followers (40:13–16). Sometimes Yahweh is pictured as anticipating a dialogue between Jeremiah and the people (5:18–19; 13:12–14; 16:10–13), or between the nations (22:8–9), in which he sets forth differing views by using quotations. And frequently the book of Jeremiah presents the beliefs or actions of the Jewish leaders or people or foreign nations as words which they themselves are speaking (17:15; 18:12, 18; 23:17; 27:9; 29:15; 31:29; 32:3–5; 33:24; 45:3; 48:14; 50:7).

Instances of dialogue between the prophet and his audiences would be quite appropriate in a book in which so many other types of dialogue are in evidence. The present paper calls attention to six examples of this phenomenon, all in the first twenty chapters of the book of Jeremiah. In some cases, the alternating speakers are identified by an introductory formula, while in others they are determined by linguistic variations and context. The present writer's understanding of the speaker(s) in each verse, group of verses, or portions of a verse is indicated along with the biblical text (usually following the RSV) by parentheses at the beginning of each section or by italics when the speaker(s) is identified in the text itself.

Jeremiah 3:21–4:4 [65]

(The prophet)[7]   3:21   A voice on the bare heights is heard,
the weeping and pleading of Israel's sons,
because they have perverted their way,
they have forgotten the Lord their God.

(Yahweh)   3:22   Return, O faithless sons,
I will heal your faithlessness.

(The people)   Behold, *we* come to thee;
for thou art the Lord *our* God.

    3:23   Truly the hills are a delusion,
the orgies on the mountains.
Truly in the Lord *our* God
is the salvation of Israel.

7. Since "the Lord their God" is named in the third person, it is likely that the prophet is the speaker. However, it also possible that Yahweh himself is the speaker, and that he refers to himself in the third person to emphasize the gravity of the situation.

3:24   But from *our* youth the shameful thing has
          devoured
       all for which *our* fathers labored—
       their flocks and their herds,
       their sons and their daughters.

3:25   Let *us* lie down in *our* shame,
          and let *our* dishonor cover *us*;
       for *we* have sinned against the Lord *our* God,
          we and *our* fathers,
       from *our* youth even to this day
       we have not obeyed the voice of the Lord
          our God.[8]

(The prophet on   4:1   If you return, O Israel, *says the Lord*,
behalf of Yahweh)   to *me* you should return.
                              If you remove your abominations from *my*
                                 presence,
                                 and do not waver,

                       4:2   and if you swear, "As the Lord lives,"
                                 in truth, in justice, and in uprightness,
                              then nations will be blessed by him[9]
                                 and in him shall they glory.

                       4:3   For *thus says the Lord* to the men of Judah
                                 and to the inhabitants of Jerusalem:
                              Break up your fallow ground,
                                 and sow not among thorns.

                       4:4   Circumcise yourselves to the Lord,
                                 remove the foreskin of you hearts,
                              O men of Judah and inhabitants of
                                 Jerusalem; [[66]]
                              lest *my* wrath go forth like fire,
                                 and burn with none to quench it,
                              because of the evil of your doings.

8. There is much discussion over the originality of portions of vv. 24–25, and over whether these lines are "poetry" or "prose." The RSV prints them as prose, but the NEB, JB, and NIV print them as poetry. The sharp distinction between biblical "poetry" and "prose" is being discussed at length at the present time. See James L. Kugel, *The Idea of Biblical Poetry: Parallelism and Its History* (New Haven: Yale University, 1981), 56–95. The rendering here follows the NIV essentially.

9. The question of whether the hitpaᶜel of ברך [['bless']] has a passive or a reflexive nuance is widely debated. For the reflexive understanding, see E. A. Speiser, *Genesis* (AB; Garden City: Doubleday, 1964), 86. For the passive interpretation, see Gerhard von Rad, *Genesis* (OTL; Philadelphia: Westminster, 1966), 156. The passive rendering adopted here follows the NIV. The RSV has 'then nations shall bless themselves in him'.

There is no agreement among scholars as to the extent of the pericope involving Jer 3:21–4:4. Some reduce it to 3:21–25,[10] while others expand it to as much as 3:1–5 + 3:19–4:4.[11] In the opinion of the present writer, J. P. Hyatt is probably correct in seeing 3:21 as the beginning, and in extending the pericope through 4:4.[12] Admittedly, there are points of contact with what precedes (as "sons" in 3:19 and 21, 22; שוב [['return']] in 3:1 [twice] and 22; 4:1 [twice]; etc.) and with what follows ("Judah and Jerusalem" in 4:3 and 5), but these appear to be redactional joins rather than integral parts of a common original pericope.

Of major concern for the present study is the nature of 3:22b–25 and its relationship to 4:1–4. Scholars have proposed three positions. First, in 3:22b–25 Jeremiah is envisioning events in the future which he thinks or hopes will occur, and describing them as if they were present. Hyatt thinks that these are words which the Israelites *should* say as they acknowledge their sin and return to Yahweh.[13] Volz believes that Jeremiah is motivated by the tendencies of his fellow-Jews to repentance, and relates to them a vision which he had in which they forsook their idolatry and returned to Yahweh, in order to encourage them to do so.[14] Harrison believes that in 3:21–25 the prophet is voicing what Judah will learn in the Babylonian captivity, namely, that man cannot serve Yahweh and Baal. Then in 4:1–2 Yahweh expresses his concern that Israel's repentance be

---

10. So A. W. Streane, *The Book of the Prophet Jeremiah, Together with the Lamentations* (The Cambridge Bible for Schools; Cambridge University Press, 1882), 32–33; and Friedrich Nötscher, *Das Buch Jeremias übersetzt und erklärt* (Die Heilige Schrift des Alten Testamentes 7/2; Bonn: Peter Hanstein, 1934), 55–56.

11. So Carl H. Cornill, *Das Buch Jeremia* (Leipzig: Tauchnitz, 1905), 42; Paul Volz, *Der Prophet Jeremia übersetzt und erklärt* (KAT 10; 2nd edn; Leipzig: A. Deichert, 1928), 35; and Guy P. Couturier, "Jeremiah," *The Jerome Biblical Commentary*, I (Englewood Cliffs: Prentice-Hall, 1968), 307. This is not the place to engage in a lengthy discussion of the various views which have been proposed and the arguments on which they are based. Here five other additional analyses are recorded for purposes of illustration. The pericope covers: (1) 3:1–5 + 19–25: Wilhelm Rudolph, *Jeremiah* (HAT 12; 3rd edn; Tübingen: J. C. B. Mohr [Paul Siebeck], 1968), 29–32; (2) 3:1–5 + 12b–14a + 19–25: William L. Holladay, *The Architecture of Jeremiah 1–20* (Lewisburg: Bucknell University, 1976), 51–52; (3) 3:19–4:2: F. Giesebrecht, *Das Buch Jeremia übersetzt und erklärt* (HKAT 3/2; 2nd edn; Göttingen: Vandenhoeck & Ruprecht, 1907), 14–17; (4) 3:21–4:2; Artur Weiser, *Das Buch Jeremia übersetzt und erklärt* (ATD 20/21; 5th edn; Göttingen: Vandenhoeck & Ruprecht, 1966), 32; (5) 3:19–4:4: Arthur S. Peake, *Jeremiah I* (The Century Bible; Edinburgh: T. C. & E. C. Jack, 1910), 112; H. Cunliffe-Jones, *The Book of Jeremiah: Introduction and Commentary* (Torch Bible Commentaries; London: SCM, 1960), 62–64; John Paterson, "Jeremiah," *Peake's Commentary on the Bible* (London: Thomas Nelson and Sons, 1962), 543.

12. "The Book of Jeremiah (Introduction and Exegesis)," *IB* V (Nashville: Abingdon, 1956), 829–30.

13. Ibid., 830.

14. *Der Prophet Jeremia*, 38–39.

genuine and lasting. These verses show that the situation envisioned in 3:21–25 was a prospect rather than a reality.[15] According to this view, the protasis of the lines beginning in 4:1 indicates that Jeremiah is thinking of the future. Second, in 3:22b–25 either the people themselves actually repent sincerely, or Jeremiah intercedes in their behalf by putting sincere words of repentance in their mouth. Then, in 4:1–2 (or 4) Yahweh assures them that he will restore them as they return to him with their whole heart.[16] But, third, it seems most likely that 3:22b–25 contains an insincere mouthing of repentance designed to avert the calamities which prophets like Jeremiah had been announcing and which recent international (and possibly natural) occurrences seemed to forewarn. These words sound staid and memorized, and probably reflect a repentance liturgy which was often stated or sung in the Jerusalem cult.[17] Further, they betray a concept of public [[67]] worship which assumes it is designed, at least in part, to attempt to soothe or appease God's anger by praising him and promising to serve him with overly extravagant expressions. Then 4:1–4 is a rejection of this insincerity, and at the same time a call for genuine repentance, stated explicitly in the terms "in truth" (v. 2), "break up your fallow ground" (v. 3), and "circumcise your hearts" (v. 4).

Jeremiah 5:12–17

(The prophet addressing the people concerning themselves, but under the guise of another group)

5:12 *They* (the people) have spoken falsely of the Lord and have said,
"He will do nothing;[18]
no evil will come upon *us,*
nor shall *we* see sword or famine.

---

15. Roland K. Harrison, *Jeremiah and Lamentations: An Introduction and Commentary* (The Tyndale Old Testament Commentaries; Downers Grove, Ill.: Inter-Varsity, 1975), 67–68.

16. Paterson, "Jeremiah," 543; Weiser, *Das Buch Jeremia,* 32–33.

17. See Paterson, "Jeremiah," 543; John Bright, *Jeremiah* (AB 21; Garden City: Doubleday, 1965), 25; Weiser, *Das Buch Jeremia,* 33.

18. The meaning of לא הוא (a hapax legomenon in the OT) is disputed. Edmund F. Sutcliffe ("A Note on לא הוא Jer 5,12," *Bib* 41 [1960], 287–90) thinks הוא is to be interpreted as a neuter (in light of 1QH 4:18 in the Qumran texts and the LXX), referring in general terms to the enunciation of God's threat of punishment. The positive form of this statement, then, occurs in 2 Kgs 15:12. Thus one should translate:
Not so! Evil will not come upon us,
neither shall we see sword or famine.
However, it seems best to take הוא as a masculine, and to read 'he (Yahweh) does not do it' (so Cornill, *Das Buch Jeremia,* 60), or 'he (Yahweh) will do nothing' (so the NIV).

5:13 The (true) prophets will become wind;
    the word is not in them.
      Thus shall it be done to them."
5:14 Therefore thus says the Lord, the God of
    Hosts:
    "Because they[19] (the people) have spoken
    this word,
    behold, I am making my words in your
    (Jeremiah's) mouth a fire, and this people
    wood,
    and the fire shall devour them.
5:15 Behold, *I* am bringing upon you a nation
    from afar,

(The prophet in
behalf of Yahweh)

    O house of Israel, *says the Lord.*
    It is an enduring nation,
    it is an ancient nation,
    a nation whose language you do not know,
    nor can you understand what they say.
5:16 Their quiver is like an open tomb,
    they are all mighty men.
5:17 They shall eat up your harvest and your
    food;
    they shall eat up your sons and your
    daughters;
    they shall eat up your flocks and your herds;
    they shall eat up your vines and your fig
    trees;
    your fortified cities in which you trust
    they shall destroy with the sword."

[68] The extent of the pericopes in Jeremiah 5 is very difficult to determine. With regard to vv. 12–17, Rudolph is the exception in making a division between vv. 13 and 14.[20] "This word" in v. 14 apparently refers back to vv. 12–13. The two most common views are to separate vv. 15–17

19. The MT reads 'you'. However, if v. 14 is the prophet's report of Yahweh's instructions to him concerning the feelings of the people expressed in vv. 12–13, as "therefore" at the beginning of v. 14 and the flow of thought suggest, it is very difficult, if not impossible, to determine whom Yahweh might be addressing directly here. 'You' could hardly refer to the people, as the prophet is speaking *about* them in vv. 12–13, and in v. 14. It can scarcely mean Jeremiah and his companions, because Yahweh is condemning those being described in v. 15b. Therefore, it is best to emend the MT to 'they' (with most scholars).

20. *Jeremia,* 39.

from what precedes,[21] or to regard vv. 10–19 as a separate pericope.[22] For the reasons given below, it seems best to follow Weiser and Couturier in considering vv. 12–17 as a separate pericope.[23]

There is a problem of identifying the speakers and of following the line of thought in this passage. Assuming that at least vv. 12–14 belong to the same pericope, five interpretations have been proposed. (1) Verse 12 contains the words of false prophets, who declare that Yahweh will not bring calamity on his people, then vv. 13–14 record Jeremiah's response condemning this view and announcing impending punishment (cf. 14:13–16; 23:16–17).[24] In this case, however, Jeremiah's response has no introduction like the words of the false prophets in v. 12, or like the words of Yahweh in v. 14. (2) The speaker in vv. 12–14 is Yahweh, who first quotes in his own words the view of the people that he is not active in his world (vv. 12b–13), then gives his reply in v. 14.[25] But it is not natural for Yahweh to refer to himself in the third person in v. 12. (3) The people are the speakers in vv. 12b–13, and Yahweh gives his response in v. 14.[26] However, this does not explain the introductory formula in v. 12a. (4) 5:12 + 14 originally formed the pericope, which consisted of two parts: a reason and an announcement of punishment. "This word" of v. 14 refers back to the announcement in v. 12, not to v. 13. Verse 13 belongs after v. 14 as the continuation of the announcement of doom on the false prophets. A redactor wrongly placed this verse between vv. 12 and 14. "The prophets" in v. 13 must be the false prophets, since this is the meaning of the phrase elsewhere in the book of Jeremiah.[27] (5) The suggestion of the present study is based on adherence to the MT, and views vv. 12–17 as a coherent pericope. Accordingly, the prophet is the speaker for Yahweh in the formulas found in vv. 12a, 14a, and at the end of 15a. He uses the third person plural in v. 12a to draw his present hearers into his snare by calling their attention

---

21. So Giesebrecht, *Das Buch Jeremia*, 30; Volz, *Der Prophet Jeremia*, 59, 63–65; Nötscher, *Das Buch Jeremias*, 68; Hyatt, "The Book of Jeremiah," 848–50; Cunliffe-Jones, *The Book of Jeremiah*, 70–71; and Bright, *Jeremiah*, 36–37, 42.

22. So Peake, *Jeremiah*, I, 126; Paterson, "Jeremiah," 544; and Harrison, *Jeremiah and Lamentations*, 76–77. Very similarly Streane (*The Book of the Prophet Jeremiah*, 47–48) thinks vv. 10–18 form a separate pericope because of the inclusio in vv. 10 and 18; and Holladay (*The Architecture of Jeremiah 1–20*, 63–64, 66) regards vv. 10–17 as a unit.

23. Weiser, *Das Buch Jeremia*, 47–48; Couturier, "Jeremiah," 308.

24. So Bright, *Jeremiah*, 40; Weiser, *Das Buch Jeremia*, 42, 47.

25. So Hyatt, "The Book of Jeremiah," 848–49.

26. So Cornill, *Das Buch Jeremia*, 60–61; Peake, *Jeremiah*, I, 130; Volz, *Der Prophet Jeremia*, 65; Harrison, *Jeremiah and Lamentations*, 76–77.

27. Giesebrecht, *Das Buch Jeremia*, 33–34; Georg Schmuttermayr, "Beobachtungen zu Jer 5,13," *BZ* n.s. 9 (1965), 215–32.

to the alleged position of some group whom he had recently heard or with whom he had had a conversation, as though his present audience would agree with him against their position. In v. 14, he related Yahweh's commission to him (note the second person singular, "*your* mouth") concerning "this people" ("they" of vv. 12a and 14b). Only in v. 15 does ⟦69⟧ he spring the trap. Yahweh suddenly addresses his audience directly, at first individually (note the plural 'you' in 'I am bringing upon you'—עליכם), and then in the rest of the pericope, collectively in the second person singular, beginning with v. 15c. One is reminded of the skillful way in which the prophet Nathan drew King David into his trap by telling the story of the little ewe lamb (2 Sam 12:1–7), or how Isaiah maneuvered his hearers into a self-condemning stance with his parable of the vineyard (Isa 5:1–7).

Now if this analysis of Jer 5:12–17 is essentially correct, again the book of Jeremiah contains a (contrived) dialogue between Jeremiah and one of his audiences, in which the prophet refutes what he considers to be an erroneous and harmful belief of his fellow-Jews.

Jeremiah 8:13–17

(The prophet in behalf of Yahweh)	8:13	When I would gather them, *says the Lord,*
		    there are no grapes on the vine,
		        nor figs on the fig tree;
		    even the leaves are withered,
		        and what I gave them has passed away
		            from them.

(The people)	8:14	Why do *we* sit still?
		Gather together, let *us* go into the fortified
		    cities and perish there;
		for the Lord *our* God has doomed *us* to
		    perish,
		    and has given *us* poisoned water to drink,
		because *we* have sinned against the Lord.

	8:15	*We* looked for peace, but no good came, for a time of healing, but behold, terror.

(The prophet)	8:16	The snorting of their horses is heard from
		    Dan;
		    at the sound of the neighing of their
		        stallions the whole land quakes.
		They come and devour the land and all that
		    fills it,
		    the city and those who dwell in it.

> 8:17 For behold, I am sending among you
>   serpents,
>   adders which cannot be charmed,
>   and they shall bite you, *says the Lord.*

[[70]] It is almost universally agreed among scholars that one pericope ends at Jer 8:17, and another begins at 8:18. However, there is little agreement as to whether the first begins with v. 4,[28] 10,[29] 13,[30] or 14.[31] In my opinion, the most likely beginning is v. 13. Then the pericope would begin and end with נאם יהוה [['says the Lord']] (vv. 13, 17). Furthermore the root אסף [['gather']] connects vv. 13 and 14.

If this is the correct analysis, Jer 8:13–17 contains some sort of dialogue. Some scholars believe v. 14 contains the people's cry of distress which Jeremiah hears in his imagination.[32] Others think vv. 14–16 represent a soliloquy placed in the mouth of the people by the prophet to indicate their terror at the approaching invader.[33] It seems more likely, however, that the picture is that of a dialogue between the prophet (speaking in Yahweh's name) and the people. While several scholars suggest that the people are the speakers in v. 16,[34] it appears to be more in keeping with the flow of the context to take Yahweh as the speaker here.[35]

Accordingly, the pericope may be analyzed in this way. Yahweh begins by expressing his desire to have an intimate relationship with his people and bring them near him as a gleaner would gather grapes or figs, but he found this impossible because they had produced no fruit even though he had blessed them richly (v. 13). The implication clearly is that they are doomed to destruction. The people respond by encouraging each other to flee for safety to the fortified cities, since Yahweh had doomed them (vv. 14–15). Yahweh replies that the enemy is indeed approaching from the north (note "Dan" in v. 16), because he is sending

28. Giesebrecht, *Das Buch Jeremia,* 53; Harrison, *Jeremiah and Lamentations,* 88–90.

29. Paterson, "Jeremiah," 545.

30. Streane, *The Book of the Prophet Jeremiah,* 74–76; Peake, *Jeremiah,* I, 158; Nötscher, *Das Buch Jeremias,* 92–95; Bright, *Jeremiah,* 66; G. P. Couturier, "Jeremiah," 311; Rudolph, *Jeremia,* 63–65.

31. Cornill, *Das Buch Jeremia,* 118–23; Volz, *Der Prophet Jeremia,* 109–12; Hyatt, "The Book of Jeremiah," 882–85; Cunliffe-Jones, *The Book of Jeremiah,* 92–94; Weiser, *Das Buch Jeremia,* 70, 73–76.

32. Paterson, "Jeremiah," 545.

33. Bright, *Jeremiah,* 65.

34. Bright, *Jeremiah,* 65; Weiser, *Das Buch Jeremia,* 74–75.

35. Following Giesebrecht, *Das Buch Jeremia,* 56; Holladay, *The Architecture of Jeremiah 1–20,* 110.

him to punish his people for their sins; therefore, it is hopeless for the people to try to escape (vv. 16–17).

Jeremiah 8:18–23 ⟦8:18–9:1⟧

(The prophet)	8:18	*My* grief is beyond healing, *my* heart is sick within *me.*

	8:19	Hark, the cry of the daughter of *my* people
		    from the length and breadth of the
		        land:
		"Is the Lord not in Zion?
		    Is her King not in her?"

(Yahweh)		Why have they provoked *me* to anger with
		    their graven images,
		    and with their foreign idols?

(The people)	8:20	The harvest is past,
		    the summer is ended,
		    and *we* are not saved. ⟦71⟧

(The prophet)	8:21	For the wound of the daughter of *my* people is *my* heart wounded, *I* mourn, and dismay has taken hold on *me.*

	8:22	Is there no balm in Gilead?
		    Is there no physician there?
		Why then has the health of the daughter of
		    my people not been restored?

	8:23	O that *my* head were waters,
		    and *my* eyes a fountain of tears,
		that *I* might weep day and night for the
		        slain
		    of the daughter of *my* people.

Scholars are virtually unanimously agreed that the pericope which begins at 8:18 continues through 8:23. This passage contains several abrupt changes of speakers, a "kind of quick conversational interchange"[36] similar to that found in 6:4–5 and 6:16–17. Some believe that this is not a genuine dialogue, but arises from Jeremiah's imagination.[37] However, the sudden change of speakers and the liveliness of word exchange suggest at least a literary presentation of the kind of oral interaction which actually occurred during Jeremiah's career. Holladay's analysis

---

36. Holladay, *The Architecture of Jeremiah 1–20*, 111.
37. Paterson, "Jeremiah," 545–46.

seems to be correct: Jeremiah begins by expressing his grief over the sin and punishment of Judah, and by quoting the cry of the people that Yahweh is in Zion (vv. 18–19b). Yahweh declares that the Judeans have aroused his anger by turning away from him to idols (v. 19c). The people concur sadly, probably quoting a well-known proverbial statement, that even though Yahweh had given them ample opportunity, they had not returned to him (v. 20). Jeremiah immediately takes up the people's remorse, yearns for some means by which they could be healed, and declares that he will weep over them incessantly, in spite of their apparently irreversible condition (vv. 21–23).[38]

A pericope such as this reveals the manner in which dialogue can be used effectively in prophetic literature to indicate the beliefs and emotions of various personalities and groups involved in a conflict or crisis situation.

Jeremiah 14:1–10[39]

(A rehearsal of Yahweh's word to the prophet)

14:1 *The word of the Lord* which came to *Jeremiah* during the drought:

14:2 Judah mourns
and her gates languish; [[72]]
her people lament on the ground,
and the cry of Jerusalem goes up.

14:3–6 ... ...

(The people)

14:7 Though *our* iniquities testify against *us*,
act, O Lord, for thy name's sake;
for *our* backslidings are many,
we have sinned against thee.

14:8 O thou hope of Israel,
its savior in time of trouble,
why shouldst thou be like a stranger in the land,
like a wayfarer who turns aside to tarry for a night?

14:9 Why shouldst thou be like a man confused,
like a mighty man who cannot save?
Yet, thou, O Lord, art in the midst of *us*,
and *we* are called by thy name;
leave *us* not.

38. *The Architecture of Jeremiah 1–20*, 110–11.
39. It is not necessary for the purposes of this paper to print all of vv. 2–6.

(The prophet)
14:10 *Thus says the Lord* concerning this people:
They have loved to wander thus,
    they have not restrained their feet;
therefore the Lord does not accept them,
    now he will remember their iniquity
    and punish their sins.

Jeremiah 14:17–15:4

(Yahweh's in-
struction to
the prophet)
14:17 You (Jeremiah) shall say to them (the
    people) this word:
Let my eyes run down with tears night and
    day,
    and let them not cease,
for the virgin daughter of my people is
    smitten with a great wound,
    with a very grievous blow.
14:18 If I go out into the field,
    behold, those slain by the sword!
And if I enter the city,
    behold, the diseases of famine!
For both prophet and priest ply their trade
    through the land,
    and have no knowledge. ⟦73⟧

(The people)
14:19 Hast thou utterly rejected Judah?
    Does thy soul loathe Zion?
Why hast thou smitten *us*
    so that there is no healing for *us?*
We looked for peace, but no good came;
    for a time of healing, but behold, terror.
14:20 *We* acknowledge *our* wickedness, O Lord,
    and the iniquity of *our* fathers,
for *we* have sinned against thee.
14:21 Do not spurn *us*, for thy name's sake;
    do not dishonor thy glorious throne;
remember and do not break thy covenant
    with *us.*
14:22 Are there any among the false gods of the
    nations that can bring rain?
    Or can the heavens give showers?
Art thou not he, O Lord *our* God?

                                    We set *our* hope on thee,
                                    for thou doest all these things.

(The prophet's   15:1   *Then the Lord said to me,* Though Moses
rehearsal of   and Samuel stood before me, yet my heart
Yahweh's instruc-   would not turn toward this people. Send
tion to him)   them out of my sight, and let them go!

                        15:2   And when they ask you, "Where shall we
                                    go?"
                                You shall say to them, Thus says the Lord:
                                Those who are for pestilence, to pestilence,
                                    and those who are for the sword, to the
                                        sword;
                                those who are for famine, to famine.
                                and those who are for captivity, to
                                    captivity.

                        15:3   I will appoint over them four kinds of
                                destroyers, *says the Lord*: the sword to slay,
                                the dogs to tear, and the birds of the air and
                                the beasts of the earth to devour and
                                destroy.

                        15:4   And I will make them a horror to all the
                                kingdoms of the earth because of what
                                Manasseh the son of Hezekiah king of Judah
                                did in Jerusalem.[40]

Jer 14:1–10 and 14:17–15:4 are strikingly similar in form and content,
and should be examined together. Several scholars have correctly argued for the coherence of Jer 14:1–15:4[41] (or 15:9[42]). But this is a redactional unity, and thus does not necessarily indicate that this whole
section comes from the same occasion or even the ⟦74⟧ same time pe-

40. It is generally agreed that all of 15:1–4 except the second half of v. 2 is in "prose."
However, notice that there is balance of thought in much of the "prose" material in these
verses, as the two statements at the end of v. 1, or the four kinds of destroyers in the last half
of v. 3. On the problem of "poetry" and "prose," see n. 8 above.

41. Volz, *Der Prophet Jeremia,* 169; Hyatt, "The Book of Jeremiah," 929–37; Bright, *Jeremiah,* 103; Rudolph, *Jeremia,* 97–99; Martin Kessler, "From Drought to Exile: A Morphologi-
cal Study of Jer. 14.1–15.4," *SBLSP* 2 (1972), 519–23; G. R. Castellino, "Observations on the
Literary Structure of Some Passages in Jeremiah," *VT* 30 (1980), 406–407.

42. Cornill, *Das Buch Jeremia,* 181; Giesebrecht, *Das Buch Jeremia,* 84–88; Peake, *Jeremiah,*
I, 199–200; Albert Condamin, *Le Livre de Jérémie* (EBib; 3rd edn; Paris: Gabalda, 1936), 123–
30; Cunliffe-Jones, *The Book of Jeremiah,* 114–21; Paterson, "Jeremiah," 548; Weiser, *Das Buch
Jeremia,* 119–27; Couturier, "Jeremiah," 314–15; Holladay, *The Architecture of Jeremiah 1–20,*
145–46.

riod. As a matter of fact, the crisis of 14:17–15:4 apparently was decidedly more intense than that of 14:1–10. Whereas the problem in 14:1–6 is a drought, that in 14:18–19 and 15:2–3 is military invasion with its attendant devastations. It appears that the redactor of this section of the book or the whole book has arranged this material in a chiastic fashion:

A   14:1–10
B   14:11–16
A'   14:17–15:4

The first and last sections follow the same sequence: (1) Yahweh instructs Jeremiah to describe for his hearers the calamity to come upon them (14:1–6 and 17–18); (2) his hearers respond, confessing their sins and asking God for deliverance (14:7–9 and 19–22); (3) the Lord rejects their pleas because he sees they are insincere (14:10 and 15:1–4).

The most controversial aspect of this sequence has to do with the precise nature of the second part. (a) Some scholars take it as Jeremiah's intercession for the people, citing 14:11 and 15:1.[43] However, Yahweh's prohibition against the prophet interceding for the people and the reference to Moses and Samuel as intercessors for Israel do not necessarily refer to the controversial verses under consideration. They could be simply forthright instructions designed to emphasize that God's people had gone so long and so deep in sin that it was vain to pray for their deliverance in view of the present condition of their hearts. (b) Others regard these passages as the prophet's concept of the ideal confession which the people should make if they are to be accepted by God.[44] But the language appears to be stronger than what would be expected if one were suggesting to others what they should do. (c) Consequently, it seems best to understand 14:7–9 and 19–22 as a literary representation of the response of Jeremiah's hearers to what he had just said in Yahweh's name.[45] And yet, their words sound too precise and unfeeling to have originated in their heart. Instead, they have the appearance of confessional or lament liturgies which the people were taught in the Jerusalem temple on fast days.

43. So Peake, *Jeremiah*, I, 202 (yet on p. 205 he states that vv. 19–22 resume the prayer of the people in vv. 7–9); Weiser, *Das Buch Jeremia*, 126–28; Kessler, "From Drought to Exile," 504–505, 513; Harrison, *Jeremiah and Lamentations*, 101–102.

44. Hyatt, "The Book of Jeremiah," 931–32 (possibly on vv. 7–9); Bright, *Jeremiah*, 102 (possibly); Rudolph, *Jeremia*, 99 (possibly on vv. 7–9).

45. Cornill, *Das Buch Jeremia*, 183; Volz, *Der Prophet Jeremia*, 163, 167–68; Nötscher, *Das Buch Jeremias*, 125, 127; Hyatt, "The Book of Jeremiah," 931–92, 935 (possibly on vv. 7–9; certainly on 14:19–22); Paterson, "Jeremiah," 548; Bright, *Jeremiah*, 102 (possibly); Rudolph, *Jeremia*, 99, 102 (possibly on vv. 7–9; certainly on vv. 19–22); Lundbom, *Jeremiah*, 44.

In such a *Sitz im Leben*, it was expected that a priest or cult prophet would respond in Yahweh's name to the people's cries. This is precisely what occurs in 14:10 and 15:1–4, except that here Yahweh rejects their pleas because the lives of the people up to this time show [[75]] that they are persistently and consistently untrustworthy, insincere, and unstable;[46] whereas normally he would be expected to respond favorably.

Concluding Observations

The analysis of these six pericopes in Jeremiah 1–20 leads to certain conclusions which are important in understanding the structure and theology of Jeremiah the prophet and of the book of Jeremiah.

First, the dialogue form reflected in these texts suggests that sometimes Jeremiah actually engaged in dialogue with his audiences, that sometimes he used a dialogue style by putting words into the mouths of his opponents for the purpose of refuting their position, and that the redactor (or redactors) of this material portrayed that dialogue or created a dialogue as a form of his own as a means of defining clearly the distinction between what he wanted his readers to believe the view of Jeremiah to be in contrast to that which he opposed. The final redactor(s) of the book of Jeremiah used the dialogue method to communicate his message to his readers, whether this was handed down to him from actual confrontations during the ministry of Jeremiah, or was one of the literary styles he adopted to communicate his message. At the same time, the frequency of the use of dialogue in the book, and the impression of a lively, sharp, compactly juxtaposed oral exchange between conflicting parties which at least some of the texts make, strongly suggest that some literary representations of these dialogues reflect actual events in the life of the prophet.[47]

---

46. See Cornill, *Das Buch Jeremia*, 183; Volz, *Der Prophet Jeremia*, 164–65; Nötscher, *Das Buch Jeremias*, 125.

47. Overholt ("Jeremiah 2 and the Problem of 'Audience Reaction,' " 253) is certainly correct when he suggests that "on the basis of his experience Jeremiah may have selected from, altered, even created 'audience reactions' to serve as foils for his indictment of the people." The problem is that it is extremely difficult to determine with certainty in each text which of these alternatives is correct. For example, Overholt (pp. 267–68) assumes that if a statement of the audience contains stereotyped material (as "Where is Yahweh?" in 2:6, 8), the audience could not have spoken these words in reality, so they must have been put in the mouths of the audience by the prophet (or the redactor). However, even this is not absolutely certain, because when the beliefs or practices of a person or group are being challenged or reproved, it is natural for them to try to defend themselves by turning to traditional, widely-accepted statements which sum up their viewpoint in succinct proverbial or conventional language. See the helpful remarks of W. Brueggemann ("Jeremiah's Use of Rhetorical Questions," 361–64), especially concerning 8:18–23 and 14:19–22.

Second, the positions of Jeremiah's audiences reflected in those passages which present them in the form of quotation provide important insights into the thinking of the Jewish leaders and masses in Jeremiah's day and the day of the redactor(s) of the book of Jeremiah. There would be no reason for the prophet or the redactor(s) of the book which bears his name to misrepresent the views of his hearers deliberately; and it is hardly likely that the prophet or a redactor would have thought he could gain the respect and confidence of hearers or readers by such practices.

An understanding of the beliefs of the audience of Jeremiah is an important aid to comprehending the message of the prophet and of the school which preserved his work, as it stood over against that of the speakers being opposed.

[[76]] Third, the words of the two or more speakers in a dialogue situation should not be isolated into separate pericopes, even if they contain a complete thought unit in themselves (as, e.g., the words of the people in 3:22b–25; 14:7–9, 19–22). Rather, the pericope includes everything within the dialogue. This usually consists of three parts: (a) a proclamation by Yahweh or the prophet, which moves the hearers to some type of reaction; (b) the response of the hearers; and (c) the counter-response of Yahweh or the prophet to the hearers' position. But it may contain as few as two parts (corresponding to items [b] and [c] here), or more than three parts (when the interchange continues through several responses and counter-responses).

Fourth, the theology of Jeremiah, or of any prophet, or of the Old Testament usually should not include the views reflected in response sections of a dialogue pericope, although sometimes these views may be the norm except for the particular (kind of) circumstance reflected in the immediate context and/or except for the way in which the hearers are interpreting or applying them, and sometimes they confirm or emphasize the view of the prophetic spokesman (as, e.g., when the princes and the people contended that Jeremiah's message was not a justifiable cause to put him to death, Jer 26:16–19). To be specific, the confession and plea for help in 14:7–9 does not represent the thought of Jeremiah. It contains several thoughts which sound tantalizingly "religious" and very conducive to a highly spiritual climate, and which might even be acceptable to Jeremiah under different circumstances. But v. 10 shows that it is rejected and denounced *in this context*, either because it suggests a naive mind-set that man's return to God is quick and simple, or because the people who are speaking are insincere and have little intention of changing their hearts and lives, as their long-established life styles have made clear, or because their purpose is not to express genuine sorrow to God for the way they have treated him by their ingratitude and disobedience, but to terminate the drought which is making their lives unbearable and possibly threatening their ability to survive. The fact that these words are probably an oft-used confession- or lament-liturgy common in the Jerusalem cult on a fast day or day of repentance lends itself to the possibility that the speakers are merely mouthing words which they know religious leaders and their followers consider to be acceptable to Yahweh in the ritual. Hence, while these verses may be said to represent the widely held theology of Judeans [[77]] in the days of Jeremiah, they do not represent the prophet's theology, and thus cannot be used as a source for determining the theology commended by the Old Testament in the context of the book of Jeremiah.

Fifth, speaking form-critically, the extent of a pericope frequently cannot be determined by the logical flow of thought, the speakers, the consistency of the use of the second or third person in referring to a certain individual or group, the coherence of the subject matter, or the adherence of the passage to elements which may be shown to belong to a certain genre from examples of that genre elsewhere in the Old Testament or in extrabiblical ancient Near Eastern literature. There are two reasons for this. First, an audience (individual or group) may interrupt the prophet before he finishes what he had intended to say, thus eliminating the elements in the genre which otherwise he might have used. Second, the response of that audience may cause the prophet to reply by going in a direction of thought which he had not originally planned and which is totally out of keeping with the message and method which at first he had intended. Accordingly, the desire for smoothness which the literarily-trained mind almost demands must not be allowed to dictate to one's understanding of the biblical text in such a way as to reduce the size of a pericope so as to destroy the living interchange between personalities which it contains, or to emend or rearrange the text so as to achieve that smoothness. On the contrary, the critic must strive to listen to the speaker or writer of the biblical text, so that he may follow his turns and irregularities, but also his absolute reverses, manifested in the voices which run counter to the messenger whose theological position is being set forth as that of the canonical book.

The Priestly Blessing and Its Aggadic Reuse

MICHAEL FISHBANE

⟦329⟧ The great priestly blessing in Num 6:23–27 concludes a cycle of priestly instructions to the people of Israel. It opens with an instruction to the Aaronids delivered by Moses, "In this manner shall you bless (תברכו) the Israelites," and then proceeds with the blessing itself:

(24)	May YHWH bless you	יברכך ה׳
	and protect you;	וישמרך
(25)	May YHWH brighten	יאר ה׳
	his countenance	פניו
	towards you	אליך
	and show you favour;	ויחנך
(26)	May YHWH raise his	ישא ה׳
	countenance towards	פניו אליך
	you and give you peace.	וישם לך שלום

At the conclusion of this blessing, there is a final instruction: "And when they shall put (ושמו) my name (שמי) over the Israelites, I shall bless them (אברכם)" (v. 27).[1] In this way, the narrative instruction in v. 27 balances,

Reprinted with permission and excerpted from "Aggadic Transformations of Non-legal Pentateuchal Traditions," *Biblical Interpretation in Ancient Israel* (Oxford: Clarendon, 1985) 329–34.

1. The Samar. reading is *wśymw* ⟦'and put'⟧, probably a plural imperative in order to balance the command/instruction in v. 23. Comparably, the LXX transposes v. 27 to the end of v. 23, and thereby tightens the nexus between the verses. However, v. 27 is resultative, and so no verse transposition is necessary; see also below for comments on the formal symmetry of the MT, which reinforces this point. In any event, the precise meaning of v. 27, and its

223

in both form and content, the instruction found in v. 23; and it further-more provides a stylistic envelope to the encased poetic blessing.[2]

In addition to this formal presentation, there are hints elsewhere in Scripture that the Priestly Blessing was enunciated by the priests on [[330]] various occasions. In what appears to be a deliberate reference to Num 6:24–26 in Lev 9:22, it is said that Aaron, after the appointment of the priests, raised his arms and "blessed" the people (cf. Num 6:23); and, similarly, it is stated in Deut 10:8 and 21:5 that the levitical priests constitute a special class, one designated to serve YHWH "and to bless (ולברך) in his name" (cf. Num 6:27). In addition to these circumspect al-lusions, and the frequently repeated requests in the Psalter for divine blessing, for the manifestation of the radiant divine countenance (cf. the refrain in Ps 80:4, 8, 20), or for grace and favour (cf. Pss 25:16; 86:16)— piecemeal expressions which may derive from common metaphorical us-age—the clustered technical terminology in Ps 67:2 leaves no reasonable doubt that its source is Num 6:24–26. In this instance, the psalmist opens his prayer with the invocation, "May Elohim show us favour (יחננו) and bless us (ויברכנו); may he brighten his countenance יאר פניו among us— selah." Not only have the priestly liturgists—or their lay imitators—been decisively inspired by the language and imagery of the Priestly Blessing, but, as is evident, they have reused it creatively. The verbs have been se-lectively chosen and regrouped innovatively, and there is a use of verbs from both halves of each of the cola.

Psalm 4 contributes another example of the impact of the Priestly Blessing on the liturgical life of ancient Israel, as reflected in the Psalter. It is particularly significant since it provides a literary form manifestly different from that found in Psalm 67. In the latter, Num 6:24–26 is first (partially) cited and only then applied (cf. v. 3). By contrast, in Psalm 4 the key terms of the Priestly Blessing are spread throughout the piece, serving simultaneously as its theological touchstone and its ideological matrix. The psalmist first calls upon YHWH to חנני 'favour me' and hear his prayer (v. 2); then, after citing those disbelievers "who say: 'Who will

---

relationship to the previous prayer, is an old crux. See the most recent review by P. A. H. de Boer, "Numbers 6:27," *VT* 32 (1982), 1–13, though his reconstruction, which claims that ʿal 'over' is a misreading of an original divine epithet "The Most High of the Israelites" is problematic and gratuitous: it is problematic because it leaves the verb without an object; and it is gratuitous because it is the divine name YHWH which recurs in the blessing itself.

2. The narrative framework is also textually linked to the blessing; cf. the stem *bārēk* [['bless']] in vv. 23–24 and the stem *śîm* [['put']] vv. 26–27. For other stylistic aspects, and a critique of certain reconstructions based on "symmetry," see my "Form and Reformulation of the Biblical Priestly Blessing," *JAOS* 103 (1983), 115 and n. 3.

show us (יראנו) good?' " the psalmist calls upon Y𝐇𝐖𝐇 to "raise over us (נסה־עלינו) the light of your presence (אור פניך)" (v. 7).³ The psalmist concludes with a reference to שלום, peace or well-being (v. 9).⁴

These and other references to the Priestly Blessing in the Psalter and, particularly, the recurrence of similar language in the Psalter and many biblical genres, suggest that such imagery as "shining the face" in favour, [[331]] or "raising the face" in beneficence, were widely diffused throughout the culture. Indeed, one may turn to the abundant use of such imagery in ancient Near Eastern literature, where it recurs in a wide range of genres, as the source for the diffusion of this imagery.⁵ In addition, several Mesopotamian documents actually indicate a remarkable linguistic and stylistic similarity to the biblical Priestly Blessing.⁶ But these parallels do not constitute instances of aggadic transformation any more than, from the strictly biblical side, Psalms 4 and 67 are aggadic transformations of Num 6:24–26. These psalms merely reuse its liturgical prototype, sometimes creatively; that is all.

The strong claim made by L. Liebreich, over a generation ago, that the entire ensemble referred to as the "Songs of Ascent" (Psalms 120–30) reuses the key language of the Priestly Blessing, falls into this general category.⁷ For although a number of key terms recur in Psalms 120–30 and, arguably, give the ensemble its coherence, the contention that all this reflects reapplication of the old Priestly Blessing for the post-exilic community ("the earliest interpretation of the Priestly Blessing, an interpretation that may be considered to be the precursor of the homilies

3. In this context *yarʿēnû* [['show us']] is a pun on PB [[Priestly Blessing]] *yāʾēr* [['brighten']]; and *nᵉsāh* is a play on *yiśśā* (if it is not simply an orthographic error). I find no basis for the emendation of M. Dahood, *Psalms*, i (AB; Garden City: Doubleday, 1966), 26, which introduces new problems.

4. Heb. *šālôm* appears to combine Akk. *šulmu/šalmu* 'be well, unimpaired, at peace' and *salīmu/sulīmu* 'be favourable, gracious'; cf. M. Weinfeld, "Covenant Terminology in the Ancient Near East and Its Influence on the West," *JAOS* 93 (1973), 191f. and n. 31, and the references cited.

5. For Ugaritic literature, cf. UT 1126:6; and for Akkadian literature, see the examples collected and discussed by E. Dhorme, "L'Emploi métaphorique de parties du corps en hébreu et en akkadien," *RB* 30 (1921), 383ff., and A. L. Oppenheim, "Idiomatic Accadian," *JAOS* 61 (1941), 256–58, "Studies in Accadian Lexicography, I," *Orientalia*, NS 11 (1942), 123f. Also cf. next note.

6. See the texts published by L. W. King, *Babylonian Boundary-Stones and Memorial-Tablets in the British Museum* (London, 1912), No. 36, and by H. Lewy, "The Babylonian Background of the Kay Kaus Legend," *An Or* 17/2 (1949), 51f. On the latter see my remarks in "Form and Reformulation," and the fundamental observations of Y. Muffs, *Studies in the Aramaic Legal Papyri from Elephantine* (Studia et Documenta ad Iura Orientis Antiqui Pertinentia 8; Leiden: E. J. Brill, 1969), 130–34.

7. "The Songs of Ascent and the Priestly Blessing," *JBL* 74 (1955), 33–36.

on the Priestly Blessing in Midrashic literature") is doubtful.[8] Given the commonplace nature of the words and verbs emphasized and, especially, given the fact that these words and verbs do not occur in clusters which either dominate or transform the meaning of the psalms in question, it is possible to observe that certain liturgical terms were used in the "Songs of Ascent" in order to convey the sense of blessing and peace so much hoped for by the post-exilic community. But it is quite another matter to assume, on the basis of these references to blessing and protection, that any one of the psalms—let alone the ensemble—is an interpretative re-use of the Priestly Blessing.[9]

[[332]] These methodological qualifications may serve to highlight the case of Mal 1:6–2:9, a remarkable post-exilic example of the aggadic exegesis of Num 6:23–27. Indeed, Malachi's outspoken and vitriolic critique of cultic and priestly behaviour is, at once, a systematic utilization of the language of the Priestly Blessing and a thorough exegetical transformation of it. With great ironic force, the prophet turns to the priests and says:

Where is your fear of Me (מוראי), says YHWH of hosts, to you, priests who despise my name (בוזי שמי).... You offer polluted meat upon my altar ... [and] bring it to your governor. Will he accept you, or will he be gracious to you (הישא פניך) ...? So, now, beseech the countenance of God (חלו־נא פני־אל) that he may show us favour (ויחננו); ... will he be gracious to you (הישא מכם פנים)? Would that there was one among you to close the door [of the Temple] that you do not kindle (תאירו) my altar in vain (חנם).... I will not accept your meal-offerings ... [for] my name (שמי) is awesome (נורא) among the nations (1:6–14).

After this condemnation, Malachi levels a harsh statement of ensuing divine doom at the priests:

If you do not hearken ... and give glory to my name (שמי), says YHWH of hosts, I shall send a curse (המארה) among you and curse (וארותי) your blessings (ברכותיכם).... Behold, I shall ... scatter

8. Ibid. 36.
9. O. Loretz, in "Altorientalischer Hintergrund sowie inner- und nachbiblische Entwicklung des Aaronitischen Segens (Num 6:24–26)," *UF* 10 (1978), 118, has claimed that the Priestly Blessing already contains exegetical expansions. But (1) his "exegetical expansions" are not exegetical in any meaningful sense; and (2) the whole enterprise rests on his reconstruction of the text's strata, which is dubious. For he isolates the "original" components from later accretions on the basis of metric criteria (cf. p. 116), though he has, thereby, introduced new asymmetries, since the *waw*-clause is retained only for the first blessing.

dung upon your faces (פניכם) . . . and raise you (ונשא אתכם) to it
(אליו).[10] For you know that I have sent you this covenant, that my
covenant be with the Levites . . . and my covenant was with them
for life and peace (השלום); and I gave them fear that they might
fear me (מורא וייראני) and . . . my name (שמי). A true Torah was
in their mouth; . . . but you have turned from the path . . . and so
I shall make you contemptible . . . for you do not guard (שמרים)
my ways; but [you rather] show partiality/favour (נשאים פנים) in
[the administration and teaching of] the Torah (2:2–9).

The foregoing indicates, boldly and decisively, that all the key terms of
the Priestly Blessing are alluded to, or played upon, in the prophet's
diatribe. On the one hand, the dense clustering of these terms makes
it clear that Mal 1:6–2:9 has more than casual, terminological similarities with Num 6:23–27. Indeed, the transformed reapplications of these
terms indicate that Malachi's oration is *exegetical* in nature. The prophet
has taken the contents of the Priestly Blessing—delivered by the priests,
[[333]] and with its emphasis on blessing, the sanctity of the divine
Name, and such benefactions as protection, favourable countenance,
and peace—*and inverted them.* The priests, the prophet contends, have
despised the divine name and service; and this has led to a threatened
suspension of the divine blessing. Even the governor will not give his gracious acknowledgement of the offerings.[11] The only hope lies in Yhwh's
favour and beneficence. The gift, articulated in Num 6:24–26, of a
brightened divine countenance which leads to divine favour (יאר ה' פניו
אליך ויחנך), and the raising of the divine countenance (ישא ה' פניו אליך)
which leads to שלום, peace or well-being, are punningly countered by the
prophet's wish that the priests will no longer ignite (תאירו) the altar in
vain (חנם), and by the anticipated divine curse (המארה וארותי). Indeed,
the priests' perversion of their sacred office is such that they who asked
Yhwh to raise his countenance (ישא ה' פניו) for the good of the people
now 'raise the countenance' (theirs and others') in overt partiality and
misuse of the Torah and its laws (נשאים פנים בתורה). In truth, says the
prophet, the priests have spurned the divine gift, entrusted to them,
of שלום [['peace']]; so that what will be 'raised' for them, or against
their 'faces' (על-פניכם . . . ונשא אתכם אליו) will be the polluted refuse of
their offerings, nothing more. Those who neglect their office, and do

---

10. The LXX reads something like *ûněśāʾtîkem* 'and I bore you'. A. Ehrlich, *Mikrâ ki
Pheschutô*, iii. 492 [Heb.], has posited the Niphal form *wěnišśěʾtem* 'und ihr werdet darauf
angewiesen sein'.

11. Ehrlich, ibid., suggested that the subject of Mal 1:9 ("will he be gracious to you")
is God, not the governor, and compared Num 6:25.

not guard (שמרים) Yhwh's ways, can hardly be permitted, implies the prophet, to invoke the Lord's blessing of protection (cf. וישמרך) upon the people of Israel.

A more violent condemnation of the priests can hardly be imagined. Nor does the ironic texture of the diatribe stop with the preceding lexical and conceptual cross-reference between Mal 1:6–2:9 and the Priestly Blessing. On closer inspection, one will further note that the prophet's speech is replete with interlocking puns that condemn the priests "measure for measure." Note, for example, the initial ironic appeal to "beseech" (חלו) God, which is countered by the reference to the priests' desecrations (מחללים),[12] or the initial reference to the 'governor' (פחה), which is echoed in the punishment of utter blasting and ruination by God (הפחתם),[13] or the failure of the priests to fear Yhwh's awesome (נורא) presence, which leads to the extinguishing of the altar lights (תאירו) and the onset of divine curses (המארה וארותי),[14] or the priestly contempt of the divine name (בוזי שמי), which leads to the contempt (נבזה) of the priestly offering and the priests themselves (נבזים).[15]

The ironic reversal of the priests' language, actions, and hopes is thus textured through a series of reworkings and plays on the liturgical [[334]] language of Num 6:23–27. In this way, the priests' cultic language is desacralized and their actions cursed. By unfolding the negative semantic range of most of the key terms used positively in the Priestly Blessing, the rotten core and consequences of the language and behavior of the priests is echoed throughout the diatribe. And further, in so far as the prophetic speech of Malachi is presented as a divine word, Malachi's speech is revealed to be no less than a divine exegesis of the Priestly Blessing, and a divine mockery of the priests who presume to bless in his name. The sacerdotal language of the Priestly Blessing is thus, by further irony, systematically desecrated and inverted by Yhwh himself. The priests, bearers of the cultic Blessing, and sensitive to its language, could not have missed the exegetical irony and sarcastic nuance of the prophet's speech.

The relationship between form and content in Mal 1:6–2:9 supports and illumines the foregoing reflections. As against the fairly balanced and symmetrical style of Num 6:23–27, the reuse of it in Mal 1:6–2:9 is unbalanced and asymmetrical. If the formalized style of the positive blessing in the old Priestly Blessing is the objective literary correlative of the hopes for protection, well-being, favour, and sustenance expressed

12. Mal 1:9, 12.
13. Mal 1:8, 13.
14. Mal 1:10, 14, 2:2.
15. Mal 1:6, 12, 2:9

therein, then the disorder of Malachi's condemnation—its narrative effusiveness, its redundancies, and its disjointed and scattered allusions to Num 6:23–27—is the literary correlative of the fracture and disruption of harmony forecast in the threats and curses. The transformation of the sacerdotal blessing into a curse is thus expressed both on the manifest level of content and on the deeper levels of structure and form. The deep ironical core of Malachi's speech inheres in its destabilizing liturgical mockery, a mockery which curses the forms and language of order, cosmos, and blessing as entrusted to the priesthood. The *Mischgattung* [['mixed genre']] created by this interweaving of liturgical language with prophetical discourse thoroughly transforms the positive assurances of the former into the negative forecasts of the latter. It may, finally, be wondered whether Malachi's diatribe does not have its very *Sitz im Leben* in an antiphonal outcry in the gates of the Temple. Viewed thus, the mounting crescendo of exegetical cacophony in the prophet's speech served as an anti-blessing, a veritable contrapuntal inversion of the sound and sense of the official Priestly Blessing simultaneously performed in the shrine.[16]

16. For the possibility that Ps 119:135 is a reinterpretation of Num 6:25, and a reapplication of it to wisdom and Torahistic piety, see M. Gertner, "Midrashim in the New Testament," *JSS* 7 (1962), 276. As I noted in "Form and Formulation," 120, it is striking that all eight verses of this acrostic Psalm beginning with the letter *pe*, of which Ps 119:135 is one, have some terminological link to the Priestly Blessing. Cf. especially vv. 130, 132, and 134 (plus v. 135). The wisdom-Torahistic exegesis in Ps 119:135 thus precedes the extended exegesis of the same type in 1 QS. ii. 2–9.

Inner-biblical Interpretation in the Prophets

JOHN DAY

[[39]] The Old Testament prophets (i.e., the latter prophets) are rich in inner-biblical interpretation. Sometimes they allude to actual biblical texts but in other cases they take up themes from the tradition which was later to become embedded in the biblical text. In considering this large topic I shall discuss first the prophets and the law, then go on to a consideration of the creation and other primeval traditions, historical and legendary traditions, the prophets and the Psalms, and prophets quoting earlier prophets, and finally I shall deal with the subject of *relectures* [['re-readings']].

The Prophets and the Law

Traditionally the law was understood as something which preceded the prophets and which was presupposed in the prophetic proclamation. With the rise of critical scholarship in the nineteenth century, as exemplified in the work of Wellhausen, the order was reversed so that the written law came to be seen as a development subsequent to the work of the pre-exilic prophets. Accordingly, the originality of the prophets became emphasised. In the present century, however, there has been a general acceptance that, though the final form of the Priestly legislation is relatively late, the tradition of law in ancient Israel antedates the prophets. Although the prophets were not constantly quoting the letter of the law,

Reprinted with permission from "Prophecy," in *It Is Written: Scripture Citing Scripture* (Barnabas Lindars FS; ed. D. A. Carson and H. G. M. Williamson; Cambridge: Cambridge University Press, 1988) 39–55.

it does appear that they were indebted to the tradition of law. Hosea, for example, could declare, "Were I to write for him my laws by ten thousands, they would be regarded as a strange thing" (Hos 8:12).

As for the decalogue, there are only two passages in the prophets which appear to contain a direct echo of it. The first is in Hos 4:2, where the prophet declares, "there is swearing, lying, killing, stealing, and committing adultery," which seems to echo the third, ninth, sixth, eighth and seventh commandments respectively. (Cf. too Hos 12:10 [ET 9] and 13:4.) Those, however, who date the decalogue later than Hosea will naturally not see an allusion to it here. The second apparent allusion to the decalogue is in Jer 7:9, where we read, "Will you steal, murder, commit adultery, swear falsely, burn incense to Baal, and go after other gods you have not known . . . ?" We find here echoes of the eighth, sixth, seventh and either the third or ninth commandments, in addition to [[40]] words which presuppose the first commandment. This verse is part of a chapter which has undergone deuteronomic redaction, but it is still possible, as Nicholson believes (1970: 69), that authentic words of Jeremiah underlie it.

Condemnation of social injustice and inhumanity is particularly prominent in the preaching of Amos, Isaiah and Micah. It is likely that the laws of social righteousness in the Book of the Covenant lie, at least in part, behind their preaching. This is particularly clear in the case of Amos, who condemned the practice of taking a man's garment in pledge (Amos 2:8), which is the subject of a specific law in Exod 22:25–27. It is to be noted that this law is in casuistic form, thus refuting the claim of Bach (1957) that Amos only appealed to apodictic law. Bach was able to maintain his position only by supposing that Amos was dependent on apodictically formed laws in Deuteronomy—manifestly later than Amos—rather than on casuistic formulations in the Book of the Covenant (cf. Exod 22:25–27 and Deut 24:17). Bergren's claim (1974) that, not only Amos, but the prophets as a whole, appealed to apodictic rather than casuistic law, is also dubious.

The influence of the book of Deuteronomy is, of course, most marked in the book of Jeremiah, a work which has clearly undergone deuteronomic redaction in its prose sermons and probably in its prose narratives. This seems unlikely to have occurred if the prophet himself was known to be anti-deuteronomic. Whatever the famous crux in Jer 8:8f. is saying, it is therefore probably not to be construed as an attack on the book of Deuteronomy *per se*. Moreover, it is interesting that Jer 3:1 appeals to the deuteronomic law on divorce, which is taken up to illustrate Yahweh's relationship with Israel. Since this is a poetic piece it may well be an authentic word of Jeremiah.

Other prophets who appear to allude to Deuteronomy are Trito-Isaiah and Malachi. In Isa 56:3–8 we find the view opposed that eunuchs and foreigners have no role in temple worship, which may be contrasted with Deut 23:2ff. (ET 1ff.), where eunuchs and certain foreigners are specifically singled out for exclusion from the sanctuary. Mal 4:4 (ET 3:22) declares, "Remember the law of my servant Moses, the statutes and ordinances that I commanded him at Horeb for all Israel." It seems that he had the law of Deuteronomy particularly in mind. Not only are the terms "law, statutes and ordinances" and "Horeb" characteristically deuteronomic, but we find in Mal 1:8 a condemnation of the offering of blemished animals to the Lord couched in terms reminiscent of Deut 15:21 rather than the Priestly legislation of Lev 22:22. Also, Mal 3:5 commends justice to the widow, orphan and sojourner (cf. Deut 14:29; 16:11; 24:17, etc.), and there are a number of other deuteronomic features.

For a prophet showing clear contacts with the Priestly tradition we need to turn to Ezekiel. In particular there are many parallels with the Holiness Code [[41]] (Leviticus 17–26). Although the Holiness Code in its final form is surely later than Ezekiel, knowing as it does the Aaronite priesthood and the high priesthood (unlike Ezekiel), it is probable that, as a priest, Ezekiel drew on the priestly tradition which was to be embodied in the Holiness Code.

Creation and Other Primeval Traditions

There are, of course, a number of references in the prophets to Yahweh as creator. Only Jeremiah and Deutero-Isaiah, however, show evidence of familiarity with the P tradition which became embodied in Genesis 1. In Jer 4:23 the prophet describes the reversal of the process of creation, and included are the words "I looked on the earth, and lo, it was waste and void" (*tōhû wābōhû*), which recalls the description of primeval chaos in Gen 1:2. According to Fishbane (1985: 321) Jeremiah is directly dependent on Genesis 1. However, in view of the widely accepted evidence that P did not attain its final form before the sixth century B.C., I incline to see here an allusion to the tradition behind the P account of Genesis 1 rather than to Genesis 1 itself.

Weinfeld (1968) has plausibly argued that Deutero-Isaiah rejected some of the ideas about creation attested in the P account. Thus, whereas Deutero-Isaiah questioned the idea that God needed assistance when creating the world (Isa 40:13f.; cf. 44:24), Gen 1:26 has God say, "Let *us* make man," which is usually thought to refer to his addressing the heavenly council. Again, Deutero-Isaiah opposed the notion that Yahweh had a physical image (Isa 40:18; 46:5), but in Gen 1:26f. we read that

God made man in his own image, a term which surely includes a physical likeness, even if this does not exhaust its meaning (cf. Gen 5:3). Further, Deutero-Isaiah rejected the idea that Yahweh needed rest (Isa 40:28), which may be contrasted with Gen 2:2f., where God is stated to have rested on the seventh day after all his labours. Moreover, Deutero-Isaiah declared that Yahweh did not create the world a waste (*tōhû*, Isa 45:18), which may be contrasted with Gen 1:2. However, whereas Weinfeld believes that Deutero-Isaiah was polemicising against the creation account in Gen 1:1–2, 4a, I think that he was opposing certain ideas in the priestly tradition underlying it, since Isa 40:13f. implicitly (cf. v. 12), and Isa 44:24 explicitly, are rejecting the notion that God needed to consult his divine council when creating the world as a whole, not man in particular (cf. Gen 1:26). If this understanding is correct, it becomes necessary to reject Whybray's claim (1971) that there is no known tradition in Israel of Yahweh's needing assistance in creation, and his postulation that Deutero-Isaiah was polemicising against Babylonian concepts is rendered questionable (cf. Day 1985: 54–56).

A variant tradition of the expulsion of the first man from Eden recounted by J in Genesis 2–3 is preserved in Ezekiel 28, where the imagery is applied ⟦42⟧ to the king of Tyre in an oracle proclaiming judgment on him. The points of comparison are as follows: in both we have a human figure who dwells in the garden of Eden, in both he is at first perfect but sin leads to his expulsion from the garden, and in both reference is made either to a cherub (Ezek 28:14, 16) or cherubim (Gen 3:24). Scholars dispute whether the king of Tyre is equated with or distinguished from a cherub in Ezekiel 28. On the former view we should read in v. 14 *ʾatt kĕrûb* ('you were a cherub') with MT but on the latter view *ʾet kĕrûb* ('with a cherub') with LXX and Pesh. The parallel in Genesis 3 enables one to decide in favour of the latter alternative, since the cherubim are there clearly set over against the first man, not equated with him. Interestingly Eden is set on a mountain in Ezek 28:14, 16, which is unattested in Genesis 2–3. It seems likely that Ezekiel was indebted to a tradition similar to, but not identical with, our J account.

There is no other reference to the first man in the prophets. It is true that the MT of Hos 6:7 reads, "But like Adam (*kĕʾādām*) they transgressed the covenant," but it is now generally agreed that, with a very slight emendation, we should read, "But *at* Adam (*bĕʾādām*) they transgressed the covenant," since the next line goes on "*there* they dealt faithlessly with me" (Day 1986: 2ff.).

There are, however, other allusions to Eden in the prophets but they are in the nature of passing references (Isa 51:3; Ezek 31:9, 16, 18; 36:35; Joel 2:3). In addition, we find paradisiacal imagery employed in the prophets in a typological sense in descriptions of the coming eschaton (Isa 11:6–8; Ezek 47:1–12; Zech 14:8).

There are two passages in the prophets which make explicit mention of Noah, namely Isa 54:9 and Ezek 14:14, 20. Ezekiel cites Noah, alongside two other non-Israelites Job and Daniel, as a righteous man who, were he to be alive in the prophet's own time, would save but his own life by his righteousness. Doubtless the prophet was familiar with the story of the flood in which Noah did deliver his life by his righteousness, just as the righteous Job was eventually delivered from his suffering, and some comparable deliverance for the Ugaritic Daniel may be presumed (Day 1980a). In Isa 54:9 Deutero-Isaiah makes a typological comparison between the exile and Noah's flood and declares that, just as God had promised never to bring such a flood on the earth again, so now he promises never again to bring judgment on the nation. Interestingly, the next verse refers to Yahweh's "covenant of peace," which suggests that the prophet was familiar with the Noachic covenant of the P tradition (Gen 9:11) and not simply with J's version (Gen 8:21), which contains Yahweh's promise without expressing it in covenantal terms. Gunn has attempted to find other implicit Noachic allusions in Deutero-Isaiah (Isa 44:27; 50:2; 51:10a; 55:13b) but, as I have argued elsewhere, these are unconvincing (Day 1985: 93).

[43] There are, however, two implicit Noachic allusions in the "Isaiah apocalypse," in Isa 24:5 and 18. The former verse declares that the inhabitants of the earth "have . . . broken the everlasting covenant." The universal context suggests that it is specifically the covenant with Noah which is in mind here (referred to as "the everlasting covenant" in Gen 9:16, cf. v. 12). This conclusion is further borne out by Isa 24:18, which reads 'for the windows of heaven (lit. on high) are opened' (*kiˀărubbôt mimmārôm niptāḥû*), thus echoing the words of the flood story in Gen 7:11, 'and the windows of heaven were opened' (*waˀărubbôt haššāmayim niptāḥû*). Since the words of Isa 24:18 describe the judgment which follows the breaking of the everlasting covenant, it would appear that the writer of Isaiah 24 regarded it as appropriate that the breaking of the Noachic covenant should result in a punishment like that of Noah's flood. This is contrary to the idea found in Genesis 9 and Isa 54:9f.

Historical and Legendary Traditions

We turn now to the patriarchs. The most extended patriarchal references in the prophets are the verses about Jacob in Hos 12:3ff., 13 (ET 2ff., 12), where a whole series of parallels with pentateuchal traditions may be found. Hosea does not cite the allusions in the same chronological sequence as in Genesis, but this need not be significant as his purpose was something other than to provide a narrative account. The series of parallels suggests that Hosea knew a tradition similar to, though not identical with, our pentateuchal narratives. Verse 4a (ET 3a), for instance, contains a play on the name of Jacob, "In the womb he supplanted (*ʿāqab*) his brother," which recalls the play on words in the birth story in Gen 25:26 (J), "Afterward his brother came forth, and his hand had taken hold of Esau's heel (*ʿāqēb*)." However, it is clear that in the Hosea passage the meaning of *ʿāqab* is 'supplant, deceive, cheat' and not 'take by the heel', because the verb is not attested with the latter meaning; consequently the parallel with Gen 25:26 is not exact. On the other hand, the verb *ʿāqab* 'supplant, deceive, cheat' is used in connexion with Jacob's taking Esau's birthright and blessing in Gen 27:36 (J). In Hos 12:4b–5a (ET 3b–4a) Jacob is said to have striven with God or an angel, and in Gen 32:22–32 (J) we read of the incident of Jacob's striving with God or a man at Penuel. Hosea's allusion to Jacob's weeping and seeking God's favour in Hos 12:5a (ET 4a) is unparalleled in our Genesis account, and must reflect some tradition not recorded there. The attempt by Holladay (1966) to see here rather a reference to Jacob's weeping before *Esau* and seeking his favour (cf. Gen 33:4, 8, 10, 15) does not seem the most natural way of construing the Hebrew text. God's meeting Jacob at Bethel in Hos 12:5b (ET 4b) presumably refers to the story in Gen 28:10–22 (J) rather than the later P ⟦44⟧ version in Gen 35:9–15. The point of the reference in Hos 12:13 (ET 12) to Jacob's fleeing to Aram and there doing service for a wife (cf. Gen 28:5 [P]; 29:15–30 [J]) is not entirely clear. The most likely explanation is that it has reference to Israel's subservience to foreign powers, which is contrasted in the following verse Hos 12:14 (ET 13) with Moses' deliverance of Israel from slavery in Egypt.

There is no universally held view about these verses. There seem no convincing grounds for supposing that the verses should be rearranged (*contra* Ginsberg 1961) or that a dialogue is taking place between prophet and people (*contra* Vriezen 1942). The dominant view is that in these verses Jacob is presented in a critical light, Israel's current deceitfulness and striving against God being regarded as of a piece with the behaviour of its ancestor. A number of scholars, however, especially Ackroyd (1963), suppose that Jacob is being presented in a positive light, and that we have here a depiction of God's providential guidance comparable to the famous passage in Deut 26:5ff. about Jacob as "a wandering Aramean." Ackroyd claims that we should not suppose that Jacob's deceitfulness was necessarily viewed in a bad light. However, this interpretation does not seem the most natural one. The allusions to Jacob are introduced in v. 3 (ET 2) by the words, "The Lord . . . will punish Jacob according to his ways, and requite him according to his deeds." In the light of this introductory reference to Jacob we expect negative, not positive, things to be said about the patriarch. Verse 4a (ET 3a) surely bears this out, for the allusion to Jacob's cheating his brother must be taken as a negative comment, *contra* Ackroyd, since deceit (*mirmâ*) is specifically singled out for criticism in connexion with Israel in nearby verses, Hos 12:2 (ET 1) and 12:8 (ET 7). Although it might seem surprising for Israel's national ancestor to be presented in a negative light, it may be noted that this attitude is not unparalleled in the prophets. Jer 9:3f. (ET 4f.) seems to be alluding to the Jacob tradition: note especially the word-play in v. 3a (ET 4a), "Let every one beware of his neighbour, and put no trust in any brother: for every brother is a supplanter (*ʿāqōb yaʿqōb*)," as well as the reference to *mirmâ* 'deceit' in v. 5 (ET 6; cf. Gen 27:35). In addition, Isa 43:27, "Your first father sinned," is generally agreed to be referring to Jacob (cf. v. 28). The prophetic attitude to Jacob appears therefore to be remarkably negative. We do find a positive reference, however, in Mal 1:2f., "Yet I have loved Jacob but I have hated Esau. . . ." There are also favourable allusions in Ezek 28:25 and 37:25 (secondary, according to Zimmerli 1969); cf. too Jer 33:26 and Mic 7:20.

Unlike Jacob, the prophetic allusions to Abraham are uniformly positive. He is referred to in Isa 29:22; 41:8f.; 51:2; 62:16 and Ezek 33:24 (cf. Jer 33:26 and Mic 7:20), all of which are exilic or post-exilic. The reference in ⟦45⟧ Isa 29:22 to "the Lord, who redeemed Abraham" is not easy to identify with any particular event, but the other allusions all cohere well with Genesis. Thus, Abraham's call is known in Isa 41:8f. and 51:2, and his coming from a distant country may be referred to in Isa 41:9. His wife's name Sarah is attested in Isa 51:2, as is Yahweh's blessing Abraham and granting him many descendants (cf. Jer 33:26; Mic 7:20). Similarly, Ezek 33:24 knows of Abraham's taking the land in possession. In this last verse, however, there is a negative note, not against Abraham himself, but against the false confidence of the people: the prophet implies that, since the people are guilty of manifold sins, they do not have the automatic right to take possession of the land like their ancestor Abraham.

An incident from the Abraham cycle which is frequently alluded to in the prophets (though no patriarchal name is mentioned) is that concerning Sodom and Gomorrah. The prophets clearly knew of them as cities of exemplary wickedness which God overthrew, and they are usually cited as an object lesson for Israel (Isa 1:9f.; 3:9; Jer 23:14; Ezek 16:46, 48f., 53, 55f.; Amos 4:11; also note Admah and Zeboim in Hos 11:8) but also for Babylon (Isa 13:19; Jer 50:40), Edom (Jer 49:18), and Moab and Ammon (Zeph 2:9). In Genesis (J) the cities are clearly regarded as wicked generally (Gen 13:13; 18:20) but special attention is drawn to the homosexual rape with which the Sodomites threaten the angels; cf. Gen 19:5, where the Sodomites say to Lot, "Bring them out to us, that we may know them." That 'know' is here being used in its sexual sense is strongly supported by Gen 19:8, where Lot replies to the Sodomites, "Behold I have two daughters who have *known* not man . . . ," and these he offers in lieu of the angels. It is therefore surprising that none of the prophetic references indicates awareness of Sodom's propensity to homosexuality. Rather, such indications as we have point in the direction of social injustice (cf. Isa 1:10ff.; Ezek 16:49f.), and, although there are sexual innuendoes in Jer 23:14 and throughout Ezekiel 16, these are of a heterosexual nature. This should not be used as an argument against the homosexual interpretation of Sodom's sin in Gen 19:5, as some apologists suppose (e.g., Bailey 1955: chap. 1). Rather we should suppose that the prophets were familiar with a version of the Sodom story in which homosexuality was not emphasised.

We turn now to the Exodus, which is frequently mentioned in the prophets, but it is not necessary to discuss every occurrence (cf. Isa 10:24, 26; 63:11; Jer 7:22, 25; 32:20f.; Hos 12:14 [ET 13]; Amos 2:10; 4:10; 9:7; Mic 6:4, in addition to passages discussed below). All the allusions are clearly paralleled in the Pentateuch, with the exception of the reference in Ezekiel to the idolatry practised by the Israelites in Egypt (Ezek 20:7f.). Fishbane (1985: 365) is wrong, however, in saying that this reference is "thoroughly unique," since, as [[46]] a matter of fact, Israel's idolatry in Egypt is clearly alluded to in Josh 24:14. There is also possibly a hint of it in Lev 18:3 (interesting in view of the evident connexion between Ezekiel and the Holiness Code).

In addition to the references to the historic Exodus, the prophets also make allusion to the Exodus in a typological sense, i.e., Exodus imagery is employed to describe the future deliverance. This is the case in Hos 2:16ff. (ET 14ff.); Mic 7:14f.; Jer 16: 14f. (= 23:7f.); and Ezek 20:33–44. But it is, of course, Deutero-Isaiah who is most renowned for his use of Exodus typology. The importance of the motif for this prophet is underlined by the fact that it occurs both at the beginning (Isa 40:3–5) and at the very end of his prophecy (Isa 55:12f.), as well as in a considerable number of passages in between (Isa 41:17–20; 42:14–16; 43:1–3, 14–21; 48:20f.; 49:8–12; 51:9f.; 52:11–12). For Deutero-Isaiah it seems that the future Exodus from Babylon is going to surpass the Exodus from Egypt (Isa 43:16–19; cf. Jer 16:14f. = 23:7f.). As well as in Isa 43:16f., the deliverance at the Sea of Reeds is also mentioned in Isa 51:9f., where it is fused with imagery drawn from Yahweh's conflict with chaos at creation. There is no explicit reference to the Plagues or Passover in Deutero-Isaiah, but in Isa 52:12 we read, "For you shall not go out in haste (*běḥippāzôn*) . . . ," the Hebrew expression being found elsewhere in the OT only in connexion with the Exodus, when the Hebrews did leave

Egypt in haste (Exod 12:11; Deut 16:3). We thus have here an anti-type
of the Exodus. Finally we read in Deutero-Isaiah that in the wilderness
wanderings water will flow from the rock (Isa 48:21; cf. 43:19f.), which of
course recalls the first Exodus (cf. Exod 17:2–7; Num 20:8).

Joshua is never mentioned by name in the prophets, but there are
two allusions to the dispossession of the Amorites (Amos 2:9; Isa 17:9, cf.
LXX). A few scholars (e.g. Sparks 1949: 135; Tournay 1965: 428) have
seen a further reference to the Joshua traditions in Hab 3:11, where we
read that "The sun and moon stood still in their habitation . . . ," which
has been taken to refer to the standing still of the sun and moon during
the battle of Gibeon in Josh 10:12b–13a. This, however, is improbable,
for just two verses later, in Hab 3:13, we read of Yahweh's saving his
anointed (i.e., the king) as part of the same course of events. This indicates that the description does not refer to the time of Joshua. There is,
admittedly, an interesting verbal similarity between Hab 3:11 and Josh
10:12b–13a, suggesting that similar phenomena may be being described
here. In Hab 3:11 the reference seems to be to the blotting out of the
sun and moon by the brightness of Yahweh's theophany in the lightning. This may lend support to the view that Josh 10:12b–13a originally
referred to the disappearance of the sun and moon as a result of an
early morning storm, which would cohere with the allusion to the hail-
storm in Josh 10:11.

There are a few references in the prophets to events of the periods of
the [[47]] Judges and early monarchy (cf. Isa 9:3 [ET 4]; 10:26; 28:21; Jer
51:1; Hos 9:9; 10:9; Amos 6:5; Zech 12:8), in addition to well-known passages anticipating an ideal future Davidic ruler (cf. Isa 9:1–6 [ET 2–7];
11:1–9; Jer 23:5f.; Mic 5:1–5 [ET 2–6]; Zech 9:9f.), a concept democrat-
ised in Isa 55:3–5, but it is not my intention to discuss these here.

The Prophets and the Psalms

That the prophets were indebted to the tradition of psalmody in ancient
Israel is clear enough. Isaiah, for example, had a theology that was firmly
rooted in the Zion Psalms (e.g., Psalm 46 is echoed in Isa 7:14 and
17:12–14) and Jeremiah's "Confessions" are clearly modelled on the Individual Lament Psalms. For reasons of space, however, I shall confine
myself to Deutero-Isaiah and that genre of hymn known as the Enthronement Psalms (Psalms 47; 93; 95–99), which both have a number of
theological themes and linguistic traits in common.

One question that has been discussed is whether Deutero-Isaiah was
dependent on the Psalms or whether the Psalms were dependent on
Deutero-Isaiah. An earlier generation of scholars believed that the En-

thronement Psalms were post-exilic and dependent on Deutero-Isaiah. While there are a few scholars who still follow this view, the majority upholds the priority of the Psalms, or at the very least of the Enthronement Psalm form. In support of this view a number of points may be made. First, Deutero-Isaiah was explicitly monotheistic, whereas the Psalms assume the existence of other gods (Pss 95:3; 96:4; 97:7). After the ringing declaration of Deutero-Isaiah that no God existed apart from Yahweh, it would be surprising for these Psalms to be dependent on him. Secondly, as Johnson has pointed out (1967: 61 n. 1), the theme of Yahweh as *gō'ēl* 'redeemer', which is important in Deutero-Isaiah, is absent from these Psalms, suggesting that they were not dependent on the prophet. Thirdly, Ps 99:1 refers to the cherubim and Ps 47:6 (ET 5) appears to presuppose the ark, neither of which existed in the post-exilic temple.

Theological echoes of the Enthronement Psalms may be detected in the declaration "Your God reigns (or has become king)" (Isa 52:7; cf. Ps 47:8 [ET 7], etc.), in the theme of Yahweh's victory over the chaos waters (Isa 51:9f.; cf. Ps 93:3f.), of Yahweh's exaltation over all other gods (Isa 45:21f.; 46:9; cf. Ps 95:3; 97:9), his creation of the world (Isa 40:12, 28; cf. Ps 95:4f.), and the appeal to nature to join in the song of praise to Yahweh (Isa 44:23; 49:13; cf. Ps 96:11f.). There are also many linguistic echoes of the Enthronement Psalms in Deutero-Isaiah, e.g., "his holy arm" (Isa 52:10; cf. Ps 98:1), "in the sight of the heathen" (Isa 52:10; cf. Ps 98:2), "clap the hands" (Isa 55:12; cf. Ps 98:8), "from of old" (Isa 44:8; 45:21; 48:3, 5, 7f.; [48] cf. Ps 93:2), etc. (see Snaith 1934: 66–69). We also find an actual quotation in Isa 42:10 from Psalms 96 and 98. Both Pss 96:1 and 98:1 begin "O sing to the Lord a new song," and these words are taken up *verbatim* in Isa 42:10. Moreover, both Pss 96:11 and 98:7 declare, "Let the sea roar and all that fills it," and it is widely accepted that Isa 42:10 should be restored thus, i.e., *yir'am hayyām ûmĕlō'ô*; as it stands MT reads *yôrĕdê hayyām ûmĕlō'ô*, 'Those who go down to the sea and all that fills it', which is clearly corrupt and appears contaminated from Ps 107:23 (cf. Allen 1971: 146–47).

Prophets Quoting Prophets

For the pre-exilic and exilic periods attempts have been made to show that Isaiah was dependent on Amos (Fey 1963), Jeremiah on Hosea (Gross 1930 and 1931), Ezekiel on Jeremiah (Miller 1955), Deutero-Isaiah on Jeremiah (Paul 1969), and Deutero-Isaiah on Ezekiel (Baltzer 1971). The strongest case can probably be made for Jeremiah's dependence on Hosea, and Lindars has written a fine article in support of this (1979).

However, it is my intention here to concentrate on the post-exilic period, for it is then that we find a really marked tendency of prophets to cite earlier prophets. The reinterpretation of earlier prophecies clearly became one of the most characteristic features of prophecy in that period, especially in those works sometimes dubbed "proto-apocalyptic." For instance, Trito-Isaiah cites Deutero-Isaiah on a number of occasions (e.g., Isa 58:8b = 52:15b; 62:11 = 40:10; 60:4a = 49:18a), and Zimmerli (1963b) has written a thorough study of this subject.

Zechariah 9–14 shows evidence of dependence on a number of earlier prophets. Earlier studies by Stade (1881) and Delcor (1952) have offered comprehensive surveys of this topic. Deutero-Isaiah has obviously been used, e.g., Zech 12:1, "Thus says the Lord, who stretched out the heavens and founded the earth and formed the spirit of man within him," which echoes Isa 42:5 (cf. 48:13). Also, Zech 9:12, "today I declare that I will restore to you double," sounds like a reversal of Isa 40:2, where Israel is said to have received double punishment for her sins. On the other hand, Lamarche's attempt (1961) to trace the influence of the servant songs on Zechariah 9–14 does not seem convincing, with the exception of the fourth song, which possibly influenced Zech 12:10–13:1. There are also echoes of other prophets, such as Amos, Jeremiah and Ezekiel. For example, in Zech 13:5, we read of a coming time when the prophet will say, "I am no prophet, I am a tiller of the soil," and it is difficult not to find here an echo of Amos 7:14. In the light of this allusion it is tempting to suppose that Amos may also be the source behind Zech 14:5, where reference is made to the earthquake in the time of Uzziah king of Judah, attested elsewhere in the OT only in 〚49〛 Amos 1:1. The influence of Jeremiah and Ezekiel may also be detected on Zechariah 9–14. Mason (1976) believes that Zechariah 9–14 was influenced by Zechariah 1–8, but I do not find the alleged parallels sufficiently striking as to warrant dependence (none of them is verbal).

We turn next to Joel. The presence of quotations from earlier prophetic works is here clearly marked. They are, in fact, one of several pointers to the relatively late date of the prophecy. Unlike a modern author, who would state when he is citing an earlier author, the OT prophets almost never admit explicitly that they are quoting. One exception to this is in the book of Joel, for in Joel 3:5 (ET 2:32) we read, "for in Mount Zion and in Jerusalem there shall be those who escape, *as the Lord has said*. . . ." When had the Lord said this? The answer is in Obadiah 17, where we read, "But in Mount Zion there shall be those that escape. . . ." Fishbane (1985: 479 n. 54) curiously thinks that Joel is here quoting Isa 4:2, but this stands much less close in wording to Joel than Obadiah 17, which he fails to mention.

In our Bibles Joel stands next to the book of Amos, presumably reflecting the belief that he was a contemporary of Amos. There are, in fact, a couple of clear citations from Amos in Joel, which may have contributed to this understanding. One is taken up from very near the beginning of Amos, Amos 1:2, "The Lord roars from Zion and utters his voice from Jerusalem," which is cited in Joel 4:16 (ET 3:16), whilst the other is taken from very near the end of Amos, Amos 9:13, "the mountains shall drip sweet wine," which is quoted in Joel 4:18 (ET 3:18).

In his depiction of the coming Day of the Lord Joel has been influenced by earlier prophecies, e.g., in Joel 1:15, where the words "for the day of the Lord is near; as destruction from the Almighty it will come!" are a quotation from Isa 13:6. Words applied to Babylon in Isaiah 13 are now applied to the Jews. This is in keeping with his tendency to reverse earlier prophecies. For example, in place of the famous prophecy of Isa 2:4 (= Mic 4:3) about men beating their swords into ploughshares and spears into pruning hooks, we read in Joel 4:10 (ET 3:10), "Beat your ploughshares into swords, and your pruning hooks into spears."

There are two striking parallels between Joel and Jonah, namely Joel 2:13 and Jonah 4:2 and Joel 2:14 and Jonah 3:9. In Jonah 4:2 the prophet declares, "for I knew that thou art a gracious God and merciful, slow to anger, and abounding in steadfast love, and repentest of evil." Of course, part of this quotation is attested a number of other times in the OT (Exod 34:6; Neh 9:17; Ps 86:15; 103:8; 145:8). However, only in the Joel and Jonah passages do we find this citation with the concluding words about Yahweh repenting of evil. This indicates that there is a clear literary relationship between Joel and Jonah, something which is supported by the fact that there is a further parallel between Jonah 3:9 and Joel 2:14. In Jonah 3:9 the king of Nineveh declares, [[50]] "Who knows, God may yet repent . . . ," and similarly in Joel 2:14 the prophet states, "Who knows whether he will not turn and repent . . . ?" Is Joel dependent on Jonah or is it the other way round? In this instance, unlike other cases I have mentioned, priority seems to lie with Joel. The classic citation about Yahweh's mercy found in Joel 2:13 and Jonah 4:2 is applied to Israel in the former and Nineveh in the latter. In the other allusions to this quotation referred to above, it is characteristically used, as in Joel, of Yahweh's mercy towards Israel. It is the use of this citation in connexion with Yahweh's attitude to the foreign city of Nineveh that is striking, and it is natural to suppose that this is a secondary derivation. It is attractive to suppose that the book of Jonah, with its universalistic message, has taken up this passage about Yahweh's mercy towards Israel from Joel and applied it instead to Nineveh. It is arguable that what we find in Jonah is a critique of the kind of proto-apocalyptic outlook attested in Joel.

Whereas Joel looks forward to God's judgment coming on the heathen, the book of Jonah makes the point that foreigners can repent, with the result that Yahweh suspends his judgment. If so, this would tend to support the thesis of Payne (1979) that the book of Jonah was directed against the growing proto-apocalyptic movement with its longing for God's judgment to come on the heathen.

Another work commonly dubbed proto-apocalyptic is Isaiah 24–27. In an earlier article (1980b) I drew attention to a series of eight parallels between Isa 26:13–27:11 and Hos 13:4–14:10 (ET 9), all of them in the same order, with one partial exception, thus strongly suggesting the dependence of the Isaiah passage on Hosea.

- (i) Israel knows no lords/gods but Yahweh
  Hos 13:4. Cf. Isa 26:13 (LXX)
- (ii) Imagery of birthpangs with child refusing to be born
  Hos 13:13. Cf. Isa 26:17f.
- (iii) Deliverance from Sheol
  Hos 13:14 (LXX, etc.). Cf. Isa 26:19
- (iv) Imagery of destructive east wind symbolic of exile
  Hos 13:15. Cf. Isa 27:8
- (v) Imagery of life-giving dew
  Hos 14:6 (ET 5). Cf. Isa 26:19
- (vi) Israel blossoming and like a vineyard
  Hos 14:6–8 (ET 5–7). Cf. Isa 27:2–6
- (vii) Condemnation of idolatry, including the Asherim
  Hos 14:9 (ET 8). Cf. Isa 27:9
- (viii) The importance of discernment; judgment for the wicked
  Hos 14:10 (ET 9). Cf. Isa 27:11

The cumulative effect of these parallels, admittedly thematic rather than [[51]] verbal for the most part, seems too much to be attributable to chance. A number of the themes are only rarely encountered elsewhere in the OT, and the fact that we find references to the birthpangs with child refusing to be born and deliverance from Sheol, occurring in successive verses in both cases, is particularly striking. The effect of all this is to question the view of those who find evidence of many redactions in Isaiah 24–27, since the fact that many of the verses in Isaiah 26–27 have their background in verses coming in the same order in Hosea 13–14, indicates that they belong together and therefore come from a single hand. However, for a detailed presentation of the case I refer the reader to my article.

Relectures

So far we have been considering instances where the prophets were indebted to other parts of the OT or at any rate to traditions which were later to be embodied in our OT. It is probable, however, that on occasions the prophetic oracles are themselves reworkings of earlier versions of those oracles. It is widely accepted, for example, that the deuteronomic prose sermons in Jeremiah were not simply created *ex nihilo* [['from nothing']] but often reflect a reworking of authentic Jeremianic logia [['sayings']] (Nicholson 1970), and Zimmerli's views on the redactional development of the Ezekiel tradition (1969) have gained some measure of support. The postulation of *relectures* [['rereadings']] is, however, something to be undertaken very warily, since some of the suggestions that have been put forward seem to reflect a high degree of subjectivity or are not sufficiently rigorously argued. Vermeylen (1977–78), for example, has written a large two-volume work giving a highly detailed redactional history of Isaiah 1–35, in which he claims to be able to plot with great accuracy when each verse or half verse was added, but the reasons are often very speculative and I do not believe such confidence is justified.

Recently, Macintosh (1980) has made a thoroughgoing attempt to apply the principle of *relecture* to a particular chapter, namely Isaiah 21. He claims that we have here an eighth-century B.C. text that has been "overwritten" in the sixth century B.C., "overwritten" in such a way that the original recension can still be perceived, so that it constitutes a kind of palimpsest. Although this is highly ingenious, I do not find the grounds for postulating an original eighth-century B.C. recension convincing. Macintosh tells us that the reference to Elam in Isa 21:2 cannot originally have referred to Cyrus (even though it did in the sixth-century B.C. revision), since Cyrus is nowhere else called an Elamite. This, however, is incorrect, since he is called an Elamite in the Babylonian Dynastic Prophecy (see Grayson 1975: 25, 33). Again, we are told that the prophet's trembling in Isa 21:3f. at the prospect of the fall of Babylon would be inexplicable in the sixth century B.C., but this overlooks the fact that Habakkuk [[52]] similarly trembles at the imminent overthrow of a power oppressing Israel, probably Babylon (Hab 3:16), even though this will mean deliverance for Israel. Or again, we are told that the lack of anti-Edomite sentiment in the Dumah oracle (Isa 21:11f.) indicates an original pre-exilic date, but this is not so, since Dumah was not Edom but a place in North Arabia (Gen 25:14; cf. 1 Chr 1:30). It is clear that Macintosh's thesis is to be rejected (cf. Day 1983). The positing of *relectures* is something that should only be done with great caution.

Bibliography

Ackroyd, P. R.
1963   Hosea and Jacob. *Vetus Testamentum* 13: 245–59.
Allen, L. C.
1971   Cuckoos in the Textual Nest at 2 Kings xx. 13; Isa xlii. 10; xlix. 24; Ps
        xxii. 17; 2 Chron v. 9. *Journal of Theological Studies* n.s. 22: 143–50.
Bach, R.
1957   Gottesrecht und weltliches Recht in der Verkündigung des Proph-
        eten Amos. Pp. 23–34 in *Festschrift Günther Dehn,* edited by W. Schnee-
        melcher. Neukirchen.
Bailey, D. S.
1955   *Homosexuality and the Western Christian Tradition.* London.
Baltzer, D.
1971   *Ezechiel und Deuterojesaja.* Beihefte zur Zeitschrift für die Alttestament-
        liche Wissenschaft 121. Berlin.
Bergren, R. V.
1974   *The Prophets and the Law.* Cincinnati.
Day, J.
1980a   The Daniel of Ugarit and Ezekiel and the Hero of the Book of
        Daniel. *Vetus Testamentum* 30: 174–84 .
1980b   A Case of Inner Scriptural Interpretation: The Dependence of Isaiah
        xxvi. 13–xxvii. 11 on Hosea xiii. 4–xiv. 10 (Eng. 9) and Its Relevance
        to Some Theories of the Redaction of the "Isaiah Apocalypse." *Jour-
        nal of Theological Studies* n.s. 31: 309–19.
1983   Review of A. A. Macintosh, *Isaiah XXI: A Palimpsest,* in *Journal of Theo-
        logical Studies* n.s. 34: 212–15.
1985   *God's Conflict with the Dragon and the Sea: Echoes of a Canaanite Myth in
        the Old Testament.* University of Cambridge Oriental Publications 35.
        Cambridge.
1986   Pre-Deuteronomic Allusions to the Covenant in Hosea and Psalm
        lxxviii. *Vetus Testamentum* 36: 1–12.
Delcor, M.
1952   Les sources du deutéro-Zacharie et ses procédés d'emprunt. *Revue
        biblique* 59: 385–411.
Fey, A.
1963   *Amos und Jesaja.* Wissenschaftliche Monographien zum Alten und
        Neuen Testament 12. Neukirchen.
Fishbane, M.
1985   *Biblical Interpretation in Ancient Israel.* Oxford.
Ginsberg, H. L.
1961   Hosea's Ephraim, More Fool than Knave: A New Interpretation of
        Hosea 12:1–14. *Journal of Biblical Literature* 80: 339–47.

Grayson, A. K.
1975   *Babylonian Historical-Literary Texts.* Toronto and Buffalo.
Gross, K.
1930   *Die literarische Verwandeschaft Jeremias mit Hosea.* Berne and Leipzig.
1931   Hoseas Einfluss auf Jeremias Anschauungen. *Neue kirchliche Zeitschrift* 42: 241–56.
Gunn, D. M.
1975   Deutero-Isaiah and the Flood. *Journal of Biblical Literature* 94: 493– 508.
Holladay, W. L.
1966   Chiasmus, the Key to Hosea XII 3–6. *Vetus Testamentum* 16: 53–64.
Johnson, A. R.
1967   *Sacral Kingship in Ancient Israel.* 2d edition. Cardiff.
Lamarche, P.
1961   *Zacharie IX–XIV.* Paris.
Lindars, B.
1979   "Rachel Weeping for Her Children": Jeremiah 31:15–22. *Journal for the Study of the Old Testament* 12: 47–62.
Macintosh, A. A.
1980   *Isaiah XXI: A Palimpsest.* Cambridge.
Mason, R. A.
1976   The Relation of Zech 9–14 to Proto-Zechariah. *Zeitschrift für die Alttestamentliche Wissenschaft* 88: 227–39.
Miller, J. W.
1955   *Das Verhältnis Jeremias und Hesekiels sprachlich und theologisch untersucht.* Assen.
Nicholson, E. W.
1970   *Preaching to the Exiles.* Oxford.
Paul, S.
1969   Literary and Ideological Echoes of Jeremiah in Deutero-Isaiah. Pp. 102–20 in *Proceedings of the IVth World Congress of Jewish Studies* 1. Jerusalem.
Payne, D. F.
1979   Jonah from the Perspective of Its Audience. *Journal for the Study of the Old Testament* 13: 3–12.
Snaith, N. H.
1934   *Studies in the Psalter.* London.
Sparks, H. F. D.
1949   The Witness of the Prophets to Hebrew Tradition. *Journal of Theological Studies* 50: 129–41.
Stade, B.
1881   Deuterozacharja: Eine kritische Studie. *Zeitschrift für die Alttestamentliche Wissenschaft* 1: 1–96.

Tournay, R.
1965   Review of A. Deissler and M. Delcor, *Les Petits Prophètes* 2, in *Revue biblique* 72: 427–29.

Vermeylen, J.
1977–78 *Du Prophète Isaïe à l'Apocalyptique.* 2 volumes. Paris.

Vriezen, T. C.
1942   La tradition de Jacob dans Osée XII. *Oudtestamentische Studiën* 1: 64–78.

Weinfeld, M.
1968   God the Creator in Gen. 1 and the Prophecy of Second Isaiah. *Tarbiz* 37: 105–32 [Hebrew].

Whybray, R. N.
1971   *The Heavenly Counsellor in Isaiah xl 13–14.* Cambridge.

Zimmerli, W.
1963a   Der "neue Exodus" in der Verkündigung der beiden grossen Exilspropheten. Pp. 192–204 in *Gottes Offenbarung.* Munich.
1963b   Zur Sprache Tritojesajas. Pp. 217–33 in *Gottes Offenbarung.* Munich.
1963c   *Das Gesetz und die Propheten.* Göttingen. English translation, *The Law and the Prophets.* Oxford, 1965.
1969   *Ezechiel.* 2 volumes. Biblischer Kommentar: Altes Testament 13/1–2. Neukirchen. English translation, *Ezekiel.* 2 volumes. Philadelphia, 1979–83.

Festal Drama

J. H. EATON

[[110]] My interpretation of Isaiah 40–55 can be correlated with other prophets in another aspect, that of cult-drama.

We have already seen that cult-drama has left its mark on these chapters—40:1–11 draws upon the messages that had launched the festal procession, chap. 53 on the choral revelation that had interpreted the ritual mystery, chaps. 49 and 50 on the speeches of the king in the rites, chaps. 46 and 47 on the cult-prophetic poetry that had been wielded as a weapon against oppressors. It is important to see more fully how the kind of dramatic prophecy reflected here is exemplified by a variety of texts from the late seventh century onwards. (For the following analyses cf. especially my *ONHZ* [[*Obadiah, Nahum, Habakkuk, and Zephaniah* [London: SCM, 1961]]].)

First of these we may mention Nahum. As in Isaiah 40–55, we have two series or sub-cycles (Nah 1:2–2:13/12; 2:14/13–3:19), consisting of varied units which together speak salvation for Judah and doom for the great oppressor. The scenes created in the imagination change swiftly. The direct addresses may switch abruptly from party to party without indication in the text, but clarified no doubt by the manner of oral delivery (e.g., 1:12–14). Each of the two series shows God challenging his foes, launching his attack, winning his victory, and each ends with a dirge over the fallen enemy; the second series differs from the first in containing no word of salvation directly to God's people, and it is more [[111]] specific about Nineveh's sin. The actuality is so vivid (one sees the bounding and jostling chariots, hears the crack of the whip, etc.) that some exegetes have been misled into thinking the composition followed the event.

In two respects we are especially reminded of Isaiah 40–55. Firstly that Yahweh's battle-march and triumph lead to a scene of messengers bringing good tidings over the mountains to Zion, launching the celebration of

Reprinted with permission and excerpted from "Relation to Other Prophetic Collections," *Festal Drama in Deutero-Isaiah* (London: SPCK, 1979) 110–14.

247

the festivities: "Behold upon the mountains the feet of the tidings-bearer announcing peace . . ." (2:1/1:15). It is apparent from this that Isaiah 40–55 follows pre-exilic precedent in envisaging the end of imperial oppression in terms of Yahweh's festal victory and advent (pp. 41, 74–75 [[not reprinted in this volume]]). The second obvious resemblance between Nahum and Isaiah 40–55 lies in the doom-words against the foe which vividly imagine the downfall of the capital city and the capture of the images (pp. 57–59 [[not reprinted in this volume]]).

Another comparable work of cultic prophecy is the Book of Habakkuk. Here we find first the familiar pattern when a prophet assisted in the meeting of God and congregation: he voices a lament about the oppression of society (1:2–4), mediates an answering oracle (1:5–11), voices a second lament (1:12–17), and after a vigil (2:1) mediates a second divine answer (2:2–4) which was also to be written as a placard of witness. And now the doom of the imperial oppressor is hastened by a divine assault through the prophetic mouth—a series of execrations, mysterious parables by which the arrows of divine justice will find their appropriate target (2:5–20). In chap. 3 we find the prophet actualizing God's battle against the arch-foe by falling into ecstasy and describing the fearful divine warfare which he sees in vision; the details here, such as the dearth in nature and the conquest of the waters, point to a setting in the autumn festival in the presence of king and assembly (3:13), as I have argued in *ZAW* (1964). The vision of Yahweh going into battle may be compared with that in Isa 42:10–17 (pp. 50–51 [[not reprinted in this volume]]); through both, promise of salvation is strengthened. Note also the comparability of the parabolic woes (Isa 45:9–10; Hab 2:6, 9, 12, 15, 19) and of the ridiculing of idols (pp. 43, 54 [[not reprinted in this volume]]; Hab 2:18–19).

The Book of Zephaniah, when seen as a whole, is also evidence of prophetic drama. The units here are mostly oracles in form with occasional variations such as prophetic announcements (1:7, 14–16, 18) and festal hymns (3:14–15, 16–17). The recital presents to the imagination in awful actuality the supreme intervention of Yahweh, his "Day." The imagined events come before us in three "acts," progressive and also having an inner symmetry. The first "act" is wholly concerned [[112]] with the terrible wrath of Yahweh against a corrupted world; two pieces see this wrath bearing against the whole earth (1:2; 1:3), then four relate it to Jerusalem (1:4–7; 1:8–9; 1:10–11; 1:12–13), then two again relate it to the whole earth (1:14–16; 1:17–18). The second "act" imagines Yahweh's victorious warfare against all oppression, both in the heathen nations and in Jerusalem; the dreadful aspect of his Day is continued here, but some elements of hope for a "remnant" begin to emerge; two pieces convey a last warning as the divine warfare commences (2:1–2; 2:3–4); in a

geographical pattern like that used by Amos 1–2, four pieces picture the
fall of God's enemies on all sides (2:5–7; 2:8–11; 2:12; 2:13–15) and two
pieces convey his attack on sinners in Jerusalem (3:1–7; 3:8). The third
"act" shows the positive result of Yahweh's Day, a purged and restored
society gathered about a glorious Zion; after the universal prospect (3:9–
10), a series of short oracles and hymns centre on Zion, singing a crescendo of joy over her transformation (3:11–20). Words of the festivals
resound most clearly in 1:7 (applied threateningly) and in 3:5, 14–15,
16–17. Resemblance to Isaiah 40–55 is most obvious in the celebration
of Zion's restoration, especially the hymnic response to the coming of
Yahweh King of Israel to his bride Zion (3:15, 17).

Especially close to Nahum and to Isaiah 46–47 is Jeremiah 50–51.
Again we find the prophet creating a vivid actuality of the future downfall of the imperial foe. The assailing armies are called to and encouraged, the axe of Yahweh is adjured and empowered, the downfall is
announced, the taunts are raised. A few extracts will illustrate the drama:

> Declare among the nations and proclaim . . . Babylon is taken! Bel is put
> to shame! Marduk is dismayed! Her images are put to shame. . . . Flee
> from the midst of Babylon. . . . Set yourselves in array against Babylon,
> all that bend the bow . . . her bulwarks are fallen, her walls thrown
> down . . . the noise of battle is in the land, and of great destruction. How
> is the hammer of the whole earth cut down and broken! How is Babylon
> become a horror among the nations. . . . Hark, they flee and escape out
> of the land of Babylon to declare in Zion the vengeance of Yahweh our
> God, the vengeance of his Temple. . . . Behold I am against you, O
> proud one, says the Lord Yahweh of Hosts. . . . A sword against the
> Chaldeans, says Yahweh . . . a sword against her warriors . . . a sword
> against their horses and chariots . . . a sword against her treasures . . . a
> drought against her waters. . . . My battle-axe are you, my weapon of
> war, with you will I break in pieces the nations . . . and with you will I
> [[113]] break in pieces the horse and his rider . . . and with you will I
> break in pieces man and woman, and with you will I break in pieces
> young man and maid, and with you will I break in pieces the shepherd
> and his flock, and with you will I break in pieces the husbandman and
> his yoke, and with you will I break in pieces the governors and com-
> manders, and before your very eyes will I requite Babylon . . . for all the
> evil they have done in Zion, says Yahweh.

And so the imagination of the terrible scenes of Yahweh's intervention
continues here at length and with sustained excitement.

Among other examples I mention only Isaiah 13–14, with resemblances to all the materials that have been adduced here, not least
Zephaniah's Day of Yahweh. Prediction passes into actualization; the
mocking elegy (14:4f.) is raised over the doomed tyrant.

From the texts just considered we learn of an important contribution of the prophetic classes at the centre of worship. In addition to the articulation of the dialogue between the manifest deity and his gathered people, the prophets contributed to another basic action in the festival, Yahweh's victory over chaos and oppression. Their words, no doubt accompanied by gestures and filling out the meaning of liturgical movements, created vivid scenes in the imagination of all participants, scenes of preparation for the war, calling out of armies, adjuring Yahweh's weapons, doom-laden condemnations, the advance of the warrior God, his challenge to combat, the din, smoke, fire, and slaughter of battle, the relief of Zion, songs of mockery, Yahweh's return to his beloved Zion, hymns of joy, visions of fertility. It was natural that these basic festal themes and scenes should be linked at times of crisis with current political experiences. At climaxes of history prophets would thus apply their traditions to the prediction of a particular tyrant's downfall and Zion's relief from a particular affliction.

In launching these dramatically imagined scenes of Yahweh's warfare, which actualize their perception of the imminent future, the prophets could achieve several aims. They prepare the people's understanding of coming events, showing them as the work of Yahweh in judgement and fidelity. Further, by drawing the assembly into their vision, they may change their present attitude: sinners may tremble (Zephaniah), pessimists regain faith. More directly, the prophets intended to assist in the battle of Yahweh, hastening on and ensuring the reality yet to come, for it was held that the prophetic word could hew peoples like a sword (Hos 6:5), devastate like a sledge-hammer (Jer 23:29), tear down [[114]] kingdoms and plant new ones (Jer 1:9f.). With such motivation the prophets' speech rose to a fierce and brilliant power, all their strength and skill being devoted to the lively actualization of the imagined scenes. The succession of units is not necessarily the result of later redaction, for it is often the series which builds up the intensity of the scenes. As the prophets functioned in groups, sometimes one ecstatic speaker will have succeeded another, carrying the visionary drama a stage further.

The Isaianic circle (pp. 106–7 [[not reprinted in this volume]]) was such a group, to judge from Isaiah 13–14, 24–27, 33, etc. Their work in 40–55 is in many respects another example of dramatic prophecy in worship to add to the specimens we have in Nahum, Zephaniah, Habakkuk, Jeremiah 50–51. Their imagination was not fatally restricted by the circumstances of the exilic period. No less than their predecessors, they were able to project in brilliant words the festal triumph of Yahweh the King and through it declare the imminent political deliverance of Israel: Yahweh the warrior goes forth to the vengeance (42:13f.), down comes the queenly tyrant-city in disgrace (47), the images and their ministers troop off into captivity (46), in triumph the King Yahweh marches to Zion (40; 52), his power of salvation and rich providence radiates to the ends of the world, his highest minister, his royal servant, is brought through greatest trials to eminence, where he shares in the glorious reign. All this salvation is dramatized in brilliant words and combined with extensive elements of argument in the tradition of the festal dialogues (§38, pp. 42, 51, etc. ⟦not reprinted in this volume⟧) to uplift the assembly with vision, faith, and hope.

A Close Reading of Zephaniah

[[55]] Chapters 1 and 2 [[not reprinted here]] provide a methodological foundation for exploring Zephaniah. The first chapter states the need for both close reading and genre analysis in a thorough literary study, and the second chapter explains genre study. This chapter attempts a close reading of Zephaniah to reveal its literary artistry and provide information about its genre. As was stated in the first chapter, "close reading" means the careful evaluation of the major aspects of a literary work. While some facets of Zephaniah are not mentioned, the points covered reflect the main elements of Zephaniah.

The Structure of Zephaniah

Edgar V. Roberts defines structure as "the organization of a literary work as influenced by its plot . . . or main idea. . . . The word is also sometimes defined as the pattern of emotions in the literary work" (1973: 119). Every literary analysis needs to deal with structure, since themes, images, ideas, and actions must be revealed through a literary framework. A work's structure should be one with the other elements of the art form. That is, it should be appropriately chosen in consideration of genre, plot, characterization, and imagery. A well-chosen structure allows these components to blend in a logical fashion. As Roberts declares, "In a good work of literature, the parts are not introduced accidentally. One part demands another, sometimes by logical requirement" (1973: 120). Finally, an effective structure is cohesive and unobtrusive. Kitto says that

Reprinted with permission and excerpted from "A Close Reading of Zephaniah" and "The Application of Genre Theory to the Close Reading of Zephaniah," in *Zephaniah: A Prophetic Drama* (Journal for the Study of the Old Testament Supplement Series 69; Sheffield: Almond, 1988) 55–61, 94–97, and 135–36.

in the best literary work "the component parts are grouped in one un-alterable way; the composition has what the Greeks called *rhythm*, and it never occurs to us that we should mentally recompose it" (1966: 16). Since structure is so interrelated with other parts of a literary piece [[56]] there is some overlap between a discussion of structure and the explana-tion of other literary aspects in this chapter. An effort is made, however, to keep such overlap to a minimum.

Biblical scholars have dealt quite inadequately with the structure of Zephaniah. Most merely posit some sort of three-part scheme, as if the book has a superstructure but no substructure. S. R. Driver reduced Zephaniah to three convenient parts: Destruction (1:1–18), Repentance (2:1–3:7), and Restoration (3:8–20) (1891: 341–42). Childs divides the book into threats against Judah (1:2–2:3), threats against the nations (2:4–3:8), and promises to each (3:9–20) (1980: 458). Other writers out-line the prophecy according to its individual threats of judgment (Ralph Smith 1984: 124), or its threats *and* its redactional layers (J. M. P. Smith, Ward, and Bewer 1911: 172–74, 182ff.). Even commentators who deal more carefully with this aspect of the work fail to notice the subtle struc-tural shifts the writer employs. In short, these commentators may deal with themes, or major movements in the text, but they hardly explain *structure*.

One must discern the intent of a structure before making statements about it. Usually, as noted above, a work's structure reflects its plot. Stated briefly, Zephaniah's plot revolves around the writer's concept of "the day of Yahweh," and the prophecy's framework is chosen to reveal this idea. Clyde Francisco (1977) recognizes that Zephaniah offers many notions about "the day of Yahweh," including that the day is imminent (1:14), a time of terror (1:15), a judgment for sin (1:17), and a disruption of na-ture (1:15). It will fall on all creatures and all nations (1:2–3, 2:4–15), and will be survived by a remnant that will enjoy the blessings of Yahweh (2:3, 3:9ff.). Bernard De Souza lists more of these characteristics, and sums up the "day" as an expression of God's wrath (1970: 12–17). Thus, it is the in-tent of the structure of Zephaniah to gradually introduce these plot ele-ments. This process allows the plot's conflict and resolution to unfold in an orderly fashion that lets tension build throughout the book.

Dialogue in Zephaniah. Zephaniah's framework is built on dialogue between Yahweh and the prophet that forms seven sets of speeches in the text. These speeches are evident because of the writer's shifting be-tween first- and third-person narration. Several commentators note the presence of two speakers in Zephaniah. Gerhard von Rad realizes that the book [[57]] displays "a continuous change in style between objective

descriptions of events and words spoken by God in the first person"
(1965: 122). Moulton states that, throughout the prophecy, God denounces Judah, but that "this denunciation is at intervals interrupted by
snatches of verse, not words of God, but lyric comments upon the divine
word at emphatic points" (1899: 124). Kapelrud correctly divides the
speeches by the use of first- and third-person designation for Yahweh.
He observes:

> Whatever the origin of the two styles of speech was, it is hard to find any
> other differences between them in Zephaniah than the purely gram-
> matical one that one speaks in the first person singular, the other in the
> third person (1975: 48).

Kapelrud argues that the presence of two speakers does not mean there
are two redactional layers of the text, one in first and one in third person (1975: 48). While this belief may be true, Kapelrud rejects the idea
that there is *any* significance in the existence of the two speakers. He
concludes that "the division between divine and prophetic speech is irrelevant in Zephaniah. It does not add anything to a better understanding of the message of the prophet" (1975: 49). Kapelrud errs at this
point, however, since these speeches are the key to the book's structure.
The speeches' presence, then, is unchallenged, but their significance
has gone unnoticed.

Each set of speeches consists of a speech by Yahweh and a speech by
the prophet, except that Yahweh, fittingly, has the last word.[1] Of course
the characters speak for a reason, since the speeches reveal plot, movement, characterization, and genre. As Holman claims about dialogue:

> (1) It advances the action in a definite way and is not used as mere or-
> namentation. (2) It is consistent with the character of the speakers, their
> social positions and special interests . . . (3) it gives the impression of
> naturalness . . . (4) It presents the interplay of ideas and personalities
> among the people conversing, it sets forth a conversational give and
> take—not simply a series of remarks of alternating speakers. (5) It varies
> in diction, rhythm, phrasing, sentence length, etc., according to the vari-
> ous speakers participating. (6) It serves, at the hands of some writers, to
> give relief from, and lightness of effect to, passages which are essentially
> serious or expository in nature (1972: 528).

Holman's survey of dialogue underscores its importance for plot, [[58]]
characterization, and themes. Holman also establishes that speeches
have many lengths and purposes. In Zephaniah the characters do not

1. It must be said at this point that every shift between first- and third-person speech
is treated as a speech except for Yahweh's brief threat in 2:5. This promise—"I will destroy
you, and none will be left"—is a quotation of Yahweh by the prophet.

speak directly to one another, but, as in early Greek drama, the characters supplement and complement each others' words (Kitto 1950: 55). All seven sets of speeches are examined to show how they form the book's structure.

Set one. Yahweh's first speech (1:2–6) establishes the tone for the first five series of speeches. Total judgment is announced. All of creation, including men, birds, and fish, is to share in the destruction. The reason given for the destruction of the earth is that the people have ceased to follow the Lord (1:6) and have begun, or continued, to serve other deities alongside Yahweh (1:4–5). God is obviously quite angry at the present state of affairs, and His words come with great suddenness and vehemence.

Recognizing Yahweh's extreme anger, the prophet's first speech (1:7) cautions the audience to be silent before the Lord. No defense for their actions is acceptable, and no protest is allowed. He also announces the prophecy's governing theme, the day of Yahweh. Thus the structure reveals plot in the initial round of comments. The prophet further mentions that a sacrifice is being prepared and that Yahweh has selected His guest. Such imagery would be familiar to early readers of Zephaniah.

Set two. His anger still raging, Yahweh interrupts the prophet and begins His second speech (1:8–13). Here He condemns everyone in Israel from "the princes and king's sons" (1:8) to men who believe God will do nothing good or bad about the nation's actions (1:12). General apathy about God exists in the land, which the writer conveys with sight and sound imagery. Yahweh is shown here as all-knowing, since He sees all the corruption in the land.

Continuing his initial theme, the prophet now elaborates on the day of the Lord (1:14–16). Three basic components of the day are revealed: its imminent nature (1:14); its terrifying aspects (1:15); and its disruptive character (1:15). Once again the sober prophet solemnly warns the audience of its fate. At this point the oblique reference to "sweeping away" is already an event with definite contours.

Set three. God's speech (1:17) is shorter and less vitriolic than the previous two, but it still declares that the people's sin will cause them to become "dust and . . . filth." In this round of orations His short speech sets the stage for the prophet's first long speech.

[59] The prophet's third series of remarks (1:18–2:7) is vital to the scheme of the play, for he inserts two more aspects of the plot, which are the possibility of escaping judgment and the condemnation of other kingdoms. To this point no hope for averting the wrath of God has been offered; rather, the entire world is to be destroyed. In the midst of this hopelessness the prophet mentions that the "humble of the land" may,

perhaps, be saved (2:3). This group of people becomes the remnant from whom God forges a new, righteous nation (cf. 3:12–13). The author uses this piece of foreshadowing to offer insight into the end of the play.

Nearly as important as the possibility of forgiveness is the knowledge that Israel's enemies will also be judged on the day of the Lord. The reader therefore learns that all nations are responsible to God. Israel is given some encouragement, for the land of the enemies is promised to the remnant (2:7). Once more the writer anticipates the last two series of speeches by speaking of the remnant's exaltation. Expectation is thereby heightened. In the midst of conflict, resolution is in sight.

Set four. Since it has been the prophet who has provided the new schematic elements, Yahweh is now in the unusual position of filling out *the prophet's* message (2:8–10). In this way the two characters work as interchangeable revealers, and the word of the two is shown as one united word. Because of the pride of Ammon and Moab (2:10) they too will receive severe punishment (2:9). Also, Yahweh himself now mentions that the remnant will plunder their enemies. More light, then, is shed on the darkness of absolute, devastating judgment. Very briefly (2:11), the prophet mentions that the nations are judged because of their idols. These gods will have to pay homage to Yahweh. This verse is to be read with 1:4–6, because both denounce foreign gods. The sin of Israel and her neighbors is linked as one and the same. This idea is renewed when Israel and Assyria are compared (cf. 2:13–3:5).

Structurally, the fourth series of comments serves as a pause in the action. No startling new factors are introduced, no further characterizations made, or clever insights offered. This set is really a lull before the storm of activity in the concluding orations. Once more anticipation is raised, this time by a lack of statements instead of an abundance of them.

Set five. Not wanting to forget even one enemy, the Lord includes Ethiopia in His judgment (2:12). Such a statement precludes the possibility of God being unaware of the nations' sins.

〚60〛 In another long speech (2:13–3:5), the second actor compares Israel with Assyria, traditionally one of her most bitter enemies. Nineveh is to be just as devastated as Moab and Ammon (cf. 2:9 and 3:14). The once-great city becomes a place despised by all. Just at the point at which the reader is enjoying the destruction of Assyria, however, the author reverses his line of thought to show how Israel is similarly wicked. Every level of society in Israel is unresponsive to God. Officials and judges are corrupt, prophets are "wanton," and priests "profane" (3:3–5).

Clearly the plot's conflict is now fully presented. It finds its summary in this fifth speech of the prophet. Israel and the nations stand together in direct opposition to God. For His part, the Lord is sending judgment on all offenders. As has been seen, however, this conflict can be resolved through repentance.

Set six. Yahweh himself begins the resolution (3:6–13). It has been His purpose to judge and destroy (3:6–8), but now the author unveils the final element of his plot, the mercy of God. The day of Yahweh will conclude with the grace of Yahweh. His grace is extended first to all the nations. They will receive the opportunity to "call upon the name of the Lord and serve Him with one accord" (3:9). In return, Yahweh will purify their speech (3:9).

More importantly, for Zephaniah's audience, the Lord will take away the shame of Israel and forgive the nation's sin. A purging process must take place, whereby the old, proud people are removed in favor of a humble, holy remnant, but this process benefits the nation (3:13). Another integral part of the plot is now in place. Yahweh's remnant has moved into the realm of reality.

Likewise, the prophet encourages the audience to rejoice in the presence of God ("in your midst") and his plans for restoration (3:14–17). Once more the two characters are partners in revelation. Both have proclaimed judgment, and now both join in the announcement of the remnant's rise and the nation's resulting restoration. God will act as warrior for Israel and rejoices over them (3:17). The prophet's final speech completes his character. At the start of the book he was a warning figure, while at the end he is an exhorter of the people. Thus, he is the complete prophet, combining judgment and salvation in his message.

The pleasant turn of events does not totally surprise the reader, for the author hints at Yahweh's redeeming work in 2:7 and 2:9. All tension built over the threatened judgment is relieved as the ⟦61⟧ foreshadowing changes to fulfilled promise. By using this method of interrelating promise and completion the book's structure is tightly bound by allusion and concrete image.

Set seven. Only Yahweh speaks in 3:18–3:20. At this point He summarizes His acts of grace by saying He will deal with Israel's oppressors, save her cripples, and bring her scattered people home. The prophecy's plot is now also complete. It seems a strange ending, for the book's beginning suggested an unhappy conclusion. The writer shows his artistic skill by changing the expected into something surprising and different. Zephaniah is not allowed to degenerate into an oracle of total doom, which saves the work from being a dreadful, hopeless mass of condemnation.[2]

---

2. This viewpoint is opposed to Moulton's assertion that "the structure . . . is entirely in the Doom form." Cf. Moulton, *The Literary Study*, 124.

Throughout Zephaniah the book's structure effectively unfolds the intended plot. Each set of speeches has an artistic purpose, whether it is to present a problem, heighten suspense or tension, or conclude the work with a satisfactory resolution. Both speakers are important, for each actor's part is versatile enough to initiate plot elements or buttress the comments of the other. These structural achievements point to an author with a definite plan for presenting his story, and one who can carry out his plan with subtlety and ingenuity.

. . . .

The Application of Genre Theory

A Comparison of Zephaniah to Drama

[94] Because of the data gathered from the close reading of Zephaniah in Chapter 3 [pp. 252–58 in this volume] it is possible to note many distinct parallels between Zephaniah and drama. Each element of the prophecy explored through close reading either has clear affinity with dramatic elements or fails to differ greatly from drama. Thus, each aspect of Zephaniah charted in Chapter 3 is now studied in the light of similarities and differences with drama. Through this comparison a clear decision regarding the dramatic nature of Zephaniah can be made.

Structure and Dialogue. Dramatic structure can take many forms. At the most fundamental level the framework of a drama is marked by scenes and acts, which are basically major movements of the story. Scenes build upon one another to form acts and the sum of these acts composes a play. Alan S. Downer realizes the importance of the scene when he writes:

> The basic unit in the dramatic structure is properly called the *scene*; but it is necessary to be aware constantly that the term has several meanings in theatrical usage. . . . As the basic unit of play construction, however, it means simply a portion of the total play in which the stage is occupied by an unchanging group of players (1955: 169–70).

Scenes end for various reasons, the chief of which is to move the plot to a different point. Each scene adds something to the overall presentation of the story. As Downer explains:

> Each of the scenes in the act is made up of varying amounts of three elements: exposition, action, and preparation. Exposition is the recounting of the past, action is the forward movement of the scene, and preparation is the hint of things to come, the unanswered question (1955: 170).

Every succeeding scene therefore is built upon previous action, functions as a present plot device, and projects future plot development.

Acts consist of scenes. Acts were originally divided in Greek drama by the appearance of the chorus in the play. The chorus normally appeared five times, creating five acts (Holman 1972: 7). Hugh Holman notes that to "varying degrees the five-act structure corresponded to the five main divisions of dramatic action: exposition, complication, [[95]] climax, falling action, and resolution" (1972: 7). Since then the acts have coalesced so that most modern plays are three acts, with some plays even portraying only one act. From Holman's survey it is obvious that acts end at major points in the plot. One significant portion of the drama ends and another begins. Acts are not superfluous, or chosen at random, but are keys to how a drama must be understood.

Effective dialogue is critical in drama, since it is the playwright's main source of communication. Good dialogue illuminates plot, characterization, themes, and all other aspects of the play. Theodore W. Hatlen sets forth several standards for dialogue when he declares:

> Discourse in drama must be clear since the language must be immediately apprehended by the listener; in the theater, there is no turning back the page, no pause to weigh and consider a line before continuing to the next. The dialogue must be interesting despite the need for simplicity and economy. It should capture the spirit of life and character. . . . The diction must be appropriate for the character and the situation. Lines do not exist in the theater as separate entities. They are always in context. They grow out of the emotionally charged incidents of the plot. The language of drama must be dynamic. As we have already suggested, speech is a form of action. The dialogue shows the character's relationship to others, reflects the progression of the action, indicates what is happening inside the characters, reveals their suffering, growth or decline. It is a means of articulating the clash of wills and the conflicting motivations (1962: 51–52).

Hatlen's statements cogently emphasize the importance of dialogue in drama. It is the major element the dramatist can use to unfold the various parts of his play. Dialogue's significance can hardly be overstated.

Zephaniah's structure parallels dramatic structure in a number of ways because it is constructed on a series of speeches. As in drama, the dialogue of Zephaniah reveals a plot, character, and themes. It moves the plot from one point to the next, always careful to hint at future events through skillful use of foreshadowing. Since the speeches in Zephaniah are arranged in pairs a sense of scenes emerges, and from the scenes grow an outline of acts.

Many scholars have noted the presence of three major parts of Zephaniah. S. R. Driver says these parts are destruction (chapter one), ⟦96⟧ repentance (2:1–3:7), and restoration (3:8–20) (1891: 341–42). Parts one and three of this scheme accurately reflect Zephaniah's emphasis, but part two over-emphasizes the role of repentance in restoration. The verse divisions are also incorrect. Childs' three portions are threats against Judah (1:2–2:3), threats against the nations (2:4–3:8), and promises to each (3:9–20) (1980: 458). Childs' three headings are basically correct, but like Driver he fails to divide the book according to the characters' speeches. While neither scholar mentions the superstructure of the book formed by the characters' speeches, both do notice the major divisions of Zephaniah. Three major divisions of the prophecy do exist, and they are fashioned by a series of provocative speeches.

The first major division of the book is 1:2–17. This section consists of five speeches, three by Yahweh and two by the prophet, that describe the general nature of the day of Yahweh. The first two speeches set forth the idea of catastrophic judgment and provide a name for that judgment. Speeches three and four state that Judah will suffer through the day of the Lord, and again state the nature of Yahweh's judgment. Yahweh concludes the first part of the prophecy by categorically saying that the sin of the people will result in condemnation (1:17).

Once a general notion of judgment is presented, the second major division of the book tells who will suffer with Judah in the great judgment (1:18–3:5). The prophet gives the first speech in this section, claiming that the "shameful nation" Judah (2:1) will be joined in judgment by Philistia. Yahweh responds by adding Moab and Ammon to the list (2:8–10). The prophet agrees with God's destruction of their idols (2:11), only to be followed by Yahweh's condemnation of Cush (2:12). Finally, the prophet condemns Assyria and concludes his sober comments as he began them—with a denunciation of Judah (3:1–5). As in the first division, the speeches of the characters create the plot in the second section.

After the second division incredible tension exists. Judah and her neighbors are to be destroyed. A third division is needed to provide some relief to the reader. Yahweh's first speech offers hope through the day of Yahweh (3:6–13). A remnant will be saved that will be joined by nations purified by judgment. This development is foreshadowed in 2:3, 7, and 9. The prophet rejoices in this resolution (3:14–17), and is followed by the Lord's promises to the remnant. ⟦97⟧ One speech logically follows another, filling out or explaining what went before and moving ahead towards the end of the book.

As was stated in Chapter 3, it is the dialogue of Zephaniah that creates the prophecy's structure. The speeches in the book are recognizable by the constant shifting between first- and third-person speech. The reason the book cannot be divided at the places Driver and Childs suggest is that their schemes interrupt unfinished speeches. Dialogue moves the prophecy's story and establishes the personality traits of Yahweh and the prophet.

It is apparent that the structure and dialogue of Zephaniah reflect the same basic principles as in drama. Sets of speeches work together to form parts of the plot, thus serving as scenes. Groups of speeches that serve as scenes constitute a section of the plot, and therefore create acts. Three basic acts are evident in the text, the first (1:2–17) consisting of three scenes, the second (1:18–3:5) of three scenes, and the third (3:6–20) of two scenes. These scenes and acts fit well with basic dramatic plot theory, as is shown below [not reprinted here].[3] Perhaps the most telling argument for the dramatic nature of Zephaniah's structure is its formation around sets of speeches. There is no doubt about the existence of these speeches grammatically or contextually, so their significance must be recognized. Zephaniah's structure and dialogue are therefore definitely dramatic.

3. Chapter 5 [not reprinted here] divides the text into acts and scenes to show how the prophecy reads as a drama.

Bibliography

Childs, Brevard
  1980   *Introduction to the Old Testament as Scripture.* Philadelphia: Fortress.
De Souza, Bernard
  1970   *The Coming of the Lord.* Jerusalem: Franciscan Press.
Downer, Alan S.
  1955   *The Art of the Play: An Anthology of Nine Plays.* New York: Holt.
Driver, S. R.
  1891   *An Introduction to the Literature of the Old Testament.* Reprinted in Gloucester, Massachusetts: Peter Smith, 1972.
Francisco, Clyde T.
  1977   *Introducing the Old Testament.* Revised edition. Nashville: Broadman.
Hatlen, Theodore W.
  1962   *Orientation to the Theater.* New York: Appleton-Century-Crofts.
Holman, C. Hugh
  1972   *A Handbook to Literature.* 3d edition. New York: Odyssey.
Kapelrud, Arvid S.
  1975   *The Message of the Prophet Zephaniah.* Olso-Bergen-Tromso: Universität-forlaget.
Kitto, H. D. F.
  1950   *Greek Tragedy.* 2d edition. Garden City, New York: Doubleday.

1966   *Poiesis: Structure and Thought.* Los Angeles: University of California Press.

Moulton, Richard G.

1899   *The Literary Study of the Bible.* Revised edition. Boston: Heath.

von Rad, Gerhard

1965   *Old Testament Theology.* Volume 2. Translated by D. M. G. Stalker. New York: Harper & Row.

Roberts, Edgar V.

1973   *Writing Themes about Literature.* 3d edition. Englewood Cliffs, New Jersey: Prentice-Hall.

Smith, John M. P., William H. Ward, and Julius A. Bewer

1911   *A Critical and Exegetical Commentary on Micah, Zephaniah, Nahum, Habakkuk, Obadiah and Joel.* The International Critical Commentary. New York: Scribner's.

Smith, Ralph

1984   *Micah–Malachi.* Word Biblical Commentary 32. Waco, Texas: Word.

Jonah from the Perspective of Its Audience

DAVID F. PAYNE

⟦3⟧ The little book of Jonah seems to hold a perennial interest and attraction for many of us; but it is amply clear from recent publications on the subject that the world of scholarship has not yet reached unanimity about Jonah, and probably never will. The uniqueness of the book is, I suppose, the chief cause of the difficulty in reaching objective and definitive conclusions about some of the questions it raises. There do seem to be fairly clear objective grounds, in a measure of linguistic evidence, for thinking that the book is relatively late; if the case for its late date is not watertight, it may at least for present purposes be assumed to be established. (Kaiser at any rate offers it as a "result" rather than a "problem" of Old Testament study.)

Most of the book's issues and problems require a more subjective approach, and it is not surprising that differing viewpoints are held. Among the unresolved questions the most important is without doubt the purpose of the book; and the overlapping problem of the book's genre is also fundamental. There are however a number of other questions, of less importance but by no means without significance; these include (i) the presentation of the prophet, (ii) the function of Nineveh in the book, (iii) the function of the pagans, and (iv) the relationship of the book to other literature.

Reprinted with permission from *Journal for the Study of the Old Testament* 13 (1979) 3–12.
    Paper (slightly revised) read at the 54th Summer Meeting of the Society for Old Testament Study, St. Andrews, 18–21 July, 1978.

These are questions which are often subordinate to the question of the author's purpose; moreover, they have often been *subordinated* to that question. That is to say, individual scholars, [[4]] having established their own standpoint on the purpose of the book, have tended to take a somewhat dogmatic approach to these lesser questions, and to offer interpretations which fit in with their more general standpoint. From a strict methodological point of view, however, each question deserves to be investigated separately; and it may be that the solution of relatively minor problems would point the way more clearly towards locating and clarifying the author's overall intentions.

In the search for objective criteria to apply to these and similar questions, I became increasingly convinced that it was vital to bear in mind the *audience* to which the book was addressed. It may be objected at once that we know all too little about that audience; and this is admittedly the case. Nevertheless, it may be that we can at least tentatively gauge the probable audience-reaction to various facets of the book; and on that basis draw certain conclusions about the book and its contents.

Jonah

First let us consider the central character of the book, Jonah himself. We are offered three data about him, as well as a portrayal of him, each of which can be briefly examined.

(i) *He was a known historical character.* If we assume that the original audience had no more information than we do, all they knew about the prophet is contained in one verse, 2 Kgs 14:25, which recounts that Jeroboam II's reconquest of lost territory had been prophesied by Jonah ben Amittai. The link between this verse and the book of Jonah has troubled many a modern exegete: indeed, Magonet in his monograph *Form and Meaning* describes the relationship between this verse and the book as one of the most difficult problems of all. The allegorical interpretation cuts the Gordian knot at a stroke, since it divorces the 2 Kings passage from the prophetic book. However, the allegorical approach commands little support today; in any case, it fails the audience-reaction criterion. No ancient reader would have readily taken as allegorical the name of a known historical figure.

But what was he known for? Some modern scholars have portrayed the Jonah of 2 Kings as the worst kind of nationalistic prophet; and so he may have been, for all we know, though the evidence is slender enough. The important question for our purposes now, however, is the impression Jonah ben Amittai would [[5]] have made on the ancient reader. I cannot think that the reader would have held any such view of Jonah on the basis of 2 Kgs 14:25, which states no more than that what he said came true, and was indeed the word of Yahweh. The presentation of Jonah in the book may have altered the reader's standpoint, but surely all that 2 Kgs 14:25 will have put into his mind was that Jonah was a genuine ancient spokesman of Yahweh. For this reason I do not see Jonah as a natural foil for Amos, *pace* R. E. Clements, or for that matter any other OT prophet whom we today may see in a strongly contrasting light. In other words, I see no grounds in 2 Kgs 14:25 for our unknown author's choice of Jonah ben Amittai as his hero or central character.

(ii) *He was a northerner.* L. C. Allen in his recent commentary considers this significant for the readers, in that they (as Judeans) would find a natural cause for resentment against a northern, nationalistic prophet. I have in effect already questioned the "nationalistic" label; the "northern" label is not historically open to doubt, of course, but it is only patent in 2 Kings 14, not in the book of Jonah (where indeed his very port of embarkation is a southerly one). He is presented just as a prophet, with no emphasis on his northern background. In any case, is it clear that opinion in Judah would have been hostile to ancient prophets from the north? There seems remarkably little hostility to them elsewhere in OT, with Hosea even getting into the Canon. The most one could deduce is that this prophet would seem rather remote from the readers, in time and perhaps in place too, if they recalled his Gath-hepher origins.

(iii) *He was a prophet.* To be precise, this is again not stated in the book (the description הנביא [['the prophet']] occurs only in 2 Kgs 14:25), but it is a clear implication and indeed presupposition. (Magonet finds significance in the omission, but I am not persuaded of this.) What sort of effect would a prophet as such have on the reader? If one accepts the reasoning of Grace I. Emmerson, the whole issue is the prophet's *authentication*—the book "finds a solution for the prophet's dilemma." It is easy to draw comparisons with say, Jeremiah, who undoubtedly did feel a desperate need for vindication. But would the book of Jonah have raised that sort of issue for the readers? There seems to me a wide gulf between the living voice of a Jeremiah, pleading to be understood, and a literary work written centuries after the prophet's lifetime. The later the book is, indeed, the more [[6]] likely it is that prophets as a whole were a thing of the past. The question of authentication can hardly have arisen, in, say, the fourth century B.C. or later. Such a view, on the criterion of audience-reaction, demands a remarkably early date for the book. A late date would produce an audience-reaction simply of remoteness once again: prophets were either rarities or else phenomena of an era past and gone.

If so, the reader would scarcely immediately identify himself with the prophet, except insofar as any reader does tend for psychological reasons to identify himself with the "hero" of a narrative. Even at an earlier period, for that matter, it may be doubted whether readers would readily identify themselves with such individualistic figures as the prophets.

(iv) *The portrayal of Jonah in the book.* This consideration leads naturally on to a fourth question about audience-reaction, but one of a rather different kind, namely, is the prophet caricatured, on the one hand, or sympathetically treated, on the other? Both possibilities have their advocates; and a middle way is not impossible, namely that the prophet is portrayed neutrally.

On this question I for one can see no ambiguity. Despite the arguments of Keller (notably), it is very difficult *not* to see elements of caricature in the portrait. Arguments to the contrary do not carry much weight: for instance, Keller's attempt to whitewash Jonah over his running away from Yahweh to the sea (which on his own confession was equally the domain of Yahweh) is less than convincing. He argues that it is merely the *cultic* presence of Yahweh from which Jonah sought to escape; but if so, the author certainly took no pains to clarify the point, and it is very doubtful if audience-reaction—especially in a post-prophetic era—would have grasped it. The general argument that some parts of the portrait are not unsympathetic is simply inadequate; there is no reason whatever to insist on a totally black picture if one affirms that the portrayal is essentially unsympathetic. (To take a NT analogy, the Parable of the Prodigal Son is a polemic against those who adopted the elder brother's general stance; but the portrait in Luke 15 is by no means totally unsympathetic to him.)

To sum up, the tentative answers to the four questions posed all seem to point in much the same direction: audience-reaction to the person of Jonah would have been neither hostile nor strongly sympathetic, but rather, objective and critical—a dispassionate ⟦7⟧ scrutiny of a rather remote character. It is unlikely that he conveyed any immediate impression, as e.g., an ardent nationalist, to the average reader. It is much more likely that Jonah's immediate and long unexplained disobedience to God depicted in the narrative would have attracted the reader's attention, and indeed shocked him.

Nineveh

By contrast, it seems impossible that Nineveh can have failed to create an immediate impression on any reader. At any time from that of the historical Jonah onwards, it stood as the epitome of everything that was cruelly hostile to Israel and Judah. Whether or not it came to symbolize foreign oppression, as the term אשור [['Assyria']] certainly seems to have done, is not clear; but it is not easy to suppose that the ancient readers of Jonah would have thought of Nineveh in any neutral fashion. To say that it symbolizes any and every city, or that the message of the book required the readers to identify their own community with it, seems not at all probable on the basis of the criterion of audience-reaction. (That is not to say, however, that an *a fortiori* argument could not have been drawn from it.)

A complicating factor, however, is the plain historical fact that Nineveh had fallen, before the end of the seventh century. The fact is not so much as hinted at in the book, but no reader from the sixth century onwards can have failed to know of it. Yet one would have thought that this knowledge would have detracted or distracted from the message of the book—even without defining that message too precisely. Would not the reader have been inclined to respond, "Yes, but Jonah's preaching of doom *did* come true, though not within 40 days"? Or to the question, "'Should not God pity and spare Nineveh?' . . . Well, the fact remains that He did *not*, ultimately"? In other words, the author might well have provoked quite the wrong audience-reaction by predicating Nineveh as the repentant city to which Jonah was sent.

There is a serious dilemma here, from which I can see only two ways of escape. The first is to argue that after all Nineveh does *not* signify any special city—a position I have already rejected. The other to my mind must be followed: namely, that for the purposes of his didactic work, the author utilized an already existing tradition as a datum, that the historical Jonah ben Amittai had preached to Nineveh and that the city had (temporarily, [[8]] to be sure) repented. (We may view this as a tradition without at all raising the question of its historicity.) I do not see this approach as a necessity for the interpretation of ch. 1, I may add; I can accept the statement of G. M. Landes that "The fish . . . is simply a beneficent device for returning Jonah to the place where he may reassume the commission he had previously abandoned." But if some tradition that Jonah had visited Nineveh lay to hand, it would do much to explain the otherwise obscure reasons for the selection of Jonah and Nineveh to figure in the story. Given this datum, indeed, the reader would find ch. 1 the more dramatically compelling: Why is Jonah rejecting his commission? What caused him to change his mind? How did he come to reverse his steps?

If the author had selected the name of Nineveh more or less at random, moreover, the reader would surely have been tempted to dismiss the story as simply too improbable. Surely God never could or would have pardoned a Nineveh, of all places. But the existence of a tradition about its repentance would have provided a counterbalance to the otherwise very awkward fact of its ultimate fate. (If it be objected that the Parable of the Good Samaritan might suggest otherwise, my answer would be that there is a world of difference between the specific and the general: even the most anti-Samaritan of Jesus' contemporaries would have to admit that *some* Samaritans must be decent, humane and kindly folk, but would any Jew of any era have expected a *Nineveh* to repent en bloc?)

Pagans

Next, the question may be raised of the likely audience-reaction to the pagans of the book, i.e., the sailors of ch. 1 and the Ninevites of ch. 3. J. Magonet in his monograph on the book maintains that the pagans are portrayed as showing "better behaviour [than the prophet] . . . in their relationship to God," and goes on to state that "the pagan world is depicted in glowing colours, in its piety, in its humanity and its readiness to come to Israel's God. That such a picture is as much a caricature of reality as the portrayal of Jonah, need hardly be said (though surprisingly enough it rarely is). . . ." Magonet's first point may be well taken; something of a contrast between untutored openness to God and Jewish disobedience may well be intended—just as the Parable of the Good Samaritan offers two or three possible models of behaviour. However, the statement that the picture of the pagans is a caricature of reality seems to me an exaggeration. My contention that the repentance of Nineveh was a preconception [[9]] of both author and audience obviously has considerable bearing on this question; let us therefore concentrate our attention rather on the sailors of ch. 1. Would the portrayal indeed have struck the readers as a caricature? We may at once concede a considerable element of drama, but can it really be said that the reader would find the picture absurdly unreal? Magonet's choice of terms may well beg the question: are the sailors displaying "piety," as he says, or is it the superstition for which sailors are often notorious? And are they truly displaying "readiness to come to Israel's God," and not rather a general and very unsurprising readiness to take any steps, religious or practical, to avert the tempest? As for their "humanity," the reason for their reluctance to throw Jonah overboard, it is clearly implied, is their fear of offending a powerful and vengeful deity, not any consideration for Jonah. The portrayal is imaginative and dramatic, but not, I think, unrealistic in Magonet's terms.

As for Nineveh, if the actual deed of repentance be not unrealistic, the portrayal is again perfectly acceptable, except perhaps for the detail that the animal kingdom too is obliged to wear sackcloth and repent. The repentance of dumb beasts may be a heightening of drama or a touch of humour, or it may be intended to demonstrate the Ninevite ignorance stressed in the last verse of the book; but the general picture is no caricature of reality, since there is evidence that in Persia animals were put into mourning garb (cf. L. C. Allen.)

The reader, then, would probably have taken sailors and Ninevites alike as a reflection of potential reality; but on the whole there does not seem to be much stress laid on either party, and it is rather doubtful whether the reader would have drawn direct moral lessons from their words and behaviour. On the whole they serve as a foil and a contrast for Jonah himself.

Earlier Literature

Part of the general difficulty in interpreting the book of Jonah is its unique character within the OT, so that it is difficult to make direct comparisons with other books. Undoubtedly there are echoes of verses here and there (especially in the psalm of Jonah in ch. 2); but there is no agreement as to the literary parallel to, or literary source of, the book of Jonah. Many have stressed the influence of Second Isaiah; Keller draws attention to Jeremiah; Clements and Fohrer emphasize Ezekiel 18 (especially [[10]] verse 21). A midrash on 2 Kgs 14:25 has also been suggested. Or, less specifically, it has been argued that the book explains the non-fulfilment of earlier divine threats of doom against foreign nations, scattered through the prophetic literature.

Whatever the author may have had in his mind, it seems relatively unlikely that the reader would have taken the book in any but its own terms. For instance, if the author had been intent on explaining away the non-fulfilment of prophetic threats, by fictional means, it would have been more effective, one would have thought, to quote some of these denunciations and refer to a much better known prophet. Moreover, once again the known subsequent fall of Nineveh would have undermined any such intention on the author's part.

If then the book was intended as an extension of, or a contrast to, any older literature the fact is well disguised. For that reason it seems a better approach to relate the book to its own historical environment, so far as we can assess it. Here we cannot but enter the realms of conjecture; or rather, we should perhaps be content to try to establish a general rather than a specific life-setting. It is probably idle, for instance, to speculate whether the book is polemic or not. If "critical orthodoxy" has tended to take it as polemic too readily, I do not think we can go so far as von Rad and say that the book does not appear to be polemical or tendentious. But for modern recognition that many of Jesus' parables are polemical by intention, we should probably have read the Parable of the Prodigal Son as didactic, simply—indeed, appeal and protest are not psychologically very far apart. By the same token, Jonah may have been written against discernible attitudes of the day, whatever precisely they may have been and wherever located.

Does the book give any hint as to its audience? A number of recent scholars have drawn parallels with wisdom literature: Kaiser, e.g., remarks that the book moves close to the question of theodicy, while Magonet emphasizes the extent to which the idea of knowledge, and especially knowledge of God, dominates the book. Was the book then issued to be put in the "Wisdom Literature" shelves of the day?

If it is true, however, that wisdom literature tends to be fairly universalistic, the wide dimensions of Jonah might suggest that if its category is simply wisdom literature, it would have been preaching to the converted to some extent. Of course, we ⟦11⟧ should avoid setting up watertight compartments, as if no book could have affinities with more than one category or genre of literature. But the category of literature which has increasingly struck me as an interesting contrast to the book of Jonah is apocalyptic, a category which has left certain representatives for us to read, but of which probably a great deal was ephemeral and has long since perished. Before exploring the contrast briefly, we may revert to the question why the author should have adopted a prophet as his central character, when prophets were possibly already rather remote figures. The current pseudonymous attribution of apocalypses to prophets might not be irrelevant; or to approach the matter in a slightly different way, the prophets may well have been viewed increasingly as predictors of doom for Israel's foes—as the Qumran *pesharim* ⟦'commentaries'⟧ prove at a somewhat later date. In part, then, the book may represent a corrective and challenge to current preconceptions about the role of the prophets.

However that may be, there is no gainsaying that the apocalyptists had a black-and-white view of good and evil, anticipated a great drama of destruction about to come, and often predicted the exact timing of it. That the book of Jonah would disappoint the apocalyptic-reading public, or the apocalyptists themselves, in these respects, is quite obvious. Here are heathen sailors who prove to be god-fearing, Ninevites who prove to be repentant, and a prophet of the Lord who is plainly no model for the righteous to follow. The prophecy of doom is clearly there, but its timing is anything but determined, once the prescribed forty days have elapsed. (Nineveh had fallen since, to be sure; but could a reader extrapolate from that fact that his own particular foe would share a like fate? Who knows?—as the book itself asks in 3:9.)

Yet interestingly, the language of determinism is there, in the repeated choice of the verb מנה of God's *ad hoc* creations: God 'appoints' indeed, not however long beforehand (as one might expect in apocalyptic), but actually in the context of encounter with the recalcitrant Jonah.

Even the great fish is conceivably an ironic contrast to the animal and monster symbolism of the apocalyptists, though this is clearly no point to be pressed.

The theme of "knowledge" is not necessarily a wisdom feature; it is part of the apocalyptic picture of the intertestamental era. The Qumran community could style itself "the knowing ones." It is ⟦12⟧ part of the description of the good, the Sons of Light. By contrast, the Isaiah "apocalypse" (Isaiah 24–27) depicts an unnamed city, about to be signally punished, in these terms:

> This is a people without discernment; therefore he who made them will not have compassion on them, he that formed them will show them no favour (Isa 27:11).

Here the very reason given for lack of compassion is lack of discernment; yet in Jonah a very contrary picture is painted, in the abysmal ignorance of Nineveh being the precise reason offered for God's pity (4:11).

Such features suggest that we have in Jonah the work of an author familiar with the apocalyptic outlook but—mildly at least—sceptical of it.

To conclude, it seems to me that a study of audience and of audience-reaction is a necessary prolegomenon to a discussion of the book's message and purpose. Certain hypotheses—I would instance C.-A. Keller's—can probably be excluded on this basis of argument alone, and others may seem more or less probable. If my arguments about the extent of traditional material in the book are acceptable, then we may better gauge the extent of the author's own material—his emphases, and perhaps the surprises he brings to his audience. And finally, if the book in some respects seems to reflect an apocalyptic milieu, we may hazard a guess at the concerns and convictions of the audience to which the author addressed himself.

Books and Articles Referred to in the Text

O. Kaiser. *Introduction to the Old Testament.* English translation. Oxford: Oxford University Press, 1975.

J. Magonet. *Form and Meaning: Studies in Literary Techniques in the Book of Jonah.* Beiträge zur biblischen Exegese und Theologie 2. Bern: Herbert Lang/ Frankfurt am Main: Peter Lang, 1976.

R. E. Clements. "The Purpose of the Book of Jonah." Pp. 16–28 in *Congress Volume, Edinburgh 1974.* Vetus Testamentum Supplements 28. Leiden: Brill, 1975.

L. C. Allen. *The Books of Joel, Obadiah, Jonah, and Micah.* New International Commentary on the Old Testament. Grand Rapids, Michigan: Eerdmans, 1976.

G. I. Emmerson. "Another Look at the Book of Jonah." *Expository Times* 88 (1976–77) 86ff.

C.-A. Keller. Pp. 263–91 in *Osée, Joël, Abdias, Jonas, Amos.* Edited by E. Jacob, C.-A. Keller, and S. Amsler. Commentaire de l'Ancien Testament 11a. Neuchâtel: Delachaux et Niestlé, 1965.

G. M. Landes. "The Kerygma of the Book of Jonah." *Interpretation* 21 (1967) 3–31.

G. Fohrer. *Introduction to the Old Testament.* English translation, London: SPCK, 1968.

G. von Rad. Pp. 289–92 in *Old Testament Theology,* volume 2. English translation, San Francisco: Harper & Row, 1965.

Part 4

Prophecy and Society

Introduction

The varying levels of relationship between prophets and their contemporaries are reflected in the material selected for this section. The very term "prophet," its currency in the time of the early "classical" prophets and its implications as regards social function and community expectation have generated some spirited discussion. For a number of recent writers the prophets of the pre-exilic period were more in the way of religious poets who were retrospectively recognized as prophets when the term began to be used of others who stood in the same succession. It is claimed that the distribution of the prophet terminology in the prophetic books suggests the redactional origins of the title where it describes the classical prophets (Auld, pp. 289–307 below; Carroll, 1983, 1988). In opposition to this it has been argued that pre-exilic Israelite society knew very well the "office" of prophet and had already developed certain expectations in terms of behavior and societal function (Overholt, pp. 354–76 below). So stated, the argument is between a reconstructed text and extrinsic anthropological evidence, but the case for the retention of "prophet" as an early designation of the eighth-century prophets (not least) can be supported from references in the prophetic books that cannot so easily be written off as redactional, even if it may be conceded that the classical prophets may have had good grounds for soft-pedalling the use of the term (Vawter 1985; Barstad 1993; Gordon 1995). The distinction between "true" and "false" prophets is firmly drawn in most Old Testament texts, yet the recognition of a prophet as one or the other could not have been so straightforward at the time (Long, pp. 308–31 below; Wilson 1980; Coggins 1993). Some recent scholars even find little use for the distinction.

It is evident, at any rate, that the canonical prophets of the pre-exilic period did not support the popular theology of the times, according to which Judah and Israel, by dint of a special relationship with God, were proof against disaster. Rather, the prophets arose to promote "righteousness," rather than "wellbeing," and for the same reason they could easily be perceived as a destabilizing element in society (Nicholson, pp. 345–53 below). Since even those who were regarded as authentic spokesmen for Yahweh could find their predictions short on fulfilment, certain tensions with their calling and with their contemporaries readily followed. The insights of modern anthropology and cognitive psychology have been summoned to help clarify this issue (Carroll, pp. 377–91 below), though the dangers involved in applying insights from societies geographically and chronologically remote from ancient Israel are apparent (Rodd 1981). Finally, the prophetic books also witness to serious community tensions after the return from Babylon, as seems to be indicated in Isaiah 56–66 and as has been noted in several recent treatments of these chapters and the period that they represent (Blenkinsopp, pp. 392–412 below; Schramm 1995).

Additional Reading

Section (i).   Were the Prophets *Prophets?*

Auld, A. G.
    1988   Word of God and Word of Man: Prophets and Canon. Pp. 237–51 in
            Ascribe to the Lord: Biblical and Other Studies in Memory of Peter C. Craigie,
            edited by L. Eslinger and G. Taylor. Journal for the Study of the Old
            Testament Supplement Series 67. Sheffield: JSOT Press.
    1990   Prophecy in Books: A Rejoinder. *Journal for the Study of the Old Testa-
            ment* 48: 31–32.
Barstad, H. M.
    1993   No Prophets? Recent Developments in Biblical Prophetic Research
            and Ancient Near Eastern Prophecy. *Journal for the Study of the Old
            Testament* 57: 39–60.
Carroll, R. P.
    1983   Poets Not Prophets: A Response to "Prophets through the Looking-
            Glass." *Journal for the Study of the Old Testament* 27: 25–31.
    1988   Inventing the Prophets. *Irish Biblical Studies* 10: 24–36.
Gordon, R. P.
    1995   Where Have All the Prophets Gone? The "Disappearing" Israelite
            Prophet against the Background of Ancient Near Eastern Prophecy.
            Bulletin for Biblical Research 5: 67–86.
Ringgren, H.
    1988   Israelite Prophecy: Fact or Fiction? Pp. 204–10 in *Congress Volume:
            Jerusalem 1986,* edited by J. A. Emerton. Vetus Testamentum Supple-
            ments. Leiden: Brill.
Vawter, B.
    1985   Were the Prophets *nābî?*s? *Biblica* 66: 206–20.
Ward, J. M.
    1988   The Eclipse of the Prophet in Contemporary Prophetic Studies.
            Union Seminary Quarterly Review 42: 97–104.

Williamson, H. G. M.
  1983   A Response to A. G. Auld. *Journal for the Study of the Old Testament* 27:
          33–39.

Section (ii). Prophetic Conflict

Coggins, R. J.
  1993   Prophecy: True and False. Pp. 80–94 in *Of Prophets' Visions and the Wis-
          dom of Sages* (R. N. Whybray Festschrift), edited by H. A. McKay and
          D. J. A. Clines. Journal for the Study of the Old Testament Supple-
          ment Series 162. Sheffield: JSOT Press.

Section (iii). Social Function of Prophecy

Buss, M. J.
  1980   The Social Psychology of Prophecy. Pp. 1–11 in *Prophecy* (G. Fohrer
          Festschrift), edited by J. A. Emerton. Beihefte zur Zeitschrift für die
          Alttestamentliche Wissenschaft 150. Berlin: de Gruyter.

Carroll, R. P.
  1989   Prophecy and Society. Pp. 203–25 in *The World of Ancient Israel: Socio-
          logical, Anthropological and Political Perspectives*, edited by R. E. Clem-
          ents. Cambridge: Cambridge University Press.
  1990   Whose Prophet? Whose History? Whose Social Reality? Troubling
          the Interpretative Community Again: Notes towards a Response to
          T. W. Overholt's Critique. *Journal for the Study of the Old Testament* 48:
          33–49.

Culley, R. C., and T. W. Overholt, eds.
  1981   *Anthropological Perspectives on Old Testament Prophecy*. Semeia 21. Chico,
          California: Scholars Press.

Davies, G. I.
  1993   Pp. 52–66 in *Hosea*. Old Testament Guides. Sheffield: JSOT Press.

Kselman, J. S.
  1985   The Social World of the Israelite Prophets: A Review Article. *Religious
          Studies Review* 11: 120–29.

Mayes, A. D. H.
  1993   Prophecy and Society in Israel. Pp. 25–42 in *Of Prophets' Visions and
          the Wisdom of Sages* (R. N. Whybray Festschrift), edited by H. A.
          McKay and D. J. A. Clines. Journal for the Study of the Old Testa-
          ment Supplement Series 162. Sheffield: JSOT Press.

Overholt, T. W.
  1979   Commanding the Prophets: Amos and the Problem of Prophetic Au-
          thority. *Catholic Biblical Quarterly* 41: 517–32.
  1989   *Channels of Prophecy: The Social Dynamics of Prophetic Activity*. Minne-
          apolis: Fortress.
  1990   It is Difficult to Read. *Journal for the Study of the Old Testament* 48: 51–54.

Rodd, C. S.
  1981   On Applying a Sociological Theory to Biblical Studies. *Journal for the
          Study of the Old Testament* 19: 95–106.

Wilson, R. R.

1980　　*Prophecy and Society in Ancient Israel.* Philadelphia: Fortress.

Section (iv).　Failure of Expectation

Carroll, R. P.

1979　　*When Prophecy Failed: Reactions and Responses to Failure in the Old Testa-ment Prophetic Traditions.* London: SCM / New York: Seabury.

1980　　Prophecy and Dissonance: A Theoretical Approach to the Prophetic Tradition. *Zeitschrift für die Alttestamentliche Wissenschaft* 92: 108–19.

Section (v).　Community Conflict

Schramm, B.

1995　　*The Opponents of Third Isaiah: Reconstructing the Cultic History of the Restoration.* Journal for the Study of the Old Testament Supplement Series 193. Sheffield: Sheffield Academic Press.

Ecstasy and Role Enactment

DAVID L. PETERSEN

Ecstasy

[[25]] The subject of role enactment is especially germane to the study of the role of the prophet. Since Duhm's commentary on Isaiah, many scholars have viewed one level of role enactment, that of ecstasy, as a hallmark of prophetic activity.[1] Hence at this point in our study, an overview of the place of ecstasy in discussions of Israelite prophecy must be undertaken. In the aforementioned volume on Isaiah, Duhm pointed to a peculiar psychological experience, ecstasy, in which the prophet received his message.[2] Gunkel, too, pointed to what he called "the mysterious experiences of the prophets."[3] Gunkel claimed that the prophets had received their visions in an elevated, almost mystical state, and that they later wrote or [[26]] spoke their message in a more normal mode of behavior. Building on Duhm's and Gunkel's recognition of ecstasy in Israelite prophecy, Hölscher proposed a much more important place for

Reprinted with permission and excerpted from "Role Theory and Prophecy," in *The Roles of Israel's Prophets* (Journal for the Study of the Old Testament Supplement Series 17; Sheffield: JSOT Press, 1981) 25–34.

1. B. Duhm, *Das Buch Jesaja* (Göttingen: Vandenhoeck & Ruprecht, 1982).

2. For a discussion of Duhm's significance, see H.-J. Kraus, *Geschichte der historisch-kritischen Erforschung des Alten Testament* (Neukirchen-Vluyn: Neukirchener Verlag, 1969) 275–283; R. Clements, *One Hundred Years of Old Testament Interpretation* (Philadelphia: Westminster, 1976) 52–56.

3. H. Gunkel, "Die geheimen Erfahrungen der Propheten Israels," *Suchen der Zeit* 1 (1903) 112–153. This essay was revised and published in *Die Schriften des Alten Testaments*, Vol. II/2, ed. H. Schmidt (Göttingen: Vandenhoeck & Ruprecht, 1915). For analysis of this material, see Kraus, *Geschichte* 360–362; Clements, *One Hundred Years* 59–61; R. Wilson, *Prophecy and Society in Ancient Israel* [[Philadelphia: Fortress, 1980]] 7.

this phenomenon in prophetic activity.[4] Invoking the psychological and religio-historical research of his own time to define what he meant by ecstasy, Hölscher maintained that ecstasy was typical of Israelite prophecy. Though Israel's prophets transformed the ecstatic mode of behavior which they had inherited from their Canaanite forebears, Hölscher claimed that the mode, ecstasy, was constitutive for Israelite prophetic activity. Of utmost importance in assessing Hölscher's work is to recognize two prominent features of his basic case. He contended that there was a particular cultural connection between Canaan and Israel which led to the development of Israelite prophecy. Ecstatic prophecy was native to the Levant and was taken over by Israel after its settlement in Syria-Palestine. The development of prophecy in Israel was one feature of its acculturation to this new setting. Further, Hölscher contended that ecstatic behavior was part of the prophet's public performance, the mode in which he delivered his message, and was not simply the private source of the prophet's call or message as Duhm and Gunkel had earlier maintained.

Hölscher's work has remained seminal. Some have denied its validity, others have incorporated insights from it. Virtually everyone has referred to it.[5] However, and somewhat surprisingly, it remained until 1962 for two full-scale and influential responses to Hölscher to be formulated. These were the volumes of Johannes Lindblom and Abraham Heschel.[6]

As for the first tome, Lindblom constructed a description of the prophet as an individual "who, because he is conscious of having been specially chosen and called, feels forced to perform actions and proclaim ideas which, in a mental state of intense inspiration or real ecstasy, have been indicated to him in the form of divine revelations."[7] As this definition demonstrates, Lindblom took pains to develop the categories of inspiration and ecstasy. "Inspiration is the more general term. Inspiration appears as mental excitement and exaltation in general. I prefer to use the term ecstasy when inspiration has grown so strong that the inspired person has lost full control of himself."[8] Using these categories, Lind-

---

4. G. Hölscher, *Die Profeten. Untersuchungen zur Religionsgeschichte Israels* (Leipzig: J. Hinrichs, 1914).

5. For brief assessments of post-Hölscher work in this regard, see Wilson, *Prophecy and Society* 5–8; Kraus, *Geschichte* 472–473.

6. J. Lindblom, *Prophecy in Ancient Israel* (Philadelphia: Fortress, 1962); A. Heschel, *The Prophets* [2 vols.] (New York: Harper Torchbooks, 1962). G. Widengren's work on the "parapsychic experience of the prophets" is, for the most part, a continuation of Hölscher's and Lindblom's insights, so his *Literary and Psychological Aspects of Hebrew Prophets*, UUÅ 10 (1948) 94–120.

7. Lindblom, *Prophecy* 46.

8. Lindblom, *Prophecy* 35.

blom was able to achieve a rather more nuanced description of intense religious experience than had Hölscher. Further, Lindblom maintained, in 〚27〛 contradistinction to Hölscher, that ecstasy was "an accessory and accidental phenomenon in the religious life of the great prophets . . . ," not an essential feature of their prophetic activity.[9]

These features, however, do not constitute the greatest difference between Lindblom and Hölscher. Rather, as Lindblom himself noted, "After more recent investigations of a religio-historical and psychological nature the ideas presented by Hölscher are hardly tenable. Ecstatic phenomena and movements are not confined to particular races, people or countries; they flourish all over the world. . . . Ecstasy with its manifestations is a general human phenomenon and based not on peculiarities of races and people but on personal predisposition in individuals."[10] For Lindblom, inspiration/ecstasy is a religio-historical universal available to all people at all times and is more the result of a personality type than it is a function of cultural or social influence.

While Lindblom's careful work in observing the variety of intense religious experience is commendable, his claim that such behavior is universal, the function of personality, tends to isolate the behavior of a prophet from the society of which he was a part. Such isolation of behavior from its social nexus is unjustified, as a recent and productive study demonstrates. Lewis, in a seminal volume entitled *Ecstatic Religion*, decries just such theories as Lindblom's as purporting a "steady state theory of mystical productivity."[11] Such an approach, Lewis argues, divorces "transcendental experience from the social environment in which it occurs. . . ." The "steady state" theory disallows much valuable evidence about intense religious experience and makes the sort of valuable conclusions which Lewis achieves—on which see below—impossible to achieve. Hence, despite Lindblom's having broadened the base for the investigation of Israelite prophetic behavior, his lack of attention to the social setting of that behavior severely hampers the use of his insight as a research model.

The other thoroughgoing response to that of Hölscher was that of Heschel. Heschel took a tack quite different from that of Lindblom. He denies systematically that Israel's prophets may be construed as ecstatics. He elaborately analyzes the literary prophets and concludes that none of the distinguishing marks of ecstasy, e.g., frenzy, merging with the god,

9. Lindblom, *Prophecy* 310.
10. Lindblom, *Prophecy* 98.
11. I. Lewis, *Ecstatic Religion. An Anthropological Study of Spirit Possession and Shamanism* (Harmondsworth: Penguin Books, 1971) 24.

extinction of self, is present in the literature of the classical prophets.[12] Having rejected ecstasy as a category with which to [[28]] understand Israelite prophecy, Heschel proposes another concept, "the divine pathos." The divine pathos signifies that "God is involved in history, as intimately affected by events in history, as living care."[13] The prophet is a person who, because of a distinctive consciousness, is able to share in the divine pathos and who is able to communicate that pathos to the human scene. Heschel writes, "The fundamental experience of the prophet is fellowship with the feelings of God, a sympathy with the divine pathos, a communion with the divine consciousness which comes about through the prophet's reflection of, or participation in, the divine pathos."[14]

By replacing ecstasy with a special prophetic consciousness, Heschel has replaced an ambiguous category with one of little analytical rigor. It is difficult indeed to know how to study either the divine pathos or a prophet's consciousness. Again, as with Lindblom, there is little attention devoted to the social setting of the prophet. Furthermore, it is difficult to deny that there is special pleading in Heschel's case since, for him, Israel's prophets appear *sui generis* [['unique']], without significant forerunners, contemporaries or descendents. Any approach which systematically excludes either the Mari prophetic material or the Deir ᶜAlla Balaam is not sensitive to important ancient Near Eastern evidence which might illumine Israelite prophecy. Heschel's tome, despite its felicitous style and its theological sensitivity, does not offer a sufficiently critical discussion of prophecy so as to allow for further research.

In an attempt to move the discussion of ecstasy forward, R. Wilson noted, as had Lindblom and Clements before him, that ecstasy has often been used to mean two quite different things: "(1) the nature of the process of divine-human communication, and (2) the behavioral characteristics arising from that process of communication."[15] Having said that, Wilson surveys anthropological studies on trance and possession behavior (anthropologists do not often use the term ecstasy). His conclusions from that survey as well as from an analysis of the stem *nbᵓ* [['prophesy']] are fundamentally fourfold: (1) some of Israel's prophets did evince stereotype possession behavior; (2) such possession behavior was not

---

12. A. Heschel, *The Prophets*, Vol. 2, 124ff. In not dissimilar fashion, I. Seierstad denied the presence of ecstasy among Israel's prophets and maintained that their experience of revelation constituted a "heightened consciousness" rather than an ecstatic loss of consciousness; Seierstad, *Die Offenbarungserlebnisse der Propheten Amos, Jesaja, und Jeremia. Eine Untersuchung der Erlebnisvorgänge unter besonderer Berücksichtung ihrer religiös-sittlichen Art und Auswirkung* (Oslo: Jacob Dybwad, 1946).

13. Heschel, *The Prophets*, Vol. 2, 11.

14. Heschel, *The Prophets*, Vol. 1, 26.

15. R. Wilson, "Prophecy and Ecstasy: A Reexamination," *JBL* 98 (1979) 324.

static, i.e., prophetic performance could vary according to historical period, place, cultural and social context; (3) possession behavior was not always the same. Prophets could deviate from the social norm for such behavior; (4) ecstatic behavior was evaluated differently by various groups inside Israel.[16] And by way of summary comment, Wilson [[29]] states, "the question of prophecy and ecstasy is far more complex than earlier scholars had supposed."[17]

One can only second Wilson's just-cited observation and welcome the careful work he has done in surveying the anthropological evidence for possession and trance behavior. Simple appeals to the work of Hölscher, Lindblom, and Heschel are no longer possible. However, one crucial question remains: is trance or possession behavior characteristic or even regularly prominent in Israelite prophetic activity.[18]

Wilson's argumentation, for one, seems to address this question in the following way. He studies the word $nb^{\jmath}$ and hypothesizes that the hithpael originally meant "to act like a prophet" whereas the niphal originally meant "to speak like a prophet." He then surveys the hithpael uses of the root as evidence for prophetic, i.e., possession, behavior.[19] One can only respond to this proposal that to speak like a prophet could be and most likely was often thought to be typical prophetic behavior. Hence, the hithpael uses could mean the same thing as the niphal occurrences. Both conjugations could mean "to speak like a prophet" since such speaking was, incontestably, typical prophetic action. Further, Wilson observes that the meanings of the hithpael and niphal uses of $nb^{\jmath}$ merged at some later point, a fact which makes the case for a distinction between these two conjugations even more difficult to evaluate. In sum, a word study of $nb^{\jmath}$ is unlikely to reveal examples of possession behavior within Israelite prophetic activity.

---

16. Wilson, "Prophecy and Ecstasy" 336–337.

17. Wilson, "Prophecy and Ecstasy" 337. Wilson builds a great deal on the observation that possession behavior may be stereotypic. For example, he suggests that the stereotypic language present in the book of Jeremiah reflects Jeremiah's behavior (*Prophecy and Society* 303). Such a contention is tantamount to asserting that any stereotypic or conventional language may be adduced as evidence of spirit possession, an inference which is unwarranted. Though possession language and behavior may be stereotypic, not all stereotypic language and behavior derive from possession behavior.

18. Some recent treatments of this question do not advance the discussion. H.-C. Schmitt reasserts Canaanite ecstasy as the source of Israelite prophecy. His thesis is difficult to sustain because he overemphasizes the Wen-Amun narrative, he underemphasizes the Mari texts, and he overlooks the Zakir inscription. Further he fails to apply higher critical methods to the texts he studies, e.g., 1 Samuel 10; 15; "Prophetie und Tradition. Beobachtungen zur Frühgeschichte des israelitische Nabitums," *ZTK* 24 (1977) 255–272.

19. Wilson, "Prophecy and Ecstasy" 330.

S. Parker, in another recent study, also treats the aforementioned
question: is possession behavior prominent in Israelite prophetic behavior? Using cross-cultural anthropological perspectives, as did Wilson,
Parker argues that there is little evidence for identifying possession
trance in Israelite prophetic activity. Possession trances are not mediumistic; i.e., there is no communication between a god and a person in
possession trances. And without such communication—a hallmark of Israelite prophecy—one can hardly speak of possession trance as a part of
the prophet's experience. Further, and more important, Parker maintains that "Yahwistic prophecy in Israel does not involve possession of any
kind."[20] Texts such as Isa 31:3–4 and Jer 23:9, texts which are often adduced as evidence for possession behavior, are better explained by appeal to ancient Near Eastern literary convention.[21] There is significant
conventionality in the portrayal of reaction to misfortune, e.g., compare
Isa 13:7–8 with Isa 31:3–4. [[30]] Further, use of terms like *mĕšuggāᶜ*
[['crazy']] is usually polemic, not a neutral description of prophetic behavior (Jer 29:24–27; 2 Kings 9; Hos 9:7). Parker does suggest that possession trance may be present in Phoenician culture, so 1 Kings 18, but it
is not part of the Israelite cultural expectation for its prophets. Parker
summarizes his position:

> I conclude that possession trance is *not* an element of Israelite proph-
> ecy, and figures in a history of Israelite prophecy only marginally in dis-
> cussions of (i) the possible impact of Phoenician prophecy on Israelite
> institutions, especially in the Omride court, and (ii) the calumny and
> mockery to which prophets could be subjected.[22]

One may only conclude that if the very presence of ecstatic, or better termed, trance or possession behavior in Israelite prophecy is moot,
and Parker's analysis surely suggests that it is, ecstasy can hardly be an essential or even regular feature of Israelite prophetic performance.
The situation with ecstasy is therefore this. Anthropological study of
trance and possession behavior allowed us to describe ecstatic behavior
in ways much more precise than was possible in earlier studies (Hölscher,
Lindblom, Heschel), volumes which have strongly conditioned the discussion of Israelite prophecy today. This new clarity enables us to ask: is
trance or possession behavior a hallmark or even a prominent feature of
Israelite prophecy? There is strong warrant for answering this question in

20. S. Parker, "Possession Trance and Prophecy in Pre-exilic Israel," *VT* 28 (1978) 281.
21. So D. Hillers, "A Convention in Hebrew Literature: The Reaction to Bad News,"
ZAW 77 (1965) 86–90, and Parker, "Possession Trance" 281–282. Cf. Wilson who maintains
that Jer 23:9 is an example of ecstatic activity, *Prophecy and Society* 7.
22. Parker, "Possession trance" 285.

the negative. Further, it is theoretically possible that only one level of role enactment intensity is characteristic of Israelite prophecy. However, since prophecy is a rather preemptive role, and since it entails a fairly complex role set, one should expect, on purely theoretical grounds, that prophecy entails more than one level of organismic involvement.

Prophetic Role Enactment

Texts which purport to describe the activity of Israel's prophets do, in fact, support the supposition that various intensities of organismic involvement are present in the behavior of Israel's prophets.[23] A survey of the prophetic corpus suggests that prophets could enact their roles in at least four different levels of organismic involvement. The first level of role enactment observable in Israelite prophetic texts is that designated by the term ritual acting. Some of the symbolic actions which Ezekiel is reported as having undertaken could [[31]] have been performed almost on cue. One may cite Ezek 4:1–3:

> And you, O son of man, take a brick and lay it before you, and portray upon it a city, even Jerusalem; and put siegeworks against it, and build a siege wall against it, and cast up a mound against it, and plant battering rams against it round about. And take an iron plate, and place it as an iron wall between you and the city, and set your face toward it, and let it be a stage of siege, and press the siege against it. This is a sign for the house of Israel.

Here Yahweh commands Ezekiel to use various materials—an air-dried brick, earth and a griddleplate—to portray Jerusalem under siege.[24] The action of the prophet in manipulating these elements is best construed as ritual acting. The gestures, the modelling of the siegeworks out of earth, required a relatively low level of organismic involvement. No one watching Ezekiel undertaking this sign act would perceive significant involvement of the prophet's self in the action. Since the action is considerably more than semiautomatic, it represents a level higher than casual enactment. And yet, since the affective component important to engrossed acting is absent, the activity entails a level lower than engrossed acting.

23. In adducing the following examples, I make no claims for the historicity of the texts. Since these examples are fully consistent with what we know about Israel's prophets, there is no reason to question the range of behavior represented in the material adduced here.

24. W. Zimmerli, *Ezekiel 1* (Hermeneia) (Philadelphia: Fortress, 1979) 161–163.

More frequent, even typical of much prophetic activity, is the level of behavior labelled engrossed acting. The actions of Nathan (2 Samuel 12), Elijah (1 Kings 21), Elisha (2 Kgs 4:8–37), Amos (Amos 7:10–17), and Isaiah (Isaiah 7) may best be understood as engrossed acting. And one may well imagine that many of the prophetic oracles without accompanying narratives would fit this paradigm. Nathan's interchange with David is a good example of engrossed acting (2 Samuel 12). Nathan operates within the strictures of conversation with the king. He does not challenge royal authority. Instead, he lets David trap himself as he responds to the parable which Nathan proffers. The picture is of a prophet maneuvering with consummate strategy, speaking with the deepest possible conviction and affecting not only the personal life of the king but issues of state as well. Clearly, the level of intensity has moved beyond that of ritual acting; with engrossed acting, the ego is fully integrated in the role performance. The prophet is not speaking "as if," i.e., as if he were Yahweh himself; hence the activity may not be classified as classic hypnotic role taking. Further, the prophet's behavior does not involve the loss of voluntary action, thus preventing the action from being termed ecstatic. [[32]] This level of behavior—engrossed acting—aptly describes much of the behavior we associate with Israel's prophets.

As for classical hypnotic role taking, it is possible to maintain that vision reports constitute the requisite "as if" behavior. A person who behaves "as if" she or he were receiving external ocular stimuli, without receiving externally observable stimuli which are reported in the vision, is involved in this type of behavior. Such behavior is especially prominent in the vision reports which Lindblom labels as "hallucinations," visions in which the perceived world does not correspond to the objects in the external world.[25] Though Lindblom does not wish to apply this category to Israel's classical prophets, it is difficult indeed to claim that either the flying scroll (Zech 5:1–4) or the flying basket (Zech 5:5–10) corresponds easily to the "real" world. Such vision reports exemplify the level of involvement represented by the term classical hypnotic role taking. One need not deny the reality of the prophet's visionary experience to make this point. Rather to classify visionary experience as classical hypnotic role taking is to observe that prophets report visions "as if" they were normal ocular experience, something which, one suspects, the prophets themselves would not claim.

Evidence for the level of organismic involvement termed histrionic neurosis also appears in Hebrew Bible texts depicting prophetic behavior. In a detailed study of the phrase, "the hand of Yahweh," J. Roberts has

25. Lindblom, *Prophecy in Ancient Israel* 122ff.

compared that Hebrew phrase with other similar ancient Near Eastern formulations. He discovered that the phrase uniformly refers to what Labat has called "the disastrous manifestation of the supernatural power."[26] In both Akkadian and Ugaritic texts, sickness and natural catastrophe are attributed to the presence, and presumably pressure, of the divine hand. Roberts claimed that the same meaning obtains in the Biblical material as well, so Exod 9:15. The use of this phrase in the prophetic literature represents a specialized usage, a meaning in large part drawn from the prophet's physical response to the divine presence. For the prophet, the presence of the divine may be perceived as illness or pain. So Jeremiah:

> I did not sit in the company of
> merrymakers,
>   nor did I rejoice;
> I sat alone, because your hand was upon me,
>   for you filled me with indignation. [33]
> Why is my pain unceasing,
>   my wound incurable,
>   refusing to be healed?
> Will you be to me like a deceitful brook,
>   like the waters that fail? (Jer 15:17–18)

Roberts suggests that in contexts such as Jeremiah 15 the expression "the hand of Yahweh" refers to "some kind of ecstatic experience of the prophet."[27] By way of making that judgment more precise, I suggest the action or state to which "the hand of Yahweh" refers be understood as the level of organismic involvement denoted by the term histrionic neurosis. There are, as Roberts makes clear, physiological symptoms without the expected pathology, a hallmark of the sixth level of organismic involvement. To make this contention is not to question the reality of the perceived illness or pain, but is rather to point to its origin in the prophet's encounter with the deity. The level of behavior labelled histrionic neurosis could be part of Israelite prophetic role enactment.

The ensuing level of organismic involvement, ecstasy, is difficult to discern among Israel's prophets. To be sure, this form of involuntary behavior seems to be present in the activity of the Baal prophets described in 1 Kings 18. However, if Parker's assessment of the Biblical material is correct, and I think it is, then there is little evidence to suggest that involuntary mediumistic behavior was present among Israel's prophets.[28] It

---

26. J. Roberts, "The Hand of Yahweh," *VT* 21 (1971) 246.
27. Roberts, "The Hand of Yahweh" 251.
28. Parker, "Possession Trance and Prophecy" 281–285.

is, of course, possible that such behavior occurred; but there is simply no unambiguous evidence for it.

In sum, Israel's prophets seem to enact their roles in at least four different levels of organismic involvement: ritual acting, engrossed acting, classical hypnotic role taking, histrionic neurosis. To speak about one level of organismic involvement as definitive for prophetic role enactment, as many have with ecstasy or possession behavior, is to ignore other important levels of Israelite prophetic role enactment. Further, to focus on ecstasy is especially inappropriate since we have been unable to discern one unambiguous example of that level of organismic involvement. Prophets could be prophets at several levels of organismic involvement.

Conclusions

In this chapter, I have attempted to suggest what role theory is about, and secondly, to demonstrate the value of this [[34]] theoretical perspective in understanding Israelite prophecy. In this latter regard, I have argued that a systematic consideration of prophetic role enactment reveals that ecstatic behavior occurs rarely, if at all, among Israel's prophets. Further, when one recognizes that prophets could enact their roles at a variety of behavioral levels, attempts to delimit one behavioral type, e.g., trance or possession behavior, as characteristic of prophetic activity are impossible to sustain. The application of role theory to a critical problem in the study of Israelite prophecy has therefore produced significant conceptual clarity.

Prophets through the Looking Glass:
Between Writings and Moses

A. Graeme Auld

Orientation: The Room This Side of the Glass

[[3]] This paper[1] seeks to extend a study on "Prophets and Prophecy in Jeremiah and Kings,"[2] and to explore some of its implications. To try to spread the blame, I should like to mention first some recent publications which appear to me to furnish the room through whose mirror I want to take you.

In his discussion of "Poetry and Prose in the Book of Jeremiah" at the Vienna Congress, W. McKane has commented on the very different approaches—and indeed presuppositions—of Thiel and Weippert to the prose tradition in Jeremiah.[3] He follows this with an examination of closely related poetry and prose in Jer 3:1–13 and 12:7–17. McKane concludes that "the kind of activity uncovered in 3:6–11 and 12:14–17 . . . is a type of enlargement and elaboration which operates within narrow contextual limits and does not have the comprehensive systematic

Reprinted with permission from *Journal for the Study of the Old Testament* 27 (1983) 3–23.

1. This is the text of a paper read to the winter meeting of the Society for Old Testament Study on 6th January 1983. It was dedicated to Professor G. W. Anderson, whose 70th birthday fell later that month. And it was drafted to stimulate discussion over a whole morning session of the meeting.

2. Forthcoming in *ZAW* 96 (1984) [[pp. 66–82]].

3. W. McKane, "Poetry and Prose in the Book of Jeremiah," *Congress Volume, Vienna 1980* (SVT 32), 220–37.

theological objectives which it is customary to ascribe to prose redactions of the book of Jeremiah." Further: "Those who claim a systematic theological activity for a [[4]] Deuteronomistic editor and identify compositions in which this is realised are perhaps professing to know more of the inner workings of his mind than can be gathered from the text." I suggest that these comments may have a wider relevance—to the production of Joshua to Kings.

In his massive Genesis-commentary, C. Westermann has strongly advanced the argument—in itself not at all novel—that much of the present text of Genesis was generated from material already within earlier forms of the book.[4] He presents a cogent case for understanding Genesis 20 as a development from Gen 12:10–20 for largely exegetical reasons. Having read the fuller subsequent account of Abraham's dealings with a foreign king over his wife, the reader becomes disposed to a "proper" approach to the briefer and possibly misleading prior text. However the generation of narrative in Genesis from narrative already in the text does not always serve local exegetical needs. The use of the same material again in Genesis 26 may have been simply to help build up an "independent" series of traditions about the middle patriarch Isaac.

E. Tov has usefully summarized his own and others' researches into the interesting textual history of the book of Jeremiah in his contribution to the Louvain Colloquium on Jeremiah: "Some Aspects of the Textual and Literary History of the Book of Jeremiah."[5] One welcomes his linkage of textual and literary matters. Tov and Bogaert are persuaded that the shorter Greek text of Jeremiah represents a first edition of that book, while our traditional Hebrew text is an expanded second edition. In somewhat similar vein to McKane's comments noted above Tov writes: "Editor II was not consistent, so that the inconsistency of his rewriting cannot be taken as an argument against our working hypothesis. In fact, very few revisions are consistent—in the biblical realm only 'inconsistent' revisers are known, such as the deuteronomistic reviser of Jos– 2 Ki and Jer, the 'Elohist' in the Psalms, the Lucianic reviser of the LXX, and, on a different level, the Samaritan Pentateuch."

H. G. M. Williamson's note on "The Death of Josiah and the Continuing Development of the Deuteronomic History" seeks to account for the differences between Kings and Chronicles in their reporting of the death by positing "a revised and expanded form of Kings, which the

4. C. Westermann, *Genesis*, BK 1, 1966–[[1982]].
5. E. Tov, "Some Aspects of the Textual and Literary History of the Book of Jeremiah," in P.-M. Bogaert (ed.), *Le Livre de Jérémie* (BETL 54), 1981.

Chronicler can at most have worked over only lightly" as "the best way of accounting for the literary development of this passage."[6]

[5] These four studies do not all tend in exactly the same direction But it may be helpful to underline some elements in them before proceeding further: (a) Poetic nucleus and prose development. (b) Narrative generated from difficult material within a corpus, then added to that corpus. (c) Greek Jeremiah as translation of an earlier version of the book than the familiar Hebrew. (d) Biblical revisers as inconsistent. (e) Development of the text of the book of Kings.

"Prophets and Prophecy in Jeremiah and Kings": Through the Glass

My own study mentioned above focuses on the usage of the noun *nābî* ('prophet') and its related verbal themes in the books of Jeremiah and Kings.

In writings associated with the Latter Prophets, the attitude to "prophets" appears to change radically during or soon after the exile. The eighth- and seventh-century figures are mostly hostile, and at best neutral, about "prophetic" contemporaries. (Hosea is the most neutral.) By contrast, post-exilic figures are readily titled "prophet" and this title is extended in the writings associated with them to earlier individuals like Elijah and Isaiah. The large books of Jeremiah and Ezekiel stand at the cross-roads.[7] There is still critique of contemporary prophets in plenty within these collections. However each book as it now stands is concerned to present its hero as a "prophet." And in addition to the plentiful criticism of prophets there is a new theme of a tradition of faithful "servants the prophets." Exploration of these two larger books helps to locate where and how the change of attitude occurred. It may be significant that Ezekiel is not directly accorded the title "prophet," although a hope is expressed concerning him twice (2:5; 33:33) that his people "will know that a prophet has been among them." If frequency of usage is significant, it may be more important to note that Ezekiel's words are introduced some thirty times by a reported command to "prophesy." Perhaps during the period when attitudes were changing the verb was more acceptable than the noun "prophet" as a designation of acceptable "prophetic" activity.

---

6. H. G. M. Williamson, "The Death of Josiah and the Continuing Development of the Deuteronomic History," *VT* 32 (1982), 242–48.

7. Full documentation is available in my *ZAW* article—see note 2 above.

These rather broad generalizations about the book of Ezekiel as a point where certain trends intersect within the Latter Prophets as a whole can fortunately be tested with a degree of objectivity in the ⟦6⟧ book of Jeremiah—with its different editions, and its blend of poetry and prose. Of course argument is legitimate over the classification of this or that element of the text as poetry or prose, over the historical conclusions that are proper from such a decision, and even over the very relevance to the biblical material of the "western" distinction between poetry and prose.[8] I still hold that such a decision is helpful—and hope that the following discussion may be held to offer it some support. However two versions of Jeremiah are objectively to hand; and the longer stresses a number of concerns which are either peripheral or much less formed in the shorter version. If the widely accepted distinction between earlier poetic nuclei and later prose development is combined with the evidence of less and more developed versions of Jeremianic prose, then three stages in the development of our inherited Hebrew text of Jeremiah are available for comparison: the poetry; the shorter prose development translated into Greek; and the familiar fuller prose development. The book of Jeremiah is doubly suited to our requirements: in the stratification of its traditions just described; and in the fact that nābî² ('prophet') and its related verbs are used as often in this book alone as in all the rest of the Latter Prophets.

Analysis of this rich stock of "prophetic" terminology in the three sections of Jeremiah produces the following results:

"Prophets" are mentioned in Jeremiah's poetry mostly to be criticized. There are a couple of exceptions in which they appear in a more neutral light.

In the prose common to Hebrew and Greek, such criticism still bulks very large; however some new features appear. The verb "prophesy" comes to be used in passages critical not just of "the prophets," but also of certain named individuals who are never so described. Even more novel, it is used positively of the activity of Jeremiah himself, and also of Uriah and Micah. Four times at this stage in the book's development Jeremiah is accorded the title "prophet"; and (perhaps more important) he is strategically designated "prophet to the nations" at the beginning of the book (1:5). And finally we meet five positive references to an otherwise obscure group termed Yahweh's "servants the prophets."

And in the extra material of the received Hebrew text we find a further small expansion of censure of "prophets"—the theme that dominates the other sections of the book. But most noteworthy is the multiple

---

8. So J. L. Kugel, *The Idea of Biblical Poetry: Parallelism and Its History,* 1981.

insistence (24 extra references) that Jeremiah is a "prophet" ⟦7⟧—not
to speak of the further six times in chapter 26 in which Hananiah too is
accorded this title.

It appears that the scattered instances of "prophetic" terminology
in other (Latter) Prophetic books can be successfully correlated with the
more abundant—relatively datable—evidence in the book of Jeremiah.
It was only after the exile that such figures became termed "prophet."
And until this development was successfully completed, it may have been
easier to use the verb "prophesy" of them (whatever that means!) than to
term them "prophet."

Kings is the other biblical book replete with talk of "prophets." Much
of this is concentrated in the middle third of the book: the Elijah/Elisha
narratives in 1 Kings 17–2 Kings 10. We find there all five instances of
the verb; 33 of the 38 occurrences of the plural noun; but only 12 of the
41 appearances of the noun in the singular. Half the usage of the singular noun is in the form of the title "prophet" with a proper name; and
this title features only in the first and last thirds of Kings—once certainly
in 1 Kgs 18:36 (MT) but *not* LXX. The only other singular prophet in
these parts of Kings is the unnamed one from Bethel in 1 Kings 13 and
2 Kings 23.

The textual leverage on this material is provided not by the LXX
version of Kings, although it does offer two significant scraps of evidence,
but by the alternative account of the monarchy in the book of Chronicles. Chronicles is also interested in the phenomenon of "prophecy"; but
what it has to report about "prophets" and "prophesying" diverges much
more from the material in Kings than the broad similarities between the
two books would lead us to expect. And variation over the title *hannābîʾ*
is as interesting here as between MT and LXX in Jeremiah. For example,
while Kings uses the title "prophet" 20 times (and never in the special Eli-
jah/Elisha material that is without parallel in Chronicles), and while part
of Chronicles that mirrors the traditions in Kings uses this title 13 times,
there is only one perfect overlap in usage: the mention of "Huldah the
prophetess" in 2 Kgs 23:22 and 2 Chr 35:18. The Chronicler's mention
of "Isaiah the prophet" in 2 Chr 32:20 is clearly related to 2 Kgs 19:1–2.
But apart from these two cases, the title is used quite differently. This
is all the more striking since the story linking the king of Israel, Jehoshaphat of Judah, and Micaiah son of Imlah, with its frequent use of
"prophet(s)" and "prophesy," appears almost identically in 1 Kgs 22:1–35
and 2 Chronicles 18.

The most economical account of the "prophetic" materials in Kings
⟦8⟧ and Chronicles—and one that accords well with our account of
"prophetic" terminology within the Latter Prophets—is that each of the

familiar books was developed from a common original that used the title
"prophet" rarely, and knew the Micaiah story.

The account of true and false prophecy in this story of Micaiah may
well emanate from circles close to those who told similar stories about
Jeremiah and his opponents. I argue that the distinctive expression in
that story, 'a prophet of the Lord' (*nābî' lĕyhwh*), in 1 Kgs 22:7, and 2 Chr
18:6, is in fact the source of the remaining limited biblical usage of the
phrase: it appears elsewhere only in the neighbouring 1 Kgs 18:22 of Elijah (where it is a later supplement), and 2 Kgs 3:11 of Elisha (within a
narrative largely dependent on the Micaiah story); at the end of the introduction to Samuel in 1 Sam 3:20 (of which more anon) and then of
Oded in 2 Chr 28:9—"a prophet of the Lord" in Samaria.

Three further appearances of the word "prophet" in the singular occur in the Naaman story in 2 Kings 5. Elisha urges his king to invite the
Syrian "that he may know there is a prophet in Israel" (v. 8). Naaman's
Israelite maid has already wished (v. 3) that her lord might be "with the
prophet who is in Samaria." These expressions are most reminiscent of
the hope that Ezekiel's people "will know that a prophet has been
among them" (Ezek 2:5; 33:33).

If many instances of the title "prophet" in Kings may have been
added after the Kings text was used by the Chronicler, and if the rare
phrase "a prophet of Yahweh" was coined in the Micaiah story with its
links with the theme of true and false prophecy in Jeremiah, and if references to Elisha in the Naaman story remind us of the presentation of
Ezekiel, then we have a plausible post-exilic context for almost all *singular* uses of "prophet" in Kings. The main group remaining are the eight
references in 1 Kings 13 (and the one back reference in 2 Kings 23) to
the unnamed prophet from Bethel who encountered the "man of God"
from Judah: another story, like the Micaiah one, that handles questions
about the true and false prophet, and may plausibly be related to those
discussions of the proper norms for "prophecy" which also shaped some
of the Jeremiah prose traditions.

Most occurrences of "prophets" in the plural are in a few localized
groups: "prophets of Yahweh," 5 times in 1 Kings 18 and 19, "prophets of
Baal (and Asherah)," 8 times and mostly in 1 Kings 18; "prophets of the
king of Israel," 7 times and only in the Micaiah story and the dependent
story of Jehoshaphat and Elisha in 2 Kings 3; "the sons of [[9]] the
prophets," 4 times in 2 Kings 2 and 6 times more in chapters 4 to 9. No
one within these prophetic groups is ever named but they all have a
clear (even if only chorus-like) role to play in the stories that feature
them.

The other "prophets" in Kings are Yahweh's "servants the prophets" who make five appearances: in 2 Kgs 9:7; 17:13, 23; 21:10; 24:2. In the last two of these passages the relevant phrase is absent from the related passage in Chronicles. And I have suggested grounds for considering Yahweh's "prophetic servants" an addition to the first three texts that mention them as well. These prophets have no narrative role—they are simply acknowledged agents of the divine "word." And it may well be the case that this acknowledgment was a theological afterthought.

The Wider Prophetic Family: Still in the Room on the Other Side

If it be granted, at least for the sake of argument, that the classical "prophets" of the Bible began to be *called* so only some time after the exile, is it possible to strip away from the Biblical traditions this *nābî'* overlay and recover the prophets' own estimate of themselves? It may be helpful to review from our new vantage point the usage of some other related biblical expressions.

"Man of God" is used to introduce or address "prophetic" figures several times in the Bible, but the usage is far from widespread. It occurs but once in the Latter Prophets: in Jer 35:4, which gives no clue why Igdaliah is so designated. The term is used most often of Elijah (5 times) and Elisha (27 times) in Kings.[9] That book uses *'îš hā'ĕlōhîm* [['man of God']] also of Shemaiah in 1 Kgs 12:22 (= 2 Chr 11:2), who bears the word of God to Rehoboam that he should not attack the north after Jeroboam's defection; and a dozen times immediately afterwards in 1 Kings 13 of the "man of God" from Judah who spoke against Bethel. Other unnamed men of God appear in Judg 13:6, 8 and 1 Sam 2:27. Samuel himself is so introduced in 1 Sam 9:7, 8, 10. The date of these passages may be variously assessed; however the remaining nine instances of "man of God" are in certainly late texts, six referring to Moses and three to David.[10]

Haggai bears the title "messenger of Yahweh" in Hag 1:13. Then it is often supposed that *mal'ākî* ('my messenger') is a title not a name—at least in Mal 3:1. And the set for our next problem is [[10]] complete when we note that in the intervening book of Zechariah a "messenger"

---

9. Of Elijah, in 1 Kgs 17:18; and 2 Kgs 1:9, 11, 12, 13. Of Elisha, 10 times in 2 Kings 4; 4 times in 2 Kings 5; 6; 7; 8; and then in 2 Kgs 13:19.

10. Of Moses, in Deut 33:1; Josh 14:6; Ps 90:1; Ezra 3:2; 1 Chr 23:14; and 2 Chr 30:16. And of David in Neh 12:24, 36; and 2 Chr 8:14.

appears some twenty times—but this time as a visionary (rō°eh) interme-diary.[11] Outside these three late books, Yahweh's "messenger" figures in the Latter Prophets only in Hos 12:5, of the opponent over whom Jacob prevailed, and in Isa 37:36 (= 2 Kgs 19:35; cf. 2 Chr 32:21) of the divine agent that disposed of large numbers of Assyrians in Judah. He re-appears as a similar agent of death in 2 Samuel 24—and even more often in the parallel 1 Chronicles 21—in the punishment that follows David's census.[12] Then apart from Pss 34:8 and 35:5, 6 the remaining scattered appearances of the "messenger" are in earlier episodes of the biblical story: from Abraham to Elijah.[13] It is often unclear whether the mal°āk was human. In the promise of Samson's birth (Judges 13), "messenger" and "man of God" are used side by side. Earlier in the same book, it seems likely that 6:7–10 was drafted to underscore that Yahweh's envoy in the following verses was in fact a human prophet. Maimonides un-derstood Exod 23:20 to refer to Moses. And we are left to speculate on what sort of being supplied food to Elijah (1 Kgs 19:5, 7) or dispatched him to King Ahaziah (2 Kgs 1:3, 15).

The regular Hebrew word for 'seeing' (r°h) is used not infrequently in the Bible of special, enhanced, second 'sight'. Quite exacting exegesis may often be necessary before deciding that such a sense is appropriate in any given occurrence of the qal theme. Of course interpretation is eased when we meet other themes of the verb with a divine subject—whether the hiphᶜil in the sense of 'show' or 'let see', or the niphᶜal in the sense of 'is seen' or 'shows himself'. God may make things seen, and may let himself be seen. The related noun mar°eh, often rendered 'vi-sion', is used of phenomena as substantial or insubstantial as are de-noted by the English 'appearance'.

Given all this, it is noteworthy that neither Amos nor Jeremiah is ever described as a 'seer' (rō°eh), although each is 'let see' things by Yah-weh and asked what they 'see'.[14] In fact the title rō°eh is used very rarely in the Bible: (a) of Samuel, first in 1 Samuel 9, from half-way through the story in which he was first styled 'man of God', then in 1 Chr 9:22; 26:28;

---

11. In fact, 20 times in Zechariah 1–6, and then once in 12:8.

12. We shall have more to say below on divergences between 2 Samuel 24 and 1 Chron-icles 21. W. E. Lemke's "The Synoptic Problem in the Chronicler's History," HTR 58 (1965), 349–63, has helpfully pinpointed the complex relationship between our inherited texts of Samuel–Kings and Chronicles.

13. See for example Genesis 16 (× 4); 21:17; 22:11, 15; 24:7, 40; 28:12; 31:11; 32:2; Exod 3:2; 14:19; 23:20, 23; 32:34; 33:2; Num 20:16; 22:22–35 (× 10); Judg 2:1, 4; 5:23; 6:11, 12, 20, 21, 22; 13:3–21 (× 12); 1 Kgs 13:18; 19:5, 7; 2 Kgs 1:3, 15.

14. Amos 7:1–8; 8:1–2; 9:1; Jer 1:11–13 (cf. 4:23–26; 23:18).

29:29; (b) of Hanani in 2 Chr 16:7, 10; (c) in the plural and paired with *ḥōzîm* of 'seers' generally in Isa 30:10.

The other 'seeing' verb, *ḥzh* is used much less frequently, and occurs only in the *qal* theme although there are several related noun forms— *ḥāzôn, ḥāzût, ḥizzāyōn, maḥ^azeh*. Some would suggest that the [[11]] word is not Hebrew at all, but a loan word from Aramaic. Many of its appearances are in technical prophetic contexts, often in close association with *nābî'*. Accordingly, to achieve some "purchase" on these, it may be helpful to review first those biblical passages in which this is *not* the case.

In one Psalm (63:3), *ḥzh* and *r'h* are used in close proximity—of gazing on God in the sanctuary. The four other Psalms in which *ḥzh* appears use it alone: in 11:4 and 17:2, of what God sees; in 11:7 and 17:15, of man seeing God; in 46:9, of seeing God's actions; while 58:9, 11 talk of the premature child never seeing the sun and the joy of the righteous at seeing vengeance. In Proverbs the verb is used of observation and discernment, twice alone and once paired with *r'h*. Then in Job *ḥzh* is used of insight in 15:17 and 34:32, and of seeing God in 19:26, 27 and 23:9. In Job the noun is always paired with 'dream', whether as a means of revelation (4:13 and 33:15), or as something ephemeral (20:8; cf. Isa 29:7), or a divine visitation in a nightmare (7:14). Prov 29:18 pairs *ḥāzôn* [['vision']] with *tôrâ* [['instruction']].[15] And Ps 89:20 recounts how God 'spoke in a vision' of his promise to the Davidic house.

The technical sense of both verb and noun which is almost standard elsewhere in the Bible is already encountered in some of these poetic texts. Indeed the only other non-technical usage is in Exod 24:11, of the elders 'seeing' God on his mountain—and even there the reading is less than certain.[16] We meet the term in only two other Pentateuchal contexts: in connection with (Aramaean?) Balaam in Numbers, and in Gen 15:1 of how the "word of Yahweh" came to Abram.

In Chronicles, as we shall see shortly, *ḥōzeh* ('seer') alternates with *nābî'* (and indeed *rō'eh*) in a quite stylized way. The situation is quite different in Samuel–Kings. 'Seer' and 'vision' make only four appearances in these books—and 'prophet' *is* part of each context, though perhaps not always an original part. In 2 Sam 24:11 and 2 Kgs 17:13 they are paired. 1 Samuel 3 opens with a comment on the state of *ḥāzôn* in Samuel's youth and closes with him designated *nābî' lĕyhwh* [['prophet of the LORD']]. And 2 Samuel 7, which introduces Nathan as 'the prophet' in

15. McKane has noted (*Proverbs*, 640–41) that LXX took *ḥāzôn* as referring to a person—a 'guide'; but retains this "solitary reference . . . to prophetic vision . . . in the book of Proverbs."

16. MT's *wyḥzw* is certainly the *lectio difficilior* [['the more difficult reading']]: LXX offers the passive 'were seen'; while some Samaritan MSS attest *wy'ḥzw* 'caught'.

v. 2 and talks of Yahweh's word coming to him by night in v. 4, describes the whole event in v. 17 as 'this vision'. Perhaps we should note that of all the patriarchs it is Abraham, with whom Yahweh had communicated 'in a vision' and by his 'word' (Gen 15:1), who bears the title 'prophet' in Gen 20:7.

[12] Within the *text* of the Latter Prophets, the "seer" enjoys the same rating as the "prophet." Amos (7:12) side-steps the title with a denial that he is a "prophet." Micah (3:7) has "seers" disgraced along with "diviners." Jeremiah mentions "visions" only twice, and both times within critique of the "prophets": in 14:14 blaming their "lying visions," and in 23:16, 17 complaining of "visions of their own hearts" which promise peace. These two themes recur in Ezekiel 13 (vv. 7 and 16); while problems of false or unrealized "vision" are handled in 12:21–28. And in 7:26 "vision" is simply what is expected of a "prophet" (just as Jer 18:18 expects of him "word"). We might note that Lamentations in much the same period mentions the "prophet" four times: twice to link him with the "priest" (2:20; 4:13), once to complain that they "obtain no vision from the Lord" (2:9), and once to blame them for their "false and deceptive visions" (2:14). Then in Zech 10:2 "diviners *see* lies," while according to 13:4 "every prophet will be ashamed of his vision." In fact in the main text of the Latter Prophets it is only in Hab 2:2, 3 and the manifestly late Joel 3:1 that "vision" is a clearly positive term—and in Joel that goes also for prophecy, dreaming and possession by the spirit.

In a final group of passages, *ḥzh* and its related nouns are used in what is certainly a technical, broadly "prophetic" context, but not in close association with the term *nābîʾ*. It is used in the title verse of many books: Isaiah, Amos, Obadiah, Micah, Nahum, and Habakkuk. Indeed in Isaiah its use is even more widespread: it heads individual sections of the book in 2:1 and 13:1; and figures also in 21:2; 22:1, 5; and 29:11—some at least of which may be post-Isaianic.

To return briefly to the *nābîʾ*, the burden of the first part of our argument was to show that the great majority of occurrences of this term belonged to the late biblical period. Although contemporary *nĕbîʾîm* [['prophets']] are often castigated in the Latter Prophets, some references to them are neutral, and even favourable.

We noted earlier that in Ezekiel and also in the earlier prose tradition in Jeremiah, the verb "prophesy" was used very much more often than the noun "prophet" in connection with these two figures. It may be appropriate to correlate this fact with two elements in the book of Amos. In the short narrative of his encounter with Amaziah, Amos refuses the appellation "prophet" but accepts the divine command to "go, prophesy" (7:14, 15). Then following the series of questions in 3:3–6, the conclusion is drawn that "prophesying" after hearing Yahweh speak is as much anyone's business as is being afraid [[13]] after hearing a lion roar. May it be that the use of the verb in connection with these now classical figures preceded and facilitated the later application to them of the title *nābî*ʾ? If so, what did the verb mean?

The verb is attested in only two themes—*niphʿal* and *hithpaʿel*—both of which themes are occasionally used in Hebrew to create verbs from nouns.[17] The use of this verb in connection with Amos, Jeremiah, and Ezekiel, but not the noun—or at least the noun only very sparingly and perhaps only afterwards—may suggest an absence of appropriate terminology for these figures, filled by the application of a denominative verb meaning 'to act like a *nābî*ʾ', 'to play the part of a prophet'.

Many of the non-redactional occurrences of *nābî*ʾ have already been noted in other contexts. The remainder of our reduced stock of evidence for plotting the earlier biblical sense(s) of our term should now be mentioned. Amos complains equally of stopping "prophets" and making "Nazirites" break their vows. The Elisha stories portray their hero in some sort of association with the "sons of the prophets." Elijah is in despair over Jezebel's treatment of Yahweh's "prophets" and is in conflict with Baal's. Saul has sought enlightenment from *ʾûrîm*, dreams, and prophets before resorting to the medium at En-Dor.[18]

The remaining passages use verb as well as noun, and are notoriously hard to interpret. In the two stories of Saul falling in with bands of "prophets", the related verb apparently denotes remarkable behaviour. Yet the interpretation of 1 Samuel 10 and 19 is immediately complicated by their offering different explanations of the same saying: "Is Saul too among the prophets?" We can be sure that "prophesy" in the intervening MT "plus" in 1 Sam 18:10 is pejorative: the second is caused by an "evil spirit." And this is equally true of the only use of this verb in Kings outside the Micah story—in 1 Kgs 18:29, of what Baal's prophets do to arouse him. The only occurrence of the verb in the Pentateuch (Num 11:25, 26, 27) describes behaviour that pillars of the community want to see stopped forthwith. We are left to ponder whether Saul's association with the prophets is evaluated in the text—or simply remarked on.

Remarkably little contemporary evidence for an estimate of preexilic "prophecy" has survived this review. "Man of God" and "Yahweh's

17. Gesenius-Kautzsch-Cowley cites for the *niphʿal* (§51g) *nzkr* [['to be born a male']] from *zkr* [['male']], *nlbb* [['to get a heart']] from *lb* [['heart, mind']] and *nbnh* [['to obtain children']] from *bn* [['child']]; and for the *hithpaʿel* (§54i) *htyhd* [['to embrace Judaism']] from *yhwd(h)* [['Judah']], and *hṣṭyd* [['to provision oneself for a journey']] from *ṣydh* [['provision for a journey']].

18. Amos 2:11–12; 2 Kgs 4:1; 6:1; 9:1; 1 Kings 18–19; 1 Sam 28:6, 15.

envoy" appear in scattered passages that may be early. On the other hand it is unlikely that $rō^{\ni}eh$ was used as a title until a later [[14]] writer used the occasion of Saul's visit to Samuel "the man of God" to equate this designation with the subsequent "seer" and "prophet." The use of $ḥāzâ$ and $ḥāzôn$ in the titles of several Prophetic books is similar to the positive development of "prophet" and "prophesy": *within* the text of several of the Latter Prophets its associations are pejorative. However non-prophetic parts of the Bible do use $ḥzh$ positively, of insight and discernment; and they may have contributed to the development.

It seems unlikely that earlier designations of these figures were suppressed by later tradition. The evidence reviewed suggests refinement by supplementation, rather than alteration or suppression of terminology already in our texts. The earlier biblical tradition may have been less interested in designation—and so too perhaps in "office."[19] It remembered some of the names: of those who had "stepped out of line"? of those whose words had a special quality? And, if this is so, then sound method requires us to start our quest from these words, and not from any institution or office.

Deuteronomist and Chronicler:
Sortie down the Corridor

This section is only partly relevant to our main theme. But perhaps you will indulge this sortie—since we are in the room through the glass anyway—down a corridor which I can never properly see from our regular side of the mirror.

It is remarkable how little communication there is between students of Chronicles and students of Joshua to Kings. In treatment of the latter, there are often few if any references to the largely parallel biblical narrative of the Chronicler;[20] while those who focus on his work assume that

---

19. Two differences between the related 2 Sam 24:11 and 1 Chr 21:9 seem relevant here—cf. note 12 above. The texts are as follows:

Sam	*wdbr-yhwh hyh*	*$^{\ni}$l-gd hnby$^{\ni}$*	*ḥzh dwyd l$^{\ni}$mr* . . .
	[['the word of the Lord came to the prophet Gad, David's seer, saying . . .']]		

Chr	*wydbr yhwh*	*$^{\ni}$l-gd*	*ḥzh dwyd l$^{\ni}$mr* . . .
	[['the Lord spoke to Gad, David's seer, saying . . .']]		

It is arguable that Chronicles preserves the earlier reading; and what we have read in Samuel has made plain that the divine communication came through the proper channels.

20. W. Dietrich's argument for three main Deuteronomistic strata in Kings (*Prophetie und Geschichte*, 1972) cites Chronicles not at all. Then neither R. D. Nelson, who advances Cross's arguments in *The Double Redaction of the Deuteronomistic History*, 1981, nor H.-D. Hoffmann, who argues for a single author of the History in *Reform und Reformen*, 1980, cites Chronicles more than a few times.

what we know as the Deuteronomistic History was available to him in substantially the shape we know.[21] The actual text the Chronicler used may differ frequently from our MT of Samuel–Kings;[22] but the basic materials were all there. However some of our observations about the distribution of "prophetic" vocabulary in the two corpora invite some reconsideration.

We have already noted that there is very little overlap between Kings and Chronicles in the way they use the title "prophet." And, with the notable exception of the Micaiah story, this is equally true of the way they use noun and verb as a whole. Chronicles uses "seer" language very much more frequently than Samuel–Kings; and it may [[15]] help if we plot this richer usage before we proceed. Chronicles agrees with its assumed *Vorlage* [['source']] *only* over titling Gad "seer" and Nathan, Isaiah, and Huldah "prophet(esse)s."[23] Half the remaining titles (24) appear in the cross-references at the end of the report of a reign to the further available information in Samuel–Kings.[24] And only the remaining 12 occur in the "main text" of Chronicles. There Samuel and Hanani are styled *rō'eh*; Jehu ben-Hanani is styled *ḥōzeh*—along with the heads of the three musical families whose business is to "prophesy"; and Elijah, Nathan, Samuel, and Jeremiah are termed "prophet."[25]

Two quite different, but equally substantial attempts have recently been made (by Hoffmann[26] and Polzin[27]) to defend Noth's view that the Deuteronomist was a single writer, his history representing a unified

---

21. T. Willi insists, *Die Chronik als Auslegung*, 1972, 54–56, that the Deuteronomistic History in its present form was the Chronicler's main source—he paid close attention even to those sections of his source he did not repeat. P. Welten, in his conclusion to *Geschichte und Geschichtsdarstellung in den Chronikbüchern*, 1973, is clear that the Chronicler wrote some 300 years after the Deuteronomist.

22. Cf. above, notes 12 and 19. Willi (*op. cit.*) and Williamson (*1 and 2 Chronicles*, 1982) are fully aware of the textual problems.

23. Cf. 1 Chr 21:9 and 2 Sam 24:11; 1 Chr 17:1 and 2 Sam 7:2; 2 Chr 32:20 and 2 Kgs 19:2; and 2 Chr 34:22 and 2 Kgs 22:14.

24. In 1 Chr 29:29 and 2 Chr 9:29; 12:15; 13:22; 26:22; 32:32; 33:18. Contrast 2 Chr 20:34 which cites Jehu ben-Hanani without a title.

25. In fact in the inherited MT the remaining dozen instances form a neat pattern: each of the three titles appears four times:

> *rō'eh* [['seer']] in I [[Chronicles]], 9:22; 26:28; II [[Chronicles]], 16:7, 10
> *ḥōzeh* [['visionary']] in I, 25:5; II, 19:2; 29:30; 35:15
> *nābî'* [['prophet']] in II, 21:12; 29:25; 35:18; 36:12

However some indications from both LXX and Syr suggest that later adjustments have been made to some of these verses.

26. Cf. above, note 20.

27. R. Polzin, *Moses and the Deuteronomist: A Literary Study of the Deuteronomistic History I*, 1980.

conception.[28] Hoffmann even enhances Dtr's achievement by ascribing
to him even more of the material in the relevant books than Noth had
done. However most scholars are persuaded by either of two main accounts that reckon with a substantial revision of the history by a second
Deuteronomist. These accounts differ in several ways, including whether
Noth was right to deem the (first) Deuteronomist exilic (so Smend,[29]
Dietrich,[30] Veijola[31]), or whether the earlier draft closed with its hero
Josiah (so Cross,[32] Nelson[33]). However both accounts ascribe "prophetic" material to their second hand. If our earlier observations have
force, then the rewriting of the "Deuteronomistic" traditions in "prophetic" terms continued long after the exile. And the absence of Judg
6:7–10 (the major reference in that book to the "prophetic" role) from
the relevant Qumran fragment of Judges[34] only serves to confirm this
conclusion.

In studies of the book of Joshua I have noted links between Chronicles and some elements of an *early* revision of the basic (Deuteronomistic?) draft of that book.[35] How much of Joshua–Kings was *not* available to
the Chronicler? And if we have reasonable ground for suspicion that the
Deuteronomistic History was far from complete before the Chronicler's
work was being composed then several new questions will have to be
asked. The more it is recognized that biblical revisers were inconsistent
and that narrative could be generated piecemeal for exegetical purposes, the harder it may be to answer many of them.

Only one simple "manipulation" of Noth's magisterial account of the
Deuteronomistic History is required if we want to remove much of the
evidence for the Chronicler having radically altered by [[16]] subtraction
what he inherited from the Deuteronomist (plus a few supplements). The
story of David in his court (2 Samuel 9–20 + 1 Kings 1–2) and the Elijah/
Elisha narratives (much of 1 Kings 17–2 Kings 10) are readily identifiable
and separable entities. Why not deem them *supplements* to the Deuteronomist's work, not *sources* for it? The Chronicler is deafeningly silent over
each corpus. But *is* he the innovator?

28. M. Noth, *The Deuteronomistic History* (JSOTS 15), 1981.

29. R. Smend, *Die Entstehung des Alten Testaments*, 1978.

30. Cf. note 20 above.

31. T. Veijola, *Die Ewige Dynastie: David und die Entstehung seiner Dynastie nach der dtr
Darstellung* (AASF B. 193), 1975.

32. F. M. Cross, *Canaanite Myth and Hebrew Epic*, 1973.

33. Cf. note 20 above.

34. Reported in R. G. Boling, *Judges*, Anchor Bible, 1975, 40—on the basis of a communication from F. M. Cross.

35. A. G. Auld, "Judges I and History: A Reconsideration," *VT* 25 (1975), 261–85 (especially 280–82); and *Joshua, Moses and the Land*, 1980 (especially 101, 108f.).

Von Rad's argument is often quoted: that repeated examples of prophecy and fulfilment form one of the structural elements of the Deuteronomistic History.[36] To the extent that the main point is true, we should now say more cautiously that (before all the prophetic titles were added) it was a narrative about the fulfilment of what Yahweh had said. Yet this is another important feature of Joshua–Kings which looks different when viewed from Chronicles. Von Rad does not make explicit that only the first two of his eleven examples of Deuteronomistic notes of fulfilment write of Yahweh 'establishing the word he had spoken' (*hēqîm ʾet-dĕbārô ʾǎšer dibber*). It is only these same two examples (1 Kgs 8:20 = 2 Chr 6:10; and 12:15 = 10:15) that reappear in Chronicles. Selection from Deuteronomistic tradition—or common source? Williamson writes that Chronicles suppressed the story of Ahab's fate from the end of the Micaiah story in part because the fulfilment of a prophecy was involved which it had not reported.[37] But *was* it in his source? . . . Is there between the "Matthew" of Samuel–Kings and the "Luke" of Chronicles a lost "Mark" that told the whole story of the Jerusalem monarchy? What relation does this "chronicle of the kings of Judah" bear to Deuteronomistic thought and style?

Between Writings and Moses: Back to the Room through the Glass

The discussion in the earlier part of this paper encourages the view that both parts of the "prophetic" canon of the Hebrew Bible received much of their distinctive and positively intended "prophetic" vocabulary over a briefer and in a later period of the biblical tradition than is regularly supposed. The process which has been sketched appears to imply recognition that these "prophetic" writings were different from the other "writings": it was on to these books and not others that "prophetic" and "visionary" terminology was grafted.

John Barton has recently discussed canonical development [[17]] relating to the "prophets," and in particular Josephus' talk of the prophets after Moses writing the history of their times in thirteen books.[38] He suggests this points to a bipartite canon of Law and Prophets—with "prophets" implying a certain level of inspiration or authority. It was a further stage that what we have inherited as Former and Latter Prophets

---

36. G. von Rad, *Studies in Deuteronomy,* 1953 (especially 78–81).

37. H. G. M. Williamson, *1 and 2 Chronicles,* New Century Bible, 1982, 286.

38. J. Barton, " 'The Law and the Prophets': Who Are the Prophets?" forthcoming in *OTS* [[23 (1984) 1–8]].

were selected from Josephus' Prophets, with the remainder assigned to Writings.

Our own discussion belongs to a rather earlier period, and appears to point in a different direction. We have noted the emergence of two standard terms, "prophets" and "seer" in Isaiah, Jeremiah, Ezekiel, and the Twelve; and an analogous proliferation of "prophetic" vocabulary in Kings, which extended into Samuel and even, in time, Judges. This process itself appears to recognize a "prophetic" *je ne sais quoi.*

To an extent our account of the "prophetizing" of Chronicles too would appear to undercut this conclusion. But the situation in that book is rather more complex. I incline to the view that the references in both Kings and Chronicles at the end of almost every king's reign to the availability of further information elsewhere are in fact cross-references between these two narratives that have diverged from their common source. This is widely recognized in the case of the Chronicler's references. But I wonder whether the references to "chronicles of the kings of Judah" within Kings are not an invitation to scrutinize the other biblical book, and not extant state archives. Be that as it may, the form of many of the acknowledgments in the present text of Chronicles of material in Samuel–Kings recognizes those traditions as "prophetic" or "visionary,"[39] or it notes that the familiar text of Kings is a development, or exposition (*midrāš*), of an earlier "book of kings,"[40] or it points to "prophetic" supplementation of a shorter account of the monarch:[41] the invitations in 1 Chr 29:29 and 2 Chr 9:29 to consult *dibrê nātān hannābîʾ* [['the Chronicles of Nathan the prophet']] for further information on David or Solomon will more likely be a reference to the "court history" which is not reflected in Chronicles, than to Nathan's dynastic oracle which is. Parts of the main text of Chronicles have received "prophetic" supplementation—and of course this may be the contribution of the Chronicler himself. However the marginal references in Chronicles as we have received the work (the references to Samuel–Kings) tend to emphasize the prophetic character of that other parallel work. Perhaps those who drafted them would not have been averse to deeming Samuel and Kings part of a restricted "prophetic" canon that excluded Chronicles.

[[18]] While late passages mainly in Jeremiah and Kings,[42] but also in some other books,[43] talk in a stereotyped way of Yahweh's "servants the prophets," the last chapter of Chronicles handles the same theme by mak-

39. Cf. note 24 above.
40. On Joash, in 2 Chr 24:27.
41. Cf. 2 Chr 26:22, and also 13:22.
42. Jer 7:25; 25:4; 26:5; 29:19 (not LXX); 35:15; 44:4; 2 Kgs 9:7; 17:13, 23; 21:10; 24:2.
43. Amos 3:7; Zech 1:6; Dan 9:6, 10; Ezra 9:11.

ing an explicit—and unique—link between "his prophets" and "his messengers."[44] I have already noted that I find this implied in Judg 6:7–10—the first prophetic passage in Joshua–Kings.[45] These verses attribute Israel's suffering under the Midianites to her spurning Yahweh's voice and revering Amorite gods. This developed understanding of a prophet's message prefaces the rather more practical approach taken to Gideon by Yahweh's messenger (6:11ff.) in response to Israel's lament over Midian. This preface deftly claims prophetic influences in other episodes of the Judges even where the actual accounts use different terminology—so helping to make explicit the prophetic character of yet another part of this whole narrative corpus.

This late addition to Judges rather takes away some of the force of 1 Samuel 3. There we encounter the heaviest concentration of words and phrases relating to the whole phenomenon of prophecy and its importance of any score of verses in the Bible. However ancient the origins of this story of Samuel's night-time audition, it seems clear that it has been redrafted to highlight the institution of biblical prophecy.[46] Noth may have been right to detect behind the present book of Judges and the opening chapters of Samuel an earlier "Deuteronomistic" conception of a period of the Judges that extended to and concluded with Samuel's transfer of power to a king. Samuel had been the last judge (cf. 1 Sam 7:15). This conception is largely neutralized by the present division of "books"—with the birth narrative and this audition underscoring a prophetic portrayal of this early leader, a view again shared with Chronicles when we read of "the days of Samuel the prophet" in preference to Kings' "days of the judges. . . ."[47]

H.-C. Schmitt has recently drawn our attention again to certain parts of the Pentateuch—or more strictly Genesis to Numbers—which have clear relations with prophetic concerns.[48] Elements of Exodus 3–4 are very like narratives of prophetic call. Chapter 4, and also the report of the act of exodus itself in chapter 14, both culminate in reports of the people's belief in Moses and his God. The terminology is that of Isa 7:9 and 2 Chr 20:20. Almost identical expressions constitute important moments in other blocks of Pentateuchal tradition: Exod 19:9 at Sinai; Num 14:11; [[19]] 20:12 in the desert; and Gen 15:6 in the time of the patriarchs—and we have already noted other prophetic links in that chapter.

---

44. 2 Chr 36:15–16.

45. Cf. p. 302 above.

46. There is further discussion of this chapter in my paper in *ZAW*—cf. note 2 above.

47. Contrast 2 Chr 35:18 with 2 Kgs 23:22.

48. H.-C. Schmitt, "Redaktion des Pentateuch im Geiste der Prophetie," *VT* 32 (1982), 170–189.

Schmitt argues that these passages are part of a "redaction of the Pentateuch in the spirit of prophecy"; and that they postdate the "priestly" strata of the Mosaic tradition. Prophets before Torah!

It is commonplace to recognize Deuteronomy too, and its figure of Moses, as influenced by prophetic conceptions. He himself proclaimed "the word of Yahweh," and promised the raising up of a *nābî^ɔ* like himself (18:15, 18). This passage is part of the same discussion of true and false prophecy as we have seen already in Jeremiah and Ezekiel. Polzin has recently attributed it to the Deuteronomist, who here claims authority equal to that of Moses for *his own* exposition of the divine will.[49] Mayes equally views 18:15ff. as a late addition to the Deuteronomistic law; and states that here Moses is not so much viewed as the archetypal prophet as the standard by which to judge the validity of the prophetic word.[50] Mayes' alternative I find puzzling: Moses is surely regarded as a "prophet"—the sort of "prophet" which Jeremiah and Ezekiel, and also Elijah and Samuel, become. He is also the standard by which they are validated and their opponents condemned. Yet this is not the Pentateuch's last word on prophecy.

There are too many uncertainties about Num 12:6–8 for us to know whether Moses is there a privileged prophet, or of a different category. God speaks to him "mouth to mouth" or "face to face," and not in vision, dream or "riddles." The clue to his categorization may lie in the words: *bĕkol-bêtî neɔĕmān hûɔ*—'in all my house it is he who is established/ faithful/trustworthy'. Now it is possible that these words have a similar force to Ahimelech's attempt (1 Sam 22:14) to reassure Saul over David's intentions towards him: "who among all your servants is faithful as David?" It could be that Moses is portrayed as *the* trusty servant. But Ahimelech's words have a deeper sense. Reinforced shortly afterwards by Abigail's "Yahweh will make of (or for) my lord a sure (or established) house" (1 Sam 25:28), they echo through Psalm 89, Samuel–Kings and Chronicles[51] as a promise of the institution of the Davidic line. Indeed we find this promise first, and rather obliquely at the end of 1 Samuel 2, concluding Eli's message from the man of God. It is surely to contrast Samuel with Eli, and to compare the institution of prophecy with that of monarchy, that the immediately following story of Samuel's call concludes with him *established* as a prophet of Yahweh.[52] Is [[20]] it fanciful to see that claim outdone in Moses' favour in Num 12:7? Be that as it

49. Cf. note 27 above.

50. A. D. H. Mayes, *Deuteronomy*, New Century Bible, 1979.

51. Ps 80:29, 38; 1 Kgs 8:26 (= 1 Chr 6:17); 11:38; 1 Chr 17:23 (n.b.: not equivalent to 2 Sam 7:25); 2 Chr 1:9.

52. Cf. 1 Sam 2:35; 3:20.

may, the concluding verses of the Pentateuch effectively neutralize the earlier promise in Deuteronomy 18. At whatever date they were penned they simply note that (despite all appearances to the contrary?) the expected prophet like Moses still has not arisen. Moses—and that means the whole Torah associated with his name—is incomparable.

They are surely right who see these verses as the end of the Pentateuch, and not just of its last book, and who hear them say something about Torah and Prophets and Canon, and not just something about Moses and historical successors.[53] Certainly, if our arguments have force, they confirm this reading. It is common to view the preaching of the prophets as one of the influences which helped form the teaching of Deuteronomy. I have attempted to show that the *nābî*, the 'prophet' who Moses is or with whom he is compared is no historical "prophet"— but the reconstructed, post-exilic "prophet" of the Prophetic Canon. The last word of the Torah knows the Prophets substantially as we know them—even the earlier Deuteronomy 13 and 18 would seem to know Jeremiah 1 and 23.

Prophets then precede—but have no precedence over—Moses. Prophets are also "Writings"—"writings" that have been redefined as "prophetic" at a quite advanced stage in the development of the earlier of them. We must leave it to another study to clarify what about these writings let them become prophetic; but conclude with an Alice-like view of the Bible—with Prophets between Writings and Moses. Torah, having been nurtured at several stages by the prophetic traditions, sought to control them—and does so in the Hebrew Bible. Yet the argument between Sadducee (Jewish or Samaritan) and Pharisee was not whether to add Prophets as new scripture beside Torah, but whether to retain Prophets once it had been ensured that Moses had said enough.

53. J. Blenkinsopp, *Prophecy and Canon*, 1977, 85–95.

Social Dimensions of Prophetic Conflict

BURKE O. LONG

[[31]] The Hebrew Bible frequently alludes to conflict involving the prophets—conflict with each other and with various other people with whom they interacted, or to whom they addressed their oracles. At the same time, because of its viewpoint which champions an impeccable Yahwistic faith, the Bible tends to view these conflicts almost exclusively in ideological [[32]] terms. It is a question of truth, and of a prophet truly sent by God: true religion, prediction, reading of events; true understanding of religious norms; true homily for a needy people, e.g., Ezek 13:1–19; Jer 23:9–15; Mic 3:5–8. Accordingly, the Bible tends to ignore, or to suppress, the societal aspects of conflict—those personal, political, social, and economic factors that would have been a part of any public display of rivalry. The Biblical traditions may even foster a slightly negative attitude toward conflict, which after all, interferes with a person's being a prophet. Conflict is something to be endured and suffered in the interest of a higher duty to one's holy calling (see 1 Kgs 22:24–28; Jer 1:7–8, 18–19; 20:7–12; Ezek 3:8–9).

Naturally, this perspective on the prophets' conflicts reflects the bias of those who collected and authored the Biblical materials. Careful study of the traditions has exposed therein a history of developing consensus among people who were convinced of the religious truth and value of *certain* individual prophets, and of the falsity of those who opposed them. We now see a stereotype in which *any* opposition to a prophet who came to be canonized is viewed simply, and simplistically, as anti-prophetic, anti-Yahwistic, as a misguided and even virulent paganism (Hossfeld and Meyer 1973: 113).

Reprinted with permission from *Semeia* 21: *Anthropological Perspectives on Old Testament Prophecy* (1981) 31–53.

Despite a few neutralist voices among historians of religion (e.g., Ringgren 1966: 215–16; Lindblom 1962: 211–12), this theological interest and commitment have remained at the center of the studies on prophetic conflict. Consequently, for most critics, the canonical tilt toward ideologically drawn pictures persists.

In one form, the bias shows up in the fixation on truth and falsity as an issue, perhaps *the* issue, in the earliest translators (Septuagint and Targum) down to the latest historical critical investigations. This stream of discussion was brought to a modern watershed by G. Quell (1952), who moved beyond *a priori* and pejorative assumptions about the moral character, motivations, and intentions of so-called "false" prophets, and set the agenda for subsequent study. It is now widely held that criteria for distinguishing true from false were, and are, illusive and subjective, quite incapable of generalization (von Rad; Osswald; Hossfeld and Meyer; Crenshaw). Nevertheless, the quest goes on, dressed recently as a problem in hermeneutics. The (true) prophet was one who turned out in time to be flexible, alive to the shifting situation, and above all sensitive of Yahweh's transcendent freedom to do a new and surprising thing with his people Israel. In ancient Israel, true or false was a matter of correct or incorrect interpretation of authoritative Israelite traditions (Sanders 1972: 73–90; 21–41; see Kaufmann 1960: 278–79; Overholt 1970: 43–44). Taking account of our skeptical and pluralistic times, one may say that in these recent discussions the Biblical claims of truth in all their boldness were suspended or, at least, muted for purposes of scholarly description, but the Biblical formulation of the problem posed by conflict was embraced. To this [[33]] extent, the social, non-theological dimensions of the prophets' conflicts were largely, if not entirely, overlooked.

Even when the focus of study is on the prophets' conflicts with the royal houses, the canonical bias dominates scholarly imagination. For example, in an exhaustive study of 1 Kings 22, Simon DeVries not only ranks the prophet's problem with the king as the most important, but he defines the problem theologically—just as do the author-editor(s) of the Biblical traditions. Micaiah ben Imlah, the hero, emerges in our mind's eye as the defender of true Yahwism over against the hubristic, self-serving royal establishment.

> It is clear that the most central conflict was the constant polarity between the spiritual power of prophecy insisting on Yahweh's absolute priority, and the political establishment—theoretically instrumental but ever prone to forsake its status as servant to Yahweh and the people. . . . Conflict is always between covenant integrity and political opportunism (DeVries 1978: 148; cf. Th. C. Vriezen 1970: 42–43).

One last example. James Crenshaw has written an admirable book in which he emphasizes that the inevitable conflict among the prophets grew out of the nature of prophecy itself. Appeals to higher transcendent authority, charges and counter charges, the inner struggles of the prophets with self-doubt, all fueled controversy. For Crenshaw, it is a theological problem theologically imagined:

> Within the two-fold task of the reception of the word of God in the experience of divine mystery and the articulation of that word to man in all its nuances and with persuasive cogency rest multiple possibilities for error and disbelief (Crenshaw 1971: 3).

And the outcome, the eventual collapse of prophecy as a viable religious institution, is evaluated theologically.

> . . . the conflict between prophets so degraded the prophetic movement that its witness was weakened and prophetic theology was too burdensome to overcome such a weakness (Crenshaw 1971: 108).

The theological approach to prophetic conflict is neither incorrect nor inappropriate. But like any method, it limits while illuminating. In order to engage overlooked, but important, aspects of the Israelite situation, we must be absolutely clear about the theological interests of both the Bible and the bulk of critical scholarship. Often in details that may escape the theologian's eye (that of the Biblical narrator as well as the commentator) lie hints of social, economic, and political currents helpful in giving us fuller historical understanding. In quest for this elusive and indirect evidence, we find some help in contemporary anthropological studies where access to a particular culture is not limited to literary texts. Such aid comes not in the form of directly comparative data, but as enriching stimulus to historical and sociological imagination. From anthropology we gain a wider range of questions, a heightened sense of the relative place of ideology (or theology) [[34]] alongside of other forms of social expression, and a feel for what might be worth investigating in ancient Israel.

This article is especially concerned with some social aspects of conflict among the Hebrew prophets. We will survey a few recent anthropological studies related to this subject, and armed with this new background material, look again at selected Biblical traditions.

At the outset, we must realize that the word "prophet" has been used in a number of different ways by ethnographers. A broad range of material discusses diviners, priests, oracle givers, shamans, witches and mediums in rather culturally specific ways. These titles, if there is a corresponding native word for such, often overlap to a considerable degree in a given society, and religious functions may blend and separate in quite specific ways. To be able to gain from these studies, a flexible stance is helpful. We follow Wilson (1980: 27–28; see Fry 1976: 30; Carley 1977: 242–43) in speaking generally of an "intermediary," that is, of a religious specialist who works in contact with the divine reality, and who brings forth for his public direct or indirect messages through which others gain access to, and benefits from, the supranatural world. From this standpoint, then, we may mention a few relevant studies. I have been selective rather than exhaustive, citing works which illuminate the social dimensions of conflict among intermediaries, and which seem to me to be particularly useful to Biblical scholars because of the specific character and history of our discipline.

As part of a thorough study of the shaman (= "master of the spirits," Eliade 1964: 3–13; Shirokogoroff 1935: 269) as a social and religious institution among the Evenks of Eastern Siberia, A. F. Anisimov provides a detailed description of a curative seance. After the disease spirit had been captured and expelled with raucous and aggressive ceremony, there followed the ritual "vengeance of the shaman and his spirits on the shaman of the hostile clan . . . (wherein) exclamations of indignation and threats descended from all sides onto the evil alien shaman" (Anisimov 1963: 105). The alien shaman, seen as the cause of disease among clan members, naturally bears the brunt of this purgation (cf. the ritualized combat among the South American Yanomamö in Chagnon). This form of conflict received social reinforcement not only in the public ritual but in the cultural mythology about the shaman himself. The master healer possesses a *marylya*, a mythical fence consisting of those spirits controlled by the shaman and built to protect his clan from the invasion of evil spirits from alien sources. Some of the protective spirits are weak, however, and sometimes an evil spirit at the behest of an alien shaman breaks through the defenses, bringing disease or misfortune. Hence, the necessity of shamanizing, and the appropriateness of a curative procedure dramatizing conflict and power; the shaman aims to drive off the spirit, and to repair the protective fence around the clan (Anisimov 1963: 111–12). Thus ritual conflict among shamans is fully expected. It is thought to be essential and is explainable in the society's world view.

[[35]] Conflict is also a positive world-maintaining social force because it is connected with healing and maintaining the equilibrium of the Evenk clan. Such social functions are entirely consistent with the highly professional, specialistic, and status conscious role of the shaman among the Evenks. Winning these important battles with the alien spirits (and their shamans) is a way to defend power and position through public works—all part of the shaman's social network which offers an extraordinarily privileged status to a chosen few (Anisimov 1963: 114–15).

Asen Balikci (1967; 1970) paints a similar picture for Netsilik Eskimo shamans. Based in part on the North American expedition reports of Rasmussen, Balikci (1967) interprets the shaman's powers and rituals as means to (1) deal with environmental threats which endangered the clan; (2) mitigate individual or group crises; (3) control interpersonal relations, including the aggressive and competitive acts by shamans against others; and (4) support and enhance the shaman's own prestige among the clan members.

Where the shaman is in conflict with members of his clan or with other shamans, it becomes a matter of competition for superior status, power, and recognition. Informants told Balikci about contests of supernatural strength which sometimes involved aggressive behavior, and often the working of miracles before an appreciative audience. People who claim to have seen such performances speak with awe and admiration about the ability of the shamans; folk tales, particularly, remember the power of some great shamans of the past (Balikci 1967: 203–204).[1]

As in the Evenk groups, this aggressive behavior seems to have been supported by belief in a hostile cosmos from which one needed powerful protection. Shamanizing and shamanistic conflict not only were expected, but in a dramatic way mirrored the hidden world of the spirits. Conflict seems therefore to reinforce both the clan's world view and the shaman's central position in society. Nevertheless, discreet criticism and skepticism of particular practitioners may be privately expressed by a few (Rasmussen 1931: 54–55).

Shirokogoroff gives us a much fuller picture of the shaman's social position among the Tungus of Siberia. In the days before extensive Russian European influence, the shaman was an important figure who stood at the head of a network of social relations built out of contacts and dealings with clients. As with the Evenks and the Netsilik Eskimos, the Tungus shaman carried out his profession against the ideological backdrop of a spirit filled cosmos from which mankind needed protection. Ironically, while regulating the social and psychological equilibrium of the clan, the shaman's own social position was, according to Shirokogoroff, delicate and in need of constant fine tuning. Lacking the absolute authority of the priest, and the political position of the clan "chief," the shaman was dependent upon public opinion, [[36]] which monitored his every step. His shamanizing in public, while supported by the group's liking for social gatherings, nevertheless faced a range of reactions—from full ap-

1. Many of the tales have been collected and translated in Rasmussen. Note also legends in Bogoras. Cf. the public shows of power and prestige among shamans in the Pacific Islands (Berndt 1946–1948: 338–344) and conflicts for status among shamans of west Nepal (Winkler 1976: 257–258).

proval to hostile interference. Success in curing and bringing on a kind of group "ecstasy" brought him status. Failure brought lowered prestige, perhaps disuse. Such public evaluations were individual matters, however, and need not weaken confidence in the institution of shamanism. Even individual failure could sometimes be explained ideologically by pointing to evil spirits which could not be fought, or to an evil shaman, a "bad person," whose aggressive and hostile powers proved too strong (Shirokogoroff 1935: 332–378 [332–334; 342–344; 376–378]).

In this context of fragile reputations and guarded positions, the Tungus knew a much more dangerous form of shamanic conflict: the "wars" between shamans who were personal rivals for power and influence, or representatives of clan hostilities. Battles in the form of competition in art and murder took place while dreaming or awake. But the results were thought to be tangible indeed—mystifying deaths, illness, bodily mutilations, intractable disease, and the like. Among certain groups of Tungus, these shamanic conflicts had a decidedly negative effect on the public attitude toward shamanizing. For most groups, however, negative feelings were directed only at individual practitioners. These "bad persons" were feared, not consulted, and in other ways were socially isolated by clansmen. They were also fought by ritual means. Shamanism as an institution thereby remained intact, supported by ideologies and social forces more powerful than individual competing shamans (Shirokogoroff 1935: 371–372).

A thorough and substantial study of mediums (= a human channel of communication from the spirits, the god, or the gods) among the Zezuru in southern Rhodesia provides yet another picture of social authority, status, and conflict (Fry). For the Zezuru medium, as among many other peoples, public success depends upon an ability to articulate common consensus, especially in politics (i.e., African nationalism), and his day to day "capacity as a diviner, his ability to foster a wide circle of adherence, his ability as a showman, and a certain amount of luck" (Fry 1976: 33–42).

Conflict with the public is built into the social order. Insofar as status rests upon public opinion, undergirded of course by certain ideologies relating to spirits and the specialists' role in mediating their influence, conflict with members of the public including other mediums may result in being dismissed as a fraud or simply down-graded. More rarely, a Zezuru medium might be *totally* discredited because of a flagrant violation of social norms (Fry 1976: 43). He might be only *partially* discredited when suspected of feigning his "trance" (Fry 1976: 44) or on the basis of a public challenge to the identity of his spirit presentation, rather than a more radical challenge to his mediumship (Fry 1976: 68–106). A particularly interesting case involved one called "Wild Man," who claimed to be the medium of the legendary spirit, [[37]] *Chaminuka*, a famous Shona oracle-giver and rainmaker (see Cripps) Another person, one Muchatera, claimed also to be *Chaminuka's* medium and pointedly observed that it was impossible for two people to act as hosts for the same spirit. A public meeting was thereby arranged. According to *Drum* magazine, the two claimants exchanged deprecatory comments with one another, and Muchatera challenged the "Wild Man" to make rain, whereupon he climbed up a small rock, waved his arms, and rain clouds appeared. The "Wild Man" and his supporters demanded the withdrawal of Muchatera, who did in fact leave, disgraced. Later, the "Wild Man" announced that Muchatera was not the medium of *Chaminuka*, but of another spirit, *Zhanje*. Fry's analysis follows:

> The import of the *Drum* article was that the "Wild Man" was the true *Chaminuka* medium whereas Muchatera was a fraud. However, such questions are relative, for the status of a particular medium depends on the population which supports him. In this case, Muchatera's authority was based on his followers who were far away in Rusape. The "Wild Man's" status as the true medium of *Chaminuka* was guaranteed by the presence of his followers at Chitungwiza [where the meeting took place]. Muchatera was partially discredited because he was "playing away" and it is quite probable that the outcome would have been reversed had the meeting taken place in Rusape [Muchatera's home] (Fry 1976: 43–44).

Conflict primarily with other mediums rather than the general public is built into the social order because claims of supernatural warrant and proper ritual initiations, even successful mediation with the spirits, are not sufficient in themselves to guarantee success and social status, both of which—contrary to the Zezuru ideology of mediumship—are in fact important to individuals (Fry 1976: 36). In practice, authority is built and maintained by creating a network of client and peer relationships. In this situation, endemic rivalry among mediums is a given, as they compete for positions of power and status relative to various factions in the populace. In Fry's words:

> The overall situation is best described in terms of networks and spheres of influence. Each medium, on being initiated, incorporates himself into the ritual network of the mediums who are involved in the initiation. If he is successful as a high level medium he in his turn will initiate new mediums who join the wider network through joining his, and so on. In this way successful mediums are able to build up networks which ramify continuously and which are not bounded. These spheres of influence reach the lay public through their contact with the mediums as

clients, as attenders of rituals, but these ritual networks are not stable or exclusive. Their stability is threatened by the competition between mediums which is endemic to the system and which may bring a medium to challenge the authority of the medium who initiated him, in order to alter relationships within the network or to establish a new network with him as center (Fry 1976: 45).

A good deal of Fry's book is in fact given over to intensive case study material which penetrates the complexities of these social networks. He was a close observer of the entry of his assistant, Thomas Mutero, into high-level ⟦38⟧ spirit mediumship, and witnessed a long and difficult process in which Mutero met not only considerable opposition in the village from the senior low level mediums in the village, but became embroiled in a long standing dispute between his full and paternal half-brother. Eventually the personal, village level disputes touched on the larger Black nationalist movement in Rhodesia, the support of which was a major source for the social strength of mediumship (Fry 1976: 68–106; 107–123).

It is clear from Fry's analysis that competition, public rivalry, and conflict were as much a part of the Zezuru medium's life as ritual performances. And equally important. Conflict served to destroy and to build status and influence, to challenge a social situation, and to adapt to changing situations—including the political movements in Rhodesia. Conflict was a constant and positive means of adjusting the "system" to the rise and fall of various mediums in the society. It seemed to have less to do with ideological differences than with social and political dynamics.

But is not conflict among intermediaries divisive rather than up-building? The answer must be in some cases, yes, in others, no, in others, both yes and no. Certainly for the Zezuru medium, conflict both builds and tears social fabric. For the Nuba peoples, of the southern Sudan, whom Nadel (1946) studied, conflict seemed more clearly divisive. Highest ranking shamans were remembered as leaders in the widest sense; they were appealed to regularly, and looked to for leadership in war. They would advise on blood feuds between clans and ordain wars to be fought. Equally, they might recommend peace and reconciliation, and negotiate on behalf of communities or kinship groups. But shamanistic leadership was fluid, irregular, localized, and often conflicting. The shamans were rivals of one another, and frequently divided the people. In Nadel's words:

> One shaman, entrusted with the supervision of some ceremonial, would unite the community in one way and on certain occasions; the war shaman would unite it in a different way and for different purposes. The leadership of each would last only while he was alive or unrivalled by the

priest [shaman] of a stronger spirit. Rival war shamans and other *kujurs* frequently divided the people. The Nyima rebellion of 1918 collapsed so easily because a *kurjur* prophesying the downfall of its leader caused a large section of the community to desert the cause (Nadel 1946: 31).

Similarly, Kingsley Garbett (1977) has noted for modern Zimbabwe the divisive effect of competition among factions which claim rival inter-mediaries and spiritual sanctions for their political programs (Garbett 1977: 86–87). On the other hand, Elizabeth Colson (1977) observed a more complex situation among the Tonga peoples of Zambia. She stud-ied conflict and tension between prophets ("possessed" oracle-givers) and custodians of local shrines (ritual officiants carrying out seasonal re-ligious duties). In the situation following government resettlement of large numbers of people, however, this tension had a double effect. When resettled prophets criticized a shrine or its ⟦39⟧ custodian, dis-puting, for example, matters of shrine maintenance, the prophets em-phasized by their actions their freedom to reassert innovative leadership in a new geographic area. On the other hand, this public conflict indi-rectly highlighted the "social maintenance" role of traditional shrines, and their importance in meeting needs for continuity among the re-settled prophets. Thus, conflict affirmed both the prophetic "free" role and status, while underlining the important conservative social functions of shrines (Colson 1977: 119–139, esp. 128–135).

Reviewing these various studies with due caution and allowing for the uneven quality of data and interpretation, we may venture a few sum-marizing comments. First, conflict among intermediaries is obviously a complex, little-studied, incompletely understood social phenomenon. Second, conflict is highly situational—that is, related to, and expressive of social dynamics in particular societies. Full understanding requires more information than we usually have for a given example. Third, con-flict in the mediational process is certainly normal, if not inevitable.[2] The potential for disputes lies in the claim to supernatural mediation—spirit possession, manipulation of the spirits, disputes over the value of, and interpretations given to, messages from these spirits. The potential for conflict lies also in the social components of such ideological matters: competition for status, influence, and power in situations where reli-gious authority tends to be pragmatically given and removed by public consensus (Fry). Fourth, it is important to conceive of such conflicts in both their ideological and social aspects. Given the variety in the ex-

---

2. Note, however, that absence of conflicts between prophets is noted by Tamoane (1977: 205) for Melanesia, and that Evans-Pritchard (1956: 305) emphasized the absence of conflict between priests and prophets among the Nuer.

amples we have seen, we may recognize, according to the weight given to various factors, different *kinds* of conflict among intermediaries, such as personal, ideological, and political. But no typology should fail to take into account the degree and extent of overlap in characteristic features and social involvements.[3] It seems appropriate always to ask about the relative weight these factors may have, and how this may differ from express comments made by participants.

The social effects of conflict among intermediaries is also complex, shifting, and varied. Although Nadel and Garbett mentioned in passing the divisive, negative consequences of disputes among shamans and mediums, other studies clarified more positive effects as well. Depending on the situation, and a given society's basic view of reality, conflict might be supportive and protective of community (Anisimov; Balikci), somewhat disruptive (Shirokogoroff), or expressive of a socially healthy and upbuilding tension between need for innovation and conservation of religious values (Colson). Disputes among intermediaries may also be important to an individual's maintaining both social position and adaptability in changing circumstances (Fry). Finally conflict may, but need not, undermine public acceptance of the mediation process (Shirokogoroff), although it may have something to do with an individual's credibility among his peers (Fry).[4]

[[40]] In the light of these anthropological studies, some of the special problems associated with trying to reconstruct social aspects of conflict among Biblical prophets are all the more obvious. The historical and social distance between text and situation to which text might refer, a point of view more theological than sociological, a one-sided, Yahweh-triumphant perspective on conflict and opposition—these are the main problems to be dealt with, but not entirely overcome. I have chosen to comment on a few major scenes of conflict in Jeremiah 26–29 and 37–38, which, because of their fullness of detail, offer the best hope of adding some important information to our understanding.

There is widespread agreement among critics that early exilic Deuteronomistic (Dtr) editors had a determinative hand in shaping the materials in Jeremiah 26; 27–29; 37–38. There is less agreement when it comes to spelling out details of that editing or isolating original traditions (see Hossfeld and Meyer; Nicholson; Seidl; Kessler). It seems the safest course, therefore, to consider first the matter of conflict from the perspective of these latest editors.

3. In contrast to a focus on ideology, see the study of "possession" as a social fact by Lewis and also Beattie and Middleton.
4. Evans-Pritchard (1937: 181–201; 245–257) was of this opinion for the healing specialists (witch doctors) among the Azande.

Jeremiah 26 highlights the fate of the divine word as spoken by Jeremiah and as resisted by King Jehoiakim. It is this king who by implication acquiesces to the priests, opposition prophets, and all the people in the hostile rejection of Jeremiah (vv. 7–9). And this same Jehoiakim is explicitly said to have spurned the word and person of yet another prophet (vv. 20–23; cf. Jer 22:13–19). These two pictures of conflict and rejection now frame a scene of apparent reprieve for Jeremiah: "This man does not deserve the sentence of death, for he has spoken to us in the name of Yahweh our God" (v. 16). The point seems to be a double one: Jeremiah is spared (vv. 16–19, 24) and yet the hopes raised in v. 3 that the divine word might achieve its end are dashed. The tradents cite no repentance by this king, but only a second instance of obstinate hostility toward a Yahweh prophet.

In Jeremiah 27–29, despite problems in some details, it is clear that we are meant to see a unit of thematic consistency. The tradition develops two events: chaps. 27–28, Jeremiah's word about the inevitable Babylonian conquest in King Zedekiah's day (after a first deportation to Babylon of certain leaders in 597 B.C.E.), and chap. 29, a letter from the prophet to these same exiles. These two events, linked by the symbol of ox yoke and Jeremiah's word, are now woven together as material about Jeremiah and prophets who rejected his message. The effect is to dramatize the singularity of Jeremiah's view—speaking for Yahweh over against many whose heads and hearts were turned to others—and to maintain the correctness and eventual triumph of Jeremiah's position. Having focused in this way on the rejection of the divine word in chaps. 26–29, the text goes on to tell of Jeremiah's rejection and violent treatment during Zedekiah's reign (Jeremiah 37–38), and his ultimate vindication in events of exile (Jer 39:1–10) and rescue (Jer 39:11–14).

[41] Clearly, we are reading in all these chapters a Dtr vision of the failure of a nation and its religion, focused like a prism on the actions of Kings Jehoiakim and Zedekiah, princes, and prophets (principally Hananiah and Shemaiah).[5] In Jeremiah 26, the issue is not so much conflict among the prophets or between Jeremiah and his public as it is the fate of Jeremiah's message, seen now as the true word of God. Will the word be heeded or ignored? True, the message provoked hostile reactions, and eventually Jeremiah escaped harm, but in the eyes of the final editors this incident along with Jehoiakim's treatment of another prophet, Uriah ben Shemaiah, seems to have been treated as illustrative of the failure of a people to turn to Yahweh alone for guidance. These scenes are paradigmatic for the editor and perhaps for his audience. One cannot

5. Nicholson (1970: 52–53, 93–100) argues that these traditions were actually composed by the Dtr editors of Jeremiah.

ignore Jeremiah and his words, preserved of course in tradition, nor should one ignore the "type" of the pious king, represented in Hezekiah (26:18–19; cf. the Dtr evaluation of Hezekiah in 2 Kgs 18:1–18).

Similarly, chaps. 27–29 defend the correctness of Jeremiah's word and the legitimacy of this particular prophet in the long line of those prophets who were sent as messengers of warning to a stubborn people (28:8–9; 29:19; cf. 2 Kgs 17:13–14, a classic Dtr text). For the editor, it is not the institution of prophecy which is on trial, but certain practitioners, just as the monarchy is not in itself religiously misguided, only certain kings. Indeed, in Jeremiah 26, the value of prophecy as a means of mediation with the deity is affirmed by citing as a positive model the earlier incident involving Micah and King Hezekiah (26:18–19). And in chap. 28, the editor must have defended Jeremiah over against his look-alike Yahweh prophet Hananiah by succinctly showing Jeremiah's word of death to Hananiah fulfilled ("In that same year, in the seventh month, the prophet Hananiah died," v. 17) and by repeating Hananiah's prophecy of a short exile (v. 3) in a tradition aimed at an exilic people who had already experienced its disconfirmation. The perspective is no different in chap. 27, where Jeremiah opposes other prophets, and where the Dtr ideology of the legitimate prophet is applied to the opposition (27:18). The institution is not questioned, but a number of practitioners *en masse* are measured and found wanting.

In this later editorial context, the *traditions* of Jeremiah's conflict functioned obviously to explain the catastrophe of exile in terms of the transgressions of king and people, mainly their refusal to heed the consistent warnings of Yahweh's messengers, especially the one called Jeremiah whom hindsight and devotion now deemed to be among those truly sent to a misguided people. The *tradition* of conflict, therefore, carried with it certain ideological claims, and this probably meant that it also was addressed to a situation of ideological confusion and/or competition following the demise of temple, monarchy, and cult in 587 B.C.E. If we might apply the categories of "cognitive dissonance" (Festinger; cf. R. P. Carroll), we might suggest that [[42]] when the basic social, political, and religious institutions were destroyed, and consequently their religious underpinnings called into question, the Dtr editors could have lessened dissonance over disconfirming facts by reinterpreting tradition in the light of new circumstances. Belief in monarchy, Yahwism, and prophecy is reaffirmed by remembering paradigmatic examples of "true" prophesying, and "right" rule, and by attributing present circumstances to improper handling of these God-given trusts.[6]

---

6. This Dtr perspective is consistent with that of Chronicles. Cf. 2 Chr 20:20, 36:11–21.

The traditions of conflict may also have served as a kind of homily in this exilic period. As paradigmatic literature, they represented a transformation of the prophetic impulse into a textual tradition of implicit warning to a later generation—those who bore and those who heard the filtered memory of the events spiraling to disaster. The Dtr ideology of prophet, as reflected in 2 Kgs 17:13–15, is embodied as it were in Jeremiah 26, 27–29. These incidents become warnings therefore, and carry with them a "prophetic" exhortation—as do the prose traditions dealing with law in the Book of Jeremiah—"turn again (to *Tôrāh*) and live" (Jer 7:1–8:3; 17:19–27; 18:1–12; 24:4–7; 29:10–14; Nicholson: 57–93). Whether or not conflict among prophets was a live issue for the Dtr editor(s) remains uncertain. The self-serving assertions found in Zechariah, ". . . you shall know that Yahweh of hosts has sent me . . ." might suggest that such conflict among intermediaries was not unknown in the exile and post-exilic periods (Zech 2:15 [= 2:11 rsv]; 6:15; see Petersen).

Can we see anything of these conflicts other than what the Dtr editor wanted us to see? Perhaps so, by focusing on elements in the tradition not directly expressive of the editor(s) apologetic and homiletic interests.

The prophet delivers oracles to Israelite kings, priests, princes and people, as well as to the kings of neighboring states (Jer 27:4–11). Even allowing for exaggeration, it seems justified to say that Jeremiah at the least worked as a highly placed oracle-giver (cf. Jer 37:3, 17; 38:14–28), who enjoyed certain influence with at least one king (Zedekiah) (37:17–20), but who was opposed by certain of Zedekiah's high ranking men (Jer 38:1–6) and sometimes even the king (such as Jehoiakim [Jeremiah 26 and 36]). We get some indication of the social and political status of these opponents from Jeremiah 38. The text, as usual, has been pointed by later interest in the eventual rescue and vindication of Jeremiah (vv. 7–13; cf. 39:15–18), but the details of name and family in 38:1 ring truly. The 'princes' (*śārîm*) who plot against Jeremiah are among the elite in the land. Gedaliah is the son of Pashhur, presumably the priest who was in charge of the temple (he is *pāqîd nāgîd bĕbêt Yhwh* ⟦'chief officer in the house of the Lord'⟧ in 20:1) and who was an opponent of Jeremiah (20:1–6). Jehucal (Jucal) turns up elsewhere in a delegation of two persons, one of whom is a priest, sent by King Zedekiah to Jeremiah for divinatory consultation during the military siege of Jerusalem (37:3). Similarly Pashhur, son of Malchiah, is one of two persons, and again the second is a priest, sent ⟦43⟧ by King Zedekiah to Jeremiah for consultation when the Babylonians first attacked the city (21:1). In both instances the priest is Zephaniah ben Maaseiah, who is the second ranking priest in the kingdom (Jer 52:24), and who possesses some kind of supervisory power over prophets in the temple compound (Jer 29:25). Shephatiah is unknown.

If there was some presumed difference in social status between Jeremiah and the princes who opposed him, there is little or no evidence that he differed in any way from his prophetic opponents. Jeremiah is opposed by another Yahweh prophet, Hananiah, in chap. 28, without any hint of social distinction. They speak with similar language, using typical prophetic forms of discourse, and ply their trade inside the temple compound in the presence of priests. In chap. 29, it is a Yahweh prophet in exile, Shemaiah, who complains to a priest in Jerusalem about Jeremiah's activities; and they are Yahweh prophets who are said by the people to have been "raised up by Yahweh" in Babylon, and who are condemned by Jeremiah (29:15, 21–22). Furthermore, both Jeremiah and his prophetic opponents are pictured as delivering oracles to the king (Jer 27:12–15). Moreover, both Jeremiah and his prophetic opponents share the common characteristic of being native to villages outside the royal and religious capital. Hananiah comes from Gibeon (28:1), Jeremiah himself from Anathoth (1:1), and Shemaiah from Nehelan. Even those prophets cited in the traditions as ideologically akin to Jeremiah, are similarly remembered to have been non-Jerusalemites (Uriah, 26:20; Micah, 26:18). None of these prophets, including Jeremiah, claims a special status because of place of birth or family associations. But they may in fact have had in common the social background and culture of village life.

Jeremiah and his prophetic opponents also appear to have been associated with priests and their cultic affairs. The Dtr editors pictured the prophets as oracle givers to both king and priest (27:16b; 28:1). They viewed Jeremiah in exactly the same way (27:16a; 28:5; 29:1). As far as we can tell, this view of the editor(s) is consistent with historical fact. In Jer 29:26, a Yahweh prophet who opposes Jeremiah appeals to a priest, Zephaniah, and thereby implies that the latter has some authority over, or at least working association with, prophets who prophesy in the temple. The exact nature of Zephaniah's authority is unclear. At the least, the tradition assumes a relationship that made a complaint before a priest a sensible course of action for disputing prophets.

From other texts, we may sketch something more of this association of priest and prophet. Jeremiah enjoyed free access to the temple (26:1; 35:2–4)[7] and speaks in the temple before priests (28:5); so does his rival,

---

7. Jer 36:5 does not necessarily imply a legal restriction on Jeremiah's movements into the temple, as RSV 'I am debarred from going to the house of the LORD' might suggest. The Hebrew is better translated, 'I am imprisoned; I am not able to go to the house of the LORD'.

Hananiah (28:1). According to Jer 26:7, Jeremiah's temple audience
consists of priests, prophets, and "all the people." These references may
be nothing more than narrative stereotyping, however. A more reliable
indication is the ⟦44⟧ oracle in 23:11, which implies that both priest and
prophet regularly operate within the temple:

> Both prophet and priest are ungodly;
>   even in my house I have found their wickedness,
>   says the LORD (Jer 23:11; cf. Lam 2:20).

Or again, Jeremiah says:

> The prophets prophesy falsely,
>   while priests make rulings[8]
>   at their direction (Jer 5:30–31).

Quite without tendentiousness, Jer 35:4 mentions a special chamber in
the temple set aside for the "sons of Hanan ben Igdaliah, the man of
God," that is, for a guild of prophets attached to Hanan ben Igdaliah. We
recall, too, that Nathan, the prophet, and Zadok, the priest, worked together in the coronation of Solomon (1 Kgs 1:26, 32–40). Similarly, in
Zech 7:1–14, both priest and prophet are involved in a cooperative effort
at rebuilding the temple. All these passages suggest a long-standing association of priest and prophet (Johnson 1962: 60–64). They further
suggest no important distinction between Jeremiah and his rival prophets in this regard. The details escape us. But apparently Jeremiah, his
rivals, and the priests are functionaries in associated systems for dealing
with the national deity.

In sum, the evidence suggests that there was little social distinction
between Jeremiah and his prophetic rivals, and they had much in common. A typology of "peripheral" and "central" to describe and/or contrast their relationships to central governmental authority does not seem
appropriate (against Wilson). On the other hand, the Dtr perspective
gives the distinct impression that Jeremiah is something of an outsider.
For example, he addresses King Zedekiah and refers to other prophets
who speak to that king as though he, Jeremiah, is not a part of the group
of prophets who regularly have the royal ear. And in that same chapter,
Jeremiah speaks to priests as though he is not regularly used to working

---

(Cf. 33:1 and 39:15, where the verb, *ʿāṣar* 'be imprisoned, bound, shut up', is used in an
identical way. Cf. 32:2; Neh 6:10.)

8. The meaning is uncertain, but demands some association between priest and
prophet.

with the cultic officials (v. 16). But, given the ample indication of Jeremiah's activities within the temple before the priests and his associations with and solicitation by royalty (37:3–5; 38:14–28; 22:1; 34:6), the impression that Jeremiah was something of an outsider likely means only that in the view of the Dtr editor Jeremiah was pitted *ideologically* against others in the society.

Precisely because of this editorial interest, it is very difficult to gain a sure sense of the ideologies of Jeremiah's opponents, or even the full range of issues in any given incident of conflict. For the prophets, we unfortunately see this matter only through the eyes of editors, who by and large have Jeremiah speak for the opposition. Any picture we have of their beliefs is very likely to be simplified, exaggerated, and hardly able to be [[45]] generalized into an ideological portrait of the opposition, despite efforts to the contrary (e.g., van der Woude; Crenshaw).

According to tradition, the opposition prophets spoke of Yahweh's unshakable attachment to Jerusalem and its well-being, *šālôm* (Jer 5:12–13; 6:14 = 8:11; cf. 14:13). This characterization of the prophets' message seems consistent with a kind of royal theology evidenced in Isaiah 36–38, a theology which rested the defense of Jerusalem on Yahweh's protective care and covenant with the Davidic monarchy (cf. Isa 7:1–9 and 2 Sam 7:1–14). However, the matter is put this way partly, perhaps largely, because the collectors of the traditions focus Jeremiah's distinctiveness in his predictions of destruction for Jerusalem, which in hindsight turned out to be correct. We really have very little basis on which to reconstruct an opposing ideological position. My guess is that the conflict between Jeremiah and these other prophets was, as the anthropological evidence would suggest, highly situational, highly geared toward particular events and circumstances to which all of these prophets addressed themselves. There must have been ideological disagreements on specific issues, and in the Book of Jeremiah we see these issues by editorial choice circling around the threat of Babylonian conquest and the fate of Jerusalem and its exiles.

We can be even less assured of the ideological positions of those princes who opposed Jeremiah. Presumably they were active in positions of authority with Zedekiah, son of Josiah. The Babylonians had taken Jehoiachin and the queen mother into exile, and instead of installing a successor in the normal line, put Zedekiah, Jehoiachin's uncle, on the throne (37:1). If not exactly a puppet government, it was a regime which stood at the pleasure of the Babylonian King Nebuchadrezzar. It must have been a government naturally sensitive to its precarious position, and to judge from Jer 38:4; 52:3, apparently secretly nationalistic as well. Perhaps it was a sign of the times that the house of a high ranking royal official, the scribe (*sôpēr*) had become a prison in Zedekiah's reign (37:15).[9] We might surmise that the princes (*śārîm*) were jealously guarding the hope of eventually resisting the Babylonian threat and surviving the siege (Jeremiah 38). Presumably, it was this reading of the situation that Jeremiah opposed (38:2–3). Here again, we must allow for the Dtr editor's filtering of the situation for his own apologetic and homiletic purposes.

What of those who supported Jeremiah in the midst of conflict? We have only indirect information of a general sort, and no information for specific situations of conflict in chaps. 26, 27–29, 37–38. According to Jer 1:1, the prophet came from Anathoth, a city which by tradition was given to the Levites (Josh 20:18). Jeremiah was possibly a descendant of the priest Abiathar, who was an early supporter of the Davidic house and part of a line of priests nearly wiped out by King Saul (1 Sam 22:11–23). Abiathar was one of David's chief priests who had been later banished by King Solomon [[46]] to Anathoth for aiding Adonijah's rebellious claim to the throne (1 Kgs 2:26–27). There at Anathoth, the priestly family continued, perhaps as earlier, variously supportive of and opposed to the monarchy. Jeremiah's father was Hilkiah, and we may wonder if this is the same Hilkiah who was the chief priest intimately connected with Josiah's reform of Israelite religion (2 Kings 22). Perhaps he was not. But in any case, Jeremiah's uncle, Shallum, was a property owner at Anathoth (Jer 32:7), and thus presumably a member of the landed Levites in that village. Shallum might be the husband of Huldah, the prophetess who was instrumental in Josiah's reform (2 Kgs 22:14). Thus one may see that tradition assigns Jeremiah blood relationships with a prominent priestly house, a house moreover that was linked to events of religious reform highly praised by the Dtr editors of the Books of Kings and Jeremiah.

The tradition also indicates that Jeremiah was closely associated with the family of Shaphan, a family also linked to the Josianic reforms. Jeremiah is protected by Shaphan's son Ahikam, who had been at court in Josiah's time (Jer 26:24; 2 Kgs 22:11, 14). The letter which Jeremiah sent to the exiles (Jeremiah 29) was carried by Elasah, a second son of Shaphan (Jer 29:3). The scroll which Baruch read to King Jehoiakim was read from the house of Gemariah, another son of Shaphan (Jer 36:10–12). From this particular passage, we learn that Shaphan himself held royal office as the king's scribe (*sôpēr*), and indeed must be the same Shaphan who bore that title for King Josiah (2 Kgs 22:3, 8). Finally, when the Babylonians crushed the Israelite monarchy, they put Jeremiah into the custody of Gedaliah, a grandson of Shaphan (Jer 39:14; 40:5).

---

9. On the royal scribe or secretary (*sôpēr*), see Mettinger (1971: 25–51).

As we have seen, Jeremiah's uncle, Shallum, was a property owner at Anathoth and presumably a Levite. His son, Maaseiah, Jeremiah's second cousin, was a priestly official, the "keeper of the threshold" (Jer 35:4; see 2 Kgs 25:18 = Jer 52:24; 2 Kgs 12:9). One of Maaseiah's sons, and second cousin to Jeremiah, was the second ranking high priest, Zephaniah (Jer 21:1; 37:3; 52:24). This same Zephaniah presumably supported Jeremiah on at least one occasion, to judge from his refusal to take Shemaiah's side in opposing Jeremiah (29:24–32).

Finally, Elnathan ben Achbor, a prince (*śar*) in Jehoiakim's court (36:12), is among Jeremiah's sympathizers. At least, he was not openly hostile to the message of Jeremiah when it was presented at court (Jer 36:25). Now Elnathan's father was linked to Josiah's reform (2 Kgs 22:12, 14). Also, this same Elnathan may have fathered Jehoiakim's queen (2 Kgs 24:8).

Thus we may catch the barest suggestion of a network of family relationships supportive of Jeremiah, and extending into the highest levels of royal and cultic service. Jeremiah is born into a priestly house, is kinsman to at least two prominent priests—the second ranking high priest and one of the three "keepers of the threshold." Jeremiah finds support with this high ranking priest Zephaniah in a dispute with another Yahweh prophet. He also ⟦47⟧ is surrounded by supporters from families whose connections with the royal court are intimate and extensive, and whose links to the religious reform movement under King Josiah are deep. Jeremiah may have been born a rural non-Jerusalemite, but his blood and social relationships are anything but lower class.

We now have another perspective on the conflicts reflected in chaps. 26; 27–29; 37–38. A scene of conflict between Jeremiah and royal princes with priests (Jeremiah 26) is essentially repeated in the following regime with a new king, and many of the same royal officials (chaps. 27–29; 37–38). We have a picture of a relatively weak king (Zedekiah) who is said to have rebelled against the Babylonians and hence to have brought on a siege of the capital city (Jer 52:3). But this king is dominated by a group of princes (*śārîm*), who at least want to offer strong resistance to the Babylonians and may stand in a general tradition of protecting national autonomy at all costs (Jer 38:5, 7–16, 24–28). Presumably, the Yahwistic theology which would have accompanied such political sentiments is reflected in the royalist theology of the Davidic dynasty (2 Samuel 7) and the divinely chosen and protected city, Jerusalem (Isaiah 36–38). On the other side, we may think of Jeremiah and his supporters from members of an aristocratic family (Shaphan) and official, priestly ranks in Judean society. Because Gedaliah, a grandson of Shaphan and a protector of Jeremiah, was eventually chosen by conquering Babylonian

authorities to be a Judean provincial governor instead of other princes in
Zedekiah's court (Jeremiah 39–40), we may presume that he and his
family associates were perceived as more or less amenable to Babylonian
authority. If so, the basis for the Babylonian perception may have lain in
their earlier political action and opinions which would have argued for
cooperation and co-existence with Babylon: ride out the storm, cooper-
ate with the foreign domination, make the best of Judah's position of
weakness following a first deportation in 597 B.C.E. In fact, Jeremiah is accused of going over to the Babylonians during the siege (37:11–15) and
of counselling others to do the same (38:2). In 29:4–9 he was said to have
advised the first deportation exiles to support their new Babylonian masters. Presumably, the theological justification for this political persuasion
would have roots in the ideals of Josianic reform, as now reflected in
2 Kings 22–23, since Jeremiah and his supporters had such deep and intimate ties with that movement. But these ideals in this particular moment in history may have been cast in terms of allegiance to Yahweh
alone and turning away from what was deemed a religiously apostate and
foolhardy course set by the noblemen around Zedekiah, the "autonomists" who apparently hoped to resist (Jer 26:4–6; 36:29). Thus within
the royal court, among people of high familial and professional connection, including Jeremiah the prophet, there apparently raged a political
struggle for the future of the nation. How much, or how little, a role personal ambitions may have played in the conflict, we cannot know.

[48] The struggle did not cease with the final blow to the monarchy
in 587 B.C.E. The Babylonians crushed the resistance, sweeping away, presumably, Zedekiah and many of those who supported the "autonomist"
position. They also chose Gedaliah, a grandson of Shaphan, and presumably heir to all those associations stretching back through Shaphan
to Josiah's reign, to be the provincial governor at Mizpah (Jeremiah 39;
52). This same Gedaliah was given custody of Jeremiah as well (39:11–
14). It looks as though the political figures who were more or less amenable to living with, rather than resisting, Babylonian power were now
placed in authority. But the remnant of Zedekiah's court resisted and
finally murdered Gedaliah (Jer 41:1–10), provoking counter violence
(Jer 41:11–12) and a plan to flee to Egypt out of fear of Babylonian re-
prisals for Gedaliah's murder. In this new situation of political division,
Jeremiah apparently was aligned with Gedaliah and the remnant in the
land who had accepted existence under Babylonian supervision as a
positive, desirable state (40:7–12). And he counsels them even in the
wake of this murder to remain where they are, not to flee to Egypt. His
line is as it was before 587: roll with the Babylonians, do not resist them,
or in this case, do not flee to Egypt.

These same basic political divisions must have been at work in the dispute between Hananiah and Jeremiah. Hananiah counsels that exile (the first deportation) will be short, that the Babylonian power is short-lived, that autonomy will be regained within two years. Jeremiah, representing the political option of "co-existence," has a different prophecy: servitude to Babylon is inevitable (28:14; cf. 27:7–8). Both men stand for opposing political options in the kingdom; both may have been closely involved in the struggles for influence. At least we know that Jeremiah was well connected; possibly Hananiah's grandson accused Jeremiah of deserting to the Babylonians (37:13); both, as Yahweh prophets, cover or reinforce their political persuasion with oracles from Yahweh.

We may see something similar in Jeremiah 29. Jeremiah's letter to the exiles, victims of the first deportation, counsels "co-existence" as a command from Yahweh:

Build houses and live in them; plant gardens and eat their produce . . . seek the welfare of the city where I have sent you into exile, and pray to the LORD on its behalf, for in its welfare you will find your welfare (29:5–7).

Apparently what we have is an attempt by Jeremiah to extend his sphere of influence to the exiles who are in Babylon—done at close to the time that he advocated to those in Jerusalem a similar conciliatory posture toward Babylon (Jeremiah 38). And just as his political advice met with opposition in the capital, so too, his advice by letter to the exiles drew forth resistance in the person and words of Shemaiah, the Babylonian Yahweh prophet (29:24–32). Again, the matter seems not to be just that two prophets opposed one [[49]] another on a specific theological issue, but that they—at least we may say this for Jeremiah—were part of a larger struggle between factions for "autonomist" or "co-existence" political action. Both factions evidently sought support in prophetic oracles.

It is surely no accident that the struggles of Jeremiah are preserved and presented so fully by the Dtr editors. We may presume from the thoroughly Dtr composition in chap. 44 that the editors were unsympathetic to those Israelites who insisted upon fleeing to Egypt after the murder of Gedaliah. Translated into political terms, the editors in hindsight favored the counsel put in the mouth of Jeremiah, that one should remain in Judah, wait out this period of exile while Jerusalem lay in ruins, and get along with the Babylonians (42:7–17; 44:1–14, 26–30). It may be that these editors were themselves survivors of that group which before exile had counselled moderation and co-existence. In any case, it appears that now, in exile, the traditions of conflict between Jeremiah and his public were serving yet another function besides explanation and homily for Yahwistic religion. Tradition of conflict may have reinforced the social and political position of the editors as well. We might suppose that they wished to mount a political argument against those who went to Egypt, sanctioned of course with theological reprobation, because their own situation in exile demanded that they remain on amicable terms with their Babylonian masters. Such a pro-Babylonian posture was in fact to be elaborated more fully by the Chronicler (Ackroyd).

We have come full circle—beginning with the latest editorial perspectives on these traditions, back to what we could learn of Jeremiah's situation, now returning to the environment of the editors. There remains much that we would wish to know: the group with which Jeremiah apparently was aligned seems hardly distinguishable in socio-economic terms from those "autonomists" around Zedekiah. But were there in fact "class" distinctions? Were there social, economic, material bases for the political options we have seen? The personal dimension remains closed to us—those human strivings for power and influence that one might imagine to be at work are never mentioned or hinted at. And the effects of those conflicts, whether over theological warrants for political action or political programs themselves, are invisible. It is difficult to say who the victors and the victims finally were, unless one assumes the story to be written by the victors, i.e., that the Dtr editor(s) carried on that earlier tradition of cooperation with Babylonian powers.

In any case, what we can see has enabled us to gain a somewhat fuller picture of the social dimensions of conflict between one prophet and his public. And certainly from the point of view of the editors, conflict in itself was not viewed as a problem, but part of a renewed proclamation of religion and (implicitly) political posture. It may have been that a consistent literary portrait of conflict along with the vindication of spokesmen for [[50]] certain political views would have been served as part of the Dtr editor(s) response to a new need in Babylonian exile, viz., to establish that there was precedent within the advocacy of pure Yahwism for a policy which, if not pro-Babylonian, was at least favorable to co-existence with that nation.

The textual tradition, tendentious as it is, nevertheless allows us a glimpse of the complex social and political situation in which this example of prophetic conflict was played out. Anthropological studies help us realize that conflict is a vital element in prophetic activity, and that it is both deeper and broader than disputes over religious beliefs. Thus, anthropological study helps us compensate for distortions which arise from isolating religious ideology from other forms of social expression.

Works Consulted

Ackroyd, Peter
1968   *Exile and Restoration.* Philadelphia: Westminster.
Anisimov, A. F.
1963   The Shaman's Tent of the Evenks and the Origin of the Shamanistic Rite. Pp. 84–123 in *Studies in Siberian Shamanism,* edited by H. N. Michael. Toronto: University of Toronto Press.
Balikci, Asen
1967   Shamanistic Behaviour among the Netsilik Eskimos. Pp. 191–209 in *Magic, Witchcraft, and Curing,* edited by John Middleton. New York: Natural History Press.
1970   *The Netsilik Eskimo.* Garden City, New York: American Museum of Natural History.
Beattie, John, and J. Middleton, eds.
1969   *Spirit Mediumship and Society in Africa.* New York: Africana.
Berndt, R. M.
1946–48 Wuradjeri Magic and "Clever Men." *Oceania* 17: 327–65; 18: 60–86.
Bogoras, Vladimir G.
1910   *Chuckchee Mythology.* The Jesup North Pacific Expedition 8/1–2. New York: American Museum of Natural History.
Carley, Keith
1977   Prophets Old and New. Pp. 238–66 in *Prophets of Melanesia,* edited by G. Trompf. Port Moresby: Institute of Papua New Guinea Studies.
Carroll, Robert P.
1977   Ancient Israelite Prophecy and Dissonance Theory. *Numen* 24: 135–51.
1979   *When Prophecy Failed: Cognitive Dissonance in the Prophetic Traditions of the Old Testament.* New York: Seabury.
Chagnon, N. A.
1968   *Yanomamö: The Fierce People.* New York: Holt, Rinehart, and Winston.
Colson, Elizabeth
1977   A Continuing Dialogue: Prophets and Local Shrines among the Tonga of Zambia. Pp. 119–39 in *Regional Cults,* edited by R. P. Werbner. Association of Social Anthropologists Monograph 16. London: Academic Press.
Crenshaw, James L.
1971   *Prophetic Conflict: Its Effect upon Israelite Religion.* Beihefte zur Zeitschrift für die Alttestamentliche Wissenschaft 124. Berlin: de Gruyter.
Cripps, A. S.
1928   *Chaminuka.* London: Sheldon.
DeVries, Simon
1978   *Prophet against Prophet.* Grand Rapids: Eerdmans.

Eliade, Mircea
  1964   *Shamanism: Archaic Techniques of Ecstasy.* Princeton: Princeton University Press.
Evans-Pritchard, E. E.
  1937   *Witchcraft, Oracles, and Magic among the Aznade.* Oxford: Clarendon.
  1956   *Nuer Religion.* Oxford: Clarendon.
Festinger, Leon, Henry W. Riecken, and Stanley Schachter
  1956   *When Prophecy Fails.* Minneapolis: University of Minnesota Press.
Fohrer, G.
  1972   *History of Israelite Religion.* Nashville: Abingdon.
Fry, Peter
  1976   *Spirits of Protest.* Cambridge: Cambridge University Press.
Garbett, Kingsley
  1977   Disparate Regional Cults and a Unitary Ritual Field in Zimbabwe. Pp. 55–92 in *Regional Cults,* edited by R. P. Werbner. London: Academic Press.
Hossfeld, F. L., and I. Meyer
  1973   *Prophet gegen Prophet.* Biblische Beiträge 9. Fribourg: Schweizerisches Katholisches Bibelwerk.
Johnson, Aubrey
  1962   *The Cultic Prophet in Ancient Israel.* 2d edition. Cardiff: University of Wales Press.
Kaufmann, Yehezkel
  1960   *The Religion of Israel, from Its Beginnings to the Babylonian Exile.* Chicago: University of Chicago Press.
Kessler, Martin
  1968   Jeremiah Chapters 26–45 Reconsidered. *Journal of Near Eastern Studies* 27: 81–88.
Lewis, I. M.
  1971   *Ecstatic Religion.* Baltimore: Penguin.
Lindblom, Johannes
  1962   *Prophecy in Ancient Israel.* Philadelphia: Fortress.
Martin-Achard, R.
  1977   Hanania contre Jérémie: Quelques remarques sur Jérémie 28. *Bulletin du Centre Protestant d'Études* 29: 51–57.
Mettinger, T. N. D.
  1971   *Solomonic State Officials.* Lund: Gleerup.
Meyer, Ivo
  1977   *Jeremia und die falschen Propheten.* Göttingen: Vandenhoeck & Ruprecht.
Nadel, S. F.
  1946   A Study of Shamanism in the Nuba Mountains. *Journal of the Royal Anthropological Institute* 76: 25–37.
Nicholson, E. W.
  1970   *Preaching to the Exiles: A Study of the Prose Tradition in the Book of Jeremiah.* Oxford: Blackwell.
Osswald, E.
  1962   *Falsche Prophetie im Alten Testament.* Tübingen: Mohr.

Overholt, Thomas
   1970   *The Threat of Falsehood: A Study in the Theology of the Book of Jeremiah.*
            Naperville, Illinois: Allenson.
Petersen, David L.
   1977   *Late Israelite Prophecy.* Missoula, Montana: Scholars Press.
Quell, G.
   1952   *Wahre und falsche Propheten.* Gütersloh: Bertelmann.
von Rad, Gerhard
   1933   Die falschen Propheten. *Zeitschrift für die Alttestamentliche Wissenschaft*
            51: 109–20.
Rasmussen, Knud
   1931   *The Netsilik Eskimos.* Report of Fifth Thule Expedition 8. Copenhagen:
            Nordisk.
Ringgren, Helmer
   1966   *Israelite Religion.* Philadelphia: Fortress.
Sanders, James A.
   1972   *Torah and Canon.* Philadelphia: Fortress.
   1977   Hermeneutics in True and False Prophecy. Pp. 21–41 in *Canon and
            Authority: Essays in Old Testament Religion and Theology,* edited by George
            W. Coats and Burke O. Long. Philadelphia: Fortress.
Seidl, Theodor
   1977   *Texte und Einheiten in Jeremia 27–29: Literaturwissenschaftliche Studie.*
            St. Ottilien: EOS Verlag.
   1978   *Formen und Formeln in Jeremia 27–29: Eine literaturwissenschaftliche
            Studie.* St. Ottilien: EOS Verlag.
Shirokogoroff, S. M.
   1935   *Psychomental Complex of the Tungus.* London: Kegan Paul / Trench &
            Trubner.
Tamoane, Matthew
   1977   Kamoi of Darapap and the Legend of Jari. Pp. 174–211 in *Prophets of
            Melanesia,* edited by G. Trompf. Port Moresby: Institute of Papua New
            Guinea Studies.
Vriezen, Th. C.
   1970   *An Outline of Old Testament Theology.* 2d edition. Oxford: Blackwell.
Wilson, Robert R.
   1980   *Prophecy and Society in Ancient Israel.* Philadelphia: Fortress.
Winkler, Walter F.
   1976   Spirit Possession in Far Western Nepal. Pp. 244–62 in *Spirit Possession
            in the Nepal Himalayas,* edited by J. T. Hitchcock and R. L. Jones. War-
            minster: Aris and Phillips.
van der Woude, A. S.
   1969   Micah in Dispute with the Pseudo-Prophets. *Vetus Testamentum* 19:
            244–60.
Zimmerli, W.
   1978   *Old Testament Theology in Outline.* Atlanta: John Knox.

Interpreting Israel's Religion:

An Anthropological Perspective on the Problem of False Prophecy

R. R. WILSON

[[67]] The use of anthropology in the critical study of Israel's religion began with the seminal work of Julius Wellhausen and W. Robertson Smith,
who attempted to apply contemporary ethnographic research to the problem of reconstructing Israelite religious history. Their work was highly
influential and inspired others to follow their lead, but enthusiasm for
this type of comparative study waned once scholars began to recognize
the methodological problems involved in setting biblical data within a
theoretical social-scientific framework.[1] Since the early part of this century, scholars have usually been reluctant to use anthropological studies
to interpret features of Israelite religion, although they have been much
more willing to use ancient Near Eastern evidence for this purpose.

Even though methodological considerations have certainly been a
major cause of this reluctance, theological factors have also been involved. Scholars who have held that Israel's faith was in some way unique
have usually argued that extrabiblical evidence is irrelevant to the study
of Israelite religion because religious phenomena in other cultures are

Reprinted with permission from *Sociological Approaches to the Old Testament* (Philadephia:
Fortress, 1984) 67–80.

1. Hahn, *Old Testament in Modern Research* [[Philadelphia: Fortress, 1966]], 44–82.

not truly comparable to those in Israel. If these scholars engage in comparative studies at all, they are usually interested in using cross-cultural data to highlight Israel's uniqueness.[2] To be sure, there is a sense in which every society's religion is unique, for it is shaped by a distinctive history and a particular set of cultural forces. However, once this uniqueness has been recognized, the fact remains that the same general religious phenomena appear in a number of different societies. Even more important, these phenomena tend to ⟦68⟧ play similar social roles in their respective cultures. For this reason comparative anthropological studies can help us to understand more clearly the interaction between religion and society in a particular culture, such as ancient Israel, without requiring that we ignore the religion's distinctive features.

One area in which the usefulness of anthropological research can be demonstrated is the study of Israelite prophecy. Israel's prophets were certainly unique individuals, and in fact they are the paradigms used to identify prophets in other cultures. However, the very existence of prophecy outside of Israel suggests that comparative studies might help us to explore the relationship between prophecy and society in the world of the biblical writers.[3] A more comprehensive knowledge of the nature of this relationship is essential if we are to understand the complexities of Israelite prophecy. This is particularly true in the case of one long-standing problem in prophetic research, the problem of false prophecy.

The Nature of the Problem

False Prophecy in the Old Testament

The possibility of false prophecy is inherent in any society that tolerates the existence of prophets. This is so because prophecy is essentially a process by which an intermediary (the prophet) facilitates communication between the human and divine realms. In various ways the prophet receives divine messages and then delivers them to human recipients. However, the prophetic experience is basically a private one, even though the prophet may describe it publicly. In the end the prophet's audience can never be sure that the experience took place as described or that the

2. A prime example of this approach can be seen in the brilliant work of Yehezkel Kaufmann (*The Religion of Israel*, trans. Moshe Greenberg [London: George Allen & Unwin, 1961]), who argued that those features of Israelite religion that had parallels in the ancient Near East were actually part of the popular folk religion and not the official religion of the nation.

3. For an example of such an exploration, see R. Wilson, *Prophecy and Society in Ancient Israel* ⟦Philadelphia: Fortress, 1980⟧.

prophet is accurately reporting the divine message. Therefore, the reliability of any prophecy can be questioned, and the threat of false prophecy
is always present.

Ancient Israel was fully aware of the difficulties involved in assessing
the truth of prophetic claims, and the Old Testament records several suggestions for dealing with the problem, none of them completely satisfactory. In Deut 18:22 Moses tells the Israelites that a false prophecy can be
recognized when it does not come true. By implication, then, true prophecies are those that do come to pass, but unfortunately this test can only
be applied retrospectively, long after the time for public decision about
the truth claim has passed. [[69]] Deut 13:1–5 proposes a limited but more
certain test by considering false any prophet who exhorts the people to
worship other gods. This test is useful as far as it goes, but it is not applicable to many prophetic oracles. According to Jer 28:8–9, Jeremiah himself suggested that prophets delivering disaster oracles are more likely to
be true prophets than those prophesying peace. This suggestion was presumably based on an observation of past examples of prophecy and
fulfillment, but it remains a calculation of probabilities. It is still possible
that prophecies of peace might turn out to be accurate, a possibility that
Jeremiah himself would surely have supported when he began delivering
salvation oracles (Jeremiah 30–32). Finally, the Greek translators of the
Old Testament at least partially solved the problem by giving some
prophets the title "pseudoprophet" (Jer 6:13; 26:7, 8, 11, 16; 27:9; 28:1;
29:1, 8; Zech 13:2), but this characterization is based on interpretations
by the translators of the Septuagint and is not present in the Hebrew text.

The prophets were also aware of their credibility problem and devised various means to solve it. Occasionally they offered the people
miraculous signs which occurred immediately to demonstrate the truth
of prophecies to be fulfilled in the distant future (1 Kgs 13:3, 5). Some
prophets also provided detailed accounts of their initial calls (Isaiah 6;
Jeremiah 1; Ezekiel 1) and described their encounters with the divine
world (1 Kgs 22:17–23) in an attempt to support the truth of their oracles.[4] However, such efforts were not always convincing, and in the end
the people received little help in adjudicating prophetic claims.

Scholarly Views on False Prophecy

Given the uncertainties that pervade the Old Testament's attempts to
deal with false prophecy, it is not surprising that biblical scholars have

---

4. The notion that the prophets cited their call visions in order to strengthen their authority has recently been challenged by B. O. Long, "Prophetic Authority as Social Reality,"
in *Canon and Authority* [[ed. G. W. Coats and B. O. Long; Philadelphia: Fortress, 1977]], 3–20.

discussed the issue at great length.[5] A number of different solutions to the problem have been proposed, but at the risk of [[70]] oversimplification we may arrange them in seven categories. First, some scholars have argued that true prophets could be distinguished from false ones on the basis of the content of their message. False prophets delivered messages of well-being and used a distinctive vocabulary, while true ones did not.[6] Second, attempts have been made to show that false prophets had revelations of lesser quality than those of the true prophets. The true prophets received their oracles through a divine word rather than through a spirit. They were closer to God and stood in the divine council.[7] Third, all cultic prophets are sometimes considered to have been false.[8] Fourth, interpreters have held that true prophets were those best able to correlate their historical and theological traditions with a perceptive reading of their current situation. In this way they knew which oracles were needed at a particular historical moment, a knowledge that the false prophets did not possess.[9] Fifth, a growing number of scholars hold that all Israelite prophets faced pressures toward falsehood. From the outside, the king, the people, and the theological tradition all tried to influence the prophet's oracles, while from the inside, the prophet's own desire for acceptance pressed him to conform to popular expectations. Only those prophets able to resist these influences were able to keep from becoming false prophets.[10] Sixth, it has been argued that false prophets could not be identified by normal people but could be recognized only by a true prophet.[11] Finally, some interpreters hold that so many factors

5. For an assessment of the scholarly discussion up to 1971, see James L. Crenshaw, *Prophetic Conflict* (Berlin: Walter de Gruyter 1971), 13–22. For additional treatments see Martin Buber, "False Prophets," in *On the Bible: Eighteen Studies by Martin Buber*, ed. Nahum M. Glatzer (New York: Schocken Books, 1988), 166–71; Thomas W. Overholt, *The Threat of Falsehood* (Naperville, Ill.: Alec R. Allenson, 1970); Ivo Meyer, *Jeremia und die falschen Propheten* (Freiburg: Universitätsverlag, 1977); Gerhard Münderlein, *Kriterien wahrer und falscher Prophetie* (Bern: Peter Lang, 1979); Frank Lothar Hossfeld and Ivo Meyer, *Prophet gegen Prophet* (Fribourg: Verlag Schweizerisches Katholisches Bibelwerk, 1973); James A. Sanders, "Hermeneutics in True and False Prophecy," in *Canon and Authority*, 21–41; and Simon John DeVries, *Prophet against Prophet* (Grand Rapids: William B. Eerdmans, 1978).

6. Gerhard von Rad, "Die falschen Propheten," *ZAW* 51 (1933): 109–20; A. S. van der Woude, "Micah in Dispute with the Pseudo-Prophets," *VT* 19 (1969): 244–60.

7. Sigmund Mowinckel, "The 'Spirit' and the 'Word' in the Pre-Exilic Reforming Prophets," *JBL* 53 (1934): 199–227; Hans-Joachim Kraus, *Prophetie in der Krisis* (Neukirchen-Vluyn: Neukirchener Verlag, 1964).

8. G. von Rad, "Die falschen Propheten," 109–20.

9. Buber, "False Prophets," 166–71; Sanders, "Hermeneutics," 21–41; Thomas W. Overholt, "Jeremiah 27–29: The Question of False Prophecy," *JAAR* 35 (1967): 241–49.

10. E. Jacob, "Quelques remarques sur les faux prophètes," *TZ* 13 (1957): 479–86; Crenshaw, *Prophetic Conflict*, 23–111.

11. Gottfried Quell, *Wahre und falsche Propheten* (Gütersloh: C. Bertelsmann Verlag, 1952).

were involved in recognizing false prophets that it is not possible to generalize about the matter.[12]

Each of these tests for false prophecy can claim some support from the Old Testament text, although some approaches are more subjective and therefore less useful than others. However, some solutions cannot accommodate all of the biblical evidence, and it is [[71]] likely that the problem is even more complex than even the most perceptive interpreters have realized.

The Choice of an Anthropological Approach

Given the difficulty of the false prophecy question, it is unlikely that any sort of comparative approach can provide a definitive solution to the problem. However, it is clear that the false prophecy issue has a sociological dimension that has not yet been fully addressed. The prophetic process involves an exchange between prophet and society, and it is within this exchange that decisions about the prophet's authenticity are made. This suggests that the problem might be clarified by examining anthropological research on the various ways that prophets interact with their societies. Because we are interested here in the way the prophet relates to all aspects of his society, the material collected by social anthropologists will again be useful.[13]

A Survey of the Anthropological Evidence

The Prophet as Intermediary

The prophet stands between the human and divine worlds and has strong ties to both. As a human being delivering divine messages to a specific audience, the prophet is intimately involved with a particular his-

---

12. Hossfeld and Meyer, *Prophet gegen Prophet*, 160–62; Eva Osswald, *Falsche Prophetie im Alten Testament* (Tübingen: J. C. B. Mohr, 1962).

13. I have discussed this material in detail in Wilson, *Prophecy and Society*, 21–88, where extensive bibliographical references may be found. The following are particularly important: John Beattie and John Middleton, ed., *Spirit Mediumship and Society in Africa* (New York: Africana Publishing Corporation, 1969); Jane Belo, *Trance in Bali* (New York: Columbia University Press, 1960); E. Bourguignon, "The Self, the Behavioral Environment, and the Theory of Spirit Possession," in *Context and Meaning in Cultural Anthropology*, ed. M. E. Spiro (New York: Free Press, 1965), 39–60; Dorothy Emmet, "Prophets and Their Societies," *JRAI* 86 (1956): 13–23; Peter Fry, *Spirits of Protest* (New York and Cambridge: Cambridge University Press, 1976); I. M. Lewis, *Ecstatic Religion* (Baltimore: Penguin Books, 1971); J. Middleton, *Lugbara Religion* [[Oxford, 1960]]; John Middleton and E. H. Winter, ed., *Witchcraft and Sorcery in East Africa* (London: Routledge and Kegan Paul, 1963); R. Prince, ed., *Trance and Possession States* (Montreal: R. M. Bucke Memorial Society, 1968); S. M. Shirokogoroff,

torical society. Yet at the same time the prophet participates in the supernatural world, which is the source of his oracles. Although both aspects of the prophet's existence must be carefully studied in order to obtain an accurate understanding of the prophetic process, scholars have often concentrated on the second.

In contemporary scholarship the prophet's relationship to the supernatural world is frequently explained in psychological or [[72]] sociological terms. Thus, for example, psychologists tend to see in prophetic behavior the symptoms of trance, a psychological and physiological state marked by a loss of control over bodily and mental processes and accompanied by altered views of reality and extreme sensitivity to outside stimuli. In extreme cases the individual loses touch with reality entirely and must be considered mentally ill. In the opinion of many researchers, certain individuals are psychologically or sociologically predisposed to become prophets. The sensitive person has a mystical experience that leads to becoming a prophet. The "charismatic" individual becomes a prophet by receiving a "call" which validates his claim to special status and authority. The psychotic or neurotic goes into a trance and is accredited as a prophet. The social misfit consciously exhibits prophetic behavior in order to enhance his social status.

The difficulty with this sort of approach is that it cannot easily be applied to all prophets. Some prophets display no symptoms of trance, and not all of them fit the paradigm of the neurotic or charismatic individual. Furthermore, the standard scholarly approach cannot explain why people with the necessary psychological characteristics do not become prophets. Mystics, charismatics, neurotics, and social misfits do not inevitably resort to delivering prophetic oracles.

A more fruitful way of exploring the relationship of the prophet to the supernatural is to look at the way the prophets and their societies describe the process. These descriptions fall into two general categories. First, many societies attribute the characteristic behavior of prophets to some form of spirit possession. During this process, a spirit from the divine realm temporarily takes up residence in the host's body. The host "clothes" or "embodies" the spirit, so that the spirit rather than the individual controls speech and action. In cases where a possessing spirit has distinctive behavioral characteristics, these will be visible in the host and permit onlookers to identify the spirit. Second, divine-human communication may take place when a prophet's soul leaves his body and travels to the divine world. There it has supernatural visions that become the basis for oracles after the prophet's experience is completed.

Psychomental Complex of the Tungus (London: Kegan Paul, Trench, Trubner, 1935); and S. S. Walker, *Ceremonial Spirit Possession in Africa and Afro-America* (Leiden: E. J. Brill, 1972).

Prophets and Their Societies

Not all societies react to prophetic claims in the same way, and even within a single society varying evaluations may be made in different cases. In some instances possession and soul migration are [73] viewed negatively. This occurs when the society does not believe in the possibility of divine-human communication or when the characteristic behavior of the prophet is considered to be socially harmful. In either case the would-be prophet is likely to be considered mentally ill or possessed by an evil or demonic spirit. The individual must then be cured or, if that is not possible, must be removed from the society through exile or execution.

Some societies view the prophetic experience negatively but believe that prophetic behavior can be regularized after an initially unwanted case of possession. In this instance, prophets are tolerated so long as their words and actions remain within the expected patterns. If these patterns are broken, then the individual is likely to be restrained and prevented from prophesying.

Finally, certain societies see the prophetic process positively, particularly when the prophet's behavior is completely controlled. In such societies prophecy is likely to play a role in the religious establishment and to have crucial social functions. Because of the importance assigned to prophecy, attempts will often be made to induce a prophetic experience, through the use of artificial stimulation if necessary. However, such techniques are not believed to affect the validity of the prophet's revelation.

In societies where prophecy is tolerated or encouraged, a prophet requires social support throughout the entire prophetic experience. If such support is lacking, the prophet will not be taken seriously and will therefore be ineffective. The process of validation begins when the prophet first claims to have a divine revelation. At this point the society must decide whether or not the prophet's experience is genuine. If the decision is favorable, then the society will tolerate the prophet or even encourage him by integrating him into the religious establishment. However, if the prophet is to continue to be effective, he must have social support throughout his career. In a sense, then, every new prophetic experience must be evaluated and validated by the society. If for some reason the society decides that the prophet's oracles are no longer genuine, it may refuse to see him as a true prophet.

The mechanisms by which societies adjudicate prophetic claims are imperfectly understood and require more extensive study. However, an important factor in the process is the role played by social expectations. Every society has certain commonly held opinions about the nature of the prophetic experience and about typical forms of prophetic behavior. All prophets must conform to these ⟦74⟧ social expectations if they are to be considered true prophets. To put the matter bluntly, societies recognize individuals as true prophets because their words and deeds fit stereotypical patterns of prophetic behavior.

The way in which societies accredit prophets puts a great deal of pressure on would-be prophets to conform to social expectations. The prophets are thus faced with a dilemma. On the one hand they must be true to the divine revelation which they have received. On the other hand they must conform to a social paradigm in order to gain a hearing for their message. Both sides of the equation must be held in a delicate balance if the prophet is to be successful. Prophets usually strike this balance by subconsciously making their speech and actions conform to expected patterns while at the same time insuring that the content of their oracles is consistent with their divine revelation. However, difficulties arise when the balance cannot be maintained because social demands conflict with the prophet's supernatural imperative. Then the prophet must decide whether to deliver the message as he understands it and risk losing necessary social support or to conform to what is expected at the risk of distorting his revelation. This problem becomes even more complex when the society contains groups having different ideas about stereotypical prophetic behavior. In this case the prophet is in the position of deciding which group's expectations to follow. The prophet cannot be accredited by the whole society, and if other groups have their own prophets, then prophetic conflict becomes inevitable.

The Social Location of Prophets

Prophets may function at any level of the social structure and may be found in connection with any group in the society. However, a useful way of talking about the social standing of a given prophet is to locate the individual in relation to the center of the society's social, religious, and political power structure. Those prophets who carry out their activities close to the centers of power may be called *central prophets*. They are likely to play regular roles in the religious establishment and to enjoy a certain amount of social prestige and political power by virtue of their important religious functions. At the other extreme, prophets may be far removed from the power centers and may operate on the fringes of the society. Such *peripheral prophets* have almost no authority within the society as a whole and are usually dispossessed individuals having little status or political ⟦75⟧ power. Prophets, of course, are not confined to the two ends of this spectrum but may appear at any point on the continuum between a society's center and its periphery. It is possible for a society at any given time to contain prophets located at various places on this continuum, and over time a prophet may move from one social location to another. Such conditions can also breed prophetic conflict.

It is important to note that placing a prophet on a social continuum is a relative matter. From the standpoint of a society's religious and political elite, prophets on the fringes of the society are indeed peripheral. They are to be tolerated but can usually be ignored because they are considered to have no political or religious power. However, from the standpoint of a peripheral group supporting a prophet, that prophet is of central importance, for he represents a means by which the group may speak to the whole society. Judgments about centrality or peripherality are therefore seldom made objectively but depend largely on the social location of the people making the judgments.

The Social Functions of Prophecy

Prophecy can have a variety of different social functions, but in general a given prophet's functions are determined by his social location. Peripheral prophecy sometimes enables individuals of low status to improve their personal situations and to obtain a hearing for their message that would not otherwise be possible. While a society might normally ignore such individuals, when they speak with the voices of the spirits they are likely to be accorded a hearing if the audience accepts the spirits' authority.

Peripheral prophets are usually interested in bringing about fairly rapid social change. As representatives of individuals who have been denied access to the society's centers of power, peripheral prophets are concerned to alter fundamental social institutions in order to end social repression and improve the situation of their support group. The social reforms sought by peripheral prophets sometimes involve a reaffirmation of traditional social values and a return to older religious practices and deities. However, the prophets are more likely to demand radical innovations aimed at restructuring the whole society.

In contrast to peripheral prophecy, central prophecy tends to be concerned with the orderly functioning of the social system. If central prophets are official members of the cultic establishment, then they [[76]] are responsible for providing access to the divine world whenever necessary. They also serve as the representatives of the spirits in affairs of state. As leaders of the society, they must supply supernatural legitimation for the existing social order and provide divine sanctions for traditional religious, political, and social views. This means that central prophets tend to be more conservative than their peripheral counterparts and are likely to oppose unnecessary innovation that might lead to social instability. However, central prophets are by no means totally opposed to social change. Rather they are concerned to regulate the speed at which change takes place. They are interested in promoting gradual and orderly change that will allow the society to maintain its traditions and preserve its stability.

Witchcraft and False Prophecy Accusations

We have seen that prophecy can be a means by which peripheral individuals seek to bring about radical changes in the social structure. Although they are rarely totally successful in this effort, their work is usually at least partially rewarded. Peripheral prophecy thus indirectly helps to maintain social stability by providing an outlet for repressed individuals to express their frustrations. However, there are limits to the amount of prophetic pressure that a society will tolerate. When the demands of peripheral prophets become too radical, they are likely to antagonize the society and invite retaliation.

Societies have several means of restraining prophetic excesses and preventing undue social friction. One of the most important is the witchcraft accusation. In most cultures witches are viewed as malevolent individuals whose aim is to destroy all forms of human and social life. So clever are these figures that they cannot be observed pursuing their evil plans, and only the final results of their work can be seen. Most societies therefore require the death penalty for witchcraft, for only in this way can the witch's power finally be curbed. When a society accuses a prophet of witchcraft, the initial judgment which the society made on the prophet is in effect reversed. Rather than attributing the prophet's behavior to benign spirit contact, the society accuses him of involvement with demonic powers. The witchcraft accusation thus goes beyond a false prophecy accusation, which simply discredits the prophet by denying a divine source for his oracles. When witchcraft accusations are made, the society is able to remove an offending prophet physically, either by killing or banishing him. This move inevitably leads to a rupture in the social structure, for by destroying the prophet the society also rejects [[77]] the prophet's support group. Most societies are not willing to go this far and instead use the *threat* of a witchcraft accusation as an effective weapon against the excesses of peripheral individuals and groups.

However, the witchcraft accusation is a two-edged sword, for it can also be used by peripheral prophets against vulnerable individuals in the central social structure. Political leaders, priests, and other prophets are likely targets for such accusations, for these figures are prominent exponents of the views that the peripheral prophet seeks to change. By using this technique the prophet not only claims supernatural support for his own views but demolishes his adversary's views by tracing them to demonic origins.

The Implications of the Anthropological Evidence

The Formulation of New Hypotheses:
The Social Roots of Prophetic Conflict

The anthropological evidence suggests that prophetic conflict may be due to a number of factors, among which social forces play a prominent role. If this is so, then we may suspect that debates about false prophecy in Israel also had sociological components and were not simply disputes over theological issues. It is thus reasonable to assume that decisions about true and false prophecy were essentially made by applying sociological criteria to determine which prophetic claims were valid and which were not. Israel presumably went about this process by employing tests similar to those that are used in modern societies. True prophets were those whose words and actions fit the stereotypical behavior of true prophets. However, because of the complexity of Israelite society, we may also assume that various groups in Israel had different notions of how prophets should act and talk. In this case there would have been no general agreement on which prophets were true and which were false, and this lack of agreement would inevitably have led to prophetic conflict. This hypothesis can be tested in a preliminary way by examining the passages in Jeremiah that deal with prophetic disputes.

The Testing of the Hypotheses:
Jeremiah and the False Prophets

Prophetic disputes play an important role in Jeremiah and are the subject of several narratives (Jeremiah 27–29) and collections of oracles (Jer 5:12–13, 30–31; 6:13–14; 8:10–11; 14:13–16; 23:9–40). However, the narratives in particular have been difficult to interpret, [[78]] for they seem to provide no firm grounds for distinguishing the true prophet from the false one. For example, in the account of Jeremiah's confrontation with Hananiah (Jeremiah 27–28), both prophets use the same basic speech forms for their oracles and employ similar symbolic actions. To be sure they deliver different messages. Jeremiah advocates surrender to the Babylonians (Jer 27:1–13), while Hananiah predicts that Jerusalem will be divinely protected from the Babylonian threat and that the previously deported exiles will soon be allowed to return. However, ancient Israelite theological traditions lie behind both of these views. Jeremiah's message consistently follows the views of the Deuteronomistic theology, which held that the election of Jerusalem and the Davidic royal house was contingent on obedience to divine law as understood by the Deuteronomists. As proof for this position Jeremiah could cite accounts of the fall of Shiloh and Samaria, both of which were destroyed as punishment for not obeying the law (Jeremiah 7; 2 Kings 17). On the other hand, Hananiah's message followed the Jerusalemite royal theology, which stressed the unconditional character of the election of the city and its dynasty and God's promise to dwell forever in Jerusalem (2 Samuel 7; Psalm 132). As proof for this position, Hananiah could cite the miraculous deliverance of Jerusalem at the time of Sennacherib's invasion, when Israel's acknowledged sins did not result in the destruction of the city or the removal of the king (2 Kings 18–19; Isaiah 10, 28–31, 33).

Given the lack of obvious distinctions between these two prophets, it is likely that the roots of the conflict lie in the fact that they are representatives of different groups, neither of which accepts the authority of the other's prophet. In this case it is not difficult to reconstruct the nature of these groups. Jeremiah is a member of one of the priestly families of Anathoth (Jer 1:1), the city to which the High Priest Abiathar and his Ephraimite priestly relatives had been exiled by Solomon (1 Kgs 2:26–27). This priestly line is traditionally associated with the old northern sanctuary at Shiloh and may be related to the carriers of the Deuteronomistic theological traditions. We have already noted that Jeremiah is a supporter of those traditions, and it is clear that he also accepted Deuteronomistic views on prophecy. This is particularly obvious in the account of his call, which portrays him as a "prophet like Moses," a particular type of prophet playing a prominent role in Deuteronomistic tradition (Jer 1:4–10; cf. Deut 18:9–22). It is therefore likely that Jeremiah's supporters were [[79]] among those groups that accepted the Deuteronomistic theology and that they viewed him as a legitimate Mosaic prophet (Jeremiah 26). However, it is clear that Jeremiah was a peripheral figure who was not part of the central religious establishment in Jerusalem. His oracles seem to have had no impact on anyone but his own supporters, and his message was strongly opposed by the Jerusalemite establishment, which saw him as a madman rather than as a true prophet (Jer 20:1–6; 29:24–28; 36:1–32).[14]

Hananiah's acceptance of the Jerusalemite royal theology and his position in the royal court suggest that he was a central prophet who was

---

14. For a more comprehensive account of Jeremiah's background and theological views, see Wilson, *Prophecy and Society,* 231–51.

a part of Jerusalem's religious establishment. His supporters were to be found in this group, which preserved the old traditions of God's eternal election of the city. He undoubtedly viewed Jeremiah as a threat to the social order whose oracles simply undermined the people's traditional faith.

The conflict between Jeremiah and Hananiah was therefore not only a conflict between different theological positions but was also a confrontation between two prophets having different social locations and different supporters. Jeremiah, the peripheral prophet, and Hananiah, the central prophet, were each unwilling to recognize the prophetic claims of the other, and their supporters were also unlikely to be persuaded by the opposition's views. Hananiah did not fit the paradigm of the Mosaic prophet and so was not likely to be accredited by Jeremiah's group, and Jeremiah did not fit the Jerusalemite picture of what a prophet ought to be.

The only way of resolving this conflict was to attempt to discredit the opponent. This is precisely what Jeremiah did by making use of false prophecy accusations. On a number of occasions he complains that the Jerusalemite prophets have spoken visions from their own minds rather than the true word of God (Jer 23:16–17). They have not stood in the Divine Council but have spoken ineffective words that did not come true (Jer 23:18, 21–22). Unlike Mosaic prophets such as Jeremiah, the Jerusalemites have relied on dreams and have copied words from one another instead of speaking the direct word of God, which can always be recognized because of its effectiveness (Jer 23:25–32; cf. Num 12:6–8; Deut 18:21–22).

However, Jeremiah's charges are more than simple false prophecy accusations, for in his theological tradition false prophecy was [[80]] punishable by death (Deut 18:20). Seen in this light, false prophecy accusations have the same function as witchcraft accusations do in modern societies. In the face of deteriorating social conditions, Jeremiah risked shattering the Jerusalemite social structure by attempting to remove Hananiah permanently from the scene. According to the biblical tradition, Jeremiah succeeded in his attempt. His false prophecy accusation ultimately led to Hananiah's death (Jer 28:12–17).

Prophecy and Covenant

ERNEST W. NICHOLSON

I

[[201]] The decisive stage in the history of this inner-Israelite controversy [[about the nature of God and his relation to Israel]] began in the eighth century with the preaching of the great prophets, and [[202]] it was from this period onwards that a radically new and distinctive Israelite world-view emerged. The resultant transformation of Israel's understanding of God and his relation to Israel provided the basis for, and found expression in, the concept of a covenant between Yahweh and Israel, as I shall argue below. But the controversy which the eighth-century prophets sharply intensified had antecedents which go further back.

Evidence for this can be found, for example, in connection with the demand for Israel's exclusive allegiance to Yahweh which is so central a feature of the covenant theology where it has the status of nothing less than a principle upon which the religious community stood or fell. It is similarly conceived of in the preaching of Hosea, most notably among the eighth-century prophets.

Controversy on this issue did not first emerge in the time of this prophet. The traditions about Elijah a century or so before Hosea bear witness to an earlier history of controversy concerning it. Indeed, it is not unlikely that it had still earlier origins. In the indisputably ancient traditions of Yahweh's deliverance of Israel's ancestors from bondage in Egypt and of his victories on behalf of the tribes of Israel against their enemies during the early generations of Israel's emergence in Canaan, Yahweh was acknowledged to be the God who alone stood at the foundation and

Reprinted with permission and excerpted from "The Distinctiveness of Israel's Faith," *God and His People: Covenant and Theology in the Old Testament* (Oxford: Clarendon, 1986) 201–10.

beginnings of Israel.[1] Traditions such as these provide the evidence for how Yahweh became the God of Israel, and it is likely that some circles in Israel from the earliest period maintained an exclusive relationship with Yahweh. But the evidence strongly suggests that for Israelites in general—not only at the level of a popular "folk religion" but also in official religion in the pre-exilic period—the worship of the national God Yahweh was not believed to be incompatible with the worship of other gods as well, and it seems highly unlikely that exclusive worship of Yahweh was regarded as of the very essence of the national religion, much less that it was the principle upon which the community stood or fell.

〚203〛 However, though controversy on this issue may have had early beginnings, in particularly heightened form and with violent consequences it erupted in the ninth century at the hands of Elijah and the circles associated with him. Such is the development which the traditions about Elijah have undergone, and such the Deuteronomistic re-working to which they have been subjected in being placed in their present context, that particular caution is required in attempting to reconstruct the events of the period and to discern the religious motivations behind Elijah's activity.

His name itself has the appearance of a sort of confessional assertion which on the basis of the declaration of the people at Carmel "Yahweh, he is God" (1 Kgs 18:39) may be rendered "Yahweh is God."[2] It may have been acquired by him as a nickname, and suggests that he belonged to conservative Yahwistic circles in Israel and now entered the scene as the leader of a movement of militantly self-conscious Yahwism. That he came from Gilead in Transjordan, and thus well away from the centre of the kingdom, has frequently been seen as also suggestive of his conservative background. The policies and behaviour of the dynasty of Omri, and most notably the role of the evidently formidable Tyrian princess and fervent patroness of Baal, Jezebel, occasioned his activity; indeed it was partly as a result of this that the dynasty met its violent end—he himself is described as having announced its rejection by Yahweh and as having inaugurated the dynasty which was to succeed it (1 Kgs 19:15–18; 21:17–24)—and that Jezebel met her bloody death.

---

1. On this period see R. Smend, *Jahwekrieg und Stämmebund: Erwägungen zur ältesten Geschichte Israels*, FRLANT 84, Göttingen 1963; E. trs. *Yahweh War and Tribal Confederation: Reflections upon Israel's Earliest History*, Nashville and New York 1970. Cf. H.-P. Müller, "Gott und die Götter in den Anfängen der biblischen Religion. Zur Vorgeschichte des Monotheismus," in *Monotheismus im Alten Israel und seiner Umwelt*, ed. O. Keel, Biblische Beiträge 14, Fribourg 1980, 99–142.

2. For this see R. Smend, "Der biblische und der historische Elia," *SVT* 28, 1975, 176–80.

It has been suggested that his stand for Yahweh was nationalistically inspired and motivated: Yahweh is Israel's God, and not a foreign deity. In the name of Yahweh, Israel's national God, it is suggested, he waged rebellion against this dynasty's recognition and patronage of foreign cults—the installation of the cult of the Tyrian Baal, Jezebel's own ancestral state god, in Samaria (1 Kgs 16:31f.), and Ahaziah's quest for a cure for his sickness not from Yahweh but from Baalzebub ("Is it because there is no God in Israel that you are going to enquire of Baalzebub, the god of Ekron?" [2 Kgs 1:3]).

Though there is some justification for such a view, it may be questioned whether the royal patronage of foreign cults was the sole [[204]] motivation of Elijah's "jealousy" for Yahweh, and whether what he represented is adequately described as a nationalistically inspired Yahwism. He is described as the "troubler of Israel" and not just of the house of Omri (1 Kgs 18:7), and it was Israelites at Mount Carmel whom he confronted with the uncompromising choice "Yahweh or Baal?." In my opinion, these elements in the traditions about him, as well as his name and background, suggest a controversy not merely between him and the ruling dynasty, but the sort of inner-Israelite controversy referred to above, a controversy between, on the one hand, a tradition that Yahweh alone stood at the foundation and beginnings of Israel's life and that to him alone Israel's allegiance was due, and, on the other, the polytheistic religion and *praxis* [['practice']] which not merely rivalled but, on the evidence of the Old Testament, prevailed against it throughout the preexilic period with at best only sporadic reversals.

Conflict within Israel concerning the nature of Yahweh and his relation to, and claims upon, Israel was not, however, confined to this issue of the worship of the one as against that of the many. In addition, though in important respects related to it, was a further issue of which the Elijah narratives again provide some evidence. It may be described as follows.

As I have suggested, Israelite religion, no less than the religions of its environment, contained a "state-ideological" component; Israel believed its social order and institutions to have been established by God and thus to be legitimated by him as permanent. The order which Yahweh willed and his actions on Israel's behalf were seen as a manifestation of the righteousness which Yahweh both possessed and safeguarded. It was not considered that the demands of Yahweh's righteousness posed any ultimate threat to Israel. When offences were committed or when there was any other sign that Yahweh's favour had been lost, the organs of the cult (lament, sacrifice, etc.) were there to restore it. Thus Israel's well-being (*šālōm*) was believed to be permanently guaranteed by Yahweh;

fundamentally Yahweh's will and Israel's well-being were identified: "Is not Yahweh in the midst of us? No evil shall befall us" (Mic 3:11).

In acute form controversy within Israel on this issue did not come until the prophets of the eighth century who turned Yahweh's righteousness against Israel, placing it at the centre and vehemently denying the belief that his will and Israel's well-being were simply identical. No one before [[205]] that period had polarized Yahweh's righteousness and Israel's offences against it to such an extent as to announce that Yahweh had rejected Israel (see further below).

Nevertheless, there is evidence that tension arose at an earlier time between, on the one hand, the "state-ideology" component of Israel's understanding of Yahweh's ordering of the world, and, on the other, the demands of Yahweh's righteousness. Thus, for example, the demands of Yahweh's righteousness were the basis of the prophetic condemnation of Ahab's violent appropriation, at the instigation of Jezebel and with her energetic help, of Naboth's land, understood as his inalienable patrimony from Yahweh. In the prophetic denunciation and condemnation of the king "Have you murdered and also taken in possession?" (2 Kgs 21:19) is already indicated the claims of Yahweh's righteousness, if not at the cost of Israel as such, then certainly at the cost of the state's dynasty. Similarly, at a still earlier time David's adultery with Bathsheba and his ensuing treacherous murder of Uriah were confronted by the divine righteousness at the hands of Nathan, and although the Davidic dynasty remained intact, lasting punishment was announced against it (2 Sam 12:10).

Just as religion in Israel was a legitimating agency, these two instances are testimony to its significant role as a "de-mystifying" agent. That is, the very institutions, in this instance kingship, which religion legitimated *sub specie aeternitatis* [['in its essential form']], religion could also relativize, "de-mystify," *sub specie aeternitatis* by declaring them in the face of God's righteousness to be devoid of inherent sanctity or divinely willed permanence.[3]

The fervent exclusivism of Elijah and the circles associated with him in the face of traditional polytheism, and the "de-mystifying" role of religion in the face of its traditional role of legitimating the social order and its institutions, bear witness to a history of controversy within Israel concerning the nature of Yahweh and his claims upon Israel. But as suggested above, there are good reasons for believing that the most decisive stage in the history of this controversy, and that which gave a qualitatively new dimension to Israel's understanding of God, man and the world, began in the eighth century with the preaching of the great prophets. The

3. Cf. P. Berger [[*The Social Reality of Religion* (London, 1969)]], esp. ch. 4.

notion of a covenant between Yahweh and Israel was conceived of at this ✓ time, both contributing to, and reflecting leading aspects of, the radically transformed world-view which now began finally to emerge in Israel.

II

⟦206⟧ Elijah announced Yahweh's rejection of the dynasty of Omri and arranged for Jehu to be anointed to rule over Israel. He did not announce the rejection of Israel, but saw its continuation under a new dynasty. In this respect he stood in the tradition of, for example, Ahijah at an earlier time. But the prophets of the eighth century, beginning with Amos *ca.* 760 B.C., announced Yahweh's rejection of Israel.

Israel believed its well-being to be permanently guaranteed by Yahweh. But if tradition declared "You only have I known of all the nations of the world," Amos added in Yahweh's name "therefore I will punish you for all your iniquities" (3:2), "The end has come upon my people Israel" (8:2; cf. 5:2). If from ancient times Israel believed itself to be Yahweh's people, Hosea now announced "You are not my people and I am not your God" (1:9). When Judaeans and citizens of Jerusalem confidently boasted that since Yahweh was in their midst "No evil shall befall us," Micah prophesied "Zion shall be ploughed like a field; Jerusalem shall become a heap of ruins" (3:11f.).[4] The Zion tradition declared that Yahweh would devastate any enemies who dared assault it (e.g. Pss 2; 46:6f.; 48:5–7), but Isaiah announced that Yahweh was about to summon enemies to execute his wrath upon its inhabitants for their sins (7:18).

The grounds of their indictment of Israel were not simply uniform. But consistently present in the preaching of all four prophets of this period is their condemnation of Israel in the ethical sphere, in the sphere of Yahweh's righteousness, that is, on the basis of Yahweh's divine "order" in the sphere of interpersonal relationships.[5] In unprecedented manner they intensively focused upon Yahweh's righteousness against which, again in unprecedented manner, they rigorously measured Israel's life and pronounced it as standing condemned by God (cf. Isa 1:16f., 21–23; 3:13–15; 5:7, 8, 23; 10:1–4; Hos 4:1; 6:6–9; 7:1–7; 8:3; Amos 2:6–8; 3:10; 4:1; 5:7, 10–15, 24; 8:4–6; Mic 2:1f.; 3:1–4, 9–12);[6] no amount of cultic religiosity (sacrifice, lament, etc.) could uphold a relationship between

4. For evidence of a possible background in controversy for some of the material in Micah see A. S. van der Woude, "Micah in Dispute with the Pseudo-prophets," *VT* 19, 1969, 244–60.

5. Cf. Schmid, *Altorientalische Welt in der alttestamentlichen Theologie* ⟦Zurich, 1974⟧ 14f., 49ff.

6. Ibid.

this ⟦207⟧ righteous God and this unrighteous people (cf. Isa 1:10–17; Hos 6:6; Amos 5:21–24; Mic 3:4). That is, these prophets sharply augmented the clash, of which there were already some signs at an earlier time, between the demands of Yahweh's righteousness and the "state-ideological" component in Israel's understanding of Yahweh's ordering of the world; not the *šālōm* ('well-being') of Israel, but Yahweh's righteousness now occupies the centre, if needs be at the cost of Israel.[7]

Put differently, in the preaching of these prophets the role of religion as a de-legitimating agent entered its most vigorous period in the history of Israel, and with far-reaching consequences. No longer merely the kingship or any other individual institution, but the social order as a whole was relativized in the face of a radicalized perception of Yahweh's righteousness.

The presupposition of such a relativizing of the social order was a radical differentiation between the divine and the human world, between God and his creation, so that the human world is not viewed as simply continuous with the divine: the divine-human continuum is split apart, so that the human world even can be viewed as being at loggerheads with its creator. In short, the transcendence of God over the human world is emphasized.[8]

Such a relativizing of the human world in the face of a transcendent God and his will for righteousness is one of the hallmarks of Old Testament religion, and the view is warranted that it was fundamentally this that effected the decisive departure of this religion from the religious thought-world of its environment, including what appears to have been the predominantly polytheistic religion of Israel in the pre-exilic period. Herein lies the justification for the description of Old Testament religion as the rationalization of life on the basis of the "disenchantment of the world," to employ the phrase made popular by Weber.[9] Such "disenchantment of the world" is represented by, for example, the decisive break with the typical creation-theology of the ancient Near East: God is not continuous with his creation, does not permeate it, is not to be identified with, or represented by, anything within it, but stands outside ⟦208⟧ his creation confronting it with his righteous will. More than anything else, more than any traditional monolatry which may have existed among some circles in Israel from early times, this emphasis upon the transcendence of God polarized the difference between Yahweh and other gods and

---

7. Ibid., 53.

8. See Berger, 115ff.

9. Cf. Berger, 111f. The description "Entzauberung der Welt" was evidently first coined by Schiller. For a brief description of Weber's use of this phrase see H. H. Gerth and C. Wright Mills, *From Max Weber: Essays in Sociology*, London 1948, 51ff.

eventually led from monolatry to monotheism proper. Further, because of this "disenchantment of the world," the world, seen as inimical to God's righteousness, becomes a world not merely to be sustained, as in the cosmogonic religions of antiquity, but a world to be transformed. Hence Israel is more and more viewed as having been called by God as a manifestation of his will for righteousness in the world, and is eventually conceived of as the divine means of bringing blessing, salvation, Yahweh's righteousness, to the world. That is, the emphasis upon the transcendence of God and the relativizing of the human world in the face of God's righteousness necessarily involved the development of soteriology.

The understanding of the role of Israel among the nations was itself a new understanding of Israel's existence: from being a state among other states, Israel was conceived of as "the people of God," performing a role for God in history among the nations. The break with traditionalism represented by the "disenchantment of the world" yielded a rationalization of life within the world. For example, all magic and ritual conceived of as a means of sustaining the world from within, of maintaining the immanent order of the cosmos, were eliminated—a more literal translation of Weber's description *Entzauberung der Welt* is 'demagicalization of the world'—and life was rationalized in terms of service to a transcendent and righteous God whose will was declared and known. This insistence upon the totality of life in the service of God imposed a "cohesive and, *ipso facto*, rational structure upon the whole spectrum of everyday life."[10]

"The prophet is significant as the initiator of a great process of rationalization in the interpretation of the 'meaning' of the world and the attitudes men should take toward it."[11] It was pre-eminently the prophets of the eighth century in Israel who broke with traditionalism by denying that Israel's life was divinely guaranteed as permanent. Such an [[209]] unprecedented relativizing of Israel's life in the face of God's righteousness was in itself a decisive advance in the perception of the nature of Yahweh as transcendent. To claim that the "disenchantment of the world" which is such a characteristic of Old Testament religion had its sole source in, or received its sole impulse from, the preaching of these prophets would be an oversimplification. But the view is justified that what they preached was crucial for its development and that without their preaching such potential as Israelite religion may already have had for such a "disenchantment of the world" would not have been fully realized. At their hands the inner-Israelite controversy to which attention

10. Cf. Berger, 120.

11. Talcott Parsons, *The Structure of Social Action*, vol. II, New York and London 1968 (originally published 1937), 567. (Parsons at this point is discussing Weber's notion of rationalization and of prophets as initiators of the process of rationalization.)

has been drawn above (concerning the nature of Yahweh and his claims upon Israel) entered its decisive stage; to the extent that the history of the development of Israelite religion was a history of two increasingly conflicting world-views, the preaching of these prophets may be said to have marked the beginning of the triumph of the one over the other.

In their condemnation of Israel and in the prophecies which some of them announced of a transformed Israel beyond judgement, they gave a qualitatively new dimension not only to the perception of the nature of Yahweh as transcendent, but also to the concept of Israel as "the people of Yahweh." Theirs was a radically theocentric understanding of Israel's existence; whether explicitly or implicitly their vision of Israel was of a people summoned to live in single-minded obedience to the claims of God: herein lay Israel's very *raison d'être*, and short of this it had none. To the extent that tension had earlier emerged in Israel between the "state-ideological" component in Israel's religion and the claims of Yahweh's righteousness, they roundly broke it in favour of Yahweh's claims, which they viewed as being uncompromisingly totalistic.

They themselves did not engage in any systematic rationalization of Israel's life on this basis. But what came to the fore in their preaching and the desacralized understanding of Israel which it embodied initiated, at the hands of others, just such a rationalization. And it was this that found expression in the notion that Israel's relationship with Yahweh was a covenant relationship.

Covenant-theology is through and through a theology of "the people of Yahweh." Appropriated by Yahweh as his own, Israel is commanded to live in exclusive allegiance and total commitment to him. As in the preaching of the prophets of the eighth century and their successors, here [[210]] too this is Israel's *raison d'être*. By its very nature the notion of a covenant between God and his people disposed of any belief that Israel's election was simply Israel's destiny in the sense that Yahweh automatically guaranteed Israel's existence. No less than in the preaching of the prophets of the eighth century, the covenant-theology opposed a false traditionalism which believed this to be so. Rather, Israel's election is understood as Israel's vocation, that is, something which had to be realized in Israel's life as a society. The making of a covenant thus involved choice and decision on Israel's part no less than on God's. The requirement of a covenant is itself the clearest evidence of this, for it may justifiably be claimed that it was addressed to an Israel which was not wont to serve Yahweh in the exclusive manner for which it calls. That is, its very formulation, the fervent imperative which it placed upon Israel's allegiance to Yahweh alone and to his will, could not simply be assumed or taken for granted: from such a people the most solemn pledge of loyalty to Yahweh alone, the solemnly binding pledge of a covenant, was evidently necessary. Further choice and decision confronted each generation of Israel, for again by its very nature the making of a covenant carried with it the possibility that the relationship between Yahweh and Israel could be terminated, something which is made explicit in, for example, the "new covenant" passage in Jer 31:31–34 (see below [[not reprinted here]]). The very fact that the making of a covenant confronted Israel with such a choice is itself an indication of the goal of the covenant-theology: the transformation of Israel from what it historically had been into what it had been summoned to be: the people of Yahweh. Put differently, the covenant-theology represented at once an indicative and an imperative: the indicative, Israel's constitution as the people of Yahweh; the imperative, Israel's vocation to be the people of Yahweh.

Prophecy in History:
The Social Reality of Intermediation

THOMAS W. OVERHOLT

[[3]] There *were* prophets in ancient Israel and Judah, and persons like Amos and Jeremiah were recognized by their contemporaries as being among them. This proposition may seem to many a banality—a piece of common knowledge and hardly something to be argued—but in recent years it has come under explicit attack by two British scholars, A. Graeme Auld and Robert P. Carroll. My proposition, then, provides an occasion to appraise their arguments and to make a modest proposal about how cross-cultural studies can contribute to our appreciation of the historical reality of biblical prophecy.

Poets, Not Prophets

The position that Auld seeks to defend is that "it [is] at least plausible that [the terms] 'prophet' and 'prophesy' only came to be attached to those whom we regard as the towering prophets of the Bible in a period no earlier than when Jeremiah and Ezekiel became similarly represented" (1984: 82). Stated in a slightly stronger way, he informs us that his "first aim is a negative one: to discount the inherited suggestion that these poets were 'prophets' in their own eyes or in the eyes of their contemporaries" (1983b: 41). Recent studies by Carroll have tended toward a similar conclusion. These two scholars have studied different material, and their arguments are not identical. Still, they are in basic

Reprinted with permission from *Journal for the Study of the Old Testament* 48 (1990) 3–29.

agreement that figures ⟦4⟧ like Amos, Hosea, and Isaiah were poets and were not thought of as prophets until exilic times. Between them, Auld and Carroll marshal four arguments in support of this "poets, not prophets" hypothesis.

The first argument is linguistic. Auld in particular has been preoccupied with what he calls the "history of terminology" (1984: 82). Several of his studies center on the noun and verb forms of *nbʾ* ⟦'prophesy'⟧ and conclude that there are three identifiable stages in the use of these terms in the prophetic and historical books of the Hebrew Bible. First, at an early stage the terms were applied to groups that were the objects of criticism. During this period, the canonical prophets—Isaiah, Micah, Zephaniah, and Jeremiah (in the poetic sections of the books)— were not referred to as "prophets." "The usage is rather more nuanced" in Amos and Hosea, but "there is no suggestion that Hosea was himself a 'prophet'; and that label is specifically rejected by Amos in 7:14" (1984: 68). The books of Jeremiah and Ezekiel represent a second, transitional stage. In addition to criticism of the prophets as a group, these books contain positive references to past prophets and apply the title "prophet" to Jeremiah and Ezekiel themselves. The latter book regularly uses the verb to describe Ezekiel's functioning. Auld concludes, however, that neither Jeremiah nor Ezekiel used the noun to describe himself or the verb to refer to his own activity (1984: 73). Finally, there is a late stage in which the view of prophets is essentially favorable and individuals—Haggai, Zechariah, and Habakkuk—are given the title prophet. The favorable attitude toward prophets in Kings is the result of late editorial additions.

In this view, Jeremiah and Ezekiel "stand at the cross-roads" of a development from eighth- and seventh-century hostility (or at best neutrality) toward "prophetic contemporaries" to the post-exilic period when persons were "readily titled 'prophet'" (Auld 1983a: 5 ⟦in this volume, p. 291⟧). The validity of this scheme can be tested with "a degree of objectivity" in the book of Jeremiah, "with its different editions, and its blend of poetry and prose" (1983a: 5–6 ⟦292⟧). References to "prophets" in the Jeremiah poetry are mostly critical. In the earliest stratum of prose (the material common to LXX and MT) there are many critical references to prophets, but Jeremiah, Uriah, and Micah are ⟦5⟧ referred to positively as prophets. The latest prose ("extra" material in MT) has a few critical references, but gives the title "prophet" to Jeremiah (24×) and Hananiah (6×). Carroll also notes the development that has taken place between the two editions of the book of Jeremiah: while the first (represented by LXX) gives Jeremiah the title "the prophet" only four times (all refer to the period after the fall of Jerusalem), the second (represented by MT) does so twenty-six times, making him "the prophet *par excellence*" (1989a: 23).

Auld observes that the verb "prophesy" seems to have been used positively earlier than the noun "prophet." For example, Amos 3:3–8 (Auld eliminates v. 7 as a later prose addition) groups prophesying with other matters of general human experience. Thus *"prophesying*. . . [is] an activity that is not confined to official *prophets*, but open to *anyone* who has heard Lord Yahweh speak" (1986: 32). This line of argumentation involves the supposition "that for the author of the narrative one did not have to be a 'prophet' in order to receive the divine imperative to 'prophesy'; and indeed that such a command did not turn one into a 'prophet'" (p. 30). Amos 7:10–17, a late addition included to explore "the nature of Amos's authority" (1986: 28), has the same tendency: "the designation 'prophet' is rejected but the activity of 'prophesying' [is] acceptable" (1984: 68). Thus, neither 7:10–17 nor 3:3–8 provides "evidence for Amos's own attitude to the business of prophecy" (1986: 35).

In another study Auld examines the use of the phrase "the Word of God" in order to call into question "the widespread confidence that in the classical Hebrew prophets we meet the quintessential bearers of the divine word" (1988: 245). He points out that the phrase rarely occurs in books associated with the eighth-century prophets. In Hosea, for example, the only two occurrences (1:1; 4:1) are in secondary editorial insertions (1988: 246). This phrase and others (like "says the Lord" in passages which on other grounds can be considered secondary) may be "used to claim authority for a later insertion to the message of the eighth-century figure," and it is doubtful that prophets like Isaiah, Hosea, or Jeremiah "ever actually said 'Hear the Word of the Lord' or 'The Word of the Lord came to me'" (1988: 246–47).

⟦6⟧ A second argument in support of the "poets, not prophets" theory follows from the observation that there is no unanimity in the Hebrew Bible on "what a prophet is or should be" or on the evaluation of prophets. Carroll points out that "the Bible offers no definition of what a prophet is (1 Sam 9:9 is a most curious statement!) nor does the biblical word *nabiʾ* ⟦'prophet'⟧ have any definite meaning in Hebrew that we can discern." It is impossible to derive from the biblical texts a clear understanding of the relationship between prophets and diviners or the cult, and attempts to delineate "the various roles specified by different terms in the Hebrew Bible" must negotiate the twin hazards of scanty data in the texts and inexact matches between ancient roles and modern activities. Furthermore, the Hebrew Bible displays "a strange tension between good reports about prophets and trenchant dismissals of them as deceivers and idolaters." All of this should make the modern interpreter beware of assuming that he or she knows what biblical prophecy was (Carroll 1989b: 209–15).

There is an obvious link here with the argument based on terminology. By stressing the distinction between the act of "prophesying" and the social role "prophet," Auld was able to argue both that Amos was not a prophet and that the book reveals nothing about Amos's attitude toward prophecy (Auld 1986: 25–35; cf. 1988: 246–50).

Carroll has suggested a third argument, namely that our association of texts with specific prophets is merely a matter of convention and cannot be substantiated with hard evidence. The poetic sections of the prophetic books, he reminds us, tend to be anonymous; they are associated with named individuals on the basis of the editorial frameworks, which serve to incorporate them into larger collections. The introductory colophons are very important in this respect, since in most cases they are the only place in a book where the prophet is named. The contents of the colophons cannot be substantiated historically, however, and "we may equally regard them as part extrapolation [from tradition] and part invention" (Carroll 1988: 28; 1989a: 26). The persons who wrote these colophons thus "helped to *invent* the ancient prophets as biographical figures" (Carroll 1988: 25).

[[7]] Finally, it is relatively clear to students of the Hebrew Bible that many of its books are the result of a long and complicated process of editorial activity. The fourth argument for the "poets, not prophets" position focuses on two aspects of this editorial process.

The first of these is that the texts of the prophetic books are products of literary activity. According to Carroll, we must think of the biblical books as conventional literary texts fabricated by their authors for particular purposes. Furthermore, "prophecy was an oral phenomenon," and the writing down of prophecy severed the originally oral text from the speaker's situation and transformed it into a "timeless reference . . . addressed to future generations." Thus, unless there is "considerable justification," to infer a social background from the text amounts to "an illegitimate transfer of meaning from story to social background" (Carroll 1989b: 206–207).

The implications of this view may be seen in Carroll's interpretation of the book of Jeremiah. Since we are basically ignorant about the formation of that book, scholars have resorted to "axiomatic assertions," for example, that the poetry contained in it had to be spoken by someone, and in view of 1:1–3 this someone must have been Jeremiah. But such assertions are "very unhelpful." In fact, it is reasonable "to accept, for the sake of argument," the view "that the book purports to be the work of a fictional character called Jeremiah and then to proceed from that point

to treat the work *as if* such a figure behaved and spoke in the ways attributed to him in the book." This is the way we understand Homer's Odysseus, Shakespeare's Macbeth, Swift's Gulliver, and Joyce's Bloom,

> and there is no good reason to treat biblical characters in a different
> fashion. What we would not do is to insist on a one-to-one correspon-
> dence between the fictional characters and any historical counterparts
> we might imagine of them. . . . A similar approach must be advocated
> for reading Jeremiah. We should treat the character of Jeremiah as a
> work of fiction and recognize the impossibility of moving from the book
> to the real "historical" Jeremiah, given our complete lack of knowledge
> independent of the book itself (1989a: 12).

At issue is not whether in their present form the prophetic books are
products of a period of editorial activity, but how this ⟦8⟧ activity is to
be conceived. In his recent commentary on Jeremiah, William McKane
proposed the idea of a "rolling corpus" to explain the process of growth.
According to this theory, poetry generally preceded prose, and expansions of the text were not systematic but were ad hoc and exegetical in
intent. Auld and Carroll both embrace this idea, which allows them to
focus on the motivations of the redactors of the books and play down
the possibility that portions of the text may reflect an original (or at least
earlier) message and social situation (Auld 1983a: 3–5 ⟦in this volume,
pp. 289–91⟧). Furthermore, Carroll draws more far-reaching conclusions than does McKane, who like many others assumes that the poetry
of Jeremiah 2–20 contains genuine words of the prophet. Though Carroll says this hypothesis is worth entertaining, he insists that "there is no
hard evidence to support it." The identity of Jeremiah actually derives
from the editorial framework of the book (1:1–3) and not from the poetry (Carroll 1989a: 37).

To speak of the motivations of redactors suggests a need to view the
texts in terms of their ideological content. This is the second aspect of
the argument from editorial activity. Carroll points out that within the
book of Jeremiah one finds "quite contrary, even contradictory" views on
matters ranging from the social situation (society is totally corrupt / it is
composed of both righteous and wicked persons) to the possibility of repentance (the people are incorrigible / repentance is possible) to the
prophet himself (in the laments he is a "depressed and depressing"
figure / in the narratives he "commands" and "confronts"; 1986: 292–95).
Such diverse views must have their origin in attitudes of the redactors.

Carroll's view of the laments indicates his inclination to look for *later*
ideological developments. These poems, often interpreted as "auto-
biographical utterances of the prophet Jeremiah," are neither collected

into a single place nor "given any editorial connections with Jeremiah's speaking," though the placement of 11:21–23 and 18:18 "suggests some connection between the laments and the life of Jeremiah." Carroll suggests that "the most natural way to read" those poems is as a stage in the development of the traditions in which the innocent who suffered at the nation's fall seek vindication—contradicting ⟦9⟧ Jeremiah's blaming of the *whole* nation for the disaster (e.g., 5:1–5; 6:13, etc.; 1989a: 46–47).

In view of the Bible's differing attitudes toward prophecy, it is less problematic to refer to the canonical figures like Amos, Isaiah, and Jeremiah as "poets" rather than "prophets." The fact that later compilers of the "anthologies" shared at least some of these poets' ideology may account for the development in the direction of correlating poet and prophet (Carroll 1983; Auld 1988: 246–50).

Prophets after All

Commenting on the organization of his study of the book of Amos, Auld says, "I have started near the end, with reports of Amos's visions and the discussion of his status, rather than at the beginning because I find that much reading of the Bible's prophetic literature is prejudiced since readers *know* in advance what a prophet or visionary *really* is—but are wrong" (1986: 10). A prominent feature of my attempt to rebut the Auld-Carroll position on prophets and prophecy will be this: historically and sociologically, religious intermediation is a very widely distributed phenomenon, and it conforms rather strictly to a particular pattern. On the basis of such comparative evidence we can indeed know in advance what "prophets" are, and we will be *right*. Let me take up their lines of argumentation one by one.

The "History of Terminology"

Amos 7, where "the designation 'prophet' is rejected but the activity of 'prophesying' acceptable" (Auld 1984: 68), is a good place to begin a consideration of the linguistic evidence. Auld's only explanation for this locution is that here (and in Amos 3:8) we have a parallel with the books of Jeremiah and Ezekiel, in which the verb develops more rapidly than the noun "in connection with the hero of a 'prophetic' book" (1984: 73). The narrative of Amos 7:10–17, however, demonstrates clearly the weakness of concentrating on terminology. Though Amos denies he is a prophet, Amaziah recognizes his public activity as "prophesying" (7:12–13) and Amos uses the same term to describe his commission from Yahweh (7:15). ⟦10⟧ Würthwein (1950) has argued that Amos's refusal to accept the title "prophet" was motivated by his desire to distinguish himself from official prophets whose primary task was intercession. This is a reasonable explanation. In any case, the important point is that regardless of what he and they were called, it is evident that both Amos and the "prophets" to whom he refers were performing a recognizable social role.

Who, according to Auld, was Amos? It appears

> that he did not regard himself as a "prophet," that he did not claim status as a "religious" functionary, that he did not require a position in popular or official religion to say what he had to say. . . . He appears rather to have held that *anyone* who had heard Yahweh speak should himself "prophesy" [cf. Amos 3:3–6, 8]: that means, speak out with the freedom prophets use. He appears to have been an agriculturalist. Yet our main evidence for him is as a communicator: and he certainly was extraordinarily skilful in his use of words (1986: 73).

But this leaves unanswered the question of what role Amos was playing in society when he uttered his wonderfully poetic words. The definition of prophecy implied here—a prophet is someone to whom Yahweh has spoken and who freely communicates the contents of this revelation to an audience—describes precisely what, according to the narrative, Amos claimed he was doing. Therefore, Amos was a prophet!

Similarly, Auld notes about Ezekiel that he is never "directly" given the title "prophet," though twice he is indirectly called that (2:5; 33:33). Still, about thirty times his "words are introduced . . . by a reported command to 'prophesy.' Perhaps during the period when attitudes were changing the verb was more acceptable than the noun 'prophet' as a designation of acceptable 'prophetic' activity" (1983a: 5 [291]). It is not clear why the noun should be unacceptable. In any case the use of the verb implies some observable behavior. It follows that the prophetic role is being performed and *recognized*. This presupposes that both the performers and the audience had a certain view of what was transpiring.[1]

The same thing is true of Auld's discussion of how the terms develop within Jeremiah. There the verb form occurs more often in the "shorter prose tradition" than it had in the poetry, and in these prose passages it can refer to "the activity of individuals [11] who are not otherwise 'prophet' *in the immediate context of the passages concerned*: eight times of Jeremiah himself—11:21; 19:14; 20:1; 26:9, 11, 12; 29:27; 32:3; twice positively of others—26:18 (Micah of Moresheth) and 26:20 (Uriah); and five times negatively of others—20:6; 28:6; 29:21, 26, 31" (1984: 71; emphasis added). The intent, of course, is to bolster the point that these individuals were not yet designated as "prophets." But again, what sense does it

---

1. This applies also to Auld's denial that Elijah was a prophet (1984: 80).

make to say audiences recognized that people were "prophesying" but did not understand them to be "prophets"? The reference to the "immediate (literary) context" is a smokescreen which obscures the fact that there must certainly have been a *social* context in which the use of the verb made sense. Notice the content of the eight references to Jeremiah: most involve other persons identifying his activity as "prophesying"; two have the narrator making the reference (19:14; 20:1), and in one Jeremiah is made to describe his own activity in this way (26:12).

There is a similar problem in his treatment of Jeremiah 28. The longer prose (= MT) uses the title "prophet" for both Jeremiah and Hananiah. On the other hand, the shorter prose (= LXX) never gives Jeremiah the title, and gives it only once (in the form *pseudoprophētēs*, 'false prophet' [v. 1]) to Hananiah. Though admitting "proof is impossible" (1984: 72), Auld infers that the short prose does not consider Hananiah a prophet. As evidence he cites the fact that elsewhere the short prose uses "prophet" only of groups mentioned in conjunction with other groups (6:13; 26:7, 8, 11; 27:9; 29:1, 8). But what sociological sense does it make to assert that persons operating in groups can be recognized to be prophets, while those operating (as far as we know) independently would not be called by the same name? The use of the verb for both implies that at the very least the individuals were recognized as performing the same social role.

As to the Jeremiah poetry, if it mostly criticizes prophets and does not refer to Jeremiah himself as a prophet, this seems only what one would expect. The poetry is preoccupied with a critique of Judean society; there is little opportunity for self-reference.

[[12]] The major assumption in my rebuttal of Auld's argument from the "history of terminology" is that the kind of religious intermediation we designate "prophet" was a social reality in ancient Israel and Judah, presumably from very early times. Furthermore, I believe it was a social role which the population as a whole understood very well. To think that prophecy developed late in the Old Testament period, or that the canonical figures were only then identified as prophets, is incorrect.

My assumption is based upon evidence that prophetic intermediation is a widely distributed and precisely describable social phenomenon and the conviction that cross-cultural research on prophecy can contribute to our understanding of the Hebrew prophets.[2] Data from a number of cultures and historical periods show that prophetic intermediation is

2. I have discussed this at length in my book, *Channels of Prophecy* (1989). Because of vast differences in time, circumstances, and geographic location, cross-cultural comparisons of prophecy require the use of a model which focuses on the social dynamics of the prophetic act itself, on how the prophetic process works. The model I have developed for this purpose contains two essential features: a set of three actors (a deity, an intermediary, and an

characterized by a regular and recognizable set of social behaviors, which are in turn made possible (and rendered plausible) by the societies' own assumptions about the relationship of the gods to the everyday world of human experience.[3]

Old Testament prophecy conforms to this pattern. It is not a unique phenomenon invented, so to speak, by the Israelites, let alone by a group of exiles late in their history. This is not merely a negative comment, since seeing the Israelite prophets within the broader context of the history of religions has the advantage of confirming and providing a clearer description of their role in Israelite society.

The pattern of behavior defined by my model of the prophetic process constitutes a kind of "program" which allows members of a society to recognize and respond to persons who seem to have taken up a certain socio-religious role (Overholt 1989: 149–62). Both the ancient Israelites and Judeans (because they lived in a society hospitable to this kind of intermediation and with a tradition of such activity) and we (because on the basis of research we can recognize the presence of the pattern) do, contrary to Carroll, "have knowledge independent of" the biblical accounts themselves.

The point is, conclusions about prophets in ancient Israel based on an examination of the use of words like "prophet" and "prophesy" err in failing to take into account a social reality clearly perceivable in (or behind) the texts. [[13]]

Consensus and Definition

The second line of argumentation had to do with the supposed lack of unanimity within the Hebrew Bible on "what a prophet is or should be." The "ancient Israelite writers," says Carroll, "had no clear image" about the prophets and often dismissed them as undesirable (1989b: 209). The statement seems hyperbolic. I have already referred to a cross-cultural account of prophecy which identifies a process of intermediation that can be precisely described (Overholt 1989). The model employed in that study, it should be noted, accommodates the variety of terms used to gloss the role of this particular kind of religious intermediation, as well as conflicts between intermediaries themselves and between intermediaries and segments of their audiences. Such conflicts are a normal part of the process (cf. Long 1981). They may be discon-

---

audience) and a pattern of interrelationships among them involving revelation, the proclamation of a message, and feedback (cf. pp. 17–25).

3. Cf. Overholt (1989: 157–59) and the discussion of "social prerequisites of intermediation" in R. Wilson (1980: 28–32).

certing to audiences faced with the need to evaluate what a particular prophet is saying, but they should not be to us.

Etymologically, it may be true that "the biblical word *nābî*" has no "definite meaning in Hebrew." On the other hand, in ancient Israel and Judah it evidently glossed a rather well-recognized social role, a religious intermediary of a specific type. If the description of this type in terms of a cross-cultural model seems somewhat ideal, it has social reality nonetheless, incorporating functionaries ranging along a continuum from prophet to diviner.

According to Auld, the notion of prophecy, "the idea of God speaking to or through mediators," came to be attached to approved figures like Amos and Jeremiah only during a late "re-formation of the prophetic traditions" (1988: 248). In his own time Amos "was a critic of the community of classic proportions . . . [but] he was not a prophet till the descendants of his community made him one, nor did he purvey the word of God till his successors discerned that quality in his words. . . . Poetic critics like Amos were deemed bearers of the divine word even before they were redefined as 'prophets'" (1988: 246–47). Amos himself was not a prophet. He and others like him, Auld says,

> come across not as men of the word but as craftsmen with words. The developed view of the prophet may be of the divine messenger or ambassador. . . . If that poetic succession from [[14]] Amos to Jeremiah was later re-presented as a series of "servants" duly acknowledged by God then this is in part a judgment that they had in fact been good advocates. It tells us how their authority for a later scriptural age was understood; but leaves unstated how they functioned in their own age. My submission is that when later generations called Amos and Isaiah "prophets," and received their words as "Word of God," they gave them an honor they had richly deserved but did not claim (1988: 250).

There is some truth in this formulation, since ultimately prophets must be recognized (authorized) by the communities in which they function; one cannot perform a social role like "prophet" unless at least some members of the society validate that performance. It is no doubt also the case that appreciation of the biblical prophets increased as time passed and some of what they said was confirmed by events. But there are problems. First, even if it could be established that Amos and the others did not claim to be prophets, we would not be entitled to conclude that *no one* understood them to be performing the role of prophets. Explicit claims are not the only, or the most important, feature of prophetic behavior.[4] Second, Auld does not seem to reckon with the possibility that

4. Cf. the account of the Melanesian prophet, Yali, in Overholt 1986: 295–308.

there existed in Israel from earliest times the assumptions that Yahweh and humans could be in contact and that persons performing certain recognized roles (generally glossed "prophets" and "diviners") were the chief channels of this intercourse.

In the same context, Auld suggests the prophets "sought to convince by argument rather than compel by authority. Amos makes his appeal to Israel not in terms of divine revelation old or new but by an invidious point to point comparison of her behaviour with that of her neighbours who she knew broke all natural norms" (1988: 250). This poet cannot be a prophet; he is too rational. But it is not clear why revelation and rational "point to point comparison" should necessarily be incompatible. Intermediaries need not be considered mere megaphones through whom an emotional deity speaks.

Identity and Invention

The third line of argumentation for the "poets, not prophets" position entailed the claim that the identity of the figures after ⟦15⟧ whom the prophetic books are named derives from the editorial material in those books and is as likely as not a late fiction. Carroll argues that the book of Jeremiah is "a highly polemical text" made up of "many different polemical pieces," coming from a variety of times and situations. It cannot, therefore, go back to a single author. Even the assumption that Jeremiah is at least responsible for the poetry depends for support upon taking secondary editorial material (e.g., 1:1–3) at face value. But "good scholarship," he says, requires that "nothing must be assumed without some evidence for it" (1986: 298–99).

The question is whether Carroll sets up a straw opponent and assaults it with too big a weapon. Who would claim that the whole book of Jeremiah goes back to a single person? Why is it necessary, in order to refute such a position, to completely dispose of the prophet Jeremiah as a human being about whom something can be known? One might just as well pose a different question about the book: Doesn't the fact that there is a major block of material bearing the name "Jeremiah" make it plausible to assume that somewhere behind, and in, that tradition is a real historical person? Carroll admonishes us that "nothing must be assumed without some evidence for it," but what passes for evidence? I am proposing that if the texts speak of behavior which confirms to a widely distributed pattern of intermediation, we should accept this as evidence that they attest in some way to actual social and historical phenomena.[5]

---

5. It is difficult for any of us to be entirely consistent in our use of biblical evidence. So it is that in a study of the introductory colophons of the Old Testament prophetic books Carroll comments, "no named prophet in the prophetic traditions and no figure in the colophons is said to have come from Jerusalem! It would appear to be the case that

Carroll claims about the colophons of the prophetic books that without them we would neither "read what follows as the utterances of specific persons," nor would we "be tempted to read what follows as the output of prophets in the first place!" (since the collections condemn prophets and "no prophet is praised" in them [1988: 33]). On the contrary, I think it quite likely we would. Thematic and stylistic coherence in prophetic books or sections thereof suggests the influence of some specific person, whether or not he or she could be identified. And if some of these texts tend to attack prophets, this should be no surprise. Prophecy is at home in times of crisis, and at such times differences of opinion are bound to arise. Polemics against prophets are easily understood as directed against *other* prophets. A response made by H. G. M. Williamson to one ⟦16⟧ of Auld's papers is pertinent here: the pre-exilic prophets do not reject their opponents "because they are *nebiʾim*, but because they are bad ones" (1983: 34).

The Literary Character of Prophetic Texts

Finally, there is the matter of the literary character of the Old Testament prophetic texts. For Carroll, the writing down of materials originally transmitted orally seems to imply a "transformation" of content: "The import of the words" has been changed, enabling them "to change beyond their immediate context and to apply to circumstances far removed from their original setting" (1989b: 208). The argument seems to be: literary texts yield reliable data only about the situation and ideological purpose of their authors; since the authors of prophetic texts are not the prophets themselves, we cannot look to these texts for reliable data about the prophets.

Again, the position seems extreme. I am perfectly in agreement with the notions that a series of editors have in all likelihood shaped our present prophetic books to fit their own understandings and the needs of their time and that what these texts "mean" does not so much reside in the books, like a precious pearl in its shell, as arise out of the process of persons ancient and modern hearing and reading them. The question is whether this on-going process of interpretation forecloses the possibility of deriving from the words themselves hints about the social situations that were the occasions for their utterance. In my opinion, it does not.

The larger issue is the extent to which a literary text (in this case a prophetic book) asserts some influence over readers' interpretations of

---

no Jerusalemite prophet was accepted in the canon of the prophets—whether for ideological, cultural or political reasons must be left to scholarly speculation" (1988: 30). It seems to me that, contrary to his own position, this statement depends upon the assumption that the books and their colophons do indeed retain *some* historical information.

it and yields useful information about the prophet and his time. This is a complex issue, much debated among recent literary theorists.

The crux of the problem lies in the peculiar relationship that exists between texts and readers. That the text of Jeremiah can be physically present on the desk in front of me like a coffee mug or a computer is obvious. But I am related differently to the Jeremiah text than to these other objects. In the words of Georges Poulet, the text offers itself to me to be read, and when I read it, its images and ideas come to reside in the "interior world" of my "consciousness" (Poulet 1972: 42–43). [[17]] The result is a "convergence of text and readers," in which the author's text stimulates a response in the reader and gives rise to a dynamic, dialectical process which "brings the literary work into existence" (Iser 1974: 50). To be sure, subsequent readings by the same or different readers may yield differing "realizations" of the text, but since "the written text imposes certain limits on its unwritten implications," the process is not entirely arbitrary (Iser 1974: 51, 57).

This view, which acknowledges the role of the reader in creating the meaning of the text while seemingly preserving the text's independent status, has been challenged by Stanley Fish. For Fish it is not the author's "intention" that determines a text's meaning. Rather, readers see in a text what the "interpretive strategies" of the community to which they belong allow them to see (1976: 176). But it seems likely that Fish has given away too much. We ought to concede to him (and others) that the text (the collection of words that confronts us on the printed page or in some other medium) is not a self-sufficient entity which contains a single, true meaning that has only to be uncovered. The proposition that meaning arises out of the dynamic, dialectical process set in motion by the "convergence of text and reader" (Iser) seems altogether reasonable. However, if the text is an occasion for the reader's experience, it also sets boundaries for that experience. Interpretations of it can be more or less warranted by the language it contains. Thus, if the aim is to interpret a text, it will be useful to be attentive to its language, for example, to the range of possible meanings of the words its author has selected.[6]

On the other hand, if the text creates a boundary or horizon that marks off the proper realm for its interpretation, it is important that this

6. Jonathan Swift's essay, "A Modest Proposal," has been understood by readers with a literalistic interpretive strategy to be a serious espousal of cannibalism, and it is possible to imagine a reader who becomes sexually aroused as a result of reading the U.S. Constitution. But most readers would agree that the warrant for such interpretations resides less in the language of the text itself than, say, in specific readers' own needs or the interpretive strategy of their community of like-minded readers.

horizon not be considered too close at hand. It must be wide enough to encompass more than a single reading of the text. The ideal, it would seem, is to avoid the two extremes on the reader-text continuum: the view that texts contain *a* meaning which one simply has to uncover, and the view that texts place virtually no limit on the meanings generated while reading them. Fish (who claims to have "made the text disappear" [1976: 183]) seems close to the latter pole.[7]

Robert Scholes agrees with Fish that interpretation enters the reading process at an early point, but insists that texts do [[18]] guide us in their interpretation. His argument has two main prongs, a rather minimalist statement of which would be that there is "some reality in the texts and some freedom in the interpreter" (1985: 159). A text is always "encoded in a particular language" and can exist "as a text only in and through its language" (1985: 152). Interpretation, therefore, assumes "familiarity with [its] linguistic code."

Codes (such as language, or the rules of chess) set boundaries for behavior, but allow freedom within those boundaries. Scholes (1985: 161–62) uses the example of Pat Kelly, a Baltimore Orioles outfielder who attributes his home runs to divine intervention, to illustrate "the major problem in Fish's theory: his refusal to see any difference between the primary system in which a text is encoded and secondary systems that can only be brought to bear by an interpreter who comprehends the primary system." Both Kelly and the sports writer share a primary system, the rules of baseball by which home runs are perceived as home runs. It is not that for Kelly the Christian view has replaced the baseball view; rather, "he grafts another interpretation onto the baseball interpretation." The dispute between the two is over the proper hierarchy and the relevance of several codes. Thus, says Scholes, "Where Fish sees interpretive communities remotely controlling acts of interpretation by individuals suffering from the illusion of freedom, I see individuals with many codes, some more and some less relevant, trying to see which ones will serve best in dealing with structures that have their own necessities."[8]

But we must not forget that our readings of a text are never neutral or innocent. Terry Eagleton's claim that every reading of a work is also

7. Cf. the critique of Scholes (1985: 147–52), and also Moore (1986). B. Long offers a reader-response interpretation of 2 Kgs 4:8–37 which demonstrates a healthy balance: there are "contrary tendencies" in the narrative, but both "rest on one's response to items in the work" (1988: 174).

8. See Eagleton's brief meditation on the word "nightingale," the point of which is that "language is not in fact something we are free to do what we like with." Despite the fact that we can easily imagine inventing any number of contexts that would permit us to make its

in some sense a re-writing of it does not refer simply to the fact that our subjective value-judgments somehow subvert the factual knowledge conveyed by the text. While it is possible for "factual knowledge . . . [to] be distorted by particular interests and judgements," the more basic point is that "interests are *constitutive* of our knowledge, not merely prejudices which imperil it." We come to a literary text, as to everything else in life, bearing a "largely concealed structure of values," beliefs, and interests which as members of a society we are "born into." Our interpretations and value judgments [[19]] are not whimsical, but are informed by an "ideology" (1983: 12–16).

I have no interest in claiming that my reading supplies the only—or even the best—interpretation of the biblical texts concerning prophecy. It is one of a number of useful ways of interpreting them. What prompts me to argue so vigorously against the "poets, not prophets" hypothesis is an interest in understanding a particular kind of human social behavior to which we may give the rather general label "prophecy." I have encountered the basic structures of this type of behavior in texts produced by or about such a wide variety of societies—including those of ancient Israel and Judah—that the attempt to eliminate it from certain biblical texts seems to me to be a misinterpretation. The biblical texts seem clearly to embody a "code"—a pattern of social behavior quite analogous to Scholes's "rules of baseball"—that was both expected and recognized as "prophetic," and that persistently points the reader in the direction of social reality. This code was evidently firmly entrenched in the ideology of ancient Israel and Judah during the whole period of the texts' production and for centuries before. That these texts are considered Scripture by two major religious traditions does not privilege them, or the society in which they were produced, in the sense of placing them off limits to non-theological interpretations or comparisons with other cultures.

One can only speculate about the "ideology" which informs the "poets, not prophets" position. It seems fair to observe that Auld's view of Amos as a great communicator has the effect of playing down spiritual claims and making him appear to be more an "enlightened" social

---

words signify what we wished, we cannot make a literary text mean whatever we want it to mean. "For such texts belong to language as a whole, have intricate relations to other linguistic practices, however much they might also subvert and violate them" (1983: 86–88). It is true, of course, that one is more constrained when reading a road sign, which supplies a ready-made context that renders the language intelligible, than when reading a literary work, which generally does not. But in no case can there be "total interpretative freedom," because "the social uses of words . . . govern my search for appropriate contexts of meaning" (p. 88). For a related criticism of the post-structuralist "dogma that we [can] never know anything at all," cf. pp. 144–45.

reformer than perhaps he was. And Carroll's choice of the phrase "deconstructing the prophet" in one of his titles invites us to assume some level of commitment to a specific theoretical position.

There is another matter which relates to the literary character of the prophetic texts. Carroll, as we have seen, has argued that we ought to understand the prophet Jeremiah as a fictional character like Homer's Odysseus and Shakespeare's Macbeth, recognizing "the impossibility of moving from the book to the real 'historical' Jeremiah, given our complete lack of knowledge independent of the book itself" [[20]] (1989a: 12). This proposal to treat the book of Jeremiah as fiction raises the issue of the role of *genre* in interpretation. Does the genre of a work allow us to infer anything about the intention of its author or put any constraints upon us as readers? For example, one assumes when reading a novel or a play, no matter how historically oriented (e.g., *Macbeth*), that the author is at liberty to create the story as he or she sees fit. One is, therefore, wary of reading history out of such texts, though there may in fact be historical information in them. One further assumes that the author intended freely to create a story; that is why the genre was chosen over another (say, a history of . . .). If, on the other hand, authors choose to write histories, we assume they intend to construct accounts of the past. This does not, of course, mean that such accounts are perfectly accurate and free from bias. Still, we will be inclined to look for historical information in them, and rightly so.

The idea that attention to genre might be relevant to biblical studies is not a new one. Since the pioneering work of Hermann Gunkel at the turn of the century and of Karl Ludwig Schmidt, Martin Dibelius and Rudolf Bultmann just after World War I, form criticism has been one of the prominent methods employed in the critical study of the Bible. Central to this approach is the idea that genres "arise and become stereotyped because of recurring situations in human life" (Tucker 1971: 2). To speak of the function, or intention, of a genre is to ask—both in general and with respect to specific examples of the genre—about the particular purpose it arose to fulfill in its ancient setting (Tucker 1971: 16).

Genre has thus been used as a tool for classifying biblical texts and reconstructing the social and historical background out of which they arose, but this is not its only significance. Genre is also important in the process by which readers come to construct the meaning of particular texts. Without it, texts would hardly be "readable." In the words of Mary Gerhart, "Genres are not only principles of categorization or identification; they are also principles of production. Understood retrospectively, genres can be said to produce, as well as to identify meanings" (1988: 33–34; cf. Buss 1979: 10).

This position has been argued at length by the literary theorist, E. D.
Hirsch, Jr. Hirsch contends that interpretation must ⟦21⟧ address itself
to the "verbal meaning" of a text, which he defines as "whatever someone has willed to convey by a particular sequence of linguistic signs and
which can be conveyed (shared) by means of those linguistic signs"
(1967: 31). Verbal meanings are "changeless" in the sense that they remain "the same from one moment to the next" (1967: 46). Language, on
the other hand, is "two-sided and reciprocal," involving both the expression and the interpretation of meaning. This confronts us with a problem for which genre will offer the solution: the "paradox" that verbal
meaning is individual but interpretations are variable is resolved when
we realize that in our acquisition of language all of us master through
repeated experience "not only [its] variable and unstable norms . . . but
also the particular norms of a particular genre."[9]

Our understanding of a text is powerfully influenced by our "meaning expectations," which in turn arise from our "conception of the type of
meaning that is being expressed," that is, from our "generic conception"
of the text (1967: 76). Therefore, a "genre conception is constitutive" of
both speaking and interpreting. Verbal meaning is "genre-bound," since
both speaking and understanding "must be governed and constituted by
a sense of the whole utterance" (1967: 78).[10]

We can now see how genre provides the key to solving another problem: If meaning is (as Hirsch insists) "an affair of consciousness," then
how can an author mean more than he or she is conscious of meaning?
The answer lies in "typification": the author conceives meaning as a
whole, and within this whole unintended meanings are possible (Hirsch
1967: 48). To conceive of verbal meaning as a "willed type" allows us to
see how it "can be (as it is) a determinate object of consciousness and yet
transcend (as it does) the actual contents of consciousness" (1967: 49).

---

9. Hirsch (1967: 68–71); in his discussion he utilizes Saussure's distinction between
langue and *parole* and Wittgenstein's idea that one must know the rules of the game being
played to know the meaning of an utterance. Later in the book Hirsch says, "At the level
of verbal meaning, all types, regardless of their earliest provenance, are learned types—
that is, they are type ideas which derive from previous experience and can subsume later
experience" (p. 269).

10. See his explanation of how "generic expectations" help us understand the early
parts of a text even before we reach its end (1967: 85). In the same vein, Alastair Fowler has
argued that the recognition of genres is "fundamental to the reading process. . . . No work,
however avantgarde, is intelligible without some context of familiar types" (1982: 259).
Genre, then, "primarily has to do with communication. It is an instrument not of classification or prescription, but of meaning" (1982: 21–22; he develops the idea of "redundancy,"
taken over from communication theory).

Terry Eagleton strenuously objects to Hirsch's position on the grounds that (under the influence of Husserl's phenomenology) his conception of authorial intention is too purely mental[11] and his defense of that intended meaning too "authoritarian," its aim being "the protection of private property" (1983: 68). Because they are "the products of language, which always has something slippery about it," authorial meanings can never be stable, and no "complete distinction" [[22]] can be made between a text's meaning and its meaning to me (1983: 69–70).

To show the flaw in Hirsch's argument "that meaning is always the intentional act of an individual at some particular point in time," Eagleton develops an example (uses of the phrase, "close the door") to make the point that "the meaning of language is a social matter: there is a real sense in which language belongs to my society before it belongs to me" (1983: 70–71). To ask about someone's intentions in using the phrase is not, as Hirsch would have it, to ask about a purely private mental act. The question is rather about the "effects the language is trying to bring about." To understand a speaker's intention is to grasp his or her "speech and behaviour in relation to a significant context. When we understand the 'intentions' of a piece of language, we interpret it as being in some sense *oriented*, structured to achieve certain effects; and none of this can be grasped apart from the practical conditions in which the language operates" (1983: 114).

One might say that Hirsch is asking for this criticism, but that in the end it is too harsh. Hirsch ultimately defines "verbal meaning" as "a *willed type* which an author expressed by linguistic symbols and which can be understood by another through those symbols" (1967: 49). The clue to the intended meaning of a text (despite even an author's subsequent change of opinion about what he or she has written) lies in the particular pattern of its language. Once written, both the language and its pattern are public. They provide both the clues and the restraints for the reader's construction of the work's meaning.

In any case, I should like to utilize Hirsch's theory in a weaker form than that attacked by Eagleton. Genre gives an indication of at least part of the meaning a text had for its author, but it does not guarantee that we can reconstruct the author's intention exactly. However, it is not crucially important that we do so, since what we need is only a broad indication of the context in which interpretation should take place.

---

11. According to Eagleton, meaning as Hirsch conceives of it is "prelinguistic... something which the author *wills*: it is a ghostly, wordless mental act which is then "fixed" for all time in a particular set of material signs" (1983: 67).

Hirsch is aware, no less than Eagleton, that there will always be a variety of interpretations of a given text. He also proposes criteria for judging how satisfactory various interpretations are. But ultimately, the constraints of genre can only be part of [[23]] our judgment. To ask which of all the possibilities available for interpreting a text is likely to be the most fruitful is to raise, of course, the question, "Fruitful for what?" "Ideology" is not something we can, or should, aspire to escape.

But what is the genre of Jeremiah? If we were to consider it an *anthology*, that would assume the activity of one or more editors, who chose materials to preserve and "edited" and arranged them. But what were the materials that the earliest editor(s) collected? Presumably, they were utterances of a prophet named Jeremiah. Clearly a great deal of the material in the book comes from persons other than Jeremiah, but the genre gives us license to believe that there was such a person as Jeremiah and that the book contains at least some evidence for his life and work. The existence of the prophet is on this account a more plausible assumption than his absence.

I am proposing that at least some of the prophetic books of the Hebrew Bible belong to a genre that we may call "anthology." Works in this genre have two prominent features: there is an opening colophon which announces that the work contains the words (or vision) of a named (male) individual and dates his activity within the reign of a specific king or kings.[12] Following the colophon is a body of material consisting of separate and discrete units which are homogeneous in neither form nor (in the judgment of many researchers) date. If we view the colophons as expressions of authorial intention, it should be immediately clear that what follows is to be understood as collections of material related to the life and work of historical figures who were active at specified times. We must not, of course, be too naive about this. The colophon to the book of Jeremiah opens with the phrase, "the words of Jeremiah," but there are extensive narratives in the book that do not fit that rubric. We can safely assume that the editor of the present book of Jeremiah worked sometime after the prophet's death and had some freedom in the choice of materials to include in his or her anthology. It is even possible that the criteria by which "words of Jeremiah" were identified for inclusion differed from those modern scholars would apply.

However, the issue is not whether some parts of the book accurately report the *ipsissima verba* [['very words']] of the prophet, or whether it is

12. Isa 1:1; Jer 1:1–3; Ezek 1:1–3; Hos 1:1; Amos 1:1; Mic 1:1; Zeph 1:1; cf. Hag 1:1; Zech 1:1.

the prophet's biography—another genre altogether.[13] 〚24〛 We are concerned, rather, with the verbal meaning of an editor's work. When the
anthologist tells us in the introductory colophon that what follows pertains to the activity of a man named Jeremiah who was active during the
reign of the last five kings of Judah and whom he or she and, presumably,
others understood to have been the recipient of revelations from Yahweh, there is no good reason to reject this broad characterization out of
hand. On the contrary, there is a very good reason to accept it as a guide
to our interpretation, since this is precisely what we expect of anthologies. By contrast, the genres implied in Carroll's own notion of the book's
fictional nature are not appropriate to the text. The book as it stands (or
even as it could conceivably be reconstructed by scholarly effort) is neither an epic nor a play nor a novel.

But is the book of Jeremiah an anthology? Unlike modern anthologies, it does not cite sources or bear the name of its editor. On the other
hand, the organization, though loose, is like many modern anthologies
roughly thematic (poetry predominates in chaps. 1–25 and narratives
in 26–45; 46–51 is a collection of oracles against the nations). As Fowler
points out, genres resist definition, and because they tend to change
over time, we must guard against imposing our up-to-date conceptions
of a genre's characteristics on older materials (1982: 40, 261).

If we recognize that the prophetic books are literary products, we
also recognize that these anthologies have an ideological content. Carroll finds evidence for this in the conflicting, even incompatible, images
of the prophet within the book of Jeremiah. For example, references to
his speaking to (26:16), even commanding (19:1), the nation's leaders
suggest that Jeremiah had great authority, but this contradicts the idea
that the nation fell because these same leaders refused to listen to him.
That he was both supported and rejected by the public are incompatible ideas that "can only be sustained at a theoretical or *textual* level";
they cannot be justified "*in real life.*" The contradiction stems from the
editors' desire to do two things: show that Jeremiah was recognized as a
true prophet and account for the fall of Jerusalem (1989a: 78–79). Certainly, this is a case of black-and-white reasoning and does not correspond to what we know both intuitively and from cross-cultural 〚25〛
studies to be social reality. Prophets must have support groups, but these
need not include the entire population. Nor need the membership of
the groups remain constant. People can change their minds; their support can blow hot and cold. We need to keep *social reality* in perspective.

---

13. Cf. the discussion of biography in Overholt (1988: 601–603).

Carroll is preoccupied with later ideological developments that may be mirrored in the prophetic texts, so he claims that "the most natural way to read" the laments in the book of Jeremiah is as an exilic attempt to vindicate the innocents among the people who suffered at the nation's fall. But if that were the intent of the laments, why would they speak of murder plots and commands not to prophesy (11:21), of the speaker's associations with Yahweh's word (15:16, 19; 17:15; 20:8–9), of intercession (18:20), and of childbirth (20:14–18)? The collective reading does not seem particularly "natural" for these laments, taken as a group. At the very least, the personal reading seems equally "natural."

Clearly, there are many details of this argument from genre that remain to be worked out. What I want to argue here is that the "meaning expectations" associated with the genre anthology, taken together with what cross-cultural research demonstrates about the social reality of prophecy, enable us to affirm that the named individuals of the Hebrew Bible actually *were* prophets, both in their own eyes and in the judgment of at least some of their contemporaries. The Bible contains many things of which critical scholars can be skeptical, but this is not one of them. The radical skepticism of Auld's and Carroll's "poets, not prophets" position is unwarranted.

Bibliography

Auld, A. G.
  1983a   Prophets through the Looking Glass: Between Writings and Moses. *Journal for the Study of the Old Testament* 27: 3–23 [reprinted in this volume, pp. 289–307].
  1983b   Prophets through the Looking Glass: A Response. *Journal for the Study of the Old Testament* 27: 41–44.
  1984   Prophets and Prophecy in Jeremiah and Kings. *Zeitschrift für die Alttestamentliche Wissenschaft* 96: 66–82.
  1986   *Amos.* Old Testament Guides. Sheffield: JSOT Press.
  1988   Word of God and Word of Man: Prophets and Canon. Pp. 237–51 in *Ascribe to the Lord: Biblical and Other Studies in Memory of Peter C. Craigie*, edited by L. Eslinger and G. Taylor. Journal for the Study of the Old Testament Supplement Series 67. Sheffield: JSOT Press.
Buss, M. J.
  1979   Understanding Communication. Pp. 1–44 in *Encounter with the Text*, edited by M. J. Buss. Philadelphia: Fortress.
Carroll, R. P.
  1983   Poets Not Prophets. *Journal for the Study of the Old Testament* 27: 25–31.
  1986   Dismantling the Book of Jeremiah and Deconstructing the Prophet. Pp. 291–302 in *"Wünschet Jerusalem Frieden": Collected Communications*

to the XIIth Congress of the International Organization for the Study of the Old Testament, Jerusalem 1986, edited by M. Augustin and K.-D. Schunck. Frankfurt am Main: Peter Lang.
1988 Inventing the Prophets. *Irish Biblical Studies* 10: 24–36.
1989a *Jeremiah.* Old Testament Guides. Sheffield: JSOT Press.
1989b Prophecy and Society. Pp. 203–25 in *The World of Ancient Israel,* edited by R. E. Clements. Cambridge: Cambridge University Press.
Eagleton, T.
1983 *Literary Theory: An Introduction.* Minneapolis: University of Minnesota Press.
Fish, S. E.
1970 Literature in the Reader: Affective Stylistics. Reprinted in Tompkins 1980: 70–100.
1976 Interpreting the *Variorum.* Reprinted in Tompkins 1980: 164–84.
Fowler, A.
1982 *Kinds of Literature: An Introduction to the Theory of Genres and Modes.* Cambridge: Harvard University Press.
Gerhart, M.
1988 Genric [sic] Competence in Biblical Hermeneutics. *Semeia* 43: 29–44.
Hirsch, E. D., Jr.
1967 *Validity in Interpretation.* New Haven: Yale University Press.
Iser, W.
1974 The Reading Process: A Phenomenological Approach. Reprinted in Tompkins 1980: 50–69.
Long, B. O.
1981 Social Dimensions of Prophetic Conflict. *Semeia* 21: 31–53.
1988 A Figure at the Gate: Readers, Reading and Biblical Theologians. Pp. 166–86 in *Canon, Theology, and Old Testament Interpretation: Essays in Honor of Brevard S. Childs,* edited by G. M. Tucker, D. L. Petersen, and R. R. Wilson. Philadelphia: Fortress.
McKane, William
1986 *A Critical and Exegetical Commentary on Jeremiah.* Volume I. Edinburgh: T. & T. Clark.
Moore, Stephen D.
1986 Negative Hermeneutics, Insubstantial Texts: Stanley Fish and the Biblical Interpreter. *Journal of the American Academy of Religion* 54: 707–17.
Overholt, T. W.
1986 *Prophecy in Cross-Cultural Perspective.* Atlanta: Scholars Press.
1988 Jeremiah. *Harper's Bible Commentary,* edited by J. L. Mays. San Francisco: Harper & Row.
1989 *Channels of Prophecy: The Social Dynamics of Prophetic Activity.* Minneapolis: Fortress.
Poulet, G.
1972 Criticism and the Experience of Interiority. Reprinted in Tompkins 1980: 41–49.

Scholes, R.
1985   *Textual Power: Literary Theory and the Teaching of English.* New Haven: Yale University Press.
Tompkins, J. P.
1980   *Reader-Response Criticism: From Formalism to Post-Structuralism.* Baltimore: Johns Hopkins University Press.
Tucker, G. M.
1971   *Form Criticism of the Old Testament.* Philadelphia: Fortress.
Williamson, H. G. M.
1983   A Response to A. G. Auld. *Journal for the Study of the Old Testament* 27: 33–39.
Wilson, R. R.
1980   *Prophecy and Society in Ancient Israel.* Philadelphia: Fortress.
Würthwein, E.
1950   Amos-Studien. *Zeitschrift für die Alttestamentliche Wissenschaft* 62: 10–52.

Ancient Israelite Prophecy and Dissonance Theory

R. P. CARROLL

[[135]] Among the dialectical structures of ancient Israelite prophecy the tension between the critique of society (threat oracles) and predictions of future wellbeing (salvation oracles) is the most striking. The trenchant criticism of society's corrupt, oppressive practices has become a hallmark of prophecy as has its equally characteristic prophesying of a golden future when Israel would live securely under a Davidic king and Jerusalem would be the focus of religious attention for the nations. In dialectical terms the elements of judgment and promise represent prophecy's No and Yes to Israelite society. Now it is generally acknowledged that the social criticism of the prophets was a percipient description of Israel's socio-political state and their predictions of doom accurately anticipated the future. But the salvation oracles, their positive hopes for the future, were a complete failure to foresee the longterm prospects with any degree of accuracy. The conventional idiom of these oracular hopes (e.g., Amos 9:11–15; Isa 2:2–4; 9:2–7; 11:1–9; Jer 31:31–34) suggests that the prophets had given little thought to the shape of the future other than to believe that there would be a future. By its very nature predicting the future is precarious yet this was considered to be the business of the prophet (cf. Deut 18:22). This failure of prophecy raises questions about the nature of prophecy and the prophet's apperception of his own work in relation to the world at large. In particular this paper is devoted to a consideration of the problem of whether the prophet was aware of his failure and endeavoured to bridge the gap between expectation and

Reprinted with permission from *Numen* 24 (1977) 135–51.

reality or simply had a different view of reality which permitted him to avoid confrontations with possible failure.

Before examining the material available for such an approach it is necessary to consider briefly some views of prophecy which would [[136]] reduce the above problem to a pseudo-problem. Thus any view of the prophetic books which maintained that only oracles of judgment were authentic in the eighth century prophets would dismiss the presence of salvation oracles in Amos, Isaiah of Jerusalem and Micah as secondary interpolations.[1] This would effectively rule out the notion of failure in these prophets and only leave the subsequent prophets open to such a criticism. The cultic approach to prophecy which sees the prophet as a cult functionary proclaiming salvation and judgment as part of his ministry of the covenant cult would make salvation and judgment purely formal elements of a sacred liturgy.[2] The cultic view of reality may be seen in the royal psalms where the often beleaguered Israelite king is regarded as the scourge of the nations (Pss 2:7–9; 45:2–5; cf. 72:8–11). Problems too difficult to solve elsewhere found resolution in a cultic context (cf. Psalm 73; Habakkuk 3). This cultic interpretation of prophetic statements can be linked to a formal linguistic approach to their utterances whereby the fulfilment of any prediction is a matter of language usage.[3] Thus a spiritual understanding of what a prophet predicted might constitute its fulfilment. Any of these three approaches would seriously modify the claim that predictions of salvation in the prophets were open to the charge of having failed to be fulfilled. However, apart from the proponents of these views, most scholars tend to reject the cultic interpretation of prophecy and many regard the salvation promises of Isa 9:2–7; 11:1–9 as not improbably from Isaiah himself.[4] There can be little doubt that Second Isaiah was a prophet of salvation who fully expected the return from exile to be a triumphalist affair. As such he is a classical example of a prophet seriously compromised by the event as it later materialised. But this view of the prophet as a foreteller of the future is in keeping with the biblical presentation of the prophet. The deuteronomistic history, Joshua–2 Kings, presents much of its history as the unfolding of the prophetic word, the deuteronomic [[137]] legislation for the

---

1. Cf. G. Fohrer, *History of Israelite Religion* (London, 1973), 223–91, esp. p. 272.

2. Cf. E. Würthwein, "Der Ursprung der prophetischen Gerichtsrede," *ZTK* 49 (1952), 1–16; H. G. Reventlow, *Das Amt des Propheten bei Amos* (Göttingen, 1962).

3. Cf. Wittgenstein's remark "It is in language that all expectation and its fulfilment make contact." *Philosophical Investigations* (Oxford, 1972), I. §445; see also §§437–45.

4. See O. Kaiser, *Isaiah 1–12* (London, 1972), 123–30; also G. von Rad, *Old Testament Theology* (Edinburgh, 1965), 169ff.

prophet concerns itself with the fulfilment of predictions (Deut 18:22), and the clash between the prophets Jeremiah and Hananiah (Jeremiah 28) is one of conflicting predictions about the future. Thus it is reasonable to pursue this line of enquiry in terms of predictive prophecy and its failures.

Where prophecy failed there must have been a gap between expectations encouraged by the prophets and the reality in which they lived without any evidence of fulfilment. This gap between belief and reality may have affected the prophet and his followers in varying ways, ranging from the ability to ignore it altogether to such loss of confidence as to silence the prophet. The real problem in dealing with this issue in Old Testament prophecy is the paucity of data about the prophet's self-awareness of such crises. In order to maximise the exploration of this subject I wish to have recourse to dissonance theory. The theory of cognitive dissonance was put forward by Leon Festinger in 1957.[5] It is essentially a psychological description of how people react to problems arising out of clashes between belief and behaviour. In simple behavioural terms dissonance is said to exist where there is a conflict between an attitude, e.g., the belief that certain indulgences are bad for one's health, and a practice, e.g., the persistent performing of such indulgences. Attempts to modify or resolve the dissonance may include refusing to think about the issue, or a denial of the existence of a conflict, or avoiding the company of people who insist on pointing out the discrepancy between belief and behaviour, or even the maintenance of the view that in spite of the harmful effects of such practices the overall gains outweigh any possible damage done to health. The intensity of dissonance resolution will depend entirely upon the degree of conflict existing in a situation and the pressures put on a person to establish an equilibrium between attitude and behaviour. In this way dissonance reduction can be seen as "the psychological analogue of the physiological mechanisms which maintain homoeostasis in the body."[6] Perhaps the most important aspect of eliminating dissonance is the role of social support, i.e., the social [[138]] group provides the individual with a context of cognitive factors with which he can identify and which can protect him from dissonance producing opinions.[7]

The theory of cognitive dissonance has had an immense impact in the field of social psychology, particularly in relation to post-decision

5. *A Theory of Cognitive Dissonance* (Evanston, 1957); Festinger was then professor of psychology at Stanford University.
6. M. L. J. Abercrombie, "Small Groups," *New Horizons in Psychology*, ed. B. M. Foss (London, 1966), 386.
7. On social support see Festinger, *op. cit.*, 177–259.

studies.[8] But it is Festinger's work on groups with specific predictive expectations which is most relevant for biblical studies. In his book *When
Prophecy Fails* Festinger and his colleagues studied a group who had received a message from outer space informing them of an imminent flood
about to destroy their part of the world.[9] When the flood failed to materialise on the expected date, instead of the group disintegrating as might
be expected, the Seekers, as they were called, went public and even began
to seek converts for their beliefs.[10] This reaction illustrates one of the
conclusions generated by dissonance theory: "when people are committed to a belief and a course of action, clear disconfirming evidence may
simply result in deepened conviction and increased proselyting."[11] However further research has suggested that this principle requires some
modification so as to take into account whether the group's environment
is hostile or friendly. Thus where there is minimal social support and the
group is ridiculed there will be a drive towards proselytising but where
there is more social support and the group is not ridiculed by outsiders
there may be little need to convert others.[12] As the function of conversion
in dissonance theory is to reduce dissonance by persuading more and
more people that the system of belief is correct and thus increase the social support within the group so there is less need for such tactics when
the public at large is not overtly hostile.

⟦139⟧ The opening chapter of *When Prophecy Fails* discusses unfulfilled prophecies and disappointed messiahs and has an obvious bearing on this study of prophecy.[13] But its main importance is the paradigm
of conditions set out for testing Festinger's thesis about increased fer-
vour following disconfirmation of a belief. For this will permit the biblical scholar to check his data to see if this approach can be used in their
analysis. Although it is specifically designed to test a particular form of
activity response to dissonance it can be used to delineate general reactions to the failure of expectations. The paradigm may be set out briefly
as follows:

8. See relevant articles in *Journal of Abnormal and Social Psychology* vols. 52–60
(1956–60); also any competent introduction to psychology, e.g., M. Manis, *An Introduction to Cognitive Psychology* (California, 1971), 239–53; E. E. Sampson, *Social Psychology and
Contemporary Society* (New York, 1971), 108–14.

9. L. Festinger, H. W. Riecken, and S. Schachter, *When Prophecy Fails* (Minneapolis,
1956; paperback edition New York, 1964).

10. *Ibid.*, 139–92.

11. *Ibid.*, 12, 28.

12. J. A. Hardyck and M. Braden, "Prophecy Fails Again: A Report of a Failure to Rep-
licate," *Journal of Abnormal and Social Psychology* 65 (1962), 136–41.

13. *When Prophecy Fails*, 3–32.

1. There must be conviction.
2. There must be commitment to this conviction.
3. The conviction must be amenable to unequivocal disconfirmation.
4. Such unequivocal disconfirmation must occur.
5. Social support must be available subsequent to the disconfirmation.[14]

Conditions 1 and 2 make the belief resistant to change, 3 and 4 suggest factors that would entail the discarding of the belief, and 5 allows a situation whereby the belief may be maintained or even used to persuade others of its truth. In the subsequent discussion Festinger looks at various millennial or messianic movements such as the second coming of Christ, the Sabbatai Zevi movement in the 17th century, and the Millerites in the 19th century. The main difficulty for his thesis is finding sufficient data to confirm or refute it. The ambiguity of the evidence also militates against a cogent exposition of the theory when applied to complex traditions such as the second coming of Christ.[15]

In applying dissonance theory to the prophetic traditions of the Old Testament it is necessary to restate the theory in such a way that it can be usefully applied to material outside the normal range of social psychology. The general theory of cognitive dissonance describes at least three responses to dissonance which can be readily adapted for biblical research purposes. These consist of avoidance of [[140]] sources likely to increase dissonance, i.e., a tendency to associate with those who hold the same opinion, or the production of rationalisations and explanations which show how the dissonance can be reduced by new evidence, or by gaining converts to the movement whose conversion will constitute new elements of cognition consonant with the belief system.[16] Thus social support is of paramount importance in providing the individual with a secure context from which he may avoid or modify all dissonant elements. To translate these responses into suitable categories for application to prophetic movements of the biblical period I would suggest the traditional notions of exclusivity of grouping, hermeneutical systems, and various forms of missionary activity. The tendency towards exclusiveness is apparent in certain periods of ancient Israelite society. The histories of Judaism and Christianity are filled with complex hermeneutical systems explaining doctrines and dogmas in such a way as to avoid charges of inconsistent or contradictory notions. Missionary movements

---

14. *Ibid.*, 216; a longer exposition of the paradigm is given on pp. 4–6.
15. This is acknowledged by Festinger, *ibid.*, 23–25.
16. See especially *A Theory of Cognitive Dissonance*, 177–202.

have been a strong feature of Christian activity over the centuries. However these elements are not in themselves responses to dissonance. But given a context of prophetic prediction their presence might indicate an area of response to the experience of dissonance among members of the group. Thus the theory may provide the researcher with another analytical probe for his material.

The paradigm set out for describing a suitable testing of the dissonance theory raises one major problem for prophecy and that is the difficulty of clearly establishing evidence for conditions 3 and 4. There are many examples of predictions in the Old Testament which have been fulfilled, e.g., Jeremiah's predictions of the destruction of Jerusalem, and predictions which have not been fulfilled, e.g., Israel's sharing power with Egypt and Assyria (Isa 19:24) or the hopes expressed in Isa 9:2–7; 11:1–9. But there is little evidence of a conscious awareness on the prophet's part that his predictions have failed to materialise. Condition 4 states "such undeniable disconfirmatory evidence must occur and must be recognised by the individual holding the belief."[17] This lack of awareness poses the question whether the prophet seriously expected these predictions of future bliss to be actually fulfilled and if so did he expect such fulfilment in ⟦141⟧ his own lifetime? It certainly seems to be the case that the prophets hardly ever anticipated the distant future (cf. Deut 18:22).[18] For them the immediate future was the stage on which would be played out the consequences of Israel's response to the prophetic message. The one clear example available of a prophet confronted by a positive response to his preaching and therefore a rescinding of the threat of doom is Jonah. And that presents a picture of a prophet shocked and disappointed by the success of his mission! It may be that the prophets were simply unaware or incapable of conceiving of the possibility of failure, in which case it becomes difficult to apply rigorously the conditions of Festinger's thesis. But it is the structure of the prophetic proclamation that poses the main obstacle to the discovering of dissonant elements in the prophetic traditions.

The basic structure of Israelite prophecy is the proclamation of a message designed to create a response in the people to whom it is addressed and thereby to influence their behaviour. Within the critique of society there is the call to return or repent, that is, a call to make a decision and change direction. This principle of repentance makes the people a moral agent capable of responding to the prophetic word. As such it means that prophecy cannot be simply thought of as predicting the future irrespective of man's action in the present time. Although

17. *When Prophecy Fails*, 4.
18. Fohrer, *op. cit.*, 272f.

the literature influenced by deuteronomic ideas (e.g., Deut 18:22; Jeremiah 28) gives the impression of the prophet as a predictor of future events this is an inadequate summary of his role in Israelite society. The kernel of the prophetic summons to transformation in society may be summed up in the words of Isaiah "cease to do evil, learn to do good" (1:16, 17). It is, of course, necessary to add a rider to the principle of repentance by pointing out that an oversimplified notion of repentance is ruled out in certain instances, e.g., Isaiah's preaching is designed to prevent the people turning and being healed (6:10), and Jeremiah recognises that public repentance can be a false form of repentance (3:10). At the other end of the scale there is the example of Jonah's preaching to the Ninevites which resulted in national fasting and repentance and averted the threatened doom (3:4–10).

This principle of repentance and its effect on the prophetic proclamation is enunciated most clearly in Jer 18:7–10:

> [142] If at any time I declare concerning a nation or a kingdom, that I will pluck up and break down and destroy it, and if that nation, concerning which I have spoken, turns from its evil, I will repent of the evil that I intended to do to it. And if at any time I declare concerning a nation or a kingdom that I will build and plant it, and if it does evil in my sight, not listening to my voice, then I will repent of the good which I had intended to do to it.

The element of response here controls the future so that whatever a prophet might declare about a nation's prospects was subject to that nation's response. So Festinger's simple paradigm of a prediction-fulfilment state of affairs will not cover the prophetic case. Furthermore there is built into this statement about response a fail-safe device for prophetic prediction. No prediction can ever really be falsified because whatever may be predicted of the future it will be subject to human reaction. If the future turns out to be other than expected then the principle expounded in Jer 18:7–10 can be utilised to show how the prediction was controlled by men's actions. There is even some evidence within the Old Testament traditions that this possibility was realised on occasion. The oracles of Jerusalem's destruction given in Micah 1–3 are shown to have been neutralised by Hezekiah's repentance (Jer 26:18, 19). A similar application of the repentance principle may also have operated in the Chronicler's account of the reign of King Manasseh (2 Chr 33:10–20; cf. the account in 2 Kgs 21:1–18 which has no mention of Manasseh's prayer). It is also possible to see the false repentance of Jer 3:10 as the reverse side of this application, namely, repentance may only be a show of repentance so if disaster follows national repentance the rule remains valid.

The prophetic call to decision which can evoke man's response and bring about what Buber calls "the extreme act: the turning to God"[19] stresses the activity of man but must not be taken to mean that God is subject to man's response in such a way that the notion of transcendence is lost. For another strand in the prophetic proclamation is the declaration of redemption, especially in Second Isaiah. Both repentance and redemption are aspects of the transformation of man, one from the human side and the other from the divine side.[20] Thus the vision of salvation in Isa 9:2–7 is anchored in the assertion "the zeal of Yahweh of hosts will do this" as if to suggest that the future is not [[143]] entirely dependent upon man's response. The reverse of this positive aspect of transcendence is Isa 6:10 where the proclamation subverts man's response in order to prevent his turning away from disaster. These signs of transcendence may well modify the principle laid down in Jer 18:7–10 and permit at some level the introduction of dissonance theory. But it must be recognised that the principles of transcendence and repentance severely qualify any application of this theory to prophetic traditions.

If the notion of repentance removes the bulk of Old Testament predictions from the possibility of falsification, particularly the salvation oracles, then the remnant motif may well protect the positive element in prophecy from total disintegration. There is, however, no agreement among scholars on the precise nature of the remnant. It is clear that in Amos 5:3 (cf. 3:12) it simply indicates the scale of the destruction and in Isa 1:8, 9 it points to bare survival. But it came to mean the nucleus of the future for later writers (e.g., Isa 11:11, 16; Hag 2:2; Zech 8:6).[21] So it became a device for retrieving the oracles of salvation from obscurity and a vehicle for new oracles of salvation. It also functioned as a hermeneutical principle in later interpretations of the prophets for a more positive evaluation of the salvation element in the canonical prophets.[22]

In practical terms the concepts of repentance and remnant expose the inadequacy of dissonance theory for dealing with the complex notions involved in prophecy. No prediction need ever fail because the repentance principle creates sufficient space for it to be modified in accordance with human behaviour. The prophetic view of human society tends to be pessimistic and critical so the proclamation of doom is dominant but because of the possibility that men will respond there is always the hope of restoration or salvation. The historical experiences of Israel and Judah reflect the disintegration of small states during the rise of the

19. *The Prophetic Faith* (New York, 1949, 1960), 104.
20. Cf. Fohrer, *op. cit.*, 273.
21. Fohrer, *ibid.*, 271.
22. Cf. G. F. Hasel, *The Remnant* (Berrien Springs, 1972).

Assyrian and Babylonian empires and this fitted in with the prophetic critique of society. But after the Babylonian exile the Jerusalem community was reconstructed along different lines and the remnant motif provided a useful approach to reinterpreting the old salvation oracles of the prophets. Thus even the salvation ⟦144⟧ oracles were not seen as failures but as new possibilities for the ongoing community. So these two levels of prediction expectation safely guard prophecy from a simplistic approach to failure response. Festinger's theory is fine for post-decision problems in modern society and for dealing with simple communities whose existence is grounded in predictions of a straightforward nature.

But dissonance theory can provide some positive insights into the prophetic tradition in the Old Testament. It can make the researcher aware of the problems facing any prophet in a given situation in which expectation of a particular nature comes under pressure from events outside the prophet. Where expectation can be falsified and where the prophet is embarrassed by his situation then it is reasonable to assume some experience of dissonance has disturbed the prophet. But the editing of the prophetic tradition has removed so many oracles from their social setting that it is extremely difficult to reconstruct any possible interaction between prophet and environment.

The prophetic tradition which yields the most positive material for this study is that associated with Isaiah of Jerusalem. The totality of judgment expressed in Isa 6:9–13 is in striking contrast to the salvation oracles elsewhere attributed to Isaiah and also to the call to turn from evil in 1:16, 17. The material in 6:9–13 looks like mature reflection on the nature of his call in the light of his subsequent experiences of an unresponsive people. This section should probably be treated as coming from a time after his failure to persuade Ahaz the king to trust Yahweh rather than the Assyrians (7:1–17).[23] Thus dissonance caused by the failure of his proclamation is resolved, or modified, by the hermeneutics of his commission which demonstrate that such a failure was his mission! This general failure of preaching eventually led Isaiah to retire from active proclamation and to seal up his teaching among his disciples (8:16–18). Here is a good example of a withdrawal from the source of dissonance and of recourse to social support among a group of sympathetic followers whose agreement with the prophet could stimulate him and detract from his failure. The response of his followers could provide him with a more positive ⟦145⟧ ministry without the intrusion of harsh dissonant elements. The tendency of prophets to congregate in groups

---

23. See H. W. Hoffmann, *Die Intention der Verkündigung Jesajas*, BZAW 136 (Berlin, 1974), 77–80; cf. Kaiser, *op. cit.*, 82.

must have facilitated the avoidance of critical elements in the general public. It is clear from Jeremiah's experience that the prophet was a particularly vulnerable target to gibes such as "where is the word of Yahweh? Let it come!" (Jer 17:15; cf. Isa 53:1).

The complex traditions surrounding the Assyrian crisis in the time of Isaiah make it very difficult to sort out both Isaiah's view of the situation and the precise nature of the event described in the legendary accounts in 2 Kings 19. How the siege of Jerusalem in 701 B.C. and its stringent consequences described in Isa 1:4–9 are to be reconciled with the triumphalist deliverance recorded in the Kings story is beyond the scope of this paper and the wit of most competent scholars. But Childs, whose study of this problem is a fine piece of form-critical work, is certainly correct in his assessment, "the oracles of Isaiah are far too complex and diversified to allow for a simple formulation of his position on Assyria which could then serve as a criterion for measuring the historical elements in the narrative material."[24] Furthermore it is not clear at all whether Isaiah held out hope for Jerusalem irrespective of whatever its people did or whether Isa 37:33–35 is a genuine Isaiah saying.[25] If it could be established that Isaiah did believe Jerusalem was inviolable and that Yahweh would defend it against the Assyrians then it would be possible to regard 2 Kings 19 as an outworking of that belief. In which case in the light of Isa 1:4–9 and the terrible deprivations of the siege it is possible to regard the legend in 2 Kings 19 as a resolution of the dissonance caused by the failure of Isaiah's hopes for his city put forward by the theologian historians who believed history to be the outworking of prophecy. However the evidence is far too meagre to maintain such a view with any degree of confidence. At the most it is a possibility, but one which reflects all the uncertainty and obscurity of the prophetic tradition at its most difficult level. In the final analysis it is not the prophet's experience of dissonance but the later community's experience which involves the prophet in the situation.

[146] Outside of the Isaiah tradition traces of dissonance reaction can be seen in the confessions of Jeremiah where the prophet considers the possibility of having been deceived by the deity (15:15–18) and in his general adamancy against the people and the other prophets (1:18; 15:20; 23:9–40). Throughout the oracles of Jeremiah there is a feeling of confusion and anxiety which suggests the prophet was struggling with inner conflicts in an attempt to resolve the problems of his role in Judean

24. *Isaiah and the Assyrian Crisis* (London, 1967), 120.
25. Cf. T. C. Vriezen, "Essentials of the Theology of Isaiah," *Israel's Prophetic Heritage*, ed. B. W. Anderson and W. Harrelson (London, 1962), 139–42; O. Kaiser, *Isaiah* 13–39 (London, 1974), 367–412, esp. 384f., 394f.

society. Further elements of dissonance can be found in the prophecies
of the post-exilic prophets Haggai and Zechariah concerning the community governor Zerubbabel (Hag 2:20–23; Zech 4:6–10; 6:9–14). Here
the expectations centring on Zerubbabel are in contrast with the reality
of Zerubbabel's failure to realise the high hopes predicted of him. Yet the
only trace of that reality would appear to be in Zech 6:11 where "crowns"
may originally have been made for both Zerubbabel and Joshua the high
priest, or what is more likely, for Zerubbabel alone. Because the expectations for Zerubbabel were never realised the high priest has been substituted for the governor in the text."[26] Again this is only a possibility and
one without further support in the text. Perhaps the case of Zerubbabel
is a good example of a problem posed for later readers of the text rather
than for the community which produced the tradition. But, at least, it is
an indication that dissonance producing events could be dealt with by
editing the text at some level so as to reflect historical outcome.

These examples drawn from Isaiah, Jeremiah and the post-exilic
prophets show that there is some evidence of factors giving rise to dissonance within the prophetic experience and reflected in the written traditions. The coenobia of the earlier prophets and the disciples of the
canonical prophets provided the prophetic movement with adequate social support to shield them from the onslaughts of their critics and the
worst ravages of dissonant experiences. The failure of so many salvation
oracles and the modifications brought about by time and reality may have
helped shape Second Isaiah's vision of Israel as a servant suffering on behalf of others (Isaiah 53) but even that vision terminated in a hint of tri-
umphalism (v. 12). The hermeneutic [[147]] process of rationalisation
and explanation is difficult to trace within the biblical tradition, though
in the later prophets there are echoes of the earlier prophets (e.g., Hab
1:5; Zech 7:7; cf. Dan 9:2, 24–27).[27] But in post-biblical times systems of
hermeneutical activity emerge which subjected the biblical text to minute
examination. Thus there is the handling of the prophetic text at Qumran
where the community tried to read itself in the predictions of the prophets. The New Testament is the beginning of multiple forms of exegesis on
the Old Testament in which the writers expound their belief that the
Christ event is the fulfilment of prophecy, and that many of the events of
that period can be expressly described as "this is what was spoken by the
prophet . . ." (e.g., Acts 2:16). Rabbinical Judaism continued to produce

26. M. Noth, *The History of Israel* (London, 1960), 312; cf. J. L. McKenzie, *A Theology of
the Old Testament* (New York, 1974), 288; P. R. Ackroyd, *Exile and Restoration* (London, 1968),
196f.

27. Cf. F. F. Bruce, "The Earliest Old Testament Interpretation," *The Witness of Tradition*,
OTS xvii (Leiden, 1972), 37–52.

exegeses of the biblical text and some of the rabbis sought in their own time the fulfilment of prophecy. Early Christian patristic interpretation followed a messianic understanding of the prophets in which all the expectations of the prophetic tradition were related to Christ and the experiences of the Christian community. Thus the failure of prophecy in its own time became the opportunity for later communities to seek in their time the unfolding of prophetic expectation.

The fundamental principle which seems to emerge from all this exegetical activity surrounding the prophetic texts is that dissonance gives rise to hermeneutic. In order to avoid the failure of prophecy or because there is a strong belief that prophecy cannot fail it becomes necessary to construct a system of explanation showing how various examples of supposedly failed predictions can be rescued by reinterpretation and reapplication. Here is the main thrust of dissonance theory for biblical studies—it allows hermeneutical systems to be seen as responses to failures in prediction. It therefore theoretically poses the assertion that where there are prophetic texts there must also be, what Barr calls, a "resultant system," i.e., "there are two systems or levels at work: the first is the text, the second is the system into which the interpretation runs out."[28] The resultant system may be any form of hermeneutical principle used by later interpreters, e.g., mystical approaches to the text or allegorical systems or typological [[148]] exegesis in Jewish and Christian theology. Perhaps the earliest attempts at reinterpreting and therefore transforming the prophetic traditions came from the apocalyptic writers who attempted to get around the basic failure of the prophetic expectation of future salvation by grounding such hopes in a transcendental act of God imposed upon mankind (cf. Dan 2:44, 45; 7:9–27).[29] The fusion of prophecy and apocalyptic eventually led to the emergence of Christianity which introduced yet another set of dissonance producing expectations.

If the structure for analysis is accepted as the text plus its interpretation within various communities embracing it as holy scripture or authoritative writ then it becomes possible for dissonance theory to be applied with fruitful results. However this means the material available for research is increased to include the fields of biblical exegesis and its history, historical theology and the multiple forms of sects deriving their existence from discrete interpretations of the Bible. It becomes a programme for historical, sociological and intellectual research and

---

28. J. Barr, *Old and New in Interpretation* (London, 1965), 108f.

29. See P. D. Hanson, "Jewish Apocalyptic against Its Near Eastern Environment," *Revue Biblique* 78 (1971), 32–58; "Old Testament Apocalyptic Re-examined," *Interpretation* 25 (1971), 454–79; and more recently his *The Dawn of Apocalyptic* (Philadelphia, 1975).

threatens to get out of hand. The difficulties of establishing the precise meaning of so much biblical material remain and therefore the legitimacy of many of the interpretations maintained in any such study is also called in question. An example of the difficulty of clearly establishing what is the nature of the case may be taken from the New Testament. On the surface it would appear that an ideal subject for dissonance analysis would be the notion of *Parousieverzögerung* 'delay of the parousia'. The New Testament certainly seems to present a community daily expecting the return of Jesus (cf. Matt 24:34; Acts 1:11; 1 Cor 7:26, 29–31; 1 Thess 4:15–17; 2 Thess 1:10; Rev 22:20). The return of Jesus is an event that appears to be easily verifiable or falsifiable. History has shown that the expected return did not materialise so there should be fairly straightforward evidence of attempts to resolve the ensuing dissonance caused by this failure. At one level this seems to be the case in that there are assertions in the New Testament which suggest that an interim period must occur before the parousia takes place, e.g., "this gospel of the kingdom must be preached throughout the whole world . . . [[149]] and then the end will come" (Matt 24:14) or "that day will not come unless . . ." (2 Thess 2:3). Thus explanations are arising which attempt to modify the expectation in the light of reality and show how the coming may still be expected but not before a period of time has elapsed in which must occur certain other events. On the other hand the Fourth Gospel gives the impression that there will be no second coming in the future because the parousia has already taken place.[30] The real problem for the researcher is to discover which view represents the authentic Christian belief and to what extent there was any one fixed view about the future. Some of the early churches may have had a strong belief in an imminent parousia but others probably identified that coming with the outpoured spirit at Pentecost, or, by regarding the church as the body of Christ, had no concept of an absent Christ requiring a return to earth. Thus it becomes very difficult to establish clearly dissonance response because of the lack of strict controls on the material.

Furthermore the early Christian communities were not simply eschatologically orientated groups so expectations of future events were open to failure without catastrophic effects for the communities. Fundamental to these communities was the emergence and development of christology which became the formative element in subsequent Christianity.[31] It is the christological *kerygma* which functions as the resultant system in

30. Cf. N. Perrin, *The New Testament: An Introduction* (New York, 1974), 41; see also A. L. Moore, *The Parousia in the New Testament* (Leiden, 1966).
31. See D. Flusser, "Salvation Present and Future," *Numen* 16 (1969), 139–55.

the New Testament.[32] Christology allied to notions of transcendence prevented Christianity becoming the slave of eschatological expectations and allowed it to develop into a complex system of transformational beliefs. Where there are dissonance producing events in the New Testament christology resolves them by hermeneutical processes. If there is cognitive dissonance in the New Testament it is created by the death of Jesus and resolved by the christology of the gospels.[33] The dissonance expressed by Luke 24:21 acquired its resolution by way of a christological interpretation of the Old Testament (vv. 25–27). It cannot be denied that communities continued to ⟦150⟧ expect some form of literal return of Jesus, e.g., the churches of Paul and the churches addressed by the Apocalypse, but slowly christological hermeneutic won its way until by the time of Augustine christology had overcome chiliasm. Yet the subsequent history of Christianity in Western Europe has been punctuated by chiliastic movements, strong in millennial expectations but rather weak in christology.[34]

Because Judaism and Christianity had strong elements of eschatological expectation within them there was always a tendency for dissonance resolving hermeneutics to emerge, but because neither structure was simply constructed around such expectations their central cores were relatively safe from the vicissitudes of failed predictions. Perhaps because Christianity has a stronger eschatological element at its roots it has been more vulnerable to millennial movements seizing it and distorting its christology. Judaism is centred around Torah and sees its existence as the way of obedience to divine commandment with the stress on the ethical mode of life. As such even prophecy was subservient to Torah and was seen as commentary on Torah. So the failure of prophecy was not a danger to Judaism, though the existence of prophetic expectation did give scope to movements within Judaism to develop messianic movements which occasionally broke away from the parent body, e.g., Qumran, Christianity, and the later stages of the Sabbatai Zevi movement.

This study has been a theoretical exploration of the possibilities of applying the theory of cognitive dissonance to the study of biblical prophecy. If it has failed to reveal startling results that is because the material to hand is strictly limited in terms of information about prophetic self-awareness and details about how the prophetic preaching was re-

32. Barr, *op. cit.*, 109.

33. See U. Wernik, "Frustrated Beliefs and Early Christianity," *Numen* 22 (1975), 96–130.

34. Flusser notes "where Christology is strong, the longing for Millennium is comparatively weak," *op. cit.*, 155; on later movements see N. Cohn, *The Pursuit of the Millennium* (London, 1970).

ceived by the people.[35] The fundamental element of repentance in the prophetic declaration also rendered clear failures of prediction rather difficult to establish.[36] Festinger's theory has great explanatory [[151]] value when applied to groups constructed around simple prediction expectations characteristic of the twentieth century but it is out of its depth when applied to complex structures of belief and hermeneutic such as Judaism and Christianity. This is not to conclude that the theory has no applicatory value to the study of prophecy but to be wary of any simplistic application of a cross-disciplinary approach. It can uncover various levels of tension within the prophetic traditions and it illustrates the complexity of the interaction between prophet and society. According to some authorities "the main virtue of dissonance theory is that its use permits so much understanding. It points to many nonobvious sources of tension."[37] As such the theory should assist in mining the multiplex nature of the Old Testament prophetic tradition given further research into specific sets of texts.

35. Some useful material is contained in H. W. Wolff, "Das Zitat im Prophetenspruch," *Gesammelte Studien zum Alten Testament* (München, 1964), 30–129.

36. On repentance see T. M. Raitt, "The Prophetic Summons to Repentance," *ZAW* 83 (1971), 30–49.

37. J. W. Brehm and A. R. Cohen, *Explorations in Cognitive Dissonance* (London, 1962), 314.

The "Servants of the Lord" in Third Isaiah:

Profile of a Pietistic Group in the Persian Epoch

JOSEPH BLENKINSOPP

[[1]] There has been a reaction in recent years among students of Israelite prophecy against the heavily intellectual and theological emphasis which has dominated the subject since the nineteenth century; let us say, since Heinrich Ewald's *Die Propheten des Alten Bundes* (1840). This has led an increasing number of scholars to look more closely at such related issues as the social location of the prophet, his (less commonly her) behavioural characteristics, possession phenomena in other cultural contexts deemed comparable to that of ancient Israel, the role of the prophetic leader in millennarian cults, and the nature of the prophet's support-group. Such questions were not, of course, entirely new. As early as 1917 Max Weber had used the comparative method in dealing with early Israelite war prophecy and those "plebeian technicians of orgiastics" (his phrase) called "sons of the prophets" in the history of the kingdoms. Even earlier the study of prophetic behaviour had been put on the agenda by Gustav Hölscher (*Die Propheten*, 1914) with the help of comparable phenomena recorded in ancient Near Eastern inscriptions and by such authors of late antiquity as Philo of Byblos and Lucian of Samosata.

Reprinted with permission from *Proceedings of the Irish Biblical Association* 7 (1983) 1–23.

An interest in social context is also implicit in form critical studies of prophetic material from the time of Gunkel and his student Mowinckel. And it goes without saying that the interminable discussion on prophecy in relation to cult was and is, in effect, aimed at determining the social context of some prophets or some aspects of prophetic activity.

The most recent phase of discussion[1] has the advantage of more sophisticated sociological and anthropological tools and can make use of a dossier of reporting on ecstatic or millennarian cults and their leaders. If it has not always found the best way to make use of anthropological theory and field-work, it has at least brought more forcibly to our attention some interesting questions which we would like to have answered. One of these, already alluded to, has to do with the prophet's support-group and his (less commonly her) role in the emergence of a cult, sect, party, conventicle or church (the terminology [[2]] is imprecise even among sociologists). We would like to know how such an entity, once it has achieved a certain degree of cohesion, understands itself in relation to the parent-body or the wider society, how the latter reacts to its emergence, the threshold of mutual tolerance involved, the kinds of conditions and situations which favour the emergence of such groups. Comparative data are also at hand, which could help us, if not to answer some of these questions, then at least to pose them in a more satisfactory way. This is particularly the case with millennarian cults and movements, the programmes embraced by their adherents, and their reaction to the disconfirmation of their belief-structures. The relevance of such studies to millennarian and/or messianic movements during the six centuries of the Second Commonwealth, including early Palestinian Christianity, has of course been noted.[2]

This brings me to the subject of this paper, namely, a prophetic-eschatological movement which emerged during the last days of the Neo-Babylonian Empire and continued on into the Persian period and perhaps even beyond. Without attempting to describe a complete historical trajectory—for which task the surviving sources are clearly inadequate—I believe it can be shown that this movement is transitional between prophetic followings of the pre-exilic period and the well-known sects of Hasmonaean and Roman times. My intent will be simply to put together what can be reasonably deduced about it from the few texts which have survived, leaving the task of sociological analysis to those more competent than I am to discharge it.

1. On which see J. Blenkinsopp, *A History of Prophecy in Israel*, Philadelphia, 1983, 38–46.
2. E.g., by R. P. Carroll, *When Prophecy Failed*, New York, 1979, especially chaps. 5 and 6; J. G. Gager, *Kingdom and Community*, Englewood Cliffs, New Jersey, 1975.

The Setting:
Palestinian Judaism in the Persian Period

After Cyrus had occupied Babylon (539 B.C.E.) he issued an edict permitting the repatriation of ethnic groups which had been relocated in Mesopotamia by the Babylonians, even subsidizing the reestablishment of native cults like that of Marduk in Babylon itself, Sin in the city of Ur, and Yahweh in Jerusalem.[3] The consequent return to the homeland of some of the deportees or their descendants, though probably not in the form of an immediate and enthusiastic *aliyah* [['immigration']] as the Chronicler would have us believe, must have created a situation in which conflict was practically inevitable. Now, for the first time, we have two distinct groups, whom for convenience we may call the Palestinians and the Babylonians, both claiming to be the genuine heirs of the old Israel destroyed in the massive [[3]] disasters of the sixth century.[4] The civic status of Jews in the small province around Jerusalem, including their title to property, was contingent on their support of and participation in the temple cult; a situation by no means unique in the Persian Empire. Hence the importance of control of the cult, and therefore of the redemptive media; an issue which was decided, not without struggle, in favour of the Zadokite faction, with other branches of the priesthood having to accept either total exclusion or demotion to the rank of *clerus minor* [['minor cleric']].[5]

The economic implications of this new situation can be detected in the claim of those who had never left the homeland that the deportees had been expelled from the cultic community (Ezek 11:14–16), a claim transparently aimed at justifying the expropriation of land and property. It is therefore hardly surprising if, again for the first time, qualification for membership in the community constituted by cultic affiliation became a problematic issue. To take only one example: the liberal dispositions relating to the status of aliens and eunuchs in Isa 56:3–5 are at variance with the disqualifications listed in Deut 23:1–8, a passage of unknown date but almost certainly not pre-exilic. Regulations concerning ritual purity (e.g., Hag 2:10–14) also came much more to the fore at that time, and continued thereafter to play an important part in the emergence of separatist and dissenting movements.

---

3. For the Cyrus cylinder see *ANET*[3], 315–16 and on Persian policy with respect to the Jerusalem temple Ezra 1:1–4; 6:4, 10; 7:15–20. For the background see J. M. Cook, *The Persian Empire*, London, 1983, 25–43.

4. It must be borne in mind that our principal source, the author of *Chronicles*, testifies on behalf of the *běnê haggôlāh*, diaspora Jews.

5. Some aspects of this struggle can be reconstructed from certain passages in P (e.g., Leviticus 10) and the Zadokite additions to Ezekiel 40–48.

Continued subjection to an alien power, though one more enlightened in its imperial policy than its predecessors, the disappearance of
the monarchy after more than four centuries, and the miserable social
and economic conditions which appear to have plagued the province of
Judah throughout the Persian period,[6] combined to favour the emergence of millennarian and, more specifically, messianic movements, not
all of them confined to peripheral groups in the province.[7] These, too,
were inevitably a source of conflict. Those which aimed at the restoration
of the native dynasty were generally linked with disturbances in other
parts of the empire, especially Babylon and Egypt.[8] But there were others
with rather different ideas and aims, and it is with one of these that we
will be concerned in this paper.

"Servants of the Lord" in Third Isaiah

We now turn to Isaiah 56–66, a collection of prophetic material [[4]]
which we take to derive mainly from the early Persian period, say from
Cyrus (550–530) to Artaxerxes I nicknamed Longhand (465–424), in
the twentieth year of whose reign Nehemiah undertook his rebuilding
programme (Neh 1:1; 2:1). After the opening passage (56:1–8), which
adopts a controversially liberal position on the status of eunuchs and
aliens,[9] a sustained anti-syncretist diatribe (56:9–57:13) clearly indicates
intra-group conflict without requiring the existence of a well-defined
sub-group within which the polemic originated.[10] As we read on, however, we become aware that the term "servants of Yahweh," which at the
beginning alludes to the entire community (56:6), begins to be restricted
to a minority within the province which is experiencing opposition and
even persecution at the hands of its opponents. We first read that, on account of his servants, those of his people who seek him, God will not destroy the entire community (65:8–12). The opponents of the group
within which this polemic originated are those who abandon Yahweh, neglect the temple cult, ignore the prophetic word while offering sacrifice
to Gad and Meni, gods of good luck. The lines are drawn even more
clearly in the following passage, addressed to the reprobates (65:13–16),
which contrasts their fate on judgment day with that of Yahweh's servants:

---

6. Hag 1:6, 8–11; 2:16–17; Zech 8:10; Mal 2:13–16; 3:10–11; Isa 58:3–4; 59:9–15;
Joel 1–2; Neh 5:1–5.
7. E.g., during the critical years following the death of Cambyses (Hag 2:6–9, 20–23).
8. See Blenkinsopp, *A History of Prophecy in Israel*, 244–45.
9. Cf. the quite different dispositions in Deut 23:1–8.
10. It appears to allude to the violent death of the righteous (*ṣaddîq*) and the devout
(*ʾanšê ḥesed*) (57:1).

> Behold, my servants shall eat,
>   but you shall be hungry;
> behold, my servants shall drink,
>   but you shall be thirsty;
> behold, my servants shall rejoice,
>   but you shall be put to shame;
> behold, my servants shall sing for gladness of heart,
>   but you shall cry out for pain of heart,
>   and shall wail for anguish of spirit.

This theme of eschatological reversal, familiar to readers of the gospels (e.g., Matt 5:3–12), presupposes division and conflict and, more specifically, the existence of a prophetic-eschatological minority which has achieved a certain degree of identity and self-definition. This impression is confirmed by the second part of the passage (vv. 15–16) which affirms that in the last days the "servants" will be given a new name—another well-attested eschatological motif. It continues: [[5]]

> So that he who blesses himself in the land
>   shall bless himself by the God Amen,
> and he who takes an oath in the land
>   shall swear by the God Amen;
> because the former troubles are forgotten
>   and are hid from my eyes.

It has become the common practice to emend "the God Amen" to "the God of truth" (RSV) or something similar.[11] But Jewish and early Christian writers did not find it implausible,[12] and no one has taken exception to the equally strange appellative *ᵓehyeh* (I will be) at Exod 3:14 and Hos 1:9. What it implies, in the context, is that "the servants" will bear this new name in the future age; they will be the Amen people, a people, that is, that says Yes to God. The conferring of such new names fits a pattern of eschatological discourse and is attested elsewhere in Third Isaiah (e.g., 62:1–5).

We now move on to a prophetic saying in the following chapter which provides the clearest evidence in Isaiah of intra-group conflict:

---

11. *ᵓĕmet* or *ᵓōmen* or *ᵓēmûn* for *ᵓāmēn*. See, e.g., C. Westermann, *Isaiah 40–66*, Philadelphia, 1969, 403, without discussion.

12. 2 Cor 1:17–20; Rev 3:14. See A. Jepsen in *TDOT* I 322–23.

> Hear the word of Yahweh,
>   you who tremble at his word.
> Your brethren who hate you
>   and cast you out for my name's sake
> have said, "Let Yahweh be glorified,[13]
>   that we may see your joy";
> but it is they who shall be put to shame (66:5).

The anonymous seer is here addressing a group which receives the prophetic word with fear and trembling, which is ostracised by their fellow-Jews on account of their association with the prophetic leader,[14] whose opponents reject their claim that they, and they alone, will rejoice in the parousia, and who believe that, notwithstanding, they will be vindicated on judgment day. The quotation put into the mouth of the opponents, which does not necessarily imply rejection of eschatological faith *tout court* ⟦'absolutely'⟧, sounds very much like their answer to the claim of the "servants," discussed earlier, that they and not "the others" would eat, drink, rejoice and sing at the parousia (Isa 65:13–14) — a typically sectarian assertion. A further implication would be that "the servants" of 65:8–16 are identical with "the quakers" (those who tremble at ⟦6⟧ his word) of 66:5, and that the opponents who are now in control but will eventually be put to shame are in both texts also identical.

Further light may be thrown on this situation by the saying, or paired sayings, immediately preceding 66:5. The first two verses (66:1–2) appear to contrast attachment to the temple with the attitude of those who are humble, contrite and tremble at God's word. This has led, not surprisingly, to an interpretation of the saying as rejecting the proposal to rebuild the temple and restore the practice of animal sacrifice; and the following verses (3–4), which read like a blunt disavowal of the temple cult, have made the temptation almost irresistible.[15] If, however, the tremblers of v. 2 are identical with those of v. 5, it must be noted that the latter look forward to an imminent parousia, and that the parousia is always associated in prophetic texts from that period with the temple.[16] The idea that God's real domain is heaven and that on earth he is present to the lowly and afflicted occurs more than once in the Isaiah scroll; and nowhere does it necessarily imply rejection of the temple and

---

13. Reading *yikkābēd* for *yikbad*.

14. The name is his, not God's; cf. Matt 10:18, 22.

15. E.g., James D. Smart, *History and Theology in Second Isaiah*, Philadelphia, 1965, 281–88: the author, the Palestinian Second Isaiah, represents a position diametrically opposed to that of Haggai.

16. Isa 60:7, 13; 62:9; 66:6, 20–21, 23; Hag 2:6–9; Mal 3:1–4.

its services.[17] The contrast between heavenly and earthly dwellings also appears in the (Deuteronomic and exilic or post-exilic) prayer of Solomon at the dedication of the first temple (1 Kgs 8:27–30, cf. 2 Sam 7:5), suggesting, in the context of Deuteronomic theology, that support of the temple is consistent with disavowal of wrong understandings of how God is present in it. As for the second part of the saying (vv. 3–4), which juxtaposes illegitimate with legitimate cultic acts (e.g., slaughter of oxen, human sacrifice), it must not be overlooked that both are performed by those who have chosen their own ways and delight in their abominations, which is to say, their idols (*šiqqûṣêhem*). It may therefore not be concluded, at least on these grounds, that the "servants"/"quakers" were opposed on principle to the temple cult.

Taking these passages together, we gather that the opponents of this prophetic minority do not heed the word of God (65:12; 66:4), which presumably means that they reject the claims of the group and the seer who speaks for them. They are also engaging in idolatrous, meaning syncretic, cults, a not uncommon complaint in post-exilic prophetic writings.[18] While the author of these chapters, unlike Malachi, does not make a special point of polemicising against the temple clergy, the opponents no doubt included [[7]] some of the latter since only they would be capable of, in effect, excommunicating them. We can therefore visualise a situation not unlike that of the Qumran sectarians who combined attachment to the temple on principle with dissociation from it in practice.

The *ḥaredim* of the Second Temple

We should now look more closely at this term *ḥārēd, ḥărēdîm* which occurs twice in Isa 66:1–5. Trembling or quaking as an expression of intense religious emotion is, of course, well attested in the literature of many cultures and especially sub-cultures. The best known examples are, perhaps, the Quakers (Society of Friends) of seventeenth century England and their offshoot the Shakers who, like their biblical predecessors, developed a strongly millennarian faith. Jewish history in the post-biblical period has also known its *ḥărēdîm*, and the term is still in use among ultra-orthodox communities. In biblical Hebrew the verb *ḥrd* occurs often with reference to fearing and one or other of its manifestations, but is used rather rarely of specifically numinous fear. Israel at Sinai trembled when it experienced the theophany (*wayyeḥĕrad kol-hāᶜām* [['and all the people

17. Isa 40:22; 57:15; 60:13; 63:15.
18. Isa 57:5–13; 65:3–5, 7, 11; 66:3–4.

trembled']], Exod 19:16). The Philistines experienced a divinely-inspired panic during an Israelite attack (1 Sam 14:15).[19] In the participial form it occurs only in Isa 66:1–5 discussed above and twice in the Ezra narrative (Ezra 9:4; 10:3).[20] While in none of these cases is it a title like Pharisee or Essene, it is arguable that it presupposes a certain fixity of usage in the contexts in which it occurs.

In the Ezra narrative we read that, shortly after his arrival in Jerusalem (the disputed date need not, for the moment, concern us), Ezra was confronted with the need to do something about the addiction of the diaspora group (*běnê haggôlāh*, Ezra 8:35, etc.) to marriage with outsiders. After his initial and somewhat intemperate reaction (rending his garments, pulling out his hair, etc.), the initiative to take appropriate action came from "all who trembled at the words of the God of Israel" (9:4). From that point on they were closely associated with him in fasting (9:5; 10:6), penitential prayer (9:6–10:1) and keeping vigil (10:6), in preparation for the covenant to put aside foreign wives, a covenant which was carried out "according to the counsel of my lord and of those who tremble at the commandment of our God" (10:3). That is all that we hear of them in this source.

[[8]] It would be natural to ask whether there is any connection between the *ḥărēdîm* [['tremblers']] of Isaiah 66 and these associates of Ezra. At first sight the answer would appear to be no. In Isaiah they are the humble and contrite in spirit and are hated and cast out by their fellow-Jews. These verbs carry a rather stronger connotation than the translation suggests. Hating involves active dissociation while *niddāh* [['cast out']], which occurs only at Isa 66:5 and Amos 6:3, comes close to the sense of excommunicating which it has in Mishnaic Hebrew.[21] Far from being an ostracised minority, the *ḥărēdîm* of Ezra 9–10 constitute an elite group in the *gôlāh* [['diaspora']] community who take the lead in initiating certain reforms. And again, what characterizes the "quakers" of Isaiah 66 is their adherence to a prophetic leader and his eschatological teaching, of the kind which has been preserved in the central section of Third Isaiah (60–62), while the distinctive mark of Ezra's support-group is their fearful solicitude for the law ("those who tremble at the commandment of our God," 10:3). It may well be, then, that the term has

19. The *ḥerdat ʾĕlōhîm* [['panic from God']] was accompanied by earthquake activity (*wattirgaz hāʾāreṣ*); the substantive occurs twice and the verb once in this verse.

20. The only exception is 1 Sam 4:13: Eli's heart was trembling (*ḥārēd*) for the (safety of) the ark; and, in fact, shortly afterwards, he suffered a fatal heart attack.

21. See the examples in M. Jastrow, *A Dictionary of the Targumim, The Talmud Babli and Yerushalmi, and the Midrashic Literature*, Philadelphia, 1903, *sub voce*.

come to be used in a quite general sense of loyal Jews during the Second Temple period.[22]

There are, notwithstanding, some indications that this conclusion is not entirely satisfactory. It is extremely important, in the first place, not to set a prophetic and eschatological orientation over against concern, even intense concern, for law observance. The example of the Qumran community will suffice to show that the one was not only compatible with but demanded the other. In view of the conventional scholarly generalizations about Ezra, it must also be said that nothing that we know of him supports the assumption of an anti-prophetic or anti-eschatological posture. There are also certain features of the *ḥărēdîm* in the two sources which positively suggest a connection. Throughout Isaiah 56–66 mourning is associated with fasting just as eschatological rejoicing is with feasting. One of the characteristics of those known as "servants" and "quakers" is that they mourn and fast in the present age in anticipation of rejoicing and feasting at the parousia—the familiar theme of the messianic banquet.[23] Now it is precisely this association which we find where the Ezra narrative describes those who supported his programme. The parallelism between "all who trembled at the words of the God of Israel because of the faithlessness of the returned exiles" (9:4) and Ezra "mourning over the faithlessness of the exiles" (10:6) suggests that trembling and mourning are being predicated of a penitential group with the *gôlāh* community. In this respect Ezra's support-group ⟦9⟧ anticipates certain features of the milieu in which *Daniel* circulated during the Seleucid epoch: mourning, fasting, penitential prayer, and intense concern for the law.[24]

There is also the fact that marriage with foreign women, which Ezra and his supporters were bent on eliminating, brought with it syncretic cults in which some of the leaders of the community, including temple personnel, were involved (Ezra 9:1–2; 10:18–24).[25] We have seen that it was precisely this situation which confronted the prophetic group within which the material in Isaiah 56–66 circulated. It may then be suggested that the mission of Ezra, backed by the authority of the Persian government which had a stake in supporting and maintaining local cults (Ezra 7:12–26), resulted in a setback for the temple authorities and an enhancement of status for the "servants" and "quakers" among whom he found his principal support in pushing through his reforms. While we do

22. "It was probably in the post-exilic period that it came to be a fixed expression describing the loyal Jew," R. N. Whybray, *Isaiah 40–66*, London, 1975, 281.

23. In Isaiah 56–66 'mourners' (*ʾăbēlîm, mitʾabblîm*) is a frequent appellative for the devout minority (57:18; 61:2, 3; 66:10).

24. See especially Dan 9:3–23; 10:1–9.

25. This is, of course, a frequent theme throughout the history; e.g., 1 Kgs 11:1–8.

not know the outcome of these measures, it would be a reasonable conjecture that they did not long survive the mission of Ezra after whose departure things probably went on much as before in the province.[26]

The Elect in Malachi 3

Towards the end of Malachi occurs a passage which may throw further light on the situation I have been trying to reconstruct on the basis of Isaiah 56–66 and Ezra 9–10. It opens with an accusation addressed by Yahweh to those who had been speaking strongly against him (3:13). What this means is that they had been wondering aloud whether, in view of the prosperity of the wicked, it was worthwhile continuing to live the holy life (vv. 13–15). The outcome was that Yahweh heeded their complaint, and a book was produced in which were written the names of those who feared him and thought on his name (v. 16). These were to form the elect community of the last days when the righteous and God-servers would be set aside from the wicked and the latter would be utterly destroyed (vv. 17–21).

To settle one problem at the outset, there can be no doubt that those addressed in the first part of the passage, who are giving strong expression to their religious doubts, are identical with the elect who can look forward to vindication on judgment day.[27] After all, they distinguish themselves from the arrogant and wicked, they serve God in spite of their doubts, they keep his commandments [[10]] and mourn.[28] The two parts (vv. 13–15 and 16–21) are therefore related as problem and solution, and they are both addressed to the same segment of the community, i.e., those who serve God (vv. 14, 16, 17, 18) even though assailed by doubt and discouragement. The solution is eschatological. The distinction between those

---

26. Much would depend on the disputed issue of the date of Ezra's mission and the identity of the Artaxerxes of Ezra 7:1ff. If Ezra came in 458 B.C., and therefore preceded Nehemiah's first mission, the probability that his success was limited and short-lived would be much greater.

27. The adverb *ʾaz* [['then']] at the beginning of v. 16 might suggest that the God-fearers who conferred together were different from those spoken of in vv. 13–15. Since, however, the context suggests otherwise, several commentators including Wellhausen, Budde, Nowack and van Hoonacker have taken their cue from LXX and emended to *zōh, kōh, kāzōʾt* [['thus']] or something similar. A better solution seems to be that of W. Rudolph, *Haggai—Sacharja 1–8—Sacharja 9–14—Maleachi*, Gütersloh, 1976, 286–87, who retains MT as *lectio difficilior* [['the more difficult reading']] but translates 'damals', 'als' [['then']]. Most, at any rate, would agree with Wellhausen, *Die Kleinen Propheten übersetzt und erklärt*, Berlin, 1893[3], 210. "Es sind die Frommen welche murren; und sie werden im Folgenden nicht gestraft sondern getröstet" [['It is the pious who grumble; and in what follows they will not be chastised but consoled']].

28. *Hālaknû qĕdōrannît* [['walking as in mourning']], v. 14.

who fear and serve God and others in the community who do not is already established, for the names of the elect are already recorded in God's directory (*sēper zikkārôn*, v. 16). They will be made public, however, only on judgment day.

This principle of eschatological discrimination, familiar to readers of the gospels (e.g., Matt 13:37–43; 25:31–46), draws an invisible line through the community, dividing the true Israel from those who are Israel only in name. This, it seems to me, is of the essence of sectarianism. Pointing in the same direction is the highly-charged term 'special possession' (*sĕgullāh*), used traditionally of all Israel in relation to Yahweh,[29] but here restricted to a faithful minority within it. This sort of language presupposes certain social facts: division within the group and, more specifically, the existence of a sub-group which could be presumed to agree with the writer's views, which was animated by the same eschatological faith and which rejected, and was no doubt rejected by, others in the group who did not share these views.

While we have no sure pointers to the date of this passage, or indeed of the book in which it occurs,[30] it makes sense to infer that those addressed are in some way related to, if not actually identical with, the "servants" and "quakers" of Isaiah 66 and Ezra 9–10. They are described as servants of God (vv. 14, 17, 18), they mourn in this age (v. 14), they are attentive to the divine Name (vv. 16, 20), obedient to the law (v. 14) and fear God (vv. 16a, 16b). What is more, they believe that they will be vindicated and will rejoice ("leaping like calves," v. 20) on the last day, as we have seen of those addressed by the anonymous seer in Third Isaiah. The connection would be even closer if, as suggested by Nowack as long ago as 1897, the crisis of faith alluded to in Malachi 3 had been precipitated by delay in the hoped-for parousia.[31] The traditional Jewish view that the anticipated messenger of Mal 3:1–4 is none other than Ezra himself, a view reflected in the Targum and Babylonian Talmud (*b. Meg.* 15a), taken over by Jerome and Calvin, and argued by at least one modern commentator,[32] may well be speculative, but no more so than competing iden-

---

29. Exod 19:5; Deut 7:6; 14:2; 26:18.

30. Most commentators date the book around the middle of the fifth century B.C., shortly before the mission of Nehemiah. Holtzmann's argument (in *Archiv für Religionswissenschaft* 29, 1931, 1–21) that the God-fearers of Mal 3:16 are identical with the *asidaioi* [['Hasidaeans']] of 1 Macc 2:42 has had few followers.

31. W. Nowack, *Die Kleinen Propheten*, Göttingen, 1922³, 405.

32. A. von Bulmerincq, *Einleitung in das Buch des Propheten Maleachi*, Dorpat, 1926; O. Eissfeldt, *The Old Testament. An Introduction*, 442–43, who is non-committal. The comment of J. M. P. Smith, *A Critical and Exegetical Commentary on Haggai, Zechariah, Malachi and Jonah*, Edinburgh, 1912, 7, is worth quoting: "The Book of Malachi fits the situation amid which Nehemiah worked as snugly as a bone fits its socket."

tifications. That 〖11〗 the book attacks the same abuses which occupied Ezra during his mission[33] at least permits the argument that the author and the God-servers addressed in this passage belonged to the number of those who rallied to Ezra's reforms.

Given the lack of precise definition, any term which we choose to employ in this kind of situation (sect, party, faction, conventicle) will probably be contested. The argument is, at any rate, that we have to do with a group which had attained a fairly well-developed sense of identity and cohesion and which may be considered intermediate between the disciples of the earlier prophets and the sects of late antiquity. It remains to be seen whether anything is known, or can be reasonably surmised, about its origins.

Second Isaiah and the So-Called "Servant Songs"

Since the late eighteenth century it has been generally accepted that Isaiah 40–66 cannot have been written by the Isaiah of the Assyrian period to whom the entire work is attributed. Critical scholarship has also, by and large, accepted Duhm's conclusion (in his commentary of 1892) that a distinction must also be made between 40–55 and 56–66, the former exilic and the latter predominantly or entirely post-exilic. It was also Duhm who singled out certain passages in the exilic portion for special attention—the so-called "Servant Songs" (42:1–4; 49:1–6; 50:4–11; 52:13–53:12) which he dated after Second Isaiah but earlier than the last eleven chapters of the book.[34] In one form or another—and the variations are legion—this too has become part of the critical consensus. As is often the case, however, these "assured results of modern scholarship" turn out, on closer inspection, to be somewhat less than certain. The division of the book into First, Second and Third Isaiah, respectively preexilic, exilic and post-exilic is, to begin with, only very roughly correct. Much of First Isaiah, and not only in the long section 13–27, cannot be dated to the pre-exilic period. Chapter 35, which speaks of the restoration of Zion, the new miracles in the wilderness, the sacred way over which the deportees are to return, belongs thematically with the second section of the book. The connection has been broken by the insertion of the biographical narrative in chapters 36–39, roughly corresponding with 2 Kings 18–20, and presenting a strikingly different Isaiah from the author of what are taken to be the genuine sayings. That this narrative

33. I.e., exogamous marriage and cultic irregularity.

34. B. Duhm, *Das Buch Jesaja übersetzt und erklärt*, Göttingen, 1902², xiii. According to Duhm, chapters 40–55 were composed, probably in Phoenicia, ca. 540; 56–66 in Jerusalem shortly before the arrival of Nehemiah.

ends with a prediction of exile in Babylon (39:5–8), thus preparing [[12]] for the announcement of return from that country in the following chapter, may help to explain its insertion at this point.

The division into Second and Third Isaiah, with a clean break after chapter 55, is also not free of problems. If it is argued on the grounds of chronology we would have to point out that, leaving aside allusions to Cyrus and the fall of Babylon, chronological indications are not abundant in these chapters. Thus, we hear of the city and temple lying in ruins not only in 40–55 but also in the following section.[35] An examination of stylistic features, especially *inclusio*, is also indecisive, and would as well indicate four "Isaiahs" as three, with an additional break after chapter 48.[36] In other respects, too, Isaiah 40–48 appears to have its own distinctive character. It focusses on the new era inaugurated by the campaigns of Cyrus and has as its centrepiece the Cyrus oracle in 44:24–45:13. The following chapters, on the contrary, concentrate exclusively on the internal affairs of the Jewish community. We shall go on to see that these two sections—40–48 and 49–55—also speak of servanthood and use the term 'servant' (*ᶜebed*) in significantly different ways, and that this fact may bear on the interpretation of Duhm's four "Servant Songs."

The setting apart of these four passages has also given rise to problems, some well known, others less so. On the number to be so designated, as well as their exact extent, there has been continual disagreement, though it must be said that Duhm's original proposal has stood up rather well. The designation itself is problematic, even curious, since whatever else they are, they are certainly not songs. To describe them for the moment very roughly, the first (42:1–4) is a public proclamation establishing a designated Servant in office, while the second (49:1–6) is an address of one so installed alluding to a new assignment. The third (50:4–9) is a kind of apologia or self-vindication, similar in some respects to the psalms of individual lamentation, while the last (52:13–53:12) is composed of two elements: a public vindication by Yahweh and a reflection on the life and mission of the one vindicated spoken by a third party, presumably a disciple. We therefore have Yahweh as speaker in the first and fourth (he is quoted in the second), the Servant himself in the second and third, and a third party (disciple) in the third and fourth.

On the assumption that the determination of speaker is an important aspect of genre study, we should perhaps look beyond the four passages

---

35. Isa 44:26, 28; 45:13; 49:16, 19; 51:3; 52:9; 54:3; 60:10; 61:4; 63:18–19; 64:10–11.

36. *Inclusio* is a common stylistic device for closing a book or pericope by recalling its opening, e.g., the Isaiah scroll ends with a reference to 'those who rebel against me' (*pōšĕᶜîm bî*, 66:24) recalling *pāšĕᶜû bî* of 1:2. 40–48 begins and ends with the theme of repatriation (40:1–5; 48:20–22) though the matter is complicated by the repetition of 48:22 at 57:21.

canonized by the critics at one or two others in the book in ⟦13⟧ which a prophetic individual speaks autobiographically, i.e., in his own name. The first occurs at the beginning of Second Isaiah (40:6–8) where such an individual receives a commission to proclaim a message, and it occurs in a passage often taken to be the prophetic call of Second Isaiah.[37] Somewhat later there occurs what appears to be a detached fragment of a first person prophetic utterance about commissioning and endowment with the Spirit: "and now Yahweh God has sent me, and his spirit . . ." (48:16b).[38] Finally, in Third Isaiah (61:1–4), we hear an individual endowed with the spirit proclaiming a mission of bringing the good news of redemption to his oppressed people. If these texts cannot necessarily be referred to the same person, the same holds, and is generally acknowledged, for the "Servant Songs" also. Throughout Isaiah 40–66, therefore, and not only in the "Servant Songs," there are allusions to a prophetic individual or individuals, and it would be reasonable to conclude, in the absence of positive indications to the contrary, that the material in these chapters derives from one and the same prophetic movement or party and its representatives over a considerable period of time.

The Language of Servanthood in the Exilic Period and After

It was noted a moment ago that the key term *ᶜebed* is employed in significantly different ways in the sections 40–48 and 49–55 (or 49–66), and that this observation may bear on the interpretation of Duhm's "Servant Songs." But before we can demonstrate this we must first say a word about the usage of the term in general. Leaving aside detailed statistical study, which anyone can do with the help of a concordance, it should be said that the consistent use of the word in specific and religiously significant ways is characteristic of the Deuteronomic school. In Deuteronomy itself, the Deuteronomic History, and those editorial additions to prophetic books, especially Jeremiah, which can be safely attributed to this school, a certain consistency of usage emerges. Along one line the servant of Yahweh is the prophet (e.g., Ahijah, Elijah,

37. Isa 40:1–8 describes "the experience which made Deutero-Isaiah a prophet," R. N. Whybray, *Isaiah 40–66*, London, 1975, 49. For the view that the speakers in vv. 1–5 are divine beings, members of the heavenly *curia*, see H. W. Robinson, "The Council of Yahweh," *JTS* 45, 1944, 151–57 and F. M. Cross, "The Council of Yahweh In Second Isaiah," *JNES* 12, 1952, 274–78. While this motif may well be in the background (cf. Isaiah 6), the command to proclaim the end of Israel's penal servitude more naturally demands human agents; cf. 35:3–4, also exilic, and 52:7–10 where an individual proclaimer is linked with a prophetic group ("watchmen").

38. See C. Westermann, *Isaiah 40–66*, London, 1969, 203, who speculates that it may have been a marginal gloss on 49:1–6 inserted in the text at the wrong place.

Jonah), while the prophetic succession as a whole is characterized in terms of servanthood—witness the recurring phrase "his servants the prophets."[39] Almost as frequent, however, is the epithet "servant" used of David or the Davidic representative, sometimes in connection with the dynastic code-name 'the Branch' (*şemaḥ*).[40] According to [[14]] the same school Moses is the servant *par excellence*, and the epithet can also be used of Joshua as succeeding to and sharing in the office of Moses.[41] The description of the entire people as Yahweh's servants is not, however, characteristic of this school, though it does occur.[42] It should be noted that in exilic compositions, and especially Second Isaiah, the entire people is often addressed as Jacob, servant of Yahweh.[43] That the context is generally that of exile and the hope of repatriation is entirely understandable in light of the traditions about the great ancestor's own exile in Mesopotamia, the servitude under which he suffered there, and his eventual return to the homeland.

It seems proper to conclude that, according to Deuteronomic theology, Moses was the fountainhead and pattern of charismatic office which, in the course of time, found distinct but related embodiments in prophecy and kingship.[44] It goes without saying that the understanding of both of these institutions would have been affected by the political disasters of the sixth century. One result, of far-reaching importance for political theory, was the redefinition of office in terms of instrumentality and service. It is therefore hardly surprising that—to return to our point of departure—the language of servanthood occurs so frequently in the literature of the exilic and restoration periods.[45]

Servanthood in Second Isaiah

It is against this background that we are to try to make sense of the usage in Second and Third Isaiah. There is no need to expatiate on the notorious difficulties of interpretation which led as great a scholar as Samuel Rolles Driver to abandon his commentary on this part of the book. The

---

39. Individual prophets: 1 Kgs 15:29; 2 Kgs 9:36; 10:10; 14:25; prophets in general: 2 Kgs 9:7; 17:13, 23; 21:10; 24:2; Jer 7:25; 25:6; 26:5; 29:19; 35:15; 44:4; Amos 3:7; also Ezek 38:17; Dan 9:6, 10; Zech 1:6; Ezra 9:11.

40. 2 Sam 3:18; 1 Kgs 8:24–26; 2 Kgs 19:34 (= Isa 37:35); Jer 33:21–22, 26; Ezek 34:23–24; 37:24–25; Zech 3:8.

41. Moses: Deut 34:5; Josh 1:2; 9:24; Mal 3:22, etc.; Joshua: Josh 24:29; Judg 2:8.

42. Deut 32:35, 43; 1 Kgs 8:23; cf. Ps 136:22.

43. Jer 30:10 = 46:27–28; Ezek 28:25; 37:25; Isa 41:8; 44:1–2, 21; 45:4; 48:20.

44. A theme developed by K. Baltzer, *Die Biographie der Propheten*, Neukirchen-Vluyn, 1975.

45. Thus, in Isaiah 1–39 ᶜ*ebed* [['servant']] occurs in religiously significant ways only twice (20:3; 22:20; 37:35 derives from 2 Kings 19–34), compared with 32 times in 40–66.

identification of the Servant in chapters 52–53 was a matter for speculation at least as early as the first century of the era (cf. Acts 8:34). The
earliest stage of interpretation is, in fact, incorporated in the Servant
passages themselves, creating what is surely not the least of the problems
confronting the modern reader. By proceeding with caution we may,
nonetheless, hope that some small progress is possible.[46]

To begin with Isaiah 40–48, it was suggested earlier that this section
has for its major theme the new order to be established by Cyrus and its
effect on the diaspora communities. In almost every instance where the
context allows a decision, ᶜebed here alludes to this people which bears
the name Israel/Jacob.[47] The first of Duhm's [[15]] "songs," the only one
in this section (42:1–4), has also been taken to have the same referent,
though there are others who have found the language of commissioning
too specific for this to be likely. As it stands, it reads like the public designation of one who has been endowed with authority—through the
spirit—to administer justice and bring the nations under his jurisdiction, but without the brutality so often associated with imperial rule. The
immediate context, and the theme which runs throughout the section,
would suggest that the agent of this new international order is Cyrus, a
view which, though not without its difficulties, is certainly possible.[48] It is
also possible, however, that the passage was read differently according to
the changing political situation; that it was, in other words, subject to an
ongoing reinterpretation. It may therefore have been taken to refer at
some point to Jehoiachin or one of his sons, alluded to but unfortunately not named in the Weidner tablets.[49] If we knew more about political events leading up to and following the conquest of Babylon in
539 B.C.E. we might be in a better position to decode these unspecific
allusions. In the absence of such information we can do no more than
speculate.

46. No attempt will be made to present in detail and document alternative explana-
tions. The full range may be studied with the help of C. R. North, *The Suffering Servant in
Second Isaiah*, Oxford, 1956² and H. H. Rowley, *The Servant of the Lord and Other Essays on the
Old Testament*, Oxford, 1965², 1–93.

47. I.e., 41:8–9; 43:10; 44:1–2, 21; 45:4; 48:20; probably also 42:19, alluding to blind
and deaf servant, in view of 43:8–10 where the people as a whole are afflicted with the same
disabilities.

48. The most serious difficulty is with the endowment with the spirit. That he is addressed as servant is not problematic since even Nebuchadrezzar is accorded this status (Jer
25:9; 27:6; 43:10), and elsewhere Cyrus is Yahweh's shepherd (44:28) and even anointed
(*māšîaḥ*, 45:1).

49. *ANET*, 308. The case for the Davidic scion is strengthened by a comparison with Isa
11:1–9 where the Davidic king is endowed with the spirit, entrusted with the task of bringing justice to nations, and putting an end to war and violence; cf. Jer 33:15 and the only reference to the Davidic king in Isaiah 40–66, namely, 55:3–4.

The situation is different with the remaining "songs," all of which occur in the following section (49–55). We now hear no more of Cyrus, the anticipated collapse of Babylonian rule and satire directed at the Babylonian imperial cults. There is little apparent order in this section. It opens with an address to the nations by one designated Servant of Yahweh who is predestined from the womb to bring together the dispersed house of Israel. Though the mission appears to have failed, the speaker is convinced that God will vindicate him, and even feels called to the further task of bringing salvation to the nations (49:1–6). In contrast to the first "song," therefore, the primary mission is to Israel, and only after the at least partial failure of that mission does the Servant look towards the nations. Though much of what is said of the Servant could apply to Israel in general—and he is in fact addressed as Israel in the words of commissioning (49:3)—the task is to be carried out on behalf of Israel (vv. 5–6), implying that the prophet must be speaking in his own name, or at least in the name of an entity within Israel to which he belongs and which he represents.[50]

A little further on we again hear an individual Servant of Yahweh speaking in his own name (50:4–9). While he is only identified as such in the editorial comment which follows (vv. 10–11), the [[16]] allusion to a mission which involves speaking, to prophetic inspiration, to opposition and ultimate vindication, justifies the conclusion that this is the same person as in the previous passage. For our present purpose the comment in vv. 10–11 is particularly significant. It consists in a violent attack on the speaker's contemporaries, none of whom fears God or heeds the Servant. They choose instead to follow their own lights down a path which will lead them to perdition. There can be no doubt that we are hearing the voice of a disciple, and that he is speaking out of a situation of conflict occasioned by the anonymous prophet and his following. On the situation envisaged by the prophetic address and its commentary we can only speculate. Allusion to punishment in the former and walking in darkness in the latter may suggest that the prophet's activities had come to the attention of the authorities, that he was in prison and waiting sentence, and that his misfortunes were being widely interpreted in the Jewish communities as a sign of the divine disfavour.[51]

---

50. "Israel" in v. 3 is perhaps best understood as an example of "serial editing" (cf. 42:1 LXX which identifies the Servant with Jacob/Israel). It anticipates the standard Jewish interpretation of these passages.

51. Cf. the two earlier prophets, Ahab and Zedekiah, whose execution by the Babylonians led to subsequent accusations of immorality and to their name being used as a curse among the Jewish communities (Jer 29:21–23).

It may be in order at this point to ask whether there are not other allusions here and there in the Isaiah scroll to the fate of this prophetic leader. At one point we hear an assurance that "he who is bowed down shall speedily be released" (51:14), an entirely possible allusion to imprisonment. In the first part of the scroll there is the mysterious reference to a teacher long hidden who will be seen again by his followers and whose words will keep them on the right path (30:20–21).[52] And—to anticipate the fourth "song"—we may note the allusion to the *ṣaddîq* [['righteous man']] whose death has gone unlamented which, since it is coupled with a reference to the devout (*ʾanšê-ḥesed*) in the plural, is probably not to be understood collectively (57:1).[53] None of these, needless to say, can with certainty be referred to a prophetic leader, but the possibility cannot be discounted.

The fourth and last of the Servant Songs appears to have been spliced into a long apostrophe to Zion, a lyric celebration of the coming redemption and the establishment of God's kingdom in the devastated city (52:1–2, 7–12; 54:1–17). It is noteworthy that the future consummation is described in the last verse of the apostrophe (54:17) as the heritage of Yahweh's servants. While there is no connotation of sect or party here, it may well have been read by the disciples of the martyred prophet as referring to themselves, and thus have suggested the insertion of the passage dealing with *his* fate and ultimate justification. Since there is no other obvious connection between the fourth "Servant Song" and its immediate [[17]] context, this is a possibility which merits consideration.

Since a verse by verse interpretation is out of the question, all that will be offered is a reading of the text as it fits into the argument of the paper as a whole. It was noted earlier that there are two speakers: Yahweh at the beginning and end (52:13–15; 53:11b–12);[54] a disciple of the Servant in the middle (53:1–11a). The divine address promises ultimate vindication of the Servant's career and mission. His eventual success, his exaltation, the saving effect of his mission on the Jewish community, will be manifest before nations and kings. Reckoned by them a reprobate— a point hinted at in the previous "song"—he took their sins, and the consequences of their sins, upon himself and thus turned away the divine anger.[55] It is not yet clear—in the divine address—how this vindication is to be effected. We are simply told that the Servant will be successful, he

---

52. The post-exilic origin of this passage has been widely recognized since Bernhard Duhm, *Das Buch Jesaja*, 221–25. In view of the final exhortation and the context in general it seems highly unlikely that the teacher (*môreh*) refers to God.

53. Cf. the Servant as *ṣaddîq* in Isa 53:11.

54. Yahweh is certainly the speaker in 11b, but it is uncertain to whom 11a is to be attributed.

55. 52:14 may have originally followed 53:2, as has often been suggested.

will be exalted, he will see light. It is also not yet certain whether this passage from *kenōsis* to *plērōsis*, from degradation to exaltation, is to take place during his lifetime or posthumously.[56]

The central part of the text is spoken by a third party, one who has come to see the significance of the Servant's mission and who must therefore be considered a convert to discipleship. Previously he had been one of the many who had interpreted the Servant's misfortunes as divine punishment; now he has come to see their true meaning (53:4–6). The intensity of the language at this point, which has given this passage an appeal unparalleled in the Hebrew Bible, arises directly out of the experience of conversion. While both the state of the text and the obscurity of the language preclude certainty, the most natural inference is that he arrived at this conviction after the death of the Servant. He speaks of him led like a lamb to the slaughter, being taken away, cut off from the land of the living, smitten to death, having his grave with those of the wicked. One or other of these expressions, taken by itself, might be patient of a different explanation. Cumulatively, however, they point as clearly as could be expected to violent death.[57] If this is so, the statement that he will see descendants and prolong his days would indicate one of two things. Either he was believed to have been miraculously restored to life or, more probably, his work and mission would be continued through those disciples who, like the speaker, had come to believe in him and were called to perpetuate his teaching.

The Servant and the Servants

[[18]] Isaiah 49–55, then, testifies to the career of an anonymous[58] prophetic figure who, far from being discouraged at the relative failure of the mission to his own people, felt himself called to an even more demanding one to the nations. If the general context of Second and Third Isaiah is a reliable guide, it is clear that his commission was understood to be in function of the imminent coming of God's kingdom. The two passages containing commentary and reflection from the immediate circle of his disciples (50:10–11; 53:1–11a) not only indicate that the Servant

---

56. "He poured out his soul (life) to death" (53:12) might be interpreted to mean that he risked his life, came close to dying.

57. R. N. Whybray, *Thanksgiving for a Liberated Prophet*, Sheffield, 1978, 92–106, is the most recent and determined attempt to prove that the Servant was alive at the time of writing.

58. It has sometimes been suggested that *mĕšullām* [['dedicated one']] (Isa 42:19) could be a proper name (Meshullam), as at 2 Kgs 22:3 and 1 Chr 3:19; see C. R. North, *The Suffering Servant*, 89–90.

had a following which continued in existence after his death, and which was the focus of dispute and conflict in the community; they also provide the vital link between the Servant and those other Servants discussed earlier in this paper.

The possibility of making this connection rests on the assumption that there is a certain continuity in the editorial history of Isaiah 40–46. This means that, while we are clearly not in a position to reconstruct that history in detail, it did not reach its present form by a process of haphazard accumulation of material from quite different sources. This seems to be the more reasonable assumption, and it is supported by the basic continuity of teaching and theological *Tendenz* [['inclination']] in these chapters. The conclusion would then suggest itself that the literary growth of Isaiah 40–46 is related in important ways to the emergence and consolidation of a prophetic-eschatological group within post-exilic Judaism which perpetuated the memory and teaching of its "founder," a martyred prophet of the exilic age.

The comment from the circle of this prophet's disciples in Isa 50:10–11 points in the same direction by describing a situation similar to the one we have reconstructed on the basis of Third Isaiah and related texts. There are, on the one hand, those who fear Yahweh (cf. Mal 3:16) and obey the prophetic word (cf. Isa 65:12; 66:4–5), and there is the prophet's own veneration for the name of Yahweh (cf. Isa 66:5; Mal 3:16, 20). The opponents are those who walk by their own lights or, in other words, go their own way (cf. Isa 66:3) and who are destined for perdition (cf. Isa 65:12, 14; 66:24; Mal 3:21). If, moreover, the titles (Servant, Servants) are the same, it is because the disciples embody the form and exemplify the consequences of the prophetic founder's ministry.

On the later history of this prophetic movement, if indeed it continued in existence beyond the time of Ezra and of Nehemiah, we [[19]] know nothing. The features which it has in common with the "hasidic" group in which the visions of Daniel circulated, alluded to briefly in the paper, suggest but of course cannot prove that there were lines of continuity. It has always been recognized that early Christian reflection on the Isaian Servant texts has contributed significantly to the presentation of the mission and death of Jesus in the gospels and elsewhere. A closer study of the movement generated by the Servant's career may serve not only to fill out some details,[59] but to suggest that the early Christian

59. E.g., persecution "for my name's sake," Isa 66:5; cf. Matt 10:18, 22; the theme of eschatological reversal, Isa 65:13–14, cf. Matt 25:31–46; Luke 6:20–26; the messianic banquet, Isa 65:13, cf. Matt 22:1–14; the names of the elect written in God's directory, Mal 3:16–18, cf.

movement, in the way it understood itself charged,[60] and the prospects which lay ahead of it, was following a pattern already at hand in the historical experience of Second Temple Judaism.

Luke 10:20; perhaps 'the Way' (*hodos*) used of the Christian movement, Acts 9:2; 19:9, 22–23; 24:14, cf. Isa 30:21 and frequently in Isaiah 40–66.

60. The sequence: mission to Israel, relative failure, mission to the Gentiles as a preparation for the parousia not only in the Servant passages but throughout Second and Third Isaiah (e.g., 66:18–21 for a Gentile mission leading to the parousia).

Part 5

The Developing Tradition

Introduction

For much of the modern period scholarly study of prophetic texts has proceeded on the basis that there is a core of original prophetic utterance that can be recovered by the application of appropriate critical methods, and that there are layers of secondary material which have to be identified and removed for the pristine prophecy to be heard to proper effect. But the prophetic books are not always approached in this stratigraphic fashion nowadays, and greater emphasis is laid upon the redactional shaping by which the text is brought more or less to its final form (Zimmerli, pp. 419–42 below). The idea of specifically Deuteronomistic editing of prophetic texts now has many advocates (Williamson, pp. 453–77 below; Seitz 1989). In academic discussion, of course, the "Deuteronomists" have long been associated with the composition of the book of Jeremiah, but now other prophets such as Isaiah, Amos and Zechariah are involved. The complex unity represented by the "Twelve Prophets" has also been studied from a redactional point of view in some recent writing. The arrangement of the books, it is argued, gives evidence of redactional shaping (House 1990), and this may have begun already before the individual books had achieved anything like their final form (Nogalski 1993).

The development of original themes and the reshaping of texts to make up the complex unity of a prophetic book are much more of a talking-point in the case of Isaiah, the subject of a large number of recent studies concerned with overarching themes and other kinds of evidence of a close linkage between the two main sections of the book (Ackroyd, pp. 478–94 below; Clements 1982, 1985; Williamson 1994, etc.). This kind of approach seeks to show how, for example, original Isaianic texts relating to the Levantine depredations of the Assyrians in the eighth century could speak to the circumstances of the Babylonian destruction in Judah in the sixth century (Clements 1980). The relationship between chaps. 1–39 and 40–55(66) has been explained in a variety of ways. Most often it is assumed that "Deutero-Isaiah" was composed independently of the earlier chapters, but the case for the formative influence of chaps. 1–39 (substantially) on the composition of "Deutero-Isaiah" has recently been argued (Williamson 1994). More conventional redactional approaches to the text of Isaiah are ably represented by Kaiser (pp. 495–512 below).

It has also been claimed that certain Old Testament and Apocryphal books bear the marks of editing by representatives of the wisdom tradition, as is suggested, for example, by the last verse of the book of Hosea, which indicates a particular (wisdom) perspective from which the words of the prophet should be read (Sheppard 1980; cf. Macintosh 1995). A further dimension is added to the redactional issue when the shaping of texts is seen as the result of a canonizing process which seeks not only to influence reader-perspective on the literature but also to establish the authority of the canonical text over its future readers (hearers) within the "community of faith" (Childs, pp. 513–22 below). While the abstractions associated with the concept of "canonical process" occasion much difficulty, the issues which Childs in particular has brought to the forefront of theological discussion are unavoidable for anyone who regards the Old (or New) Testament as "Scripture."

Additional Reading

Section (i).   Prophetic Redaction

Clements, R. E.
   1993   Jeremiah 1–25 and the Deuteronomistic History. Pp. 93–113 in *Understanding Poets and Prophets* (G. W. Anderson Festschrift), edited by A. G. Auld. Journal for the Study of the Old Testament Supplement Series 152. Sheffield: JSOT Press.
Collins, T.
   1993   *The Mantle of Elijah: The Redaction Criticism of the Prophetical Books.* The Biblical Seminar 20. Sheffield: JSOT Press.
House, P. R.
   1990   *The Unity of the Twelve.* Journal for the Study of the Old Testament Supplement Series 77. Sheffield: JSOT Press.
Nogalski, J.
   1993   *Literary Precursors to the Book of the Twelve.* Beihefte zur Zeitschrift für die Alttestamentliche Wissenschaft 217. Berlin: de Gruyter.
   1993   *Redactional Processes in the Book of the Twelve.* Beihefte zur Zeitschrift für die Alttestamentliche Wissenschaft 218. Berlin: de Gruyter.
Person, R. F.
   1993   *Second Zechariah and the Deuteronomic School.* Journal for the Study of the Old Testament Supplement Series 167. Sheffield: JSOT Press.

Schmidt, W. H.
    1984   Pp. 173–80 in *Old Testament Introduction*. London: SCM / New York: Crossroad. (English translation of pp. 174–81 in *Einführung in das Alte Testament*. 2d edition Berlin: de Gruyter, 1982.)
Seitz, C. R.
    1989   The Prophet Moses and the Canonical Shape of Jeremiah. *Zeitschrift für die Alttestamentliche Wissenschaft* 101: 3–27.
Tollington, J. E.
    1993   *Tradition and Innovation in Haggai and Zechariah 1–8*. Journal for the Study of the Old Testament Supplement Series 150. Sheffield: JSOT Press.

Section (ii). Isaiah Studies

Beuken, W. A. M.
    1991   Isaiah Chapters LXV–LXVI: Trito-Isaiah and the Closure of the Book of Isaiah. Pp. 204–21 in *Congress Volume: Leuven 1989*, edited by J. A. Emerton. Vetus Testamentum Supplements 43. Leiden: Brill.
Carr, D.
    1993   Reaching for Unity in Isaiah. *Journal for the Study of the Old Testament* 57: 61–80.
Clements, R. E.
    1980   The Prophecies of Isaiah and the Fall of Jerusalem in 587 B.C. *Vetus Testamentum* 30: 421–36.
    1982   The Unity of the Book of Isaiah. *Interpretation* 36: 117–29.
    1985   Beyond Tradition-History: Deutero-Isaianic Development of First Isaiah's Themes. *Journal for the Study of the Old Testament* 31: 95–113.
Clifford, R. J.
    1993   The Unity of the Book of Isaiah and Its Cosmogonic Language. *Catholic Biblical Quarterly* 55: 1–17.
Davies, G. I.
    1989   The Destiny of the Nations in the Book of Isaiah. Pp. 93–120 in *The Book of Isaiah / Le Livre d'Isaïe. Les Oracles et Leurs Relectures: Unité et Complexité de l'Ouvrage*, edited by J. Vermeylen. Bibliotheca ephemeridum theologicarum lovaniensium 81. Louvain: Louvain University Press.
Macintosh, A. A.
    1980   *Isaiah XXI: A Palimpsest*. Cambridge: Cambridge University Press.
Sweeney, M. A.
    1988   *Isaiah 1–4 and the Post-exilic Understanding of the Isaianic Tradition*. Beihefte zur Zeitschrift für die Alttestamentliche Wissenschaft 171. Berlin: de Gruyter.
    1993   The Book of Isaiah in Recent Research. *Currents in Research* 1: 141–62.
Tomasino, A. J.
    1993   Isaiah 1.1–2.4 and 63–66, and the Composition of the Isaianic Corpus. *Journal for the Study of the Old Testament* 57: 81–98.

Vermeylen, J.
   1989   L'unité du Livre d'Isaïe. Pp. 11–53 in *The Book of Isaiah / Le Livre
            d'Isaïe. Les Oracles et Leurs Relectures: Unité et Complexité de l'Ouvrage,*
            edited by J. Vermeylen. Bibliotheca ephemeridum theologicarum
            lovaniensium 81. Louvain: Louvain University Press.
Williamson, H. G. M.
   1994   *The Book Called Isaiah: Deutero-Isaiah's Role in Composition and Redac-
            tion.* Oxford: Clarendon.

Section (iii).   The Prophets and the Canon

Macintosh, A. A.
   1995   Hosea and the Wisdom Tradition: Dependence and Independence.
            Pp. 124–32 in *Wisdom in Ancient Israel* (J. A. Emerton Festschrift),
            edited by J. Day, R. P. Gordon, and H. G. M. Williamson. Cambridge:
            Cambridge University Press.
Sheppard, G. T.
   1980   Pp. 129–36 in *Wisdom as a Hermeneutical Construct: A Study in the Sapi-
            entializing of the Old Testament.* Beihefte zur Zeitschrift für die Alttesta-
            mentliche Wissenschaft 151. Berlin: de Gruyter.

From Prophetic Word to Prophetic Book

WALTHER ZIMMERLI

[[481]] Amos has conspired against you in the midst of the house of Israel; the land is not able to bear all his words. For thus speaks Amos: "Jeroboam will die by the sword, and Israel must go into exile away from its own land" (Amos 7:10–11).

This, according to Amos, was the high priest's report at the national sanctuary of Bethel to King Jeroboam II of Israel. The report was followed by Amos's immediate expulsion from the land at the priest's own initiative. We read in Jer 26:8–9 that priests and prophets seized Jeremiah at the temple in Jerusalem after one of his speeches, saying:

You are doomed to die! Why did you prophesy in the name of Yahweh that this temple will be like Shiloh [an earlier sanctuary in Northern Israel that lay in ruins in the days of Jeremiah] and the city will be desolate and without inhabitants?

Translated and reprinted with permission from "Vom Prophetenwort zum Prophetenbuch," *Theologische Literaturzeitung* 104 (1979) cols. 481–96. Translation by Andreas Köstenberger.

This paper was originally read as a lecture on November 8, 1978, as part of the "Theological Days" of the "Theology Section" of the Karl Marx University in Leipzig, with the overall theme: "Prophecy: Historical and Present Reality." For the lively discussion about "oral tradition" especially during the decades between 1930 and 1950, see the introduction and critique by A. H. J. Gunneweg, *Mündliche und schriftliche Tradition der vorexilischen Prophetenbücher als Problem der neueren Prophetenforschung* (FRLANT 73; 1959).

As both of these passages from the Old Testament prophetic books demonstrate—and more examples could easily be given—a prophetic word entails a concrete reference to history. Prophecy is critically spoken into a particular context and, in turn, generates a specific response at a given time in history.

By the same token, the prophetic commission is always subordinate to the sovereignty of God, who sends when and where he desires and who always remains lord over the content of the prophetic message. It is evident from Isaiah's words that this prophetic commission might be configured very differently if the historical circumstances were different. Indeed, the wording may actually appear to be almost the opposite of what had been said earlier.[1] Thus the commission cannot simply be used word for word in an attempt to apply it to a new historical situation.

Jeremiah 28 shows how the prophet Hananiah reuses a word of the prophet Isaiah, who had prophesied more than 100 years earlier. Faithful to his predecessor, Hananiah uses Isaiah's message in the Jerusalem Temple during the final decade prior to Jerusalem's destruction. He confronts the prophet Jeremiah, who was running around with a yoke on his back, proclaiming,

> You should bear the yoke of Nebuchadnezzar's foreign rule according to the will of God.

In an impressive symbolic gesture, Hananiah tears the yoke from his neck, breaks it, and announces,

> This is what Yahweh says, "Thus I will remove the yoke of Nebuchadnezzar, the king of Babylon, from the neck of all nations and break it" (v. 11).

This, of course, is very similar to Isa 9:3, which reads,

> As on the day of Midian, I will shatter the yoke that burdens them, and the bar across their shoulders, [[482]] and the rod of their oppressors.

And Isa 14:25:

---

1. Compare, for instance, the harshness of the announcement of judgment in the early days of the prophet, typified by Isaiah 6, with the exhortation to rest and confidence that is anchored in the apodictic promise of the crisis of 733: "It shall not happen, and it shall not come to pass" (7:7). Likewise, the two children's names in 7:3 and 8:3 seem to be accentuated entirely differently in different situations.

His yoke will be taken from them, and his burden from their shoulders.

In response, however, Jeremiah confronts what appears to be firmly grounded in the prophetic word by saying:

Listen, Hananiah, Yahweh has not sent you, and you have given false confidence to this people. Therefore Yahweh declares, "Behold, I am sending (sweeping) you away from this country. You will die this very year."

This is followed by the laconic statement,

And the prophet Hananiah died in the seventh month of that year (vv. 15–17).

What all of this shows is that a prophetic word is always a message that is highly relevant to a given historical context, a message that is invariably characterized by the freedom of God. It can turn into a treacherous lie, if someone lifts it out of its context by even the most pious biblicism in an attempt to perpetuate the word merely by quoting it without sharpening his ear to hear God's will anew for his own time.

But now we have books in our Bible that do not merely tell us what happened to the prophets in ages past. The books of the so-called classical prophets of the eighth through the sixth centuries are for the most part collections of the prophets' words that were simply recorded without comment and transmitted in written form. What benefit can we derive from this word that was written down and transmitted for later times? Should not the fate of a Hananiah raise suspicion in us—indeed, be a warning for us not to take up these words in a different time? (It should, of course, be self-evident that our present is in many respects different from the times of the prophets in ancient Israel and Judah.) What, we continue to ask, occasioned the writing down of these words, words that clearly had relevance for a particular point in time? Are they not robbed of their actual life by having been written down? Does the recorded prophetic message not take on an archival character, that is, material that is of interest to the historian but irrelevant for the life of the later community?

All of these questions introduce the topic of the following discussion. [[483]] What can be said regarding the progression from the oral, situation-bound prophetic word to the written message, which was lifted out of its original context and has apparently become timeless? Moreover, what can be said regarding the relevance of the written prophetic word for the community that has transmitted this word in its holy Scriptures and doubtless will continue to pass it on in the future?

I

Here, then, is the first question: Can we learn something regarding the recording of the prophetic word from the wording of the writings of classical prophecy of the eighth to the sixth centuries? In the following discussion, we will focus on the prophecies that were collected in the actual prophetic books of the Old Testament. Our answer will indeed be in the affirmative. It will be shown that there is clear evidence in the prophets' own contemporary proclamation.

Isa 8:1–2 records a peculiar event. The prophet reports,

> And Yahweh told me, "Take a large tablet and write on it with a human pen: Maher-shalal-hash-baz" [this has been translated as 'rob soon, hasten spoils']. And I took two trustworthy witnesses, Uriah the priest and Zechariah the son of Jeberechiah.

The particular issue of what is meant by "human pen"—that is, whether one should read, with Wildberger[2] (following Gressmann), with a slight change of vocalization, 'with (a) hard (pen)' or 'with a pen of destruction'—does not need to be discussed further at this point. Morenz[3] has plausibly suggested that this curious expression that Isaiah was told to write down originated in the language of Egyptian soldiers, referring to the spoils won in a quick victory. I consider it probable that this emphatic expression, posted publicly with the aid of witnesses, originally was intended to be a message of calamity directed toward Judah by the prophet Isaiah. However, when the text continues to read,

> Then I approached the prophetess, and she became pregnant and gave birth to a son. And Yahweh said to me, "Give him the name Maher-shalal-hash-baz; for before the boy will be able to say 'father' or 'mother,'[4] the wealth of Damascus and the spoils from Samaria will be carried before the king of Assyria,"

a son of Isaiah is given a symbolic name in a second act that was apparently accomplished some time after the first, and this second act is, in changed circumstances, turned polemically against both of the enemies of Judah who are approaching Jerusalem in the Syro-Ephraimite War. We may note here that the prophet himself is urged by Yahweh to write down a terse, initially mysterious, but unmistakably calamitous message

---

2. BKAT 10/1.312 note b on Isa 8:1.

3. S. Morenz, "Eilebeute," *ThLZ* 74 (1949) columns 697–99 (= *Religion und Geschichte des alten Ägypten: Gesammelte Aufsätze* [ed. E. Blumenthal and S. Herrmann; 1975] 395–400).

4. These terms refer to the first babbling words: "Papa, Mama."

that has relevance for anyone who reads the words written on the tablet. The use of witnesses, one of whom is also named as a high priest of the Jerusalem Temple in 2 Kgs 16:10–16, underscores the importance of this tersely phrased, written pronouncement.

The account in Isaiah 8 finds a parallel in Hab 2:1–4, where a prophet of the second half of the seventh century reports,

> I will stand at my watchpost and station myself on the rampart in order to keep watch and to see what he will tell me and what answer "he" will give to my complaint [previously, in Habakkuk 1, there had been a complaint by the prophet regarding the misery of his people]. Then Yahweh answered and said, "Write down the vision and engrave it on tablets in order that whoever reads it can act accordingly. For there is still a limit set for the vision (that is, revelation), but its time has come, and it does not lie. If it tarries, wait for it, for it will surely come and not delay."

When this is followed by the statement,

> Behold, the unrighteous person languishes [thus the Zürcher Bibel (commentary); the text has not been determined with certainty], but the righteous person will live by his faithfulness,

what is at issue once again is the announcement of a crisis in which only that person can be saved who remains faithful to God. Standing on the rampart and watching for the divine revelation, which is called a "vision," may reveal [[484]] something of a stereotyped prophetic office. We may perceive that, as in Isaiah, the revealed word is recorded and publicly posted, so that everyone is able to read it.[5] The people are not merely to hear the prophets' message from God with their ears, but to read it with their own eyes. In both cases, we find a divine message that is to be proclaimed into a particular situation, a message that is valid even if its fulfillment is delayed, as appears to be the case in the present circumstance. God wants people to know his word, in any event, and ensures that the message is written down for the purpose of unmistakable proclamation.

In another place in Isaiah, one finds another motif regarding the writing down of the prophetic message. Isa 8:16 provides a possible example of this. We find here the final pronouncement of a series of

---

5. We seem to have encountered here an almost institutionalized form of questioning Yahweh and of the announcement of prophetic information, which should then also have a retrospective effect on the evaluation of the position of Isaiah.

statements made by Isaiah in the context of the Syro-Ephraimite War. In a surprising development, the prophet is authorized at this point by his God to promise to Judah, to whom he had previously announced judgment, deliverance from the threat represented by a coalition of the two kings of Aram and Northern Israel. This promise has only one condition, which is that Israel's king must be prepared to rely on Yahweh's promise:

> If you do not believe, you will not remain (7:9).

The king, however, is not ready to do this. The assistance of the Assyrian king, who had been summoned to help, seems more reliable to him. Thus Isaiah views the Assyrians as the more dangerous enemy of his people, and the danger is imminent. The prophet himself feels condemned to silence and waiting. His final message in these days is:

> I will bind up the testimony and "seal" the instruction among my disciples; I will wait for Yahweh, who hides his face from the house of Jacob, and I will hope in him.

Duhm, Smend, and others find in this verse a hint regarding the writing down of the prophetic words from this time and their committal to the prophet's circle of disciples. But it is not impossible that this is merely a symbolic reference to the fact that Isaiah no longer appeared or spoke but felt compelled to remain silent. However the message may have been preserved by his disciples, it remains a living indictment of a disobedient people.

The subject of Isa 30:8ff., on the other hand, is clearly the writing down of a message from the prophet's later period. Yahweh says to the prophet,

> Go in now, write it on a tablet before them and inscribe it in a book, so that it may forever be a testimony regarding the future. For they are an obstinate people, treacherous sons, sons who do not want to hear the instruction of Yahweh. They say to the seers, "Do not see [visions]. Do not see what is straight [i.e., the truth]. Speak of pleasant things, see deception, leave the way, stray from the path, remain silent regarding the Holy One of Israel."

Once again, the topic of discussion is the writing down of a prophetic word. Opinions differ regarding the precise content of what is to be written down.[6] But one thing is clear, namely, that we are dealing with

---

6. See, for instance, O. Kaiser (ATD 18; 1973) 234 on 30:8.

something other than a person's memoirs. When the prophet is instructed to 'go in', that is, probably to retreat from public proclamation and to write down his message, the purpose is different from the purpose in Isaiah 8 and Habakkuk 2. The prophet is to be a concealed accuser and witness of the people's guilt for "the latter day." When calamity finally strikes, the nation will not be able to resort to the excuse, "We never heard of it." In the form of written word, God will be present even in the later hour of judgment.

At this point one may ask whether or not this may also have been the motive for recording the prophetic word in other instances. Amos was banished from the Northern Kingdom. People did not want to listen to his message any longer. Should one perhaps interpret the recording of, say, the cycle of visions in Amos 7–9 in this way, which, despite expansions, [[485]] can still be recognized? There the prophet speaks in the first person, so that it is reasonable to assume that he was personally responsible for the writing down of his message. It may be assumed that Amos obeyed the command to leave the country. In the hour of calamity, however, the word recorded by him will accuse the people. No one will be able to say at that time that Yahweh had not spoken. Yahweh himself will stand before the nation as its accuser by his written prophetic word. The disaster is not a result of destiny but of guilt. God has spoken actively in history.

The passage regarding the Syro-Ephraimite War in Isaiah 7–8, which probably has as its basis the prophet's own records, is preceded by Isaiah 6, another section that is told in the first person. Since the unit of Isaiah 6:1–9:6[7] clearly interrupts a previously existing context of so-called strophic poetry and perhaps also a collection of seven cries of woe, one should consider it to be an already-formed, coherent, subsection. The placement of the prophetic commission before the pronouncements of the year 733 thus appears to conform to the prophet's own preference. This, however, leads to the fact that not even the writing of the commissioning narrative in the first person should be seen as the writing of memoirs. This call narrative with its mysterious statements confirms Isaiah's realization that the failure of his proclamation and his lack of success in the offer of divine grace do not constitute an incidental mishap caused by the prophet's own incompetence. The lack of response is rather an integral component of the judgment, which was why Yahweh had sent him to "this people." It was precisely the offer of grace that hardened the nation all the more toward its God.

---

7. The problem of the expansion of the subsection beyond the "final word" of 8:16 cannot be discussed here.

Thus the prophet reports how he was already told the following message at the hour of his call by Yahweh, the one whom he had seen in the temple and who had sent him thence to his people as his messenger:

> Go and tell this people: "Keep listening and do not understand, and keep seeing and do not perceive! Harden the heart of this people and stop their ears, blind their eyes that they will neither see with their eyes nor hear with their ears nor comprehend with their hearts and turn and be healed" (Isa 6:9–10).

This is the message given to the prophet by Yahweh on the occasion of his call. As Isaiah himself experiences his own impurity and cries out when entering the light of the Holy One at the hour of his call in the temple,

> Woe is me! I am lost,[8] for I am a man of unclean lips and live among a people of unclean lips, for my eyes have seen the king, Yahweh of hosts (6:5),

it is precisely the message regarding God's gracious suspension of judgment in the year 733 that reveals the people's profound obduracy. That the latter is already revealed at the prophet's call is probably the most profound motive underlying the prophet's narration of his call. The written account does not seek to confront the reader with the prophet as an individual or with his life story but rather with God himself, before whom God's people can only be revealed in all of their faithlessness and guilt.

From here, we may turn to the other prophetic call narratives, asking whether or not similar motives led to their being recorded in writing. Amos does not give an account of his call. The information that Yahweh had taken him from his flock and had given him a prophetic commission (Amos 7:15) is part of an extraneous report that originates from the circle of his followers. The cycle of visions, however, even though one should not interpret it as a call narrative, indicates nonetheless that the severe message of Yahweh's judgment upon his people should be distinguished from the backdrop of his initial willingness to forgive, which is still perceptible in the first two visions in chap. 7. Should not the writing down of this personal experience of visions serve the intention of recording irrevocably the inexcusable condition of the nation against which Amos prophesies? Once again, this occurs by means of the written word, since the people refused to listen to the prophet's oral message.

---

8. The translation suggested by KBL (and also, for example, by Wildberger), 'Ich muß schweigen' [['I must remain silent']], hardly reflects the depth of the prophet's cry of terror.

> The lion is roaring, who is not afraid? ⟦486⟧ The Lord God is
> speaking, who can but prophesy?

This word, likewise recorded by Amos (3:8), manifests the total unavoid-
ability of the prophetic mandate, as well as the menace posed by the
Lord who approaches the people with his word.

One could make similar observations regarding the investigation of
the call narratives of Jeremiah and Ezekiel, whose records also betray,
apart from the validation of the prophetic call, the purpose of confrontation with the Lord, who approaches for the purpose of judgment. But
regarding the issue of the recording of the prophetic word, we may
instead look at the curious episode reported in Jer 51:59–64. There
we learn that Jeremiah sent his prophetic words against Babylon with
Seraiah, the quartermaster of King Zedekiah, when he accompanied the
king to Babylon in the fourth year of the latter's reign.

> Jeremiah wrote in a scroll all the disasters that would come over
> Babylon . . . and Jeremiah said to Seraiah: "When you come to
> Babylon, see that you read all these words aloud. And when you
> have finished reading this scroll aloud, tie a stone to it, throw it
> in the midst of the Euphrates, and say: 'Thus Babylon will sink
> and never recover from the calamity I am bringing upon it.'"

The written prophetic word therefore has a dual function. In the first
place, it is in the possession of the man who is going to Babylon. It can
be read there by him on location, in the country of the recipients of the
prophetic word. Second, it is the subject of a symbolic prophetic act,
that is to be enacted vicariously by the king's companion, who is sent on
his journey with the written prophetic word. The sinking of the scroll in
the Euphrates, which is accomplished by weighting it with a stone, surely
does not serve only the function of the diligent destruction of a document that is dangerous for its bearer to possess in Babylon itself. The
scroll's lowering in the Euphrates, the great river of Babylon, also represents the imminent total destruction of Babylonian power, which will
never be restored. And since symbolic prophetic acts are more than
mere graphic illustrations, since they always also exercise an influence
of their own in the form of a kind of anticipation of the coming event,
so all the power of the written prophetic word casts its shadow forward
by this act. One might be tempted to speak of a kind of magical act if it
were not that, especially in Jeremiah, the divine word that touches him
personally also reveals itself to him as a crushing force.

> "Is my word not like fire," says Yahweh, "and like the hammer that
> shatters the rock?" (23:29),

the prophet hurls toward those who think they can disguise their own dreams as God's word. Thus Jeremiah himself, by his own admission, when considering whether to remain silent, experienced God's word in his heart like burning fire shut up in his bones.

> I am weary of holding it in, and I cannot (20:9).

The episode recounted in Jeremiah 51, of course, raises a number of questions. How can Jeremiah, who in his letter to the exiles (Jeremiah 29) urges them to pray for the well-being of their captors' country and who predicts that they would live in the land of their exile for a long time, at the same time speak harsh words of warning against Babylon? Consequently, these must be words that would only take effect in the distant future seventy years on (25:11, 29:10), after the time of Nebuchadnezzar, his son, and his grandson (27:7). On the other hand, the fact that it is Seraiah (the brother of Jeremiah's closest associate, Baruch) who features as the king's companion during a trip by Zedekiah to Babylon (which is not mentioned elsewhere, though Zedekiah's motives may be easily explained) instills confidence in this report as the narration of an actual event in the prophet's life.

With the account of Jeremiah 36, we enter historically secure territory. According to this narrative, Jeremiah had already, in the fourth year of Jehoiakim, the second predecessor of Zedekiah, received the divine command [[487]] to dictate to Baruch the scribe all the words Yahweh had commanded him during the last few years. A day of repentance was held some time later in connection with the unexpected invasion by Nebuchadnezzar of the world of Syria and Palestine, which only recently had been controlled by the Egyptians. On this day, Jeremiah commissioned Baruch to read the words of the scroll in the temple. Jeremiah himself could not enter the temple; whether this was due to temporary ritual impurity or to a permanent prohibition on entering the temple is unclear. At this point, we may discern a further reason for the writing down of the prophetic word that had initially been spoken orally. We see here nothing of the intrinsic power of the written word of Jeremiah 51. Nor does the writing down serve the purpose of recording an accusation of inexcusable disobedience at the hour of imminent judgment, in the sense of Isaiah 30. The word read by Baruch to the community gathered in the temple was instead designed to shake them, just like the orally spoken prophetic word, so that the people might still be induced to return to Yahweh through a fresh hearing of Yahweh's prediction of judgment. Here as well, it is entirely clear that the divine word, which had been proclaimed at an earlier time, is designed to address the circumstances of the community directly and to confront the people with their

God. Therefore the recording of the word is not understood in terms of a historicizing documentation of earlier proclamation but as an attack on the present, this time by the mediation of a third party who holds the written prophetic word in his hands and reads it. One can see, then, that this form of transmission of the word stirs up excitement among the people, that the royal government officials themselves are touched, and that they ensure that the king himself is informed. However, the word has no effect on the king. What is more, Jehoiakim commits the blasphemy of throwing the divine word in its written form into the fire. And only the fact that both Jeremiah and Baruch hide themselves saves the prophet and the mediator who read his word from sharing the fate of the written divine word at the hand of the king.

Jeremiah 36 signals a new stage of the prophet's ministry through his word. He is no longer merely entrusted with prophetic speech in the form of direct, oral discourse, which may or may not be reasserted in concise, public, written form, but he also issues written summaries of messages that had been delivered in a variety of contexts and now can be read by a third party. This shift marks a gradual change in the prophetic ministry at the end of the seventh century in relation to the prophecy of the eighth century.[9] One should not conceive of this as an abrupt change. The transmission of words that had originally been written down for different reasons, and also the collections of the messages of the eighth-century prophets, may have been significant in this regard. But it is the end of the seventh century that illustrates the attempt of contemporary prophecy also to reach its audience by way of written proclamation. Whether the introduction of the so-called "Book of Comfort for Ephraim" in Jeremiah 30–31, where Jeremiah is commanded by Yahweh to "write all the words I have told you in a book," is indeed original with Jeremiah is doubtful in the light of the strong Deuteronomic form of the final collection.[10] What cannot be disputed, however, is the fact that Jeremiah, after Jeremiah 29, proclaimed Yahweh's command that the people accept obediently the divine judgment in a letter that was written by him, taken to Babylon by a royal delegation, and there read by a third party to the Judeans who had been deported to Babylon in the year 597.

The call narrative of the prophet Ezekiel furnishes clear proof that the prophetic word was normally understood in terms of a written word at the beginning of the sixth century. When the prophet is commissioned

9. This change of form that becomes visible in the texts has not, in my view, been adequately considered in the whole discussion regarding "oral tradition."

10. S. Böhmer, *Heimkehr und Bund: Studien zu Jeremia 30–31* (1976).

by Yahweh who calls him to eat a scroll [[488]] handed to him (2:9–3:3), it is evident that the prophet was already familiar with scrolls of this kind, inscribed with the prophetic word. When Jeremiah, in one of his confessions before Yahweh, admits, "When your words were found, I devoured (ate) them" (15:16), it should be understood metaphorically. In Ezekiel, the word written in a book becomes tangible reality that is experienced in the form of a vision.[11] Prophetic writing has become a visible entity. Did Ezekiel the priest perhaps see with his own eyes the dramatic scene in which Baruch read Jeremiah's scroll in the temple? When he more closely describes the scroll that lay before him with the words, "It was inscribed on the front and on the back, and laments, sighs, and woes were written on it," it becomes apparent that the word he is to proclaim will likewise be the word of judgment that needs to be announced harshly at that very hour, only a few years before the complete destruction of Jerusalem. This calamity will evoke nothing but "laments, sighs, and woes" in the house of Israel. But when it is determined immediately thereafter that the scroll devoured by the prophet becomes "sweet as honey," one is reminded initially of the continuation of the sentence quoted in Jeremiah's confession: "Your word became the delight and joy of my heart." While the message is harsh, the prophet delights in the very fact that God is speaking at all, even though the word uttered by God may lead the prophet himself into suffering and misery, as can be observed immediately thereafter in Jeremiah.

If we wanted to pursue these thoughts further, it would now be necessary to extablish to what extent written material can be found in the books of the prophets from Neo-Babylonian to Persian times. It would also be necessary to consider to what extent faithful records of a prophet's oral address to the people surrounding him can be found in this written version, which may even have been composed by the prophet himself. We dare not overlook the fact that the book of Ezekiel, which is consistently portrayed as a report by the prophet himself, clearly reflects a later revision, as is the case, for example, in the words by which Yahweh initially addresses the prophet himself before he commissions him to speak to the "house of Israel." Thus in 37:1–14, for example, the prophet is authorized to proclaim to the nation, which languishes and sighs in the throes of the death of political destruction, the coming awakening to new life and the return to the land in the incredible vision of the raising of the dead bones. Here the detailed narration of the visionary experiences is placed prior to the three final verses that contain the actual commission to deliver the prophetic message. The explicit

11. On this phenomenon, which appears not only here in Ezekiel, see BKAT 13.78.

message the prophet is given to proclaim is very short (vv. 12–14). In 36:16–22a, the announcement Yahweh commands Ezekiel to make to the people—that Yahweh would make a new beginning for the sake of his own name, that he would bring the nation back from exile, and that he would purify it and give it a new heart—is preceded by a recapitulation, directed personally to the prophet, of the past evil history of the desecration of the divine name among the nations. Can anyone imagine all of this as the prophet's primarily oral proclamation? The extent to which Deutero-Isaiah's message of salvation in Isaiah 40–55 contains a simple reproduction of an oral prophetic word,[12] without at least occasionally containing the reflected-upon written deposit of the prophet's word, is disputed. (Should we in this case think of a pamphlet-like transmission of the prophetic word?) And in the case of the great, systematically arranged cycle of night visions[13] of Zechariah, later expanded from seven to eight, we can barely avoid the supposition of a conscious literary composition that was probably never proclaimed orally in this form. This fact cannot conceal the notion that, in Zechariah as well, brief individual expressions are repeatedly interjected among the visions and may best be interpreted as oral proclamation using the same style.

With this we turn to the second kind of question that will be entertained in the following discussion: What can be said regarding the [[489]] process by which the prophetic word was transformed into a definitive book, a process in which the original features of the proclamation are clearly removed far from the original occasion of their utterance? That is, what can be said about the formation of the unified book and the theological implications of this?

II

With this second thought, we enter the arena of the method called "redaction criticism." This approach no longer asks regarding the *ipsissima vox* [['very voice']] of the individual prophet, that is, regarding what is "genuine" (as is often said in ambiguous language) in the individual prophetic book. Instead, it starts with the entirety of the book's text and asks what the book's redactor or redactors themselves sought to emphasize. The method first became familiar to us from the New Testament Gospels: What is the particular *kerygma* of Mark, Matthew, or Luke that is recognizable in their respective shapings of the Jesus tradition? In recent times, the prophetic books have increasingly been approached with

12. For example, E. von Waldow, *Anlaß und Hintergrund der Verkündigung des Deuterojesaja* (Ph.D. diss., Bonn, 1955).

13. Chr. Jeremias, *Die Nachtgesichte des Sacharja* (FRLANT 117; 1977).

this kind of question. Does not the book have a dignity of its own in the form in which it was received into the canon of biblical literature? Can one not discern a particular message of the book in its entirety beyond the things explained by historical criticism and beyond the things said by the prophet who gives the book its name? We may start with the book of the oldest prophet of scripture, Amos, whose work has already been analyzed frequently in this regard.[14] Without aiming at comprehensiveness, we may select three facts.

The first pertains to the observation that can be made regarding the first part of the book. The first two chapters of the book of Amos contain the so-called "Cycle of Foreign Nations." Here, in a peculiarly stereotypical style, words of judgment are assembled against a number of Israel's neighbors. Such warnings against neighboring nations may constitute an ancient prophetic practice. Prophetic discourse of this kind is found in the story of Elisha, during the period before the writing prophets. There the promise of victory for Israel implies the defeat of Israel's enemies (2 Kgs 3:18–19; 7:1–20; 13:14ff.; but cf. 8:11–13).[15] The novel element in Amos's "Cycle of Nations," however, consists in the fact that the charges against the neighboring nations develop into an initially similar, but eventually incomparably broader, word of accusation and judgment against Northern Israel, to which Amos had been sent as a prophet. Israel must not presume that it will escape Yahweh's judgment and expectantly and complacently look for Yahweh's judgment on its neighboring nations.

> You alone I have known from all the generations of the earth;
> therefore I will visit all your evil deeds upon you.

This is how the prophet expressed the same idea in a different passage (3:2). Today one can still read in the "Cycle of the Nations," immediately before the stanza concerning Israel, a stanza regarding Judah that reads:

> Thus says Yahweh: "On account of three transgressions of Judah and on account of four I will not revoke the punishment: because they despised Yahweh's instruction and did not keep his statutes, and because their lying idols, which their fathers had followed, led them astray, I will send fire to Judah, and it will devour Jerusalem's palaces" (2:4–5).

14. See, for example, H. W. Wolff, BKAT 14/2 (1969) 129–38: §5 "Die Entstehung des Buches."

15. Here also belong the words of the unnamed prophet or man of God from 1 Kgs 20:13, 28, which have the form of a "word of proof," a form especially common in Ezekiel (BKAT 13.55*–61*).

Linguistic usage and conceptual development clearly distinguish this
stanza from Amos's style and conceptual world elsewhere and place it in
the sphere of Deuteronomic speech and thought, which had spread
widely in post-Josianic times.[16]

However, the most important thing has not been said with the mere
assertion that the stanza is "inauthentic" within the framework of Amos's
ancient "Cycle of Nations." Rather, we encounter here a later Judean addition that lends the entire cycle a new direction at a later time and in a
different environment: Let no one in Judah (after the Northern Kingdom has been subdued, while Judah, for the time being, survived) point
to the Northern Kingdom, saying, "There is the sinful kingdom that has
rightly been judged." Your case, Judah, is likewise addressed by Yahweh
in all of this! This is how the Judean addition applies the older prophetic word to more recent circumstances or to [[490]] a different group
of listeners. Yahweh's word does not die when the situation that had
originally been addressed ceases to exist. A similar case is Amos 6:1,
where a reference to those living in Jerusalem is placed prior to the
word that attacks the blasphemous self-confidence of those living in luxury in Samaria: "Woe to those who feel secure in Zion." Since Amos
never attacks Jerusalem elsewhere in his own words, we should see this
as an expansion, which turns against Jerusalem the threatening word
that was once spoken by the prophet against Samaria.

Similar traces of an *interpretatio Judaica* [['Judean interpretation']],
which document how the written prophetic word receives new relevance
in changed circumstances, can be found in the book of the prophet Hosea, who also prophesied in the Northern Kingdom. Thus when Hosea
in 5:5 speaks of Israel's stumbling over its guilt and adds the statement,
"Judea also stumbles with them," the message of the prophet of the
Northern Kingdom, when read in book form in the Southern Kingdom,
turns with surprising directness against the Judean audience as well. As
the living judge, God unexpectedly steps out of his ancient word in new
immanence. This is also the case in Mic 1:5 where, in a context originally
directed against the Northern Kingdom, the question is asked, "What is
the sin of Jacob? Is it not Samaria (that is, the capital of the Northern
Kingdom)?" and the question put right beside it is, "And what is the sin
of Judah (according to the LXX)? Is it not Jerusalem?" Thus the prophetic word in the prophetic book illumines new contemporary circumstances that transcend the original prophet's historical situation.

---

16. The attempt of Rudolph (KAT 13/2; 1971) 120 to consider only 2:5bß to be a later
expansion is unconvincing.

A second observation can be made regarding the book of Amos. In three different locations, brief, entirely different hymnic pieces are inserted into the prophetic words. These pieces speak of Yahweh's creative power, describing it participially, and all climaxing in the phrase, "Yahweh is his name" (4:13, 5:8, 9:5–6). Drawing on Josh 7:19, F. Horst has rendered plausible a very specific life-setting for these doxologies.[17] In this passage in Joshua, after the taking of Jericho, a man named Achan transgressed the strict prohibition and secretly took a bar of gold from the spoils. Joshua says to Achan, "Give honor to Yahweh, the God of Israel, and confess him (literally: give him praise), and confess now to me what you have done," a statement that is followed by Achan's confession of guilt. It becomes clear from this statement that a confession of guilt before God could take on the form of praise. According to Horst, in such expressions of praise, which seem like lost fragments in the book of Amos, we encounter the fact that the later community that reads and hears the prophetic word here confesses its own guilt and thus praises Yahweh. However doubtful the theory of H. W. Wolff, that these doxologies always occur when Yahweh's judgment has previously been threatened against the altar at Bethel and that, specifically, in these doxologies one is able to hear the voice of the community at a time when the altar of Bethel was destroyed under Josiah,[18] we nonetheless have found another instance where an older prophetic word is affirmed as valid in a new setting contemporary with its transformation into a book, at a time when praise is given to God by a later community. People confess that Yahweh deserves honor and glory precisely when he acts as a judge.

After these partial observations regarding individual additions to the book, we may note a third element pertaining to the book in its entirety. In his own words, Amos announced judgment over Israel without mercy. The book named after him, however, climaxes in 9:11–15 in two words from Yahweh that promise future salvation. Amos 9:11–12 speaks of the fact that Yahweh will restore the fallen booth of David, that he will repair the breaches in its wall and restore the ancient rule over Edom and over all nations belonging to Yahweh; in other words, Amos refers to the restoration of the Davidic kingdom. In the second word (9:13–15), on the other hand, it is the blessing of nature that is in view alongside the promise of restoration and the people's return to the land.[19] In both cases, the

17. F. Horst, "Die Doxologien im Amosbuch," *ZAW* 47 (1929) 45–54 (= "Gottes Recht," *ThB* 12 [1961] 155–66).

18. Wolff, BKAT 14/2.135–36.

19. W. H. Schmidt, "Die deuteronomistische Redaktion des Amosbuches," *ZAW* 77 (1965) 168–93; U. Kellermann, "Der Amosschluß als Stimme deuteronomistischer Heilshoffnung," *EvTh* 29 (1969) 169–83.

one who speaks is someone who already has in view God's judgment of his people and of the house of David. How should one evaluate these two final sections of the book of Amos? The mere assertion that we are [[491]] dealing here with later additions does not suffice, and neither does their simple removal from the book of Amos. This expansion has been consciously added to the book of Amos during the course of the book's further development. The explanation that is frequently given, that the intention was to give a more positive ending to the book of Amos in the light of all the warnings it contains, is unduly superficial. Rather, this expansion, whoever may have formulated it, seeks to place Amos's proclamation in a larger context and wants it to be read in the light of a more comprehensive knowledge of God's will for his people.

This comprehensive knowledge of Old Testament faith, however, entails the assurance that Yahweh is committed to his promise, even when he must proclaim only death and judgment in Amos's particular context. This also entails the knowledge that Yahweh will fulfill his promise to the house of David, even though it has collapsed into a heap of rubble. This is without doubt maintained at this point entirely within the framework of Old Testament faith. Yahweh will once again say a decided "yes" to the kingdom of David, which reaches beyond the mere borders of Israel. The second addition (9:13–15) affirms this "yes" of God to his people with regard to the blessing of all of nature as well. Yahweh asserts anew that "the mountains will drip wine and all hills will flow (with abundance that grows on their slopes)."

This arrangement of a prophetic book, by which words of salvation follow the complete collection of the prophet's words of doom, can also be discerned in the book of Hosea. The words of salvation cling to the divine promise that remains valid for Israel even in the midst of and beyond the calamity. Hosea 14 gives a preview of the eventual return of Israel to her God and God's renewed provision of salvation. Once again, this may stem from the later hand of a redactor. And in the book of Micah, we note that this change, from a proclamation of doom to a proclamation of salvation, can be found twice in the juxtaposition of chaps. 1–5 and 6–7. It should also be noted that we find at the very end of the book of Hosea the pensive remark of a man speaking in the style of wisdom, saying,

> Who is wise to understand this, understanding so that he may discern it? For Yahweh's ways are right (straight), and the righteous walk in them, but the wicked stumble on them (Hos 14:10).

In both expansions, the ones who speak are the individuals who are directly affected: first, the one affected by the imminent judgments of

Yahweh, the one who looks beyond the judgment into the future; then, the one who wisely meditates and ponders everything, the pensive pious one, who maintains that everything that has been said in the preceding book should not be seen as archival history but as a message that calls for proper understanding.

Alongside the two-fold structure of the prophetic book, one also finds a tripartite structure that likewise entails a very definite message and that can be clearly discerned in the books of Ezekiel, Isaiah, and Zephaniah, and also in the Greek version of the book of Jeremiah. It can be seen most clearly in the book of Ezekiel. The first large main section, Ezekiel 1–24, the *pars destruens* [['destructive section']], in which primarily words of judgment are found, is followed by a collection of words against foreign nations in chaps. 25–32, directed against seven addressees. The fact that the last of these seven groups, that is, the collection of words against Egypt and the Pharaoh, comprises within itself another seven units, is evidence of the deliberate arrangement of the entire collection. This middle section is followed by a third part, chaps. 33–48, the *pars construens* [['constructive section']], which contains for the most part promises of salvation for the house of Israel, particularly, in its long concluding section, chaps. 40–48, the great vision of the new temple and the new land. It is not hard to understand the message of this arrangement: the words referring to Yahweh's intervention against the nations surrounding Israel announce, together with Yahweh's judgment against Israel's neighbors, Yahweh's renewed turning to his own people.[20] The rich details found in conjunction with the words against Egypt in the book of Ezekiel show that five of the six units where a specific date is given belong in their original state precisely to the period of Judah's final days. The order [[492]] "words of doom / words of salvation" is marked also in Ezekiel's message by the date of the comprehensive judgment of Israel in 587. Thus the order "proclamation of doom / words against the nations / proclamation of salvation" suggests itself to Ezekiel by the chronological sequence of his proclamation. The book of Ezekiel could therefore have provided the example par excellence for the arrangement of additional prophetic books, such as the books of Isaiah and Zephaniah, where this historical sequence and the distribution of proclamations of doom and of salvation cannot be demonstrated as clearly and where the material organized by the redactor, especially in the case of the book of Isaiah, proves to be rather resistant to this kind

---

20. Regarding the sequence "destruction for the nations / salvation for Israel," we may recall the structure of the messages to the foreign nations in pre-classical prophecy, which has been discussed above.

of arrangement. As mentioned, this principle of arrangement also penetrated very late into the Greek transmission of the words of Jeremiah.
The words against the nations that are found almost at the end of the
Hebrew text (chaps. 46–51) have been inserted in connection with Jeremiah 25.

It should further be mentioned that final narrative elements were
added to the books of First Isaiah (chaps. 1–35) and Jeremiah during a
later stage. In Isaiah, this unequivocally represents a borrowing from
2 Kings 18–20. Jeremiah 52 likewise betrays a proximity to the final narratives of 2 Kings. The driving force behind these two additions is not
the contemporization of the message, but rather an historical interest
that led to expansions of the books with portions that further illumine
the times and circumstances of the prophetic proclamation. In the expansion of the book of Isaiah it is also no doubt a matter of the completion of the prophetic message with clearly legendary traditions from the
Isaianic school.

While the factors just mentioned pertain to the total conception of
the prophetic book, we now need to draw attention to the internal expansion of the collections of original prophetic words as a feature of
subsequent history and ponder its theological significance. We are dealing with a phenomenon that can especially be found in the book of
Jeremiah but that is also not entirely absent from other prophetic books.
Regarding the book of Jeremiah (the book that is at present probably
the most difficult prophetic book to interpret), it was noted as early as
the turn of the century that it consists of peculiarly disparate parts. Subsequently, in 1914, Mowinckel[21] sought to explain this lack of homogeneity by demonstrating that four entirely different collections or sources
are brought together: Source A, which contains the prophet's original
words; Source B, including narratives about Jeremiah that could come
from the pen of his friend Baruch; Source C, discourses of Jeremiah in
deuteronomic revision; and Source D, the so-called "Book of Comfort
for Ephraim" in Jeremiah 30–31. The sayings regarding the nations in
chaps. 46–51 are not included in this analysis. Mowinckel's theory has
stimulated Jeremiah research in many ways and has remained a major
subject of discussion until Rudolph's commentary.[22] It was Mowinckel's
Source C that particularly attracted attention. What was one to think of
the words of the book of Jeremiah that reveal such an unmistakable
proximity to deuteronomic language and conceptuality? A stage of
research that focussed on the mere delimitation of deuteronomically

---

21. S. Mowinckel, *Zur Komposition des Buches Jeremia* (1914).
22. HAT 12.3 (ed. 1968).

colored chapters was followed by a period of more detailed analysis of
this material. This analysis now seeks to identify potential Jeremianic
material within the deuteronomically colored sections. The analysis of
Winfried Thiel[23] represents a showcase of this kind of work. Thiel dealt
with this subject in part of his dissertation, which treated the entire book
of Jeremiah. The question that is significant for the present discussion
can be crystallized on the basis of the partial publication of Thiel's work.
I would like to illustrate this in the case of Jeremiah's temple discourse,
which has already been mentioned, and by its revision by deuteronomic
redaction.

Chapter 26, a chapter that belongs to the second part of the book of
Jeremiah, that primarily contains narratives, reports the events surrounding Jeremiah's discourse in the temple. The juxtaposition of a discourse section (chaps. 1–25) and a narrative section (chaps. 26–46) may
possibly reveal a structural principle of the deuteronomist which does
not, however, appear to contain any particularly profound theological
implications, as also applies [[493]] to the addition of Jeremiah 52 to
chaps. 1–51 in a later connection. The narrative of Jeremiah 26 indicates the commotion that was caused by Jeremiah's proclamation when
he equated the coming fate of the Jerusalem Temple with the fate of the
temple at Shiloh. Jeremiah's life is threatened by the irate priests and
prophets in the temple, who are initially also followed by the people
gathered there. He only escapes with his life because the government
officials intervene, forcing an orderly hearing, and because elders of the
land remind others that, in the days of Hezekiah, Micah of Moresheth
had likewise proclaimed,

> Thus says the Lord of hosts: "Zion is plowed like a field, and
> Jerusalem is a pile of rubble, and the temple mount a wooded
> height."

Hezekiah did not kill Micah but sought to appease Yahweh. The entire
context, like the reference to the word of Micah in Mic 3:12, indicates
that Jeremiah openly proclaimed the temple's destruction. Thiel's freeing of the text of Jeremiah 7 from the redactional additions of the deuteronomist reveals this apodictic proclamation. It reads:

> Do not trust in lies by saying, "Yahweh's temple, Yahweh's tem-
> ple, Yahweh's temple is here." How? Lying, murder, adultery, the
> bearing of false witness, sacrifices to Baal—and then you come
> and approach me in this house and say, "We are saved." Is this

23. W. Thiel, *Die deuteronomistische Redaktion von Jer. 1–25* (WMANT 41; 1973).

house a den of robbers in your eyes? ... Go to my holy place in Shiloh ... and see what I did to it on account of the evil of my people Israel. Therefore I will do what I did to Shiloh to this house in which you trust.

This original text experienced a telling change during the time of the exile, when the deuteronomic redaction did not merely arrange the text but also revised it. Thus the charge of false confidence in the temple was further developed by the following pronouncements:

If you earnestly change your ways and your deeds, if you promote righteousness between a man and his neighbor, if you do not oppress the foreigner, the widow, and the orphan ... and if you do not run after foreign gods to your own calamity, then I will allow you to dwell in this place, in the land I have given to your fathers, from eternity to eternity.

What has happened here? The apodictic prophecy of doom has been transformed into a hypothetical threat. Thiel coins the term "preaching of alternatives" for this. The people are offered an alternative to calamity. Salvation will be the reward for obedience, and calamity will be the consequence of disobedience. One may initially object that this destroys the original prophetic message and that the original apodictic word of Jeremiah is no longer heard. The historian who reads the text with the intention of reconstructing the past proclamation of Jeremiah cannot avoid this verdict. Once again, however, it would be completely wrong to close the case regarding this word and to consider the message of Jeremiah to be material for the archives.

In reality, something totally different has happened. The redactor who revised the transmitted text lived during the time of the exile. The judgment has occurred, the temple has been destroyed, the nation's sovereignty was lost. In the midst of these circumstances, the bearer of the tradition of Jeremiah's word adapts it by clinging to the divine promise (in the way of those who added the conclusions to Amos and Hosea) that God's dealings with his people are not a thing of the past, even at this point of apparent complete hopelessness.

He also knows, however, that the word of the living holy God, spoken by his prophet, is nothing but abiding truth. Thus he continues to transmit this message. At the same time, he knows that this message is not done away with by the events of the year 587 but rather has abiding validity, since it is the word of the living God. In 587, God spoke in history and proved the truth of his word. A person endangers his life if he does not heed God's righteousness. Thus he expands [[494]] the transmitted discourse of Jeremiah by a direct appeal in a conditional formulation. Only when the people of Yahweh are willing to listen to Yahweh's requirements can they receive a future. This results in a peculiar parallel to Ezekiel 18, a word probably spoken by the prophet himself after the collapse of 587. This word, likewise, albeit in stronger priestly coloring, ties the possibility of "life" to the call to repentance, which needs to find concrete expression in the keeping of God's commandments.[24]

Did the deuteronomic redactor falsify the divine word? For the historian, it is clear that he changed Jeremiah's original message. For the one who attempts to hear the divine call anew from that earlier word, it should be clear that the redactor provides Yahweh's truth with new relevance in his new circumstances. Once again, the text of the book of Jeremiah, at this as well as at other places where the apodictic proclamation turns into the "preaching of alternatives," becomes evidence for the fact that the valid call of Yahweh to his people was maintained in a new and different situation. And no doubt whatsoever is cast on the knowledge that God is the same today as he was yesterday. The issue is listening to the prophetic message in a new day.

We should say a brief word regarding one final phenomenon that is evident as we consider the development from prophetic word to prophetic book. Again, we can merely illustrate the general principle, and the book of Isaiah may serve as an example. O. Kaiser, in his treatment of Isaiah 13–39,[25] when considering the development of the prophetic word, initially maintained that one should distinguish between an eschatological, a proto-apocalyptic, and an apocalyptic period. Expectations "that reckon with a decisive turn in the destiny of Israel and of the nations without ceasing to be historically grounded are 'eschatological.' They are called 'apocalyptic' when they expect a change of people's circumstances by way of supernatural or cosmic intervention, while the connection to specific historical powers remains obscure or fanciful, or finally calculations regarding the time of the last events are made." In the majority of the Isaiah texts analyzed, one finds an intermediate layer "that pertains to the transitional stage between historical-eschatological and cosmic-apocalyptic elements."[26]

At this point the issue is not the analysis of individual texts in order to determine whether or not Kaiser's specific interpretations are supported by the text in every case. We must be content with determining the basic tendency that can doubtless be observed in several instances.

---

24. On the problem of whether Ezekiel 18 is original to Ezekiel or not, see W. Zimmerli, "Deutero-Ezechiel?" *ZAW* 84 (1972) 501–16.

25. Kaiser, ATD 18.234.

26. Ibid., 2.

This coincides with comments made by Paul D. Hanson,[27] from a different perspective, regarding texts in Trito-Isaiah and in Deutero- and Trito-Zechariah. Thus, for example, the so-called "Isaiah Apocalypse" in Isaiah 24–27 joins onto the collection of oracles against the nations in chaps. 13–23. Yahweh's activity regarding the individual nations expands there to the great assize of the nations and the description of the earth-shattering doom of Israel's enemies. This is followed in context by a description of the great meal that Yahweh will prepare on his mountain for the nations, when the veil will be taken away from the faces of the nations. The collection of chaps. 28–35, in turn, leads in chaps. 34–35 from the wrath of Yahweh, which is described as his great day over the entire world of nations as demonstrated by the destruction of Edom, to the description of salvation, which is narrated in the clear colors of Deutero-Isaianic proclamation. Lebanon and the desert are transformed when Yahweh brings salvation to his people. The conclusion of the entire book of Isaiah speaks expansively of the divine judgment upon all flesh and of the new heavens and the new earth that God will create for the well-being of his people.

> Every new moon and every Sabbath, all flesh will come to cast itself down adoringly before Yahweh

—while the enemies will perish in eternal fire (66:23–24). This is the final image in the book of Isaiah. Similar things can also be seen in the postexilic book of Joel and in the book of Zechariah, which was treated by Hanson. They likewise [[495]] conclude with a worldwide perspective of a final judgment and final salvation.

In conclusion, while we cannot discuss this in detail, we need to ask the principal question, which concerns the inner legitimacy and theological validity of this redaction of certain parts of prophetic books or of entire books. Traces of this can already be detected in the early prophecy of Amos regarding a day of Yahweh, a proclamation that continues through Isaiah, Zephaniah, and Ezekiel, all the way to Joel and Malachi. In this way, the prophetic word is interpreted as a phenomenon that is relevant for all the world. In the historical Isaiah as well as in Amos, this prophetic word proclaims Yahweh's presence in the judgment of his people, addressing very concrete times and circumstances. This is certainly not merely a matter of sketching a worldwide historical framework that people can complacently acknowledge, just as Ezekiel's audience could say to him, "The visions he sees are in the distant future, and he prophesies regarding times that are far from now" (12:27). Rather, the

---

27. Paul D. Hanson, *The Dawn of Apocalyptic* (1975).

apocalyptic expansion in the arrangement of the final elements of certain prophetic books seeks to show that the world in its entirety will be confronted with Yahweh's presence not on a distant day, but soon—a presence by which Yahweh, through his judgment, brings salvation to his own. This is a final unleashing of the prophetic message, which is relevant even in a new situation.

Even more à propos, we may say that it is an unleashing that comes about because of the knowledge that Yahweh will continue to accomplish a work of judgment and salvation that cannot be escaped by any realm, people, or period. However much apocalypticism may later become entangled in the thicket of calculations, in the end it is rejuvenated by the confidence that the Lord of all the world and of all of history is committed to his word, the word initially spoken by the prophets, addressing clearly demarcated circumstances in the life of the people of Israel.[28] The increasing significance of the world's confrontation with its God—which can never be addressed as a thing of the past, however much past events may reveal traces of his activity regarding his people and the world—can be revealed to us when we pay attention to the path of development from the prophetic word to the prophetic book in all of its various stages. The transformation of the divine word into a book never sent into retirement the living call of the living Lord. It is able to speak unexpectedly to a new day. God never retires.

28. W. Zimmerli, "Alttestamentliche Prophetie und Apokalyptik auf dem Wege zur 'Rechtfertigung des Gottlosen,'" in *Rechtfertigung: Festschrift für E. Käsemann* (1976) 575–92.

Prophets, Editors, and Tradition

Ronald E. Clements

The Prophetic Editors as Creative
Originators of Tradition

[[210]] It is not unfair to claim that, after half a century of studies of the Book of Jeremiah in the wake of the work of Duhm and Mowinckel, scholarship found itself faced with as much of an impasse at the end of it as it had at the beginning. It appeared to be equally possible to arrive either at a very positive estimate of the degree to which Jeremiah's editors had preserved his actual words and pronouncements or at a rather negative one. The nature of the problem of the divergent types of material which was in question was what such divergencies implied. New approaches were called for and we may single out certain of them as indicating a significant shift in the line of scholarly questioning.

The first of these, by E. W. Nicholson,[1] was concerned primarily with the material which Mowinckel had identified as "source C," and which took the form of prose sermons scattered throughout Jeremiah 1–25. The very title of Nicholson's book, *Preaching to the Exiles*, indicates much of the argument regarding the content. The prose sermons were seen not to be from Jeremiah himself but rather to represent fresh creative addresses delivered to the small community of Judaean exiles in Babylon.[2] They used the name of Jeremiah because they addressed the situation of

Reprinted with permission and excerpted from "The Prophet and His Editors," in *The Bible in Three Dimensions: Essays in Celebration of Forty Years of Biblical Studies in the University of Sheffield* (ed. D. J. A. Clines, S. E. Fowl, and S. E. Porter; Journal for the Study of the Old Testament Supplement Series 87; Sheffield: JSOT Press, 1990) 210–20.

1. E. W. Nicholson, *Preaching to the Exiles. A Study of the Prose Tradition in the Book of Jeremiah* (Oxford: B. H. Blackwell, 1970).

2. Nicholson, *Preaching to the Exiles*, 116ff.

exile which his prophecies had served to interpret and foretell, but they
bore little other effective relationship to Jeremiah himself. Their importance was to be found in the way in which they brought new messages to
bear upon the situation which formed the aftermath of the events which
had formed the background to Jeremiah's prophetic activity. In particular, the loss of confidence that had survived in Judah after 587 B.C.E. became a dominant feature of their message.

What was important regarding this fresh line of questioning was that,
in spite of some attention still to the question of whether or not they represent part of the preserved Jeremiah tradition, these prose sermons
were viewed as creative attempts to address a situation subsequent to that
of [[211]] Jeremiah's prophetic activity. They expanded further upon the
meaning of the Babylonian exile which Jeremiah's own prophecies had
addressed in an earlier, and still emergent, phase. In other words it was
the situation which had arisen subsequent to Jeremiah's own preaching
that had elicited the concern to elaborate and expand upon his own pronouncements. The prophet's editors had done more than simply strive to
preserve his own words. They had added words of their own to make the
prophet's sayings more meaningful! It is true that a living connection
could still be traced between Jeremiah and the work of these exilic
preachers, but it was far too oblique for it to be classed simply as that of
the transmission of a body of sayings.

Nicholson's work explored the connections and overlap between the
style and content of the Jeremianic "prose sermons" and the vocabulary
and theological interests of the Deuteronomistic literature. This connection formed the central focus of attention for the two volumes from
W. Thiel[3] which sought to demonstrate the point that Jeremiah's literary
editors can be seen, on the basis of literary and theological evidence, to
have belonged to the circle of the Deuteronomistic "School." The importance of this observation, which had become part of the investigation
into the literary make-up of the Book of Jeremiah since the work of
Duhm and Mowinckel, was only now beginning to be fully appreciated.
What was abundantly clear was that Jeremiah's editors had assimilated
his prophetic message into the framework of the aims and theological
ideals of a dominant scribal group of the sixth century B.C.E.[4] Accordingly, it was not the relationship of the preserved literary tradition to

3. W. Thiel, *Die deuteronomistische Redaktion von Jeremia 1–25* (WMANT 41; Neukirchen-
Vluyn: Neukirchener Verlag, 1973); *idem, Die deuteronomistische Redaktion von Jeremia 26–45*
(WMANT 52; Neukirchen-Vluyn: Neukirchener Verlag, 1981).

4. Cf. also J. P. Hyatt, "The Deuteronomic Edition of Jeremiah," *Vanderbilt Studies in the
Humanities I* (ed. R. C. Beatty, J. P. Hyatt and M. K. Spears; Nashville: Vanderbilt University
Press, 1951), 71–95 (= *A Prophet to the Nations* [[Winona Lake, Ind.: Eisenbrauns, 1984]] 247–67).

Jeremiah the prophet that mattered, but rather the ideological circle into which the prophet's message had been incorporated.

[[212]] With Thiel's work, combined with that of other scholars, the relationship between a prophet and his editors could be set in a fresh light which made the assumption of a group of prophetic "disciples" an increasingly irrelevant one. The tradition of Jeremiah's preaching had evidently been "adopted" into a major scribal and reforming circle of Judaean leaders at the time that Judah collapsed in its attempts to resist Babylonian imperial control. The same basic assumption, that the editors of Jeremiah's prophecies belonged, in significant measure, to the same scribal circle that had produced the law-book of Deuteronomy and the Deuteronomistic History, was fundamental also to P. Diepold's study of the concept of "The Land"[5] during this vitally important period of the collapse of the Judaean state. He could build upon the recognition that the editing of the prophecies of Jeremiah represented the third of the major literary productions of this Deuteronomistic "School."

A further major attempt to re-evaluate the aims and methods of the editors who had been responsible for producing a book, or more accurately, a scroll of Jeremiah's prophecies has been forthcoming from Robert Carroll.[6] We should note, however, that even before the appearance of Carroll's studies, P. R. Ackroyd had addressed very directly the question of how we should understand the nature of the preserved Jeremiah tradition.[7] In particular he focused attention upon the recognition that written prophecy, based upon a preserved collection of a prophet's spoken words, could be used to legitimate changes in cultic and political institutions. Such a written prophetic testimony could appeal to the prophet's words as divine authorization for political changes which had been made inevitable by events, or to bolster the claims of particular religious groups over against those of rival groups. Written prophecy could become a literature of legitimization affecting the political and religious shape of a community in a very different [[213]] way from that in which the original spoken words of the prophet had done.

In a number of respects Carroll's work has developed very extensively the contention that written prophecy, in his judgment often only very tenuously related to the work of the prophet to which it was ascribed, served to legitimate developments within a community.[8] By claiming divine fore-

---

5. P. Diepold, *Israels Land* (BWANT 5/15; Stuttgart: W. Kohlhammer, 1972).

6. R. P. Carroll, *When Prophecy Failed. Reactions and Responses to Failure in the Old Testament Prophetic Traditions* (London: SCM, 1979).

7. P. R. Ackroyd, "Historians and Prophets," *SEÅ* 33 (1968), 18–34 (= his *Studies in the Religious Tradition of the Old Testament* [London: SCM Press, 1987], 121–51).

8. Carroll, *From Chaos to Covenant* [[New York: Crossroad, 1981]], 249ff.

knowledge in advance of events, the prophetic tradition sought to affirm that a divine purpose had shaped those events. The starting-point of Carroll's study *When Prophecy Failed* is to be found in Leo Festinger's analysis of the responses shown by millennial prophetic movements to the experience of disappointed hopes.[9] Hence rather extreme forms of disappointed hope provide a norm of comparison for community responses to prophecy more generally. At the same time a psychological concern with the phenomenon of cognitive dissonance, where reality stands at some distance from prior expectations, occupies the central field of attention. Written prophecy is then seen by Carroll as one way by which the ancient Israelite community learned to cope with the frustration and disappointment of its expectations.

It is not surprising that, in the light of this broad social setting for prophetic activity, Carroll adopts a rather dogmatic scepticism over many aspects of the Jeremiah tradition in his study entitled *From Chaos to Covenant*. He remains doubtful whether we may at all know if the material ascribed to Jeremiah derived in any recognizable sense from his actual sayings. Rather, all attention is devoted to the question of how a community responded to the catastrophic events which took place during Jeremiah's lifetime and how they used the figure of Jeremiah as a prophet to interpret their own confusion and despair. To this extent, with Carroll's work, the question of whether or not Jeremiah's editors had faithfully preserved and recorded the tradition of his sayings has largely become an irrelevance. Their concern is assumed to have been throughout one of understanding and interpreting the disasters [[214]] and despair which followed the prophet's period of activity. Prior hopeful expectation and painful historical reality had given rise to a situation of cognitive dissonance which only a prophetic hermeneutic could dispel.

We can certainly recognize that Carroll's studies provide an important corrective to the earlier work which took it for granted that all that mattered in examining the relationship between a prophet and his editors was whether or not they had painted his theological and spiritual portrait faithfully. This was never their intention, and in most respects the very nature of prophecy indicates that its concerns were far too urgent and existential for such a careful literary proceeding to have been their aim. Nevertheless to explain the origin of a major part of the Book of Jeremiah on the basis of a need for a hermeneutic arising out of the experience of cognitive dissonance is to lose sight of the uniqueness and inspired charisma which lent a very distinctive divine authority to the

---

9. L. Festinger, H. W. Riecker and S. Schachter, *When Prophecy Fails* (Minneapolis, 1956).

prophet's words in the first place. Carroll's picture of Jeremiah is one of a figure so lacking in definition that he appears virtually lost altogether behind the tradition that has made use of his name.

Clearly there is a need for recognizing that the relationship which existed between the prophet and his editors, and which led to determined efforts to record a prophet's actual words, was a more genuinely reciprocal one than this. The prophet did stand apart from other men, and he was believed to possess an inspiration accorded to only a very few individuals which made his actual words memorable and vital. At the same time there was evidently a need, as the complex literary structure of all the biblical prophetic collections reveals, to edit, record and interpret those words with the help of some additional material and supplementation. If an emphasis upon the prophetic editors as preservationists erred in one direction, the attempt to present them as freelance writers who used the prophet's name simply for their own convenience erred in another.

The Prophetic Editors as Interpreters

If we are to look for some guidance as to the overall role which the editors of the prophetic literature adopted for themselves [[215]] then we find some helpful guidelines in Max Weber's basic studies of prophetic tradition.[10] In this he placed strong emphasis upon the role of the prophet as an inspired individual. The prophet's charisma was personal to himself and lent him a unique divine authority, not transferable to others. Yet against this his messages, often brief and sometimes cryptic, needed to be interpreted to make them more effective and meaningful for the life of the ongoing religious community to which he belonged. Accordingly, what the prophet's words meant for the future of established religious leaders and institutions needed to be spelled out. Weber described this process as one of "routinization" in which the implications of what the prophet had said were adapted and interpreted in more precise and concrete terms and in relation to organized religious life. The

---

10. M. Weber, *The Sociology of Religion* (tr. Ephraim Fischoff; Boston: Beacon Press, 1963), 60–79; cf. especially pp. 60–61: "Primarily, a religious community arises in connection with a prophetic movement as a result of routinization (Ger. *Veralltaglichung*), i.e., as a result of the process whereby either the prophet himself or his disciples secure the permanence of his preaching and the congregation's distribution of grace, hence insuring the economic existence of the enterprise and those who man it, and thereby monopolizing as well the privileges reserved for those charged with religious functions." Cf. also "The Sociology of Charismatic Authority," in *From Max Weber. Essays in Sociology* (ed. H. H. Gerth & C. Wright Mills; London: Routledge and Kegan Paul, 1947), 245–52.

prophet's message was perceived to lend direction and support to some groups, while he brought reproof, and sometimes outright rejection, to others.

So far as the theory of cognitive dissonance is concerned, it is noteworthy that Weber discerned an element of tension between the religious meaning of what a prophet declared and the empirical experience of what actually happened to the groups the prophet addressed. However this is peripheral to the more substantive feature that the "routinization" of prophecy marked its integration into the life of a community. Its meaning was spelled out in terms of priestly administration, pastoral care and the spiritual development of the individual's life. Revealed truth became embodied in the institutional life of a larger group and spelled out in ethical rules and support for specific forms of administrative authority.

Our argument is that this process of "routinization" is the most appropriate one to describe the nature of the relationship [[216]] between a prophet and his editors. Especially does it highlight the difference in status and perceived authority between the individual *persona* of the prophet and that of the editors and interpreters who transmitted his sayings. It explains the aims and characteristics of the editorial supplementation which shaped and adapted the prophet's words in order to give them a more permanent and practical meaning. Most especially such a process serves to show why it was important to retain some recognizable portrait of the prophet himself, together with a record of his actual words so far as this was possible, and to relate these words to the events which formed the sequel of the situation to which the prophet had originally spoken. In such a context the uniqueness and individuality of the prophet was of the very essence of his charismatic authority to which his editors needed to appeal. At the same time it was clear to these editors that the actual import of the prophet's words would be lost if their implications were not spelled out with great clarity to those who held the prophet in high regard as the spokesman of God.

We may contend therefore that this process of "routinization" best describes the relationship between the prophet and his editors. Certainly this is so in the case of both Jeremiah and Ezekiel where the connections between the editorial word and more central circles of Jewish life have long been recognized.[11] In regard to the complex literary histories of the books of Isaiah and of the Twelve Prophets the situation is not so obvi-

---

11. Some initial observations along these lines were presented in my essay, "The Ezekiel Tradition, Prophecy in a Time of Crisis," *Israel's Prophetic Tradition* (ed. R. Coggins, A. C. J. Phillips and M. Knibb; Cambridge: Cambridge University Press, 1982), 119–36.

ously clear, although in these also many facets of the routinization process are evident. In the case of Jeremiah this routinization has taken place in very direct application to central concerns of what we have broadly come to identify as a Deuteronomistic party, or group. These concerns show themselves in regard to three major features of Judah's national life: temple, kingship and national sovereignty.

So we find that the meaning of Jeremiah's prophecies has been spelled out very forcefully in respect of the temple as the primary religious institution of the nation, the Davidic kingship [[217]] as its foremost political pillar, and the future of the remnants of the nation, in Judah and in Babylon, under a prolonged period of Babylonian political control.

It is not difficult to see how the fact of the destruction of the temple in Jerusalem has exercised a formative effect upon the literary shaping of the Jeremiah tradition. A conditional warning of the destruction of the building is set out in Jer 7:1–15 in a unit which has long been recognized as showing traces of editorial reworking. It heads a substantial section dealing with false worship extending down to Jer 10:25. Furthermore a repetition of this warning of the temple's destruction commences the narrative section in Jer 26:1–15, where it is highlighted as a major cause of conflict between Jeremiah and the Jerusalem authorities. It is then noteworthy that this threat of the destruction of the temple is coupled with threats concerning the fall of the city of Jerusalem (cf. Jer 7:34; 8:1–3; 9:12; 25:29; 38:3, 23). This is given such emphasis as to suggest that the presence of the temple there had provided the basis for the belief that the city as a whole would be spared for the temple's sake.

Since the book of Jeremiah, unlike the comparable books of Isaiah, Ezekiel and the Twelve, contains no explicit promise regarding the temple's restoration, the way in which the prophet himself envisaged the future of the cultus is never made wholly clear. It is often assumed that he advocated a very inward and spiritual form of worship which needed no formal cultus.[12] Nevertheless it has to be kept in mind that this is not made formally explicit. Rather, the staunch advocacy, undoubtedly by the scroll's editors, of a necessary role for the levitical priests in the future (Jer 33:18, 21–24) suggests that a restored temple was certainly not precluded.

Significantly too the ambiguity of this situation is left even more marked by the inclusion of an assurance that the loss of the ark would

---

12. Cf. the classic exposition in J. Skinner, *Prophecy and Religion* (Cambridge: Cambridge University Press, 1922), 165–84.

not inhibit the divine blessing of all Jerusalem in future years (Jer 3:15–17). This loss, and the fact that it would not be replaced, appear at a point where we should readily have expected the temple itself to have been mentioned. Nor ⟦218⟧ can we leave out of reckoning the very surprising fact that the return of the temple vessels to Jerusalem, with the implication that they embodied much of the holiness of the temple itself, is introduced in Jer 27:16–22, once again by the prophet's editors, as a major point.[13] Obviously such a concern for the temple vessels could only have meaning on the assumption that the temple itself would eventually be restored.

Overall the question of what Jeremiah's prophecies implied about the future of the temple was evidently a major point of concern for his editors. The end result is more than a little ambiguous as to what it discloses both about the attitude of Jeremiah to the matter and about the role a restored temple might have for a renewed and re-united Israel. Clearly a strong concern was felt to show why the temple had to be destroyed, and how Jeremiah had declared as much. At the same time this had to be set out in such a way as not to preclude the expectation that, in future, Jerusalem would once again become the spiritual centre of Israel's life. The absence of any prophecy concerning the rebuilding of the temple suggests that this had still not been raised as a major issue by the time the editing of the prophetic scroll was completed. At the same time such a rebuilding is clearly not ruled out.

The future of the kingship also becomes an issue where a significant level of tension exists between what appears to have been Jeremiah's own attitude and the expectations that were nursed by his editors. The finality with which Jeremiah ruled out any possible return to the throne of Jehoiachin, or his descendants (Jer 22:24–27, 28–30), contrasts strikingly with the forthright assurance about the future of the Davidic dynasty set out in Jer 33:14–26. The latter must certainly be the work of the editors, and this must also be true of the even more enigmatic prophecy of Jer 23:5–6, with its play on the name of Zedekiah. Uncertainty about Jeremiah's hope for Zedekiah is shown up by 38:17–23, with its muted words of hope which events evidently refuted. Because the kingship was the central political institution of Israel's life, and because ⟦219⟧ the return to the throne of Jerusalem of an heir of David's line became so important an aspect of the exilic hope (cf. Isa 11:1–5; Ezek 37:24–28), editorial work on Jeremiah's prophecies has endeavoured to give room to it.

13. Cf. P. R. Ackroyd, "The Temple Vessels: A Continuity Theme," *Studies in the Religion of Ancient Israel*, VTSup 23 (1972), 166–81 (= his *Studies in the Religious Tradition of the Old Testament*, 46–60).

It seems unlikely that Jeremiah personally attached much importance to the issue of restoring the Davidic monarchy after Zedekiah's removal from his throne. Since such a restoration in any case did not eventually take place, in spite of evident hopes that the survival of Jehoiachin's family in Babylonian exile would make it possible (as is suggested by 2 Kgs 25:27–30), it is striking that it is the editorial work which has generated an element of dissonance. It is Jeremiah's editors who, in upholding Jeremiah's condemnation of Judah's last kings, have nevertheless sought to show that the Davidic monarchy would play an important role in the future of a renewed Israel, even though actual events turned out contrary to this.

The third point that has deeply affected the editorial shaping of the Jeremiah scroll was evidently that of Judah's national sovereignty under the suzerainty of Babylon. This comes most startlingly into the forefront in the narratives of Jeremiah 40–43 which contain so much valuable and detailed information about the events in Judah under Gedaliah's brief governorship. What stands out is the repeated emphasis upon the necessity for continued submission to Babylon for the time being (Jer 40:5, 7; 41:2, 18). This is spelled out so affirmatively as to insist that there was nothing to fear under such Babylonian jurisdiction:

> Gedaliah the son of Ahikam, son of Shaphan, swore to them and their men saying, "Do not be afraid to serve the Chaldeans. Dwell in the land and serve the king of Babylon, and it shall be well with you" (Jer 40:9).

Similarly Jeremiah could be presented as affirming as God's word:

> Do not fear the king of Babylon, of whom you are afraid; do not fear him, says the Lord, for I am with you, to save you and deliver you from his hand. I will grant you mercy, that he may have mercy on you and let you remain in your own land (42:11–12).

〚220〛 Clearly the Jeremiah scroll has been the subject of an editorial shaping which has made a very major issue of the necessity for the remnant in Judah to remain subservient, for an indefinite period, to the rule of the king of Babylon (cf. Jer 25:11–14, 17, 26; 27:1–7; 29:10; 38:2). This has been felt to stand wholly in line with Jeremiah's personal advocacy of surrender to the Babylonian forces at the time of the siege of Jerusalem in 587 B.C.E. (Jer 38:2, 17–23). It clearly also had much to do with the condemnation of those prophets who declared the fall of Babylon and the return of the exiles to be imminent.

K. F. Pohlmann's tracing of this "pro-Babylonian" editing in Jeremiah places it very late,[14] whereas all the indications are that it arose as an urgent issue affecting the survival of Judaean exiles very much closer to the time consequent upon Gedaliah's murder.[15] There seems little reason for dating it much later than the middle of the sixth century B.C.E. However our primary concern is to note how it was the emergence of such a basic political issue, and its evident relationship to a position which Jeremiah himself had adopted, which has elicited extensive treatment by Jeremiah's editors. It falls fully within the process which we can identify as that of the routinization of prophecy. This necessitated the elaboration and clarification of an inspired prophet's message in relation to concrete political and religious issues. The message itself was sensed to lack the specificity which was needed if its import was to be fully heeded by the community which looked back with genuine trust and confidence to the prophet who was the interpreter of their times. Hence we can claim that a genuine and positive relationship existed between the prophet and his editors. In no way were these latter trying to compensate for the limitations, or even errors, of the prophet whose heirs they felt themselves to be. Rather, their profound respect for him made them eager and anxious interpreters of his words, spelling out in detail how they could be applied to the situation which his warnings and reproof had forewarned them of.

14. K. F. Pohlmann, *Studien zum Jeremiabuch. Ein Beitrag zur Frage nach der Entstehung des Jeremiabuches* (FRLANT 118; Göttingen: Vandenhoeck & Ruprecht, 1978).
15. Cf. C. R. Seitz, "The Crisis of Interpretation over the Meaning and Purpose of the Exile: A Redactional Study of Jer. xxi–xliii," *VT* 35 (1985), 78–97.

The Prophet and the Plumb-Line:
A Redaction-Critical Study of Amos 7

H. G. M. WILLIAMSON

[[101]] There is a widespread measure of agreement among scholars that the account of Amos's visions in Amos 7–8[1] is interrupted by the story of the prophet's encounter with Amaziah in 7:10–17. Beyond the general similarity between the four visions, typified by the common introductory *kōh hir'anî* [['thus [he] showed me']][2] followed by *wĕhinnēh* [['behold']], they further fall into two closely parallel pairs. In the first pair, for instance, the account of Amos's successful intercession is retold in virtually

Reprinted with permission from *In Quest of the Past: Studies on Israelite Religion, Literature and Prophetism* (ed. A. S. van der Woude; Oudtestamentische Studiën 26; Leiden: Brill, 1990) 101–21.

1. The most substantial study of the vision cycle is G. Bartczek, *Prophetie und Vermittlung. Zur literarischen Analyse und theologischen Interpretation der Visionsberichte des Amos* (Europäische Hochschulschriften 23/120. Frankfurt am Main, 1980). However, its concerns are rather different from those of the present article.

2. In the MT of the first two and last visions, this is extended to include the words *'ădōnāy yhwh* [['Lord God']] (7:1, 4; 8:1). Some commentators wish to restore this phrase in 7:7 also; Nowack, p. 156, for instance, transposes *'dny* from its position two words later in the verse and restores *yhwh* on the basis of the LXX, while Rudolph, pp. 232 and 234, who thinks that the phrase was lost by a double haplography, suggests that the word's second occurrence in v. 4 is a misplaced marginal gloss which was intended to restore the loss in v. 7. Alternatively, Wolff, pp. 337f. and 366 = ET, pp. 291–93 and 317, uses the evidence of the LXX to restore *yhwh* alone in each of the four introductions. However, the shorter introduction in v. 7 may be original, based on the fact that, unlike in the other three cases, the Lord himself is part of the vision which immediately follows.

identical language (vv. 2b–3 and 5–6), the most significant variation being the addition of *gam hî* ⟦'this also'⟧ in v. 6, which only serves to link the two visions even more closely together. Similarly, the second pair displays a number of close parallels, which Wolff (p. 366 = ET, p. 318) summarises as the vision proper, Yahweh's question concerning the catchword, Amos's answer, and Yahweh's interpretation. Again where content allows, identical phraseology is used. This is especially noteworthy in the case of the concluding clause, *lō* *'ôsîp* *'ôd* *'ābôr lô* ⟦'I will never again pass by them'⟧ (7:8; 8:2), which additionally shows, of course, that this pair cannot be understood without reference to the first pair. It is thus difficult not to suppose that at some stage in the development of the collection the four visions belonged together as a single unit.[3]

⟦102⟧ This conclusion is reinforced by the different style and form of 7:10–17. The use of third person narrative, unprecedented in the book of Amos except for the editorial introduction (1:1), is only the most obvious point that could be made,[4] but it is sufficient for our purposes in that it causes the reversion to the first person in 8:1 to jar in the present form of the text.

By contrast with the general agreement which this conclusion commands, however, there is a considerable diversity of opinion concerning how and why this interruption has occurred. In the first place, there are some who argue that the editor's purpose was to reflect the historical course of events. Watts,[5] for instance, has developed an elaborate hypothesis in which Amos is thought originally to have recounted his first three visions at Bethel, after which he was expelled from the Northern Kingdom. A year later, he repeated his account with the addition of a fourth vision "at some Judaean sanctuary," and then after a further year he repeated the exercise yet again, this time adding the fifth vision. "Thus, each succeeding year Amos recited the earlier visions as reports of the message which had been given to him and added the latest one as a verification and confirmation" (p. 34). Watts then links this two-year

---

3. *Pace* R. Gordis, "Studies in the Book of Amos," *Proceedings of the American Academy for Jewish Research* 46–47 (1979–80), 201–64. Gordis's four arguments on pp. 251–52 for the separation of 8:1–2 from 7:1–8 are very weak, and in one case factually incorrect. He states, "In the first three visions, the question is put to Amos, 'What do you see, Amos?' There is no such interrogation in the fourth vision." On the contrary, the words *māh-'attâ rō'êh 'āmôs* ⟦'What do you see, Amos?'⟧ in 8:2 are precisely one further reason for keeping the four visions together.

4. Cripps, p. 311, however, perhaps exaggerates the grammatical disjuncture that this causes at the start of the pericope.

5. J. D. W. Watts, *Vision and Prophecy in Amos* (Leiden, 1958), 27–50.

period to the date given in 1:1, "two years before the earthquake," whose fulfilment he sees as being recounted in the destruction of the sanctuary in 9:1. In this way he seeks to do justice both to the literary evidence we have already described and to the present ordering of the material.

It may be questioned, however, whether this theory adequately accounts for the phenomena, quite apart from the broader issue of whether it is right to look for biographical intent behind such prophetic narratives.[6] Watts's view assumes that 7:10–17 was specifically written for its present setting,[7] and yet for the reasons already outlined that is the very point which is most difficult to accept. If it became a part of Amos's recapitulation of his past experiences as an introduction to his fourth (and later fifth) vision, we should expect it both to be cast in the first person and to be more smoothly integrated into its context. Even if Watts's historical reconstruction is correct (which is doubtful), it cannot be used to resolve what is essentially a literary-critical problem.

A more common approach to our passage assumes that 7:10–17 was originally situated elsewhere in the book of Amos and that it has been moved to its present position only secondarily. Indeed, some commentaries abandon the [[103]] order of the Massoretic Text at this point in order to restore the original continuity of the vision reports.[8] Suggestions as to where the passage first stood include (a) with the editorial introduction to the book, following 1:2;[9] (b) at the end of chapter 3;[10] (c) at the end of chapter 6;[11] and (d) at the end of the book.[12] All seem to be agreed, however, that it owes its present setting to the catchword principle, since v. 9b (*wĕqamtî ᶜal-bêt yorobᶜām behārēb* [['and I will rise against the house of Jeroboam with the sword']]) is echoed in v. 11 (*bahērēb yāmût yorobᶜām* [['Jeroboam shall die by the sword']]). Indeed, Rudolph (p. 237) regards this argument as sufficient to demonstrate that

6. See, for instance, R. E. Clements, *Prophecy and Tradition* (Growing Points in Theology. Oxford, 1975), 24–40; B. O. Long, "Reports of Visions among the Prophets," *JBL* 95 (1976), 353–65. To deny biographical intent does not, of course, imply any necessary denial of the historicity of the events recorded.

7. It is thus not at all clear what Watts means by his statement in a footnote that "7:10–17 is different from the vision accounts and secondary to them" (p. 32).

8. For instance, Weiser, pp. 180–205, Rudolph, pp. 228–78, and Soggin, pp. 112–45, all treat this section in the order 7:1–9; 8:1–3; 9:1–6; 7:10–17; 8:4–14; and 9:7–10.

9. K. Budde, "Zur Geschichte des Buches Amos," in K. Marti (ed.), *Studien zur semitischen Philologie und Religionsgeschichte* (FS J. Wellhausen, BZAW 27. Giessen, 1914), 65–77, with the further suggestion that the paragraph was abbreviated when it was moved; Nowack, pp. 154 and 158.

10. Cripps, p. 311.

11. Van Hoonacker, pp. 261 and 267.

12. Sellin, p. 253 (following 9:6); Weiser, p. 130, Rudolph, p. 252.

v. 9 must have been an integral part of the third vision from the start, since otherwise there would be no sufficient explanation for the present position of vv. 10–17.

This simple catchword principle, however, does not adequately account for the close connection between verses 9 and 10–17. In addition to the repetition already mentioned in verses 9 and 11, we should also observe first the unexpected use of *yiṣḥāq* [['Isaac']] in verses 9 and 16 as a parallel to Israel. This name is not used anywhere else in the book of Amos, and it further stands out because of the very rare spelling with *ś*[13] instead of the normal *ṣ*. Second, *miqdāš* [['sanctuary, temple']] occurs in verses 9 and 13, but again nowhere else in the book of Amos. Third, the catchword *baḥèrèb* [['by the sword']] occurs not only in verses 9 and 11, as already noted, but also in verse 17. In the case of so common a word, this might be considered insignificant. However, in the present context it should be allowed to carry greater weight. That verses 11 and 17 are closely related is evident from the verbal identity of their concluding clauses (*wĕyiśrā'ēl gālōh yiglèh mē'al 'admātô* [['and Israel must go into exile away from its land']]) and because they alone in the present passage are introduced by the messenger formula *kōh 'āmar* [['thus says']] (*'āmôs* [['Amos']] in v. 11, *yhwh* in v. 17). Since there can thus be no disagreement that verses 9 and 11, and 11 and 17, cannot be separated from one another, it seems plausible to assume in addition that the use of *baḥèrèb* in all three verses is consciously intended. Fourth, it will be obvious by now that I agree with the case put forward by Ackroyd[14] when he argues for a considerable degree of word-play in this passage. Many of the points that Ackroyd makes relate only to verses 10–17, and so cannot be used directly as evidence that verse 9 is an integral part of the paragraph, but insofar as that verse contributes, as we have seen, to this literary [[104]] style which characterises the paragraph as a whole, it becomes less easy to regard it as having once stood in isolation. In conclusion, since there is no clear verbal connection between verse 9 and the visions of 1–8 but every indication that it is all of a piece with verses 10–17, it is evident that the so-called catchword between verses 9 and 11 is not sufficient to explain the position of (9)10–17 in their present context.[15]

13. Elsewhere only at Jer 33:26 and Ps 105:9.

14. P. R. Ackroyd, "A Judgment Narrative between Kings and Chronicles? An Approach to Amos 7:9–17," in G. W. Coats and B. O. Long (eds), *Canon and Authority. Essays in Old Testament Religion and Theology* (Philadelphia, 1977), 71–87 (esp. 73–77), reprinted in *Studies in the Religious Tradition of the Old Testament* (London, 1987), 195–208; see also J. Morgenstern, *Amos Studies* (Cincinnati, 1941), 81–82.

15. It should be emphasised at this point that this does not, of course, resolve the problem of how vv. 9–17 originally developed, a discussion that would inevitably be highly speculative. It is sufficient to establish that these verses must have become a single literary unit before their inclusion into their present context.

If neither historical nor formal literary explanations for the positioning of Amos 7:9–17 are satisfactory, then it is inevitable that we should move thirdly to a consideration of possible redactional intention. Surprisingly, this approach appears to have been seriously adopted only by Wolff.[16] He sees a two-way relationship between the vision reports and the third person material. On the one hand, the third and fourth visions explain how the experience of 7:15 came about; this reading makes 7:15 the effective climax of the section as a whole. On the other hand, Amos's expulsion from Bethel (7:12) explains why Amos wrote down his visions (p. 341 = ET, p. 295). With regard to v. 9, it should be noted in passing, Wolff adopts a mediating position. He does not think it was part of the original vision report, but equally he does not regard it as of a single piece with vv. 10–17. Recognising nevertheless the close verbal links with the following paragraph, he suggests that it was inserted precisely to facilitate the introduction of vv. 10–17. Understanding the third vision to mean that God's intervention is inevitable, it spells out what that will mean in certain specific cases.

Wolff is surely right to seek to interpret 7:9–17 in the wider context provided by the vision reports, but it has to be asked whether his suggestions are adequate or go far enough. First, even if the eviction from Bethel explains why Amos wrote down his visions, it is unlikely that the editor was concerned to convey such information, or was even interested by it. Certainly, there is no hint in the text to suggest that such a modern, scholarly preoccupation played any part in the shaping of the passage. Second, Wolff offers no explanation as to why the interruption came between the third and fourth visions rather than following the fourth, as might have been expected on his interpretation. As an authentication of the prophet's call, the visions might be considered to function more effectively in their original unity; the question therefore remains why the series was interrupted. Furthermore, Wolff's explanation of v. 9 would also seem more suitable if it had followed 8:1–2, where the end of Israel is explicitly announced. Thus he fails to ⟦105⟧ account for the present position of 7:9–17. Third, the consequence of Wolff's interpretation is to place the emphasis of both visions and narrative on the prophet's call, whereas most scholars today would stress rather (as

16. I pass over Amsler's opinion (p. 228) that the paragraph's position is purely accidental, and also K. Koch's suggestion that "In the editing process the account of the dramatic outward events accompanying Amos' appearance in Bethel have been coupled with the visionary accounts about dramatic 'inward' events in chs. 7f., so that as we read them, the two contrasting sides of the man Amos appear vividly before our eyes" (*The Prophets. Volume One: The Assyrian Period* [London, 1982], p. 39 = ET of *Die Profeten I. Assyrische Zeit* [Stuttgart, 1978], 50). Though this may be the *effect* of the combination of the material, it is highly unlikely that it was also its sole motivation.

Würthwein did long ago[17]) that this call is itself recounted in order to add weight to the prophet's pronouncements. It would seem preferable, then, to seek a solution to the problems of 7:9–17 in terms which both justify its present literary setting and which do so on the basis of the content rather than the fact of the visions.

In the case of 8:1–2, there is no great difficulty for our present purpose; the vision leads to the categorical and unqualified statement that "the end has come upon my people Israel." 7:7–8 is far more problematic, however, because of uncertainty surrounding the meaning of ʾănāk. While an exhaustive survey of opinions is out of the question here, we should at least outline some of the major options which have been canvassed during the present century.[18]

Condamin[19] insisted that ʾănāk referred to some kind of metal—without being certain as to precisely which sort—and so saw in the wall an impregnable rampart and in that which the Lord held in his hand a military weapon. The vision thus represented an approaching war which (v. 9) would lead to the destruction of Israel.

Van Hoonacker (pp. 265–67) raised a number of objections to Condamin's proposal, and favoured instead an approach by way of the metaphor used elsewhere (cf. Isa 1:25; Ezek 22:17ff.) of Israel as a metal in need of purification. In this vision, however, the Lord was himself adding an impurity (whether lead or tin); "il s'agirait naturellement de la condition à laquelle Israël devait être réduit par le châtiment divin" [['it would naturally refer to the state to which Israel had to be reduced by the divine punishment']]. Consequently, Van Hoonacker speculated further that instead of ḥômat 'wall of' in v. 7, which plays no further part in the vision or its explanation, we should read ḥammat, the consequent phrase 'heat of lead' meaning 'plomb brûlant'.

---

17. E. Würthwein, "Amos-Studien," ZAW 62 (1950), 10–52 (especially pp. 19–24 and 28–35).

18. Earlier opinions are concisely presented by G. Brunet, "La vision de l'étain; réinterpretation d'Amos vii 7–9," VT 16 (1966), 387–95. As others have done, he reminds us that the familiar translation 'plumb-line' is not attested before the mediaeval period (Rashi and Kimḥi; Ibn Ezra simply has 'lead'). The ancient versions offer various translations: LXX and Symmachus, adamantinos 'adamantine, of steel', and adamas 'adamant', probably 'steel' (Peshitta's ʾdmos is simply a loanword from the Greek); Aquila, ganōsis 'varnishing, plastering'; Theodotion, tēkomenon 'molten'; Vulgate, litum 'plastered', and trulla cementarii 'building trowel'; Targum interprets throughout as dyn 'judgement'. In view of what follows, it is extraordinary that neither the first fascicle of the revised Koehler-Baumgartner lexicon (3d ed. Leiden, 1967), 69, nor the recent 18th edition of Gesenius' Handwörterbuch, edited by R. Meyer and H. Donner (Berlin, 1987), 81, even so much as indicates that there is a problem concerning the meaning of ʾănāk.

19. A. Condamin, "Le prétendu 'fil à plomb' de la vision d'Amos," RB 9 (1900), 586–94. He has been followed in particular by Marti, pp. 210–11.

In 1965, B. Landsberger added an important contribution to the discussion when he argued strongly that the Akkadian cognate *anaku* must mean tin.[20] He [[106]] showed that the reason why some previous lexicographers had thought of lead was precisely because of the passage in Amos rather than internal Akkadian evidence. Landsberger does not offer a translation of our passage, but his comment that *ʾănāk* = 'tin' was used here as "a symbol of (a) softness, (b) uselessness, unless alloyed to another metal, (c) perishability" (p. 287) suggests that he saw in it a symbol of Israel herself.[21]

Like Landsberger, Ouellette also regarded *ʾănāk* = tin in a negative light.[22] Believing that Amos's visions all depicted metaphysical realities and illustrating that neither in Israel nor elsewhere in the ancient Near East was the idea of a metal wall in any way strange,[23] he maintained that in some Mesopotamian rituals connected with the placing of foundation deposits tin had a decidedly negative value ('valeur negative'). Thus when God says that he is going to "put some tin in the midst of my people Israel," "Amos voyait dans l'étain un mauvais présage pour le peuple d'Israël" [['Amos saw in the tin an evil omen for the people of Israel']] (p. 328). Ouellette was thus able to exploit the presumed word-play between *ʾnk* and *ʾnḥ* 'to sigh', 'groan', which had already been proposed by Horst.[24]

Ouellette's theory seems questionable, however. We may doubt whether his starting point—the "reality" of Amos's visions—can be justified in the light of the second vision, and whether the point of the third vision as he understands it would have been appreciated by Amos's audience; but more importantly, we must insist that, on the basis of the texts adduced as evidence, the ill-omen reputedly associated with tin is grossly exaggerated. His first example comes from the series *iqqur-īpuš*, on which Ellis comments, "One section gives the prognosis if a man, in building his house, finds various metals in the old foundations. The materials listed are silver, gold, copper, (a) stone, tin, lead, 'something hard(?),' and something which cannot be removed(?)."[25] Here we should

20. B. Landsberger, "Tin and Lead: The Adventures of Two Vocables," *JNES* 24 (1965), 285–96. He has been widely followed by specialists in Assyriology; cf. *CAD* A/2, 127–30.
21. Landsberger's understanding of Amos 7:7–8 itself has not been generally accepted, but cf. H. R. Cohen, *Biblical Hapax Legomena in the Light of Akkadian and Ugaritic* (SBLDS 37. Missoula, 1978), 137.
22. J. Ouellette, "Le mur d'étain dans Amos, vii, 7–9," *RB* 80 (1973), 321–31.
23. H. Gese, "Komposition bei Amos," in J. A. Emerton (ed.), *Congress Volume. Vienna 1980* (SVT 32. Leiden, 1981), 74–95, adds further examples from the classical world; cf. pp. 80–81, n. 18.
24. F. Horst, "Die Visionsschilderungen der alttestamentlichen Propheten," *EvTh* 20 (1960), 193–205 (201).
25. R. S. Ellis, *Foundation Deposits in Ancient Mesopotamia* (New Haven and London, 1968), 103.

note that the ill-omen is associated with the finding, not laying, of the foundation deposit and that tin is only one of a number of materials, others of which certainly do not in themselves carry negative overtones. Ouellette's other main example is drawn from the ritual of the *kalû* priest in the repair of a temple. The relevant section reads, "The builder of that temple shall put on clean clothes and put a tin bracelet on his arm; he shall take an axe of lead, remove the first brick, and put it in a restricted place."[26] Whatever be the [[107]] significance of this obscure ritual, there is no evidence here that the tin bracelet formed part of a foundation deposit. Indeed, in the few cases where tin is mentioned along with other items in such deposits, there seems to be no reason to isolate it from their positive purpose which Ellis has summarised as sanctification, protection, commemoration, and elaboration (pp. 165–68). Ouellette's theory cannot, therefore, be accepted as an explanation of Amos's third vision.

The year following the publication of Landsberger's article, Brunet[27] offered a more satisfactory contextual interpretation of *ʾănāk* in the sense of tin. Observing that tin was a necessary component of bronze in order to make it sufficiently hard for the manufacture of arms, he argued that in the vision God was shown as having an inexhaustible supply of this comparatively rare mineral,[28] a veritable "wall of tin." This is reinforced by the reference to a sword at the climax of v. 9. Thus the enemies of Israel, God's agents in judgement, would be able to come against the people with "innumerable bronze swords manufactured with the help of the vision's wall of tin" (p. 394).

Rudolph (pp. 234–35) endorsed most of Brunet's criticisms of earlier solutions, and agreed that the metal in question must be tin, but argued that his own proposal foundered on its interpretation of v. 8b (see below). He therefore suggested that *ʾănāk* represented a destructive tool such as a crowbar[29] with which the Lord was about to demolish the "walls" of his people Israel, these "walls" being further specified by v. 9 as the cult centres and kingdom of Israel. It should be noted in passing that Rudolph's interpretation of *ʾănāk* = tin is the only one which still

26. Ellis, p. 184; cf. *ANET*, p. 340b.

27. See above, n. 18. Brunet's opinions were emphatically endorsed by W. L. Holladay, "Once more *ʾănāk* = 'tin', Amos vii 7–8," *VT* 20 (1970), 492–94; see also in similar vein C. van Leeuwen, "Quelques problèmes de traduction dans les visions d'Amos chapitre 7," in *Übersetzung und Deutung* (FS A. R. Hulst. Nijkerk, 1977), 103–12, and Bartczek (above, n. 1), 119–21.

28. By maintaining that *ʾănāk* refers to the mineral rather than the metal, Brunet was able to explain why this word was used in preference to the normal word for tin, *bĕdîl*.

29. Rudolph, p. 235, is mistaken when he implies that he is following Marti in this, and van Leeuwen (above, n. 27) is even further from the mark in adding Condamin to Marti. In fact, Marti closely followed Condamin's different proposal which was outlined above. Perhaps Rudolph intended a reference to Sellin (p. 251).

requires emendation of *ḥômat ᵓănāk* [['wall of tin']] to *ḥômat ᵓēbèn* [['wall of stone']] or the like because of the demands of the context as he understands it, and that he also feels obliged to emend *bĕqèrèb* [['in the midst of']], v. 8, to *bĕqîrōt*: 'I am setting a crowbar in the walls of my people Israel'.[30] But fatal to Rudolph's theory is that neither tin nor lead is a suitable material for a crowbar. Only as part of an alloy does tin form a hard metal, but of that the context gives no hint.

The general approach adopted by Condamin and Brunet was taken a stage further by Gese.[31] Earlier in his discussion, he asserts that neither in Jer 1:11–12 nor in Amos 8:1–2 does the significance of the vision depend solely on word-play. [[108]] In each case that which is seen carries its own symbolic meaning within it, and this is only reinforced and made explicit by the word-play. Similarly in our passage; the wall of tin, that necessary component in the manufacture of hard bronze, represents overwhelming military potential, and this is reinforced by the fact that God is seen holding some of this material in his hand. Furthermore, Gese finds it significant that Amos should have chosen to use the normal Akkadian word for tin rather than the regular Hebrew *bĕdîl*; it serves as a pointer to the military power which God is preparing to use. Finally, in line with his overall approach, Gese also finds a word-play in *ᵓănāk* which stands in pronunciation between *ᵓănāḥ* and *ᵓănāq*.

More recently, W. Beyerlin has devoted a whole monograph to the interpretation of Amos's third vision.[32] He too takes as his starting point the conviction that *ᵓănāk* means tin, but unlike the views just described he believes that the tin wall with the Lord stationed above it represents initially God's defence of his people against attack, as would have been popularly believed by Amos's contemporaries. Moreover, being seen in a vision, this shimmering wall would have had overtones of a theophany. Beyerlin is closer to Brunet over the meaning of tin in the Lord's hand except that in the first place it does not just represent a sword (he regards v. 9 as a later redactional interpretation of the vision) but, being again in a vision context, "in Gottes Hand ist es Andeutung enormer Waffengewalt, der Menschen nicht standhalten können" [['in God's hand it is an indication of a great armed force against which humanity cannot stand']] (p. 35); and in the second place this power is still set for the defence of the nation. At this point, however, Beyerlin finds a reversal of the expected, such as is typical of Amos, for when God speaks

---

30. Following K. Budde, "Zu Text und Auslegung des Buches Amos," *JBL* 44 (1925), 63–122 (76).

31. See above, n. 23. He has been followed enthusiastically by A. G. Auld, *Amos* (Old Testament Guides. Sheffield, 1986), 18–21.

32. W. Beyerlin, *Bleilot, Brecheisen oder was sonst? Revision einer Amos-Vision* (OBO 81. Freiburg and Göttingen, 1988).

again it is to affirm that now he is going to set tin 'in the midst of' his
people (*bĕqèrèb*, i.e., inside the protective wall); the power once thought
to be Israel's protection will now be turned against them.

In the course of this survey of *ʾănāk* = tin, I have already offered
some objections to the theories of Ouellette and Rudolph. It is now necessary to examine the more closely related views of Condamin, Brunet
and Gese, and of those who follow them.

First, they agree that in some way the wall of v. 7 is to be regarded as
threatening from Israel's standpoint. This seems unlikely, however, because of the parallel between this verse and 9:1, which introduces the
fifth vision. There too the Lord is seen *niṣṣāb ʿal* 'standing over/against',
followed in that case by the altar, which, of course, is about to be destroyed. Now, in view of the close relationship between the five visions of
Amos, a relationship for which Gese himself has added further new arguments, it is preferable to take identical phraseology in the same way.
In that case, the wall of 7:7 should be regarded as under threat from the
Lord, not part of his offensive weaponry.

Second, it may be questioned whether this approach provides an
adequate ⟦109⟧ explanation for part of v. 8, namely *hinĕnî śām ʾănāk*
bĕqèrèb ʿammî yiśrāʾēl ⟦'Behold, I am setting *ʾănāk* in the midst of my
people Israel'⟧. Brunet, it will be recalled, virtually sees *ʾănāk* as a synonym for *ḥèrèb* ⟦'sword'⟧. Indeed, although in one place he translates
the phrase in question as 'Voici que je mets l'étain dans le sein de mon
peuple Israël', he immediately goes on to explain what this means: "*Je*
mets l'épée dans le sein de mon peuple, cela le confirme bien, c'était dire: *je*
mets l'épée, je plonge l'épée dans le sein de mon peuple" ⟦'*I put the sword into*
the breast of my people . . . I put the sword, I thrust the sword into the breast of
my people'⟧ (p. 394). But here, it must be objected, Brunet allows
himself to be carried away with his theory, for even if *ḥèrèb* had actually
stood in place of *ʾănāk*, the use of the root *śym* ⟦'put, set'⟧ could not
justify the translation 'je plonge', even though such a meaning is demanded by Brunet's approach. For the meaning Brunet wants, we
should expect a verb like *tqʿ* (cf. Judg 3:21). With less dramatic force,
the hiphʿil of *bwʾ* ⟦'come'⟧ is quite frequently used for the Lord "bringing the sword" against his people. The only example I have been able to
find of *ḥèrèb* as the object of *śym* used in an aggressive sense is Judg 7:22,
but there the meaning is different: 'the Lord set every man's sword
against his fellow'. It thus seems improbable that the verb *śym* should
have been chosen at Amos 7:8 if it had the meaning which Brunet
thinks.

It must be asked, however, whether it is in any case justified to understand *ʾănāk* as sword in this verse. Brunet does not face this question
beyond pointing to the climactic use of 'sword' in v. 9 (which we have

already argued does not belong originally with the vision), but van Leeu-wen attempts an explanation: "l'étain représente—pars pro toto—les armes ennemies, par lesquelles Dieu accomplira sa punition au milieu de son peuple" [['the tin represents—[using the] part for the whole—the enemy weapons through which God will accomplish his punishment in the midst of his people']].[33] The difficulty here is the sudden switch in the meaning and use of ʾănāk which this view presupposes, but for which nothing in the context has prepared the reader. How can 'tin' as a nec-essary component for the manufacture of bronze arms suddenly repre-sent those arms themselves when they have not been referred to at any point in the narrative? "Pars pro toto" [['part for the whole']] seems to be an inappropriate principle to apply in response to this difficulty. Thus the use both of śām... bĕqèrèb and of ʾănāk in v. 8 poses difficulties for Brunet's approach.

Gese, of course, avoids this latter problem by retaining throughout the sense of tin for ʾănāk. Unfortunately, however, this does nothing to clarify the meaning of our phrase; whereas it is possible to understand that a tin wall might be understood as a threat and that the availability of tin in God's hand might indicate his ability to produce high-quality weapons, there is no threat whatever involved in his 'placing some tin in the midst of my people'. It may be significant that Gese offers no trans-lation of this phrase at any point in his discussion.

Thirdly, in addition to these two specific points regarding the mean-ing of niṣṣāb ʿal [['stationed beside']] and of śām ʾănāk bĕqèrèb, there must remain serious doubt whether the vision and its explanation as thus understood would have been intelligible to Amos's readers or listeners. At the very least, it is highly cryptic by [[110]] comparison with the un-equivocally blunt bāʾ haqqēṣ ʾèl-ʿammî yiśrāʾēl [['the end has come upon my people Israel']] of 8:2. But beyond that, I am not aware of any evi-dence that the mention of tin on its own—even as an Akkadian loan-word—would be sufficient to trigger the train of thought that tin is a component of bronze but is rarer than copper, so that if the Lord has plenty of tin he can make plenty of bronze with which to supply the enemy with plenty of weapons to use against us.[34] To be blunt, it seems far-fetched.

---

33. C. van Leeuwen (above, n. 27), 110.

34. Brunet, p. 391, suggests as a modern equivalent the impact that would be made by referring to a "wall of uranium," but the analogy is not exact. The word uranium itself has threatening overtones, and is used directly in connection with weapons. 'Tin', however, was useless on its own, and could equally be used in positive contexts, as noted above. Thus there is no evidence that merely to refer to tin would be enough to conjure up threatening images.

I shall refrain here from a full discussion of Beyerlin's monograph, because that would take us far beyond the confines of this article; suffice it to say, therefore, that although his understanding of the wall is different from that of Brunet and Gese, the use of *niṣṣāb ʿal* [['stationed beside']] in the light of 9:1 is as damaging to his view as it is to theirs, and that he effectively rejoins them in the interpretation of the second half of v. 8, so that my criticisms of them at that point are equally applicable to him.

Alongside approaches to the problem of *ʾănāk* by way of the meaning tin or the like, there have continued to be many who still favour the traditional interpretation of 'plumb-line'.[35] None that I know of, however, has tried systematically to answer the objections to this view which have been raised by adherents to alternative positions. This should be a worthwhile exercise, in order to test how strong these objections are and hence whether they categorically rule out the meaning 'plumb-line'.

(i) It is often observed that the meaning 'plumb-line' is not attested earlier than the mediaeval Jewish commentators. This argument is only of very limited weight, since it is usually raised by those who in fact wish to support an even more recent, if not totally novel, suggestion. Naturally, it is reassuring to find ancient support for a suggested interpretation, but the fact remains that the meanings of words were sometimes forgotten in the intervening centuries and, as we have noted (above, n. 18), there is in the present instance no unified versional tradition. That being so, a rendering which has commended itself since the middle ages is, at least, likely to be contextually appropriate.

(ii) Opponents of the plumb-line theory make much of the fact that in Akkadian (as in some other languages) the cognate word means tin. Two points [[111]] deserve mention here. The first is that, without wishing to challenge the Assyriological evidence, that fact alone does not necessarily settle the issue so far as Hebrew is concerned, especially since, as is well known, Hebrew has its own regular equivalents for both tin (*bĕdîl*) and lead (*ʿōpèrèt*). The two metals were undoubtedly

---

35. Confining ourselves to some prominent examples since Landsberger's article in 1965, we may note among the commentators that Hammershaimb and Mays still write without any reference to the possibility of *ʾănāk* meaning tin, while Wolff dismisses Brunet's proposal on the grounds that 'tin wall' and 'tin in his hand' are incompatible, that tin should not have been used if sword were meant, and that 7:9 is not part of the original vision report. Of these objections, the latter two are cogent, but Wolff does not grapple with the difficulties of *ʾănāk* = plumb-line nor present fully the alternative point of view. He appears to be unaware of Landsberger's article, unlike Soggin, who nevertheless retains the meaning plumb-line on the questionable evidence of *AHw* that *anāku* can also mean lead. Without independent discussion, Wolff is followed in particular by S. Niditch, *The Symbolic Vision in Biblical Tradition* (HSM 30. Chico, 1983), 22.

confused sometimes in antiquity:[36] in Arabic, the cognate *ʾanuk* covers both tin and lead,[37] while in Latin *stagnum* only came to mean tin in the late period. Before that it meant 'a mixture of silver and lead', tin being designated at that time by *plumbum album*, literally 'white lead'.[38] In Egypt there also appears to have been occasional confusion, though the evidence for this is disputed.[39] There can thus be no certainty, only a probability in the light of the nearer cognates, that *ʾănāk* does not after all mean lead in Amos 7:7–8.

(iii) A further consideration in this regard, however, is that even if *ʾănāk* is tin, that does not (paradoxically!) necessarily rule out the meaning plumb-line. In Zech 4:10 there is mention of "*hāʾèbèn habbĕdîl* in the hand of Zerubbabel." Several modern commentators regard this as part of a foundation deposit or other such item relating to a building ritual.[40] Whether or not this is true, the fact remains that it was understood as a plumb-line by several of the ancient versions (as well as many other commentators since[41]): this is quite certain in the case of the Targum's *ʾèbèn mišqôlētāʾ*, very probable in the case of the Vulgate's *lapidem stagneum* (*stagnum*: an alloy of lead with variable amounts of silver[42]), and

36. See generally R. J. Forbes, *Studies in Ancient Technology* (Leiden, 1964), vol. 8, pp. 200–201, and vol. 9, pp. 155–59; and, with particular attention to the difficulties of identifying *bĕdîl*, G. R. Driver, "Babylonian and Hebrew Notes," *WO* 2 (1954–59), 19–26 (21–24).

37. See the Lexicons of G. W. Freytag and E. W. Lane. It was by way of Arabic that Kimḥi justified his understanding of *ʾănāk* as lead, plumb-line. I am grateful to my colleague Professor M. C. Lyons for his comments on the matter: "The examples of usage quoted—or the early ones—suggest lead to me (as being poured into the ears of various unfortunates on the Day of Judgement). The common Arabic word for lead is *raṣāṣ*, and so [*ʾanuk*] may either be regional or used by a particular group. . . . In certain contexts, the word does cover both lead and tin" (personal communication of 27. iv. 1988).

38. Cf. J. D. Muhly, *Copper and Tin. The Distribution of Mineral Resources and the Nature of the Metals Trade in the Bronze Age* (Hamden, Connecticut, 1973), 240.

39. See, for instance, J. R. Harris, *Lexicographical Studies in Ancient Egyptian Minerals* (Berlin, 1961), 66–68, whereas Muhly, pp. 244–46, argues that there was no such confusion. It is of interest to note that *ʾn3wk* appears once in Egyptian, apparently as a loan-word from Akkadian, with the probable meaning tin; cf. Harris, pp. 62–63.

40. E.g., A. Petitjean, *Les oracles du Proto-Zacharie* (Études Bibliques. Paris and Louvain, 1969), 226–36; D. L. Petersen, "Zerubbabel and Jerusalem Temple Reconstruction," *CBQ* 36 (1974), 366–72; B. Halpern, "The Ritual Background of Zechariah's Temple Song," *CBQ* 40 (1978), 167–90 (esp. 171–73); S. Amsler in S. Amsler, A. Lacocque and R. Vuilleumier, *Aggée, Zacharie, Malachie* (CAT 11c. Neuchâtel and Paris, 1981), 95; C. L. and E. M. Meyers, *Haggai, Zechariah 1–8* (Anchor Bible 25B. Garden City, 1987), 253–54 and 272.

41. E.g., Keil, p. 570; H. G. Mitchell, *A Critical and Exegetical Commentary on Haggai and Zechariah* (ICC. Edinburgh, 1912), 191; L. G. Rignell, *Die Nachtgesichte des Sacharja. Eine exegetische Studie* (Lund, 1950), 161–62.

42. Cf. P. G. W. Glare, *Oxford Latin Dictionary* (Oxford, 1982), 1813; J. F. Healy, *Mining and Metallurgy in the Greek and Roman World* (London, 1978), 178–81. As noted earlier, *stagnum* came to mean tin only later; Muhly (above, n. 38) cites as an example Isidore, *Origines*, 16.22 (i.e., seventh century).

thus likely too in the case of LXX's (and Aquila's) ⟦112⟧ more literal *ton lithon ton kassiterinon* ⟦'the tin stone'⟧.[43] This seems sufficient to establish that a number of writers in antiquity saw no problem in using tin as part of a plumb-line—and if they did not, presumably Amos need not have either.

(iv) It is sometimes objected that those who translate *ʾănāk* as plumb-line are forced to emend the text at v. 7, and that this theory is therefore inferior to one which does not need to resort to such emendation.[44] Now it is true that various emendations have been proposed: some omit *ʾănāk* on its first appearance and read the absolute *ḥômâ* ⟦'wall'⟧,[45] while others emend *ʾănāk* to *ʾèbèn* ⟦'stone'⟧ or the like.[46] The intrusive *ʾănāk* is explained as a result of scribal dittography, in view of the three occurrences of the word later in the passage. However, no emendation is in fact necessary. It is well known that the construct relationship can be used to express relationships between nouns which go far wider than a simple genitive, and if *ʾănāk* means plumb-line, then there is no reason why *ḥômat ʾănāk* should not mean 'a wall built with a plumb-line'.[47] Admittedly, this passage is not discussed in the standard reference grammars, nor do the commentators I have consulted offer a detailed syntactical justification, but there is no need to look further than 1 Kgs 19:6—*ʿuggat rĕṣāpîm* 'a cake baked on hot stones'—for a close analogy. (Good illustrations of the wide and varied use of the construct state can be easily provided, though they do not furnish so close an analogy, e.g., Ps 51:19, *zibḥê ʾĕlōhîm* 'sacrifices which are acceptable to God'; 2 Chr 24:6, *masʾat mōšèh* 'the tax prescribed by Moses'. The point is that in each case it is necessary to supply appropriate words for a translation into English on the basis of the context; cf. GK §128f–q.) On this view, *ḥômat ʾănāk* does not mean a wall that is now true to the plumb-line; that is the misunderstanding which has led to the need for emendation because it contradicts what follows. Rather the picture is of a wall once straight that has become out of line (by no means a rare occurrence! cf. Isa 30:13). As such it furnishes a fine illustration of Amos's understanding of Israel (e.g., 2:6–12; 3:1–2) and v. 8 provides a close interpretation of the vision. The passage thus becomes fully intelligible without the need to include v. 9.

43. For the different understanding of the other ancient versions, cf. W. Rudolph, *Haggai—Sacharja 1–8—Sacharja 9–14—Maleachi* (KAT 13/4. Gütersloh, 1976), 111.
44. See, for instance, Holladay (above, n. 27), 493; it is worth observing that Rudolph's approach is also conditional upon emendation at this point.
45. E.g., Harper, p. 165, with further references.
46. E.g., Sellin, p. 251; Rudolph, p. 234; V. Maag, *Text, Wortschatz und Begriffswelt des Buches Amos* (Leiden, 1951), 43–44.
47. So most recently Soggin, but cf. Keil; Driver.

In the light of these remarks, it has to be concluded that discussion of the meaning of ʾănāk has reached an impasse. The word is a *hapax legomenon* in the sense of a word which occurs in only a single context in the Bible.[48] Faced with a *hapax legomenon*, scholars generally appeal to (i) ancient traditions of interpretation, as attested principally in the versions, (ii) comparison with other [113] Semitic languages, and (iii) suitability to the context.[49] We have seen that (i) is not particularly weighty or helpful here, (ii) favours tin but does not rule out lead/plumb-line, and (iii) argues against tin and is compatible with lead/plumb-line. What is missing, of course, is clear evidence from antiquity in favour of the contextually superior reading. We are thus faced with an inevitable difficulty in returning to our main discussion of the reason why 7:9–17 was inserted at just this point. I propose to proceed to suggest an explanation on the basis of ʾănāk = plumb-line, but in view of the uncertainties I shall also indicate at the end how basically the same explanation might be satisfactory if ʾănāk = tin. Though this is not my primary purpose, it will be hard to resist bearing in mind throughout the question whether any of this can at the same time shed additional light on the dilemma just outlined.

Since W. H. Schmidt's celebrated article of 1965,[50] it has been widely recognised that during the course of its transmission the book of Amos underwent some form of Deuteronomic redaction. Schmidt's discussion focussed only on various verses in Amos 1–2 and on 3:1, 7 and 5:25f., though Wolff (pp. 137–38 = ET, pp. 112–13) would add parts of 6:1 and possibly 8:11–12. However, since we have established that 7:9–17 probably owes its present position to redactional activity, it seems worthwhile asking whether this too is not part of the same or a related process.[51] In formulating this proposal, I should add that I am well aware of the dangers of "pan-deuteronomism" in current Old Testament scholarship.

48. See the discussion in Cohen (above, n. 21), 6–7.

49. This, of course, presupposes that the *hapax legomenon* is not removed by emendation. Various emendations have been proposed for Amos 7:7–8, though none would remove all references to ʾănāk; see especially Morgenstern (above, n. 14), 80–88, and H. Graf Reventlow, *Das Amt des Propheten bei Amos* (FRLANT 80. Göttingen, 1962), 36–42.

50. W. H. Schmidt, "Die deuteronomistische Redaktion des Amosbuches. Zu den theologischen Unterschieden zwischen dem Prophetenwort und seinem Sammler," *ZAW* 77 (1965), 168–93.

51. Subsequent to formulating the broad outline of the present proposal, I discovered that in some respects I had been anticipated in this by R. B. Coote, *Amos among the Prophets. Composition and Theology* (Philadelphia, 1966), especially pp. 60–62. However, apart from other differences of emphasis, I seek in what follows to ground the proposal rather more fully than Coote does in the context of what is avowedly a more introductory study (cf. p. v). J. Vermeylen, *Du prophète Isaïe à l'apocalyptique. Isaïe, i–xxxv, miroir d'un demi-millénaire d'expérience religieuse en Israël* (Études Bibliques. Paris, 1978), vol. 2, pp. 565f., finds evidence of the hand of the Deuteronomists in this paragraph but without considering the question of its setting in the chapter as a whole.

The question of who the Deuteronomist(s) may have been raises a number of hitherto unanswered questions into which I cannot enter here. It will be sufficient for my purpose to try to demonstrate that Amos 7:9–17 owes its present position to an editor who shared many of the views normally characterised as Deuteronomic. My use of such terms as "Deuteronomic circles" in what follows should not be taken to mean anything more than a form of shorthand for this rather general position.

The role of the prophets was self-evidently a matter of great interest to the Deuteronomists in the composition of the historical books, and a number of ⟦114⟧ studies have been devoted to varying aspects of this subject.[52] Our concern in the present context is not with the various accounts about prophets which have been incorporated into the work on the basis of earlier material, but rather with the summary statements which reflect the editor's appreciation of the role and function of prophecy and the prophets as a whole, and which thus illustrate the programmatic statement about them in Deut 18:15–19.

These passages comprise especially (i) 2 Kgs 17:13, in which the prophets collectively are said to have warned Israel to keep the law which "I sent to you by the hand of my servants the prophets" but which the people nevertheless rejected (v. 14); (ii) 2 Kgs 17:23, where the exile of the northern kingdom is said to have been foretold by "all his servants the prophets"; (iii) 2 Kgs 21:10–15, in which in the context of Manasseh's sin the prophets foretell the end of Judah and Jerusalem; and (iv) 2 Kgs 24:2, where the attacks of bands of Chaldaeans and others, leading to the destruction of Judah, are said to have been "according to the word of the Lord, which he spake by the hand of his servants the prophets."

The precise status of these passages within the redactional history of the Deuteronomic History is disputed, though most if not all of them are generally agreed to be amongst the latest layers of the work. For Noth himself, of course, the issue hardly arose, since he conceived of the History in its entirety as an exilic composition providing a theological rationale for the fall of the Israelite kingdoms.[53]

Two main alternatives to Noth's unified approach have been proposed. The first, often characterised as that of the Göttingen school, is best represented for our purposes in the work of Dietrich, who ascribes

---

52. In addition to the works of Dietrich, Seeligmann and Campbell cited below, cf. G. von Rad, *Deuteronomium-Studien* (FRLANT 58. Göttingen, 1947), 52–64 = ET "The Deuteronomic Theology of History in *I* and *II Kings*," in *The Problem of the Hexateuch and Other Essays* (Edinburgh and London, 1966), 205–21; O. H. Steck, *Israel und das gewaltsame Geschick der Propheten* (WMANT 23. Neukirchen, 1967); A. G. Auld, "Prophets and Prophecy in Jeremiah and Kings," *ZAW* 96 (1984), 66–82.

53. M. Noth, *Überlieferungsgeschichtliche Studien* (Halle, 1943). Noth regarded 2 Kgs 17:21–23, however, as a later addition to the work of Dtr; cf. p. 85.

all but 2 Kgs 17:13 to the work of his DtrP redactor.[54] It will be recalled that Dietrich's analysis does not start from these passages, but from four others in which in relative degrees ⟦115⟧ of isolation from their contexts a prophet utters a threat against the dynasties of the Northern Kingdom: 1 Kgs 14:7–11; 16:1–4; 21:20bβ–24; and 2 Kgs 9:7–10a. Similarities of form and terminology between these passages are certainly noteworthy, and they may be drawn into our present discussion by the reference to "my servants the prophets" in 2 Kgs 9:7. Clearly, the role of the prophets in these passages is not far removed from those we have already considered, but they may be most conveniently left out of account for the moment because of their application to specific dynasties rather than to the fate of the nation as a whole. In addition, not all scholars would agree in attributing them to the latest stage in the work's composition.[55]

The second alternative to Noth's understanding of the Deuteronomic History is that of Cross.[56] This view envisages the history receiving its basic shape in the reign of Josiah and then being updated during the exile. While Cross himself included 2 Kgs 21:10–15 and 24:2 in this exilic redaction, he retained the bulk of 2 Kings 17 in his first edition. Those who have subsequently developed and refined his position, however, have generally ascribed the parts of that chapter with which we are concerned to the exilic edition.[57]

There is thus a widespread measure of agreement[58] that at more or less the latest stage in the development of the Deuteronomic History (and thus largely determinative of its final outlook) there emerged the view that the fall of the kingdom was as much due to the rejection of the

---

54. W. Dietrich, *Prophetie und Geschichte. Eine redaktionsgeschichtliche Untersuchung zum deuteronomistischen Geschichtswerk* (FRLANT 108. Göttingen, 1972). Dietrich ascribes 2 Kgs 17:13 to the even later DtrN precisely because of its different view of prophecy (41–46). Dietrich is closely followed by, for instance, G. H. Jones, *1 and 2 Kings* (NCB. Grand Rapids and London, 1984), 543, 594 and 634. E. Würthwein, *Die Bücher der Könige. 1. Kön. 17–2. Kön. 25* (ATD. Göttingen, 1984), differs only in that he ascribes the bulk of 2 Kgs 17:21–23 to DtrG, the primary stratum of the Deuteronomic History. He accepts, however, that the reference to the prophets in v. 23 is an addition by DtrP (p. 395). For some searching criticism of Dietrich's views as a whole, see, for instance, A. D. H. Mayes, *The Story of Israel between Settlement and Exile. A Redactional Study of the Deuteronomistic History* (London, 1983), 113–20; I. W. Provan, *Hezekiah and the Books of Kings. A Contribution to the Debate about the Composition of the Deuteronomistic History* (BZAW 172. Berlin, 1988), 24–27.

55. For instance, A. F. Campbell, *Of Prophets and Kings. A Late Ninth-Century Document (1 Samuel 1–2 Kings 10)* (CBQMS 17. Washington, 1986).

56. F. M. Cross, *Canaanite Myth and Hebrew Epic* (Cambridge, Mass., 1973), 274–89.

57. See, for instance, R. D. Nelson, *The Double Redaction of the Deuteronomistic History* (JSOTSS 18. Sheffield, 1981), 53–63; Mayes, *The Story of Israel*, 125–27.

58. A partially dissenting voice is that of Provan, *Hezekiah and the Books of Kings*, 70–73, who regards 2 Kgs 17:21–23 as much earlier. He does not, however, consider Würthwein's

prophetic word as it was to the offences which themselves gave rise to that word. Through the prophets, the Lord had repeatedly warned both Israel and Judah of the dire consequences of disobedience (2 Kgs 17:13), thus reflecting the paradigm of Deut 18:18f. itself.[59] The implication is that at this stage repentance remained open as a possibility,[60] and no doubt many of the stories concerning the prophets which are included in the History will have been read in that light. Once that possibility was rejected, however, it fell to the prophets also to announce the now inevitable and irrevocable judgement.[61]

[[116]] This same pattern of thinking, I suggest, is reflected in the positioning of Amos 7:9–17 between the prophet's third and fourth visions. After the first two visions, in which Amos's intercession succeeds in averting the threatened judgement, matters take a turn for the worse in the third vision. Now, as the interpretation in v. 8b makes clear, Israel is portrayed (on the understanding we are following here) as a wall that had been originally built with the aid of a plumb-line, and now God was to test it with the same instrument to see if it was still true. Thus far, judgement is not inevitable, though the closing words of the vision—"I will not again pass by them any more"—suggest that in the original vision cycle the outcome of the test was regarded as a foregone conclusion.[62] In the fourth vision, as we have already noted, the position has advanced to the point where there is no longer any doubt: the end is announced without any possibility of qualification.

Given this state of affairs, it would not seem unreasonable for an individual or editorial circle, concerned to pass on the words of Amos in a new situation, to ask what exactly was this "plumb-line" in God's hand

---

view, noted earlier, that the reference to the prophets in v. 23 might have been added later in view of the fact that he certainly regards all the other passages under consideration (including 2 Kgs 17:13) as exilic.

59. On the significance of this passage in the History as a whole, cf. Clements, *Prophecy and Tradition*, 41–57.

60. Cf. H. W. Wolff, "Das Kerygma des deuteronomistischen Geschichtswerk," *ZAW* 73 (1961), 171–86.

61. It is of interest to note that this pattern which the Deuteronomists saw in the history of their people as a whole was interpreted later by the Chronicler as applying to each separate generation and individual king as well; cf. my *1 and 2 Chronicles* (NCB. Grand Rapids and London, 1982), 32; S. Japhet, *The Ideology of the Book of Chronicles and Its Place in Biblical Thought* (Hebrew; Jerusalem, 1977), 154–66.

62. There is thus an ironic contrast with Amos 5:17, where, when God says *ʾeʿĕbōr bĕqirbĕkā* [['I will pass through the midst of you']] (both words occurring in 7:8), he also means it as a threat. That judgement falls when God both does and does not 'pass through/ by' his people is possible, of course, only because of the elastic meaning of *ʿbr* [['pass']] on which it appears Amos is playing. On 5:17, see further M. J. Hauan, "The Background and Meaning of Amos 5:17B," *HTR* 79 (1986), 337–48.

that he was about to set in the midst of his people. More recent commentators have not given an explicit answer to this question, but their exegesis seems to imply something along the lines of righteousness, justice, or covenant law, a view of which the author of Isa 28:17 would no doubt have heartily approved ('And I will make [*wĕśamtî*!] judgement the line and righteousness the plummet [*mišqālèt*]').[63] I suggest instead, however, that the editors saw the person and mission of the prophet himself as embodying God's plumb-line. Sent to the people to warn of future judgement, his rejection was the final seal on Israel's fate. And it was an account of this rejection which the Deuteronomic editors thus appropriately (on their view) placed deliberately between the third and the fourth visions.[64]

Although we cannot hope here to enter into the multitudinous difficulties surrounding many aspects of the interpretation of Amos 7:9–17,[65] several points stand out which would have made it suitable to serve the Deuteronomists' purpose at this point. First, the reader's attention is primarily focussed on the discussion between Amos and Amaziah. This is framed in verses 11 and [[117]] 17 by a pronouncement of judgement on the king (v. 11) and the priest (v. 17) who acts as his spokesman. Seeligmann[66] has drawn attention to the fact that whereas in the prophetical books the people as a whole, or groups within the people, are primarily addressed, in the Deuteronomic History prophets normally address the king individually. The encounter in Amos 7:9–17 clearly stands within the latter category, and so is distinguished in this regard from the bulk of Amos's recorded preaching.

Secondly, this judgement on the king and priest is linked with identical phraseology in both vv. 11 and 17 with the exile of Israel from its land.[67] This would no doubt have appealed to the Deuteronomists both because of the close association throughout the History between the

---

63. See, for instance, Wolff, Mays, and Soggin.

64. Insofar as this implies the possibility of repentance, it suggests that the editor responsible for positioning 7:9–17 was closer to the Deuteronomic editors of Jeremiah than of the History itself; cf. I. L. Seeligmann, "Die Auffassung von der Prophetie in der deuteronomistischen und chronistischen Geschichtsschreibung (mit einem Exkurs über das Buch Jeremia)" (SVT 29. 1978), 254–84. See also Auld, above, n. 52.

65. It must suffice here to refer to the bibliography of A. van der Wal, *Amos: A Classified Bibliography* (Amsterdam, 1983), to the survey of R. Martin-Achard, *Amos. L'homme, le message, l'influence* (Geneva, 1984), esp. 17–37, and to Soggin, 125–26.

66. Seeligmann, above, n. 64.

67. Cf. G. Pfeifer, "Die Ausweisung eines lästigen Ausländers Amos 7, 10–17," *ZAW* 96 (1984), 112–18; rather differently, A. J. Bjørndalen, "Erwägungen zur Zukunft des Amazja und Israels nach der Überlieferung Amos 7, 10–17," in R. Albertz, H.-P. Müller, H. W. Wolff, and W. Zimmerli (eds.), *Werden und Wirken des Alten Testaments. Festschrift für Claus Westermann zum 70. Geburtstag* (Göttingen and Neukirchen-Vluyn, 1980), 236–51.

conduct of the king and the fate of the nation as a whole, and in particular because it highlights the form of Israel's judgement which, although present elsewhere in Amos (cf. 5:5, 27; 6:7), was one that was far more prominent in their own thinking.

Thirdly, there can be little doubt that, as has been described in particular by Tucker,[68] a major focus of the pericope concerns the issue of prophetic authenticity. Not all would be willing to go so far as to say "The center of the story and its key are found in verse 15, Amos' affirmation of his vocation and commission" (p. 428), but certainly the story cannot be read without due attention to this affirmation, as well as to its rejection by Amaziah. The passage would thus have been easily taken by the Deuteronomists as paradigmatic of their own generalised statements about the role of the prophets already enumerated.

Finally, and very tentatively, the possibility should at least be raised that the emphatic threefold repetition of the first person singular pronoun *ʾānōkî* [['I']] in Amos's statement in verse 14 was viewed as a word-play on the *ʾănāk* of the third vision.[69] That there is word-play involved in the fourth vision is obvious. [[118]] By analogy, several attempts have been made to detect it also in the third,[70] though this is by no means

---

68. G. M. Tucker, "Prophetic Authenticity. A Form-Critical Study of Amos 7:10–17," *Interpretation* 27 (1973), 423–34. See also Reventlow, *Das Amt des Propheten bei Amos* (above n. 49), 14–24; and T. W. Overholt, "Commanding the Prophets: Amos and the Problem of Prophetic Authority," *CBQ* 41 (1979), 517–32.

69. I decline here to speculate on the suggestion first advanced by F. Praetorius, "Bemerkungen zu Amos," *ZAW* 35 (1915), 12–25 (23) and again (apparently independently) by Coote, *Amos among the Prophets*, 92–93 (and with which, again independently, I also toyed at one stage), that within the original account of the third vision itself there was intended a play on the first person pronoun at v. 8b. Since in Phoenician and Moabite the pronoun was actually spelt *ʾnk* (cf. *DISO*, p. 19), there would then be the further possibility that this was more apparent in a northern dialect than in Judah, as also with *qayiṣ/qēṣ* in the fourth vision (on the latter, cf. Rudolph, 239; Gese, 79; and compare the spelling of *yyn* [['wine']] as *yn* in the Samaria ostraca, e.g., *KAI* 185 and 187). If this were the case, the significance of the vision would have been that God was about to presence himself in judgement in Israel (cf. 5:17), this being then reinterpreted by the Deuteronomists in terms of the prophet as his authoritative representative. Rudolph, p. 235, rejects the possibility on grammatical grounds (*ʾnk* could not be the object of *śām* [['set, put']]), though it is not certain that this is decisive in the case of a word-play. I also pass over the conjectural emendation proposed by S. Dean McBride, as reported by D. L. Petersen, *The Roles of Israel's Prophets* (JSOTSS 17. Sheffield, 1981), 77–78, to run *śm* and *ʾnk* together and so to read *śām(ʾ)ēn(n)āk* 'I am setting you'. One should note, however, that if a word-play was originally intended within the vision of 7:7–8, it would explain why the unusual word *ʾănāk* was chosen to express something which, on all views, could have been said with the use of more familiar vocabulary.

70. E.g., by W. Riedel, *Alttestamentliche Untersuchungen* I (Leipzig, 1902), 32–33; Praetorius (see previous note); Horst (above, n. 24); Morgenstern (above, n. 14); and Gese (above, n. 23).

universally agreed. Is it then inconceivable that the Deuteronomists should also have seen in this device a means of drawing attention to their own interpretation of *ʾănāk* as the prophet himself?

A different line of support for our contention may come from the somewhat analogous situation between the fourth and fifth visions in 8:3–14.[71] There is in this passage an extraordinary density of repetition of phrases and motifs from elsewhere in the book of Amos; in particular, compare v. 4 with 2:6b–7a, v. 6 with 2:6b, v. 7 with 6:8, v. 8 with 9:5, vv. 11–12 with 4:6–8, and vv. 13 + 14b with 5:1–2.[72] In addition, among various minor points of contact, we may note that "the announcement of funerary lamentation in 8:9–10 takes up not only the general theme of 5:1–2 and 16–17 but also the catchwords *qynh* ('lamentation') and *ʾbl* ('mourning')" (Wolff, p. 374 = ET, p. 325). A good case can be made for the view that all these are reapplications of authentic words of Amos by the Deuteronomists. (i) That 8:11–12 is such a reinterpretation of 4:6–8 in the light of Deut 8:3 seems clear enough: physical hunger and thirst which God had allowed in order to goad his people into repentance will now be transformed into a hunger for the word of God. (ii) What is less frequently observed, however, is that vv. 4–6 offer a similar "spiritualising" application of 2:6–7 whereby the sin of the rich is not simply oppression and injustice as such but now in addition they begrudge the time that the religious observance of new moon and sabbath demands. Furthermore, the new crime that is introduced here of using false weights and measures echoes the law of Deut 25:13–15. (iii) A similar point can be made concerning vv. 13–14, despite the textual obscurities in v. 14. The citation of 5:2 (together with probable allusions in v. 13) regarding the fall of the nation is now justified on the religious ground of idolatry.[73]

The tendency of 8:4–14 is thus to reinterpret the words of Amos in terms that seem to have been most at home in Deuteronomic circles, and to parallel [[119]] in particular the kind of accusation to be found in the Judah oracle at 2:4 (not to speak of 2 Kings 17!). All this is appropriately inserted between Amos's fourth and fifth visions, perhaps to

71. There is comparable disagreement about the relationship between 8:1–2 and 3 as there is about 7:7–8 and 9, with most commentators following the same view here as they do there. It should be noted, however, that, unlike 7:9, 8:3 does not represent God speaking in the first person; to that extent it is even less connected with what precedes than is 7:9.

72. Dr. G. I. Davies, for whose comments on a draft of this article I am grateful, further suggests that 8:10 may be an elaboration of 8:3; whether this is a comparable situation with those discussed above will depend on the original relation of 8:3 to the vision immediately before it (see previous note).

73. For further Deuteronomic echoes in these verses, cf. Vermeylen, *Du prophète Isaïe à l'apocalyptique*, 567–68.

explain and justify to a later Judaean audience the transition from announcement of the end (8:1–2) to description of the destruction of the sanctuary (9:1ff.). It is thus easier to believe that the same circle could have been responsible for the insertion of 7:9–17 which serves a similar purpose between the third and fourth visions.

Finally, it is worth noting that links of various kinds have been discerned between Amos 7:9–17 and other parts of the Deuteronomic History. My purpose in adducing these is not necessarily to support the various arguments which these links are said to favour but rather to observe that they lend weight to the view that this paragraph would at the least have been congenial to, and could have served the purposes of, the Deuteronomists, and furthermore that it may well in fact have influenced them in certain parts of their work.

(i) Though denied by some scholars,[74] a link between 1 Kings 13 and Amos 7 seems very probable. Wellhausen[75] observed the coincidences that, like the prophet in the Kings narrative, Amos also came from Judah to Bethel during the reign of a king Jeroboam in order to announce the destruction of the altar, and that in both stories there is considerable significance laid on where the prophet should "eat bread." In addition, Crenshaw saw a point of correspondence over the dispute whether each prophet was truly a *nābîʾ* [['prophet']],[76] and Ackroyd pointed to the use of *bāmôt* [['high places']] in both passages, significant because the word is not used with this sense elsewhere in Amos.[77] Although Ackroyd himself speculates that the two stories existed side-by-side before they were taken over into their present literary contexts, the majority of those who have examined the issue think rather of either literary or traditio-historical influence of Amos on Kings in this particular. Since 1 Kings 13

74. E.g., A. Jepsen, "Göttesmann und Prophet," in H. W. Wolff (ed.), *Probleme biblischer Theologie. Gerhard von Rad zum 70. Geburtstag* (Munich, 1971), 171–82.

75. J. Wellhausen, *Die Composition des Hexateuchs und der historischen Bücher des alten Testaments* (3d ed., Berlin, 1899), 277–78. He has been followed by, *inter alia*, Sellin, p. 182; O. Eissfeldt, "Amos und Jona in volkstümlicher Überlieferung," *Kleine Schriften* (Tübingen, 1968), 4, pp. 137–42; Dietrich, *Prophetie und Geschichte*, 118.

76. J. L. Crenshaw, *Prophetic Conflict. Its Effect upon Israelite Religion* (BZAW 124. Berlin, 1971), 41f. Crenshaw also notes some points of correspondence between 1 Kings 13 and other sections of the book of Amos as well as a number of significant differences before concluding that "despite these differences the probability is that Amos is the prophet behind 1 Kings 13" (p. 42).

77. Ackroyd, "Judgment Narrative," 79. After a judicious review of the evidence, W. E. Lemke concludes with the possibility that "while our story did not originate in the Amos tradition, it may have been partly influenced by the latter"; cf. "The Way of Obedience: 1 Kings 13 and the Structure of the Deuteronomistic History," in F. M. Cross, W. E. Lemke, and P. D. Miller (eds.), *Magnalia Dei: The Mighty Acts of God. Essays on the Bible and Archaeology in Memory of G. Ernest Wright* (Garden City, 1976), 301–26 (325, n. 95).

is widely agreed to be amongst the latest additions to Kings, it could well be held that the same Deuteronomists were at work here as in locating Amos 7:9–17 in its present position. As Lemke has observed, 1 Kings 13 displays very much that same theological outlook with regard to prophets and obedience to the divine word [[120]] which we have noted earlier, thus further underlining the probable connection between these passages and Amos 7.

(ii) H. Schmid has argued for a link between Amos 7 and 2 Kings 9 on the basis of the use of the root *qšr* [['conspire']] in Amos 7:10 and 2 Kgs 9:14, where it occurs in connection with Jehu's rise to power at the instigation of "one of the sons of the prophets" (9:1) working on Elisha's instructions.[78] Ackroyd has extended this observation with reference to the fact that Jehu's dynasty, of which Jeroboam II was a scion, came to an end in the same way (2 Kgs 15:10), and speculates that Amos 7:9–17 may once have been a judgement narrative on Jeroboam II, the absence of which from 2 Kings 14 he finds noteworthy.[79] This latter suggestion seems to outstrip the available evidence, but the observations about "conspiracy" in Amos 7:10 and in the account of Jehu's dynasty in 2 Kings may not have been lost on the Deuteronomic editors. It might conceivably help account for the more historically accurate reference to "the house of Jeroboam" in 7:9 by contrast with 7:11.

(iii) The need for completeness rather than a sense of conviction demands a reference to the suggestion that the account of Jeroboam's reign in 2 Kgs 14:25–27 was drafted explicitly to negate Amos's announcement of the end of Israel at that time.[80] However, apart from the absence of any verbal correspondence, the fact of Deuteronomistic editing indicates that this school was by no means inimicable to the work of Amos, but saw its message as being of abiding value.

(iv) Most recently, Gosse has undertaken a detailed study of the influence of some of the oracles against the nations in Amos 1–2 on the editors of the Deuteronomic History and *vice versa*.[81] He argues, for

---

78. H. Schmid, "Nicht Prophet bin ich, noch bin ich Prophetensohn," *Judaica* 23 (1967), 68–74. 2 Kings 9, it will be recalled, also includes a passage (vv. 7–10) from which Dietrich set out in his pursuit of DtrP.

79. Ackroyd, "Judgment Narrative," 78.

80. Cf. F. Crüsemann, "Kritik an Amos im deuteronomistischen Geschichtswerk," *FS von Rad* (above, n. 74), 57–63. See also K. Koch, "Das Profetenschweigen des deuteronomistischen Geschichtswerks," in J. Jeremias and L. Perlitt (eds.), *Die Botschaft und die Boten. Festschrift für Hans Walter Wolff zum 70. Geburtstag* (Neukirchen-Vluyn, 1981), 115–28, and C. T. Begg, "The Non-mention of Amos, Hosea and Micah in the Deuteronomistic History," *BN* 32 (1986), 41–53, who makes a similar point with specific reference to Amos 7:10–17.

81. B. Gosse, "Le recueil d'oracles contre les nations du livre d'Amos et l'histoire deutéronomique,'" *VT* 38 (1988), 22–40.

instance, that the writers of 2 Kgs 16:8–9 were endeavouring to demonstrate the fulfilment of Amos's words in 1:5, whereas the Deuteronomists' application of the lessons of Israel's downfall to Judah in 2 Kgs 17:13–15 is reflected in the substance of the Judah oracle in Amos 2:4b. In this connection, it is of particular interest to observe the links between Amos 7:11 and 17, *wěyiśrā'ēl gālōh yiglêh mē'al 'admātô* [['and Israel must go into exile away from its land']], and 2 Kgs 17:23, *wayyigèl yiśrā'ēl mē'al 'admātô* [['Israel was exiled from its own land']], and 2 Kgs 25:21, *wayyigèl yěhûdâ mē'al 'admātô* [['Judah was exiled from its own land']]. Whatever may be concluded about some of the details of Gosse's theory, which appear to be based on similarities of vocabulary that some will regard as no more than coincidental, the link in this case seems clear and convincing and to underline the association of Amos 7:9–17 with Deuteronomic thought. [[121]]

(v) In the light of this evidence (admittedly reasonably certain only in the first and last instances cited) for the influence of Amos 7 on the work of the latest editors of the History, we may return to one of our key passages and ask whether there is not comparable evidence there too. In 2 Kgs 21:10–15, where God's "servants the prophets" announce the forthcoming downfall of Judah, they include in their announcement the prediction that "I will stretch over Jerusalem the line of Samaria, and the plummet of the house of Ahab." Although the vocabulary here may have been drawn from Isa 28:17, the meaning is quite different: judgement, not hope; past, not future; Samaria, not Zion. If the Deuteronomist was inspired by the imagery of any passage known to us, it must have been Amos 7, in which case, we must observe in passing, it would also furnish the early evidence for an interpretation of *'ănāk* = plumbline which we saw earlier was lacking hitherto.

In this paper, I have argued (i) that previous explanations for the positioning of Amos 7:9–17 are unsatisfactory; (ii) that contextual considerations favour the interpretation of *'ănāk* as 'plumb-line' and that philological arguments do not rule this out; and (iii) that, in line with their view of the role of prophets as known from elsewhere, the Deuteronomists, or at any rate a writer very much in tune with their thought, inserted this paragraph to interpret God's plumb-line as Amos himself, whose rejection then led to the final announcement of the end of Israel.

But what if after all *'ănāk* should simply mean tin? Would that immediately rule my main proposal out of court? Not necessarily! Since on this approach the emphasis of the vision shifts somewhat on to the wall of v. 7, it should be observed (as proponents of this view have so far failed to point out) that two of the three Biblical examples of "iron walls" come from Deuteronomistically influenced passages in the book of Jeremiah (1:18; 15:20), and that in both cases the reference is to the person of the prophet himself. The outworkings of this observation, however, would be better left to those more sympathetic to the "tin wall" theory.

List of Commentaries Cited by Author's Name Only

Amsler, S. in *Osée, Joël, Abdias, Jonas, Amos*. Edited by E. Jacob, C.-A. Keller, and S. Amsler. Commentaire de l'Ancien Testament. Neuchâtel, 1965.

Cripps, R. S. *A Critical and Exegetical Commentary on the Book of Amos*. 2d edition. London, 1955.

Driver, S. R. *Joel and Amos*. The Cambridge Bible for Schools and Colleges. Cambridge, 1901.

Hammershaimb, E. *Amos Fortolket*. 3d edition. Copenhagen, 1967 = ET, *The Book of Amos: A Commentary*. Oxford, 1970.

Harper, W. R. *A Critical and Exegetical Commentary on Amos and Hosea*. International Critical Commentary. Edinburgh, 1910.

Van Hoonacker, A. *Les douze petits prophètes*. Études bibliques. Paris, 1908.

Keil, C. F. *Die zwölf kleinen Propheten*. 3d edition. Leipzig, 1888.

Marti, K. *Das Dodekapropheton*. Kürzer Handcommentar zum Alten Testament. Tübingen, 1904.

Mays, J. L. *Amos: A Commentary*. Old Testament Library. London, 1969.

Nowack, W. *Die kleinen Propheten*. Handbuch zum Alten Testament. 3d edition. Göttingen, 1922.

Rudolph, W. *Joel-Amos-Obadja-Jona*. Kommentar zum Alten Testament. Gütersloh, 1971.

Sellin, E. *Das Zwölfprophetenbuch*. Kommentar zum Alten Testament. 3d edition. Leipzig, 1929.

Soggin, J. A. *The Prophet Amos: A Translation and Commentary*. London, 1987.

Weiser, A. *Das Buch der zwölf kleinen Propheten*, volume 1. Das Alte Testament Deutsch. 2d edition. Göttingen, 1956.

Wolff, H. W. *Dodekapropheton 2: Joel und Amos*. Biblischer Kommentar: Altes Testament. Neukirchen-Vluyn, 1969 = ET, *Joel and Amos*. Hermeneia. Philadelphia, 1977.

Isaiah 36–39:
Structure and
Function

P. R. ACKROYD

[[3]] It would, I believe, be not inappropriate to give this study the alternative title of "Isaiah: Prophet of the Exile." Such a title would readily relate to the earliest attested *external* exposition of the prophecies of Isaiah. I am distinguishing this from our primary *internal* evidence, within the book itself, evidence which is, as is well known, very difficult to interpret with precision. This earliest external witness is Jesus ben Sira (Sir 48:17–25). It is, significantly for our discussion of Isaiah 36–39, bound up with a primary consideration of Hezekiah who, with Josiah and David, is listed as a faithful king (cf. 49:4). The passage notes the following elements of Isaiah's activity: it was by his hand that God delivered Judah from the Assyrians (48:20); Hezekiah stood firm in the ways of David "as Isaiah the prophet commanded him, the great and faithful prophet, in his vision" (48:22); "by his (Isaiah's) hand the sun stood" (48:23);[1] "he added to the life of the king" (48:23); and finally:

Reprinted with permission from *Von Kanaan bis Kerala: Festschrift für Prof. Mag. Dr. Dr. J. P. M. van der Ploeg O. P. zur Vollendung des siebzigsten Lebensjahres am 4. Juli 1979* (ed. W. C. Delsman et al.; Alter Orient und Altes Testament 211; Neukirchen-Vluyn: Neukirchener Verlag / Kevelaer: Butzon & Bercker, 1982) 3–21 (= P. R. Ackroyd, *Studies in the Religious Tradition of the Old Testament* [London: SCM, 1987] 105–20).

R. E. Clements' *Isaiah and the Deliverance of Jerusalem* (JSOTSup 13, 1980) discusses these same chapters, but primarily in relation to their function in the Deuteronomic History. Chap. III on "The Isaiah Narratives" has particular relationship to matters discussed here, and I am indebted to Dr. Clements for kindly lending me a copy of the manuscript.

1. So the Hebrew *bydw ᶜmd hšmš*; Greek ἐν ταῖς ἡμέραις αὐτοῦ (? *bymyw*, namely, Hezekiah) ἀνεπόδισεν ὁ ἥλιος [['in his days the sun stepped backwards']].

> With a spirit of power he saw the future
>   and he comforted the mourners of Zion;
> To the end of time he shewed things to be,
>   and hidden things before their coming (48:24–25).

It is clear that the selection of allusions here is geared to the figure of Hezekiah; we cannot deduce from it any lack of knowledge on Ben Sira's part of other elements in the book of Isaiah. But what is significant is that while he draws his understanding from that presentation of Hezekiah which is to be found both in 2 Kings and in Isaiah, he reads the story of Hezekiah not primarily in the context of 2 Kings but in the context of the message of Isaiah, the prophet of consolation and of the future.

The Position of Isaiah 36–39

[[4]] R. F. Melugin, in his study *The Formation of Isaiah 40–55* [2] sets out some points concerning the relationship between those chapters and what precedes. 40–55 were "never meant to stand alone." He argues that "The closest thing to a setting for chaps. 40ff. is the prophecy of Isaiah to Hezekiah in chapter 39 concerning the exile to Babylon,"[3] and he cites in support an unpublished lecture by Brevard S. Childs and my own study of 2 Kings 20 / Isaiah 38–39.[4] Melugin believes—though of this I am very doubtful—that there has been a *deliberate* removal of all traces of a historical setting from chaps. 40ff.[5] In fact, as he concedes, this is not entirely true: there are two references to Cyrus, and there is enough reference to the fall of Babylon in prospect, to the gods of Babylon and to the general situation, for it to be clear that the historical background is what it has for long now been recognized to be. We may, however, observe that very large tracts of prophetic material lack historical reference. Such references, other than of a very imprecise kind, are very sparse in the whole book of Isaiah (apart from 6:1–9:6 and 36–39), as also, for example, in Jeremiah 1–20. Should we suppose that there has been a general "deliberate removal" of historical reference; or should we not rather suppose that this is a side-effect of the processes of prophetic exposition underlying the formation of our prophetic books? Precision may have given place to reapplication.

2. *BZAW* 141 (1976), 176–178.

3. Op. cit., p. 177.

4. Op. cit., p. 177n. Cf. my "An Interpretation of the Babylonian Exile: A Study of 2 Kings 20, Isaiah 38–39," *SJT* 27 (1974), 329–352, esp. 349.

5. Cf. also B. S. Childs, "The Canonical Shape of the Prophetic Literature," *Interpretation* 32 (1978), 46–55: "drained of its historical particularity" (p. 50); and "The Exegetical Significance of Canon for the Study of the Old Testament," *VTS* 29 (1978), 66–80.

But the main point that Melugin makes is important. By placing chaps. 40ff. and 36–39 adjacent to one another, the compiler has enhanced the significance of 36–39 in a quite new direction—and this is not a direction immediately discernible in 2 Kings—and the context of 40–55 (or 40–66) is given as that of the message of Isaiah, in the dire threat and in the victory over the Assyrians in 36–37, in the threat and promise of 38, with the alleviation of death in life underscored by the psalm incorporated in that [[5]] form of the text, and in the consequences of Hezekiah's actions in 39 which, as it were, guarantee the exile, and thereby provide an appropriate occasion for 40ff.

Melugin goes further in another part of his study, though alluding to the point in his conclusion.[6] He stresses the clear relationship between 40:1–8 and the material of chap. 6.[7] He recognizes the degree to which both are concerned with actions taking place in the heavenly council,[8] seeing in the plural verbs of the opening of 40 a reference to its members.[9] He comments that "the 'I' who is commanded to 'cry' (v. 6) is not unambiguously the prophet."[10] He might have added to this the verbal coincidence of 40:3 in its reference to the *qwl qwrᵓ* [['voice (of one) crying out']] and 6:4 which refers to the earthquake effect of *qwl hqwrᵓ* [['the sound of the one who cried out']].

We may, I believe, suggest that this reference in 6:4 to *qwl hqwrᵓ* is to the deity rather than to the seraphim of 6:3. Such a suggestion can only be tentative and qualified by the recognition that not infrequently in biblical material no sharp distinction is made between the deity and his messenger or his attendant beings.[11] The description in 6:4 is clearly enough of the accompaniments of a theophany: it is when God speaks, at the sound of his thunder (cf. also Ezekiel 1), that there is a shattering

---

6. Op. cit., p. 176.

7. Op. cit., pp. 87ff.

8. H. Cazelles, "Jesajas kallelse och kungaritualet," *SEÅ* 39 (1974), 38–58; French version "La vocation d'Isaïe (ch. 6) et les rites royaux" in *Homenaje a Juan Prado* (Madrid, 1975), 89–108, criticises the view that Isaiah 6 does refer to the heavenly council, observing the absence of *šmym* [['heaven']] from the text (see p. 38, Fr. 89f.). But this is surely to take too literalistic a view of the wording. It is true that the description of Isaiah 6 makes direct reference to the temple (so vv. 1, 4, 6); but the comparability of this description with that of 1 Kgs 22:19–22 makes it clear that the appearance of the enthroned deity is pictured in terms of the correlation between heavenly dwelling and earthly temple.

9. Cf., e.g., R. N. Whybray, *Isaiah 40–66*, New Century Bible (London, 1975), p. 48.

10. MT *wᵓmr*; 1QIsᵃ *wᵓwmrh*. The often proposed acceptance of the first person form (supported by LXX [Vg.] εἶπα) cannot be regarded as certain. MT may be treated as an indefinite form.

11. Cf., e.g., J. Barr, "Theophany and Anthropomorphism in the Old Testament," *VTS* 7 (1960), 31–38.

effect.[12] [[6]] Isaiah's reaction of unacceptability is appropriate to his realisation of the presence of the deity and the effect which this produces. The Hebrew would then anticipate in v. 4 what becomes explicit as a description of auditory experience in v. 8. God speaks, the earth moves, man is convicted of impurity; when purification has taken place, he hears again the words of God this time articulated into the demand for response to an already designated office.[13] If the *qwl hqwr*ʾof 6:4 is in reality that of the deity, then the correspondence of this to chap. 40 makes good sense of the latter too. There the opening verses convey the message of comfort (vv. 1–2), and this is continued after the phrase *qwl hqwr*ʾ; vv. 3–5 are a further declaration of what is to be done, and the plural subjects of the imperatives would appear to be the same in both cases—members of the heavenly court. Both the almost parenthetic *qwl qwr*ʾ[14] and the final "for the mouth of Yahweh has spoken" underline the point that it is the divine word which we are hearing. With great skill the opening of v. 6 plays on the phrase: *qwl* ʾ*mr* [['a voice says']]—surely the same voice that speaks—with its command *qr*ʾ [['proclaim']]which echoes the *qwl qwr*ʾ. The rhetorical question: "What should one say?" ushers in not a reply, but a reflection on the contrast between the ephemeral quality of life and the solely enduring quality of the word of God (vv. 6–8), and this in its turn brings out the word of hope in the succeeding verses.[15]

This suggested relationship between chap. 40 and chap. 6 is one pointer towards the understanding of the position of 36–39. With chap. 40 we are thereby presented with what we could call a renewal of the Isaianic commission. But clearly the matter is more complex than this. In a study of Isaiah 1–12,[16] I [[7]] have pointed out, in considering general questions about the structure of the whole book of Isaiah, that

12. Since chap. 6 clearly rests upon earlier material and is itself an elaborate construct, there seems to be no good reason for a merely literal reading of the text.

13. Again an oversimple reading of the text might seem to suggest that Isaiah responds to a wholly unexpected call; but the purificatory ritual already described implicitly designates the prophet as the chosen recipient of the divine command. This is surely the full significance of the analogies seen by I. Engnell, *The Call of Isaiah,* UUÅ 1949, 4 (Uppsala, 1949), 42 in the magical texts which he cites, but incompletely, from K. L. Tallqvist, *Die assyrische Beschwörungsserie Maqlû, ASSF* 20, 6 (Helsinki, 1895).

14. The continuity of thought between vv. 1–2 and 3–5 strongly suggests that the opening words *qwl qwr*ʾ in v. 3 should be seen as an underlining of the declaration, rather than as the designation of a new speaker.

15. Cf. chap. 6 too where the succeeding verses as they now stand draw out the wider implications of the divine message.

16. "Isaiah i–xii: Presentation of a Prophet," *VTS* 29 (1978), 16–48, see 18–21. Cf. also R. Lack, *La Symbolique du livre d'Isaïe: Essai sur l'image littéraire comme élément de structuration,* Anal. Bibl. 59 (Rome, 1973), 76. Lack treats 36–39 as an appendix which may be left on one side in his discussion, though he notes in it themes of confidence (especially *bṭḥ*), Assyrian

there is no adequate basis for the common supposition that these chapters were added to an already completed first book of Isaiah. Such a book is generally described as being 1–35, though this may well be qualified by the recognition that some parts of those chapters are evidently late—this is particularly claimed for 24–27. It is then assumed that the section 36–39 was extracted from 2 Kings and placed at the end of the current form of 1–35. This, as generally presented, does less than justice to the complex structure of 1–35, and takes too little account of the degree of interrelationship of language, thought and structure between the various parts of the whole book of Isaiah. It also often takes as analogy the appearance of Jeremiah 52 as a concluding appendix to the book of Jeremiah, without noting the degree of difference between Isaiah 36–39 and that chapter; namely that Jeremiah 52 is virtually a straight variant of the last part of 2 Kings, whereas Isaiah 36–39, while clearly closely related to 2 Kings 18–20,[17] shares with that passage and with Jeremiah 37–44 the interweaving of the activity of the prophet with the narrative of the events.[18] Analogy for the placing of these narrative chapters at this point in the book of Isaiah must be sought in the consideration generally of why narratives are placed in prophetic material, and what function they perform. This is a general matter which cannot be undertaken here. It must also for each example be done with a due examination of the nature of the material, its particular structure, the function it performs in the context in which it is placed.[19]

[8] If the simple explanation—36–39 added to 1–35, 40ff. added conveniently after 36–39—will not do justice to all the evidence, we must consider other aspects of the positioning of this section. Various attempts have been made at re-opening the question of Deutero-Isaiah.[20] The orthodox view that treats 40–55 + 56–66 as two additional bodies of

---

presumption (*šᵓnn*), and Yahweh's protection of Zion and David. "The failed siege of Sennacherib became in the Israelite tradition the concretisation of the Völkersturmmotiv [['popular storm motif']]. In the book of Isaiah, it is the paradigm of the inviolability of Zion" (my translation. On this point, cf. R. E. Clements [see p. 3 n. 1 [[p. 478, author's note in this reprint]]]). But such a comment invites us to ask whether "appendix" is the appropriate term for so important a section.

17. While some reference is made in this discussion to the question of the relationship between these two closely similar but not identical texts, the major questions of a textual kind are not here considered.

18. Cf. my "Historians and Prophets," *SEÅ* 33 (1968), 18–54, see 43–50.

19. Cf., e.g., my "A Judgment Narrative between Kings and Chronicles? An Approach to Amos 7:9–17" in G. W. Coats and B. O. Long (ed.), *Canon and Authority: Essays in Old Testament Religion and Theology* (Philadelphia, 1977), 71–87.

20. Cf., e.g., C. C. Torrey, *The Second Isaiah: A New Interpretation* (New York, 1928); J. D. Smart, *History and Theology in Second Isaiah* (Philadelphia, 1965); J. L. McKenzie, *Second Isaiah*, Anchor Bible, 20 (New York, 1968).

prophetic material, added to the book of Isaiah, though not without recognition of elements of relatedness, does not resolve all the problems. Most often there has been the recognition that 34–35 have affinities with 40ff. A recent detailed discussion of Isa 35:8–10[21] argues for an updating at this point directed towards the hope of a return from exile, superimposed on a text concerned with "an eschatological renewal of (Palestine)," but not with return and therefore pre-exilic in date. The suggestion is made that it is the position of this particular passage which has led to its being so reinterpreted to provide "a pronouncement which would lead excellently into the prophecy of Deutero-Isaiah."[22] More broadly, we may recognize the wealth of material in 28–33 not unrelated to 40–55;[23] much in 28–33 is concerned with the fate of Jerusalem, and clearly goes well beyond the situation of Isaiah,[24] culminating in 33, a passage, which, however described, clearly brings out the theme of the glorification of Zion.[25] The placing of 36–39 underscores this prospect of a restored Jerusalem. That hope is expressed also in a variety of comments in prophetic collections associated with words of Isaiah both in the opening chapters of the book and in 28–32; it is drawn out more fully in 33, 34–35. [[9]] And 36–39 gives to it the firm basis of a complex prophetic narrative in which the message of Isaiah is held in a historic context and geared to the personage of Hezekiah. That it is then followed in 40ff. by the confirmation of that message of hope in immediate assurance, shows the link between what are presented as aspirations and what appear now as immediate realities. There is further sequel to this in the warning notes which echo through 40–55 but come especially to be heard in 56–66.

The Structure of Isaiah 36–39

The placing of 36–39 may be seen to be most opportune for creating a context in which 40ff. offer a response and show the use in fuller form of

21. F. D. Hubmann, "Der 'Weg' zum Zion. Literatur- und stilkritische Beobachtungen zu Jes. 35,8–10" in *Memoria Jerusalem. Freundesgabe Franz Sauer zum 70. Geburtstag* (Akad. Druck- und Verlagsanstalt, Graz, 1977), 29–41. Some doubt must be expressed on this interpretation in view of the metrical structure of the verses; cf. also for a different view of the text, J. A. Emerton, "A Note on Isaiah xxxv 9–10," *VT* 27 (1977), 488–489.

22. Loc. cit., p. 41.

23. Cf., e.g., McKenzie, op. cit., p. xxii.

24. Cf., e.g., O. Kaiser, *Der Prophet Jesaja Kapitel 13–39*, ATD 18 (Göttingen, 1973), 187f.; E.T. *Isaiah* 13–39, OTL (London, 1973), 234–236.

25. On the relation of Isaiah 33 to Psalm 46, cf. H. Gunkel, "Jesaja 33, eine prophetische Liturgie," *ZAW* 42 (1924), 177–208, a theme further developed in an unpublished paper by R. Murray of Heythrop College, London, given to a seminar at King's College, London, in November 1977 (to be published in 1982).

themes which are present in passages in the preceding chapters. We may then ask whether the structure of 36–39 contributes to this function. It is immediately apparent that there is no satisfactory chronological sequence in these chapters, and only a minimum of precise information. All the incidents are associated with the reign of Hezekiah, but beyond that no clear picture emerges of the order of events. Discussion of the complex problems of 36 and 37 is not here necessary. The literature on this theme is immense; and I refer simply to Brevard Childs' *Isaiah and the Assyrian Crisis*[26] for his discussion of the problems of the divergent material and their relationship both to the events that may be discerned in them and in the Assyrian records and to the shaping and functioning of the material.

A. K. Jenkins has attempted to get behind the present association of the narratives with Sennacherib and the year 701, to raise questions about a possible different origin for the material.[27] Whether or not this particular attempt can be regarded as proved, it underlines the importance of recognizing the degree to which the material in these chapters has been modified to reach its present form. Jenkins takes seriously the date at 36:1, the "fourteenth year" of Hezekiah, assuming the correctness of the synchronic dating of Hezekiah's accession in the third year of Hoshea (2 Kgs 18:1); the text thus provides a chronological scheme, though not necessarily a correct one. The materials of 36 and 37 would on this basis be associated with that fourteenth [[10]] year—i.e., about 714 B.C.—and originally linked to a deliverance of Jerusalem under Sargon II; the illness theme of 38, which guarantees Hezekiah fifteen further years of rule would—on the basis of 29 years of his reign—belong to that same moment or shortly after (38:6 indeed associates it with deliverance from the power of Assyria and protection of Jerusalem); and while 39 could belong somewhat later, the precise relation to the activities of Merodach-baladan being difficult to determine, it would be possible to take more precisely the "at that time" of 39:1 as meaning that all three component parts of this section could belong to almost the same moment. Jenkins accepts such a chronology, and his major concern is to suggest the plausibility of associating the material primarily with the period of Sargon II and to indicate how, in an on-going reinterpretation, the major narratives came to be associated with the period of Sennacherib. There is difficulty here. It is not easy to see why, on this assumption, such a supposed deliverance under Sargon did not hold its place, especially since it is so evident that Judah suffered very heavily under

---

26. *SBT* 2, 3, 1967; and cf. R. E. Clements (see p. 3 n. 1 [[478, author's note]]).

27. "Hezekiah's Fourteenth Year: A New Interpretation of 2 Kings xviii 13–xix 37," *VT* 26 (1976), 289–294.

Sennacherib. Why transpose a deliverance theme from the earlier to the later moment? Is it sufficient to point to the capture of Lachish and to see the non-capture of Jerusalem as a point of such reassurance as to invite the updating of the older materials to this? Jenkins has strong evidence for suggesting that the literary history of this section is even more complex than has often been supposed; I am less sure that he has resolved the problems of chronology.[28]

If we look at the material as it stands, we observe the difficulties of supposing a chronological order. We may see the rough chronological notes: *bymym hhm* [['in those days']] (38:1), *b^{c}t hhy$^{\circ}$* [['at that time']] (39:1), as comparable to other link phrases in the book of Kings.[29] They are not to be treated as precise evidence, but rather as devices by which the compiler draws together what he believes to be significantly related material. We recognize that the fourteenth year of 36:1 and the fifteen years of 38:5 tie the narratives with the tradition of a rule of 29 years by Hezekiah. This could mean that the illness preceded the attack by Sennacherib in 36–37. Similarly, if we suppose that Merodach-baladan's ambassadors were in Judah, not really to inquire after the king's health or to offer congratulation, but to gain support [[11]] for alliance against Assyria, then this would appear likely to belong to the early years of Sennacherib's reign, when Merodach-baladan was active, rather than to a period after the Sennacherib campaign had in effect brought about the subjection of Judah. If this is so, then the order of the materials as now presented is lacking in true chronology, and we may ask whether the order is not dictated by interests other than chronological or historical.

The twofold narrative of 36–37—and I leave on one side the analysis and interrelationship of what are clearly two parallel forms—is concentrated on two themes. The one is the theme of divine victory over the claims of the Assyrians; the other is that of the piety of Hezekiah and his response to the emergency. There is overlap and we may recognize that in the combining of the two strands, there has been some conflation. The first narrative presents the *hybris* of the Assyrian king: in the highly stylised wording of 36:4–10 there is a clear pattern. Where do you trust? Is it in military power? Is it in Egypt? Is it in Yahweh whose shrines Hezekiah has abolished? (vv. 4–7). The last three are then repeated in divergent form: You have no military power. Egypt is unable to help. It is Yahweh who has sent the Assyrian (vv. 8–10). After an interlude (vv. 11–12), the second speech of the Rabshakeh elaborates the theme of the uselessness

28. R. E. Clements (see p. 3 n. 1 [[p. 478, author's note]]) devotes much attention to the impact of 701 B.C. on the ongoing interpretation of Judah's experience.

29. Cf. J. A. Montgomery, "Archival Data in the Books of Kings," *JBL* 53 (1934), 46–52.

of trust in Yahweh, developing it first in terms of an offer of a new promised land (vv. 16–17) in which the Assyrian speaks the language of Deuteronomy, and second in terms of the failure of the gods to deliver any
land from Assyrian power (vv. 18–20). Significantly in v. 21 the officials
give no answer, with the comment "for it was a royal command: Do not
answer." I believe the significance of this lies not in any supposition that
Hezekiah was trying to gain time, or that he did not trust his officers to
make wise replies: but that there is no answer from men to a blasphemer:
the answer comes from God. This would suggest that this motif is here
used for a specific theological purpose; and the same may be said of the
preceding material too. The remainder of this part of the material portrays the appropriate ritual of approach to the deity, through the prophet
Isaiah, and the pronouncement of reassurance and deliverance by the
prophet (36:22–37:7). The Assyrian has claimed divine warrant for his
actions, and has—somewhat inconsistently—claimed the impotence of
Yahweh to deliver: he is answered simply by direct divine word.

The second part of the material is introduced by what appears now
as an interlude in 37:8–9, in which we may detect the joining of the two
narratives. [[12]] This second part begins with the same theme of the
powerlessness of the gods, Yahweh included (vv. 10–13). The central
part of this narrative, introduced by vv. 14–15, is the prayer of Hezekiah
(vv. 16–20): it is on the theme of the creative power of Yahweh, the recognition that the Assyrian Sennacherib has indeed been able to overthrow the gods of the nations, but they are non-gods. It is Yahweh who
can respond to the prayer by delivering Judah from Assyrian power so
that all the nations may know that he is Yahweh alone. The prayer is
markedly related to psalm passages and to Deutero-Isaiah. The answer
comes in a message from the prophet Isaiah (vv. 21–22a) to which the
real sequel appears only at v. 33 in the assurance that the city will not be
taken, the Assyrian will withdraw (vv. 33–35). The final verses (vv. 36–
38) describe disasters to the Assyrian army and to its king. These verses
may represent the true ending of the first narrative; but I think it more
important to observe here, as elsewhere within this section, the skill with
which divergent elements have been drawn together.

This is also apparent in the inclusion within chap. 37 of two further
elements. The first is the poem of 37:22b–29, clearly also at certain points
closely related to Deutero-Isaiah and providing a broader comment on
the *hybris* of the Assyrian ruler. It employs ironically the self-glorifying
style of the royal inscriptions. The second is the element of reassurance
and hope in vv. 30–32, underlined by the final words *qn²t yhwh ṣb²wt t°śh
z²t* [['the zeal of the Lord of hosts shall bring this to pass']] (cf. 9:6 and see
below). This promises miraculous restoration, and is described as being

a sign (*ᵓwt*, v. 30). These two elements are not fully integrated; they represent an extension of the narrative material. The latter of them is related to 4:2–6 and more closely still to 10:20–23 (24–26).

What we may remark as of considerable interest in this whole section is the degree to which, while the material is at some points linked with Isaiah, who appears as the spokesman of Yahweh, there are contacts with the wider Isaianic tradition, and beyond that with Deuteronomy and the Psalms.[30]

[[13]] I have treated the themes of 38 and 39 already in my 1974 study of those chapters, calling them "an interpretation of the Babylonian exile."[31] The theme of 38, the illness and recovery of Hezekiah, is verbally linked with the preceding section, in the use of *gnn* [['defend']] of the protection of Jerusalem in 37:35 and 38:6, alongside the difference of usage of *yšᶜ* [['deliver']] and *nṣl* [['rescue']] in the same verses. 37:35 and 38:5 are also linked by their Davidic reference. The illness narrative incorporates the theme of deliverance from Assyria alongside that of deliverance from death, and it is this latter theme that is more fully elaborated in the psalm, where images of death, of the pit of Sheol, are employed to contrast with the restoration to life and well-being.

Significant in the Isaiah 38 treatment of this theme is the absence of the medical procedures adopted by the prophet in 2 Kgs 20:7; 38:21 is clearly an addition designed to recall this element. Of further importance is the absence from this form of the material of any element of choice or deliberation on the part of Hezekiah. The prophet declares— using exactly the same words as are found in 37:30—"this is the sign (*ᵓwt*) to you." The piety of Hezekiah is expressed, as in 37, in the offering of a prayer, the style of which is much simpler, emphasising the loyalty and right life of the petitioner. It is noteworthy that the whole of the narrative is compressed so that the divine answer comes as an immediate response to the prayer.

By contrast, Isaiah 39 presents the story of the ambassadors virtually exactly as it appears in 2 Kings. Its theme is of submission to Babylon, the inevitability of exile, the downfall of the Davidic monarchy. The comment of Hezekiah, as I have argued elsewhere,[32] represents the acceptance of

---

30. This must inevitably raise questions about the function of the corresponding section in 2 Kings 18–19 and about the underlying problem of how that particular section within the Deuteronomic History came into being. Cf. R. E. Clements' discussion (see p. 3 n. 1 [[p. 478, author's note]]). The contacts with the wider Isaianic tradition and particularly with Deutero-Isaiah are more easily intelligible in the context of the book of Isaiah; their significance for the Deuteronomic History is partly considered by Clements.

31. Cf. p. 4 n. 3 [[p. 479 n. 4]].

32. "An Interpretation" (see p. 4 n. 3 [[p. 479 n. 4]]), 335–338.

the rightness of divine judgement. The pious king is thus portrayed as the one to whom the future judgement is disclosed through what may be described as the inadvertence of his conduct. As the material stands, no blame is attached to Hezekiah. We may legitimately suspect that underlying the present form of the material there is an older narrative in which Hezekiah comes under divine judgement through Isaiah because of his involvement with a foreign power—a theme more fully developed in regard to Egypt in Isaiah 30–31; but this is now unstated. The king discloses exactly what he has done and accepts as right what the prophet has pronounced. The final phrase may be [[14]] seen as a pious comment: doom cannot come in the time of righteous Hezekiah. The absence of this in LXX[B] in 2 Kgs 20:19 may indicate it as a later addition,[33] but it serves that purpose just the same, and may represent one further indication of the growth of the Hezekiah legend.

Set alongside 36 and 37, these two chapters present a further theme. The assurance of deliverance from Assyria of the first two chapters, continued by overlap into 38, is to be seen as a contrast to the handing over of all Judah and its royal house into the power of Babylon. But the one is not to be read without the other. The overwriting of the Assyrian narratives with the assurance of divine power, of the overthrow of the *hybris* of an alien ruler, indeed of the impropriety with which he has offered a new promised land to God's people, make it clear that there are pointers forward to the promise of restoration which in the book of Isaiah follows immediately. It is a point at which we may again ask how far in handling the form of the material in 2 Kings we must consider the relationship to the Isaiah presentation. It remains a problem to know why there is so little cross-reference to the prophetic material in the Deuteronomic History, though no lack of reference to prophecy.[34] We may perhaps consider whether sufficient of cross-linkage is to be found in these chapters to the book of Isaiah for the reader to be, as it were, invited to consider the narratives in the light of their other context. Is he perhaps already being invited to read the story of Hezekiah as it is to be found read in

---

33. The Versions, except the Targum, interpret the phrase as precative: so LXX[B] γενέσθω (LXX γενηθήτω) δὴ εἰρήνη; Vg. "sit pax et veritas in diebus meis." The Isaiah text has *ky yhyh šlwm w°mt bymy* [['let there be peace and security in my days']] where *ky* may be understood as emphatic. 2 Kings has *hlw° °m šlwm w°mt yhyh bymy* [['Will there not be peace and security in my days?']] rendered literally by LXX[A] as μὴ οὐκ ἐὰν εἰρήνη καὶ ἀλήθεια ἔσται ἐν ἡμέραις μου.

34. For an explanation related to a view of the growth of the canon, cf. D. N. Freedman, "The Law and the Prophets," *VTS* 9 (1962), 250–265, and more recently in "Canon of the Old Testament," *IDBS* (1976), 130–136, see 131–133. The view he propounds is inevitably almost entirely hypothetical.

Ben Sira, with a full consciousness of the disclosure of hidden things before they come about?[35]

The Function of Isaiah 36–39

Structure and function overlap, and in the previous part of this discussion a number of pointers to function have been suggested. A somewhat ⟦15⟧ fuller statement may now be attempted of the function of this whole section 36–39 within the book of Isaiah.

We cannot, of course, forget that this passage appears in another, closely similar, form in 2 Kings 18–20; but, however important for textual questions and indeed for points of interpretation the comparison of such duplicate texts may be, we must not be led away from consideration of the question: What function does this text perform in this particular context? It is the failure to deal with this which often mars commentaries where the commentator elects to omit altogether or to handle only sketchily a text which appears elsewhere. When writing the commentary on Isaiah for the *Interpreter's One-Volume Commentary*,[36] I found myself put under restraint in writing on Isaiah 36–39, because, in the common view, these chapters belong in 2 Kings, and it is there that they will be fully handled.[37] I was limited virtually entirely to points of difference, which meant little more than commenting on the psalm in 38. But this is to ignore what these chapters do to the book of Isaiah, how they function within it. How they affect the book in which they stand is a legitimate subject of study.

On the common view that 36–39 have simply been extracted from 2 Kings and added to an already complete book of Isaiah (1–35), we might at the very least say that they provide some supplementation to our knowledge of Isaiah and of his utterances; delicate problems will arise as to how far we may extract elements of the original message from this material. The discussion of that question is not my intention. But even that simple purposeful level of the insertion of the material raises further questions about the effect produced in the book, and the more clearly we detect cross-linkages with other parts of the book, the more evident it is that there is a much more significant function being performed here.

---

35. Again this makes clear that the relationship of the two texts to one another and to their contexts raises difficult questions.

36. (Nashville, New York, 1971), 329–371, see 352f.

37. Cf., e.g., O. Kaiser, op. cit., p. 291; E.T., p. 367.

My discussion of Isaiah 1–12[38] was directed towards attempting some
elucidation of the question why so large a body of prophetic material has
come to be associated with Isaiah, and answering this partly by consideration of the particular presentation to be found in 1–12 which, alone with
[[16]] 36–39, is a clearly demarked collection in the book. In some respects the title given to that study: "Presentation of a Prophet" could
be applied to 36–39: it is in part concerned with portraying the nature
and function of Isaiah in relation to a particular series of narratives. We
might equally observe the converse: it presents a series of narratives,
linked in part by the illumination of their meaning in the presentation
within them of the prophet. In that respect there is a valuable parallel to
be drawn with the material of 2 Kings 16 and its analogous material in
Isaiah 7–8.[39] The former presents the reign of Ahaz with no mention of
Isaiah; the latter utilises some elements of the same material but uses
them to provide a lead in to the activity of the prophet. A perfectly legitimate deduction from this—and one that may be seen to be confirmed
in the detailed examination of the material—is that a form of 36–39 /
2 Kings 18–20 can be postulated in which the events are recounted without any mention of the prophet. A full discussion would involve fuller
consideration of that hypothetical *Urtext* [['original text']]. It is a hypothesis which raises questions also about the reason for there being in 2 Kings
this one lengthy section involving Isaiah, but no such presentation of him
in relation to Ahaz.[40] The clue, I suspect, lies in the figure of Hezekiah,
and this is a point to which I want to devote further attention.

While I have suggested that 36–39 may be held to resemble 1–12 as
a presentation of the prophet, it can be more closely argued that it resembles one section within 1–12, namely 6:1–9:6. This has been generally agreed to be a unit, though not a unity. It is marked off by the
occurrence before and after of material of the same kind—the poem

38. Cf. p. 6 n. 4 [[p. 481 n. 16]].
39. Cf. "Historians and Prophets" (see p. 7 n. 2 [[p. 482 n. 18]]), 22–33.
40. Cf. also "Historians and Prophets," 43–50 on the presence in Jeremiah 37–44 of a
text which is in some respects a variant form of the main part of 2 Kings 24–25. In the
former, Jeremiah appears in some, though not in all, sections of the material; in the latter,
there is no mention of the prophet. The absence of the Jeremiah material from 2 Kings
could provide one pointer to a view somewhat like that of D. N. Freedman (see p. 14 n. 2
[[p. 488 n. 34]]); if the prophetic corpus, eventually Isaiah-Malachi, was intended as a supplement to the narrative works, then there would be no need to include such a large body
of prophetic material in 2 Kings. Freedman makes no use of this point. We should still, however, need to explain the presence of 2 Kings 18–20; Freedman's comment (*IDBS*, 132) that
the overlap of 2 Kings 18–20 / Isaiah 36–39; 2 Kings 24–25 / Jeremiah 52 suggests "that the
two works were in some sense distinct" is too vague to be helpful.

with refrain of 5:25–30 [[17]] and 9:7–20,[41] itself contained with the woes of 5:8–24 and 10:1–4.[42] It resembles 36–39 in that it offers the only substantial section of the Isaiah compilation in which direct connection with narrative material is provided. Indeed the only other sections which contain elements of narrative are to be found in 20 and in 22:15–25; and the only other date, apart from the evidently prefatory 1:1 is in the curious 14:28 on which a further comment will be in order later.

More significant are points of relationship between 6:1–9:6 and 36–39 which may be briefly noted:

1. The historical note, with its chronological indication, in the opening of 6:1 and 7:1 and again in 36:1. Of these the latter two are related to 2 Kgs 16:5 and 18:13. Apart from 1:1 and 14:28, these are the only precise chronological notes in the book of Isaiah.
2. Both events, in 7:3ff. and 36:2ff., are located at the same place, by the water conduit. In neither case does this play any further part in the narrative; arguably it is connected with the siege situation in both instances. It provides an incidental point of cross-reference.
3. The use of the sign ($^{\gamma}wt$) in 7:11, 14 is very similar to that in 38:7 (22), and further to that already mentioned in 37:30. In fact, the wording of the offer of a sign in 7:11—'go deep' (h^cmq) and 'on high' (lm^clh)— could well be compared to the use of the roots ^clh [['go up']] and *yrd* [['go down']] in 38:8, which also incorporates repeated use of the word m^clwt [['steps']] (5 times).[43] Furthermore, we may observe that the offer of a [[18]] sign in 38—and here the Isaiah text differs from that of 2 Kings—resembles the offer to Ahaz in chap. 7. A contrast may be seen between Ahaz' refusal of the sign and Isaiah's insistence on it in chap. 7, and the willing acceptance of the sign by Hezekiah with no hint in the narrative of a request. Did the compiler responsible for the

41. This is the standard view of the relationship; often the texts are rearranged to bring the poem with refrain together, with 5:25–30 (or part of it) treated as the original final stanza. But may this not be too facile a view? The occurrence of the refrain—also rather oddly in 10:4—does not prove that the passages belong together. The style of 5:25–30 is in a number of respects markedly different from that of 9:7–20.

42. The same problem appears in the woes as is noted in the previous footnote. Is 10:1–4 really another woe originally belonging with 5:8–24? Its opening may seem to support the view, but of greater interest is the marked shift in 10:3–4a. This looks like an exilic comment pointing to the relentlessness of doom and the inevitability of either submission (4aα) or death (4aβ).

43. Should we also see in ^clmh [['young woman']] (7:14) a play on m^clh [['high']] (7:11)? This would provide an additional underlining of the latter, and would raise some interesting questions regarding the unending speculation about the identity of the ^clmh. Could it be that ^clmh was used simply to provide a wordplay?

Isaiah form of this text modify the story to remove elements from its already familiar (? 2 Kings) form which he felt to be unsuited to its function in the book of Isaiah, to draw out this contrast between Ahaz and Hezekiah?

This use of the sign theme is picked out by Melugin as a link between various elements in the book of Isaiah. He extends the point more broadly, noting 8:18, which is of interest as falling within the same section as 7:11, 14. He also comments on the further examples in 19:20; 20:3; 37:30, and the way in which this is taken a stage further in 44:25; 55:13 and 66:19. Of these, 8:18, with the theme of *yldym* [['children']] as signs (using both *ʾwt* [['sign']] and *mwpt* [['portent']]), provides an extension of 7:14. 37:30, within the section 36–39, helps to bind together the two sections 36–37 and 38. The other occurrences are less close. The sign of 19:20, with reference to the divine deliverance of the Egyptians who turn to Yahweh, may be seen to be echoed in 66:19 which similarly deals with the gathering of the nations (though neither appears to be related to the use in either 6:1–9:6 or 36–39). 20:3 is also less close, though like 8:18 it uses the two terms *ʾwt* and *mwpt*. 44:25 is disconnected, being concerned with false signs. 55:13 forms a colophon to the chapter, perhaps to the larger unit also; it is possible, though less clear, that it is intended to echo the Davidic theme of 6:1–9:6. Melugin's comment goes rather further than the evidence: "The place of Deutero-Isaiah in the collection may well be related to the redactor's theology of the place of signs in the prophetic word."[44] But though there is too little ground for such a sweeping statement, there is evidence of relationship between the sign theme in chaps. 7 and 8 and 37 and 38.

4. The climax of 9:6 and that of 37:32, already noted, are unique in the phrase *qnʾt yhwh ṣbʾwt tꜥśh zʾt* [['the zeal of the Lord of hosts shall bring this to pass']]. It occurs only in these two passages (and the 2 Kings parallel). The use in both shows its ambivalent [[19]] quality, to be found in other examples of the use of *qnʾh* [['zeal']]: Yahweh shows his concern both in his wrath at Israel and at the nations, and in his mercy and salvation. (The theme is aptly summed up in Joel 2:18: *wyqnʾ yhwh lʾrṣw wyḥml ꜥl ꜥmw* [['the Lord was zealous on behalf of his land and had compassion on his people']]). Both these narrative or partly narrative sections, which alone in the book provide a full contextual setting for the activity and message of Isaiah, are evidently concerned with themes of judgement and of deliverance. The former plays its part in the presentation of Isaiah in 1–12; the latter

44. Op. cit., p. 178.

has a comparable function in relation to the chapters which precede and follow it.

5. The reference to $m^c lwt$ $^{\jmath}hz$ (38:8)—whatever it denotes—provides another link.[45] If, as has been argued,[46] the phrase is a gloss in 2 Kgs 20:11, the Ahaz reference appears only in the Isaiah form of the text. Is there yet again here a small modification in the Isaiah form of the material designed to draw out the contrast between Ahaz and Hezekiah? The point would be clearer if we had a better idea of the precise meaning of the allusion, but if, as is often supposed, it refers to a supposedly idolatrous shrine erected by Ahaz, the reference could carry with it the further implication of the contrast between pious Hezekiah and impious Ahaz.

6. To this last, we may add other indications of the contrasting of Hezekiah and Ahaz. Modifications in the text in Isaiah 7 as against that of 2 Kings 16 make the point that the threatening forces of Israel and Aram are in fact powerless, and the fears of Ahaz and his court are groundless. Isaiah 7:2 and 4 bring out this theme of unnecessary panic. By contrast, the text of Isaiah 36 preserves the theme of Assyria's power, omitting 2 Kgs 18:14–16 in which Assyria is bought off by Hezekiah. The effect is thus to stress the propriety of the conduct of Hezekiah, whose response to the Assyrian threat is a ritual of penitence, and an appeal to the deity; at no point is fear directly associated with Hezekiah or his officers; only the reply of Isaiah, in markedly liturgical terms, tells the king $^{\jmath}l$ $tyr^{\jmath}$ [['do not be frightened']]. The contrasting picture of these two kings is already discernible within the 2 Kings material; it is taken a stage further by the presentation of the one [[20]] without reference to Isaiah in 2 Kings 16 and of the other with full-scale reference in 2 Kings 18–20. Yet other developments are detectable in Isaiah 7 and 36–39. The later stage still is to be seen in the Chronicler, where the contrast is of the most extreme kind.[47] We may also note here that Isa 14:28 as it stands refers to the death of Ahaz. It may be right to emend the text, but the MT contains a possible further hint. The death of Ahaz marks the accession of Hezekiah,

45. I am indebted to my colleague R. J. Coggins for pointing this out to me.

46. So, e.g., *BHS* ad loc.; J. A. Montgomery and H. S. Gehman, *The Books of Kings*, ICC (Edinburgh, 1951), 512.

47. So most recently in H. G. M. Williamson, *Israel in the Books of Chronicles* (Cambridge, 1977), 114–118 on Ahaz and 119–125 on Hezekiah. Williamson offers some criticisms of the details of the earlier presentation of the theme by R. Mosis, *Untersuchungen zur Theologie des chronistischen Geschichtswerk* (Freiburger theologische Studien, 92, 1973). Mosis presents the contrast of the two rulers very forcibly (186–92); cf. also my discussion in *I and II Chronicles, Ezra, Nehemiah* (TBC London, 1973), 174–196, esp. 179.

and who better than such an ideal king to bring overthrow to Philistia and the establishment of Zion in security (14:29–32)?[48]

In my study of 2 Kings 20, I drew attention to some aspects of this growth of the figure of Hezekiah, both within the biblical material and beyond. We may now add a little more to this in the recognition that the message of hope for the future, which in Ben Sira is linked to the Hezekiah references, as we saw at the outset, is already, by the placing of 36–39 where it stands in the book of Isaiah, used to provide a contextual basis for the prophecies of chaps. 40ff. The basis for those prophecies is shown to rest in the relationship between Hezekiah and Isaiah, idealised king and prophet of judgement and salvation. And to this we may add the further consideration that 6:1–9:6 is ordered around the theme of the Davidic monarchy, its failure (and hence the failure of the people— so in 6, 7 and 8) and its future prospect, expressed in the concluding oracle in 9:1–6.[49] We cannot in this resolve the question of the child in 7:14; but if he is a royal child, or was interpreted as such a one, has he come to be associated with Hezekiah in the process of reinterpretation? And what more fitting than to conclude the section in 9:1–6 with a royal oracle designating a new and ideal Davidic king, and to suppose that here too the operative factor in interpretation has been the growth of the idealisation of Hezekiah. The link then [[21]] from 6:1–9:6 to 36–39 would be even stronger. Hope for the future, to be expressed in Davidic terms only once in the later chapters (55:3), is nevertheless associated with Davidic promise. Have we here one element in the process by which Davidic hope, in royal terms, comes to be transformed, as appears to be the case in the Chronicler, into a theologised concept?

Much of this exposition is of necessity tentative. It is an attempt at exploring more fully the possible links of 36–39 with the book as a whole, to give more ground for Melugin's claim than is, I believe, to be found in his brief discussion of the point. The basis for the words of hope and salvation is here declared to rest in the realities of a historic situation—no longer to be unravelled fully—in which deliverance is portrayed, new life out of death is granted, the Babylonian exile is foretold. It is another aspect of that process by which the acceptance of the disaster provides a basis for a new hope, a stage towards the further reassessments of that disaster and hope which are to be found in early and later post-exilic writings.

48. "An Interpretation" (see p. 4 n. 3 [[p. 479 n. 4]]), 350–352. See also A. K. Jenkins, "Isa. 14:28–32: An Issue of Life and Death" (to appear in *Folio Orientalia*) [[21 (1980) 47–63]].

49. Cf., e.g., A. Schoors, "Isaiah, the Minister of Royal Anointment?" in *Instruction and Interpretation* (*OTS* 20, 1977), 85–107; and H. Cazelles, op. cit. (see p. 5 n. 3 [[p. 480 n. 8]]).

Literary Criticism and *Tendenz*-Criticism:
Methodological Reflections on the Exegesis of Isaiah

OTTO KAISER

I

[[55]] Christof Hardmeier's report on Isaiah scholarship in the last decade bears the apt title "Radical Change in Isaiah Research."[1] Anyone comparing older treatments with the work produced since the beginning of the 1970s is likely to agree with this assessment. Historical-critical research at the end of the nineteenth and in the first half of the twentieth centuries, carried out under the prevailing paradigm of literary criticism, had attained some degree of stability by the 1950s and 1960s, owing to the influence of tradition criticism. This followed Bernhard Duhm's largely conservative conclusions regarding the Isaianic nature of chapters 1–39.[2] However, since the beginning of the 1970s one can observe a growing restlessness in the study of the prophets in general and in Isaiah

Translated and reprinted with permission from "Literarkritik und Tendenzkritik: Überlegungen zur Methode der Jesajaexegese," in *The Book of Isaiah / Le livre d'Isaïe. Les Oracles et leurs Relectures: Unité et Complexité de l'Ouvrage* (BETL 81; Louvain: Peeters, 1989) 55–71. Translated by Andreas Köstenberger.

1. C. Hardmeier, "Jesajaforschung im Umbruch," *VF* 31 (1986) 3–31.

2. Primarily E. Rohland, *Die Bedeutung der Erwählungstraditionen Israels für die Eschatologie der alt. Prophetie* (Ph.D. diss., Heidelberg, 1956); S. Herrmann, *Die prophetischen Heilserwartungen im Alten Testament: Ursprung und Gestalt* (BWANT 85; Stuttgart, 1965). See further especially G. von Rad, *Theologie des Alten Testaments II: Die Theologie der prophetischen Überlieferungen Israels* (Munich, 1960; 5th ed. 1968) 154–81; and the monumental commentary of H. Wildberger, *Jesaja* (BKAT 10/1–3; Neukirchen-Vluyn, 1965–82).

research in particular and, at the same time, a moving away from conventional questions and answers. While classical research on the prophets was primarily interested in the determination of the *ipsissima verba prophetarum* ⟦'very words of the prophets'⟧ and, beyond this, in the reconstruction of their religious and ethical characteristics, later, under the influence of the so-called dialectic theology, interest in the message of the prophets, as well as redaction-critical, sociology-of-religions, politics-of-religions, and literary concerns came to the fore. For the present we shall put aside questions as to what part the spirit of the age[3] played in this change of focus and what presuppositions it reflects. At any rate, one may describe the situation as a whole by observing that the pluralism characteristic of the entire period has also left its mark on the most recent Isaiah research.

⟦56⟧ This pluralism in formulating questions and methods, however, has not merely had an enriching effect on scholarship. It has also contributed to a rising sense of insecurity on the part of many regarding the effectiveness of current methods and their (in part) revolutionary results. In the Christian world, and particularly in fundamentalist and pietistic circles, this pluralism has reinforced long-standing prejudices against the historical-critical method.[4] Today every academic teacher is confronted with these tendencies in his lectures and seminars. This, of course, should not cause us to capitulate but rather to reflect on the relationship between the various parts of our method. Occasionally we may even be led to greater modesty in formulating our necessarily hypothetical conclusions and at the same time to a clarification of fundamental, inherently theological, issues. In this process, however, the scholar committed to the ethos of critical research will not allow his conclusions to be dictated by conventional, more or less dogmatic or pseudo-dogmatic, premises, but rather will bring these before the forum of his critical judgment, thus making his own contribution to the discussion of fundamental theological methods, particularly regarding the doctrine of Scripture and the Word of God.

Permit me in this context more modestly to address the problems posed by the widely shared insight that the writing down of prophecy constituted a complex process. In my view, as well as in the opinion of others, this process did not merely involve genuine writings of the

3. See also N. Hartmann, *Das Problem des geistigen Seins* (3d ed.; Berlin, 1962) 175–91, especially 188–91.

4. Paradigmatically, J. N. Oswalt, *The Book of Isaiah: Chapters 1–39* (NICOT; Grand Rapids, 1986) 17–28, especially 20–21 and 24–25. On this topic see also J. Barr, "The Problem of Fundamentalism Today," in *Studies in Isaiah* (ed. W. C. van Wyk; OTWSA 22–23; Pretoria, 1979–80) 1–25; idem, *Holy Scripture, Canon, Authority, Criticism* (Oxford, 1983) 105–26; and finally, idem, *Escaping from Fundamentalism* (London, 1984).

prophets but also, to a much greater extent than previously assumed, secondary documents produced at various times and even redactional revisions of the original material. Moreover, since the prophetic books formed in this way were passed on for centuries without the protection of being esteemed as holy writings that were complete in themselves and thus not to be altered in their wording, it is in principle possible that those who transmitted these prophetic books were themselves participants in the process of actualizing revision of the text.

What has been said should essentially be acceptable when applied to the book of Isaiah. Since the beginnings of historical-critical research in the final decades of the eighteenth century, it has been recognized that no genuine words of Isaiah are found subsequent to chapter 39 [[57]] and that the sayings regarding foreign nations predominantly represent material that was added at a later time. One may also recall the liberty with which Bernhard Duhm attributed individual texts even to the period of the Hasmoneans at a time when he was not burdened by the results of the most recent Septuagint research or knowledge of the discoveries at Qumran. The application of such insights has a provocative effect only when it is tested on texts that have been regarded as Isaianic since Duhm. For such texts one is still more inclined to take into account "alterations by the prophet Isaiah,"[5] or one proceeds on the basis of the prophet's certainty regarding the ultimate saving will of Yahweh[6] rather than dealing with the question of whether or not it is possible to attribute the tensions found in material considered to be Isaianic to the alternation of voices from different periods. After all, for the last decade and a half, an encouraging consensus—that the texts referring to the Assyrians should be considered redactional—has existed, even though differences of opinion remain regarding the dating of this redaction (or, as the case may be, redaction*s*), owing to differing estimations of the dating of the original material.[7]

5. See G. Fohrer, *Studien zu alttestamentlichen Texten und Themen (1966–1972)* (BZAW 155; Berlin and New York, 1981) 11–23.

6. See W. H. Schmidt, "Die Einheit der Verkündigung Jesajas," *EvT* 37 (1977) 260–72.

7. See also, on the one hand, O. Kaiser, *Der Prophet Jesaja: Kapitel 13–39* (ATD 18; Göttingen, 1973; 3d ed. 1983) 39–42, 70–74, 209–14, 242–47; idem, *Das Buch des Propheten Jesaja: Kapitel 1–12* (ATD 17; 5th ed.; Göttingen, 1981) 22–23; F. Huber, *Jahwe, Juda und die anderen Völker beim Propheten Jesaja* (BZAW 173; Berlin and New York, 1978) 35–82; W. Werner, *Eschatologische Texte in Jesaja 1–39: Messias, Heiliger Rest, Völker* (FB 46; Würzburg, 1982) 149–95; R. Kilian, *Jesaja 1–39* (ErFor 200; Darmstadt, 1983) 98–106; idem, *Jesaja 1–12* (NEB; Würzburg, 1986) 16; and, on the other hand, H. Barth, *Israel und das Assyrerreich in den nicht-jesajanischen Texten des Protojesajabuches* (Ph.D. diss., Hamburg, 1974); idem, *Die Jesaja-Worte der Josiazeit: Israel und Assur als Thema einer produktiven Neuinterpretation der Jesajaüberlieferung* (WMANT 48; Neukirchen-Vluyn, 1977); W. Dietrich, *Jesaja und die Politik*

When in the following pages we consider how the individual steps of the largely retained arsenal of the historical-critical method should be applied and how *Tendenz*-critical considerations are at work in this process, what is said can only convince if it does not remain at the level of theory. Rather, it is important that [[58]] the proper interplay of individual exegetical steps be demonstrated by concrete examples.

The classical point of departure remains the delimitation of the original textual units. In this procedure the established perspectives of a form-critical and a content-related nature complement one another. If there is a tension in form or content, one may conduct an investigation of the use of language, of the motives, and in some instances even of the traditions utilized. In this process the exegete's argumentation necessarily moves in a hermeneutical circle,[8] for in these investigations the interpreter inevitably relies on his own preunderstanding of the book's presumed original state and on his ideas about the course of Israel's literary and religious history. However, it is equally true that this preunderstanding is modified by each piece of work on the text. For this, if for no other reason, exegesis has proved to be an essentially unfinished process both for the individual and for the entire scholarly community. Anyone who deplores this merely reveals that he has failed to give adequate consideration to the nature of "human understanding and its horizon that changes with every new experience."[9]

II

Initially, I have selected a relatively straightforward example. Some among you will recognize in the following treatment that I have meanwhile learned from your arguments. I am referring to the woe in 31:1-3, which reads:

(BEvTh 74; Munich, 1973) 208–12; R. E. Clements, *Isaiah and the Deliverance of Jerusalem* (JSOTSup 13; Sheffield, 1980; 2d ed. 1984) 28–51; idem, *Isaiah 1–39* (NCBC; Grand Rapids and London, 1980) 5–6; but now see also Clements' contribution in this volume [[not reprinted here]]; F. J. Gonçalves, *Sennachérib en Palestine dans la littérature hébraïque ancienne* (Ebib n.s. 7; Paris, 1986) 289-327, especially 326–27; and finally also J. Vermeylen, *Du prophète Isaïe à l'apocalyptique: Isaïe 1–35, miroir d'un démi-millénaire d'expérience religieuse en Israël* (Ebib; 2 vols.; Paris, 1977–78) 2.678–88.

8. See H.-G. Gadamer, *Wahrheit und Methode* (Tübingen, 1960) 250–83; also R. Bultmann, "Das Problem der Hermeneutik," *Glauben und Verstehen II* (Tübingen, 1952) 211–35.

9. On the concept of horizon coined by Husserl, see G. Keil, *Gott als absolute Grenze* (Beihefte zur Zeitschrift für Philosophische Forschung 23; Meisenheim am Glahn, 1971) 16–24.

1. Woe to those who go down to Egypt for help
   and thereby rely on horses.[10]
   They trusted[11] in chariots since there were plenty
   and in horsemen since they were numerous.
   They did not look to the Holy One of Israel
   nor consult Yahweh.
2. Yet he also was wise and brought about calamity
   and did not retract his words. [[59]]
   And he rose[12] up against the house of evildoers
   and against help for those working iniquity.[13]
3. But the Egyptians are human beings, and not God,
   and their horses are flesh and not spirit.
   Yahweh will stretch out his hand,
   and then the helper and the one who is helped will stumble,
   and they will perish together.

In terms of genre, this constitutes a woe-cry that is developed into a well-substantiated warning. It contains a whole series of anomalies or, at least, noteworthy features. To begin with, one may ask whether or not the prophetic woe-cry represents a coherent genre. It already contains the announcement of destruction in the woe and therefore needs no further development into a word of warning.[14] Owing to these considerations, one should, in my view, suppose that the traditional saying contains a subsequent development of the prophet's cry of woe, which had originally been given primarily in oral terms. The second peculiarity consists in the consistent use of past tenses in v. 1b. In this case, likewise, one may detect a further development, be it in the original writing or in a later revision. Thus the kernel could be reduced to v. 1a and, if appropriate, to v. 3a, if the controversial v. 2 should turn out to be redactional. We must direct our attention to the latter.

---

10. On the use of the imperfect in the following colon with a preceding preterite to indicate an accompanying action in the past, see H. Bobzin, *Die "Tempora" im Hiobdialog* (Ph.D. diss., Marburg/Lahn, 1974) 30–42.

11. With this I open up for discussion my interpretation of the imperfect construction in ATD 18, ad loc.

12. See also Gesenius-Kautzsch, *Hebräische Grammatik* (28th ed.; Leipzig, 1909) §§112e and h.

13. On the objective genitive, see ibid., §128h.

14. On this see Kaiser, in ATD 17, p. 102, and the corresponding analysis of the woes in 5:8–24 (ibid., pp. 100–114), as well as in Kilian, *Jesaja 1–12*, 42–44; see also W. Werner, *Studien zur alttestamentlichen Vorstellung vom Plan Jahwes* (BZAW 173; Berlin and New York, 1988) 11–32. See also Vermeylen, *Du prophète Isaïe*, 1.169–76.

Herbert Donner already had noted in 1964 that v. 2 interrupts the reproach by introducing a sudden change in subject, from those scolded, to Yahweh. He vacillated on the question of whether the tenses should be understood as future or past. Likewise, he took no firm position on the issue of whether Yahweh's activity was directed against Judah or Egypt. He even pointed already to the conspicuous conceptual pair of *bêt mĕrē‘îm // pō‘ălê ’āwen* [['house of evildoers' // 'those who practice iniquity']], recognizing also the dependence of v. 2aβ on Isa 9:7, 11b.[15] Similarly, Brevard S. Childs objected that v. 2 breaks the continuity between vv. 1 and 3, which consists in the contrast between trusting in Egypt and trusting in Yahweh.[16] Both of these scholars drew from these observations the justifiable conclusion that v. 2 constitutes a later addition.

This example therefore reveals with particular clarity the combination of different issues raised by the historical-critical method. Certain difficulties arise regarding the most fundamental consideration, that of grammar and syntax. On the one hand, it appears that the Masoretic Text in v. 2a is undoubtedly correct. The narrative *wayyābē’* [['and he brought']] in v. 2a finds its confirmation in the term *hēsîr* [['called back']] in v. 2aβ. Verse 2b, with *wĕqām*, then poses the difficult problem of the *wĕqātal* [[verb construction]] in the continuation of a narrative perfect. Gesenius-Kautzsch explained this particular expression as a frequentative perfect.[17] Especially in view of the late provenance of the verse that will be explored further below, it cannot be excluded that this already constitutes a softening of the classical tense system, a softening that is, in my view correctly, traced to the influence of Aramaic.[18] If one looks back to v. 1b with its exclusively preterite verb forms, it is evident that it is possible only to a very limited extent to form a judgment regarding the provenance of the verse merely on the basis of the verbal structure in v. 2. The reason for this is the controversial nature of the *wĕqātal* clauses.[19]

Thus we are compelled to look for further evidence in order to confirm or to refute our hypothesis. Accordingly, we need to deal with the vocabulary and the particular concepts found in this verse. Herbert Donner's reference to the conceptual pair *bêt mĕrē‘îm // pō‘ălê ’āwen* proves to be useful in this endeavor. While the *mĕrē‘îm* appear in 1:4 and

---

15. H. Donner, *Israel unter den Völkern* (VTSup 11; Leiden, 1964) 135–36.

16. B. S. Childs, *Isaiah and the Assyrian Crisis* (SBT 2/3; London, 1967) 34.

17. See n. 12 above.

18. See R. Meyer, *Hebräische Grammatik III: Satzlehre* (Sammlung Göschen 5765; 3d ed.; Berlin and New York, 1972) §101.7a/p. 55.

19. On this problem see the recent, detailed, but hardly final, contribution by H. Spieckermann, *Juda und Assur in der Sargonidenzeit* (FRLANT 129; Göttingen, 1982) 120–30.

14:20 in the context of a reference to the *zera^c̆ měrē^c̆îm* [['seed of evil-doers']], a *bêt měrē^c̆îm* [['house of evildoers']] is found only in the present passage. When one attempts to make the admittedly difficult decision about whether one should take the *bêt měrē^c̆îm* as a reference to Egypt or to the people of God, 1:4 and the context suggest that it is a reference to the people of God. In accordance with the parallelism, then, one should interpret the genitive in v. 2bβ as an objective genitive, as is advocated by our translation, since in this way Egypt is included in the calamity described in the context.

Turning to the formulaic *pō^c̆ālê ʾāwen* [['those who practice iniquity']], we find further evidence against the original inclusion of v. 2, evidence that can be adduced independently from the evaluation of 1:4. Indeed, there is no further reference to the *pō^c̆ālê ʾāwen* in Isaiah. Apart from Hos 6:8, the phrase does not occur elsewhere in the prophetic books, while it is found sixteen times in the Psalms, three times in the book of Job, and twice in Proverbs.[20] Nevertheless, since the reference in Hos 6:8 has gone unchallenged, as far as I know, [[61]] further observations are needed to arrive at a clear conclusion. We are helped by the observation of Hans-Peter Müller that "the designation of God as wise is (rare and) late."[21] Moreover, since Jacques Vermeylen has presented well-founded objections to the portrayal of the prophet as deriving from wisdom circles,[22] we will not consider the introductory *wĕgam hûʾ ḥākām* [['moreover he also is wise']] in v. 2 to be an exception to the rule observed by Müller but rather regard it as confirmation of the suspicion that v. 2 is not original, in the light of what was said regarding the *pō^c̆ālê ʾāwen*.

In order to confirm his findings, we first recall once again Herbert Donner's correct reference to the relationship between this verse and the poem regarding the out-stretched hand of Yahweh in Isa 9:7ff. If we now return to the material regarding the structure of verb tenses presented above, we should be able to make a decision. A later author impresses upon his contemporaries the notion that Yahweh's words (of judgment) were always fulfilled in the past. History testifies to the fact that the apostates were struck by Yahweh's words of judgment, and thus we may assume that he will continue to act similarly in the future. The context may

---

20. In this regard, Otto Plöger's treatment of Prov 10:28 in *Die Sprüche Salomos (Proverbien)* (BKAT 17; Neukirchen-Vluyn, 1984) 130, lends support to the notion that the origin of this phrase is to be found in the language of the Psalms.

21. H.-P. Müller, in *TWAT* 2.934a.

22. See idem, *Le Proto-Isaïe et la sagesse d'Israël,* in *La Sagesse de l'Ancien Testament* (ed. M. Gilbert; BETL 51; Gembloux and Louvain, 1979) 39–58, especially 57–58.

further suggest that the interpolator sought to counsel his audience not to rely on external help even in the present but rather to place their firm trust in Yahweh. It would not imply any contradiction to suspect at the same time an inner-Jewish tension between the pious Jews who waited for God's decisive intervention and an upper class that preferred political intrigue. With this, however, we have reached the limit of what we can glean from the verse in question without lapsing into speculation.

Nevertheless, it appears possible, with caution, to determine the spiritual provenance of the redactor. His recourse to the language of Wisdom and of the Psalms and the simultaneous opportunity to effect changes in the traditional text of the book of Isaiah suggest that he belonged to a period in which the preservation of prophetic and Wisdom literature, as well as the collection of psalms, occurred in the same vicinity. In the interest of greater precision, one may perhaps resort to Josephus (*Ant.* 12.142), who indicates that there existed in pre-Maccabean times in Jerusalem priestly temple scribes who were responsible for the production of copies of biblical books.[23] But at this point we become painfully aware of the fragmentary nature of our knowledge of the transmission process.

One final observation may confirm that we have not erred [[62]] materially or with regard to time. As we tackle the question that has been deferred until now—that is, with reference to what contrary assertion the *wĕgam hûʾ ḥākām* at the beginning of v. 2 was formulated—we should not resort to the expedient of unexpressed intermediate ideas but look for an antecedent text in the preceding chapters. Such a text is in fact found in the claim of being *bĕn-ḥăkāmîm ʾănî ben-malkê qedem* [['I am a wise man, a son of the kings of yore']] placed on the lips of Pharaoh's advisers in 19:11bβ. By this our redactor confronts the claim of the wise counselors of Egypt with the claims of the true wise person, Yahweh, who demonstrated his wisdom in fulfilling the prophetic words and allowing his people's hopes, wrongly placed in the Egyptians, to fail. Since even the original version of the oracle regarding Egypt in Isaiah 19 should probably be placed in Persian times,[24] we have every reason to date the allusion no earlier than the final years of Persian rule or in the early Hellenistic Era. We shall not hesitate to view the redactor as a legitimate interpreter of the transmitted Isaianic message. He interpreted Isa 31:1, 3 together with 28:16 and 30:15 for his contemporaries in the light of changed circumstances. Moreover, we should note the certainty with

23. See E. J. Schnabel, *Law and Wisdom from Ben Sira to Paul* (WUNT 2/16; Tübingen, 1985) 63–69, especially 65.

24. On this see Kaiser, in ATD 18, pp. 81–82; and against Wildberger's attribution to Isaiah, Clements, *Isaiah 1–39*, 166–67.

which he was able to assume that his readers and listeners would be able to identify his allusion to an ancient text.[25]

In sum, our conclusion that 31:2 represents a late interpolation is supported by the methodical interplay of grammatical-syntactical, form-critical, lexical, conceptual, and *Tendenz*-critical research and considerations. Apart from extrabiblical information, it is a surprising reference to another passage in the book of Isaiah that has proven to be the means of securing our conclusion. One should not expect greater certainty from a redaction-critical investigation, nor is such clarity always achievable.

III

As we turn to the second paradigm, the analysis proves to be considerably more complex. Above all, we are confronted with the question that is decisive for an understanding of Isaiah, that is, whether or not the original layer contained in the book already has received a post-Isaianic [[63]] revision. In order to answer this question we select what is now the large unit of 30:6–17, which in turn finds a parallel in 28:1–18 (22). It will not be our purpose to present a complete analysis of this text but merely to call attention to the kinds of observations that are relevant for our considerations. It will therefore again be critical to conduct the argumentation in methodically verifiable steps and to remain faithful to the principle that a redaction-critical judgment needs to be supported by various kinds of observations.

Before we enter into a discussion of the data, it should first be recalled that there are conspicuous analogies between the external political condition of the Judean nation during the years of the rebellion of Hezekiah and the final stages of the Davidic empire. These parallels hardly need to be presented here. One merely needs to recall a text such as Isa 30:6–7 or the third Lachish Letter (*KAI* no. 193) to become aware of these parallels. It would indeed be curious if these correspondences had been overlooked by the stewards of the Isaianic legacy without finding expression in a later interpretation that ensured that the prophet's legacy would be interpreted authoritatively for later generations who lived in the shadow of the catastrophe of 587 B.C.E. The interpretation of the calamity and of its effects would intuitively have suggested itself as a consequence of the rejection of the prophetic message, and the lessons derived from it as signposts for the present and future conduct of Israel.

---

25. I wish to thank R. Rendtorff for his contribution to the discussion, which underscores this fact.

In formulating the possibilities for application after 587 B.C.E. (in the broadest sense), 28:12b, 30:9b, 30:12aβ, and 30:15b, with their hints of re- fusing obedience to Yahweh's word and command, stood just as much in the background as the words contained in 28:12a, 28:16aβb, and 30:15a, which I would classify as axiomatic *tôrôt* [['instructions']]. The curious connection between the *tôrâ* [['instruction']] and the formula of rejection in 28:12 and 30:15, in the first case with the additional introduction of the divine word by means of a relative clause, serves to provoke the question of whether the situation should in fact be explained by assuming that the prophet wrote down the oracles subsequently (cf. 30:8) or by assuming that there was a secondary revision of the original words of Isaiah. We ap- proach the answer by first calling attention to the interconnections within the larger unit of 30:6–17, which clearly indicate that we are here dealing with a redactional composition: 30:6–7 are introduced by the *maśśā*²- heading [['oracle'-heading]], which is certainly secondary. Since we are compelled to assume that vv. 6aβ–7 and v. 8 represent words of Yahweh, the primary introduction, for example in the form of a messenger for- mula, must have been lost. The original oracle [[64]] in vv. 6–7 is linked to the command to write down the oracle in v. 8 by way of an *ᶜattâ* [['now']]:

> Now go and write it on a tablet (with them)[26]
> and engrave it on a writing-tablet[27]
> that it may serve for future days
> "as a witness"[28] forever.

We may assume that a genuine Isaianic word forms the core of vv. 6–7 as well as of v. 8. As Walter Dietrich has expressed so poignantly and as is widely held by interpreters today,[29] the substance of the passage may be found most naturally in what precedes, that is, in the terse *rahab ham šābet* [['Rahab, who sits still', RSV (meaning uncertain)]][30] of v. 7bβ.[31] This

---

26. In accordance with the parallelism and contra G. Fohrer (*Das Buch Jesaja II* [ZB; Zurich, 1962] 94) and Kaiser (in ATD 18, p. 231), *lûaḥ* [['tablet']] should not be emended. On the other hand, the term *ᵓittām* [['before/with them']], not represented in the LXX, is suspected of being a secondary interpretation.

27. On the meaning of this word, see W. H. Irwin, *Isaiah 28–31: Translation with Philo- logical Notes* (BibOr 30; Rome, 1977) 79–80.

28. See BHS, ad loc., as well as, for example, H. Ewald, *Die Propheten des Alten Bundes I* (Stuttgart, 1840) 270.

29. Dietrich, *Jesaja und die Politik*, 142.

30. I now read the received *hēm* as *ham*, stative construct of a verbal noun *hām* derived from the verb *hûm* 'to bellow'; see also Irwin, *Isaiah 28–31*, 77–78.

31. Franz Delitzsch, *Der Prophet Jesaja* (Biblischer Commentar über das Alte Testament 3/1; 2d ed.; Leipzig, 1869) 355; Hans Schmidt, *Die großen Propheten* (Die Schriften des Alten

command then receives its substantiation in vv. 9-11 in the form of a reproach, by way of the *kî* ⟦'for'⟧ at the beginning of v. 9. Although another threat with its own explanation follows in vv. 12–14, it is likewise connected with what precedes, this time by way of a *lākēn* ⟦'therefore'⟧. One finds a similar pattern in the structurally complex explanatory threat of vv. 15–17.[32] Once again, it is linked to the preceding passage by an explanatory *kî*.

A look at this sequence immediately reveals a formal difference between the indirect reproach in vv. 9–11 and the direct reproach of the two following units. Nevertheless, the basic units of vv. 9–11, 12–14, and 15–17 share the same formula of rejection (cf. vv. 9b, 12aβ, 15b). Regarding the question of whether or not one should place an absolute break between vv. 9–11 and 12ff. on the basis of these observations, caution seems advisable, since the form ⟦65⟧ of the indirect reproach in vv. 9–11 results from its function as an immediate substantiation of the preceding command to write down the oracle. On the other hand, the [*bad*]*dābār hazzeh* ⟦'this word'⟧ in v. 12aβ peculiarly lacks a clear antecedent. An antecedent could be gained by eliminating vv. 9–11, for the phrase then would refer back to vv. 6–7 or 7bβ, but this conclusion proves, on further examination, to be less clear than it first appears.

In order to question this conclusion we turn to 28:7–18. We find that v. 12a cannot be understood apart from v. 16aβb. Only the latter ensures that the *mĕnûḥâ* ⟦'rest'⟧ refers to Zion as the place that provides rest for the weary. The word of rest and the word regarding the cornerstone are mutually interpretive. The peculiar placement of the two *tôrôt* ⟦'instructions'⟧ in their respective contexts deserves special attention in this regard. On the one hand, the divine word in v. 12 is strikingly linked with the preceding threat by way of a relative clause. On the other hand, as has been frequently observed (albeit also frequently disputed)[33] since Otto Procksch and Reinhard Fey, at least v. 16aβb is not firmly rooted

---

Testaments 2/2; 2d ed.; Göttingen, 1923) 88; O. Eissfeldt, *Einleitung in das Alte Testament* (Neue Theologische Grundrisse; ed. R. Bultmann; 3d ed.; Tübingen, 1964) 425; Kaiser, in ATD 18, p. 234; Dietrich, *Jesaja und die Politik*, 142; and Vermeylen, *Du prophète Isaïe*, 1.411.

32. On its form, see R. F. Melugin, "The Conventional and the Creative in Isaiah's Judgment Oracles," *CBQ* 36 (1974) 304.

33. See O. Procksch, *Jesaia I* (KAT 9; Leipzig, 1930) 356–57; R. Fey, *Amos und Jesaja* (WMANT 12; Neukirchen-Vluyn, 1963) 120–22 and 124–25; Herrmann, *Die prophetischen Heilserwartungen*, 142; Childs, *Isaiah and the Assyrian Crisis*, 30–31; Dietrich, *Jesaja und die Politik*, 165–66; Vermeylen, *Du prophète Isaïe*, 1.392–96; see already K. Fullerton, "The Stone of Foundation," *AJSL* 27 (1920–21) 40. With a differing view, see recently Barth, *Die Jesaja-Worte*, 121–22; Wildberger, *Jesaja*, 1069–71; Clements, *Isaiah 1–39*, 229; Gonçalves, *Sennachérib*, 197–99. J. D. W. Watts (*Isaiah 1–33* [WBC 24; Waco, Tex., 1985] 365–73) does not address this problem.

in its context. Whatever its structural composition may be,[34] this well-established saying, which has the character of a conditional promise, breaks the connection between reproach and threat. There is no refuge for the accused from the outpouring flood of v. 18. Moreover, the idea of a selective judicial activity of Yahweh can hardly be considered probable for the preexilic period.

Once the connection between 28:12 and 28:16 is recognized, one needs to question the origin of both verses. Hans Wildberger (whose passing we remember at this point with great respect for his life work, which was devoted to proto-Isaiah) had no tradition-critical problem regarding 28:12. He proceeded directly from the assumption that Psalm 132 represents an ancient ascent psalm that testifies in its own right (v. 8) to the antiquity of the concept of *měnûḥâ* [['rest']] related to Zion.[35] While everything that has to do with the preexilic tradition of Zion constitutes an extremely complex problem that requires further careful investigation,[36] I may nevertheless appeal in this context to the judgment of Tryggve D. Mettinger and Timo Veijola, both of whom believe Psalm 132 to be a comparatively late composition, because of its links with deuteronomic theology.[37] If Ps 132:8 may indeed be considered a further development of the deuteronomic concept of *měnûḥâ* under the influence of Zion theology (cf. in this regard Deut 12:9 and 1 Kgs 8:56 // 1 Chr 22:9), it seems reasonable to consider the form-critically unique oracle in 28:12 to be a secondary echo of the deuteronomic concept.[38]

The assessment of the saying regarding the cornerstone is, of course, dependent on the judgment regarding Isa 7:9b. It would be beyond the scope of the present discussion to repeat my earlier position and, at the same time, to modify it in certain details.[39] I limit myself therefore to the remark that 7:1–9 should be considered a secondary account that is

---

34. See also on this Gonçalves, *Sennachérib.*

35. See Wildberger, *Jesaja,* 1060.

36. On this see now, for example, Jörg Jeremias, *Das Königtum Gottes in den Psalmen: Israels Begegnung mit dem kanaanäischen Mythos in den Jahwe-König-Psalmen* (FRLANT 141; Göttingen, 1987) 149–65; and E. J. Waschke, "Das Verhältnis alttestamentlicher Überlieferungen im Schnittpunkt der Dynastiezusage und die Dynastiezusage im Spiegel alttestamentlicher Überlieferungen," *ZAW* 99 (1987) 157–79.

37. See T. N. D. Mettinger, *King and Messiah* (CBOTS 8; Lund, 1976) 256–57; and T. Veijola, *Verheißung in der Krise* (AASF B. 220; Helsinki, 1982) 161. But see also O. Loretz, *Die Psalmen,* vol. 2 (AOAT 207/2; Neukirchen-Vluyn, 1979), who on p. 288 refers to vv. 6–8 as a quotation from an earlier song of the Ark. His comments on pp. 290–91 show that he considers the psalm as a whole to be post-exilic.

38. On the history of the idea, see also H. D. Preuss in *TWAT* 5.304b–306. Only Gen 49:15 stands out as pre-deuteronomic evidence.

39. See Kaiser, *ATD* 17, pp. 135–49.

given a dual thrust in v. 9b. On the one hand, it serves the purpose of evaluating past history; on the other hand, it is opened out to the addressee.[40] In the end, however, the assessment of the present context and its saying does not depend on our judgment regarding 7:1–9, since our observation that 28:12 and 28:16 are mutually interpretive and that v. 12 could reasonably be suspected of a post-deuteronomic origin can assuredly stand on its own. At this point it seems appropriate to draw attention to the astonishing fact that it is precisely the keynote words that are transmitted to us in such an unhomogeneous context that they lack any information regarding their possible life-setting in the prophet's proclamation and demand to be read in context in order to be fully understood.

After this excursus, we return to our passage, 30:6–17. The observations regarding 28:12 and 28:16 ⟦67⟧ suggest that 30:12aβ and 30:15 are likewise mutually interpretive, so that the *dābār* ⟦'word'⟧ referred to in v. 12 is first quoted in v. 15. Let us see whether we can find further evidence to justify our suspicion that these also represent later interpretive pronouncements. As for v. 12aβ, the concordance indicates a conspicuous similarity to 1 Sam 15:23, which has *yaʿan māʾastā ʾet dĕbar Yhwh* ⟦'because you rejected the word of the LORD'⟧.[41] A search for possibly related Isaianic references indicates that 5:24b is redactional and should therefore be eliminated,[42] while 8:6 should be considered Isaianic according to Wolfgang Werner and Rudolf Kilian.[43] The process of the transmission of the book of Isaiah would indeed remain a mystery if it is not understood as a further development of an Isaianic core tradition. The so-called "legends of Isaiah" are in fact unable to account for the genesis of the book of Isaiah, because of their peculiarity and their presumed age.[44] If we consider the possibility that the *dābār* in 30:12aβ

---

40. See ibid., 141. In this I concur with Chr. Hardmeier, ("Gesichtspunkte pragmatischer Erzählanalyse," *Wort und Dienst* 15 [1979] 50), though differing with him in evaluation of the text in other respects.

41. On 1 Samuel 15, see T. Veijola, *Die ewige Dynastie: David und die Entstehung seiner Dynastie nach der deuteronomistischen Darstellung* (AASF B. 193; Helsinki, 1975) 102 n. 156; and idem, *Das Königtum in der Beurteilung der deuteronomistischen Historiographie* (AASF B. 198; Helsinki, 1977) 81.

42. See Vermeylen, *Du prophète Isaïe*, 1.138; Clements, *Isaiah 1–39*, 66; Kaiser, in ATD 17, pp. 113–14; and Kilian, *Jesaja 1–12*, 44.

43. See W. Werner, "Vom Prophetenwort zur Prophetentheologie: Ein redaktionskritischer Versuch zu Jes 6:1–8, 18," *BZ* n.s. 29 (1985) 11–12; and Kilian, *Jesaja 1–12*, 63. Both consider 8:6a to be part of the Isaianic material in 8:5–8*.

44. See also Kaiser, in ATD 18, p. 4, and in ATD 17, p. 21. On the Isaiah narratives in 2 Kings 18–20 parallel to Isaiah 36–39, there remain the analyses of Clements, *Isaiah and the Deliverance*, 52–71; E. Würthwein, *Das Buch der Könige: 1. Kön. 17 – 2. Kön. 25* (ATD 11/2;

relates to v. 15 and is linguistically nurtured by 8:6 and 1 Sam 15:23, it seems reasonable to assume that it owes its existence to a redactor.

It could, of course, be argued on the basis of 8:6 that v. 12 reflects Isaianic language. We therefore need further evidence within the following context that we are dealing with a post-Isaianic redaction. Thus we turn to the reproach found in vv. 9–11. I will refer here to my own work but especially to the work of Jacques Vermeylen, who has thoroughly examined and further developed my own thesis.[45] I will be as succinct as possible and will focus, appropriately, on methodological issues, for one may demonstrate once more precisely by this example how it is only the combination of linguistic, conceptual, and *Tendenz*-critical observations that leads to assured results. If we place the *Tendenz*-critical ⟦68⟧ element at the beginning of our investigation, it is evident that these verses deal no longer with the rejection of Isaiah's message but with the rejection of the prophets' message in general (cf. vv. 10–11). Here it is of particular significance that the motif recurs in the deuteronomic redactional addition to the stanza on Israel in Amos's poem on the nations, namely, Amos 2:11–12.[46] The possibility of an echo of a deuteronomic prophetic-theological motif in the present passage can therefore not be excluded.

In the second instance we turn to the discourse regarding the *tôrat Yhwh* ⟦'instruction of the LORD'⟧ in v. 9bβ. The context indicates that the phrase refers, as in 5:24 (cf. 1: 10), to the prophetic message. Nevertheless, that this phrase demonstrably constitutes a late deuteronomic development of Exod 13:9, 2 Kgs 10:31, and Amos 2:4 deserves attention.[47] For an assessment of the book of Jeremiah, I refer to Christoph Levin, who claims that the term *tôrâ* only occurs in late contexts, when referring to the Law of Yahweh.[48] Levin regards Jer 8:8, a piece of evidence that is of particular importance for the present discussion, as an

---

Göttingen, 1984) 413–38; E. Vogt, *Der Aufstand Hiskias und die Belagerung Jerusalems 701 v. Chr.* (ed. L. Alonso Schökel; AnBib 106; Rome, 1986) 24–59; and Gonçalves, *Sennachérib*, 331–487. See now also I. W. Provan, *Hezekiah and the Book of Kings* (BZAW 172; Berlin and New York, 1988).

45. See Kaiser, in ATD 18, pp. 233–35; Vermeylen, *Du prophète Isaïe*, 1.411–24.

46. See also W. H. Schmidt, "Die deuteronomistische Redaktion des Amosbuches," *ZAW* 77 (1965) 180–81; and, for example, H. W. Wolff, *Dodekapropheton 2: Joel und Amos* (BKAT 14/2; Neukirchen-Vluyn, 1969) 172 and 207.

47. On Exod 13:1–16, see M. Noth, *Exodus* (ATD 5; Göttingen, 1959; 7th ed. 1984) 97; on 2 Kgs 10:31, Würthwein, *Das Buch der Könige*, 343; and on Amos 2:4, for example, Vermeylen, *Du prophète Isaïe*, 2.533–35.

48. See Chr. Levin, *Die Verheißung des Neuen Bundes* (FRLANT 127; Göttingen, 1985) 259 n. 11.

addition to v. 7, an assessment with which Robert Carroll concurs.[49] In this passage we are given information regarding a discussion between the stewards of the Torah and the stewards of the prophetic message.

Since major objections have been raised against the attribution of 5:24 to Isaiah,[50] we also may in good conscience assign the phrase featured in 30:9 to post-deuteronomic language. The further observation, that the phrase *sûr min derek* [['turn from [the] way']] in v. 11a is exclusively found in deuteronomic or post-deuteronomic contexts, can be added without further ado.[51] The impression gained up to this point, that is, that vv. 9–11 represent a post-deuteronomic redaction, does, however, appear to be contradicted by the prophets' designation in v. 10 as *rōʾîm* [['seers']] and *ḥōzîm* [['visionaries']]. By referring to passages such as 1 Sam 9:9, the inscription of king Zakkur of Hamath (*KAI* no. 202 A 12), and possibly also Amos 7:12,[52] we might think that we have found an important objection to the emerging assessment of the reproach. A look at the concordance, however, is sufficient to invalidate the objection, since the designation of the prophets as *rōʾîm* or *ḥōzîm* occurs nowhere as frequently as in Chronicles.[53]

Not until we have come this far do we dare to cite as further evidence of deuteronomic influence the obvious linguistic correspondences between v. 9 and the deuteronomic law against the rebellious son in Deut 21:18–21. If we had taken this observation as our starting point, we would doubtless have been open to the charge of prematurely attributing to dependence a related semantic field that is represented there as well as in the present passage.

In review, we realize that *Tendenz*-critical factors and linguistic and conceptual arguments cohere. We have sufficient reason to consider 30:9–11 to be a post-deuteronomic text. It remains our task to refer to the *Tendenz*-critical component and thus to emphasize the redactor's intention. For him, Isaiah has become a paradigm for the preexilic prophecy of doom in general. If we take into account his place in history, he

49. See R. P. Carroll, *Jeremiah* (OTL; London, 1986) 228–29; contrariwise W. McKane, *Jeremiah* (ICC; Edinburgh, 1986) 185–86.

50. See above, n. 42.

51. See Exod 32:8 and also J. Vermeylen in *ZAW* 97 (1985) 5; Deut 9:12, 16; 11:28; 31:29; Judg 2:17; and Mal 2:8.

52. On the discussion regarding Amos 7:9–17, compare on the one hand P. R. Ackroyd, "A Judgment Narrative between Kings and Chronicles? An Approach to Amos 7:9–17," in *Canon and Authority: FS W. Zimmerli* (ed. G. W. Coats and B. O. Long; Philadelphia, 1977) 71–87; and on the other hand G. Pfeifer, "Die Ausweisung eines lästigen Ausländers Amos 7:10–17," *ZAW* 96 (1984) 112–18.

53. See 1 Chr 9:22, 26:28, 29:29; 2 Chr 16:7, 10 or 2 Chr 9:29, 12:15, 19:2, 29:30. On 2 Kgs 17:13, see Würthwein, *Das Buch der Könige*, 392.

presents his proof of guilt in the present situation by means of a charge
that is phrased in such a comprehensive way that his recipients would
immediately be able to discern that the issue was not merely the events
of Hezekiah's revolt or the rejection of Isaiah's message by his contemporaries, but at the same time the rejection in general of prophecies of
doom that would lead to calamity for the kingdom of Judah. It is evident
by this that he considers their time to have come to an end.

Permit me now to return to the pronouncements of 28:12, 16, and
30:15 in order to examine whether or not their content can be brought
within the framework of the date determined for 30:9–11. Proof may be
readily furnished for the saying regarding the cornerstone. If we read,
with the MT, *hinĕnî yissad* [['behold, I am laying']] as the *lectio difficilior*
[['more difficult reading']],[54] Jacques Vermeylen's suggestion, that we
consider the community gathered around the Second Temple[55] to be the
recipients of this passage, no longer appears implausible. This would
also agree in principle with the results of our earlier careful determination of the dates of 28:12 and 30:9–11, 12aβ. However painful this result
may be for us—after all, these passages belong, together with 7:9b, to the
few pronouncements by which faith is able to live—from the standpoint
of *Tendenz*-criticism, the conclusion that has emerged during the course
of our investigation [[70]] is unobjectionable: it is particularly the basic
passages of the so-called "Assyrian Cycle" that represent the formulations of a redactor from the time of the Second Temple, who retrospectively and prospectively actualizes and interprets the Isaianic legacy.
While the prophet hurled his cries of woe into a concrete political situation of his nation, the Isaianic legacy is now, after an interval, reduced to
a principle and that principle is impressed upon the Second Temple
community: the future of this community is contingent, not on aroused
expectations or repeated revolts against the community's overlords in
the context of its foreign policy, but on calm confidence in the help of
the God whose presence among his people was guaranteed by Zion. Isa
30:15 can be easily harmonized with this interpretation. If the introductory *šûbâ* (or perhaps even lQIsaᵃ *šybh*; cf. 2 Sam 19:33) may be derived
from the root YŠB [['to sit']] (see Francolino J. Gonçalves[56] for details),
and if we translate, with Friedrich Huber, *biṭĕḥâ* 'calmness',[57] the result is
a perfect parallelism:

54. See also Irwin, *Isaiah 28–31*, 30–31; and on the construction, Gesenius-Kautzsch
§115f.

55. In Vermeylen, *Du prophète Isaïe*, 1.392.

56. Gonçalves, *Sennachérib*, 171–74; and further especially H. Ewald, *Ausführliches Lehr-
buch der Hebräischen Sprache* (8th ed.; Göttingen, 1878) §153b/p. 396; also see Irwin, *Isaiah
28–31*, 86.

57. Huber, *Jahwe, Juda und die anderen Völker*, 143.

In restfulness and composure lies your salvation,
in quietness and calmness is your strength.

The picture is completed if we add that the weary needing rest in 28:12, like those in 40:29, are probably those who have lost hope in Yahweh's help. By all these words the nation is called to place its hope in the God whose presence is indicated by Zion, to trust in his promises and not to despair, and not to risk the future once more by political conspiracies. A passage such as Zech 8:6 documents this kind of situation in the early postexilic period. On the other hand, it is possible that the Ionic rebellion, the Persian defeat at Marathon, or the Egyptian revolt that was only finally put down by Xerxes, led also to thoughts and expectations of conspiracy in Jerusalem.[58]

IV

[[71]] We break off our investigation at this point, even though we are conscious of the fact that our remarks have in no way exhausted what may be said regarding the larger redactional units of the "Assyrian Cycle." The task of the redaction criticism of the original layer of the proto-Isaianic collection has therefore not yet come to an end. Conclusions need to be examined and results refined, but above all we continue to be confronted with the task of extracting from later interpretations the kernels of original Isaianic tradition. In this we may be further assisted by the technique of "colometry" developed by Oswald Loretz and Ingo Kottsieper, even though this method remains subject to refinement.[59]

Our discussion has had the goal of confronting the skepticism toward historical-critical work on Isaiah that was triggered by methodological pluralism by demonstrating that it is indeed possible to arrive at relatively assured results even in the case of complex literary issues by skillful use of a combination of all of the exegetical tools. If these considerations are judged coherent, a new portrait of the classical prophet

58. On this, see O. Kaiser, "Der geknichte Rohrstab: Zum geschichtlichen Hintergrund der Überlieferung und Weiterbildung der prophetischen Ägyptensprüche im 5. Jahrhundert," in *Wort und Geschichte: FS Karl Elliger* (AOAT 18; ed. H. Gese and H. P. Rüger; Neukirchen-Vluyn, 1972) 99–106, especially 101–2 = idem, *Von der Gegenwartsbedeutung des Alten Testaments* (ed. V. Fritz, K.-F. Pohlmann, und H.-Chr. Schmitt; Göttingen, 1984) 181–88, especially 183–84.

59. See O. Loretz and I. Kottsieper, *Colometry in Ugaritic and Biblical Poetry: Introduction, Illustrations and Topical Bibliography* (Ugaritisch-Biblische Literatur 5; Altenberge, n.d. [1987]) 57–63.

would begin to emerge. Rather than using extended discourses, he appears to have spoken concisely with memorably formulated words that he may later also have recorded, at least to a limited extent. The distinction between what the prophet himself added at a later point and what was added by the witnesses of his ministry or by the chain of later bearers of tradition leads us through the history of Israel's troubled faith from the eighth-century prophet to the early Hellenistic Period. And this perhaps compensates us for the insight that the great personalities in this history are not merely to be sought among the prophets but, as we have suggested, also among the bearers of tradition.

The Canonical Shape of the Prophetic Literature

BREVARD S. CHILDS

The Debate over Methodology

[[46]] The study of the prophetic literature of the Old Testament has gone through several important phases within the modern period. One thinks of the development of the methods of literary, form, and redactional criticism, as well as the use of comparative materials from the field of history of religions, psychology, and sociology.[1] From this history of modern research a wide consensus has emerged that the present literature is the product of a long history of development, a portion of which can now be successfully reconstructed through critical methodology. It is also generally agreed that the recovery of this prehistory has greatly illumined the study of the biblical literature by bringing into sharp focus the historical milieu of the prophets and in providing criteria [[47]] for interpreting the peculiar oral and literary forms in which the message was couched.

Reprinted with permission from *Interpretation* 32 (1978) 46–55.

1. Cf. the most recent survey of the history of research by Ronald E. Clements, *One Hundred Years of Old Testament Interpretation* (Philadelphia, Westminster Press, 1976), 51–75. Walther Zimmerli's *The Law and the Prophets* (Oxford, 1965) also has some pertinent observations on the history of scholarship. Moreover, the specialized treatments of the major figures remain invaluable: E. Sehmsdorf, *Die Prophetenauslegung bei J. G. Eichhorn* (Göttingen, 1971); H. J. Kraus's interesting analysis of G. H. A. Ewald's contribution to the study of the prophets in *Geschichte der historisch-kritischen Erforschung des Alten Testaments* (Neukirchen Kreis Moers, Verlag der Buchhandlung des Erziehungsvereins, 1956); Werner Klatt, *Hermann Gunkel. Zu seiner Theologie der Religionsgeschichte und zur Entstehung der formgeschichtlichen Methode* (Göttingen, Vandenhoeck und Ruprecht, 1969).

However, in my opinion, in spite of some impressive gains, the application of historical-critical methodology has resulted in serious weaknesses in the handling of the biblical literature. First of all, the legacy of the literary-critical method in distinguishing between "genuine" and "non-genuine" oracles has continued to interject a pejorative category into the discussion. Secondly, the form-critical analysis has increasingly atomized the literature and continued to rest much of its analysis upon fragile and often highly speculative theories of original settings. Thirdly, the redactional and sociological methods have tended to politicize the biblical material and render it into a type of political propaganda.[2] As a result, little success has been achieved in interpreting the prophetic books as Scripture of the church which accords to the Bible an authoritative role in the formation of the Christian life.

The purpose of this essay is to suggest a different approach to the biblical material, which I shall try to illustrate in terms of the prophets. It begins with the recognition that a major literary and theological force was at work in shaping the present form of the Hebrew Bible. This force was exerted during most of the history of the literature's formation, but increasingly in the postexilic period exercised its influence in the collecting, selecting, and ordering of the biblical traditions in such a way as to allow the material to function as authoritative Scripture for the Jewish community. In the transmission process, tradition, which once arose in a particular milieu and addressed various historical situations, was shaped in such a way as to serve as a normative expression of God's will to later generations of Israel who had not shared in those original historical events. In sum, prophetic oracles which were directed to one generation were fashioned into Sacred Scripture by a canonical process to be used by another generation.

The reason for treating the final form of Scripture with such seriousness lies in the peculiar relationship between text and people of God which is constitutive of canon. The shape of the biblical text reflects a history of encounter between God and Israel. Canon serves to describe this unique relationship and to define the scope of this history by establishing an end to the process. It assigns a special quality to this particular segment of history which is deemed normative for all future generations of this community of faith. The significance of the final form of the biblical literature is that it alone bears witness to the full

---

2. Examples of this approach can be found in the works of Otto Plöger, *Theocracy and Eschatology*, trans. by S. Rudman (Richmond, John Knox Press, 1968); Morton Smith, *Palestinian Parties and Politics that Shaped the Old Testament* (New York, Columbia University Press, 1971); P. D. Hanson, *The Dawn of Apocalyptic. The Historical and Sociological Roots of Jewish Apocalyptic Eschatology* (Philadelphia, Fortress Press, 1975).

history of revelation. Within the Old Testament neither the process of the formation nor the [[48]] history of its canonization is assigned an independent integrity. These dimensions have been either lost or purposely blurred. Rather, canon asserts that the witness to Israel's experience with God is testified to in the effect on the biblical text itself. It is only in the final form of the biblical text in which the normative history has reached an end that the full effect of this revelatory history can be perceived.

Certainly earlier stages in the development of the biblical tradition were often regarded as canonical prior to the establishment of the final form. In fact, the final form frequently consists of an earlier, received form of the tradition which has been transmitted unchanged from its original setting. But to take canon seriously is also to take seriously the critical function which it exercises in respect to the earlier stages of the literature's formation. A critical judgment is exercised in the way in which the earlier stages are handled. At times the material is passed on, complete with all of its original historical particularity. At other times the canonical process selects, rearranges, or expands the received traditions. The purpose of insisting on the authority of the final form is to preserve the canon's role of providing this critical norm. To work with the final stage of the text is not to lose the historical dimension, but rather it is to provide a critical theological judgment regarding the process. A reconstructed depth dimension may aid in understanding the interpreted text, but it does not possess an independent integrity for the exegetical task within the context of the canon.

Then again, the final form of the text performs a crucial hermeneutical function in establishing the peculiar profile of a passage. Its shaping establishes an order in highlighting certain features and subordinating others, in drawing elements to the foreground, and in pushing others to the background. To work with the final form is to resist any method which seeks critically to shift the canonical ordering. Such an exegetical move occurs when an overarching category such as *Heilsgeschichte* [['salvation history']] subordinates the unique canonical profile, or when an historical or rhetorical reconstruction attempts to refocus the picture according to its own standards of historical accuracy or literary aesthetics.

The canonical process was not simply an external valorization of successive stages of literary development, but was an integral part of the literary process. Beginning in the preexilic era, and increasing in significance in the postexilic era, a canonical force was unleashed by Israel's religious use of her traditions which resulted in a collecting, selecting, and ordering process. The motivations behind the canonical process were diverse and seldom discussed in the biblical material itself. However, a major concern was that a tradition from the past be transmitted in such a way that its authoritative claim was laid upon all future generations of Israel.

It is an axiom of many redactional critics that the layering within a biblical [[49]] book derives from a desire to "update" an original tradition. While this description occasionally applies, the canonical approach to the Old Testament offers a very different model of interpreting the growth of multi-layered texts. The major issue turns on how one understands the process by which a biblical text is actualized. It is constitutive of the canonical process that texts have been shaped to provide the community of faith with guidelines for its appropriation. The hermeneutical task of actualizing past traditions for each successive generation lies at the heart of the process. Theological reflection on its actualization has been built into the structure of the canonical text. The modern hermeneutical impasse has arisen in large measure by disregarding the canonical shaping. The usual critical methodology of restoring an original historical setting often involves stripping away the very elements which constitute the canonical shape. Little wonder that once the text has been anchored in the historical past by "decanonizing" it, the interpreter has difficulty applying it to a modern religious context!

The Canonical Shaping of the Prophets

The effect of the canonical shaping of the prophetic literature reveals an enormous variety in the manner by which the traditions were rendered as Sacred Scripture. A few examples from the canonical process can be briefly sketched:

(1) An original prophetic message was expanded by being placed in a larger theological context. The Book of Amos provides a classic example of this frequent canonical move. An important problem within the Book of Amos turns on how to interpret the sudden shift from a message of total judgment of Israel to one of promise for Israel in chapter 9. Often the shift in tone has been understood as an attempt to soften Amos' harsh message by a later generation who was either offended at the severity or who tried to make room for the later restoration of Judah. However, the editors of chapter 9 did not soften Amos' message of total judgment against sinful Israel by allowing a remnant to escape. The destruction is fully confirmed (9:9–11). Rather, the tradents effected a canonical shaping by placing Amos' words in a broader, eschatological framework which transcended the historical perspective of the prophet. From God's perspective there is a hope beyond the destruction seen by Amos. The effect of chapter 9 is both to confirm the truth

of Amos' original prophecy and to encompass it within the larger theological perspective of divine will which includes hope and final redemption. To distinguish between genuine and non-genuine oracles is to run in the face of the canon's intent.

(2) The shaping process changed the level on which the original prophecy functioned in order to afford the witness a new metaphorical role. The original [[50]] message of Hosea was directed to the inhabitants of the Northern Kingdom in the mid-eighth century. The prophet's word constituted a sustained attack on Israel's syncretistic religious worship which had changed the worship of Yahweh into a fertility cult. Hosea appropriated the language of his opponents to claim all the areas of fertility, land, and kinship for Yahweh, Israel's faithful lover. The sign acts of chapter 1 functioned as a history-creating act of divine judgment which actualized the threat in the giving of names of judgment. But in its collected form the original material has been arranged to reflect an important hermeneutical shift in the function of Hosea's witness. The prophet's realistic language is now understood metaphorically. Regardless of the prehistory behind the sign acts in chapters 1 and 3, the present shape of these chapters has given the material a symbolic interpretation. It is quite impossible to reconstruct a history of Hosea's marriage from these two chapters. Rather, the intent that the sign acts be understood metaphorically is made explicit in both chapters 1 and 3 (cf. 1:2, 4f., 6f., 9; 3:1, 4, 5). Moreover, the placing of chapter 2 as an extended metaphor in between these two chapters provides the editor's symbolic key for interpreting them.

(3) A collection of prophetic material has been detached from its original historical moorings and subordinated to a new theological context. The classic example of this canonical move is so-called "Second-Isaiah." Critical scholarship has made out a convincing case for dating chapters 40–55 (some scholars include the remaining chapters of the book as well) to the period of the Babylonian exile. Yet in their present canonical position these chapters have been consciously loosened from their original setting and placed within the context of the eighth century prophet, Isaiah of Jerusalem. Moreover, the original historical background of the exilic prophet has been drained of its historical particularity—Cyrus has become a theological construct almost indistinguishable from Abraham (cf. Kissane)—and the prophetic message has been rendered suitable for use by later generations by transmitting it as a purely eschatological word.

(4) A body of prophetic tradition has been edited in the light of a larger body of canonical literature. From the perspective of literary criticism, the message of Jeremiah has been cloaked in the later prosaic

language of the Deuteronomic school. But from a canonical perspective, Jeremiah's words have been preserved in conjunction with a commentary which sought to understand his ministry as part of a chain of divine messengers who were loyal to the law of Moses and who warned of Jerusalem's coming destruction. Thus, the ordering of Jeremiah's message within the tradition of the preachers of the law provides the later community with a prophetic interpretation of how the law properly functions within the divine economy.

[51] Closely allied with this move is the dovetailing of traditions from the oracles of Isaiah and Micah (cf. Isa 2:1–4 and Micah 4:1–4). From an historical perspective one could argue for a common circle of tradents who transmitted both sets of tradition. But from a canonical perspective the effect of the process is to provide each prophetic book with a commentary in the light of which a mutual enrichment is to be drawn.

(5) By means of a radical theocentric focus in the ordering of a book, the original historical sequence of a prophet's message was subordinated to a new theological function. The Book of Nahum is introduced by a hymn; the Book of Habakkuk concludes with one. But the effect on the material is similar. This shaping process did not require a de-historicizing of the original oracles. Rather, the material was left virtually untouched, yet a new role was assigned the oracles: They now function as a dramatic illustration of the eschatological triumph of God—whose divine nature is celebrated in a hymn—over his adversaries. In Nahum the destruction of the enemy is explicitly derived from the nature of God—a "jealous God," "avenging and wrathful," "keeping wrath for the enemy"—who claims dominion over the entire world. The threat against Nineveh does not stem from the personal hatred of a Hebrew prophet against Assyria, nor is it evoked by some particular historical event of the seventh century. Rather, the biblical tradents use the initial psalm, even shattering its earlier acrostic form, to establish the true theological context for understanding the prophecy. Nineveh has become a type of a larger recurring phenomenon in history against which God exercises his eternal power and judgment.

The prophecy of Ezekiel has continued to baffle its readers. The book appears to lack the sharp contours of a definite geographical locality with a concrete group of hearers. The prophet oscillates back and forth between Babylon and Jerusalem. The traditional forms of prophetic oral speech are largely missing; but the book abounds in allegory, sign acts, and visions. Surely the canonical key to understanding this unusual book lies in the radical theocentric perspective of the prophet which has deeply affected its final literary shape. Thus even when his oracles are fixed within a chronological framework, these temporal moorings are immediately transcended when the prophet testifies to the plan of God in terms freed from any such human limitations. Similarly the spatial distinction between Babylon and Jerusalem is completely relativized whenever the people of God are viewed from the divine perspective as one entity.

(6) The original prophetic message was placed within a rule-of-faith which provided the material with an interpretative guideline. It is generally recognized by critical scholarship that two appendices have been fixed to the conclusion of the Book of Malachi. To dismiss these verses as a "legalistic corrective" stemming [[52]] from some disgruntled priestly editor is to misunderstand the canonical process utterly. Rather, the first appendix reminds the whole nation that it still stands under the tradition of Moses. The imperative to "remember the law of my servant Moses" does not weaken Malachi's attack on the nation's sins, but it sets a check against any misuse of the prophet's words which would call into question national solidarity in the name of additional requirements for the pious. The canonical effect of the first appendix to Malachi testifies that the law and the prophets are not to be heard as rivals but as an essential unity within the one divine purpose. The effect of the second appendix (4:5–6) is to balance the memory of the past with the anticipation of the future.

In a similar way, the ending on the Book of Ecclesiastes is another example of a rule-of-faith which would also order a wisdom book from a perspective informed by God's commandments (12:13) and the coming judgment (v. 14).

(7) Oracles which originally functioned in a variety of historical settings have been arranged into set patterns which serve a new typological role in relation to the coming rule of God. The clearest examples of a patterning schema are the alternative blocks of oracles of judgment and salvation in the Books of Isaiah (compare 1:1–31; 2:6–22; 3:1–26, with 2:1–5; 4:2–6) and Micah (cf. chaps. 1, 2, 6 with 2:12f.; 4 and 5). The effect of this move is that a typological sequence subordinates the original historical one and refocuses the material on the dominant theological purposes undergirding all prophetic proclamation.

(8) Prophetic symbolism has been given a radical new eschatological interpretation by shifting the referent within the original oracles. Scholars have long recognized that the visions in Zechariah 1–6 appear once to have functioned independently of each other and to have been addressed to particular historical situations both preceding and following the return from the exile (cf. Galling). But the tension between the original visions and their present framework points to an intentional

theological shaping. The prophetic visions of Zechariah are now set in the second year of Darius, that is to say, some twenty years after the return from Babylon. The deliverance from the exile now lies in the past. Although the traditional language of the second exodus from slavery has been retained, it has been given a new reference. The language of hope now points to a still future event in which Israel's redemption lies. The original focus has been eschatologized and projected once more into the future. The community of faith which lives after the return still anticipates the future in the language of the past. Israel will still "flee from the land of the north," "escape to Zion," and God will dwell in her midst (3:6ff.).

The Book of Joel offers another example of a radical eschatologizing of an original oracle (chaps. 1–2) which had only faintly adumbrated the full dimension [[53]] of the End in the locust plague, but Israel learned to understand it as the prelude to the Day of Yahweh when God would hold the final assize (chap. 3).

To summarize, these examples of canonical shaping of the prophetic literature in the history of ordering Israel's tradition as Scripture do not begin to exhaust the richness of Old Testament interpretation, but at least they give a hint of the creative dimension involved in the collecting process.

Theological Implications of the Canonical Shaping

(1) The task of Old Testament exegesis is the interpretation of the canonical text as it has been shaped in the history of Israel's experience with God. The prophetic books show many signs of a growth in their composition and different layers are often discernible. But the tradents of the tradition have sought to hide their own footprints in order to focus attention on the canonical text itself and not on the process. The content of the prophets' message is first and foremost a theocentric word. Concern with Israel's own identity is always secondary and derivative from a prior understanding of God.

(2) Since the Reformation period there has been a tendency among Protestants, especially from the Reformed wing, to deprecate tradition as a threat to the integrity of the divine word; however, Scripture and tradition belong together. The active participation of the tradents in transmitting and shaping the biblical witness in no way calls into question its divine source. Rather, Israel registered the word of the prophets along with its own reception and saw in both the Spirit of God at work. To speak of the Bible as canon is to emphasize its function as the Word of God in the context of the worshiping community of faith. The canon

seeks to preserve the authority of the whole witness and to resist all attempts to assign varying degrees of theological value to the different layers of Scripture on the basis of literary or historical judgments.

(3) To assume that the prophets can be understood only if each oracle is related to a specific historical event or located in its original cultural milieu is to introduce a major hermeneutical confusion into the discipline and to render an understanding of the canonical Scriptures virtually impossible.[3] Rather, the true referent of the biblical witness can only be comprehended from within the biblical literature itself. In the ongoing experience of Israel, as the addressee of God's judgment and redemption, the divine purpose with his creation is revealed. [[54]] Canon sets the parameters to this unique history which has both a beginning and an end.

(4) Biblical texts are made relevant to today's community of faith and to the world, not by first decanonizing them in a claim of establishing an original setting, but by faithfully hearing the intent of the literature which has already been shaped to confront its hearers with the divine imperative. Canon serves as a guarantee that the biblical material has not been collected for antiquarian reasons, but as an eternal Word of God laying claim on each new generation.

(5) Any attempt to write a theology of the prophets which disregards the canonical shaping, whether in a search for the prophets' *verba ipsissima* [['very words']] or in a pursuit after prophetic self-understanding, can only end up with a formulation which has little to do with the prophets of the Old Testament. Thus even if it were possible to reconstruct an original Amos, the portrayal would have little in common with the prophetic message which both the synagogue and church heard from his book.

(6) Much of the problem of understanding the New Testament's use of the Old Testament prophets lies in the failure to take seriously the canonical perspective held in common by both Jews and Christians of the first century. Thus, the New Testament understands "Second-Isaiah's" message eschatologically as the proclamation of the immanent fulfillment of the promised new age. It interprets Joel's visions in the radical eschatological terms of the kingdom. It hears Hosea's promise of a divine reconciliation in which God restores to himself a new people. It is quite impossible to read the Old Testament prophets through the eyes of Duhm and Hölscher and yet understand what the New Testament is hearing in the Old!

3. Hans Frei's critique of a referential reading of the Bible which emerged in the 18th century and gained hegemony in the 19th marks a major advance in biblical hermeneutics (cf. *The Eclipse of Biblical Narrative* [New Haven, Yale University Press, 1974]).

(7) A final word is in order regarding the effect of canon on the larger exegetical enterprise of interpreting the Old Testament. The approach which I am advocating has been described by others as "canonical criticism."[4] I am not happy with this term because it implies that the concern with canon is viewed as another historical-critical technique which can take its place alongside of source criticism, form criticism, rhetorical criticism, and the like. I do not envision the approach to canon in this light. Rather, the issue at stake in canon turns on establishing a stance from which the Bible is to be read as Sacred Scripture.

The concern with canon plays both a negative and a positive role in delineating the scope of biblical exegesis. On the one hand, its negative role consists in relativizing the priority claims of the historical-critical method. It strongly [[55]] resists the assumption that every biblical text must first be filtered through an established historical-critical mesh before one can even start the task of interpretation. On the other hand, its positive role seeks to challenge the interpreter to look closely at the text in its received form, and then critically to discern its function for a community of faith. Attention to canon establishes certain boundaries within which the tradition was placed. The canonical shaping serves not so much to fix a given meaning to a particular passage as to chart the arena in which the exegetical task is to be carried out. Attention to canon is not the end but only the beginning of exegesis. It prepares the stage for the real performance by clearing away unnecessary distractions and directing the audience's attention to the main show which is about to be experienced.

In one sense the canonical approach sets limits to the exegetical task by taking seriously the traditional parameters. In another sense the method seeks aggressively to liberate the interpreter. By insisting on viewing the exegetical task as constructive as well as descriptive, the interpreter is forced to confront the authoritative text of Scripture in an ongoing theological reflection. By placing the canonical text within the context of the community of faith, a variety of different exegetical models, such as the liturgical or dramatic, are freed to engage the text. In sum, the canon establishes a platform from which exegesis is launched rather than a barrier by which creative theological struggle is cut off.

---

4. To my knowledge the term first appeared in J. A. Sanders' *Torah and Canon* (Philadelphia, Fortress Press, 1972).

Part 6

Prophecy after the Prophets

Introduction

Various important issues are suggested by the excerpts and additional reading for this section. The line of canonical prophets stops a century or so into the post-exilic period, but is that the end of prophecy? It might appear from certain rabbinic statements that prophecy was judged to have ceased with the post-exilic prophets Haggai, Zechariah and Malachi, but prophetic figures and prophesying did not die out so soon (Overholt, pp. 527–38 below; Neusner 1994). It is much more likely that the rabbis were saying that a particular type of prophecy had ended, and this out of a concern to deny current practitioners the possibility of laying claim to prophetic authority (Greenspahn 1989). For Overholt, indeed, prophecy, viewed anthropologically, remains "a continuing potentiality in a given society." An unusual angle on this question is offered by Dick (1984), who suggests that the committal of prophecy to writing led to its being treated as a verbal icon. As such it fell victim to the prophets' own fulminations against idolatry, which development contributed to its eventual cessation. More often the writing down of the words of the prophets is seen as a step in the direction of the cessation of prophecy in the respect that the creation of a corpus of prophetic literature that was both permanent and authoritative rendered "active" prophecy less necessary. And, if Ezekiel was the "writing" prophet that Davis (1989) claims him to have been, he might even be said to have participated in the process by which prophecy of the classical sort reached its conclusion.

Another issue is that of the interpretation of the prophets in early post-biblical Jewish literature and in the New Testament. A common tendency, highlighted by Barton (1986), was to value the prophets not so much for their moral and ethical teaching as for their powers of prediction. Qumran, Josephus, the New Testament and rabbinical sources are united in this respect (see also Begg, pp. 547–62 below; Sawyer, pp. 563–75 below; Gray 1993). This arose not just from assumptions about the prophets as miraculous predictors of the future but also from the conviction that Scripture speaks about the last times (cf. Bruce on LXX, pp. 539–46 below), which the interpreting individual or community usually reckoned themselves to be witnessing. The works listed as additional reading also raise points of interest for the biblical period as well as for the post-biblical, in relation to the use of "prophet" as a title. These are (i) the more relaxed use of the term, in the New Testament, Josephus and rabbinic literature, to describe individuals not normally regarded as standing in the prophetic succession (Barton 1986), and (ii) the restrained use of the term by Josephus in connection with individuals whose prophetic status he would not have questioned (Gray 1993).

Additional Reading

Barton, J.
   1986   *Oracles of God: Perceptions of Ancient Prophecy in Israel after the Exile.* London: Darton, Longman & Todd.
Davis, E. F.
   1989   Pp. 127–40 (endnotes 164–66) in *Swallowing the Scroll: Textuality and the Dynamics of Discourse in Ezekiel's Prophecy.* Journal for the Study of the Old Testament Supplement Series 78. Sheffield: Almond.
Dick, M. B.
   1984   Prophetic *poiēsis* and the Verbal Icon. *Catholic Biblical Quarterly* 46: 226–46.
Gray, R.
   1993   *Prophetic Figures in Late Second Temple Jewish Palestine: The Evidence from Josephus.* Oxford: Oxford University Press.
Greenspahn, F. E.
   1989   Why Prophecy Ceased. *Journal of Biblical Literature* 108: 37–49.
Heinemann, J.
   1982   A Homily on Jeremiah and the Fall of Jerusalem (Pesiqta Rabbati, Pisqa 26. Pp. 27–41 in *The Biblical Mosaic: Changing Perspectives*, edited by R. M. Polzin and E. Rothman. Philadelphia: Fortress.
Neusner, J.
   1994   What "the Rabbis" Thought: A Method and a Result—One Statement on Prophecy in Rabbinic Judaism. Pp. 303–20 in *Pursuing the Text* (B. Z. Wacholder Festschrift), edited by J. C. Reeves and J. Kampen. Journal for the Study of the Old Testament Supplement Series 184. Sheffield: Sheffield Academic Press.

The End of Prophecy:
No Players without a Program

THOMAS W. OVERHOLT

[[103]] The problem of the "end of prophecy" has in recent years been a topic of interest to students of the Hebrew Bible. The dominant opinion on this matter seems to be that Israelite prophecy came to an end in the early post-exilic period. At the very least, prophecy was after that time transformed into something else. Such a view does not seem to me altogether satisfactory, however, and my intention in this paper is to move the discussion of the "end of prophecy" onto somewhat different ground.

One difficulty with many approaches to the problem of prophecy's end is that they focus on a search for bearers of a particular social role, "classical Israelite prophet." Since with the possible exception of Haggai and Zechariah none is to be found in the post-exilic period, the problem is to determine what became of prophecy. But one might ask whether the fact that the surviving literature preserves the utterance of no such prophets means that there *were* none. Further, one wonders how to account for the fact that a society which for centuries had assumed and acknowledged the existence of prophets could suddenly find itself without bearers of that social role.

The approach I intend to take to the problem of prophecy's end may be illustrated by an analogy. At the theatre, a concert, or an athletic contest, it is common to be provided with a program booklet, the function of which is to enable members of the audience to identify performers by name. But whether one knows these names or not, the play or

Reprinted with permission from *Journal for the Study of the Old Testament* 42 (1988) 103–15.

concert or game goes on. Even without a program, there are players. What the title of this paper is intended to suggest is that in the case of a social process like "prophecy" there may be no performance at all, and consequently no identifiable "prophecy," ⟦104⟧ apart from a conceptual "program" in the collective consciousness of a society which allows a given "performance" to be recognized, and which, therefore, authorizes it. Even obvious and unavoidable social roles, such as "parent," are subject to judgments, based on such conceptual "programs," about the competence of individual bearers of them. Is, for example, an adult observed administering a severe beating to one of his offspring recognizable as a "parent"?

I

It seems appropriate to begin with a review of some recent discussions of the "end of prophecy." Inevitably, these have had to take into account the fact that "classical" Israelite prophecy seems to have existed only during and immediately after the period of the Israelite monarchy. If the prophetic tradition continued at all thereafter, it was only by virtue of its transformation into something new. In particular F. M. Cross's elaboration of these ideas has had an important influence on the subsequent debate. Cross sees prophecy as coterminous with, and generally functioning as a limitation upon, the monarchy, both "offices belong[ing] to the Israelite political structure which emerged from the conflict between league and kingdom."[1] When the kingdom fell, classical prophecy, which for Cross is "prophecy *sensu stricto*," ceased, undergoing a transformation into apocalyptic.[2] Haggai and Zechariah "are only apparent exceptions," a "last flicker of the old prophetic spirit" at the time of a royal "pretender," Zerubbabel.[3]

P. D. Hanson took up this theory about prophecy's transformation and developed it systematically. His thesis is that "the rise of apocalyptic eschatology . . . follows the pattern of an unbroken development from pre-exilic and post-exilic prophecy," apocalyptic eschatology being "the mode assumed by the prophetic tradition once it had been transferred to a new and radically altered setting in the post-exilic community."[4] The

---

1. F. M. Cross, *Canaanite Myth and Hebrew Epic* (Cambridge: Harvard University Press, 1973), 223.

2. *Ibid.*, 343. Cross suggests that in Ezekiel's oracles, which coincide with the fall of the monarchy, one can see "the transformation of classical prophecy into proto-apocalyptic" (p. 223 n. 15).

3. *Ibid.*, 343.

4. P. D. Hanson, *The Dawn of Apocalyptic* (Philadelphia: Fortress Press, 1975), 7–8, 10.

crucial distinction here is between prophets, who affirmed history as a suitable context for Yahweh's activity and understood their task as translating their visions from the cosmic to the historical-political sphere, and "visionaries," who abandoned this "prophetic task of translation" as a result of pessimism over their social-historical circumstances.[5] The resulting "polarization" of a vision and pragmatic program signalled "the demise of prophecy."[6] The social and historical "matrix" of this [[105]] demise was "an inner-community struggle" that raged in post-exilic Judah, especially during the years 520–420 B.C.E.[7] During this period, prophecy became "democratized," with the result that "the individual office of the prophet develop[ed] toward a collective office."[8]

We can observe that what this finally boils down to is an evaluation of prophetic figures in terms of the *content* of their utterances. Visionaries are said to "stem in an unbroken succession from the prophets."[9] How is this so? Presumably, the continuity lies in their *vision* of Yahweh's sovereignty.[10] But the prophet differs from the visionary in how he reports his vision: he translates "the activities of the divine council into the categories of the historico-political realm."[11] To speak in this way is the prophet's "mission."[12] Indeed, prophetic "activity" is recognizable in the early church, at the time of the Protestant Reformation, and even today in the struggle of individuals "to maintain the vital creative tension between vision and realism which is the heart of genuine ethical religion."[13] We should note the implication of this last statement: no preacher of apocalyptic themes can be a "prophet." Probably, no one who is not a Jew, Christian, or Muslim can be.

Given this emphasis on their utterances, it is not surprising that Hanson's concern with the social dynamics of prophecy is limited to a proposal about how the social status of the visionaries motivated them to adopt their peculiar theological/interpretive perspective on events (a perspective which *he* then evaluates by the standard of pre-exilic prophecy, especially Isaiah). This leaves open other questions relating to the social dynamics of prophecy. For example, were there persons (support groups) within the Jewish community who believed that these men actually *were* prophets?

5. *Ibid.*, 12, 26; cf. 409.
6. *Ibid.*, 210; cf. 219–20, 246–47, 354, 406.
7. *Ibid.*, 29, 409.
8. *Ibid.*, 69.
9. *Ibid.*, 10 n. 8.
10. See, for example, *ibid.*, 12.
11. *Ibid.*, 304.
12. *Ibid.*, 406.
13. *Ibid.*, 31.

As a recent panel discussion of the topic shows, even when there is disagreement with Hanson on specifics, there tends to be a consensus that prophecy underwent a transformation in the post-exilic period.[14] E. Meyers, for example, sees a transformation in the direction of priestly activity and concerns. In a situation where there was "no realistic opportunity to reinstate the office of kingship" Haggai and Zechariah "presuppose[d] the hegemony of Persian authorities in all local affairs and never question[ed] the appropriateness of the office of governor or high priest." In Zechariah the high priest is the principal actor in the drama of the temple's refoundation (3; 6:9–15), "while the Davidic scion . . . is relegated to an eschatological status" (3:8; 4:6b–10a; 6:12). Haggai, who was closer to the rebellions and [[106]] problems of succession occurring at the beginning of Darius's rule (522– 486 B.C.E.), repeatedly mentions Zerubbabel and "reflects a more heightened eschatology" (2:20–23). On the other hand, his exhortation and use of a priestly ruling (2:10–14) "presages a new role for the post-exilic prophet, one that is drawn more and more closely to the priesthood."[15]

In W. Harrelson's view,[16] the transformation of prophecy after the exile is to be seen mainly as an eschatological reinterpretation of prophetic traditions addressed to a believing community. This allows him to propose the thesis that "prophecy in the period following the return from Babylonian Exile continues to exercise a highly significant function

14. I refer to the "Social Roles of Prophecy in Israel Group" at the Society of Biblical Literature meeting in Anaheim, CA (November, 1985), which featured papers by E. M. Meyers ("The Persian Period and the Judean Restoration: From Zerubbabel to Nehemiah," forthcoming in the F. M. Cross *Festschrift*, Fortress Press [[1987, pp. 509–21]]), D. L. Petersen ("The End of Prophecy: Perspectives from Deutero-Zechariah and Malachi"), W. Harrelson ("Post-Exilic Prophetic Eschatology and the End of Prophecy"), and S. B. Reid ("The End of Prophecy in the Light of Contemporary Social Theory," in K. H. Richards, ed., *SBL 1985 Seminar Papers* [Atlanta: Scholars Press, 1985], 515–23). R. Wilson responded to the papers.

15. Elsewhere Meyers has written that the "unique usage of *tora* in [Hag] 2:11 demonstrates . . . [that] post-exilic prophecy went hand-in-hand with priestly concerns and provided the critical linkage between two disparate loci of society which come together in the Restoration period for a little while but remain together forever in the history of Judaism, where the sage or rabbi is the true inheritor of the biblical prophet" ("The Use of *tora* in Haggai 2:11 and the Role of the Prophet in the Restoration Community," in C. L. Meyers and M. O'Connor, eds., *The Word of the Lord Shall Go Forth: Essays in Honor of David Noel Freedman* . . . [Winona Lake, IN: Eisenbrauns, 1983], 70). Important to Meyers's view of the transformation of prophecy in the direction of priestly instruction is the assumption that "Darius' attempts to have the laws of conquered Persian territories codified" gave impetus to the canonical process which ultimately defined as authoritative the collections of the Pentateuch and Former Prophets. The law occupied center stage; the great period of prophecy was acknowledged to be in the past. See the forthcoming "Anchor Bible" commentary on Haggai and Zechariah 1–8 by C. L. Meyers and E. M. Meyers [[AB 25B; New York: Doubleday, 1987]].

16. See note 14.

in the political, social, and religious life of the Israelite community." We can, therefore, speak of the end of prophecy only in the "limited" sense that we no longer encounter individual prophets like those of the pre-exilic and exilic periods and that the collections of material named for these earlier prophets are brought to completion. Harrelson in fact suggests that

> never is prophecy more alive ... than when the collections entitled Isaiah ... [etc.] ... have definitely taken shape and begun to be the reference-points for a community that wishes to know what the prophets of Israel have said and taught, or what message God has to speak through God's servants the prophets.

The collectors of the prophets' words "did not merely edit them," but "added to them striking prophecies of their own" (he discusses Isa 4:2–6; 19:23–25; 35:1–10).

Harrelson's proposition is that if "prophetic eschatological texts" added to the collections in the post-exilic period "offer guidance in the here and now for a faithful community ... then prophecy is by no means at an end." I take him to be suggesting that until the arrival of the "End" (i.e., the consummation of God's work in the world), prophecy cannot be said to have come to an end, though by the standards of classical Israelite prophecy it underwent a change in form: "Once the great prophetic collections are assembled, the prophetic office consists largely in the interpretation of these prophetic texts." One virtue of this position is that it does not tie the definition of "prophecy" to the specific manifestation of that phenomenon. The problem seems to me to be its ambiguity about the nature of prophetic activity. What separates this type of on-going interpretation from homiletics practiced by persons making no claim [[107]] to be prophets and not believed by their audience to be such? Would such persons be performing actions recognizable by their contemporaries as those of a prophet?

This situation seems to be ambiguous. Israelite prophecy in its pre-exilic form apparently disappears, but not entirely! D. Petersen reviews the evidence for this in a series of "propositions" about the end of prophecy. The first of these is that "there is a radical polemic against prophetic activity in the Persian period" (cf. Zech 13:2–6 and Jer 23:34–40), which seems a more "broad-based" and "generic" condemnation than had existed before the exile. Second, there is evidence for a variety of activities during the Persian period which the various writers define as prophetic (e.g., the Levitical singers in Chronicles and the prophets and prophetess in Neh 6:1–14), but which seem somewhat different from the behavior of pre-exilic prophets. Third, evidence for literary connections between pre- and post-exilic prophets indicates both continuity and discontinuity.[17]

Like others, Petersen identifies the monarchy as "the political-religious locus of the prophet as mediator." To speak of "the end of classical Israelite prophecy" means that at some point "no one uttered oracles or wrote tracts in the way that Isaiah or Jeremiah had," or at least no such efforts were accepted by "the canonical process."[18] At the end of the monarchy there was a "transition from classical prophecy to an organically connected but profoundly different enterprise."[19] Indeed, prophecy was conceived differently by different groups within the society.[20] In the deutero-prophetic literature, for example, identifiable individuals functioning as prophets can no longer be discerned,[21] and the oracles depend upon and interpret the classical prophetic traditions. In Chronicles prophecy is conceived of as an activity that Levitical singers could perform. His conclusion is that "prophecy in the post-exilic period did not develop unilaterally into apocalyptic."[22]

There is an important caveat here: our judgment that prophecy in the classical Israelite mode came to an end in the period after the fall of the monarchy is dependent upon knowledge preserved for us by the canonical process. It is one thing to say that such prophecy was no longer officially (canonically) recognized, another to say it no longer existed, and yet another to say that there were no longer any performers of the prophetic role. As long as classical prophecy is tied by definition to the monarchy, the first and second of these are plausible, though not without some ambiguity (Haggai and Zechariah [[108]] must be understood to be "a last gasp of classical prophecy").[23] The third is very much open to question.

What we have seen in the Hebrew Bible is that one type of prophecy ("classical") has been transformed, sometimes in ways which (by the standard of pre-exilic forms) look somewhat strange. But this does not necessarily require us to believe that the phenomenon of prophecy itself came to an end. As Petersen notes, those post-exilic groups who denied the existence of prophecy in their own times had strong motivations for doing so (e.g., the desire "to protect the past ideal of classical prophecy

17. See note 14.

18. D. L. Petersen, *Late Israelite Prophecy* (SBLMS 23; Missoula: Scholars Press, 1977), 5.

19. *Ibid.*, 6.

20. *Ibid.*, 8; Petersen uses the notion of "theological streams" in this context.

21. For example, Deutero- and Trito-Isaiah, Jer 23:34–40, Zech 13:2–6, Joel 3:1–5, Malachi.

22. *Ibid.*, 102.

23. *Ibid.*, 97.

from spurious encroachment in the present," or in the case of the Chronicler the desire to appropriate the title and features of classical prophecy for Levitical singers).[24] Furthermore, he suggests that the deutero-prophetic critique in fact "established the formative pattern in which prophecy would be viewed in the future; the return of prophecy either in the form of an individual or as the spirit of prophecy given to the entire religious community."[25] Theoretically, for *these* persons prophecy was still *possible*, only not in their present situation.

R. Wilson has also noted the ambiguity involved in speaking about prophecy's end. After Haggai and Zechariah, no biblical book claims to be prophetic. Furthermore, late prophetic material is in some respects different from its pre-exilic and exilic counterparts, e.g., in its stronger connection with the priesthood. Yet in a later period one encounters Christian prophecy and Rabbinic materials in which the teaching priesthood is considered to be spirit-inspired. Though *we* tend to understand certain texts from the Hebrew Bible to say that prophecy had ceased, the Essenes, Christians, and Rabbis obviously did not read them that way.[26]

Wilson criticizes Hanson's distinction between visionaries and priests as being too sharply drawn, arguing that one cannot draw a direct line from a single tradition or movement in Israel to apocalyptic. Ultimately, the shape of apocalyptic religion and literature depended on the unique characteristics of each apocalyptic group.[27] One implication I draw from this criticism is that when dealing with the problem of prophecy's end/transformation, difficulties are likely to arise when one focuses too much on the content of what the figures say.

Finally, we may note that J. Blenkinsopp shares this general view of the development of Israelite prophecy, namely that it "did not come to an end during the Babylonian exile, though it did undergo [[109]] rather profound transformations."[28] Among these he lists the Deuteronomists' making "prophecy serviceable to their contemporaries by reading a message of judgment as one of salvation through judgment," the prophetic subgroup which owed allegiance to Deutero-Isaiah and which by the time of Trito-Isaiah was on the way to becoming a sect, prophecy's "reabsorption into the cult" (Joel, Chronicles), and the "eschatological

24. *Ibid.*, 98–100.
25. *Ibid.*, 102.
26. See note 14.
27. R. R. Wilson, "From Prophecy to Apocalyptic: Reflections on the Shape of Israelite Religion," *Semeia* 21 (1981), 82–83, 93.
28. J. Blenkinsopp, *A History of Prophecy in Israel* (Philadelphia: Westminster Press, 1983), 178; cf. p. 188.

reinterpretation of prophecy" by persons who did not consider themselves to be prophets (additions to Joel and Zechariah).[29]

II

One obvious feature of this discussion has been the emphasis on the
"transformation" of prophecy into something else. Implicit in this notion is the identification of the phenomenon of "prophecy" with one of
its possible manifestations, the "classical" prophecy of the Israelite monarchy. Having adopted "classical Israelite" as the norm by which prophecy is to be discussed, questions about the social and religious status of
post-exilic, biblical figures who seem to stand in some continuity with
the prophetic traditions arise as a matter of course. Nor is it easy to see
how instances of authentic prophecy could be thought to exist in post-
biblical times.[30]

At base what we have is a tendency to define the "end of prophecy"
as the last visible manifestations of a specific type of prophetic performance. After Haggai and Zechariah (at the latest), the tradition shades
off into other forms, and such evidence as we have for this development
comes to us shaped by the biases of specific groups within post-exilic
Judean society. And the bias does not end there, since researchers' own
methodological assumptions can shape their interpretation of the scant
data on the "end of prophecy."[31]

D. Petersen[32] points in the direction of another approach to this
problem when he suggests that attention to social context may reveal
"givens" which enable prophecy to occur, the absence of which "might
allow us to speak about a time in which prophecy was not important,"
and proposes that we accept as these givens the four "social prerequisites
of intermediation" outlined by R. Wilson in *Prophecy and Society in Ancient
Israel*: for intermediaries to be able to function in a society there must be
"a belief in the reality of a supernatural power or powers"; there must be
the further belief that these powers can influence affairs in this world
and can in turn be influenced by [[110]] humans; the society has to view
intermediaries positively, encouraging, or at least tolerating, them; and
"social conditions" must be such that "the services of an intermediary"
are required.[33]

29. *Ibid.*, 192, 249–51, 252, 263.
30. W. S. Towner has addressed this problem ("On Calling People 'Prophets' in 1970,"
Int 24 [1970], 492–509).
31. See S. Reid, note 14.
32. See note 14.
33. R. R. Wilson, *Prophecy and Society in Ancient Israel* (Philadelphia: Fortress Press,
1980), 28–32.

Figure 1

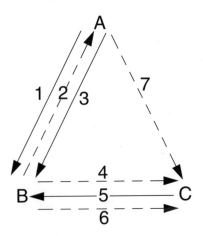

Post-exilic Judaism obviously qualifies on the first two counts. On the third, Petersen notes that Zechariah 13 and Jeremiah 23 indicate the presence of at least one group which did not encourage or tolerate prophetic behavior. As to the fourth, the 6th–5th centuries B.C.E. were "a period without significant international interference in Syria-Palestine" during which Yahwistic prophetic activity could be expected to decline in importance.[34] He concludes that "classical Israelite prophetic behavior" ended, but veneration of the words of the prophets continued, agreeing in substance with Wilson that prophetic support groups metamorphosed into apocalyptic groups.[35]

In short, prophecy came to an "end" when prophets lost their base of support within society. As Wilson has put it, "There can be no socially isolated intermediaries."[36] This, I believe, is the key which allows us to move the discussion onto different ground.

When thinking about the "end" of prophecy, we need to remember that prophets were purveyors of a particular message only by virtue of being performers of a certain recognized and accepted social role. Their speech was but one aspect of a specific pattern of social interaction. In previous publications I have proposed a model of how this social interaction works, a version of which appears in Figure 1.[37] This model seeks

34. Thus Wilson, *ibid.*, 32: "Even in societies which are supportive of intermediation in general, intermediaries tend to be forgotten or disappear when they have no social function."

35. Cf. Wilson, "Prophecy to Apocalyptic," and *Prophecy and Society*, 308.

36. Wilson, *Prophecy and Society*, 30.

37. Cf. my "Prophecy: The Problem of Cross Cultural Comparison," *Semeia* 21 (1981), 55–78; reprinted in B. Lang, ed., *Anthropological Approaches to the Old Testament* (Philadelphia: Fortress Press, 1985), 60–82.

to represent the social dynamics of prophetic activity as a set of interactions among a god (A), a prophet (B), and the prophet's audience
(C). These interactions occur along three axes: the god's revelation to
the prophet (1, 3) and the prophet's response (2), the prophet's speech
to the audience (4, 6) and its response (5), and direct manifestations
from the god to the prophet's audience (7).[38] Any component of this set
can occur many times.

I want now to ask the question: What, according to this model of
the prophetic process, would pass as the "end" of prophecy? Theoretically, the absence of any element primary to social interaction (1, 4, 5)
would be sufficient to render prophecy non-existent. However, both
prophecy and its "end" are social phenomena, and the question needs
to be re-phrased to take that reality into account: Of which element(s) of
the prophetic process could it be said that its (their) absence would necessarily be apparent, and thereby sufficient to bring prophecy to an end?

⟦111⟧ If the problem is phrased in this way, it is clear that we cannot
rely on the interactions along the revelation axis to signal prophecy's
end. Since revelation (1) is in essence a private matter not normally (or
ever fully) observable by persons other than those who are its recipients,
its presence can be *claimed* even in its absence. Furthermore, its presence
may be *attributed* even in the absence of such a claim, as the case of Yali,
a social reformer of sorts whose audiences interpreted his activity as
that of an inspired cargo cult leader though he made no claims along
those lines, shows.[39] Elements 2 and 3 are not structurally necessary for
an act of prophecy; element 1 is the critical component on this axis. On
the prophet-audience axis element 4, the statement of a message from
the god to the people, is theoretically necessary, and its absence would
be easily noticed. But there can be mitigating factors. The audience, for
example, can *understand as prophecy* that which was not intended to be
such (the case of Yali), leaving the primary A-B-C-B sequence intact. On
this axis 4 is primary, so the absence of 6 (additional proclamations) is
not a reliable signal that there is no prophecy. Element 7 is basically an
enhancer of prophetic activity, and is not necessarily present.

Element 5, feedback from the audience to the prophet, turns out to
be the key. Though a speaker may claim to have received a revelation
from the god and to be a prophet by virtue of proclaiming it, the failure

38. For example, acts of power or "miraculous" occurrences judged to be "supernatural confirmations" of the prophet's authority. Cf. my "Seeing Is Believing: The Social Setting of Prophetic Acts of Power," *JSOT* 23 (1982), 3–31.

39. An account of Yali's activities may be found in Thomas W. Overholt, *Prophecy in
Cross-Cultural Perspective: A Sourcebook for Biblical Researchers* (Atlanta: Scholars Press, 1986),
295–308.

of the audience to acknowledge, in effect to authorize, this ⟦112⟧ activity means that the A-B-C-B chain is truncated, losing its final stage. Prophecy comes to an end. But for how long? To what does the "end" of prophecy refer? In my view it refers in the first instance to the absence of persons who are acknowledged by members of their society as performing the role of a prophet. To say that in a given social context prophecy came to an end is not to deny the *theoretical possibility* of valid prophetic activity, but rather to note the failure of members of that society, at least for the moment, to credit (authorize) specific instances of prophetic behavior. Within a given society prophecy cannot be said to come to an absolute end until such time as the "social prerequisites" for this type of inter-mediation have ceased to exist. Until that happens, prophetic behavior it-self will always (at least potentially) be with us; societal acknowledgment and toleration of such behavior, however, may wax and wane and even sometimes disappear altogether. In this respect we can note that while Zech 13:2–6 polemicizes against prophetic behavior on the grounds that those currently indulging in it were speaking falsehood in Yahweh's name (v. 3), it does not claim that visions *themselves* have ceased (v. 4). Similarly, Jer 23:34–40 seems to acknowledge the *possibility* of divine-human com-munication (vv. 35, 37), while disapproving of current instances of pro-phetic *behavior* (vv. 34, 36, 38–40).

It must be assumed that within Judaism and Christianity prophecy has remained a *possibility* down virtually to the present. Evidence for this is not difficult to find in the time of Jesus (Mark 8:28),[40] the early Church (Montanists), or even in contemporary America (David Wilkerson's *The Vision*).[41] The conceptual structure of the faiths allows for its continued existence.

Now, it seems reasonable to assume that if the role of "prophet" is possible (conceptually available) within a society, some will feel them-selves drawn towards performing it. How, then, are we to account for the apparent absence of a continuing sequence of generally accepted per-formers of this role? The most obvious answer is society's (periodic) lack of interest in (or hostility toward) the role, resulting in its performers

40. Cf. R. A. Horsley, " 'Like One of the Prophets of Old': Two Types of Popular Proph-ets at the Time of Jesus," *CBQ* 47 (1985), 435–63.

41. D. Wilkerson, *The Vision* (Old Tappan, NJ: Fleming H. Revell, 1974). Wilkerson's claims to a prophetic role are implicit, but nonetheless real. In the "Introduction" to the book he speaks of a recurring vision which he experienced during the summer of 1973, and says, "In spite of my fears and apprehensions, I can no longer shake off a conviction that this vision must be published. If I understand divine guidance at all, God has instructed me to speak out" (pp. 11–12). In addition the text is sprinkled with phrases like, "I sense a kind of divine obligation to warn ministers and church organizations . . ." (p. 21), and "The mes-sage I have received for all true believers is . . ." (p. 29).

not being credited with an authentic performance. That is to say, they may be ignored, or credited with performing other roles than that which they intend (e.g., preacher, evangelist, "crazy person," "religious fanatic"). The bias of the audience clearly comes into play. In scholarly and many religious circles Wilkerson's *The Vision* is probably either unknown or rejected ⟦113⟧ out of hand as a record of prophetic activity (something like the canonical process is still at work), but this is not the case in all circles. In response to a question, some of my students suggested it immediately as an "obvious" example of contemporary prophetic literature. The reticence of the actors themselves may also be part of the answer. Some may have been reluctant to announce themselves as prophets, though they have performed, or attempted to perform, that role. Some, of course, were no doubt unnoticed by those who have preserved the past for us.

In my view, then, it is not correct to say that Israelite prophecy ended with the exile, either in the sense that it ceased or that it was transformed into *something else*. If my understanding of the social dynamics of prophecy is correct, we ought to conceive of it as a continuing potentiality in a given society, based on that society's particular religious beliefs and past experience. This view allows for the intermittent appearance of prophets within the society, defining the conditions under which prophecy can be said to "end," as well as begin again. In short, it provides a "program" which enables us to identify prophetic "performance" and, therefore, prophets.

Prophetic Interpretation in the Septuagint

F. F. BRUCE

A General Tendency

[[17]] In turning the prophetical books from Hebrew into Greek, the Septuagint translators were quite ready to conform the wording to their own religious outlook or otherwise to adapt it to an interpretation which was accepted in the circles to which they belonged.

One of the best known examples is provided by the oracle of Amos 9:11f., where the prediction of the reincorporation of Edom into David's kingdom becomes a prediction of the conversion of the Gentiles to the worship of the God of Israel: 'that they may possess the remnant of Edom' (where the subject 'they' denotes the rulers of David's line) becomes 'that the remnant of mankind may seek [me]' (ὅπως ἐκζητήσωσιν οἱ κατάλοιποι τῶν ἀνθρώπων). No doubt this change is helped by the revocalization of ʾĕdôm [['Edom']] as ʾādām [['mankind']] and by the misreading of yîrĕšû [['possess']] as yidrĕšû [['seek']] (with the ignoring of ʾet [[definite object marker]] before šĕʾērît [['remnant']]), but the total effect is more than the sum of these textual variants: it chimes in with the hope of many Jews of the dispersion that Gentiles would seek and find the true God.

Other Septuagint renderings seem to reflect less far-reaching interpretations known to the translators.

Reprinted with permission from *Bulletin of the International Organization for Septuagint and Cognate Studies* 12 (1979) 17–26.

The Figure of Gog

The figure of Gog, of the land of Magog, who in MT appears only in Ezekiel 38–39, is identified by Ezekiel himself with similar invaders of the holy land depicted by earlier prophets: "Thus says the Lord Yahweh: 'Are you he of whom I spoke in former days by my servants the prophets of Israel, who in those days prophesied for years that I would bring you against them?' " (Ezek 38:17). Ezekiel may have had in mind Jeremiah's [[18]] unnamed "destroyer of nations" bringing evil from the north (Jer 4:5ff.), or even more certainly Isaiah's Assyrian, who threatens Jerusalem from the north (Isa 10:27b–32) but is brought to a halt by Yahweh and forced to turn back on the way by which he came (Isa 37:29), ultimately falling by no human hand (Isa 10:33f.; 31:8).

What Ezekiel did with invading figures portrayed by his predecessors was done in turn by later interpreters with Ezekiel's portrayal of Gog. The last campaign of Antiochus IV against Egypt, to which the author of Daniel looked forward (Dan 11:40–45), is modelled on Gog's campaign: the king will be compelled to turn back from Egypt, and in the holy land "he shall come to his end, with none to help him" (Dan 11:45). Later still, Gog is one of the figures of Hebrew prophecy whose embodiment the Qumran writers (especially in 1QM 11:15ff.) recognize in Israel's last Gentile oppressor, the Kittim, presumably the Romans (cf. 4QIsaᵃ), while the seer of Patmos envisages Gog and Magog as enemies who are to assail the people of God at the last horizon of time (Rev 20:7–10).

This process of reinterpretation, which was begun by the Hebrew authors, is carried on by their Greek translators. If in MT Gog appears only in Ezekiel, in the Septuagint he appears more often.

What, for example, are we to make of Amos 7:1, where the prophet's vision of locusts is rendered as follows in the Septuagint: 'there was a swarm (ἐπιγονή) of locusts coming at dawn (ἑωθινή), and behold one "hopper" (βροῦχος) was Gog, the king'? (I have rendered βροῦχος by 'hopper' quite conventionally; 'hopping locust' is the RSV rendering of Heb. *yeleq* in Joel 1:4, where LXX gives βροῦχος as the equivalent.) Why should the locust king be called Gog?

The reason seems to be that the Greek translator, and perhaps the school of interpretation to which he belonged, identified the locusts of Amos' vision with those of Joel's vision. In the Septuagint Joel's [[19]] locusts are more than ordinary locusts: they are treated as a figure of speech for a real army of invasion from the north, which was identified with the horde that follows Gog. The fate of Joel's "northerner," rotting between the western and eastern sea (Joel 2:20), is quite similar to the fate of Gog's horde, as described in Ezek 39:4ff. As Joel's locust army rots away in the waterless wilderness (εἰς γῆν ἄνυδρον), so Gog's army falls in the open field and is buried in a desert wadi east of the Dead Sea.

To the Septuagint translators the prophetical books formed one sacred canon, and it was natural for them to consider that the same subject might be treated, perhaps in varying terminology, in different parts of the canon. Joel's vision thus constitutes a middle term between Ezekiel's Gog and Amos' locust king: if Joel's locusts are identified with Gog's followers, then the king of Joel's locusts must be Gog (although he is not named in the Hebrew or Greek text of Joel), and if Amos' locusts are identical with Joel's, then *their* king must be Gog (and he is accordingly so named in the Greek text of Amos).

If the Greek text of Amos 7:1 be compared with MT, it may be said that the translator understood *leqeš* ('latter growth') as *yeleq* [['locust']] (rendered βροῦχος [['hopper']] in Joel 1:4) and misread *ʾaḥar* ('after') as *ʾeḥād* ('one'). Did he also misread *gizzê* ('mowings') as *gôg*? Was his *Vorlage* sufficiently faded to make the mistake a pardonable one? Perhaps, but it would not have occurred to him to find Gog in this text unless he already had in mind the association between these locusts of Amos and Joel's locusts, and the identity of Joel's locusts with Gog's army in Ezekiel. An interpretative tradition along these lines may already have been established, in the light of which it was easy for the translator to mistranslate as he did.

[[20]] (We may recall the horde of locusts in Rev 9:1–11. They too have a king, whose "name in Hebrew is Abaddon, and in Greek he is called Apollyon"—but they are demon locusts.)

Another Septuagint reference to Gog comes in Balaam's oracle in praise of Israel (Num 24:3–9) where he sees the patriarch (in the person of his descendants) reaching such a level of prosperity that (verse 7):

> water shall flow from his buckets,
> and his seed shall be in many waters;
> his king shall be higher than Agag,
> and his kingdom shall be exalted.

According to the Septuagint version:

> a man shall come forth from his seed,
> and shall rule over many nations;
> his kingdom shall be more exalted than Gog,
> and his kingdom shall be increased.

The 'man' (ἄνθρωπος) of the Septuagint version is most probably to be identified (in the tradition which it represents) with the "star out of

Jacob" and the "man (ἄνθρωπος) out of Israel" foreseen by Balaam in Num 24:17—that is, with the expected son of David who would restore his great ancestor's fortunes. (The Hebrew text probably referred originally to David himself.)

In the primary setting of the Balaam oracles, the Amalekite king Agag was presumably a fitting standard of comparison for an Israelite ruler (in Num 24:20 Amalek's former greatness as "the first of the nations" is attested). But before we assume without further question that the "Gog" whom the Greek version puts in place of Agag is the Gog of Ezekiel's prophecy, we must bear in mind that Γώγ is one of the Septuagint transcriptions for ʿôg—that is, Og, king of Bashan (so in Deut 3:1, 13; 4:47 B* as against Ὤγ in Num 21:33 et passim). But that the Γώγ of Num 24:7 is not Og is confirmed by the Samaritan Bible, which agrees with MT in the spelling of Og, but in this verse reads gwg and not [[21]] (with MT) ʾăgag. The Septuagint version and the Samaritan text here share an interpretative tradition in which Balaam's visions are given a fulfilment in the end-time. In such an interpretative tradition Agag is no longer relevant, but Gog, himself an eschatological figure, might well appear highly relevant. The coming son of David will be exalted high above Gog, because Gog will be subdued under him.

There is one further occurrence of Γώγ in the Septuagint, but it has nothing to do with Ezekiel's invaders. In Sir 48:17 Hezekiah is said to have "fortified his city, and brought Gog into the midst thereof" (καὶ εἰσήγαγεν εἰς μέσον αὐτῶν τὸν Γώγ). The Hebrew text says that he 'fortified his city by diverting water into the midst of it', and it seems fairly clear that Γώγ in this verse is a corruption of ἀγωγόν ('conduit'), which indeed is the reading of א[c.a].

Mass-Burial in the Valley

A digression may be in place here, with regard to the burial-place of Ezekiel's Gog and his followers. In Ezek 39:11a Yahweh promises to appoint them as a grave in Israel 'the valley of the passers by' (gê hā-ʿōběrîm). 'The valley of the passers by' appears in the Septuagint as τὸ πολυάνδριον τῶν ἐπελθόντων. The rare word πολυάνδρ(ε)ιον might be expected to mean a place of any kind where many men are gathered together, but in actual usage it means 'communal cemetery' (as in 2 Macc 9:4, 14; 4 Macc 15:20). It is doubtless used to render Heb. gê in Ezek 39:11a because the valley in question is actually the cemetery of Gog's army: not inappropriately, its new name 'the valley of Hamon-gog' (Ezek 39:11b[LXX 12], 15) is rendered τὸ γαὶ τὸ πολυάνδριον τοῦ Γώγ [['the valley of the cemetery of Gog']], where πολυάνδριον corresponds to *hāmôn* ('multitude'), as it does to Hamonah in verse 16. In the curious reading of B in verse 11b[LXX12], καὶ κληθήσεται τὸ τέ, the meaningless τέ is evidently a corruption of γέ (actually found [[22]] in Q here, and in B in verse 15), which is a transcription of *gê*ʾ (cf. τὸ γαί in A).

But there are a few other places in the Septuagint (all in Jeremiah) where πολυάνδριον appears as the rendering of *gay*ʾ or *gê*ʾ. Thus, in the denunciation of Israel's idolatry in Jer 2:23f., where Yahweh says,

> How can you say, "I am not defiled,
> I have not gone after the Baals"?
> Look at your way in the valley . . .

the Septuagint rendering of the last clause is ἰδὲ τὰς ὁδούς σου ἐν τῷ πολυανδρίῳ. But why should the valley be referred to as a cemetery? The answer seems to be that the translator identified this 'valley' with the valley of the son(s) of Hinnom which, according to other oracles of Jeremiah, was to become a place for the disposal of corpses. Thus, in Jeremiah's temple discourse, he announces that because "the high place of Topheth, which is in the valley of the son of Hinnom," has been polluted by human sacrifice, the days will come when it will be renamed 'the valley of slaughter' (*gê*ʾ *hahărēgāh*), on account of the many bodies of the killed which will be dumped there (Jer 7:31f.)—a prophecy later repeated in the valley itself (Jer 19:6–11). In Jer 7:31f. *gê*ʾ is rendered φάραγξ [['ravine']] in both phrases ('the valley of the son of Hinnom' and 'the valley of slaughter'), but in Jer 19:6 it is rendered πολυάνδριον in both phrases: the place will no longer be called πολυάνδριον υἱοῦ Ἐννώμ [['cemetery of the sons of Hinnom']] but πολυάνδριον σφαγῆς [['cemetery of slaughter']]. But it is only in the light of the future use of the valley as a mass grave that it can be referred to, proleptically, as πολυάνδριον υἱοῦ Ἐννώμ, and it is because the unnamed valley of Jer 2:23 is identified by the translator (perhaps rightly) with the valley of the son(s) of Hinnom that it is called the πολυάνδριον without qualification.

The Time of the End in Daniel

[[23]] The author of Daniel, as has been said, drew upon Ezekiel's Gog oracle to fill in the as yet uncompleted career of Antiochus Epiphanes (Dan 11:40–45). This is not the only instance of his reinterpretation or reapplication of earlier prophecies.

What the author of Daniel began in this regard, his Greek translator continued. Here we are concerned with the earlier Greek version of Daniel, commonly called the Septuagint as distinct from the

Theodotionic version. The earlier version, as is known, is extant only in codices 88 (Chisianus) and 967 (Chester Beatty) and (indirectly) in the Syro-Hexaplar.

Instead of giving a fairly literal rendering, this translator shows how he interpreted the allusive language of Daniel. In the outline of Seleucid and Ptolemaic conflict in Dan 11:5ff. 'the king of the south' regularly appears as 'the king of Egypt' (and this rendering is not a mere inference from the explicit mentions of Egypt in the MT of verses 42f.). On the other hand, 'the king of the north' remains βασιλεὺς βορρᾶ, but the fact that he and the king of Egypt invade each other's territories leaves no doubt about his identity. The translator knows very well the course of history outlined by the author, as is seen outstandingly in his rendering of 'ships of Kittim' in Dan 11:30 as Ῥωμαῖοι. This was what the apocalyptist meant, but his reference to the Roman flotilla in the harbour of Alexandria as 'ships of Kittim' was probably due to his seeing in the events of 168 B.C. the fulfilment of Balaam's prophecy about "ships" which "shall come from Kittim and shall afflict Asshur and Eber" (Num 24:24) — Assyria (Asshur) and Syria being readily interchangeable in late Hellenistic and Roman times. Balaam's words are interpreted in this sense in the Targum of Onqelos, 'troops will be called together from the [[24]] Romans', and in the Latin Vulgate, 'uenient in trieribus de Italia' (echoed in Dan 11:30 Vulg. 'uenient super eum trieres et Romani').

If the author of Daniel saw the prophecy about Gog fulfilled in the closing phase of the reign of Antiochus, how did the Greek translator view it? He wrote after the death of Antiochus, but while he translates the last six verses of Daniel 11 fairly literally, he presumably identified the βασιλεὺς βορρᾶ in those verses with a later Seleucid king, who would be alive καθ' ὥραν συντελείας and who, after clashing with the king of Egypt and devastating his realm, would meet the ὥρα τῆς συντελείας αὐτοῦ in the holy land (as Gog was fated to do).

The translator's estimate of the interval which had to elapse before this συντέλεια may be hinted at in his treatment of Daniel's oracle of the seventy heptads. This oracle is the best-known example of Daniel's reworking of older prophecies: here Jeremiah's prediction of seventy years' duration for the desolations of Jerusalem (Jer 25:11f.) is stretched by reinterpretation to seventy heptads of years, in such a way that half a heptad (three and a half years) intervenes between the setting up of the abomination of desolation and the establishment of the divine kingdom. In fact, less than three and a half years elapsed between the setting up of the abomination and the restoration of Israel's true worship in the Jerusalem temple, but that restoration did not bring in the divine kingdom. Therefore, just as Daniel's oracle represents a reinterpretation of Jeremiah's prediction to bring it into line with the historical process, Daniel's oracle itself was to receive the same reinterpretative treatment (in some parts of the exegetical underworld this exercise is still pursued). The first known attempt to reinterpret it was made by the Greek translator.

In the Greek version of Dan 9:26 the χρῖσμα (MT *māšîaḥ*) is to be removed not after 62 heptads (a reference to the deposition or death of [[25]] Onias III) but μετὰ ἑπτὰ καὶ ἑβδομήκοντα καὶ ἑξήκοντα δύο, after 77 + 62 = 139—not necessarily 139 heptads, but more probably 139 years. Greater precision marks the restatement of the calculation in verse 27: "after 77 times (καιροί) and 62 years (ἔτη)"; in the light of Dan 12:7 (cf. 4:29[32]) καιρός should be taken here as a synonym of ἔτος. A total of 139 years is implied, and the reference is probably to the Seleucid era (beginning 311 B.C.). According to 1 Macc 1:10 Antiochus IV began to reign in the year 137 of that era, and the translator may have dated the deposition or death of Onias III two years later. The event is the same as that indicated by MT as the terminus of the 62 heptads (434 years), but the translator, viewing it from a longer perspective, dates it more exactly.

In MT only one heptad separates the removal of the anointed one from the establishment of everlasting righteousness. The Greek translator knew that the interval was much longer than that. In his hands, the one heptad becomes many: 'the desolation shall be taken away ἐπὶ πολλὰς ἑβδομάδας'—that is, many heptads would intervene between the removal of the idolatrous installation (which for the translator, though not for the original author, lay in the past) and the final consummation (which was now deferred to a more indefinite future). The first of these many heptads is the seventieth heptad of the Hebrew text; but whereas in MT the daily burnt-offering was to be abolished half-way through that heptad, in the Greek version it is abolished ἐν τῷ τέλει τῆς ἑβδομάδος. The replacement of the Jewish ritual by the cult of Olympian Zeus is dated in 1 Macc 1:54 in year 145 (of the Seleucid era), and this is much closer to the end than to the halfway point of a heptad which started in year 139. The Greek wording of the last part of the verse (Dan 9:27) becomes rather vague—'at the end of the heptad sacrifice and libation will be taken away, and on the temple there will be an abomination of desolations [[26]] until the end (συντέλεια), and an end (συντέλεια) will be granted for the desolation'—but its purport seems to be that, while the consummation of the divine purpose is certain, it cannot be dated.

The other calculations in Dan 7:12 are not revised with the same thoroughness. The "time, times and half a time" of Dan 7:25 and 12:7 are rendered almost identically: both Aram. *ʿiddān* in the former passage and Heb. *mô^cēd* in the latter passage are represented by καιρός. The 2300 "evenings and mornings" of Dan 8:14 become explicitly 2300 *days* (as also in the Theodotionic version); "then the sanctuary will be cleansed." The time-notes of Dan 12:11f. remain unchanged.

In short, a study of the Septuagint version of the prophets and related scriptures confirms the view that variants are not to be explained solely by the ordinary causes of textual alteration but sometimes reflect new ways of understanding the prophecies in the light of changing events, changing attitudes and changing exegetical methods.

The "Classical Prophets" in Josephus' *Antiquities*

CHRISTOPHER T. BEGG

Introduction

⟦341⟧ In the consciousness of contemporary Bible readers/hearers the so-called writing or classical prophets[1] (hereafter CPs) surely rank among the best known and most appreciated figures of ancient Israel's history. In light of this observation, it is of interest to examine the role assigned these personages in the two great OT narrative complexes covering the period of their activity, i.e., the Deuteronomistic and Chronistic Histories. The rather surprising result of such an investigation is that neither work, notwithstanding their obvious interest in the phenomenon of prophecy, accords any particular prominence to the CPs. Of this group the Deuteronomistic History (Dtr) cites Isaiah and Jonah alone,[2] the Chronistic History (Chr) only Isaiah, Jeremiah, Haggai and Zechariah.[3]

Reprinted with permission from *Louvain Studies* 13 (1988) 341–57.

1. To this category I reckon Isaiah, Jeremiah, Ezekiel and "the twelve" (Hosea–Malachi). I exclude Daniel in line with Jewish tradition which places the book associated with him among, not the "Latter Prophets," but the "Writings."

2. It should of course be borne in mind that, on the standard datings of their activities, the Deuteronomist who concluded his work with the 560 release of Jehoiachin (2 Kgs 25:27–30) would not have had occasion to mention the post-Exilic CPs Joel, Obadiah, Haggai, Zechariah, and Malachi. The Deuteronomist's mention of the CP Jonah is likewise a special case in that this citation is clearly the source for the prophetic book named after him rather than *vice versa*.

3. I abstract here from the question whether or not Chronicles and Ezra–Nehemiah stem from the same redactor/editor. They are at one, in any case, in the rather minimal attention they give the CPs.

Moreover all the mentions in question are rather brief and *en passant*; in no case does a CP stand at the center of attention. In a series of previous publications I have discussed this state of affairs and offered some suggestions as to how it might be explained.[4] In the present article I wish to extend this line of [[342]] inquiry by examining how the CPs are handled by a prominent post-Biblical Jewish historian.

The author in question is the famous and many-sided figure Flavius Josephus (ca. 37–ca. 100 A.D.), priestly descendant, world traveler, military commander, Roman citizen/pensioner, and man of letters. Of Josephus' four extant works, *The Jewish War*, *The Jewish Antiquities*, *The Life* and the *Against Apion*, it is the *Antiquities* which is of relevance for the purposes of this study. Written about 93 A.D. and comprising twenty "books," the *Antiquities* offers what might be called an "apologetic history," directed to a potentially sympathetic Hellenistic audience, of the Jewish people from Creation down to the start of the Great Revolt of 66. For the "biblical segment" of his history Josephus gives basically a sometimes closer, sometimes looser paraphrase of the relevant OT documentation, including that concerning the CPs, whose treatment by Josephus in Books 9–11 of the *Antiquities* will be the focus of what follows.[5]

At the outset of my projected study, two preliminary observations seem in order. First, Josephus clearly did know the corpus called the "Latter Prophets" in Jewish tradition in its entirety.[6] Thus, in instances where he omits mention of a given CP, this cannot be attributed (as conceivably could be the case for the absence of one or other of these figures in Dtr or Chr) to simple ignorance of their existence. Secondly, a reading

4. See C. T. Begg, "A Bible Mystery: The Absence of Jeremiah in the Deuteronomistic History," *Irish Biblical Studies* 7 (1985) 139–164; "The Non-mention of Amos, Hosea and Micah in the Deuteronomistic History," *Biblische Notizen* 32 (1986) 41–53; "The Non-mention of Ezekiel in the Deuteronomistic History, Jeremiah and Chronicles," *Ezekiel and His Book* (BETL 74; ed. J. Lust; Leuven: University Press/Peeters, 1986) 340–343; "The Non-mention of Zephaniah, Nahum and Habakkuk in the Deuteronomistic History," forthcoming in *Biblische Notizen* [[38–39 (1987) 19–25]]; "The Classical Prophets in the Chronistic History," forthcoming in *Biblische Zeitschrift* [[32 (1988) 100–107]].

5. I cite the writings of Josephus according to the edition of Henry St. J. Thackeray, Ralph Marcus, Allen Wikgren and Louis H. Feldman, *Josephus* (9 vols.; LCL; Cambridge, MA: Harvard University; London: Heinemann, 1926–1963). For more details concerning Josephus' life and writings see, e.g.: John Strugnell, "Josephus, Flavius," *New Catholic Encyclopedia* 9 (New York: McGraw-Hill, 1967) 1120–1123; Shaye J. D. Cohen, *Josephus in Galilee and Rome: His Vita and Development as a Historian* (Leiden: Brill, 1979); Tessa Rajak, *Josephus, the Historian and His Society* (London: Duckworth, 1983).

6. E.g., in *Contra Apionem* 1,40 Josephus refers to the post-Mosaic prophets' writing the history of their times in "thirteen books." This would seem to include the books of Isaiah, Jeremiah (with Lamentations), Ezekiel and "the Twelve"; see the note by Thackeray in *Josephus*, 1.179 n. b.

of the *Antiquities* makes clear that Josephus shared the Deuteronomist's and Chronist's interest in "prophecy"; indeed he even goes beyond these authors in highlighting the "prophetic factor" in Israel's history.[7] Accordingly, however else one may explicate Josephus' handling of the CPs, above all his non-mention ⟦343⟧ of certain of them (see below), one may rule out from the start the supposition that his procedure in their regard was simply a function of a general indifference (or even hostility) towards the prophetic phenomenon as such.

Passing now to the text of the *Antiquities* itself, I begin with some "statistical" observations. Of the fifteen CPs, *Antiquities* makes no mention of seven, i.e., Hosea, Joel, Amos, Obadiah, Habakkuk, Zephaniah and Malachi. In addition, however, Josephus hardly allots "equal time" to the eight CPs he does cite. Most minimal is the handling of Micah; he is mentioned only once (*Ant.* 10,92) in Josephus' version of the allusion to his announcement of Jerusalem's destruction (see Mic 3:12) in Jer 26:18. Ezekiel, Haggai and Zechariah likewise get little more than stray allusions. Thus, it is only Jonah, Nahum, Isaiah and Jeremiah among the CPs for whom Josephus offers anything like a full-scale presentation. And even here, it is really Jeremiah alone who receives a degree of attention comparable to that given by Josephus to such "non-classical prophets" as Samuel, Elijah, Elisha and Daniel.[8]

At this point an initial question arises. Why is it that Josephus cites just those CPs whom he does? Conversely, why should it be precisely Hosea *et al.* whom he leaves unmentioned among the CPs? A definitive answer to such a question is, of course, hardly possible. One might, however, offer the following surmise: *Antiquities* is a narrative work. Accordingly, it could be expected that Josephus would tend to draw on those prophetic books

---

7. Indicative in this regard is the fact that Josephus several times speaks of the intervention of a prophet where the Bible does not do so explicitly; see e.g.: *Ant.* 6,271 (David inquires of God through a prophet, compare 1 Sam 23:2); *Ant.* 7,7 (David consults God through a prophet, compare 2 Sam 2:1); *Ant.* 7,294.296 ("prophets" convey instructions to David concerning the case of the Gibeonites, compare 2 Samuel 21); *Ant.* 7,321 (David's repentance regarding the census is prompted by "prophets" informing him of God's anger, compare 2 Sam 24:10); *Ant.* 8,198 (a "prophet" warns Solomon about his misdeeds, compare 1 Kgs 11:11).

8. For overviews of Josephus' treatment of the phenomenon of prophecy, see, e.g.: E. Gerlach, *Die Weissagungen des Alten Testaments in den Schriften des Flavius Josephus und das angebliche Zeugniss von Christo* (Berlin: Hertz, 1863) 20–40; M. Dienstfertig, *Die Prophetologie in der Religionsphilosophie des ersten nachchristlichen Jahrhunderts* (Breslau: Shatzky, 1982) 24–33; Paul Krüger, "Würdigung der Propheten im Spätjudentum," *Neutestamentliche Studien Georg Heinrici zu seinem 70. Geburtstag* (Leipzig: Hinrichs'sche, 1914) 1–12; Gerhard Delling, "Die biblische Prophetie bei Josephus," *Josephus-Studien . . . Otto Michel zum 70. Geburtstag gewidmet* (ed. O. Betz et al.; Göttingen: Vandenhoeck & Ruprecht, 1974) 109–121.

which offered him narrative material regarding a given prophet since such material could be most readily incorporated into the flow of his presentation. And, in fact, this supposition is, to a considerable extent, validated by Josephus' actual procedure; he cites for example, Jonah, Isaiah, Jeremiah, and Ezekiel, that is, precisely those CPs whose respective books contain the most amount of narrative material.[9] Of course, this still leaves the problem of Josephus' citation of Nahum, seeing that ⟦344⟧ his book totally lacks such material.[10] The positive factors behind Josephus' decision to make room for Nahum in his work will be discussed subsequently. Here, however, attention might be called to the remark made by Josephus in connection with his reference to Nahum since it may help explain the absence of Hosea *et al.* from his account. In *Ant.* 9,242 Josephus states:

> And many more things beside did this prophet (Nahum) prophesy about Nineveh, which I have not thought it necessary to mention, but have omitted in order not to seem tiresome to my readers.

The above statement, when coupled with the fact that Josephus generally avoids extended, direct quotation of the actual words even of those CPs he does mention, seems to indicate that Josephus viewed the Biblical prophetic oracles as something his intended audience would find tedious and/or obscure. It is then understandable that Josephus would tend to pass over those CPs whose books consisted entirely of oracular material, as is the case, it will be noted, with most of the seven "unmentionables" cited above.[11]

Given the preceding remarks, I now turn to Josephus' presentation of those CPs he does mention, treating them in the order of their appearance in the *Antiquities*. In my exposition I shall concentrate on identifying and elucidating the differences whether of omission or commission between Josephus' portrait of a given figure and that of the MT.[12]

9. Also in the case of Haggai and Zechariah, Josephus could draw on narrative notices, i.e., those of Ezra 5:1 and 6:14.

10. The case of Micah whose book likewise lacks any narrative component is not relevant here since Josephus' reference to him is drawn, not (directly) from the Book of Micah, but from the narrative context of Jeremiah 26.

11. The one significant exception in this regard is Amos whose book relates the episode of his confrontation with Amaziah, Amos 7:10–17. Here, however, it may be remarked that Josephus would not have found the "social justice emphasis" that pervades the Book of Amos particularly congenial, given his conception of the prophetic role (see above in the text).

12. I cannot enter here into the exceedingly complicated question of the nature of Josephus' "sources"—whether Biblical or extra-Biblical—for the Biblical segment of his *Antiquities*, see the relevant literature cited and critically summarized by L. H. Feldman, *Josephus and Modern Scholarship (1937–1980)* (Berlin/New York: de Gruyter, 1984) 121–191. My assumption is that, in relating the history of the period of the CPs, Josephus had before him,

Jonah

⟦345⟧ The first of the CPs Josephus presents is Jonah (*Ant.* 9,206–214). In this presentation Josephus, as often elsewhere, works together material which the Bible gives in distinct books or contexts into a continuous account. Specifically, he juxtaposes items deriving from the two Biblical references to Jonah, that is, the notice of 2 Kgs 14:25 about his predicting the conquests of Jeroboam II and the book bearing his name.[13] In his version of the Kings' notice, Josephus (*Ant.* 9,206) leaves unmentioned its references both to Jonah's paternity and his place of origin. Conversely, he specifies Jeroboam himself as the addressee of Jonah's prophecy, whereas Kings leaves the recipient indeterminate.

More remarkable are the divergences between the Book of Jonah and the Josephian version of it. What first strikes one in comparing the two texts is how drastically the latter compresses the former. In particular, Josephus has no parallel for the entire segment Jonah 3:5–4:11 concerning Nineveh's repentance, God's relenting and the ensuing dialogue between prophet and deity (see below). Josephus likewise reproduces Jonah 1:1–3:4 itself in highly abridged form and with certain peculiarities, some of which, especially those involving his portrayal of the prophet, I wish to note here. First, in contrast to Jonah 1:2a (". . . go to Nineveh . . . and cry against it . . ."), Josephus makes Jonah's commission more specific: he is to preach in Nineveh "that it would lose its power." Conversely, however, he provides no equivalent to the motivation for God's decision cited in Jonah 1:2b "for their wickedness has come up before me." As in Jonah 1:3–4 Josephus has the prophet[14] run away from his mission. In line with his characteristic "psychologizing" interest, Josephus adds a motivation, lacking in the Bible, for his doing so, i.e., Jonah's

---

inter alia, a Bible text which did not differ significantly in content (which is my concern throughout this investigation), as opposed to details of wording, from our MT. I further believe that, as the present study will bear out, in the majority of cases where a contentual discrepancy, whether of commission or omission between the *Antiquities* and MT occurs, this can be explained in terms of Josephus' editorial *Tendenzen*. Finally, it should be kept in mind that even where a particular discrepancy between MT and the *Antiquities* is not original with Josephus himself, being taken over rather by him from a variant (non-MT) source, whether Biblical or non-Biblical, by the very fact of incorporating that divergent item Josephus signifies his acceptance of it as conformable with his intentions and viewpoint. This last observation serves to relativize the whole problem of Josephus' sources, just as it helps legitimate a comparison, like ours, between the *Antiquities* and MT both taken in their present form.

13. Note how he makes the transition from the former to the latter: "But since I have promised to give an exact account of our history, I have thought it necessary to recount what I have found written in the Hebrew Books concerning this prophet (Jonah)" (*Ant.* 9,208a).

14. Note that in contrast to the Book of Jonah itself (although see 2 Kgs 14:25), Josephus repeatedly designates Jonah as "prophet."

being "afraid" of what is not stated. Likewise in contrast to the "Tarshish" of Jonah 1:3, Josephus makes Jonah's intended destination "Tarsus in Cilicia."[15]

[346] Subsequently, while Jonah 1:5b speaks of Jonah's being already asleep at the onslaught of the storm and of the captain's rousing him with the summons to invoke his god as well, Josephus depicts the prophet as deliberately refusing to join in the crew's entreaties: "Jonah, however, covered himself and lay there, not imitating any of the things that he saw the others doing." Next, while in Jonah 1:8–9 Jonah evades the crew's question about his occupation, Josephus' Jonah does answer that query, designating himself as "a prophet of the Most High God." Contrary to what his off-cited "rationalism" might lead one to expect, Josephus does retain the Bible's reference to the fish swallowing Jonah, although prefacing it with the quizzical formula "the story has it."[16] He concludes this reference by introducing the specification that it was "on the shore of the Euxine sea" that the fish deposited Jonah (compare Jonah 2:11). He likewise goes his own way in having Jonah address his prayer to God after, rather than before, his release from the fish. Similarly, he compresses the poetic words of that prayer as given in Jonah 2:2–10 into a brief prosaic allusion to Jonah's asking "pardon for his sins," something which the Biblical Jonah does not do in his prayer as such. Josephus' presentation next returns to its starting point with Jonah finally directing his God-given message to the Ninevites. He does this "where all could hear him" (Josephus makes no mention of the fabulous dimensions of the city or of Jonah's progress through it as reported in Jonah 3:3–4), and thereupon disappears from the scene without awaiting a response. The whole account concludes with the ingenuous affirmation: "I have recounted his story as I found it written down."

What is one to make of Josephus' portrayal of Jonah? First of all, it is clear that, like the prophets in general, Jonah interests Josephus primarily as the bearer of accurate predictions, *in casu* concerning Jeroboam's conquests and the overthrow of Nineveh. On a secondary level, however, Josephus was undoubtedly sensitive to the interest-arousing possibilities of the Biblical story of Jonah's adventures, and so makes room for an abridged version of it in his own account. At the same time, however, he studiously ignores the climactic element of the Bible's narrative, that is, the city's repentance and the divine decision to relent. One might think of several factors influencing Josephus' procedure here: unwillingness to admit the possibility of repentance by a pagan city as well as his belief in

15. On this point, see Marcus' note to *Ant.* 9,17 (*Josephus*, 6.10–11 n. b).

16. On the question of Josephus' stance towards the Biblical "miracles," see the literature cited and evaluated by Feldman, *Josephus*, 477–480.

⟦347⟧ the irreversibility of divine decrees like that pronounced against Nineveh.[17] Recall too that, historically, Nineveh did suffer annihilation, and Josephus may have wished to avoid the apparent discrepancy between God's relenting as recounted in the Book of Jonah and the city's actual, eventual fate. As to Josephus' passing over the interplay between Jonah and God related in Jonah 4, one might see here an example of his tendency to leave aside, perhaps out of concern for divine transcendence, Biblical accounts relating intimate exchanges between the deity and the CPs (see further below).

While Josephus' reworking of the Biblical portrait of Jonah can thus be made understandable (at least to some degree), it also may be conceded that his version lacks much of the theological depth and satiric bite of the original.

Nahum

The next CP Josephus cites is Nahum (*Ant.* 9,239–242). In order to work this figure into his narration, Josephus had to "invent" a dating for his ministry since the Book of Nahum itself provides no direct chronological indications concerning him; he associates Nahum with the reign of Jotham of Judah presented in *Ant.* 9,236–238. Conversely, however, Josephus fails to cite the locality Elkosh with which Nah 1:1 links the prophet (compare his similar non-mention of Jonah's hometown). What Josephus thereafter has to relate regarding Nahum is a free and condensed, but nevertheless recognizable "citation" of the obscure poetic oracle Nah 2:9–13 concerning the fall of Nineveh. Following this quotation, Josephus continues, in the words cited previously, by noting that Nahum made numerous additional prophecies concerning Nineveh which, however, he leaves aside so as not to bore readers. He concludes the presentation with the generalizing affirmation that everything predicted about Nineveh did find fulfillment after an interval of more than a century.[18]

Both the fact that Josephus should mention Nahum at all and his actual treatment of this prophet are somewhat puzzling. In the first place, the absence of any narrative element concerning Nahum in the Biblical sources would seem to militate against an inclusion of him ⟦348⟧ (see above). Moreover, while Josephus typically turns the poetry of the CPs' oracles into a rather flat, prosaic paraphrase, here he retains Nahum's

---

17. See, e.g., his formulations on this point in *Ant.* 10,34.142.

18. 115 years to be exact. Josephus gives no indication as to how he arrived at this figure—the Bible itself provides no dating for Nahum's prophesying and does not even recount the fall of Nineveh, much less date that event.

obscure, metaphorical language. On the other hand, however, Josephus' Nahum plainly does fit the pattern of the prophets as long-range (and accurate) prognosticators which Josephus is especially concerned to inculcate. In addition, citation of Nahum's oracle gave Josephus the opportunity—in line with his characteristic stress on the agreement among "true prophets" (see below)—to confirm and reinforce the announcement about Nineveh's overthrow made by Jonah earlier.

Isaiah

Isaiah is the next CP to surface in the *Antiquities*. In *Ant.* 9,276 Josephus makes a first, passing reference to this prophet which, however, already suggests his particular perspective concerning his ministry. The reference occurs in an explanation of Hezekiah's disregard of Assyria's threats: this is attributed to his "confidence . . . in the prophet Isaiah, by whom he was accurately informed of future events."

In line with this indication, Josephus in *Ant.* 10,1–35, selectively utilizes the "Isaiah legends" of 2 Kgs 18:17–20:19 // Isaiah 36–39 in developing the portrait of a prophet whose primary activity is to inform Hezekiah about the future, that is, the repulse of the Assyrian menace, the king's recovery from sickness and the Babylonian deportation. In comparing the Josephian and Biblical versions of the "Isaiah legends," one is struck, once again, by the extent to which the latter is compressed in the former. This feature extends also to the data concerning Isaiah in the two versions.

The most salient illustration of this "reduction" of Isaiah's role occurs in Josephus' handling of the account of Hezekiah's cure, 2 Kgs 20:1–11 // Isa 38:1–8. Especially noteworthy here is Josephus' omission of the Biblical reference to Isaiah's initial approach to the stricken king, announcing his certain, imminent death (2 Kgs 20:1b), and to God's subsequent remanding of that announcement (2 Kgs 20:4) in response to Hezekiah's appeal. In Josephus (*Ant.* 10,24–29), the prophet first comes on the scene following Hezekiah's sickbed appeal in order to inform him that God has heard him. In this instance, it seems clear that Josephus' version reflects his conviction that a "true" prophet does not make inaccurate predictions, any more than God changes his mind, compare his treatment of the Jonah story.

[349] Josephus likewise omits 2 Kgs 20:6's promise of delivery for Jerusalem from the Assyrian assault in his version of Isaiah's words of assurance to the king (*Ant.* 10,27). His doing so is understandable seeing that this promise does appear somewhat extraneous in its immediate context. Thereafter, in contrast to 2 Kgs 20:7 (but cf. Isaiah 38), Josephus

refrains from mentioning Isaiah's directive about the use of a "cake of figs" as a curative—perhaps finding the procedure too magical. Finally, in relating the "sign" with which the incident closes, Josephus compresses the presentation in a way that plays down the prophet's role *vis-à-vis* the king's: while in Isa 38:7–8a Isaiah simply informs Hezekiah concerning the sign he will receive and in 2 Kgs 20:8–10 enumerates the possibilities available, in Josephus (*Ant.* 10,28–29) the king takes the initiative both in asking for a sign and determining its actual character, Isaiah's role being limited to asking Hezekiah what sign he desires.

Josephus does not, however, simply abridge the Biblical "Isaiah legends." On occasion, he also introduces distinctive features of his own in retelling these. The most noteworthy item in this regard occurs in *Ant.* 10,12 where, in the context of the Assyrian siege, Hezekiah sends to ask Isaiah, not only to "pray" for the people, as in 2 Kgs 19:4, but also to "offer sacrifice for the common safety." This peculiarity seems to reflect Josephus' tendency to assimilate the prophetic and priestly roles.[19] Likewise in his version of Hezekiah's cure, Josephus focusses both the king's appeal (*Ant.* 10,25–26) and the prophet's reassuring word (10,27) on a matter not mentioned in the Bible as such, that is, the sick king's current lack of progeny. Possibly, he does this with an eye to the following narrative of the "Isaiah legends" complex, that is, the account of the Babylonian embassy to Hezekiah with its concluding reference to the fate of the king's "offspring" (see 2 Kgs 20:18 and compare *Ant.* 10,33).

Josephus rounds off his version of the "Isaiah Legends" with a summary notice on the prophet's activity:

> As for the prophet, he was acknowledged to be a man of God and marvelously possessed of truth, and, as he was confident of never having spoken what was false, he wrote down in books all that he had prophesied and left them to be recognized as true from the event by men of future ages (*Ant.* 10,35).

[[350]] Several features about this formulation might be underscored. First, it reflects Josephus' characteristic emphasis on the "truth" of prophetic utterance as a matter of an accurate foretelling of the (distant) future. Characteristic too (see below) is the depiction of the CP here as a writer who sets down the whole body of his oracles in fixed form. In thus referring to Isaiah's "writing" Josephus is, of course, inspired by

---

19. As an indication in this regard, note Josephus' non-Scriptural references to prophesying on the part of various priestly figures: *Ant.* 5,120 (the High Priest Phineas "prophesies"); *Ant.* 6,254.257 (the High Priest Abimelech "prophesies" for David); *Ant.* 7,72 (the unnamed High Priest "prophesies" for David). See further Joseph Blenkinsopp, "Prophecy and Priesthood in Josephus," *JJS* 25 (1974) 239–262.

such Biblical attestations of the prophet's literary activity as Isa 30:8; 2 Chr 26:22; 32:32. At the same time, he has clearly generalized those references in a way that assimilates Isaiah to Jeremiah who, according to Jeremiah 36, wrote down the whole body of his words.

The above notice also mentions "the men of future ages" who would read Isaiah's written words. One such, according to Josephus, was the pagan king Cyrus. Specifically, *Ant.* 11,5–6 states that Cyrus' decree permitting the Jewish return was inspired by the Persian ruler's "reading" the words concerning his mission—Josephus obviously has Isa 44:28–45:1 in mind here—Isaiah had written over two centuries before. This notice, which is, of course, peculiar to Josephus (recall that in 2 Chr 36:22 = Ezra 1:1 Cyrus' deed is said to fulfill a word of Jeremiah), is of interest in more than one respect. First, it evidences, once more, his concern with pointing up the fulfillment of prophecy over long expanses of time (recall his notice on the realization of the predictions about Nineveh's downfall more than a century after their delivery). In addition, the notice attests that the book of Isaiah known to Josephus did include the material of chapters 40–66.

Another, still later "reader" of Isaiah's words in Josephus' presentation was Onias IV, refugee son of the high priest. According to *Ant.* 13,63 it was the prediction of Isa 19:19 about a future inauguration of Yahwistic worship in Egypt which inspired this figure to request permission from the Egyptian monarchs Ptolemy Philometor and Cleopatra to build a Jewish temple at Leontopolis (just as it prompted them to assent to the request, *Ant.* 13,68). Thus for Josephus, Isaiah's predictions have their effect not only across the centuries, but also outside the land of Israel and on non-Jewish figures.

In concluding my exposition on Josephus' treatment of Isaiah, I note that he does leave unused much of the relevant Biblical material, confining himself almost exclusively to the data of the "Isaiah Legends." In particular, Josephus makes no mention of Isaiah's preaching on social justice (see, e.g., Isa 1:10–20; 5, etc.), his call (Isaiah 6), confrontation with Ahaz (Isaiah 7), or the "sign" of his nakedness (Isaiah 20). Such "omissions" make Josephus' Isaiah a ⟦351⟧ rather one-sided figure in comparison with the Biblical personage. On the other hand, each of them does seem explicable in terms of one or other of the overarching tendencies of Josephus' work. Like the Deuteronomist and Chronist before him, Josephus evidences little interest in the prophet's role as castigator of social ills.

As to his failure to relate the call of Isaiah, we have already noted, in our discussion on Jonah, Josephus' tendency to shy away from Biblical accounts of intimate exchanges between God and a prophet. Josephus is interested in recording the missions received by the prophets from God, much less in the "reception process" itself.[20] Likewise his passing over the Isaiah-Ahaz encounter of Isaiah 7—even though this involves a royal-prophetic interaction of the sort he favors elsewhere—is explainable on the consideration that this narrative culminates in the "Emmanuel announcement" (7:14) which Josephus might well have found problematic given the disastrous effects of politico-eschatological (Messianic) expectations in his people's recent history and his own commitment to Rome.[21] Finally, as we shall see with Jeremiah and Ezekiel, Josephus' non-mention of Isaiah's "symbolic action" recounted in Isaiah 20 accords with his usual procedure in treating the CPs.

Jeremiah

This brings us to Jeremiah.[22] As noted, Jeremiah is the CP to whom Josephus devotes the most attention. In his treatment, Josephus cites, more or less *in extenso*, a wide range of Biblical passages concerning the prophet, mostly from the Book of Jeremiah itself,[23] which he freely combines.

A first question that might be raised is why, among all the CPs, Jeremiah should be singled out for so extensive a presentation. Various factors may be cited in explanation. First of all, Jeremiah is [[352]] the CP for whom the Bible offers the most narrative material, and as noted, it was material of this kind which Josephus would have found most readily usable. In addition, however, it seems that a "personal" consideration influenced Josephus in giving Jeremiah so much space in his work, i.e., a feeling of kinship with a figure who, like himself, suffered opprobrium for his efforts to preserve Jerusalem from destruction by the Gentiles. Indeed, David Daube has pointed out that various features specific to Josephus' presentation of Jeremiah which lack a Biblical *Vorlage* as such (e.g., his telling Zedekiah that the Temple will be spared if he surrenders, *Ant.* 10,126 or his appeal to the Babylonians for Baruch's release, *Ant.* 10,158)

---

20. Note, however, that in *Ant.* 5,348–351 Josephus does give a version of the Biblical account of the call of the prophet Samuel, 1 Sam 3:2–18.

21. Note that he likewise makes no use of the "Messianic" texts Isa 9:1–6 and 11:1–9. On eschatology/Messianism in Josephus, see the literature cited and critically analysed by Feldman, *Josephus*, 484–489.

22. On Josephus' treatment of Jeremiah, see Christian Wolff, *Jeremia im Frühjudentum und Urchristentum* (TU 118; Berlin: Akademie, 1976) 10–15.

23. *Ant.* 10,79 ≅ 2 Chr 35:25; 10,88–93a ≅ Jeremiah 26; 10,93b–95 ≅ Jeremiah 36; 10,112–131 ≅ Jeremiah 37–38; 10,156–158 ≅ Jer 40:1–6; 10,176–177 ≅ Jeremiah 42; 10,178–179 ≅ Jeremiah 43–44.

can be seen as "retrojections" of Josephus' own actions during and after the Roman siege of Jerusalem.[24]

Given the expansiveness of Josephus' account of Jeremiah, I cannot treat all its aspects here. Rather, I shall concentrate on its distinctive features. I begin with the summary remarks Josephus appends (*Ant.* 10,79–80) to his initial mention, drawn from 2 Chr 35:25, of Jeremiah as the author of a lament for Josiah. Here, right at the start of things, Josephus presents Jeremiah as a writer of both short and long-range predictions, that is, the coming miseries of Jerusalem (including its "recent capture," i.e., in 70 A.D.[25]) and the overthrow of Babylon.

He further refers to Jeremiah's being seconded in his predictions by Ezekiel with whom, as Josephus recalls from Jer 1:2 and Ezek 1:1, he shared a priestly ancestry.[26] In what follows the various points made concerning Jeremiah in this introductory sequence are reiterated. At the same time, Josephus subsequently devotes—in this systematizing various Biblical presentations—great attention to an additional feature, that is, the prophet's interactions with various groups at different points in his ministry.

He begins, in free dependence on the narratives of Jeremiah 26 and 36, developing this theme while relating the reign of Jehoiakim (*Ant.* 10,88–95). Twice during that reign, that is, in Jehoiakim's third and fifth years, Josephus shows Jeremiah threatened with death for [[353]] his predictions, but not without sympathizers and protectors. In the first instance, "people and rulers," incensed at his announcement of Jerusalem's coming fall, arraign Jeremiah on the charge unmentioned in Scripture of having "used divination against the king." Noteworthy here is the deterministic affirmation Josephus prefaces to his account of the episode: "... he (Jeremiah) spoke to no avail, since there were none who were destined to be saved, for both the people and the rulers disregarded what they heard. ..." In this situation, Jeremiah is delivered by the "elders." Just as in Jer 26:19a they do so evoking the precedent of the CP Micah whose word of doom against Jerusalem (see Mic 3:12) brought him, not punishment, but honorable recognition. On the other hand, Josephus passes over the reference in Jer 26:19b to Hezekiah's turning to God in response to Micah's preaching and God's decision to relent—recall his omission of analogous features of the Book of Jonah.

24. David Daube, "Typology in Josephus," *JJS* 31 (1981) 26–27; see too Gary L. Johnson, "Josephus: Heir Apparent to the Prophetic Tradition?" *SBL 1983 Seminar Papers* (Chico, CA: Scholars, 1983) 345. Note that in the *Jewish Wars*, 5,391–392 Josephus invokes Jeremiah's role in the siege of Jerusalem as a precedent for his own.

25. On this reference, see Marcus' note in *Josephus*, 6.200–201 n. c.

26. On the problematic text here, see Daniel R. Schwartz, "Priesthood and Priestly Descent: Josephus: Antiquities 10,80," *JTS* 32 (1981) 129–135.

Unintimidated by his narrow escape, Jeremiah, in Josephus' subsequent presentation, drawn from Jeremiah 36, immediately proceeds to set down his words of doom in a book which he (rather than Baruch as in Jer 36:10) reads to the people. Later, that book is destroyed by the enraged Jehoiakim who orders Jeremiah's and Baruch's arrest. They escape, nonetheless, thanks to advance warning by "the leaders." Subsequently, however, the influence of Jeremiah's words makes itself felt even on Jehoiakim. Josephus (*Ant.* 10,96) goes beyond Scripture both in citing a "surrender" by that king to the Babylonians who are advancing against him (compare the divergent accounts of what happened with Jehoiakim in the siege of 597 in 2 Kgs 24:6 and 2 Chr 36:6) and in attributing this action to Jehoiakim's "fear of what had been foretold by the prophet."

Jeremiah figures even more prominently in Josephus' account of Zedekiah's reign. Here too the varying responses to Jeremiah's message receive special attention. In this period Jeremiah's preaching finds a certain—if not consistent—acceptance on the part of the king, whose sympathy for Jeremiah Josephus accentuates beyond the Biblical evidence,[27] as well as of the mass of the people who—again without Biblical warrant, compare Jer 37:2—are said to "believe" him (*Ant.* 10,114). On the other hand, he meets with persistent rejection and hostility from various prominent groups, that is, the "false prophets," the royal "friends," the leaders and magistrates. [354] These groups defame Josephus as "insane" (*Ant.* 10,104.114, cf. Jer 29:26), falsely accuse him of desertion (*Ant.* 10,115, see Jer 37:13), imprison him under the harshest conditions (*Ant.* 10, 115.121, see Jer 37:15) and pressure Zedekiah to execute him (*Ant.* 10,119, cf. Jer 38:4–5). Through all this, however, Jeremiah is preserved, above all through the initiatives of Zedekiah (*Ant.* 10,123, cf. Jer 38:10).

Beyond these general indications concerning Josephus' portrayal of Jeremiah's ministry under Zedekiah, several of its more specific distinguishing features might be noted. In *Ant.* 10,104—seemingly under the remote influence of 2 Chr 36:12—Josephus presents Jeremiah, not now simply as predictor, but as a preacher of morality who calls on Zedekiah "to leave off his various impieties and lawless acts, and watch over justice. . . ." Thereafter in *Ant.* 10,112–113 he has Jeremiah address Zedekiah with an extended forecast of the people's future down to the rebuilding of the Temple (compare on *Ant.* 10,79–80 above). This prospective lacks a Biblical basis as such. It has, however, been worked up out of elements culled from various Scriptural contexts (see, e.g., 2 Chr 36:20; Jer 29:10)—evidently with the intention of magnifying Jeremiah's

---

27. Note the (unscriptural) mention of Zedekiah's "believing" Jeremiah in *Ant.* 10,105 and the notice that the king "wished to do what Jeremiah advised" in *Ant.* 10,127.

predictive capacities. Finally, attention should be drawn to the only reference to Jeremiah's inner response to his experience in Josephus, that is, his (unscriptural) admission of "fear" to Zedekiah (*Ant.* 10,125).

As Scripture does, Josephus prolongs his account of Jeremiah's ministry to cover the period just subsequent to the fall of Jerusalem. Here too, his highlighting of the contrasting responses evoked by Jeremiah is apparent. On one side are the Babylonians who leave Jeremiah free to dwell where he wills and whose benignity towards the prophet Josephus accentuates beyond the Biblical data (they are explicitly said to release him from prison, give him large gifts, and, it seems, accede to his request for Baruch's release, *Ant.* 10,156–158, compare Jer 40:1–7). Opposed to them are the remnant of the Jews whose posture of unbelief, false accusations, and eventual denial of the prophet's liberty (they force him to accompany them to Egypt, see Jer 43:6–7) recall the behavior of the Jerusalem leaders prior to 587. In this concluding depiction of the prophet who fares better at the hands of the pagan conqueror than he does at the hands of his own people, one may surely see a deliberate "prefiguring" of Josephus' own experiences.

Until this point I have been considering the relatively large-scale utilization of the narratives of the Book of Jeremiah by Josephus. Conversely, however, there is much in that book which Josephus simply passes over. These omissions appear consistent with options [[355]] taken by Josephus with regard to Biblical data on other CPs. As with Isaiah, Josephus refrains from recounting Jeremiah's "call" (Jer 1:4–10). Even more instructive, as illustrative of Josephus' disinterest in portraying the God-prophet interplay, is his total ignoring of the "complaints" of Jeremiah—this notwithstanding his emphasis on the prophet's tribulations! (In Josephus, as noted, the only indication of Jeremiah's emotional state is his confession of fear which he makes, however, not to God, but to the king.) Josephus likewise leaves aside the Biblical accounts concerning Jeremiah's various "sign actions," thereby providing further evidence of his one-sided preoccupation with the verbal dimension of prophetic activity, that is, speaking and writing. Finally, Josephus' account of Jeremiah's future hopes appears quite "reductionistic" when compared with the Biblical record as a whole. On this point Josephus confines himself to citing Jeremiah's prediction of the destruction of Babylon, the Jewish return and rebuilding of the Temple (*Ant.* 10,112–113). Conversely, he says nothing about the prophet's announcements of an inner transformation of the people (see, e.g., Jer 31:31–34; 32:39–40) or of the emergence of a "Messianic" figure (see Jer 23:3–5; 33:14–17). Thereby, he manifests anew his understandable wariness *vis-à-vis* everything "Messianic" and "eschatological."

Ezekiel

Josephus' treatment of Ezekiel stands out especially in its minimalness, above all when compared with his detailed account of the contemporary Jeremiah. In fact, while Josephus does cite various particular items concerning Ezekiel not recorded in Scripture as such (e.g., his authorship of "two books," *Ant.* 10,79;[28] his being a "boy" at the time of his deportation to Babylon, *Ant.* 10,98, and his dispatching written prophecies of doom from Babylon to Jerusalem, *Ant.* 10,106), he seems basically uninterested in the experience of Ezekiel and his message in their individuality. Rather, he consistently represents Ezekiel as simply a confirmatory echo of Jeremiah's preaching. Their agreement extends to such matters of detail as the post-capture fate of Zedekiah, as Josephus goes to considerable lengths to point out in his harmonization of the seemingly divergent [[356]] predictions of Ezek 12:13 (Zedekiah will not "see" Babylon) and Jer 34:3 (Zedekiah will go to Babylon) in *Ant.* 10,106–107.141.[29]

The question that naturally arises is why Josephus should treat Ezekiel in this way—especially since the Bible offered him a relatively large body of readily usable narrative material concerning this prophet. One reason might be that Josephus simply found much less to identify with in Ezekiel—whose earlier removal from Jerusalem precluded his direct involvement in the events of Judah's final years—than in Jeremiah (see above). In any event, consistent with his treatment of the Biblical data on Jeremiah, Josephus leaves unutilized such material of the book of Ezekiel as the prophet's call and sign actions, as well as his predictions of an inner transformation of the people or of a future "Messiah" (for this see, e.g., Ezek 34:23–24; 37:25).

Haggai and Zechariah

Josephus twice makes brief mention of Haggai and Zechariah in connection with his account of the rebuilding of the Temple (*Ant.* 11,96.106). In the first and more elaborate of these references, Josephus sums up the pair's message in terms of their assuring the people that the Persians will not interfere with their finishing the Temple. He goes beyond the explicit statements of Scripture in his reference to the people's "having faith" in the two prophets (although cf. Ezra 5:1; 6:14 where such a "belief" is implied); in this, perhaps, he intends a contrast with Jeremiah whose efforts to preserve the first Temple met with unbelief. Also to be

---

28. On this enigmatic allusion see Marcus' note in *Josephus*, 6, p. 201 n. e.

29. With this compare the analogous stress on the agreement between the predictions of Elijah and Micaiah concerning Ahab's death in *Ant.* 8,408.417–418.

noted is Josephus' characteristic silence concerning the "Messianic element" of Haggai's and Zechariah's preaching (compare Hag 2:20–23; Zech 3:8; 4:6–8; 6:9–14).

Conclusion

I conclude by briefly summing up my findings, positive and negative, on Josephus' handling of the CPs. Positively, the CPs are for Josephus, above all else, accurate predictors of coming events in the religio-political sphere. He is especially concerned to point out how their individual predictions do, in the long-term, get realized and [[357]] inspire prominent figures to act as they do (e.g., Cyrus, Onias IV and his Egyptian patrons). In their predictions the CPs further agree among themselves (see Jonah and Nahum, Jeremiah and Ezekiel, Haggai and Zechariah). Typically, they write down the whole body of their words for the edification of posterity (Isaiah, Jeremiah, Ezekiel). In terms of the response they evoke, there is a great difference between Isaiah, Haggai, and Zechariah on the one hand and Jeremiah on the other, although even the latter never lacks supporters. All these features do have some basis in the Biblical record itself; they also (largely) correspond to the emphases in Josephus' presentation of his "non-classical prophets."

Negatively, for reasons suggested in the course of this presentation, Josephus simply ignores much of the Scriptural data concerning the CPs. He is not concerned to relate their call experiences or their intimate interactions with God, as is most evident in his non-utilization of Jeremiah's complaints. Little is said by him about the CPs' inner responses to their experiences (although he does mention Jonah's and Jeremiah's "fear"). The Josephian CPs do not perform "symbolic acts" (Hezekiah's cure which Josephus does relate is rather a "miracle"). Similarly, they are not, to any significant degree, either inculcators of morality and social justice or—given the irreversibility of God's decisions—of repentance (see Jonah). Their announcements concerning Messianic figures and of the end times in general are largely censored out. Josephus likewise passes over the *kult-kritisch* [['critical of the cult']] utterances of the Biblical Isaiah (see Isa 1:10–20) and Jeremiah (see Jeremiah 7); the former is called on to "sacrifice," while the latter repeatedly expresses concern for the preservation of the Temple.

In light of the above, one might venture the following generalization/evaluation concerning the treatment of the CPs in the *Antiquities*: without adding anything essentially new or distinctive to the Biblical portrayal of these figures—various of whose features he simply systematizes and accentuates—Josephus, for a variety of reasons, fails to do full justice to the richness of his Scriptural model's presentation of them.

Prophecy and Interpretation

JOHN F. A. SAWYER

Prophecy and Fulfilment in the Bible and the Early Church

[[139]] As we saw, the main criterion for distinguishing true prophecy from false in biblical tradition is fulfilment. This view of the nature [[140]] of prophecy is not confined to the Mosaic law in Deuteronomy 18. It is clear from that passage, from the historical books Joshua to Kings and 1 and 2 Chronicles, and from numerous passages in the prophetic literature itself, that the argument from prophecy was a major expression of faith in God. Isa 55:10–11 is perhaps the best statement:

> For as the rain and the snow come down from heaven,
>   and return not thither but water the earth,
> making it bring forth and sprout,
>   giving seed to the sower and bread to the eater,
> so shall my word be that goes forth from my mouth;
>   it shall not return to me empty,
> but it shall accomplish that which I purpose,
>   and prosper in the thing for which I sent it.

Ezekiel 12 contains another example in which the prophet answers the people's doubts by arguing that fulfilment is imminent:

> Son of man, what is this proverb that you have about the land of Israel, saying, "The days grow long, and every vision comes to naught"? Tell them therefore, "Thus says the Lord God: I will

Reprinted with permission from *Prophecy and the Biblical Prophets* (second edition; Oxford: Oxford University Press, 1993) 139–53 and 165–66.

put an end to this proverb, and they shall no more use it as a
proverb in Israel." But say to them, "The days are at hand, and
the fulfilment of every vision" (Ezek 12:22–23).

Of course, without actual fulfilment, without the hard evidence of
experience, such prophetic claims seldom convince. Arguments from experience, therefore, after the event, when the words of the prophets have
been fulfilled for all to see, are crucial. The passionate conviction that a
prophecy will be fulfilled very soon (e.g., Ezekiel 12) or at the end of
time (e.g., Daniel 12) is one thing; the fact that it has been is a different
matter altogether. Let us look at some examples.

In the first place, the whole structure of Israel's history is presented,
both in Joshua–Kings and in Chronicles, in such a way as to highlight
this phenomenon. The fate of cities, for example, is meticulously related
to prophecy (e.g., Josh 6:26; cf. 1 Kgs 16:34; 2 Chr 36:21). Needless to say,
literary invention is an integral ⟦141⟧ part of this process. It was easy to
insert the story of an unnamed prophet appearing on the scene and
predicting an event some time later (e.g., 1 Kgs 13:1–10; cf. 2 Kgs 16:23),
or to adjust such details as the date in order to match prophecy and
fulfilment more perfectly (e.g., Isa 7:8). On the other hand, an event
could be invented or at least elaborately embroidered to match a well-
documented prophecy that was already in existence. This is what happened in the case of the return of the exiles in Ezra 1–2. One reason why
the author of that passage presents us with the totally unhistorical picture
of 42,360 exiles besides their servants of whom there were 7,337, plus 200
male and female singers, returning to Jerusalem and Judah each to his
own town (Ezra 2:1, 64–65), is that he wanted to show how prophecies
like Isa 51:11 were fulfilled, even if they had not been:

> And the ransomed of the Lord shall return,
>   and come to Zion with singing
>   everlasting joy shall be upon their heads . . .

Perhaps the frequent mention of "singers" (Ezra 2:41, 65, 70; 3:10–11)
among the returning exiles alludes to this and other Isaianic prophecies
(cf. 51:3; 52:8–9; 54:1–3; 55:12), and the reference to the exclusion of
unclean priests (Ezra 2:62–63) is linked to Isa 52:11:

> Depart, depart, go out thence,
>   touch no unclean thing;
>   go out from the midst of her, purify yourselves,
>   you who bear the vessels of the Lord.

The Ezra passage illustrates the power of prophecy to create its own fulfilment in spite of the evidence. Haggai also saw beyond the same facts to glories that transcend them (e.g., 2:9). These are theological statements expressing faith in God, whatever happens.

Another popular device is the attribution to an ancient prophet of prophecies concerning events that have recently occurred or are actually unfolding in the author's own day. Thus in eighth-century B.C. Samaria Amos was able to prophesy that Jerusalem would be [[142]] rebuilt after the Babylonian Exile, and Isaiah from eighth-century B.C. Jerusalem predicted with the same accuracy events that took place 200 years later, such as the appearance of Cyrus on the international scene (44:28; 45:1), the presence of Jews in Syene in Upper Egypt (49:12), and the fall of Babylon (47:1).

Daniel 11 provides an even more spectacular example in which a prophet living in sixth-century B.C. Babylon foretells in massive detail the events leading up to and including the Maccabean crisis of 168–164 B.C. (cf. p. 114 [[not reprinted here]]). By substituting ciphers for actual names (e.g., "king of the south" for Ptolemy; "king of the north" for Antiochus; "Kittim" for the Romans in 11:30) the author heightens the mysterious effect of Daniel's prophecy, as do the repeated references to his extraordinary visionary experiences (e.g., 8:27; chap. 10). The tense in such prophecies remains in the future, but fulfilment is implied by the author who deliberately matches the prophet's words to historical events, familiar to his readers. The purpose is the same as in the simpler examples: he is declaring that history is controlled by God, and that he reveals his will to his prophets. In the words of an earlier prophet:

> Surely the Lord God does nothing,
> without revealing his secret
> to his servants the prophets (Amos 3:7).

The traditional division of the Christian Bible into an "Old Testament" and a "New Testament" has tended to break the continuity that manifestly exists there, from the first book to the last, from the vision of the prophet Moses in the Pentateuch to the vision of John of Patmos in the book of Revelation. The "Old/New" division also suggests a relationship between the two parts, not only of prophecy and fulfilment, but of supersession, with the risk of damaging consequences for Christian perceptions of the "Old" parts of scripture, and, regrettably, of Jews and Judaism. Continuity might be better expressed by grouping Isaiah, known to Christians since early times as the "Fifth Gospel," and the other

Prophets, with the Gospels and Paul, rather than with the Pentateuch, Historical Books, Psalms and Wisdom. Texts providing scriptural authority for the Virgin Birth (Isa 7:14), the Suffering ⟦143⟧ Messiah (Isaiah 53), the Mission to the Gentiles (Isa 49:6), the New Covenant (Jer 31:31) and countless other fundamental Christian beliefs, appear already in the Prophets.

In addition to the arrangement of the books, pointing upwards and forwards to fulfilment (see p. 1 ⟦not reprinted here⟧), a further expression of this continuity is the custom, so well documented in the later books of scripture, of Christian writers and preachers to use passages from the earlier books to give authority to what they are saying, or to explain it or give it some added effect. This imposes a structure upon the whole Christian Bible, exactly parallel to that of the so-called Deuteronomic history (Joshua–Kings) discussed in the previous section. Integral to that structure is the element of prophecy and fulfilment.

Two routes led to this use of scripture. Some passages were read and interpreted regularly in Jewish homes and synagogues, and must have become familiar throughout the Jewish world. In such cases the question was: what does this mean? or when is this prophecy going to be fulfilled? Luke 4:16–21 seems to be an example. Jesus is given the book of Isaiah and, in response to the congregation's questioning looks, he explains what it means: "Today this scripture has been fulfilled in your hearing." This type of exegesis starts from the text, and seeks to explain its meaning in such a way as to make it come alive for contemporary readers or listeners. It occurs in commentaries, such as the Jewish Midrashic literature, and the *pesher* literature from Qumran (cf. p. 151 ⟦in this volume, pp. 572–73⟧), and in homilies based on a lectionary. But it is rare in the early Church.

Early Christian writers normally use scripture in a quite different way. Their object is seldom to discuss the meaning of a text. They wish only to use it as a vehicle to express their own beliefs or describe their own experiences. Instead of working through the books of the Bible, commenting on the continuous texts, they "search the scriptures" (John 5:39) to discover isolated texts to build into their narrative or discourse. Thus, for example, in Matthew 1, Isa 7:14 is divorced from its context in the book of Isaiah and applied to the birth of Jesus, not because the author has been wondering what it meant, but because it expresses his belief that (1) Jesus was born of a virgin, (2) in Jesus "God is with us" ⟦144⟧ (= Immanuel) in a special way, and (3) the coming of Jesus is a fulfilment of prophecy. In its original context the woman is not described as a virgin (unless Matthew knew only the Greek translation which he quotes), and the prophecy is one of judgement not salvation. But, taken out of context, it is a marvellously rich prophecy of the coming of Jesus Christ, and has functioned as such in Christian tradition ever since.

Place-names provide an easy point of contact between Scripture and contemporary events. Thus Mic 5:2 speaks of Bethlehem as the future birthplace of a Davidic Messiah and so provides an ideal expression of the author's belief that Christ was born there (Matt 2:6). The same applies to his use of Isa 9:1, which originally referred to the Assyrian invasions of northern Israel, in 734–732 B.C., but is brilliantly applied to the appearance of Jesus in Nazareth, Capernaum, and other parts of Galilee (Matt 4:12–16). Many other details in the story of the life of Jesus are described in this way: e.g., riding into Jerusalem on an ass (Zech 9:9; Matt 21:5; John 12:15); Judas's thirty pieces of silver (Zech 11:12–13; Matt 26:15; 27:9); the piercing of Jesus' side (Zech 12:10; John 19:27). The teaching of Jesus is similarly presented as "fulfilling" Scripture: e.g., the cleansing of the Temple (Jer 7:11; Matt 21:13); his attacks on hypocrisy (Isa 29:13; Matt 15:8–9). The Psalms of David are often used in this way, especially because, for the early Christian writers, they too are about a Davidic Messiah: e.g., speaking in parables (Ps 78:2; Matt 13:35); lots cast for his clothing (Ps 22:18; John 19:24); the cry of dereliction on the cross (Ps 22:1; Mark 15:34).

What has been said about the life and teaching of Jesus applies also to theological discussion about him. Thus he is the prophet foretold in Deut 18:15–16 (Acts 3:17–26); the son of God (Ps 110:4; Gen 14:17–20; Heb 5:6; 7:1–3); "the first and the last" (Isa 48:12; Rev 22:13). The same method is used in the discussion of other doctrines and beliefs as well. For example, Hosea's poignant tale of disloyalty and reconciliation with God's people is applied by Paul to the Gentiles: "Those who were not my people I will call 'my people,' and her who was not beloved, I will call 'my beloved'" (Rom 9:25). Isa 65:1, which had a universalist meaning from the start, is cited in the next chapter [[145]] (10:20). More scriptural authority for such universalist teaching is found by Jesus, rather unexpectedly, in the figures of Elijah and Elisha:

> But in truth, I tell you, there were many widows in Israel in the days of Elijah, when the heaven was shut up three years and six months, when there was a great famine over all the land; and Elijah was sent to none of them but only to Zarephath, in the land of Sidon, to a woman who was a widow. And there were many lepers in Israel at the time of the prophet Elisha; and none of them was cleansed, but only Naaman the Syrian (Luke 4:25–27).

The resurrection of the dead was not a major theme in Scripture: the Sadducees denied it altogether on scriptural grounds. But Paul, firmly within rabbinic tradition, identifies two passages which, whatever their original meaning, he uses to good effect at the conclusion of his discussion of the subject in 1 Cor 15:54–55: "Death is swallowed up in victory" (Isa 25:8); "O death where is thy victory? O death where is thy sting?" (cf. Hos 13:14).

The process continues on into the early Church, where not only was scriptural authority sought for every doctrine, but scriptural language and imagery was assumed to be the preferred medium for all Christian teaching. The doctrine of the Trinity, for example, was recognized in the "Trisagion" ('thrice holy') (Isa 6:3): "Holy, holy, holy is the Lord of hosts." Isa 9:6 confirmed the divinity of Christ, and Isaiah 53 the atoning significance of his death. Isa 66:24 (cf. Sir 7:17 Greek) gives rare biblical authority for hell-fire.

The ox and the ass found their way into the nativity story from Isa 1:3:

> The ox knows its owner,
>   and the ass its master's crib;
> but Israel does not know,
>   my people does not understand.

This readily took on a polemical tone, drawing an invidious comparison—similar to the one the original prophet intended—⟦146⟧ between the Jews who did not accept that Jesus was God ("owner . . . master") and the dumb animals who did. Isa 49:16 foretold the stigmata on Christ's hands, and the enigmatic "rich man" in Isa 53:9 was naturally Joseph of Arimathea; the fourth man who appeared in the burning furnace "like a son of the gods" (Dan 3:25) was understood to be the risen Christ. Details of the shepherd image were drawn from Isa 40:11, and invitations like Isa 55:1—"Ho, everyone who thirsts"—applied to Christ's invitation to the Last Supper (cf. Isa 12:3; Gen 14:18; Prov 9:5). The canonization of a text means its removal from the context where it originated and its application to the beliefs, stories, and experiences of the living Church.

Two final examples will illustrate how the history of biblical prophecy continued into the early Church. No verse had more impact on the phenomenon than Joel 2:28 (Hebrew, 3:1) with its prediction that in the new age men and women, young and old, would receive the gift of prophecy. According to Acts, this is what happened, first in Jerusalem at Pentecost (Acts 2), and then later at Ephesus where gentiles first received the gift too (10:44ff.). Within the new community certain men and women were recognized as "prophets" in the sense that, like Stephen, they were "full of grace and power and did great wonders and signs among the people" (6:8). Barnabas was another (cf. 11:24) and Philip (cf. 8:4–8). Philip's four unmarried daughters are described as prophets too (21:9), and they provided scriptural inspiration and authority for the second century apocalyptic/ascetic movement founded by Montanus and his two associates Prisca and Maximilla.

Some have argued that Paul himself should be described as a prophet, taking into account his election "from the womb" (Gal 1:15; cf. Isa 49:1; Jer 1:5), his call (e.g., Acts 9; cf. Ezekiel 1–2; Dan 7:9ff.), his heavenly vision (2 Cor 12:2–4; cf. Isaiah 6; Jer 23:18), and the like. He is compared to the biblical prophets, both in Acts (e.g., Acts 13:47) and in his own writings (e.g., Gal 1:15f.), and perhaps he has himself in mind when he contrasts "prophetic powers" with the power of love in 1 Corinthians 13.

The Prophets in Ancient Judaism

⟦147⟧ In the mainstream of orthodox Judaism, the Prophets have never attained the same central role as they did in Christianity. An early example of this contrast is to be found in Ben Sira (ca. 180 B.C.), whose great hymn in praise of famous men from Adam to Nehemiah (Ben Sira 44–49) devotes only a few verses to the Latter Prophets (Isaiah to Malachi), while from the Former Prophets (Joshua–Kings), Samuel, Elijah, and Elisha receive only slightly more extended treatment. The custom of reading portions of the Prophets immediately after the reading of the Torah on sabbaths and feast-days ('haftarahs') goes back to the time of Christ (cf. Luke 4:17), and the lectionary, for feast days and fasts at any rate, was fixed by the middle of the second century A.D. But of the eighty or so relatively short passages thus annually read out and occasionally preached upon, less than half come from the Latter Prophets, twenty from Isaiah and the rest divided equally between Jeremiah (nine), Ezekiel (ten), and the Twelve (fourteen). This means that many passages, like Isaiah 53, familiar to Christians, are much less familiar to the orthodox Jew. There is much less emphasis on the "Immanuel prophecy" (Isa 7:14), for instance, the Messianic hymn in Isa 9:1–6 ("the people that walked in darkness have seen a great light"), the Pentecost passage in Joel (2:28), and all the Zechariah passages cited above as prophecies about Christ (9:9; 11:12ff.; 12:10). On the other hand, Isaiah's vision in the Temple (Isaiah 6), "Comfort, comfort my people" (Isa 40:1–26), the vision in the valley of dry bones (Ezekiel 37), Micah's "What does the Lord require of you . . ." (Mic 6:8), and other passages are equally familiar to both.

Telling examples of the Jewish use of the Prophets in the liturgy are the association of Jonah with Yom Kippur, Zechariah's vision of the golden lamp (Zech 2:14–4:7) with Hanukkah (1 Macc 4:49–50), Ezekiel's chariot vision (Ezekiel 1) with the Sinai theophany (Exod 18:1–20:23) on the first day of the Feast of Weeks, and a powerful selection of Isaianic material (Isa 10:33–12:6) with the last day of the Passover celebrations. The daily Prayer Book draws heavily on the prophetic traditions too: for example the "Eighteen Benedictions," one of the oldest and best [[148]] known parts of the daily liturgy, contains prayers for the resurrection of the dead, the rebuilding of Jerusalem, the return of the exiles, and the coming of the Messiah, all in language drawn directly from the Prophets, especially Isaiah. Random verses from the Prophets are cited frequently as proof texts in the Talmud, as though they possess scriptural authority equal to the Torah. A rare reference to Isaiah 53, in a discussion of the concept of a suffering Messiah, will illustrate this: "Our teachers have said: His name shall be the Leprous One, as it says, 'Surely he bore our sicknesses, and carried our pains: yet we esteemed him as one stricken with leprosy, and smitten of God' [Isa 53:4]" (Sanh. 98b).

Another indication of the relatively low priority given to the Prophets in Judaism is to be found in the midrashic literature. Of the vast numbers of ancient Jewish commentaries, known as midrashim, only a fraction is devoted to the Prophets. Many midrashim on the Torah, or parts of it, have survived, as also on the Five Scrolls (Ruth, Esther, Song of Songs, Ecclesiastes, and Lamentations) and Psalms, but almost none on the Prophets. Jonah is the one exception, being, like the works just listed, regularly used in the liturgy. For systematic commentaries on the Prophets we have to rely on medieval collections, the best known of which is Yalkut Shimoni, a midrashic thesaurus of the whole of the Hebrew Bible probably composed in Germany in the first half of the thirteenth century. A modern "yalkut" in English is Louis Ginzberg's *Legends of the Jews.*

There are also the medieval Bible commentaries on the Prophets by Rashi, David Kimhi, and Ibn Ezra, printed in all rabbinic Bibles alongside the biblical text. These are the most widely consulted Jewish commentaries in use today. Like Yalkut Shimoni, they are not available in English, but the Soncino commentaries on the Bible regularly quote them and are helpful. For examples of midrashic comments on the Prophets, see above on Elijah, Jeremiah, Jonah, and Malachi. Finally, the mystical Hekhalot literature takes as its starting-point the "chariot vision" of Ezekiel 1 (see pp. 104–5 [[not reprinted in this volume]]), and speculates on such passages as Isaiah 6, but can hardly be described as a systematic commentary on the prophetic literature.

Not until relatively modern times has Judaism discovered the [[149]] Prophets. Nearly all the poetry of Bialik (1873–1934) abounds with allusions to the Bible, but especially the Prophets, e.g., "What is my offence, what is my strength? I am not a poet nor a prophet, but a woodcutter" ('My soul has sunk down'; trans. T. Carmi). The allusion to Amos 7:14 is very effective. Martin Buber and Avraham Joshua Heschel are two other modern writers whose works on the Prophets broke new ground in the history of Jewish exegesis.

A rich source of information on how Jewish communities in ancient times interpreted the Prophets and applied them to events and conditions in their own experience is translation into the vernacular. Some examples from the Greek translation of the Prophets will illustrate how events in second-century B.C. Jewish history were related to the prophecies of Isaiah and Amos. Isaiah 19 ends with a remarkable blessing of "my people Egypt" and, since the Greek version of the Hebrew Bible was produced primarily for the thriving Greek-speaking Jewish community in Egypt, it is no surprise to find that a Greek translator has added the preposition 'in' to change 'my people Egypt', to 'my people in Egypt', thereby redirecting the blessing away from Egypt in general to his own community there. He does a similar thing in 11:16 and 28:5, where he adds 'in Egypt' to references to 'the remnant': 'In that day the Lord of hosts will be a crown of hope, and a diadem of glory to the remnant of his people in Egypt' (28:5 Greek).

Similarly the reference in Isa 19:18 to "the city of the sun" (RSV), a city in Egypt which will "swear allegiance to the Lord of hosts," was identified with Heliopolis where, according to Josephus (*Antiquities*, 13:68), Jews believed the exiled High Priest Onias built a New Jerusalem "as the prophet Isaiah had foretold" (see also p. 151 [[572]]).

Amos 3:12 illustrates another type of contemporary application: the Greek version alters what was originally a bitter attack on affluent Samaria in the days of Amos into a twofold sectarian assault on his contemporaries: 'As a shepherd pulls out of the mouth of a lion two legs and a piece of an ear, so shall the people of Israel who dwell in Samaria . . . and those priests in Damascus be pulled out' (Amos 3:12 Greek). The polemical allusions to the [[150]] Samaritans and the Zadokite sect, best known to us today from the Dead Sea Scrolls, are unmistakable (cf. Sir 50:25–26).

The ancient Aramaic versions of the Hebrew Bible, the Targums, go further in the direction of interpreting and explaining the text in terms of the beliefs and circumstances of their own day. Thus, for example, Messianism as it had developed by the first century A.D. at the very latest has left its mark very strongly on the Targum of Isaiah. The term 'the Messiah' is inserted after 'my servant' in Isa 52:13 (also in 53:10) and the meaning of the poem radically adapted to more conventional Messianic language:

> And it was the will of the Lord to refine and purify the remnants
> of his people in order to cleanse their soul from sins. They shall

> look upon the kingdom of their Messiah: they shall multiply
> sons and daughters, they shall prolong days, and those who per-
> form the law of the Lord shall prosper in his good pleasure (Isa
> 53:10 Targ.).

Notice how much longer the Aramaic version is and how far from the
Hebrew text. It comes closer to Daniel (e.g., 11:32–35) than to the
eighth-century prophets. But given that Scripture is intended to speak
to every age, then what it originally meant may often have a low priority
in the context of a religious community that canonized it.

The Qumran Scrolls provide us with an interesting sample of a sectarian interpretation of the same prophetic texts. Composed for the most
part during the last two centuries B.C. by an ascetic Jewish sect which, like
Christianity, broke away from the Jerusalem hierarchy, the Qumran literature includes not only manuscripts of all the books of the Hebrew
Bible (except Esther) and many of the Apocryphal works canonized by
some branches of the Christian Church (e.g., Enoch), but also a quantity
of sectarian writings, commentaries on Scripture, hymns, manuals, laws,
and the like, which give us a unique insight into the history, organization, life, and beliefs of an alternative to rabbinic Judaism. Like virtually
all other varieties of Judaism, including Christianity, the sect, probably a
form of Essenism, was heavily dependent on the Hebrew Bible which its
members interpreted by their own distinctive methods and for their own
religious purposes. We shall look [[151]] briefly at examples from three
types of material: biblical manuscripts, especially the complete Isaiah
Scrolls; commentaries on the text, in particular the Habakkuk *pesher*;
and other texts, especially the Damascus Rule, in which isolated biblical
texts are cited and interpreted.

Biblical manuscripts, written about a thousand years before our
other Hebrew manuscripts of the Bible, prove how extraordinarily successful the Jewish scribes have been in preserving the text of the Bible almost unchanged for so many centuries. But in some passages, often
where there are difficulties of some kind, they show how a scribe could
choose a reading which agreed with the beliefs of the sect. In Isa 19:18,
for example, the reading is 'city of the sun' instead of the official 'city of
destruction' (MT; AV). 'City of the sun' represents opposition to Jerusalem shared both by the Qumran sect and by Onias, exiled High Priest
who founded a new Jerusalem at Leontopolis in the district of Heliopolis
('city of the sun'), at about the same time as the Qumran sect broke away
from the Jerusalem hierarchy. A variant reading in Isa 6:13 is another example. By simply spacing the words differently, the meaning is changed
from a prophecy of hope for David's Messianic descendants in Judah (cf.
RSV) to a dismissive question: 'How could its stump be the holy seed?'

The few *pesher* commentaries that have survived from Qumran are preoccupied with the fulfilment of prophecy in the experience of the community, in particular with regard to their escape from the corrupt hierarchy at Jerusalem and the imminent end of the present age. In his commentary on Hab 2:1–2, for example, the author explains that God told Habakkuk to write down what would happen to the final generation ("write down the vision . . .") and that "he who reads it . . ." refers to the Teacher of Righteousness (one of the leaders of the community) "to whom God made known all the mysteries of the words of His servants the prophets." The famous line "But the righteous shall live by his faith" (2:4; cf. Rom 1:17) is interpreted as referring to "all those who observe the law in the House of Judah, whom God will deliver from the House of Judgment because of their suffering and because of their faith in the Teacher of Righteousness." The subsequent verses, describing arrogance, greed, and violence, are interpreted as [[152]] referring to the "Wicked Priest" at Jerusalem who "forsook God and betrayed the precepts for the sake of riches" (on 2:5), and pursued the Teacher of Righteousness to the house of his exile, where he burst in on the community on the Day of Atonement "their sabbath of repose" (on 2:15). In 2:17 "Lebanon" means the Council of the Community, the "beasts" are the poor of Judah who keep the law, and the "city" is Jerusalem where the Wicked Priest committed abominable deeds and defiled the Temple of God (Vermes 1975: 235–43).

Sometimes actual historical persons are named: thus the lion in Nah 2:11 is interpreted as "Demetrius, king of Greece," probably Demetrius III Eukairos, king of Syria during the reign of Alexander Jannaeus (103–76 B.C.) (Josephus, *Antiquities*, 13:370–78). But normally the "code names" are left unexplained, perhaps originally because they were well enough known, but later probably because interest was theological rather than historical. Decipherment is a peculiarly modern preoccupation.

The third example of Qumran exegesis comes from a continuous narrative, in which frequent quotations from the Prophets are given and explained. The first part of the Damascus Rule tells the story of how the remnant of Israel escaped from the corruption of Judah and entered into a New Covenant "in the land of Damascus." At every stage prophecies are fulfilled; and it is particularly noteworthy how in this process passages originally intended as prophecies of judgement are transformed into prophecies of salvation for the new community. Isa 7:17 and Amos 5:26–27 illustrate this. In the first case, the split in Israel into north and south, when Ephraim departed from Judah, is understood to refer to the time when "those who held fast escaped to the north and all the apostates were given up to the sword." The Amos passage develops this line of thought in some detail: "I will exile the tabernacle of your king and the bases of your statues from my tent to Damascus." This is interpreted as a prophecy that the Law (tabernacle) and the Prophets (bases of the statues) will one day be taken away from Jerusalem (tent), and entrusted to the congregation (king) and "the Interpreter of the Law" (star) in the new community (Damascus). Ezek 45:15 can readily be interpreted in a similar way, while Hos 5:10 contains a particularly vicious and ⟦153⟧ appropriate attack on the "princes of Judah." The Qumran sect, like the early Christians, shows a particular fondness for quoting the Prophets. Outspoken criticism of Jerusalem and Judah is another feature common to both Christianity and Qumran.

A final example of Qumran exegesis provides further links with early Christian thinking, in this case in the Epistle to the Hebrews. In a remarkable document, unfortunately badly damaged, Melchizedek (cf. Hebrews 7) appears "at the end of days" as a heavenly saviour figure, proclaiming liberty to the captives and comfort to those who mourn (Isa 61:1): "as it is written concerning him, *who says to Zion: Your ELOHIM reigns* (Isa 52:7). *Zion* is . . . those who uphold the Covenant, who turn from walking in the way of the people. And your ELOHIM is Melchizedek, who will save them from the hand of Satan" (Vermes, 1975: 265–68). ELOHIM is the Hebrew word for 'God' or 'angels', in such passages as Ps 8:4.

Bibliography

Alexander, P. S. *Textual Sources for the Study of Judaism.* Manchester: Manchester University Press, 1984.

Barrett, C. K. "The Interpretation of the Old Testament in the New." Pp. 377–411 in *Cambridge History of the Bible,* volume 1. Cambridge: Cambridge University Press, 1970.

Barzel, H. "The Last Prophet: The Biblical Ground of Bialik's Poetry." *Biblical Patterns in Modern Literature.* Edited by D. H. Hirsch and N. Ashkenasy. Chico, California: Scholars Press, 1984.

Blenkinsopp, J. *Prophecy and Canon: A Contribution to the Study of Jewish Origins.* Notre Dame: University of Notre Dame, 1977.

Brooke, G. J. *Exegesis at Qumran.* Sheffield: JSOT Press, 1985.

Carmi, T., editor. *The Penguin Book of Hebrew Verse.* London, 1981.

Childs, B. S. *Introduction to the Old Testament as Scripture.* Philadelphia: Fortress, 1985.

Coggins, R. J., and J. L. Houlden, editors. *A Dictionary of Biblical Interpretation.* London: SCM, 1990.

Cohn, N. *The Pursuit of the Millennium.* London: Paladin, 1970.

Danby, H. *The Mishnah.* Oxford: Oxford University Press, 1936.

Ginzberg, L. *The Legends of the Jews.* 7 volumes. Philadelphia: Jewish Publication Society, 1909; 1 volume. New York, 1956.

Sawyer, J. F. A. *The Fifth Gospel: Isaiah in the History of Christianity.* Cambridge: Cambridge University Press, 1993.

Scholem, G. *The Messianic Idea in Judaism.* New York: Schocken, 1971.

Stenning, J. *The Targum of Isaiah.* Oxford: Oxford University Press, 1949.

Stone, M. *Scriptures, Sects and Visions.* Philadelphia: Fortress, 1980.

Vermes, G. *The Dead Sea Scrolls in English.* Revised edition. London: Penguin, 1975.

_____. "Bible and Midrash: Early Old Testament Exegesis." Pp. 199–231 in *Cambridge History of the Bible,* volume 1. Cambridge: Cambridge University Press, 1970.

Part 7

Future Directions

Contemporary Issues

WERNER H. SCHMIDT

[[188]] Since the prophets use a variety of literary forms, where is the essential and decisive element of their proclamation to be located: in the announcement of the future, in the analysis of the present situation (including criticism of society), or in the exhortation with the call to repentance as its climactic form? Let me at least call the reader's attention here to some basic questions in contemporary study of the prophets (the list might easily be extended).

1. To what extent may the message of the writing prophets be "derived" from Israel's earlier traditions, whether these have to do with cult or law or wisdom? The prophets certainly adopt various literary forms, themes, traditions, and representations, which they remodel in the context of their own message and use in order to address their hearers in the actual situation of the moment. But is it possible that in their announcement of the future, to the effect that God is cancelling his communion with his people (Amos 8:2; Hos 1:9; Isa 6:9ff.; Jer 1:13f.; 16:5; etc.), the writing prophets are likewise continuing an ancient idea? Or in this discernment of the future are they rather contradicting the very substance of the tradition, which professes this very communion of God and the people (Genesis 15; Exodus 3; etc.)?

2. Conversely, in their discernment of the future, in the literary forms they adopt (announcement of disaster with justification for it, woe cry, lament or dirge, etc.) and in their themes (criticism of cult, of society, and so on), the writing prophets have so much in common with one another that they can hardly have come on the scene in complete independence of one another. Despite individual traits and despite unmistakable differences even on major points, their messages are closely related.

Reprinted with permission and excerpted from "The Form of Prophecy," *Old Testament Introduction* (trans. M. J. O'Connell; New York: Crossroad, 1984) 188–90. Originally published as *Einführung in das Alte Testament* (Berlin: de Gruyter, 1979).

How, then, are we to account for these common characteristics? A direct dependence, and in particular a dependence on written sources, cannot be demonstrated. Is there, however, a link [[189]] through oral tradition (see the citation of Mic 3:12 in Jer 26:18), possibly one mediated by disciples of the prophets (Isa 8:16)?

In any case, the writing prophets only rarely associate themselves explicitly with other prophets (Hos 6:5; cf. Jer 28:8). Groups of prophets are more often critical of one another (Amos 7:14; Mic 3:5ff.; etc.).

3. Announcement of the future and analysis of the present usually go together. But there is disagreement on how the connection is to be interpreted. Does the premonition of the future arise out of profound insight into the present condition of the people, or is the demonstration of guilt rather a consequence of prophetic certainty about the future?

Latent here is also the problem of the connection between individual utterance and revelation. Are a prophet's individual utterances concrete applications, which he himself has worked out, of his general insight into the future, an insight gained in visions? Or is every utterance that is presented as God's word based on a new act of revelation?

4. The question of the relation between future and present arises anew when the attempt is made to understand utterances about the future. Are the prophetic announcements of disaster to be interpreted in the light of the exhortations, or, on the contrary, are the exhortations (which are rather infrequent, at least in the earlier period) in the service of the eschatological proclamation (see, e.g., Amos 5:5)? In fact, are even the announcements of judgment meant only as threats, that is, final warnings, the purpose of which is to have the people avert the judgment by their manner of life? Or is the prophetic message, whether of disaster or salvation, meant as the announcement of a future that will certainly come and is already at hand?

A more limited problem within this larger question is the following: Are such radical statements as the "obduration commission" of Isaiah (6:9f.) formulated only after the fact and on the basis of the hearers' reactions to the prophetic proclamation?

5. Apart from Amos, the "prophets of disaster" do not at all seem to have prophesied only disaster, but rather to have announced salvation as well. If it is not possible to explain the promises of salvation as by and large "inauthentic" (§13a3 [[not reprinted here]]), then the questions arise, Is the prophetic message ultimately lacking in harmony? Is it even inconsistent, inasmuch as at different times and to different audiences a prophet could convey divergent and even contradictory messages? Or are the announcements of judgment and of salvation objectively coherent?

According to one view, the two types of messages are linked by hope of a "remnant" that will survive the judgment (1 Kgs 19:17f.). ⟦190⟧ But in prophetic words that are accepted by all as "authentic" the remnant can be a sign of the catastrophe: a vestige that is no longer pregnant with the future and may even itself be threatened and that bears witness to the extent of the destruction (Amos 3:12; 8:10; 9:4; Isa 17:5f.; 30:17; etc.; cf. Job 1:15ff.). Conversely, it is often in disputed oracles that the remnant appears as a "holy seed," that is, as ulterior goal of the judgment and as bearer of a new salvation (Isa 6:13; 4:3; earlier, Amos 5:15; 9:8; etc.).

Similarly, was it only in retrospect that later times looked upon the call to repentance as recapitulating the prophetic message (2 Kgs 17:3; Zech 1:3f.)? Not infrequently the prophets observe that repentance has not ensued (Amos 4:6f.; Isa 9:13; 30:15) or is even impossible (Hos 5:4; Jer 13:23). Correspondingly, they may promise a conversion effected by God himself (Hos 14:5; Ezekiel 37; etc.). There is room here even for a call to repentance within the context of promised salvation (Hos 14:2; Jer 3:12; cf. Isa 55:6; etc.). In the eyes of the prophets, then, can human beings not preserve salvation but only receive it as a constant new gift from God?

Such differences as these receive quite divergent answers in contemporary study of the prophets. Since every interpretation of prophecy presupposes decisions about the "authenticity" or "inauthenticity" of texts, each picture of the prophets differs widely from the others.

The Prophets: Are We Heading for a Paradigm Switch?

FERDINAND E. DEIST

[[1]] Kuhn, in his *The Structure of Scientific Revolutions* (1970^2), pictures the history of the natural sciences as going through periods of "normal science" and "revolution." One of the basic concepts in Kuhn's thought is that of "paradigm," i.e., the complex of convictions, values, and world view shared by a scientific community which provides its philosophical framework for valid academic inquiry, or any element of such a complex that has to do with the strategy, technique, or method for solving scientific puzzles and that is accepted as effective and valid within that community. Normal science, then, in Kuhn's terminology, is that stage in the history of academic inquiry at which scholars in a particular field generally accept the validity of a particular paradigm of thought and apply it unquestioningly. The outcome of normal science is not so much the discovery of something new as a gradual refinement and articulation of elements of the paradigm of thought and/or more precise description of previous findings obtained through the application of that model.

This stage ends with the advent of a scientific revolution. A scientific revolution occurs when a dominant paradigm of thought (or an element of such a paradigm) is found to be inadequate and is eventually abandoned in favour of a new paradigm from which proceeds a new view on the problems involved in the field of study. Scholars convinced of the superior relevancy of the new set of questions and of the superior explanatory power of the new paradigm then experience a paradigm

Reprinted with permission from *Prophet und Prophetenbuch: Festschrift für Otto Kaiser zum 65. Geburtstag* (ed. V. Fritz, K.-F. Pohlmann, and H.-C. Schmitt; Beihefte zur Zeitschrift für die Alttestamentliche Wissenschaft 185; Berlin: de Gruyter, 1989) 1–18.

switch. A paradigm switch can thus be defined as the process of acknowledging the inadequacy and, therefore, the failure of a given academic approach to ask relevant questions and/or suggest valid solutions to problems in an academic field and that leads to the replacement of the old paradigm of thought by a more relevant/valid and/or promising approach. Since such a replacement does not simply imply the application of new techniques, but a complete change in outlook, it is also called a *conversion*—which may be an ironically relevant term when speaking about the prophets.

To my mind we are at present (at least in my part of the world) in the midst of such a paradigm switch with regard to the scholarly appreciation of the Old Testament prophets in general and the so-called "writing prophets" in particular.

The Dominant Paradigm

[[2]] Prior to the rise of historical criticism it was believed that the thoughts and times of the Old Testament prophets could be "read" from the texts they produced and that these words had to be understood against the historical background in which they had been spoken. On the basis of these premises, historical critics during the 19th and early 20th century initiated the quest for the very words of the individual prophets.

Historical critical procedures, especially literary criticism, provided the method for reconstructing the *ipsissima verba* [['very words']] of the prophets, while the histories of Israel and of (Israelite) religion provided the background for understanding these words as utterances of specific individuals in specific circumstances. The introduction of form criticism assisted researchers in refining their tools considerably, since this procedure allowed them to understand the unique speech forms employed by the prophets in specific *Sitze im Leben* [['life situations']]. In a similar manner tradition and redaction criticism enabled them to appreciate more fully the exact "twist" a prophet gave to a received tradition, e.g., the covenant tradition,[1] so as to assess each prophet's individual contribution to the formation of Israel's ethical monotheism. All along the prophets have been viewed as *the* makers of Israelite (ethical and monotheistic) religion.[2] The idea of *lex post prophetas* [['the law after the prophets']] helped

---

1. Cf. W. L. Holladay, "The Background of Jeremiah's Self-Understanding," *JBL* 83 (1964), 153–164; D. R. Hillers, *Covenant: The History of a Biblical Idea*, 1969, 120–142.

2. Cf. B. Duhm, *Die Theologie der Propheten*, 1875, 1–34; J. Wellhausen, *Prolegomena to the History of Ancient Israel*, 1885, 414–419; 467–477; 484–491. Both picture the "writing prophets" as proponents of the purest form of monotheism and ethics. G. von Rad, *The*

picture the prophets as historical giants in the history of (Israelite) religion. They were thought of as bearers of a divinely instituted office and viewed as individuals conscious of a unique divine calling causing them to be opponents of the kings, the rich, the priests and false prophets. Their books provided the basis for many an Old Testament theology of the day.

⟦3⟧ The high regard for the prophets is typically Christian. A mere comparison of the relative frequency of quotations from the Latter Prophets in the Mishna with that in the New Testament[3] will illustrate the point:

Quotations in: → from:	The Mishna	The New Testament
The Torah	67%	32%
The Former Prophets	5%	11%
The Latter Prophets	11%	34%
The Writings	17%	28%

Stated in different terms: for every six times the Mishna quotes from the Torah it quotes from the Latter Prophets once, while the relation in the New Testament is 1:1.

In Jewish Tradition the Prophets presented readers with a kind of *hă-lākâ* ⟦'practical rule'⟧ (compare the Haphtarah ⟦'prophetic lection'⟧), with a key to understand the time the readers were living in (as in Qumran),[4] or to understand God's mysteries.[5] The "canonicity" of the Proph-

---

Message of the Prophets, 1968, 9, referred to Israelite prophecy as "the most astonishing phenomenon in the whole of Israel's history" and to their contribution as "a volcanic re-emergence of Yahwism." Cf. also H. W. Wolff's question ("Prophecy from the Eighth through the Fifth Century," *Int* 32 [1978], 17) how prophecy came to be a unique phenomenon within the history of Israel and within biblical proclamation, and F. J. Stendenbach ("Was macht den Propheten aus? Zum Erscheinungsbild des Prophetischen," *BiKi* 31 [1976], 5), who speaks of the writing prophets as people "in denen die Prophetie ihren höchsten Gipfel erklommen hat" ⟦'in whom prophecy has reached its highest peak'⟧. The picture thus drawn of the prophets may even become "romantic" in the non-technical sense of the word. See, for instance, E. Hernando's remark in his otherwise sober article ("The Sin of the 'False' Prophets," *TD* 27 [1979], 37–40) that a "true prophet" was someone "loving his people more than himself," and a person with "selfless love."

3. These calculations are based on the textual indexes of Danby's English translation of the Mishna and the Nestlé-Aland New Testament text.

4. Although this is not an exclusive Jewish hermeneutic. See R. T. France, "Old Testament Prophecy and the Future of Israel," *TB* 26 (1975), 53–78, according to whom many Christians still "search its (i.e., a prophetical book's) pages for predictions of events in twentieth century politics, with a view to plotting the future course and, often, calculate the nearness of the final denouement" in a Qumran-like fashion, a practice very popular in millennarian groups.

5. See C. S. Rodd, "Talking Points from Books," *ExT* 98 (1986), 66–68.

ets did not put these writings on a "higher level" than, say, official *hălākâ.*[6] For instance, although the Samaritans totally rejected the Prophets, their idea of "canon" played no part in the Jewish-Samaritan dispute. In Christian circles, however, references to the Prophets provided the basis of the argument for the legitimacy of Christianity over against Judaism. This preoccupation with the Prophets formed part and parcel of 18th- and 19th-century Christian scholarship. But it explains neither the typical *questions* asked at the time nor the *method* employed in answering these questions.[7]

[[4]] The search for the *ipsissima verba* of the Old Testament prophets and the emphasis on their uniqueness[8] were the direct result of romantic historicism. Romantic historiography, in its opposition to naturalism and rationalism, emphasized the importance of *original sources* and the understanding of every age, person and phenomenon in its *uniqueness*. One only has to think of Ranke's historiographic approach[9] and of the subsequent *Methodenstreit* [['argument over method']] to appreciate that it was their scholarly environment that suggested to 19th-century Old Testament scholars what the relevant questions were and that supplied them with a methodology that could answer those questions. That frame of mind (and hermeneutic) must obviously have remained (culturally and historically) relevant ever since, because historical-critical methods have constantly been refined and are still applied widely today, even though their relevance has since the 1960s from time to time been questioned.

The reasons for the continued relevance of these questions are to be found in a number of assumptions of classical historical criticism coinciding with those of the "final text" approach, of which I mention only three. Firstly, the Christian theological community continued to proceed from the premise of the uniqueness of either ancient Israelite or Christian religion, or of both, so that the search for the "unique" (revelation) in the Old Testament tradition remained a relevant undertaking.[10]

6. Cf. A. G. Auld, "Prophets through the Looking Glass: Between Writings and Moses," *JSOT* 27 (1978), 20: ". . . the argument between Sadducee (Jewish or Samaritan) and Pharisee was not whether to *add* Prophets as new Scripture beside Torah, but whether to *retain* Prophets once it had been ensured that Moses had said enough" (my emphasis) [[see p. 307 in this volume]].

7. For a brief review of different methodologies and the typical questions raised by a particular paradigm, see F. E. Deist, "Currents in the History of Historiography," in F. E. Deist and J. H. le Roux, *Revolution and Reinterpretation. Chapters from the History of Israel,* 1987, 1–31.

8. Cf. G. Fohrer, *History of Israelite Religion,* 1973, 223, 237; W. H. Schmidt, *Alttestamentlicher Glaube in seiner Geschichte,* 1975², 226.

9. See W. P. Fuchs, "Was heißt das: Bloß zeigen wie es eigentlich gewesen?" *Geschichte in Wissenschaft und Unterricht* 30 (1979), 665–667.

10. Cf. H. Wheeler Robinson, *Redemption and Revelation,* 1942, 143f.: ". . . a prophet of the classical period would not have dared to prophesy without an inaugural vision such as

Secondly, the idealistic philosophy underlying historical-critical hermeneutics remained the philosophical basis of even the critics of historical
criticism: the (divinely inspired, and hence a priori and unique) intellectual world[11] remained to be viewed as the force that steered history: "text
production" was and still is explained with reference to a priori thought
categories (e.g., "tradition" in historical criticism, or "deep structure" in
structuralism), or with reference to inherent textual [[5]] structures (e.g.,
in discourse analysis). Therefore, the type of question prompted by the
underlying philosophy remained relevant, e.g., the quest for the intellec-
tual/spiritual force of prophetic theology that shaped human destiny
and that provided the driving force in religious evolution. Thirdly, the
essentialistic view of texts inherent in historical-critical methodology,
and according to which texts are *reflections* of reality, thought processes
and/or deposits of meaning, remained the basis of biblical research.[12]
The "controversy" over historical-critical methods therefore has more to
do with the search for other (and more appropriate) *procedures* (structuralism, close reading) for uncovering the *inherent meaning* of a text, than
with asking different questions prompted by a different *paradigm*.

The Undermining of the Dominant Paradigm

No respected model suddenly and inexplicably disappears from the
scene. It is first "undermined" by a number of factors, among which the
following are relevant to us here. Firstly, *new evidence* may come to light
which cannot be adequately explained in terms of the assumptions of the
dominant model. Secondly, the *assumptions of the scholarly world may
change* to such an extent that the premises of the dominant model are seriously called in question. Thirdly, certain *new questions* may arise which
cannot be adequately researched and answered by the procedures of the
dominant model. Fourthly, the *proponents of the dominant model may dis-*

Isaiah's . . . or an audition such as Jeremiah's, or such a characteristically peculiar experience as that of Ezekiel."

11. I am not quite sure whether Carroll's term "intellectual" for "prophet" should be
understood in its idealistic meaning, or in the "Leninist" sense of "conscientizer" (R. Carroll, "Poets Not Prophets. A Response to 'Prophets through the Looking Glass,'" *JSOT* 27
[1983], 26), although his concurring remarks regarding Weber's designation of the prophets as "pamphleteers" and "demagogues" seem to suggest the latter rather than the former
sense. Perhaps Auld's suggestion that "prophets" should not be contrasted too sharply with
the traditional "wise men" defines the term "intellectual" better: A. G. Auld, "Poetry,
Prophecy, Hermeneutic: Recent Studies in Isaiah," *SJT* 33 (1980), 581.

12. Cf., for instance, G. F. Hasel, "Major Recent Trends in Old Testament Theology,"
JSOT 31 (1985), 53.

appear from the scene and a new generation of scholars (that grew up under different circumstances) may take over.

Once such factors come into play the reigning model is steadily eroded and becomes more and more questionable until such time as it is experienced as irrelevant—at least by a section of the scholarly community. In the meantime other models start competing for acceptance until one of them succeeds in becoming the dominant model within (at least) a respected section of the scholarly community.

New Evidence That Undermined the Dominant Model

Two sorts of "evidence" began calling in question the dominant romantic-idealistic model of interpreting the Old Testament prophets. First, there was the evidence from archaeology, and second, the results of continued historical critical research.

The discovery that the phenomenon of "prophecy" was wide-spread in the ancient Near East called in question the assumption that Old [[6]] Testament prophecy was "unique" in its environment.[13] While some scholars hailed the discovery as the "missing link" in our knowledge[14] and some virtually identified the Old Testament prophets with ecstatics and mantics,[15] others spent much energy in demonstrating the real uniqueness of the individual Old Testament prophets in comparison with their Mesopotamian, Syrian and Canaanite "counterparts."[16]

The role assigned to archaeology in these debates tallies with and highlights the methodological assumptions of the model of rationality concerned. Archaeology, defined as "biblical archaeology," merely served to elucidate the (inherent meaning of the) biblical text, or to explain some or other phenomenon mentioned in the text,[17] while the text itself

13. The debate was opened with G. Dossin's "Une révélation du dieu Dagan à Terqa," *Revue d'assyriologie et d'archéologie orientale* 42 (1948), 125–134. See, for instance, H. B. Huffmon, "Prophecy in the Mari Letters," *BA* 31 (1968), 101–124; W. L. Moran, "New Evidence from Mari on the History of Prophecy," *Bib* 50 (1969), 15–56.

14. Cf. M. Noth, *Gesammelte Studien zum Alten Testament*, 1966³, 24: "Jetzt tritt uns in den Texten von Mari die ganz eindeutige Gestalt eines Gottesboten entgegen . . ." [['Now the quite unmistakable form of a divine messenger meets us in the Mari texts']].

15. The "road" to this equation was already paved by G. Hölscher, *Die Propheten*, 1914. But see H. H. Rowley's sceptical remarks in this regard in his "Ritual and the Hebrew Prophets" in: *From Moses to Qumran: Studies in the Old Testament*, 1963, 114–115.

16. Cf. Y. Kaufmann, *The Religion of Israel*, 1960, 212–216.

17. Typical of this approach is the question: "Who borrowed from whom?" and the consequent definition of "culture" as a list of "traits" that can easily be compared to cultural "traits" of other cultures. See, for instance, A. Haldar, *Associations of Cult Prophets among the Ancient Semites*, 1945; V. W. Rabi, "Origins of Prophecy," *BASOR* 221 (1976), 125–128, who still works with the old "cultural parallels concept." See already the warning of H. Frankfort, *The Problem of Similarity in Ancient Near Eastern Religions*, 1951, against the drawing of "parallels" between religious institutions.

remained the main source of (historical) information.[18] So, for instance, the Mesopotamian prophets, having been professional or "cult prophets," explained the phenomenon of "false prophets" mentioned in the Old Testament. Debates therefore tended to focus on the "prophetic consciousness" of the "true" prophets, and on their calling to the *office* of prophet, an office which scholars took great pains to sever from any known traditional (social) institution.[19] The prophets were now pictured as God's ambassadors[20] and as "lonely figures" without followers and friends.[21] In this way (the notion of) the "uniqueness" of the Old [[7]] Testament writing prophets could be retained—even if by way of a "conventional twist" or "No-true-Scotsman argument."

But the picture of the prophets thus drawn seemed to be without sociological foundation, since no idea can survive without the aid of support groups.[22] To counter this problem the idea of "prophetic disciple circles" was advanced—a rather *ad hoc* invention for which there is neither firm (contemporary) textual nor sociological evidence[23]—and which once more threatened the notion of the uniqueness of the prophets.[24] Moreover, this use of archaeological data and (ad hoc) assumptions

18. Cf. K. V. Flannery, "Culture History vs. Culture Process: A Debate in American Archaeology," *Scientific American* 217 (1967), 119–122.

19. Cf. Th. C. Vriezen, *Hoofdlijnen der theologie van het Oude Testament*, 1966², 250ff.; W. H. Schmidt, *Alttestamentlicher Glaube*, 224.

20. Cf. F. Ellermeier's critique of the notion of the prophets as "messengers" in his *Prophetie in Mari und Israel*, 1968, 190–193.

21. So H. W. Wolff, op. cit., 21f.

22. Cf. R. R. Wilson, "Early Israelite Prophecy," *Int* 32 (1978), 8: "Without support from the society, or at least from a group within it, prophets can find no permanent place within the social order and are likely to be regarded simply as sick individuals who must be cured or expelled."

23. The same applies to quite a number of assumptions with regard to the social role of prophets. So, for instance, F. J. Stendenbach, op. cit., 3 explains the relationship of the *nābîʾ* [['prophet']] to the *ḥōzæh* [['seer of visions']] with reference to social institutions of sedentary and nomadic cultures respectively. But it is a wide open question whether the "nomadic origin theory" with regard to Israel is legitimate. (For further theories on the relationship between these two concepts, see G. Fohrer, "Neue Literatur zur alttestamentlichen Prophetie (1961–1970)," *ThR* 40 [1975], 365–369.) The common notion of the "nomadic" society as "egalitarian" has been challenged by G. Palumbo, "'Egalitarian' or 'Stratified' Society? Some Notes on Mortuary Practices and Social Structure at Jericho in EB IV," *BASOR* 267 (1987), 43–59.

24. In like manner different cultural "parallels" of the prophetic "office" have been suggested, e.g., the prophet as "messenger" or "herald" (J. S. Holladay, "Assyrian Statecraft and Prophets in Israel," *HTR* 63 [1970], 29–51) of the "heavenly council" (F. M. Cross Jr., *Canaanite Myth and Hebrew Epic*, 1973, 189 n. 187). Without a specific model of the relevant society to guide the hypotheses it was fairly easy to "invent" the role of the prophet. Cf., for

about the workings of Israelite society came in for some serious criticism since the late 1960s.[25] In the meantime continued historical critical research eroded the *textual* basis on which the classical picture of Old Testament prophets had been based. Firstly, although its extremism and somewhat "wild" assumptions prevented it from becoming a serious contender of literary criticism, the "Scandinavian" emphasis on the role of oral transmission and the consequent idea of the exilic (even post-exilic) *Verschriftlichung* [['putting into writing']] of pre-exilic traditions did cause scholars to have second thoughts about [[8]] the "originality" of the *written* prophetic words.[26] Yet, in some sense the idea of oral transmission came as a relief. It now seemed possible to reconstruct the *ipsissima verba* of the prophets in cases where literary criticism failed to do so. The prophets were, after all, speakers, not writers. But the relief was short-lived, since a serious debate on "oral literature," which has up to this day not rebated, questioned this solution.[27] The anthropological fact that each instance of oral transmission of (part of) a tradition, rather than producing a faithful copy of that tradition, constitutes a new *performance*, seriously queried the reliability of such reconstructions.[28]

Secondly, research into the speech forms employed by the prophets showed that they, for nearly three centuries, must have been employing stereotyped expressions and forms,[29] and that many of these forms were borrowings from or modelled upon speech forms employed in other

---

instance, the way in which Huffmon ("The Origins of Prophecy" in F. M. Cross Jr., *Magnalia Dei*, 1976, 171–186) simply assumed that the role of *šōpēṭ* [['judge']] had been "redistributed" into the roles of the *nābîʾ* [['prophet']] (the charismatic messenger) and the *mælæk* [['king']] (the permanent war leader).

25. Cf. C. L. v. W. Scheepers, *Argeologie en die Abrahamtradisies: 'n Wetenskapsfilosofiese beoordeling van die metodologie van John van Seters*, Th.D. thesis (University of South Africa), 1988, 46–86.

26. Cf. the fairly "harsh" clash between I. Engnell and S. Mowinckel on this issue in S. Mowinckel, *Prophecy and Tradition. The Prophetic Books in the Light of the Story of the History and Growth of the Tradition*, 1946, 88, and Eissfeldt's concurrence with Mowinckel's views in O. Eissfeldt, "Zur Überlieferungsgeschichte der Prophetenbücher des Alten Testaments," *ThLZ* 73 (1948), 532. Yet, Mowinckel (op. cit., 87, 112) regarded Eissfeldt's efforts to disentangle the original words of Jeremiah from the "Urrolle" as "without prospects."

27. Cf. A. H. J. Gunneweg, *Mündliche und schriftliche Tradition der vorexilischen Prophetenbücher als Problem der neueren Prophetenforschung*, 1959, and the debate on oral forms published in *Semeia* 5 (1976).

28. See R. Finegan, *Oral Poetry. Its Nature, Significance and Social Context*, 1977, who discusses the complex interrelations between performance, composition, transmission and publication.

29. Which is peculiarly "uncreative" for men who are supposed to have been driven by the Spirit and to have been "unique" figures.

spheres of life, e.g., juridical and wisdom spheres.[30] Thirdly, it became apparent that the typical linguistic shape of many of the prophetical books and thought forms occurring in them show strong affinity with typically Deuteronomistic forms,[31] while other (non-prophetic) texts show signs of a post-exilic "prophetic" redaction.[32] It became clear that [[9]] the prophetic texts provide us neither with a mirror of genuine prophetic thought nor with a picture of their times.[33] Even the *Denkschrift* [['memoir']] of Isaiah, which had been a *locus classicus* [['classic passage']] for "unique prophetic consciousness,"[34] for "prophetic calling," and for the existence of "circles of disciples" was shown to be a Deuteronomistic creation of exilic times.[35] Moreover, even the *term* "prophet," which formed the corner stone of the whole quest, was shown to have been a late, even *ex post factum* [['after the fact']] (exilic–post-exilic) interpretation of fig-ures of pre-exilic times. And then this interpretation varies between, for instance, Deuteronomistic and Chronistic circles.[36]

Changing Assumptions

Although the terms of reference keep on changing, the medieval debate of nominalism versus realism remains an issue at the basis of many

---

30. See R. R. Wilson, op. cit., 7f., 15; G. M. Tucker, "Prophetic Speech," *Int* 32 (1978), 33. Many "parallels" of prophetic speech have been suggested, the most popular of which was the so-called "messenger speech" (cf. C. Westermann, *Basic Forms of Prophetic Speech,* 1967, 64–70).

31. See J. Muilenburg, "The 'Office' of the Prophet in Ancient Israel" in: J. Philip Hyatt (ed.), *The Bible and Modern Scholarship,* Nashville, 1965, 74–97; A. G. Auld, op. cit., 15. Cf. also L. Brodie, "Creative Writing: Missing Link in Biblical Research," *BTB* 8 (1978), 34–39.

32. Cf. H.-C. Schmitt, "Redaktion des Pentateuchs im Geiste der Prophetie," *VT* 32 (1982), 170–189. Cf. also O. Eissfeldt, *Kleine Schriften.* Bd. IV, 1968, 137–142, according to whom the prophets gained in "stature" the further history moved away from the actual time of the prophets.

33. More and more studies tended to find "reinterpretation" of prophetic words within the book published under the name of the relevant prophet. See, for instance, H. Barth, *Die Jesajaworte in der Josiazeit: Israel und Assur als Thema einer produktiven Neuinterpretation der Jesajaüberlieferung,* 1977; J. Vermeylen, *Du Prophète Isaïe à l'apocalyptique: Isaïe I–XXXV, miroir d'un demi-millénaire d'expérience réligieuse en Israël,* Vol. II, 1978 (who finds seven layers of text in Proto-Isaiah); J. Blenkinsopp, *Prophecy and Canon: A Contribution to the Study of Jewish Origins,* 1977 (who finds that 75% of "Isaiah's" book is editorial in nature). See also A. Rofé, "The Classification of the Prophetical Stories," *JBL* 89 (1970), 432–440.

34. So still J. Asurmendi, "Isaïe dans son temps: Isaïe et la politique," *MDB* 49 (Mai–Juin–Juil. 1987), 32–34, 36–37.

35. See A. G. Auld, "Poetry, Prophecy, Hermeneutic: Recent Studies in Isaiah," *SJT* 33 (1980), 575, who refers to Isaiah 6–8 as "an elaborate portrait, not a lightly touched-up personal memoir." O. Kaiser, *Das Buch des Propheten Jesaja, Kapitel 1–12,* ATD 17, 1981[5], 117–209 goes much further. According to him the complete "Memoir" is a Deuteronomistic creation.

36. See B. Vawter, "Were the Prophets Nabîʾs?" *Bib* 66 (1985), 206–220, and especially A. G. Auld, *JSOT* 27 (1978), 3–23 [[reprinted in this volume, pp. 289–307]].

a scholarly controversy. It also presented itself in the opposition Hegel-Marx: is "spirit" the basic driving force of human evolution or is it "matter"? Do we have to think in terms of human freedom or in terms of determinism? Since 19th- and early 20th-century historical-critical scholarship had (as an outcome of the *Methodenstreit*?) mainly been based on idealistic philosophy it was inevitable that its basic assumptions (idealism-freedom) would be taken to task by the rival model of materialism-determinism.

⟦10⟧ The rise of the social sciences contributed a great deal to the questioning of the dominant model of rationality. Sociology, with its empirico-positivist slant, and (ethno-)anthropology in particular, sped up the "controversy." The work of the *Annales* school of historiography, materialist critique of religion, Marx's concept of "ideology," Weber's treatise on Israelite religion, and Mannheim's sociology of knowledge epitomized the formation of an alternative model of rationality.

Another movement which questioned the dominant model, although it was not that directly opposed to (romantic) idealism as was materialism, was the rise of the (phenomenological) concept of *Gestalt* or holism-functionalism, according to which it is not the parts that contribute to the meaning(fulness) of the whole, but the whole that imparts meaning to its constituent members. Within this frame of mind it is not evolution but function that constitutes meaning. This approach gave rise to the so-called "systems theories" in the social sciences and to the so-called "immanent" reading of texts in the literary sciences.

As long as the proponents of the idealistic model of rationality remained the (only) leaders of the Old Testament scholarly community that model remained the dominant one. But once the basis of Old Testament scholarship was broadened and internationalized, "rival" models started presenting themselves, and notably so since the 1960s. It is since those years that historical criticism as an *exegetical procedure* was coming under fire and has been criticized for "asking the wrong questions." Since much of the earlier criticism could be countered by pointing out its fundamentalist assumptions its impact has not been that strong. When criticism of a more sound theoretical nature was later launched, its impact was "absorbed" by the (perhaps somewhat uncritical) acceptance of the distinction diachronic-synchronic[37] and by viewing this duality in approach as a "necessary supplementation" of traditional historical critical methods.

---

37. Cf. F. E. Deist, "Relatiwisme en absolutisme: Kan dit oorkom word? Oor 'Bybelse' en 'dogmatiese' teologie" in W. S. Prinsloo and W. Vosloo (eds.), *Ou Testament Teologie: Gister, Vandag en Môre*, 1987, 4, 7f.

Perhaps the most unacknowledged, yet most serious, challenge to the dominant model of rationality emanated from the political process of de-colonialization, which started in the 1960s and "produced" the so-called "Third World" with its peculiar socio-economic problems. These problems necessitated an emphasis on society-oriented academic work and gave birth to liberation theology.[38] The dominant model of rationality in this part of the world is of a Marxist-materialist orientation, [[11]] according to which it is not ideas that shape a people's socio-political destiny, but socio-political realities that shape ideas (ideologies). This emphasis on the creative role of everyday social realities was a major factor in the emergence of a *real* alternative to the dominant model of rationality.

Linked to the influence of the emerging "Third World" are three other (series of) events that helped shape an alternative model of rationality. Firstly, mention has to be made of the demand of European student movements during the late 1960s and early 1970s for "democratization" of (at least) educational institutions. These socially engaged movements shared in the basic philosophy which has since become dominant in the Third World. Secondly, there was a gradual realization in the First as well as in the Third World of the effects of colonialization and decolonialization on the lives of millions of people around the world, and linked to that, the experience in the Third World of neo-colonialism's economic hegemony which led to the rejection of liberal Western values. Thirdly, there was the (First World) disillusionment with the effects of (capitalist) "civilization" on the environment and on the world's natural resources.[39] It is argued that idealistically conceived policies caused most of the environmental problems we are confronted with. Whether criticism launched against the "First World" from these angles is legitimate, is not important here. What is important, is that this *conception* of the effects of First World policies contributed to the serious questioning of the dominant model of rationality.

New Questions That Caused Uneasiness

The results of ongoing textual research within the framework of the dominant model posed questions that could hardly be satisfactorily answered within that framework. For instance, if the texts published under the prophets' names contain very few real "prophetic words," if the re-

38. To be mentioned here as well is the rise of feminist theology. See, for instance, C. Landman, "A Profile of Feminist Theology" in W. S. Vorster (ed.), *Sexism and Feminism in Theological Perspective*, 1984, 1–30.

39. T. A. Matias, "The Bible, Ecology, and the Environment," *ITS* 22 (1985), 5–27; K. Nürnberger, "Ecology and Christian Ethics in a Semi-industrialised and Polarized Society" in W. S. Vorster (ed.), *Are We Killing God's Earth?* 1987, 45–67.

construction of "oral tradition" from literary texts is not really reliable, if the picture of a "prophet" in Deuteronomistic texts differs fairly substantially from that in Chronistic texts, if "prophet" really is an *ex post factum* [['after the fact']] title, if the distinction between "true" and "false" prophets was only possible *ex eventu* [['after the event']] and if the designation of the "classical prophets" as "true prophets" is to be ascribed to Deuteronomistic editors and not to prophetic consciousness as such, what then was a *prophet*? Did the "prophets" occupy any office in society? How are the "prophetic words" regarding social, economic and political issues [[12]] to be evaluated? What was the real role of those figures in the shaping of Israelite religion? In what sense are they to be regarded as "unique"? And can we really speak of "prophetic circles" and of a prophet's "disciples" if the *locus classicus* [['classic passage']] for these assumptions is not "genuine"? Why would the Deuteronomists, whose theology so extensively "called in" corroborating prophetic words, keep silent about prophets like Amos, Hosea and Micah?[40]

These *historical* questions cannot be answered effectively unless one has a clear idea of the societies in which the "prophets" lived and in which the prophetic texts had been produced. But the dominant model cannot really supply the answers to such questions, because it does not look at a phenomenon (such as prophecy) or at a text from the side of social realities.[41] Even the concept of *Sitz im Leben* [['life situation']] has far too narrow a scope to answer these questions.

It is perhaps for this reason that lateral, rather than vertical, thought has been applied to the problem, that is, scholars tended to "side-step" the (socio-anthropological) problem by focussing more and more on the finished product, the "final/canonical text."[42] The clearer it became that *these questions* threatened to invalidate the model of rationality the more *that kind of question* was made suspicious or labeled "unanswerable." Perhaps these questions cannot be answered adequately by merely (or even primarily) focussing on the *texts*. Research in, for instance, the growth of the text of the Septuagint showed that the concept "final/canonical text"

---

40. Cf. C. Begg, "The Non-mention of Amos, Hosea, and Micah in the Deuteronomistic History," *BN* 32 (1986), 41–53. If the Deuteronomists could ignore some prophets because their message did not fit in with their theology—as Begg argues convincingly—they could as well have "blown up" others beyond all proportion, so that their picture of "prophets" cannot be historically reliable.

41. See, for instance, W. McKane, "Prophecy and the Prophetic Literature" in G. W. Anderson, *Tradition and Interpretation. Essays by Members of the Society for Old Testament Study,* Oxford, 1979, 163–188, whose review of scholarly study on the prophets reflects the typically idealistic interest of the dominant model in the "intellectual" side of prophecy.

42. Cf. R. P. Carroll, "Poets Not Prophets," 28.

is a very problematic one,[43] and that one needs to have some idea of the religious communities in which texts were being edited to get a clearer picture of the processes involved in textual production.[44] ⟦13⟧ An "escape" into the "final" or "canonical text" thus neither enables us to answer the questions thrown up by the dominant model itself, nor to answer the question of prophetic authority.[45]

Another pressing question is this: Given the fact that the prophets and their message have over decades been reinterpreted within, and therefore familiarized with, the framework of the typically Western thought categories of the dominant model, can their words and actions really still *challenge* the Western World?[46]

The Disappearance of Proponents of the Dominant Model

In the context of Old Testament studies there are two factors to be mentioned in this regard. Firstly, whereas the scene had pretty well been dominated by German scholarship until the 1960s,[47] Old Testament scholarship has become a much more international affair since. American scholars entered the debate on a much larger scale, especially so after the dominance of the "Albright school" has to a large extent been overcome in that part of the world. It was chiefly the English writing world (with its less philosophical and more pragmatic slant) that stimu-

43. See, for instance, E. Tov, "Recensional Differences between the MT and LXX of Ezekiel," *ETL* 62 (1986), 89–101; H.-D. Neef, "Der Septuaginta-Text und der Masoreten-Text des Hoseabuches im Vergleich," *Bib* 67 (1986), 195–220; E. Tov, "Some Differences between the MT and LXX and Their Ramifications for the Literary Criticism of the Bible," *JNSL* 13 (1987), 151–160.

44. See F. E. Deist, *Witnesses to the Old Testament. Introducing Old Testament Textual Criticism*, 1988, where the question regarding the "identity" of the concepts "Old Testament" and "Hebrew Bible" and its implications for the concept of "canon" are discussed extensively.

45. For instance, B. S. Childs, "The Canonical Shape of Prophetic Literature," *Int* 32 (1978), 47 speaks about an (anonymous) "force" that shaped prophetic literature, a force that was exerted in especially the post-exilic period and that "allowed" the material to function as authoritative Scripture and to serve as a normative expression of God's will to later generations. Earlier generations linked that "force" to the inspiration of the prophets themselves. What do we have to understand under this "canonical force"? The problem with this approach seems to be little different from the problem F. Hesse ("Kerygma oder geschichtliche Wirklichkeit? Kritische Fragen zu Gerhard von Rads 'Theologie des Alten Testaments, I. Teil,'" *ZThK* 57 [1960], 17–20) had with von Rad's concentration on the "vom Glauben Israels erstelltes Bild" ⟦'picture supplied by Israel's faith'⟧ (*Theologie des Alten Testaments*, 1969, Bd. 1, 112).

46. See, especially, L. Newbigin, *Foolishness to the Greeks. The Gospel and Western Culture*, 1986.

47. See J. Rogerson, *Old Testament Criticism in the Nineteenth Century*, 1984, for an elaborate argument to this effect.

lated interest in the application of anthropological and sociological insights to Old Testament studies, including prophecy.

Secondly, the old masters, such as Alt, Noth, von Rad, Eissfeldt and other prominent exponents of the dominant model of rationality, passed away the one after the other. It is perhaps significant that no really comprehensive and fundamentally *new* history of Israel or Old ⟦14⟧ Testament theology has appeared after the death of the masters.[48] Even on the front of exegetical methods and introductions to the Old Testament the scene remained relatively unchanged, except for more precision in the description of the various exegetical procedures involved[49] and for difference of opinion regarding the redactional history of the different books of the Bible—although the later dating of most of the Old Testament in the newer introductions tended to undermine the foundations of the dominant model, especially with regard to prophetic texts.

An Alternative Paradigm?[50]

If we have traced the history of Old Testament research correctly it shows all the signs of a fundamental questioning of a dominant paradigm. This does not mean that the dominant paradigm has lost its credibility altogether, nor that it is on its way out, or that a new paradigm will (in the near future) be substituted for it. Even in liberation theological circles the classical writing prophets are sometimes still being interpreted in terms of a romantic-historicist paradigm. What it does mean, is that, because of its philosophical basis and consequent ideological bias, the dominant model is (at least in certain parts of the world) experienced as incapable of asking meaningful questions and of suggesting credible solutions to pressing existential problems.[51] It is for this reason that an alternative paradigm, based on different assumptions, is in the making.

Given a different experience of reality, world view and model of rationality it is inevitable that new questions will arise, for instance, questions such as the following: What did the Israelite society of the 8th, 7th

---

48. What N. P. Lemche said about the classical paradigm of critical historiography ("Rachel and Lea. Or: On the Survival of Outdated Paradigmas in the Study of the Origin of Israel," *SJOT* 2 [1987], 128), namely that people like Alt and Noth, while producing the classical "histories," also undermined the paradigm they had been utilizing, also applies here.

49. The classical example here is W. Richter, *Exegese als Literaturwissenschaft*, 1971.

50. See, in this regard, J. K. Hadden and A. Shupe (eds.), *Prophetic Religions and Politics. Religion and the Political Order*, Vol. 1, 1984, and especially the contribution to the volume by T. E. Long, "Prophecy, Charisma, and Politics: Reinterpreting the Weberian Thesis," 3–17.

51. See R. Robertson, "Liberation Theology in Latin America: Sociological Problems of Interpretation and Explanation" in J. K. Hadden and A. Shupe, op. cit., 73–102.

and 6th century look like?[52] What societal model would best [[15]] describe those societies?[53] What were the material conditions under which people had to live?[54] What exactly prompted prophets to speak out?[55] Who made up their audiences? From which "layer" of society did they come? Was there a social institution such as "prophet"? If so, where did this office fit into the structure of society? If not, who were these prophets? What was the prophet's position with regard to socio-economic and political hegemony/oppression/ideology, i.e., what made up their ideology? If they really were people from the "middle classes" who could read and write, can they then be viewed as "liberators" and "champions of the poor"?[56] Or is such a view merely suggested to us by the liberal values of modern readers? Who were the readers/makers of the "prophetic books"? Why were these figures pictured so differently by the Deuteronomists and the Chronist? Is there any ideological reason for this difference? Who were "the Deuteronomists" and who was "the Chronist" and what were their respective positions in society?[57] These questions have to do with the societal forces that "produced" the people who later became known as "prophets" and with the ideological nature of their pronouncements.

52. Cf. G. Ravasi, "Old Testament Political Theology," *TD* 31 (1984), 3–7, who empha-sizes the complicated nature of Israelite politics and the plurality of methods used in that society to seize power. Also E. Haag, "The Prophet: Yahweh's 'opposition,' " *TD* 31 (1984), 33–36, who speaks of quite a number of "pockets of opposition" that resisted kingship and its adherents. It would thus be naive to work with a simple classical Marxist model of "class conflict" to explain the workings of Israelite society. Cf. Deist's criticism of Hanson's "bi-nary" classification of exilic Israel into just two groups in F. E. Deist, "Prior to the Dawn of Apocalyptic," *OTWSA* 26 (1983), 13–38.

53. Cf. S. H. Lindar and B. G. Peters, "From Social Theory to Policy Design," *Journal of Public Policy* 4 (1984), 251, where they warn against what they call "nominal functional titles" used to label problems. The complexities of any society call for models that reflect such complexities and nuances and that allow for more precise description.

54. Cf. C. C. Smith, "The Birth of Bureaucracy," *BA* 40 (1977), 24–28 for the impact of bureaucratization on the Assyrian society. See also N. E. Andreasen, "Town and Country in the Old Testament," *Enc* 42 (1981), 259–275—although one has to be careful not to over-emphasize this social distinction.

55. Cf. R. R. Deutsch, "Why Did the Hebrew Prophets Speak?" *SEAsiaJT* 18 (1977), 26–36, who comes to the conclusion that the "driving force" behind prophetic speech has to be sought in the individual's *conscious reflection* on the people's total (historical, economic, so-cial, spiritual) situation, and that a particular *understanding* of this situation forms the basis of the "prophetic consciousness."

56. See I. J. Mosala, "The Use of the Bible in Black Theology" in I. J. Mosala and B. Tlhagale, *The Unquestionable Right to Be Free*, 1985, 194ff.

57. See R. P. Carroll, "Poets Not Prophets," 27: ". . . the role of the redactor's ideology will . . . be seen as having a much more creative and constructive part to play in the emer-gence of the traditions than has often been allowed in the past."

These questions also prompt other, critical, questions regarding the accepted view of Old Testament prophets. For instance: Was "prophecy" really a "unique" phenomenon? Was the prophets' main concern really [16] with theoretical religious issues such as monotheism,[58] and concepts such as the covenant? What are the social referents of words like justice, righteousness, sin, iniquity, etc.[59] in the mouth of a prophet like Amos, or Isaiah, or Jeremiah?

Since the concern of these questions is with the relevant *societies* and (changing) *societal structures* of Old Testament times and with the everyday *socio-economic* life of those days, another strategy is called for to answer them. And the necessary strategies are being supplied by sociological and anthropological models.[60]

This does *not* imply that historical critical *exegetical procedures* are being rejected.[61] On the contrary, literary criticism and redaction criticism are still necessary procedures for reconstructing the growth of the prophetical books. But the results of the application of these procedures to the texts may differ from "classical" results, because the model of rationality of the exegete now differs from that of exegetes operating within the classical model.[62] Moreover, the results are now also being interpreted within the framework of a different hermeneutical model and employed to answer a different set of questions.

The rise of an alternative paradigm is not only indicated by new questions put and alternative heuristic strategies employed in respect of the biblical text. It is also epitomized by a radical change in direction from "old archaeology" to "new archaeology."[63] "Biblical archaeology" has emancipated itself from the position of adding footnotes to the

58. See, for instance, E. Haag (Hrsg.), *Gott der Einzige. Zur Entstehung des Monotheismus,* 1985, where the debate is continued.

59. See J. T. Bunn, "Sin, Iniquity, Transgression: What Is the Difference?" *BibIll* 12 (1986), 77–79.

60. Cf. R. R. Wilson, *Sociological Approaches to the Old Testament,* 1984; F. S. Frick, "Social Science Methods and Theories of Significance for the Study of the Israelite Monarchy," *Semeia* 37 (1986), 9–52; J. H. le Roux, "Some Remarks on Sociology and Ancient Israel," *Old Testament Essays* 3 (1985), 12–16; G. A. Herion, "Sociological and Anthropological Methods in Old Testament Study," *Old Testament Essays* 5 (1987), 43–64. Given the fact that the Israelite society was in a process of constant change it is evident that the application of one model will not provide "the answer" with regard to that society. See C. Hauer (Jr.), "From Alt to Anthropology: The Rise of the Israelite Monarchy," *JSOT* 36 (1986), 3–15.

61. Cf. W. H. Schmidt, "Grenzen und Vorzüge historisch-kritischer Exegese. Eine kleine Verteidigungsrede," *EvTh* 45 (1985), 469–481.

62. Cf. F. E. Deist, "Idealistic *Theologiegeschichte,* Ideology Critique and the Dating of Oracles of Salvation. Posing a Question regarding an Accepted Methodology," *OTWSA* 23 (1980), 53–78.

63. Cf. K. W. Whitelam, "Recreating the History of Israel," *JSOT* 35 (1986), 45–70.

biblical text to a position of a fairly independent 〚17〛 discipline.[64] New archaeology equally asks questions about the (changing) social, economic and political *systems* in which *ordinary* people lived in ancient days, and about the forces that changed those systems. And it is in the results of new Syro-Palestinian archaeology that the alternative paradigm is interested in the first place. The application of this or that anthropological and sociological model to relevant archaeological findings provides the answers to the question as to what sort of society functioned in a particular period.

The rise of an alternative paradigm is also witnessed to by a steadily increasing body of literature over the past decade or so on the sociological interpretation of Old Testament texts, also prophetic texts.[65] Much depends, of course, on what kind of sociological or anthropological theory is employed in answering the new questions—just as much depends on what kind of literary theory is employed in order to reconstruct the supposed (inherent) meaning of the (final/canonical) biblical text. Much of the criticism launched against the application (or even applicability) of sociological and anthropological models in Old Testament studies comes from academics working within the dominant model of rationality.[66] Such criticisms may be to the point, but may also miss the point completely, because the mere questions asked within the alternative model may seem irrelevant from the viewpoint of the dominant model. Moreover, within the Kuhnian view, there is something like the incommensurability of models, i.e., the questions, procedures and answers of one model cannot simply be compared with those of another, transferred from the one to the other, or evaluated in terms of one another.

64. Cf. W. G. Dever, "Syro-Palestinian and Biblical Archaeology ca. 1945–1980" in D. A. Knight and G. M. Tucker, *The Hebrew Bible and Its Modern Interpreters*, 1982; R. B. Coote and K. W. Whitelam, *The Emergence of Early Israel in Historical Perspective*, 1987, especially the first and last chapters.

65. Cf. J. S. Kselman, "The Social World of the Israelite Prophets. A Review Article," *RelSRev* 11 (1985), 120–129; M. L. Chaney, "Systemic Study of the Israelite Monarchy," *Semeia* 37 (1986), 53–76; N. K. Gottwald, "The Participation of Free Agrarians in the Introduction of Monarchy to Ancient Israel: An Application of H. A. Landsberger's Framework for the Analysis of Peasant Movements," *Semeia* 37 (1986), 77–106. Also W. Brueggemann, "Theodicy in a Social Dimension," *JSOT* 33 (1985), 3–25.

66. This remark does, of course, not refer to all such criticism. See, for instance, R. P. Carroll, "Prophecy and Society," in R. E. Clements, *The World of Ancient Israel: Social, Anthropological and Political Perspectives*, to be published 1989 〚Cambridge: Cambridge University Press〛, who is very sceptical about the reconstruction of Israelite society from the biblical *texts*—and perhaps rightly so, but who devotes little attention to the possible contribution of new and regional archaeology in this regard. See also P. Laslett, "The Wrong Way through the Telescope: A Note on Literary Evidence in Sociology and in Historical Sociology," *British Journal of Sociology* 27 (1976), 319–342.

⟦18⟧ Although this "new look" at Israelite society is still in the making and although much work still has to be done, the prophets, if studied within this framework, may undergo a sort of "personality change."[67] For instance, the prophet Elijah has traditionally been pictured fairly "deuteronomistically" as *the* bold giant among the prophets,[68] and as *the* proponent of ethical mono-Yahwism/monotheism. But a reconstruction of his life along the lines of the alternative paradigm pictures him as an honest, but naive, spokesman for an alienated section of Israelite society, and as a person who, without any insight into the sociological forces he was unleashing by his activities, caused the downfall of exactly those people (and ideals) he sought to serve.[69]

This picture of Elijah, if valid, may suggest that the sharp distinction between prophet and priest,[70] and between "true" and "false" prophets,[71] as well as the traditional picturing of the priests and the "professional prophets" as the villains, may be in need of serious rethinking. It may also be calling for a serious rethinking not only of the nature of (early) prophecy, but also of the so-called "prophetic task" of the church in modern society—an accepted role which is fairly exclusively modelled on the romantic picture of the prophets created by the dominant model.

---

67. See already J. Negenman, "Het interpreteren van de profetische literatuur," *Tijdschrift voor Theologie* 15 (1975), 117–140, who defined "a prophet" as "een perzoon die zich geroepen voelt om te zeggen wat *volgens hem* authentieke religie inhoud" ⟦'a person who feels himself called to say what *according to him* is the content of authentic religion'⟧ (p. 124—emphasis added), and who already drew the lines between "true" and "false" prophets much less boldly than had been the case in Old Testament scholarship in general. See also T. R. Hobbs, "The Search for Prophetic Consciousness," *BTB* 15 (1985), 136–140, who thinks it fit to seek along social lines for the "origin" of prophetic consciousness.

68. Cf. R. Rendtorff, "Erwägungen zur Frühgeschichte des Prophetentums in Israel," *ZThK* 59 (1962), 145–167.

69. F. E. Deist, "Israel in a Period of Change," in F. E. Deist and J. H. le Roux, op. cit., 47–103.

70. Cf. P. Volz's very sharp distinction between priest and prophet in his *Prophetengestalten des Alten Testaments*, 1938, 56.

71. Although H. H. Rowley, op. cit., 130, already warned against an all too neat distinction between these two "groups."

Present Trends and
Future Directions

ROBERT P. GORDON

Any attempt to forecast the direction of prophets study in the next few decades is likely to consist mainly of extrapolation on present trends, and risks steering a wavering course between the speculative and the mildly prescriptive. Let us therefore concentrate in the first instance on the defining of what has been happening recently, with the help of the two "essayists" who have already featured in this section (pp. 579–99).[1] Schmidt and Deist, whose contributions are separated by no more than a decade, given that the German original of Schmidt's book was published in 1979, show an immense difference in their agendas for prophets study. It is not simply a question of chronology, since many academic studies of the prophets would still proceed on the assumption of the legitimacy of Schmidt's interests, prominent among which is the recovering of the words in which the original prophets expressed their ideas. For his part, Schmidt, without actually using the jargon of speech act theory, is asking the kind of question which forms part of its stock-in-trade, namely at what level (announcement? critique? exhortation?) the prophetic oracles of judgment were supposed to operate. But the question remains essentially an historical-critical one, being based on an assumption which is certainly unexceptionable from the present writer's point of view, namely that there are authentic prophetic words to be analyzed in this way.

Deist, who represents the "new broom" approach to the prophets, deals mainly in methodology as he explains his talk of a paradigm shift (or "switch") in the subject. The older paradigm was concerned with "uncovering the *inherent meaning* of a text," and naturally could not ask the

---

1. Schmidt's contribution, of course, represents a small part of a larger discussion in his chapter entitled "The Form of Prophecy."

newer type of question facilitated by a newer paradigm (in this volume, p. 586). Under the old rules the text itself remained the main source of historical information (in this volume, pp. 587–88), and it is this question of historical information, which the older text-based model of inquiry is judged incapable of supplying, that governs Deist's conception of the recent paradigm change. More surprisingly, even text-immanent approaches which bypass the historical questions are consigned to the older paradigm. The new is represented by socio-anthropological approaches and by "new archaeology," which is able to fulfil a similar role and is trustworthy because it does not attempt to confirm the biblical picture in a way that "biblical archaeology" is accused of doing. Sociology and anthropology are, of course, disciplines that are inclined to produce information that is capable of more than one interpretation, and, depending upon the sociologist or anthropologist, could even be found to be supportive of the biblical picture on occasion. Nor would it be difficult to find supporters of the new paradigm objecting to a socio-anthropological interpretation of evidence on the ground that it was agreeing with the biblical account rather than with a preferred reconstruction of it. The concern of the "new archaeology" with the socio-economic framework within which the prophets (for example) functioned cannot be other than welcome, but *a priori* conclusions about "new archaeology" being constitutionally subversive of the biblical data would be wrongheaded, whatever agreements or conflicts there were in practice. Moreover, the choice is not between "die Bibel hat doch recht" [['the Bible is right after all']] and a subversive alternative, as the fairly recent ventures into archaeological commentary on prophetic books show.[2] The program in this instance is not necessarily to prove the correctness of the biblical data but to illuminate the text by comparison (or conceivably contrast) with the material finds of archaeology.

Nonetheless, the idea of a paradigm shift in Old Testament prophets studies in the past couple of decades fairly reflects the situation as it is perceived by a good number of scholars. But "paradigm shift" as used here differs from what Deist means by the term, for the division is not simply between the text-related and the "text-extrinsic" (as anthropology, sociology, "new archaeology"), since that leaves the text-immanent approaches on the wrong side of the dividing-line. If the "paradigm shift"

2. Cf. P. J. King, *Amos, Hosea, Micah: An Archaeological Commentary* (Philadelphia: Westminster, 1988); *Jeremiah: An Archaeological Companion* (Louisville: Westminster/John Knox, 1993); G. I. Davies, "An Archaeological Commentary on Ezekiel 13," *Scripture and Other Artifacts* (ed. M. D. Coogan, J. C. Exum, and L. E. Stager; Louisville: Westminster/John Knox, 1994) 108–25. See also J. A. Burger, "Amos: A Historical-Geographical View," *JSem* 4 (1992) 130–50.

involves the abandoning of the text as a source of historical information, then the non-referential literary approaches currently much in vogue. belong with the "text-extrinsic" grouping. There are clear advantages in making the division in this way, first because the advent of the text-immanent approaches is sometimes also seen in terms of a paradigm shift,[3] and confusion is best avoided, secondly because discussion in terms merely of historicity is reductionistic, and thirdly because the present situation in prophets study is not to be seen simply as a response to a methodological or epistemological crisis. The current scholarly interest in the prophetic books as literature is not just in compensation for the alleged failure of the biblical text to supply the historical data which it purports to give. On the contrary, the impulse for much of the recent literary emphasis comes from outside the world of biblical studies, and, though the timing may be regarded as fortuitous, it did not come about as a crisis subvention intended to augment the dwindling returns of the historical-critical approach. If the talk of a paradigm shift is justified, as it probably is, it is not because old questions are being dressed up as new, but because new (generically different) questions are being made possible by newer approaches to the text. It is also good to remember that the "eclipse" of the older paradigm can be only partial, and that both the older and the newer approaches will be subject to scrutiny from either side.

The current phase of prophets study is, therefore, a multifaceted one, and it is difficult to imagine the discipline ever again being hogged by a single dominant approach as was the case for large areas of biblical scholarship in the era of the historical-critical method *solus*. In the present era of "older new" and "newer new" approaches[4] it is important that traditional interests have an assured place. To take but one example: our developing awareness of Near Eastern prophecy, already well advertised in the present volume, makes the limiting of attention to the final form of the prophetic texts difficult to defend. The formal comparisons that can be made between divination in Mesopotamia and certain aspects of Israelite prophecy also call for further investigation, in ways both traditional (e.g., form-critical) and modern (e.g., sociological). Again, it is a fine coincidence, if such it is, that the nation oracles of the earliest of the Israelite classical prophets (see Amos 1–2) assume internationally accepted standards of civilized behavior, and that the Mari prophecies

3. Cf. M. A. Powell, *The Bible and Modern Literary Criticism: A Critical Assessment and Annotated Bibliography* (New York: Greenwood, 1992) 3.

4. For the distinction see D. J. A. Clines and J. C. Exum, "The New Literary Criticism," in *The New Literary Criticism and the Hebrew Bible* (ed. J. C. Exum and D. J. A. Clines; JSOTSup 143; Sheffield: JSOT Press, 1993) 11–25.

have sufficient ethical content to support the idea of a "natural law" governing the attitudes of both Israel and her neighbors. While the chronological gap between Mari and Israel is large and the physical distance not insignificant, there will have been other "Maris" (e.g., Emar, Hamath) geographically and chronologically interposed between Zimri-Lim's Euphratean kingdom and first-millennium Israel. At the same time, there is point to Margaret Barker's claim that it makes more sense to try to establish "the inner nature of Israel's religion" from within the Israelite cultural domain, rather than by almost exclusive parallelism with non-Israelite tradition.[5] That her own findings are radical and controversial does not invalidate the inquiry or remove the possibility that, for example, some of the imagery used by Israelite prophets and psalmists may be better understood as a result of such inquiry.

If we consider the question of the *mode* of prophecy in recent discussion it will be to discover that several studies have emphasized in their different ways the written origin of parts of the Old Testament prophetic tradition.[6] This affects the later phase of the prophetic era and, if the several claims are taken together, would add up to a consistent picture of the way in which prophecy, and not just the work of individual prophets, developed in this later period. Floyd's conclusion, on the basis of his study of Hab 2:1–5, that "mantic writing" was one of the basic forms of prophetic activity[7] gives formal recognition to what has sometimes been envisaged for individual books or parts of them, but also opens up the possibility of a wider-ranging discussion. Written prophecy is preponderantly in the form of declamation—unidirectional speech in the name of God to the prophet's target audience—but, as already indicated in part 3 of this book, there are portions of the prophetic books that are dialogical in form. Jeremiah and Haggai have both been discussed from this standpoint.[8] There is also dialogue where changes of speaker are not indicated, but the proof of this in a given case may be more open to debate,

5. *The Older Testament: The Survival of Themes from the Ancient Royal Cult in Sectarian Judaism and Early Christianity* (London: SPCK, 1987) 125.

6. E. F. Davis, *Swallowing the Scroll: Textuality and the Dynamics of Discourse in Ezekiel's Prophecy* (JSOTSup 78; Sheffield: Almond, 1989); M. H. Floyd, "Prophecy and Writing in Habakkuk 2, 1–5," *ZAW* 105 (1993) 462–81; J. E. Tollington, *Tradition and Innovation in Haggai and Zechariah 1–8* (JSOTSup 150; Sheffield: JSOT Press, 1993); H. G. M. Williamson, *The Book Called Isaiah: Deutero-Isaiah's Role in Composition and Redaction* (Oxford: Clarendon, 1994).

7. Cf. Floyd, "Prophecy and Writing," 481 (summary).

8. See D. L. Petersen, "The Prophetic Process Reconsidered," *Iliff Review* 40 (1983) 13–19; J. T. Willis, "Dialogue between Prophet and Audience as a Rhetorical Device in the Book of Jeremiah," in this volume, pp. 205–22; L. Alonso Schökel, *A Manual of Hebrew Poetics* (Subsidia Biblica 11; Rome: Pontifical Biblical Institute, 1988) 170–77.

and the evidence so far is found mainly in Jeremiah and Micah.[9] More thorough investigation of this aspect of prophecy, which is presumably not just a literary device, may help towards a more accurate picture of the *modus operandi* of certain of the prophets, giving insight into the relationship between prophet and audience. There may also be advantage to be gained from further examination of those parts of the prophetic books that deal in narrative, not now out of interest in source or redactional questions but in order to establish how such sections function as narrative. Amos 7:(9)10–17, for example, has been much discussed in recent literature from a number of different angles, but its inclusion in a collection of visions and oracles should not disqualify it from a narratological reading, which, moreover, could affect our appreciation of its internal coherence and—though this does not automatically follow—its value as a tradition about the prophet Amos. There is possibly scope for further narratological study of otherwise well-trodden areas of prophetic narrative in Isaiah and Jeremiah especially, even if the results are not necessarily as striking as with the little book of Jonah, whose few chapters have inspired a remarkable amount of recent writing. Whether narrative study of this sort can in any way be related to the "implied narrative" that Gottwald finds running through the whole prophetic corpus is perhaps worth investigating.[10]

Future study of the prophetic books will doubtless continue to encompass the language of the books, whether from the standpoint of a broadly descriptive linguistics approach or with attention focused on a particular form of speech such as metaphor. Neither interest is special to the prophetic literature, of course, though the prophets are very free with metaphor and some recent studies have dealt illuminatively with the subject, not least in Ezekiel where interest generally has been growing steadily after the book's long-standing neglect in comparison with Isaiah and Jeremiah. The fundamental questions about what the prophets intended by their use of declamatory language in judgment speeches are also still highly discussible, and, since basically the same issue is raised in connection with the symbolic acts of the prophets, a broader discussion embracing both the spoken and the acted seems a logical development.

Approaches to the biblical text that fall into the category of "reader response" vary in their usefulness (*sic*—for why otherwise should a personal or community reading be published?), as will be the case in any

9. Cf. Willis, "Dialogue" (in this volume, pp. 205–22); Alonso Schökel, *A Manual of Hebrew Poetics*, 172–73; A. S. van der Woude, "Micah in Dispute with the Pseudo-Prophets," *VT* 19 (1969) 244–60 (esp. 249–55).

10. N. K. Gottwald, "Tragedy and Comedy in the Latter Prophets," *Semeia* 32 (1984 [1985]) 83–96.

branch of the discipline. But what their practitioners and all students of the prophets should consider seriously is not just the extent to which a method employs currently accepted reading strategies but also in what ways the implementation of the particular approach or method helps Old Testament study to make its contribution to the larger theological enterprise. This is one important reason why the more traditional approaches must not be submerged in a deluge of self-indulgent new readings of texts, strong in whimsy and individualistic observation, but offering no solid planks leading from the Old Testament to adjacent territory. Post-biblical Judaism, New Testament studies and Christian theology, to name but three, are areas of scholarly endeavor that will habitually look to the Old Testament, courtesy of its specialists, for some account of its own institutions and beliefs as a starting-point for their pursuit of their respective agendas.

INDEX OF AUTHORITIES

INDEX OF SCRIPTURE

Scripture is indexed according to English chapter and verse divisions; where the Hebrew versification differs, Hebrew chapter and verse are supplied in brackets.

Old Testament

Malachi (cont.)
  1:12 228 n. 12,
      228 n. 15
  1:13 228 n. 13
  1:14 228 n. 14
  2:2 228 n. 14
  2:8 509 n. 51
  2:9 228 n. 15
  2:13–16 395 n. 6
  3 402
  3:1 295
  3:1–4 397 n. 16, 402

Malachi (cont.)
  3:5 232
  3:10–11 395 n. 6
  3:13 401
  3:13–15 401,
      401 n. 27
  3:14 401, 401 n. 28,
      402
  3:16 401, 401 n. 27,
      402, 402 n. 30, 411
  3:16–18 411 n. 59
  3:16–21 401

Malachi (cont.)
  3:17 401–2
  3:17–21 401
  3:18 401–2
  4:2[3:20] 402, 411
  4:3[3:21] 411
  4:4[3:22] 232,
      406 n. 41
  4:1–6 24
  4:5–6 519

Deuterocanonical Books

Ben Sira
  7:17 568
  48:17 542
  48:17–25 478
  48:20 478
  48:22 478
  48:23 478
  48:24–25 479
  49:4 478

Ben Sira (cont.)
  50:25–26 571

1 Maccabees
  1:10 545
  1:54 545
  2:42 402 n. 30
  4:49–50 569

2 Maccabees
  9:4 542
  9:14 542

4 Maccabees
  15:20 542

New Testament

Matthew
  1 566
  2:6 567
  4:12–16 567
  5:3–12 396
  5:15–16 396
  10:18 397 n. 14,
      411 n. 59
  10:22 397 n. 14,
      411 n. 59
  13:35 567
  13:37–43 402
  15:8–9 567
  21:5 567
  21:13 567
  22:1–14 411 n. 59
  24:14 389
  24:34 389
  25:31–46 402,
      411 n. 39

Matthew (cont.)
  26:15 567
  27:9 567

Mark
  8:28 537
  15:34 567

Luke
  4:16–21 566
  4:17 569
  4:25–27 567
  6:20–26 411 n. 59
  10:20 412 n. 59
  15 266
  24:21 390
  24:25–27 390

John
  5:39 566

John (cont.)
  12:15 567
  19:24 567
  19:27 567

Acts
  1:11 389
  2 568
  2:16 387
  3:17–26 567
  6:8 568
  8:4–8 568
  8:34 407
  9 569
  9:2 412 n. 59
  10:44 568
  11:24 568
  13:47 569
  19:9 412 n. 59
  19:22–23 412 n. 59